EVALUATION MODELS

Viewpoints on Educational and Human Services Evaluation
Second Edition

Evaluation in Education and Human Services

Editors:

George F. Madaus, Boston College,
  Chestnut Hill, Massachusetts, U.S.A.
Daniel L. Stufflebeam, Western Michigan
  University, Kalamazoo, Michigan, U.S.A.

Other books in the series:

EVALUATION MODELS
Viewpoints on Educational and Human Services Evaluation
Second Edition

edited by

Daniel L. Stufflebeam
Western Michigan University

George F. Madaus
Boston College

Thomas Kellaghan
The Educational Research Centre, Dublin

KLUWER ACADEMIC PUBLISHERS
Boston / Dordrecht / London

Distributors for North, Central and South America:

Kluwer Academic Publishers
101 Philip Drive
Assinippi Park
Norwell, Massachusetts 02061 USA
Telephone (781) 871-6600
Fax (781) 681-9045
E-Mail <kluwer@wkap.com>

Distributors for all other countries:

Kluwer Academic Publishers Group
Distribution Centre
Post Office Box 322
3300 AH Dordrecht, THE NETHERLANDS
Telephone 31 78 6392 392
Fax 31 78 6546 474
E-Mail <services@wkap.nl>

 Electronic Services <http://www.wkap.nl>

Library of Congress Cataloging-in-Publication Data

Evaluation models: viewpoints on educational and human services evaluation / edited by
Daniel L. Stufflebeam, George F. Madaus, Thomas Kellaghan.—2nd ed.
     p.cm.—(Evaluation in education and human services)
     Includes bibliographical references and index.
     ISBN 0-7923-7884-9
     1. Educational surveys.   2. School management and organization—Evaluation.   3. Curriculum
evaluation.   I. Stufflebeam, Daniel L.   II. Madaus, George F.   III. Kellaghan, Thomas.   IV. Series.

LB2823 . E87 2000
379.1'58—dc21

                                                                                            00-034804

Printed on acid-free paper.

Printed in the United States of America

**The Publisher offers discounts on this book for course use and bulk purchases.
For further information, send email to <michael.williams@wkap.com>.**

CONTENTS

PREFACE

Any attempts to formally evaluate something involves coming to grips with a wide range of concepts such as value, merit, worth, growth, criteria, standards, objectives, needs, norms, client, audience, validity, reliability, objectivity, practical significance, accountability, improvement, inputs, process, product, formative, summative, cost, impact, information, credibility, and, of course, the term evaluation itself. To communicate with colleagues and clients, evaluators need to be clear about what is meant by such concepts. Moreover, it is necessary to integrate the concepts and their meanings into a coherent framework that guides all aspects of their work.

The conceptualization of evaluation is not a once-off activity, nor is it static. Rather, the ideas that guide evaluation work should keep pace with the growth of theory and practice in the field. Further, the design and conduct of any particular study will involve a good deal of thought focused on the job in hand, in which it will be necessary to identify and define audiences and information requirements; the object to be evaluated; the purposes of the evaluation; inquiry procedures; concerns and issues to be examined; variables to be assessed; bases for interpreting findings; and the standards to be invoked in assessing the quality of the work.

It is no small wonder, then, that attempts to conceptualize evaluation have been among the most influential works in the fast-growing literature on the topic, and the contents of this anthology attest to the existence of a rich array of theoretical perspectives. These perspectives vary in many respects, which is not surprising given the complexity of evaluation work; the wide range of situations and political contexts in which it is carried out; its service orientations; and the varied backgrounds and beliefs of those who write about evaluation. The ways in which evaluation is conceptualized will differ according to the role assigned to objectives in the process; the extent to which it is thought desirable to present convergent or divergent findings; the corollary preference for constructivist or objectivist findings and inter-pretations; the use or absence of experimental controls; the extent to which theory is used to determine the variables and the interrelationships to be examined; and the role that hard and soft data play in arriving at conclusions. It is understandable that evaluators will sometimes follow one approach in one kind of evaluation assign-ment, and a quite different approach in another setting. Given the variety of con-texts in which evaluations take place and the range of philosophical perspectives reflected in evaluations, it is fortunate that evaluators can find in the literature a variety of ways to conceptualize the evaluation process in their search for the one that best suits a particular context.

From this diversity of conceptual approaches to evaluation, however, a consensus has begun to emerge regarding the principles that should undergird all evaluations. The consensus is embodied in the standards issued by the Joint Committee on Standards for Educational Evaluation. Basically, these standards require that evalua-tions be useful, feasible, ethical, and accurate. The appearance of the standards, and the associated mechanism for regularly reviewing and revising them, signify the maturing of evaluation as a profession. While the standards were developed for use in educational evaluation in North America, they have also been usefully applied, or at least consulted, in fields outside education and in countries around the world.

The present volume is a revision of an anthology that was published in 1983. Two major considerations governed the selection of material for the revision. First, it was decided to retain papers that were regarded as seminal in the history of evaluation as well as ones that described models adequately. Some chapters were dropped because the relevance of their messages had decreased over time. Second, papers which represented developments in evaluation since 1983 were added. We increased the coverage of material that had application outside the field of educa-tion and of naturalistic evaluation. These considerations led to the retention of seven papers, the revision of three, and the addition of fifteen.

The result is a book that is an up-to-date reflection of the conceptual develop-ment of evaluation, particularly program evaluation, and is divided into five major sections. The first section includes essays on the history of evaluation; models, metaphors, and definitions; and alternative approaches. The second, third, and fourth parts contain articles that represent the current major schools of thought about evaluation, written by leading authors in the field. In Part II, papers are categorized in terms of their questions/methods orientation. They cover objectives-oriented evaluation, outcome evaluation, the role of testing in evaluation, discrepancy evalu-ation, experimental design, cost analysis, clarification hearings or judicial evaluation, case studies, the technology of criticism, and theory-based evaluation. Papers in Part III address improvement/accountability-oriented approaches: consumer-oriented evaluation, decision-oriented evaluation, and accountability. The entries in Part IV relate to social agenda-directed/advocacy evaluation models, and cover responsive evaluation, constructivist evaluation, empowerment evaluation, and deliberative democratic evaluation. In the final section, three overarching topics are addressed: utilization-focused evaluation, standards for evaluations, and the methodology of metaevaluation.

The evaluation models described in the book are not models in the sense of mathematical models used to test given theories, but they are models in the sense that each one characterizes its author's idealized view of the main concepts and structure of evaluation work, which form the basis of guidelines which are used to arrive at defensible descriptions and judgments. We are aware that some writers in the field have urged against according alternative perspectives on evaluation the status of models. However, we think the suggestion that they be called something else, such as persuasions or beliefs, might do little more than puzzle readers. We are comfortable in presenting the conceptualizations, not as models of what occurs, but as models for conducting studies according to various authors' beliefs about evaluation. In this sense, they are idealized or "model" views of how to sort out and address the problems encountered in conducting an evaluation.

We wish to emphasize that the presented models should not be considered as discrete options. While they may differ in important aspects, such as in the treatment of objectives and the use of experimental controls, they also overlap. For example, all call for examination of outcomes and most include an examination of process. Clear examples of overlap can be seen in the models proposed by Scriven, Stake, and Stufflebeam when they emphasize the importance of a comprehensive assessment of relevant criteria to illuminate, as well as present judgments of the merit of a program or other object. However, these models also differ in notable ways, such as in the relative importance accorded to an improvement orientation versus a focus on reaching a summative judgment. The practical implication of the concept of overlapping models is that users may combine elements of different models as they design particular evaluations.

We owe an enormous debt to the authors of the articles that appear in the book. We would like to thank those that gave us permission to reprint their publications and those who prepared articles specifically for this volume. We also are grateful to Zachary Rolnik and Michael Williams of Kluwer-Nijhoff Publishing, who consistently supported our effort. Further thanks are extended to Seamus Ó hUallacháin, Brian Carnell, Marguerite Clarke, John Coyle, Ida Holmstedt, Catherine Horn, Diane Joyce, Amandine Passot, Sally Veeder, Hilary Walshe, and Lori Wingate, for their competent editorial, technical, and clerical assistance throughout this project.

We believe this book will be of interest and assistance to the full range of persons who are part of any evaluation effort, including the clients who commission evaluation studies and use their results, evaluators, and administrators and staff in the programs that are evaluated. We also believe the book should be useful as a text for courses in program evaluation and for workshops. Further, it should prove to be an invaluable reference source for those who participate in any aspect of formal evaluation work. We hope that it will assist significantly all involved in program evaluation to increase their awareness of the complexity of evaluation; to increase their appreciation of alternative points of view; to improve their ability to use theoretical suggestions that appear in the literature; to increase their critical appraisal of various approaches; to increase their adherence to the field's professional standards; and, ultimately, to improve the quality and utility of their evaluations.

I. PROGRAM EVALUATION: AN INTRODUCTION

This opening section of *Evaluation Models* introduces program evaluation in three overview chapters. The lead chapter reviews the history of program evaluation. It begins by summarizing 19th century efforts to judge and pay school personnel by their students' achievements; to accredit schools; and also to examine certain policy issues, such as the value of spelling instruction. The chapter subsequently traces the development of the program evaluation field from its roots in education to its current status. Program evaluation is shown to be a maturing discipline with a rich literature and one that serves health, human services, community development, housing, military operations, law enforcement, government, and education, plus many other fields. Rather than being described as mainly an American enterprise, the chapter portrays program evaluation as an expanding profession that now has evaluation societies in more than 20 countries. The second chapter reviews models, metaphors, and definitions, which are different ways of conceptualizing evaluation. Finally, the foundational models chapter identifies and examines 22 approaches to program evaluation, culminating in a consumers report type ranking of the most promising models. The chapter identifies two pseudoevaluation approaches to evaluation as illegitimate and categorizes the 20 legitimate approaches as Questions/ Methods-Oriented, Improvement/Accountability-Oriented; and Social Agenda-Directed. These latter categories are employed in the remainder of the book to partition the presented evaluation models.

1. PROGRAM EVALUATION: A HISTORICAL OVERVIEW

GEORGE F. MADAUS and DANIEL L. STUFFLEBEAM

Program evaluation is often mistakenly viewed as a recent phenomenon. Many people date its beginning from the late 1960s with the infusion by the federal government of large sums of money into a wide range of human service programs, including education. However, program evaluation has an interesting history that predates by at least 150 years the explosion of evaluation during the era of President Johnson's Great Society and the emergence of evaluation as a maturing profession since the sixties. A definitive history of program evaluation has yet to be written and in the space available to us we can do little more than offer a modest outline, broad brush strokes of the landscape that constitutes that history. It is important that people interested in the conceptualization of evaluation are aware of the field's roots and origins. Such an awareness of the history of program evaluation should lead to a better understanding of how and why this field has developed as it did.

Where to begin? For convenience we shall describe seven periods in the life of program evaluation. The first is the period prior to 1900, which we call the *Age of Reform*; the second, from 1900 until 1930, we call the *Age of Efficiency and Testing*; the third, from 1930 to 1945, may be called the *Tylerian Age*; the fourth, from 1946 to about 1957, we call the *Age of Innocence*; the fifth, from 1958 to 1972, is the *Age of Development*; the sixth, from 1973 to 1983, the *Age of Professionalization*; and finally the seventh from 1983 to 2000 the *Age of Expansion and Integration*.

D.L. Stufflebeam, G.F. Madaus and T. Kellaghan (eds.). EVALUATION MODELS. Copyright © 2000. Kluwer Academic Publishers. Boston. All rights reserved.

THE AGE OF REFORM 1792–1900

We begin this period in our history of program evaluation in 1792 because that is the year in which William Farish invented the quantitative mark to score examinations (Hoskins, 1968). Replacing qualitative assessments of student performance with a mark for a "correct" answer permitted the ranking of examinees and the averaging and aggregating of scores. This was the first development in the field of psychometrics as we know it today (Madaus & Kellaghan, 1992). In fact Farish revolutionized testing, a technology that plays an important role in the history of program evaluation to the present.

The 19th century was the era of the Industrial Revolution with all of its attendant economic and technological changes. The very structure of society was transformed. Major social changes occurred. There was drastic change in physical and mental health and outlook, in social life and social conscience, and in the structures of social agencies. There was the laissez-faire philosophy of Bentham and the humanitarian philosophy of the philanthropists (Thompson, 1950). There were continued but often drawn out attempts to reform educational and social programs and agencies in both Great Britain and the United States.

In Great Britain there were continuing attempts to reform education, the poor laws, hospitals, orphanages, and public health. Evaluations of these social agencies and functions were informal and impressionistic in nature. Often they took the form of government-appointed commissions set up to investigate aspects of the area under consideration. For example, the Royal Commission of Inquiry into Primary Education in Ireland under the Earl of Powis, after receiving testimony and examining evidence, lamented over the progress of the children in the national schools of Ireland. The Powis Commission recommended the adoption of a scheme known as payment by results, already being used in England, whereby teachers' salaries would be dependent in part on the results of annual examinations in reading, spelling, writing, and arithmetic (Kellaghan & Madaus, 1982; Madaus & Kellaghan, 1992). Another example of this approach to evaluation was the 1882 Royal Commission on Small Pox and Fever Hospitals, which recommended after study that infectious-disease hospitals ought to be open and free to all citizens (Pinker, 1971).

Royal commissions are still used today in Great Britain to evaluate areas of concern. Rough counterparts in the United States to these commissions are presidential commissions (for example, the President's Commission on School Finance), White House panels (e.g., the White House Panel on Non Public Education), and congressional hearings. Throughout their history royal commissions, presidential commissions, and congressional hearings have served as a means of evaluating human services programs of various kinds through the examination of evidence either gathered by the Commission or presented to it in testimony by concerned parties. However, this approach to evaluation was often only emblematic or symbolic. N. J. Crisp (1982) captures the pseudo nature of such evaluations in a work of fiction. One of his characters discusses a royal commission this way: "Appoint it, feel that you've accomplished something, and forget about it, in the hope that by the time it's reported, the problem will have disappeared or been overtaken by events" (p. 148).

In Great Britain during this period when reform programs were put in place, it was not unusual to demand yearly evaluations through a system of annual reports submitted by an inspectorate. For example, in education there were school inspectors that visited each school annually and submitted reports on their condition and on pupil attainments (Kellaghan & Madaus, 1982; Madaus & Kellaghan, 1992). Similarly the Poor Law commissioners had a small, paid inspectorate to oversee compliance with the Poor Law Amendment Act of 1834 (Pinker, 1971). The system of maintaining external inspectorates to examine and evaluate the work of the schools exists today in Great Britain and Ireland. In the United States, external inspectors are employed by some state and federal agencies. For example, the Occupational Safety and Health Administration (OSHA) employs inspectors to monitor health hazards in the workplace. Interestingly, the system of external inspectors as a model for evaluation has received scant attention in the evaluation literature.

Two other developments in Great Britain during this period are worthy of note. First, during the middle of the nineteenth century a number of associations dedicated to social inquiry came into existence. These societies conducted and publicized findings on a number of social problems that were very influential in stimulating discussion (for example, Chadwick's 1842 Report on the Sanitary Condition of the Laboring Population of Great Britain [Pinker, 1971]). Second, often in response to these private reports, bureaucracies established to manage the programs sometimes set up committees of enquiry. These were official, government-sponsored investigations of various social programs, such as provincial workhouses (Pinker, 1971). Both these examples are important in that they constitute the beginnings of an empirical approach to the evaluation of programs.

In the United States perhaps the earliest formal evaluation was in 1815 when the Army Ordnance Department drew up a system of regulations for the "uniformity of manufacture of all arms ordnance" (Smith, 1987, p. 42). To accomplish this it became clear that the engineering of people was as important as the engineering of materials. The idiosyncrasy of the skilled craftsman had to yield to uniformity. Over several decades the Ordnance Department developed the administrative, communication, inspection, accounting, bureaucratic, and mechanical techniques that fostered conformity and resulted in the technology of interchangeable parts and the eventual manufacture of a host of mass-produced products in the 20th century (Smith, 1987). These early efforts by the Ordnance Department foreshadowed Frederick Taylor's Scientific Management movement discussed below.

The first formal attempt to evaluate the performance of schools took place in Boston in 1845. This event is important in the history of evaluation because it began a long tradition of using pupil test scores as a principal source of data to evaluate the effectiveness of a school or instructional program. Then, at the urging of Samuel Gridley Howe, written essay examinations were introduced into the Boston grammar schools by Horace Mann and the Board of Education. Ostensibly the essay exam, modeled after those used in Europe at the time, was introduced to replace the viva voce or oral examinations. The latter mode of examination had become administratively awkward with increased numbers of pupils and was also seen as unfair because it could not be standardized for all pupils. The interesting point in terms of program evaluation was the hidden policy agenda behind the move to written examinations; namely, it was the gathering of data for inter-school comparisons that could be used in decisions concerning the annual appointment of headmasters. Howe and Mann attempted to establish differential school effects and used these data to eliminate headmasters who opposed them on the abolition of corporal punishment. This is an interesting early example of politicization of evaluation data.

Between 1887 and 1898, Joseph Rice conducted what is generally recognized as the first formal educational program evaluation in America. He carried out a comparative study on the value of drill in spelling instruction across a number of school districts. Rice, like Mann and Howe before him, used test scores as his criteria measures in his evaluation of spelling instruction. He found no significant learning gains between systems which spent up to 200 minutes a week studying spelling and those which spent as little as ten minutes per week. Rice's results led educators to re-examine and eventually revise their approach to the teaching of spelling. More important from the point of view of this history of program evaluation is his argument that educators had to become experimentalists and quantitative thinkers and his use of comparative research design to study student achievement (Rice, 1914; 1897). Rice was a harbinger of the experimental design approach to evaluation first advanced by Lindquist (1953) and extended and championed by Campbell (Campbell & Stanley, 1963; Campbell, 1969) and others in the 1960s and 1970s and by Mosteller and his colleagues in the mid 1990s (see Chapter 8).

Before leaving this very brief treatment of the age of reform, another development should be mentioned. The foundation of the accreditation or professional judgement approach to evaluation can be traced directly to the establishment of the North Central Association of Colleges and Secondary Schools in the late 1800s. The accreditation movement did not, however, gain great stature until the 1930s when six additional regional accrediting associations were established across the U.S. Since then the accrediting movement has expanded tremendously and gained great strength and credibility as a major means of evaluating the adequacy of educational institutions. (See Floden, 1983 for a treatment of the accreditation approach to evaluation.)

THE AGE OF EFFICIENCY AND TESTING 1900–1930

During the early part of the twentieth century the seminal work by Fredrick Taylor launched the scientific management movement, an early form of personnel evaluation. Taylorism continues to affect almost all aspects of American life to this day. (For a detailed treatment of Taylor's impact on society see Doray, 1988 and Banta, 1993.) Taylor's ideas became a powerful force in administrative theory in educational and industrial circles (Biddle & Ellena, 1964; Callahan, 1962; Cremin, 1962). The emphasis of this movement was on systemization, standardization, and, most importantly, efficiency. Typifying this emphasis on efficiency were the titles of the fourteenth and fifteenth yearbooks of the National Society for the Study of Education (NSSE), which were, respectively, *Methods for Measuring Teachers' Efficiency* and the *Standards and Tests for the Measurement of the Efficiency Of Schools and School Systems*.

Surveys done in a number of large school systems during this period focused on school and/or teacher efficiency using various criteria (for example, expenditures, pupil dropout rate, promotion rates, etc.). By 1915, thirty to forty large school systems had completed or were working on comprehensive surveys on all phases of educational life (Kendall, 1915; Smith & Judd, 1914). A number of these surveys employed the newly developed "objective" tests in arithmetic, spelling, handwriting, and English composition to determine the quality of teaching. (For a detailed treatment of the history of mathematics and arithmetic tests during this time see Madaus, Clarke & O'Leary, in press.) These tests were often developed in large districts by a bureau or department set up specifically to improve the efficiency of the district. For example, the Department of Educational Investigation and Measurement in the Boston public schools developed a number of tests that today would be described as objective referenced (Ballou, 1916). Eventually tests like those in Boston took on a norm-referenced character as the percentage of students passing became a standard by which teachers could judge whether their classes were above or below the general standard for the city (Ballou, 1916). In addition to these locally developed tests there were a number of tests developed by researchers like Courtis, Ayers, Thorndike, and others, which were geared to measuring a very precise set of instructional objectives. These tests by famous researchers of the day had normative data that enabled one system to compare itself with another (Tyack & Hansot, 1982).

Many of these early twentieth-century surveys were classic examples of muckraking, "often initiated by a few local people who invited outside experts to expose defects and propose remedies" (Tyack & Hansot, 1982, p. 161). Another problem associated with these early surveys—a problem not unknown to evaluators today— was that the "objective" results obtained were often used as propaganda "to build dikes of data against rising tides of public criticism" (Tyack & Hansot, 1982, p. 155). However, researchers at the time did recognize that such surveys could and should avoid muckraking and public relations use. Many of them were indeed constructive, done in cooperation with local advisors, and designed to produce public support for unrecognized but needed change (Tyack & Hansot, 1982).

With the growth of standardized achievement tests after World War I, school districts used these tests to make inferences about program effectiveness. For example, May (1971) in an unpublished paper described the history of standardized testing in Philadelphia from 1916 to 1938. He found that commercially available achievement tests, along with tests built by research bureaus of large school districts, were used to evaluate the curriculum and overall system performance, in addition to being used to make decisions about individuals. Throughout its history, the field of evaluation has been closely linked to the field of testing. Test data have often been the principal data source in evaluations; this use of tests has been a mixed blessing as we shall see presently.

It is important to point out that studies of efficiency and testing were for the most part initiated by, and confined to, local school districts. In contrast to the national curriculum development projects of the late 1950s and early 1960s, curriculum development before the 1930s was largely in the hands of a teacher or committee of teachers. It was natural, therefore, that evaluations of that period were addressed to localized questions. This focus or emphasis on local evaluation questions continued into the 1960s despite the fact that the audience for the evaluations was state-wide or nation-wide; this resulted in many useless educational evaluations being carried out during the 1960s. It was only in the 1970s that educators and evaluators recognized and began to deal with this problem of generalizability. And, it wasn't until the 90s with the advent of standards based reform that the focus shifted from local to state level control over many aspects of the curriculum.

During the late 1920s and 1930s, university institutes specializing in field studies were formed and conducted surveys for local districts. The most famous of these institutes was the one headed by George Strayer at Teachers College (Tyack & Hansot, 1982). These institutes could be considered the precursors of the university centers dedicated to evaluation that grew up in the 1960s and 1970s.

THE TYLERIAN AGE 1930–1945

Ralph W. Tyler has had enormous influence on education in general and educational evaluation and testing in particular. He is often referred to, quite properly we feel, as the father of educational evaluation. Tyler began by conceptualizing a broad and innovative view of both curriculum and evaluation. (Cf. Chapter 4.) This view saw curriculum as a set of broadly planned school experiences designed and implemented to help students achieve specified behavioral outcomes. Tyler coined the term "educational evaluation" which meant assessing the extent that valued objectives had been achieved as part of an instructional program. (This development is the foundation of today's outcome evaluation described in Chapter 4). During the early and mid-1930s, he applied his conceptualization of evaluation to helping instructors at Ohio State University improve their courses and the tests that they used in their courses.

During the depths of the Great Depression, schools, as well as other public institutions, had stagnated from a lack of resources and, perhaps just as importantly, from a lack of optimism. Just as Roosevelt tried through his New Deal programs to lead the economy out of the abyss, so too John Dewey and others tried to renew education. The renewal in education came to be known as the Progressive Education Movement, and it reflected the philosophy of pragmatism and employed tools from behavioristic psychology.

Tyler became directly involved in the Progressive Education Movement when he was called upon to direct the research component of the now-famous Eight Year Study (Smith & Tyler, 1942a). The Eight-Year Study (1932–1940), funded by the Carnegie Corporation, was the first and last large study of the differential effectiveness of various types of schooling until well after World War II. The study came about when questions were asked in the early 1930s about the efficacy of the traditional high school experience relative to the progressive secondary school experience. As a result of these questions, leading colleges began to refuse progressive school graduates admittance because they lacked credits in certain specific subjects. To settle the debate, an experiment was proposed in 1932 in which over 300 colleges agreed to waive their traditional entrance requirements for graduates from about 30 progressive secondary schools. The high school and college performance of students from these secondary schools would be compared to the high school and college performance of students from a group of traditional secondary schools.

The Eight-Year Study introduced educators throughout America to a new and broader view of educational evaluation than that which had been in vogue during the age of efficiency and testing. Tyler conceptualized evaluation as a comparison of intended outcomes with actual outcomes. His view of evaluation was seen by advocates as having a clear-cut advantage over previous approaches. Since a Tylerian evaluation involves internal comparisons of outcomes with objectives, it need not provide for costly and disruptive comparisons between experimental and control groups, as were required in the comparative experimental approach that Rice had used. Since the approach calls for the measurement of behaviorally defined objectives, it concentrates on learning *outcomes* instead of organizational and teaching *inputs*, thereby avoiding the subjectivity of the professional judgment or accreditation approach; and, since its measures reflect defined objectives, there was no need to be heavily concerned with the reliability of differences between the scores of individual students. Further, the measures typically cover a much wider range of outcome variables than those assessed by standardized norm-referenced tests.

Clearly by the middle of the 1940s Tyler had, through his work and writing, laid the foundation for his enormous influence on the educational scene in general and on testing and evaluation in particular during the next 25 years.

THE AGE OF INNOCENCE 1946–1957

We have labeled the period 1946–1957 as the *Age of Innocence*, although we might just as well have called it the *Age of Ignorance*. It was a time of poverty and despair in the inner cities and in rural areas, but almost no one except the victims seemed to notice. It was a period of extreme racial prejudice and segregation, to which most white people seemed oblivious. There was exorbitant consumption and widespread waste of natural resources with little apparent concern about the depletion of these resources. It was a period of vast development of industry and military capabilities with little provision for safeguards against the many negative side effects.

More to the point of this review, there was expansion of educational offerings, personnel, and facilities. New buildings were erected. New kinds of educational institutions, such as experimental colleges and community colleges emerged. Small school districts consolidated with others to be able to provide the wide range of educational services that were common in the larger school systems, including mental and physical health services, guidance, food services, music instruction, expanded sports programs, business and technical education, and community education. College enrolments increased dramatically and enrolments in teacher-education programs ballooned. Throughout American society, the late 1940s and 1950s were a time to forget the war, leave the depression behind, build and expand capabilities, acquire resources, and engineer and enjoy a "good life."

This general scene in society and education was reflected in educational evaluation. While there was great expansion of education there was no particular interest on the part of society in solving social and education problems and holding educators accountable. There was little call for educators to demonstrate the efficiency and effectiveness of any of the many developmental efforts. Educators did talk and write about evaluation, and they did collect considerable amounts of data (usually to justify the need for expansion or for broad, new programs). However, there is little evidence that these data were used to judge and improve the quality of programs or that the data could have been used for such a purpose.

We have labeled the period 1946 to 1947 The Age of Innocence, not because work in evaluation did not proceed but because the work seemingly had no social purpose. The great deal of technical development in evaluation was just that. It was not geared to identifying beneficiaries' needs and critically examining society's response to the needs.

During this period there was considerable development of some of the technical aspects of evaluation; this was consistent with the then-prevalent expansion of all sorts of technologies. Chief among these developments was the growth in standardized testing. Many new nationally standardized tests were published during this period. Schools purchased these tests by the thousands and also subscribed heavily to machine scoring and analysis services that the new technology made available. The testing movement received another boost in 1947 with the establishment of the Educational Testing Service.

By the 1950s, the standardized testing business had expanded tremendously, and the professional organizations concerned with testing initiated a series of steps designed to regulate the test-related activities of their members. In 1954, a committee of the American Psychological Association prepared *Technical Recommendations for Psychological Tests and Diagnostic Techniques* (APA, 1954). In 1955, committees of the American Educational Research Association and the National Council on Measurements Used in Education prepared *Technical Recommendations for Achievement Tests* (AERA and NCMUE, 1955). These two reports provided the basis for the 1966 edition of the joint AERA/APA/NCME *Standards for Educational and Psychological Tests and Manuals* (APA, 1966) and the 1974 revision entitled, *Standards for Educational and Psychological Tests* (APA, 1974). The latter report recognized the need for separate standards dealing with program evaluation. A revision of the Standards in 1985 contained a chapter on the use of tests in program evaluation, as did a further revision in 2000.

The rapid expansion of testing was not the only technical development related to program evaluation during this period. Lindquist (1953) extended and delineated the statistical principles of experimental design. Years later, many evaluators and educators found that the problems of trying to meet simultaneously all of the required assumptions of experimental design (for example, constant treatment, uncontaminated treatment, randomly assigned subjects, stable study samples, and unitary success criteria) in the school setting were insurmountable.

During the 1950s and early 1960s there was also considerable technical development related to the Tylerian view of evaluation. Since implementing the Tyler approach in an evaluation required that objectives be stated explicitly, there was a need to help educators and other professionals to do a better job articulating their objectives. Techniques to help program staffs make their objectives explicit, along with taxonomies of possible educational objectives (Bloom et al., 1956; Krathwohl, 1964), were developed to fill this need. The Tyler rationale was also used extensively during this period to train teachers in test development.

During this period evaluations were, as before, primarily within the purview of local agencies. Federal and state agencies had not yet become deeply involved in the evaluation of programs. Funds for evaluation that were done came from local coffers, foundations, voluntary associations such as the community chest, or professional organizations. This lack of dependence on taxpayer money for evaluation would end with the dawn of the next period in the history of evaluation.

THE AGE OF DEVELOPMENT 1958–1972

The age of innocence in evaluation came to an abrupt end with the call in the late 1950s and early 1960s for evaluations of large-scale curriculum development projects funded by federal monies. This marked the end of an era in evaluation and the beginning of profound changes that would see evaluation expand as an industry and into a profession, focused on helping meet society's needs and dependent on taxpayer monies for support.

As a result of the Russian launch of Sputnik in 1957, the federal government enacted the National Defense Education Act of 1958. Among other things, this act provided for new educational programs in mathematics, science, and foreign language; and expanded counseling and guidance services and testing programs in school districts. A number of new national curriculum development projects, especially in the areas of science and mathematics, were established. Eventually funds were made available to evaluate these curriculum development efforts.

All four of the approaches to evaluation discussed so far were represented in the evaluations done during this period. First, the Tyler approach was used to help define objectives for the new curricula and to assess the degree to which the objectives were later realized. Second, new nationally standardized tests were created to better reflect the objectives and content of the new curricula. Third, the professional-judgment approach was used to rate proposals and to check periodically on the efforts of contractors. Finally, many evaluators evaluated curriculum development efforts through the use of field experiments.

The best and the brightest of the educational evaluation community were involved in efforts to evaluate these new curricula; they were adequately financed, and they carefully applied the technology that had been developed during the past decade or more. Nonetheless, by the early 1960s it became apparent to some leaders in educational evaluation that their work and their results were neither particularly helpful to curriculum developers nor responsive to the questions being raised by those who wanted to know about the programs "effectiveness."

This negative assessment was reflected best in a landmark article by Cronbach (1963; cf. Chapter 14). In looking at the evaluation efforts of the recent past, he sharply criticized the guiding conceptualizations of evaluation for their lack of relevance and utility, and advised evaluators to turn away from their penchant for post hoc evaluations based on comparisons of the norm-referenced test scores of experimental and control groups. Instead, Cronbach counseled evaluators to reconceptualize evaluation—not in terms of a horse race between competing programs but as a process of gathering and reporting information that could help guide curriculum development. Cronbach was the first person to argue that analysis and reporting of test item scores would be likely to prove more useful to teachers than the reporting of average total scores. When first published, Cronbach's counsel and recommendations went largely unnoticed, except by a small circle of evaluation specialists. Nonetheless, the article was seminal, containing hypotheses about the conceptualization and conduct of evaluations that were to be tested and found valid within a few years.

In 1965, guided by the vision of Senator Hubert Humphrey, the charismatic leadership of President John Kennedy, and the great political skill of President Lyndon Johnson, the War on Poverty was launched. These programs poured billions of dollars into reforms aimed at equalizing and upgrading opportunities for all citizens across a broad array of health, social, and educational services. The expanding economy enabled the federal government to finance these programs, and there was widespread national support for developing what President Johnson termed the Great Society.

Accompanying this massive effort to help the needy came concern in some quarters that the money invested in these programs might be wasted if appropriate accountability requirements were not imposed. In response to this concern, Senator Robert Kennedy and some of his colleagues in the Congress amended the Elementary and Secondary Education Act of 1964 (ESEA) to include specific evaluation requirements. As a result, Title I of that Act, which was aimed at providing compensatory education to disadvantaged children, specifically required each school district receiving funds under its terms to evaluate annually—using appropriate standardized test data—the extent to which its Title I projects had achieved their objectives. This requirement, with its specific references to standardized test data and an assessment of congruence between outcomes and objectives, reflected the state-of-the-art in program evaluation at that time. More importantly, the requirement forced educators to shift their concern for educational evaluation from the realm of theory and supposition into the realm of practice and implementation.

When school districts began to respond to the evaluation requirement of Title I, they quickly found that the existing tools and strategies employed by their evaluators were largely inappropriate to the task. Available standardized tests had been designed to rank order students of average ability; they were of little use in diagnosing needs and assessing any achievement gains of disadvantaged children whose educational development lagged far behind that of their middle-class peers. Further, these tests were found to be relatively insensitive to differences between schools and/or programs, mainly because of their psychometric properties and content coverage. Instead of measuring outcomes directly related to the school or to a particular program, these tests were at best indirect measures of learning, measuring much the same traits as general ability tests (Madaus, Airasian, & Kellaghan, 1980).

There was another problem with using standardized tests: such an approach to evaluation conflicted with the precepts of the Tylerian approach. Because Tyler recognized and encouraged differences in objectives from locale to locale it became difficult to adapt this model to nation-wide standardized-testing programs. In order to be commercially viable, these standardized-testing programs had to overlook to some extent objectives stressed by particular locales in favor of objectives stressed by the majority of districts. Further, there was a dearth of information about the needs and achievement levels of disadvantaged children that could guide teachers in developing meaningful behavioral objectives for this population of learners.

The failure of attempts to isolate the effects of Title I projects through the use of experimental/control group designs was due primarily to an inability to meet the assumptions required of such designs (Guba, 1966). Further, project-site visitation by experts—while extensively employed by governmental sponsors—was not acceptable as a primary evaluation strategy because this approach was seen as lacking the objectivity and rigor stipulated in the ESEA legislation. When the finding of "no results" was reported, as was generally the case, there were no data on the degree to which the "treatment" had in fact been implemented; the evaluator had overlooked the messy "black box" that constituted the "treatment." Further, we encased the word treatment in quotes advisedly since the actual nature of the treatment rendered to subjects was generally unknown. The technical description was nothing more than a vague description of the project. For example, the term Title I itself was often used to describe an amorphous general treatment. In any event, the emphasis on test scores diverted attention from consideration of the treatment or of treatment implementation.

As a result of the growing disquiet with evaluation efforts and with the consistent negative findings, the professional honorary fraternity Phi Delta Kappa set up a National Study Committee on Evaluation (Stufflebeam et al., 1971). After surveying the scene, this committee concluded that educational evaluation was "seized with a great illness" and called for the development of new theories and methods of evaluation as well as for new training programs for evaluators. At about this same time many new conceptualizations of evaluations began to emerge. Provus (1969 & 1971), Hammond (1967), Eisner (1967), and Metfessel & Michael (1967) proposed reformation of the Tyler model. Glaser (1963), Tyler (1967), and Popham (1971) pointed to criterion-referenced testing as an alternative to norm-referenced testing. Cook (1966) called for the use of the systems-analysis approach to evaluate programs. Scriven (1967), Stufflebeam, (1967 & 1971, with others), and Stake (1967) introduced new models of evaluation that departed radically from prior approaches. These conceptualizations recognized the need to evaluate goals, look at inputs, examine implementation and delivery of services, as well as measure intended and unintended outcomes of the program. They also emphasized the need to make judgments about the merit or worth of the object being evaluated. (Overviews of these developments can be found in Chapter 3.)

The late 1960s and early 1970s were vibrant with descriptions, discussions, and debates concerning how evaluation should be conceived; however, this period in the history of program evaluation ended on a down note. A number of important evaluations reported negative findings. First, Coleman's famous study, *Equality of Educational Opportunity* (1966, with others), received considerable notice. Particular attention went to his famous conclusion that "schools bring little influence to bear on a child's achievement that is independent of his background and general social context" (Coleman et al. 1966, p. 325). Title I evaluations (Picariello, 1968; Glass et al., 1970; U.S. Office of Education, 1970) argued against the efficacy of those programs. The Westinghouse/Ohio University Head Start investigation (Cicirelli et al., 1969) turned up discouraging results. Likewise, the results of the evaluation of *Sesame Street*—when critically analyzed—were discouraging (Ball & Bogatz, 1970; Bogatz & Ball, 1971). These disheartening findings raised serious questions about evaluation in general and certain methodologies in particular. For many supporters of these programs, this set the stage for our next period, which we call the Age of Professionalization.

THE AGE OF PROFESSIONALIZATION 1973–1983

Beginning about 1973 the field of evaluation began to crystallize and emerge as a profession related to, but quite distinct from, its forebears of research and testing. While the field of evaluation has advanced considerably as a profession, it is instructive to consider this development in the context of the field in the previous period.

Before this period evaluators faced an identity crisis. They were not sure whether they should try to be researchers, testers, administrators, teachers, philosophers, or iconoclasts. It was unclear what special qualifications, if any, they should possess. There was no professional organization dedicated to evaluation as a field, nor were there specialized journals through which evaluators could exchange information about their work. There was essentially no literature about program evaluation except unpublished papers that circulated through an underground network of practitioners. There was a paucity of pre-service and inservice training opportunities in evaluation. Articulated standards of good practice were confined to educational and psychological tests. The field of evaluation was amorphous and fragmented—many evaluations were carried out by untrained personnel, others by research methodologists who tried unsuccessfully to fit their methods to program evaluations (Guba, 1966). Evaluation studies were fraught with confusion, anxiety, and animosity. Evaluation as a field had little stature and no political clout.

Against this backdrop, the progress made by educational evaluators to professionalize their field during the 1970s was quite remarkable indeed. A number of journals, including *Educational Evaluation and Policy Analysis, Studies in Educational Evaluation, CEDR Quarterly, Evaluation Review, New Directions for Program Evaluation, Evaluation and Program Planning*, and *Evaluation News* were begun; and most of these journals have proved to be excellent vehicles for recording and disseminating information about the various facets of program evaluation. Numerous books and monographs dealing exclusively with evaluation were published. The May 12th Group, Division H of AERA, the Evaluation Network, and the Evaluation Research Society came into being and afforded excellent opportunities for professional exchange among persons concerned with the evaluation of education and other human service programs.

Many universities began to offer at least one course in evaluation methodology (as distinct from research methodology); a few universities—such as the University of Illinois, Stanford University, Boston College, UCLA, the University of Minnesota, and Western Michigan University—developed graduate programs in evaluation. Nova University was perhaps the first to require an evaluation course in a doctoral program. The U.S. Office of Education sponsored a national program of inservice training in evaluation for special educators (Brinkerhoff et al., 1983), and several professional organizations offered workshops and institutes on various evaluation topics. Governmental and university centers were established for research and development related to evaluation. The state of Louisiana established a policy and program for certifying evaluators (Peck, 1981).

Increasingly, the field looked to metaevaluation (Scriven, 1975; Stufflebeam, 1978; cf. Chapter 25 for a treatment of metaevaluation) as a means of assuring and checking the quality of evaluations. A joint committee appointed by 12 professional organizations issued a comprehensive set of standards for judging evaluations of educational programs, projects, and materials (Joint Committee, 1981b), and established a mechanism (Joint Committee, 1981a) by which to review and revise the standards and assist the field to use them. These standards were revised in 1994. (Cf. Chapter 24 for an overview of these standards.) In addition, several other sets of standards with relevance for educational evaluation were issued during this period (cf. *Evaluation News*, May 1981).

During this period, evaluators increasingly realized that the techniques of evaluation must achieve results previously seen as peripheral to serious research; serve the information needs of the clients of evaluation; address the central value issues; deal with situational realities; meet the requirements of probity; and satisfy needs for veracity. While the field had yet to develop a fully functional methodology that meets all these requirements, there were during this period some promising developments, including goal-free evaluation (Scriven, 1974b; Evers, 1980); the CIPP Model (Stufflebeam, 1967, Stufflebeam et al., 1971, cf. Chapter 16); adversary/advocate teams (Stake & Gjerde, 1974; cf. Chapter 10); advocate teams (Reinhard, 1972); meta analysis (Glass, 1976; Krol, 1978); responsive evaluation (Stake, 1975b; cf. Chapter 18); and naturalistic evaluation (Guba & Lincoln, 1981; cf. Chapter 19). Under the leadership of Nick Smith (1981a; 1981b), a large number of writers examined the applicability to evaluation of a wide range of investigatory techniques drawn from a variety of fields. Eisner (1975) and his students applied the techniques used by critics in evaluating materials from the arts (cf. Chapter 12). Webster (1975) and his colleagues have operationalized Stufflebeam's CIPP model within the context of a school district. Stake (1978; cf. Chapters 18 and 11) has adapted case study methods for use in evaluation. Roth (1977; 1978), Suarez (1980), Scriven & Roth (1978), Stufflebeam (1977) and others began to make both conceptual and operational sense of' the crucial yet elusive concept of needs assessment. Personnel of the Toledo Public Schools, in collaboration with Bunda (1980) and Ridings (1980), devised catalogues of evaluative criteria and associated instruments to help teachers and administrators tailor their data collection efforts to meet their information requirements. Finally, a great deal of work was done to encourage the use of objective-referenced tests in evaluation studies (Chase, 1980; Bloom, Madaus, & Hastings, 1981; cf. Chapter 6).

This substantial professional development in evaluation produced mixed results. First, while there was undoubtedly more, and certainly better, communication in the field, there was also an enormous amount of chatter (Cronbach, 1980). Second, while progress was made in improving the training and certification of evaluators to ensure that institutions obtain services from qualified persons, some observers worried that this development could result in a narrow and exclusive club (Stake, 1981). Third, even though there was increased communication between those advocating positivistic/quantitative approaches to evaluation and proponents of phenomenological/qualitative approaches, a polarization developed between these camps. The roots of this polarization are not primarily methodological, but instead reflect ideological and epistemological differences (cf. Chapter 2). Finally, in spite of growing search for appropriate methods, increased communication and understanding among the leading methodologists, and the development of new techniques, the actual practice of evaluation changed very little in the great majority of settings.

THE AGE OF EXPANSION AND INTEGRATION 1983–2001

The final period in our abbreviated history of program evaluation begins with the publication of the first edition of this book and ends with the publication of the second edition. A lot happened in the field during these eighteen years. Despite the positive title we chose for this last period it began on somewhat of a down note as there were considerable cut backs in the funding of evaluations during the Reagan years. Many evaluations during this period were geared toward cost cutting and cost benefit issues.

As the economy grew however, evaluation as a field expanded and became considerably more integrated. The expansion is seen especially in the development of professional evaluation societies in more than twenty countries and in the coming together, communication, and collaboration of evaluators from various disciplines.

In education the reform movement has had a profound effect on program evaluation. Proposed reforms—such as charter schools, vouchers, and privatization of schools—all predicated on the belief that introducing competition into the system will lead to improvement, are currently being evaluated (Miron, 1999; Horn and Miron, 1999; Peterson, 1998; Peterson, 1996). Tennessee carried out a true experiment on reducing class size and the results have influenced policy in a number of states (cf. Chapter 8). Accountability and outcome evaluations have become commonplace across the United States (cf. Chapters 5 and 17). However, these accountability systems need to be independently evaluated as many set unrealistic improvement goals based on student test performance. The standards based reform movement has now reached 49 states. Curriculum frameworks are developed, as are tests to measure progress on reaching the standards contained in the frameworks. A number of states have linked student performance on these state level tests to graduation and retention decisions. Kentucky and Vermont have had excellent evaluations of their state testing programs, which experimented with the substitution of performance measures for the traditional multiple-choice tests. (See for example Koretz et al., 1993; Koretz, 1997; Kortez & Barron, 1998). But not all states have embraced an independent evaluation of their testing programs partly for financial reasons, partly for political reasons and partly because they do not want to hear bad news. The Ford Foundation has funded the start up of the National Board on Educational Testing and Public Policy located at Boston College. The Board's mandate is to evaluate the technical adequacy of high stakes tests used in educational policy and to monitor and evaluate the impact of such testing programs on school systems, schools, teachers and students.

The Evaluation Research Society, which was composed mainly of evaluators from the social sciences, amalgamated with the Evaluation Network, comprised mainly of educational evaluators, to form the new "ecumenical" American Evaluation Association (AEA). The result has been an integration and cross-fertilization of evaluation ideas and methods across the disciplines. This is well described in Scriven's (1994a) article on evaluation as a transdiscipline.

In addition, there has been great expansion of the professional field of evaluation. In 1995, AEA focused its convention on international cooperation in evaluation and invited evaluators from around the world to attend. The meeting was a great success and spawned a continually growing involvement of internationals in AEA's meetings and other work. Additionally, more than 20 evaluation associations have been established across the world, with a concomitant increase in evaluation journals emanating from other countries.

There has also been increased activity in the development and use of professional standards for evaluation (cf. Chapter 24). Building on *The Program Evaluation Standards*, the Joint Committee on Standards for Educational Evaluation has developed standards for personnel evaluation (Joint Committee, 1988) and at this writing is developing standards for evaluations of students, especially in classroom settings.

CONCLUSION

Evaluators need to be aware of both contemporary and historical aspects of their emerging profession, including its philosophical underpinnings and conceptual orientations. Without this background, evaluators are doomed to repeat past mistakes and, equally debilitating, will fail to sustain and build on past successes.

We have portrayed program evaluation as a dynamic, yet immature, profession. While the profession is still immature, there can be no doubt that it has become increasingly an identifiable component of the broader governmental and professional establishment of education, health, and welfare, and an international entity. The prediction commonly heard in the 1960s that formalized program evaluation was a fad and soon would disappear proved false, and there are strong indications that this field will continue to grow in importance, sophistication, and stature. The gains over the past 18 years are impressive, but there are many obvious deficiencies, and we still lack sufficient evidence about the impact of evaluations on education and human services. There is a need to improve research, training, and financial support for program evaluation. Leaders of the evaluation profession must ensure that efforts to improve their profession are geared to the service needs of their clients, not merely designed to serve their private or corporate needs. Ultimately the value of program evaluation must be judged in terms of its actual and potential contributions to improving learning, teaching and administration, health care and health, and in general the quality of life in our society and others. All of us in the program evaluation business would do well to remember and use this basic principle to guide and examine our work.

2. MODELS, METAPHORS, AND DEFINITIONS IN EVALUATION

GEORGE F. MADAUS and THOMAS KELLAGHAN

The purpose of this chapter is threefold. The first is to explain what we mean by the term evaluation models. The title for the first edition of this book used the term models because that was the term in vogue at that time to describe approaches to program evaluation. But the word "model" obviously has other connotations that we need to clarify so that the reader does not over-interpret the phrase. The second purpose is to describe how the metaphors used in talking about education, implicitly and explicitly, influence the model we consider when faced with the task of evaluating a program. (Metaphors also influence evaluations in other human services programs but here we confine ourselves to education.) The third purpose is to discuss how the conduct and nature of any evaluation is affected by how one defines the process of evaluation, in education or in human services more broadly. As we shall see, the many ways in which people define the process bear dramatic witness to the pluralistic nature of the field, as well as to deep epistemological differences that underlie the various models.

THE MEANING OF MODELS

In one sense, the core of this book presents a set of alternative evaluation models. These are not models in the sense of mathematical models used to set given theories, but they are models in the sense that each one characterizes its author's view of the main concepts and structure of evaluation work, while at the same time serving the exemplary function of providing guidelines for using these concepts to

D.L. Stufflebeam, G.F. Madaus and T. Kellaghan (eds.). EVALUATION MODELS. Copyright © 2000. Kluwer Academic Publishers. Boston. All rights reserved.

arrive at defensible descriptions, judgments, and recommendations. We are aware that some writers have urged against according alternative perspectives on evaluation the status of models. However, the alternative, that some other terminology be used, such as persuasions or beliefs, would, we believe, do little more than puzzle readers. We are comfortable in presenting the alternative conceptualizations of evaluation in the book, not as models of evaluation as it occurs, but as models for conducting studies according to the beliefs about evaluation that are held by the authors of the models. In this sense, they are idealized or "model" views of how to sort out and address problems encountered in conducting evaluations.

The *Oxford English Dictionary* (Simpson & Weiner, 1989) contains a number of definitions for the term model that coincide with the way we use the word in the phrase models of program evaluation. First, a model is a *summary, epitome, or abstract* of the way a particular evaluator conceptualizes and describes the evaluation process. Another meaning that approximates our usage is *any article made by a recognised designer, e.g., a dress or a motor car.* Each of the chapters in this volume is by a recognized designer, if you will, in the field of "models" evaluation. Still another meaning congruent with our usage is *to give shape to (a document, argument, etc.).* This is what the various models do: each gives shape to the author's way of describing and doing an evaluation. Then there is the simple definition: *to organize (a community, government, etc.).* The authors' prescriptions and advice serve to "organize" a program evaluation. Finally, there is the meaning *to train or mould (a person) to a mode of life.* Chapters in the book can be regarded as a first step in training or moulding future generations of evaluators according to particular viewpoints of what constitutes evaluation and how to go about the act of evaluating.

METAPHORS INFLUENCING EDUCATIONAL EVALUATION

The way we perceive education in general and schools in particular is greatly influenced by prevailing metaphors. Metaphors give shape to ideas and concepts; they are linguistic tools for seeing, understanding, and experiencing one kind of thing in terms of another (Lakoff & Johnson, 1980). Our metaphors and figural language influence the way we understand and talk about education; they create mind-sets and influence behavior towards school and teachers; they also influence the kinds of questions we ask about educational programs. Most importantly, in terms of this chapter, metaphors influence the way we think about and design evaluations of educational programs.

The Factory Model

Since the middle of the nineteenth century, a consistent and powerful class of defining metaphors for schooling has been that associated with factories, engineering, assembly lines, production, machines, and, more recently, technology. The metaphor of *schools as factories* emerged from a defining social movement of the early nineteenth century: industrial capitalism's developing commitment to standardization, uniformity, precision, clarity, quantification, and rational tactics. This movement began with the development of the technology of interchangeable parts by the Army Ordnance Department, and eventually spread to the manufacture of a host of mass-produced products in the twentieth century (Smith, 1987; Staudenmaier, 1985, 1989). The factory model, with its techniques of conformity and "the perpetual supervision of behavior and tasks" (Kritzman, 1990), eventually came to be held in high esteem by educational administrators. As one observer has commented, "Like the manager of a cotton mill, the superintendent of schools could supervise employees, keep the enterprise technically up to date, and monitor the uniformity and quality of the product" (Tyack, 1974, p. 41). (This description sounds like a precursor to the decision-oriented evaluation model.) Within this view of schools, standardized testing became an important technique for superintendents to monitor output and hold students and educators accountable.

The factory metaphor plays out like this:

- The curriculum is the means of production.
- The student is the raw material to be transformed into a finished and useful product.
- The teacher is a highly skilled technician.
- The outcomes of production are carefully plotted in advance according to rigorous design specifications.
- Certain means prove wasteful and are discarded in favor of more efficient ones.
- Great care is taken to see that raw materials of a particular quality or composition are channelled into the proper product system.
- No potentially useful characteristic of the raw material is wasted.
- Prospective employers are the consumers of the finished product. (Kliebard, 1972)

The factory metaphor of schooling persists to this day, not in the "dumbed down" assembly line of the past where teachers perform routine repetitive acts, but in a new kind of factory metaphor, the "high tech assembly line," where teachers troubleshoot and problem-solve (Doyle, 1991). This post-modern conceptualization can be regarded as a bow to the movement from an industrial society to that of a post-industrial, global information-based society; but the root metaphor has changed little. Not surprisingly, and rooted in the metaphor, business and commercial terms such as outputs, bottom line, deregulation, accountability, destandardization, competition, and free market forces permeate current educational reform proposals.

The factory metaphor, and its close cousin technological production, have embedded in them the mind set of instrumental rationality. This view of the world influences the way in which people who subscribe to either of these related metaphors think about social programs in general, and schools and teachers in particular. In this world view, reality is based on empirical knowledge and is governed by technical rules; we can make predictions about physical or social events; we can manipulate and control the environment; no part of the work/curriculum process is unique and each part is reproducible; everything in the curriculum can be analysed into constituent, interdependent parts; and a worker's/teacher's activity can be evaluated in quantifiable terms (Bowers, 1977; Ewert, 1991).

Such a mind set tends to view education as a means to an end, e.g., as producing an educated workforce or making the country more competitive. Further, teaching and learning are seen as means to desired ends, elements in a system that can, in principle, be controlled. In this world view, teaching is regarded as a skilled craft based on technical expertise; problems with student learning can be dealt with by applying appropriate techniques; and education can be improved by a more complete mapping of cause and effect relationships in the teaching learning process (Ewert, 1991).

Factory or technology metaphors, however, appear to fall short when we consider the reality of schools. Schools are not places where things are mass-produced; teachers are not assembly-line workers (hi-tech or otherwise), trouble-shooters, or robots; educated persons are not stamped out or assembled, and they do not come with warrantees. Books such as Tracy Kidder's *Among Schoolchildren* (1989), Philip Jackson's *Life in Classrooms* (1990), and Ted Sizer's *Horace's School* (1992) provide convincing testimony that schools are extremely complex, organic, densely-packed social systems. As one of these observers put it,

[The teacher] is engaged in a process that is qualitatively unlike the descriptions implied in learning theories and in . . . the engineering view of educational progress. . . . As typically conducted, teaching is an opportunistic process. That is to say, neither the teacher nor his students can predict with any certainty exactly what will happen next. Plans are forever going awry and unexpected opportunities for the attainment of educational goals are consistently emerging. The seasoned teacher seizes upon these opportunities and uses them to his and his student's advantage. (Jackson, 1990, p. 166)

Nonetheless, the factory metaphor continues to shape the way we think about educational programs and the way we evaluate these programs. The goal-oriented approach, which is the oldest and perhaps most widely used model of program evaluation in education (see Chapters 4 & 5, this volume), fits in this mold. It focuses on the intuitively appealing concept that the function of evaluation is to determine the extent to which an educational program has achieved predetermined goals or objectives. The experimental or field trail model for evaluation (see Chapter 8, this volume) with its randomized assignment of subjects to standard treatments to assist causal inferences about the efficacy of treatments also fits comfortably within production and technological metaphors of schooling. Various decision-oriented or management-oriented evaluation models which focus on inputs, processes, and products (see Chapters 7 & 16, this volume) also embody many of the concepts underlying the production/technological metaphors used to describe schools.

Alternatives to the Factory Model

Dissatisfaction with quantitative and mechanistic approaches to evaluation—with their emphasis on paper-and-pencil techniques to measure operationally-defined objectives and the decomposition of programs into inputs, processes, and out-comes—eventually spawned a number of new approaches which are generally referred to as naturalistic or responsive. In effect, proponents of the naturalistic approach start out from a different set of metaphors for schooling than do tradi-tionalists and would be more comfortable with other metaphors of schooling.

As an antidote to the factory metaphor, and to illustrate how an alternative metaphor would demand a different conceptualization of schooling and the evalu-ation process, we might explore the metaphor of *schooling as travel*[1]. The metaphor suggests that the curriculum is a route over which students travel; the teacher is an experienced guide and companion; each traveller will be affected differently by the journey; effects are at least as much a function of the predilections, intelligence, interests, and intent of the traveller as of the contours of the route; this variability is not only inevitable, but wondrous and desirable; no effort is made to anticipate the exact nature of the effect on the traveller, but a great effort is made to plot the route so that the journey will be as rich, as fascinating, and as memorable as pos-sible (Kliebard, 1972).

If one uses the metaphor of travel rather than that of the factory to describe education, the ways in which we think about evaluation—the questions we ask, the nature of evidence and how we gather it—change radically. For example, consider a new district-wide whole-language program, where language arts instruction is integrated into a theme-based curriculum. Among the explicitly stated program goals are improved reading and writing skills. An evaluator whose views of the educational process are strongly colored by the factory or production metaphor will focus the evaluation effort almost exclusively on the stated bottom line: Did reading and writing skills improve? He/she will strive to reach a summary judgment by first operationalizing the program goals (that is, defining the goals in measurable terms) and then measuring their degree of attainment for all students in a uniform manner. This is the goals-oriented approach to evaluation.

An evaluator who likens education to travel will adopt a different approach. Since his/her view of education celebrates the uniqueness of each individual's educational experience and recognizes the unpredictability of the effects of education, he/she will not focus the data collection and analysis on reaching a summary statistic about overall accomplishment of predetermined goals. Rather he/she will show a concern with program processes and with differential impacts on different individuals and groups of individuals. Data will be collected in an ongoing manner, perhaps through in-depth observation or interviews. Such an evaluation might, for example, report multiple indicators of multiple program effects at different sites and for different groups. It might include a detailed case study of how the program was implemented at several sites in the district, so that a reader could understand why the program did or did not work well, with what groups, and under what conditions. Such procedures characterize the naturalistic or responsive approach to evaluation (see Chapters 12, 18, 19, & 20, this volume).

Naturalistic evaluations center on activities, transactions, and effects occurring within the program rather than on program goals. Their focus is not determined in advance, as it is in goal-oriented, experimental, and certain aspects of the decision-oriented models (which have, for that reason, been termed "preordinate" models). Rather, evaluation design and focus emerge through observation of program transactions; eventually, through an iterative process, themes or issues surface that the evaluator and other interested parties agree should be addressed. Naturalistic models of evaluation develop evidence on both sides of an issue and are sensitive and responsive to different information needs and to the value positions of different audiences. They attempt to describe the characteristics and nature of engagements between program participants—students and teachers, for example. They strive to provide a rich, thick, illuminating, comprehensive, qualitative description of the program—one aimed at awakening audiences to unseen dimensions of the program. Their intent is to illuminate and clarify what is actually going on, so that program participants can discern and reflect on what they are doing (Denny, 1978; Eisner, 1983, 1991).

Methods employed by naturalistic evaluators differ from the quantitative, statistical methods typically used in preordinate evaluations. Naturalistic evaluators use techniques that have long been associated with disciplines such as anthropology: long-term, direct observation; open-ended interviews; document or artefact analysis; and in-depth case studies. Indirect paper-and-pencil data collection is not taboo, and might be employed to confirm conclusions drawn from qualitative data.

Ways of Knowing

The following two quotations, neither from the world of formal evaluation or philosophy, may help illustrate the deep-seated nature of contrasting worldviews on what is important to know. The first from the writings of Romano Guardini is general in nature. He points out that:

> ... there are two ways of knowing. The one sinks into a thing and its context. The aim is to penetrate, to move within, to live with. The other, however, unpacks, tears apart, arranges in compartments, takes over and rules. ... [this] knowledge does not inspect; it analyzes. It does not construct a picture of the world, but a formula. Its desire is to achieve power so as to bring force to bear on things, a law that can be formulated rationally. ... the first way of ruling began with investigation, then noted connections, unleashed forces, realized possibilities, emphasized what it desired, and, stressing this, repressed other things. It was a knowing, validating, stimulating, directing, and underlining of natural forces and relations. (Guardini, 1994, pp. 43–45)

The second excerpt is from the world of ethnomusicology and is more specific and poignant. The folk song collector A. L. Lloyd offers this description of conflicting worldviews:

> One afternoon in a sombre room of the Ethnographical Museum of Budapest a well-known folklorist . . . played his visitor a recording of a Csango-Magyar ballad singer from Moldavia.

Her song was tragic and she performed it with a fine contained passion, in a way that showed she was totally immersed in the sense of the song. The visitor remarked on the poignant quality of the rendition and the learned professor gave him a sharp look and said: "Surely by now you know that the sound of folkmusic is meaningless? It's not until we have it down in precise notation and can see what's happening inside the mould of the melody that it comes to have any significance at all." For him, what the song meant to the singer was irrelevant; that it brought her almost to tears was a detail not worth inquiring into; the woman was a mere accessory and her heart, mind, voice were superfluities, unnecessary to take into account; pitch and duration were all that mattered. He was a good man for Kelvin's principle: What we measure can be understood. (Lloyd, 1967, p. 17)

Which Model Should We Choose?

The moral in the examples we considered is that one should carefully consider the implications of using a particular metaphor in talking about schooling since it will affect how one considers evaluation. This can be difficult since our metaphors are often not explicit but are embedded deep within our consciousness. Nevertheless, it is worth the effort to examine the language one uses for linguistic traps when one talks about educational programs.

Which model then should we choose for the evaluation of our education projects? The emphatic answer is, "None of the above; that's the wrong question to ask." Rather than starting from a pet approach, we should begin with a consideration of the evaluation questions that could be addressed, the issues that must be addressed, and the available resources. Each evaluation approach has its particular strengths that can help illuminate different aspects of a program. Within the limitations of the budget, pick and choose features from various models that can provide the best evidence to answer questions about the project. For example, consider combining test data from a goals-oriented approach, resource allocation data from the decision-oriented approach, and observational and interview data from the naturalistic approach.

Such eclecticism can be seen in the musical analogy of schools or classrooms as a maqam which in music [substitute teaching] is:

. . . a kind of skeleton or, better, scaffolding of melody which the musician [teacher] observing certain rules, is able to fill in for [him/herself] according to [his/her] fantasy and the mood of the moment. For westerners, the clearest, most familiar example of the maqam principal is provided by the Blues, always the same yet always different, a well-known, well-worn frame apt for any extemporization . . . unfixed by print or other control, nourished by constant variation, having no single "authentic" form but somewhat altering from singer to singer [teacher to teacher] and even from verse to verse [lesson to lesson or pupil to pupil] are made on the maqam principle, with its balance of constraint with freedom, fixed model with fluid treatment, communal taste with individual fantasy, traditional constancy with novel creative moments, sameness with difference. (Lloyd, 1967, p. 63)

Only an evaluation drawing on the best from various models can document the effects of the complexity of the teaching maquim: constraint with freedom, communal taste with individual fantasy, fixed model with fluid treatment, traditional constancy with novel creative moments, sameness with difference.

DEFINITIONS OF EVALUATION

We now present a collection of definitions of program evaluation culled from the writings of evaluation theorists and practitioners, past and present. The definitions are grouped under the model name or evaluation approach from which they came. The range of definitions is meant to show the diversity of ideas within the field on the fundamental concept of what constitutes "program evaluation." It is not meant to be inclusive or definitive and, despite the fact that there are numerous definitions, in the interest of space only one definition in each category is offered. This is not to imply that it is necessarily the best definition for that category, but it is representative. The definitions run the gamut of viewpoints from:

- modernity to post-modernity
- rationalistic to naturalistic
- elementistic/reductionist to holistic
- meta-narratives to no such thing as meta-narratives
- prediction to illumination
- knowing to feeling
- control to empowerment
- knowledge producing to experience producing
- evaluative inquiry to evaluative technology
- measurement/quantification to qualitative description
- proof to persuasion
- evaluator makes judgement of merit or worth to client makes such judgements

The definitions reveal the range of epistemological and ideological positions that exist among theorists on the nature of evaluation, how to conduct one, and how to present and use results. These positions are analogous to the range of theological and doctrinal positions that characterize Christianity and split the field into competing major denominations and minor sects. While we will not comment individually on the definitions, the reader is invited to think about the underlying world-view contained in each definition, the prevailing metaphor(s) for human services or education that the theorist might implicitly embrace, what does the definition reveal about the probable techniques that would be used in the conduct of the evaluation, what kinds of evidence would be valued or denigrated, and what uses might be made of the evaluation findings?

Objective/Goals-Based

Goal-Achievement Model (of evaluation). The idea that merit of the program (or person) is to be equated with success in achieving a stated goal.

   Goal-Based Evaluation (GBE) is based and focused on knowledge of the goals and objectives of the program, person or product. (Scriven, 1980a, p. 59)

Experimental/Field Trials

In its simplest form, the experimental method may be characterized as a three-stage process. Initially, two groups of people . . . are drawn at random from a single, well-defined popula tion. Then, one group is administered the treatment (program) of interest while the second group is not. . . . Finally, measurements are made to determine how some relevant aspects of behavior following treatment differ from that of the non-treated or comparison group. (Airasian, 1983, p. 166)

Decision Oriented

Decision-oriented educational research (DOER) is designed to help educators as they consider issues surrounding educational policy, as they establish priorities for improving educational systems, or as they engage in the day-to-day management of educational systems.

DOER is not designed to clarify or defend particular theoretical notions but, rather, is a very applied research designed to inform the day-to-day guidance of educational systems. It does involve what the verb "research" implies: "to search or investigate exhaustively," but it is not what is generally considered to be scientific research. (Cooley & Bickell, 1986, pp. 3 & 13)

Consumer Oriented

The purpose of a consumer study is to judge the relative merits of alternative educational goods and services and, thereby, to help taxpayers and practitioners to make wise choices in their purchase of those goods and services. (Stufflebeam & Webster, 1983, pp. 33–34)

Cost-Based Evaluation

A Cost Feasibility Analysis informs decision makers of the resources necessary for implementation and continued operation of a particular program. The relevant question addressed in a cost-feasibility analysis is "Can we afford to implement and operate this particular program?" Estimating cost to determine the cost feasibility of a program is an essential step in deciding whether the initiative is a reasonable alternative to consider given the resource base of the community.

Cost-Effectiveness Analysis is the systematic process of integrating information on the costs and effects of various alternatives to identify the option that most efficiently utilizes limited resources to produce a particular outcome or set of outcomes. This type of analysis answers the question: "Should we support one program rather than another?"

Cost-Benefit Analysis can be conducted for a single program to provide information on the degree to which an intervention is worth the investment. Here the relevant question is: "To what degree do the benefits of this program outweigh the costs?" Using this approach, costs and benefits are presented in monetary units, and are combined in a cost-benefit ration. If benefits outweigh costs (cost-benefit ratio is less than one), the program is economically desirable. If costs outweigh benefits (ratio is greater than one), the program is not economically desirable (Rice, 1997, pp. 309 & 310).

Legal Model

Based on the evidence presented, the panel deliberates and makes it recommendations. (Wolf, 1983, p. 194)

Management Theory Based

The "Balanced Scorecard" for motivating and measuring business and performance [embodies] four perspectives—financial, customer, internal business processes, and learning and growth—[to] provide a balanced picture of current operating performance as well as the drivers of future performance. . . . The Balanced Scorecard provides executives with a comprehensive framework that can translate a company's vision and strategy into a coherent and linked set of performance measures. The measures should include both outcome measures and the performance drivers of those outcomes. By articulating the outcomes the organization desires as well as the drivers of those outcomes, senior executives can channel the energies, the abilities, and the specific knowledge held by people throughout the organization towards achieving the business's long-term goals. (Kaplan & Norton, 1996, pp. 1, 3 & 4)

Internal Evaluation

Internal evaluation is characterized by the use of internal staff or of contractors closely bound to an organization to conduct evaluation activities. The usual focus of internal evaluation is programs or problems of direct relevance to the organisation's internal management. In contrast to external evaluations, those responsible for internal evaluations are often charged with remedying problems, not only with diagnosing them and developing recommendations. (Love, 1983, p. 1)

External Evaluation

An external evaluator is someone who is at least not on the project or program regular staff. . . . It is better if they are not even paid by the project or by any entity with a prior preference for the success or failure of the project. Where or to whom the external evaluator reports is what determines whether the evaluation is formative or summative, either of which may be done by external or by internal evaluators . . . and both of which should be done by both. (Scriven, 1980a, pp. 70 & 54)

Formative/Summative Evaluation

Formative evaluation is conducted *during* the development or improvement of a program or product (or person, etc.). It is an evaluation which is conducted *for* the in-house staff of the program and normally remains in-house; but it may be *done by* an internal *or* an external evaluator or (preferably) a combination. The distinction between formative and summative has been well summed up in a sentence of Bob Stake: "When the cook tastes the soup, that's formative; when the guests taste the soup, that's summative."

Summative evaluation of a program is conducted *after* completion and *for* the benefit of some *external* audience or decision-maker (e.g., funding agency, or future possible users), though it may be *carried out* by either internal or external evaluators or both. For reasons of credibility, it is much more likely to involve external evaluators than is a formative evaluation. (Scriven, 1980a, p. 129–30)

Social Science Theory Based

The concept of grounding evaluation in theories of change takes for granted that social programs are based on explicit or implicit theories of change and about how and why the program will work. . . . The evaluation should surface those theories and lay them out in as fine detail as possible, identifying all the assumptions and sub-assumptions built into the program. The evaluators then construct methods for data collection and analysis to track the unfolding of the assumptions. The aim is to examine the extent to which program theories hold. The evaluation should show which of the assumptions underlying the program break down, where they break down, and which of the several theories are best supported by the evidence. (Weiss, 1995, pp. 66–67)

Merit Oriented

Evaluation is the systematic and objective determination of the worth or merit of an object.

Merit: The excellence of an object as assessed by its intrinsic qualities or performance.

Worth: The value of an object in relationship to a purpose. (Joint Committee, 1994, pp. 205, 207 & 210).

Responsive

An educational evaluation is responsive if it orients more directly to program activities than to program intents, if it responds to audience requirements for information, and if the different value perspectives of people are referred to in reporting the success and failure of the program. (Stake, 1983, p. 292)

Inquiry Oriented

Investigative journalism is journalism focused on processes that requires the exposure or explication of elements or aspects that are wholly or partly secret, less accessible, less observable, or more logistically burdensome to ferret out, that seeks to redress imbalance inimical to the public interest, and that results from the personal efforts of the journalists involved. (Guba, 1981b, p. 183)

Empowerment Evaluation

Empowerment evaluation is the use of evaluation concepts, techniques, and findings to foster improvement and self-determination. It employs both qualitative and quantitative methodologies.

Empowerment evaluation has an unambiguous value orientation—it is designed to help people help themselves and improve their programs using a form of self-evaluation and reflection.

Empowerment evaluation is necessarily a collaborative group activity, not an individual pursuit. (Fetterman, 1996, p. 4–5)

Naturalistic Evaluation

Naturalistic (evaluation or methodology) is an approach which minimizes much of the paraphernalia of science e.g. technical jargon, prior technical knowledge, statistical inference, the effort to formulate general laws, the separation of the observer from the subject, the commitment to a single correct perspective, theoretical structures, causes, predictions and prepositional knowledge. Instead there is a focus on the use of metaphor, analogy, informal (but valid) inference, vividness of description, reasons, explanations, inter-activeness, meanings, multiple (legitimate) perspectives, tacit knowledge. (Scriven, 1980a, p. 59)

The Critic/The Connoisseur

I conceive the major contribution of evaluation to be a heightened awareness of the qualities of classroom life so that teachers and students can become more intelligent within it. Connoisseurship plays an important role towards this end by refining the levels of apprehension of the qualities that pervade classrooms. To be a connoisseur of wine, bicycles, or graphic arts is to be informed about their qualities; it means being able to discriminate the subtleties among types of wine, bicycles, and graphic arts by drawing upon a gustatory, visual, and kinaesthetic memory against which the particulars of the present may be placed for purposes of comparison and contrast. Connoisseurs of anything—and one can have connoisseurship about anything—*appreciate* what they encounter in the proper meaning of that word. Appreciation does not necessarily mean liking something, although one might like what one experiences. Appreciation here means an awareness and an understanding of what one has experienced. Such an awareness provides the basis for judgment.

If connoisseurship is the art of appreciation, criticism is the art of disclosure. Criticism, as Dewey pointed out in *Art as Experience*, has at its end the re-education of perception. What the critic strives for is to articulate or render those ineffable qualities constituting art in a language that makes them vivid. (Eisner, 1983, pp. 339–40)

Expository Storytelling

Portraiture is a genre whose methods are shaped by empirical and aesthetic dimensions, whose descriptions are often penetrating and personal, whose goals include generous and tough scrutiny. It is a sensitive kind of work that requires the perceptivity and skill of a practiced observer and the empathy and care of a clinician. (Lightfoot, 1983, p. 369)

Illuminative Evaluation

The primary concern of illuminative evaluation is with the description and interpretation rather than measurement and prediction. Its aims are to study the innovatory program: how it operates; how it is influenced by the various school situations in which it is applied; whose those directly concerned regard as its advantages and disadvantages; and how students' intellectual tasks and academic experiences are most affected. It aims to discover and document what it is like to be participating in the scheme, whether as a teacher or pupil; and, in addition, to discern and discuss the innovation's most significant features, recurring concomitants and critical processes. (Parlett & Hamilton, 1977, p. 10)

Evaluation As Persuasion

Evaluation
Is an act of persuasion
Persuades rather than convinces
Argues rather than demonstrates
Is credible rather than certain
Is variably accepted rather than compelling
Is less certain, more particularized. (House, 1983, pp. 45–64)

NOTE

1. Two other metaphors that underlie some views of the educational process are *gardening* and *medicine*. If schools are gardens, then teachers are gardeners, whose job it is to nurture each individual

student/plant by giving it individualized care (that is, the right amount of water, appropriately timed pruning, staking if necessary) and ensuring that it enjoys ideal conditions (sunlight, proper soil acidity) so that it can bloom and thrive (Kliebard, 1972). In marked contrast is the medical metaphor, in which the teacher/doctor diagnoses what is wrong with the student/patient, and prescribes remedying treatment/instruction. The medical metaphor, like the factory one subscribes to the concept of instrumental rationality.

3. FOUNDATIONAL MODELS FOR 21st CENTURY PROGRAM EVALUATION*

DANIEL L. STUFFLEBEAM

INTRODUCTION

Evaluators today have available many more evaluation approaches than in 1960. As they address the challenges of the 21st century, it is an opportune time to consider what 20th century evaluation developments are valuable for future use and which ones would best be left behind. I have, in this chapter, attempted to sort 22 alternative evaluation approaches into what fishermen sometimes call the "keepers" and the "throwbacks." More importantly, I have characterized each approach; assessed its strengths and weaknesses; and considered whether, when, and how it is best applied. The reviewed approaches emerged mainly in the U.S. between 1960 and 1999.

20th Century Expansion of Program Evaluation Approaches

Following a period of relative inactivity in the 1950s, a succession of international and national forces stimulated the expansion and development of evaluation theory and practice. The main influences were the efforts to vastly strengthen the U.S. defense system spawned by the Soviet Union's 1957 launching of Sputnik I; the new U.S. laws in the 1960s to equitably serve minorities and persons with disabilities; Federal government evaluation requirements of the Great Society programs initiated in 1965; the U.S. movement begun in the 1970s to hold educational and social organizations accountable for both prudent use of resources and achievement

* This chapter is a condensed version of a manuscript prepared for the Western Michigan University Evaluation Center's Occasional Papers Series.

of objectives; the stress on excellence in the 1980s as a means of increasing U.S. international competitiveness; and the trend in the 1990s for various organizations, both inside and outside the U.S., to employ evaluation to ensure quality, competitiveness, and equity in delivering services. In pursuing reforms, American society has repeatedly pressed schools and colleges, health-care organizations, and various social welfare enterprises to show through evaluation whether or not services and improvement efforts were succeeding.

The development of program evaluation as a field of professional practice was also spurred by a number of seminal writings. These included, in chronological order, publications by Tyler (1942b, 1950, 1966), Campbell and Stanley (1963), Cronbach (1963), Stufflebeam (1966, 1967), Scriven (1967), Stake (1967), Suchman (1967), Alkin (1969), Guba (1969), Provus (1969), Stufflebeam et al. (1971), Parlett and Hamilton (1972), Weiss (1972), Eisner (1975), Glass (1975), Cronbach and Associates (1980), House (1980), and Patton (1980). These and other authors/scholars began to project alternative approaches to program evaluation. Over the years, a rich literature on a wide variety of alternative program evaluation approaches developed (see, for example, Cronbach [1982]; Guba and Lincoln [1981, 1989]; Nave, Miech, and Mosteller [1999], Nevo [1993]; Patton [1982, 1990, 1994, 1997]; Rossi and Freeman [1993]; Schwandt [1984]; Scriven [1991, 1993, 1994a, 1994b, 1994c]; Shadish, Cook, and Leviton [1991]; Smith, M. F. [1989]; Smith, N. L. [1987]; Stake [1975b, 1988, 1995]; Stufflebeam [1997]; Stufflebeam and Shinkfield [1985]; Wholey, Hatry, and Newcomer [1995]; Worthen and Sanders [1987, 1997]).

Evaluation Models And Approaches

The chapter uses the term *evaluation approach* rather than *evaluation model* because, for one reason, the former is broad enough to cover illicit as well as laudatory practices. Also, beyond covering both creditable and noncreditable approaches, some authors of evaluation approaches say that the term *model* is too demanding to cover their published ideas about how to conduct program evaluations. But for these two considerations, the term *model* would have been used to encompass most of the evaluation proposals discussed in this chapter. This is so because most of the presented approaches are idealized or "model" views for conducting program evaluations according to their authors' beliefs and experiences.

Need to Study Alternative Approaches

The study of alternative evaluation approaches is important for professionalizing program evaluation and for its scientific advancement and operation. Professionally, careful study of program evaluation approaches can help evaluators legitimize approaches that comform with sound principles of evaluation and discredit those that do not. Scientifically, such a review can help evaluation researchers identify, examine, and address conceptual and technical issues pertaining to the development of the evaluation discipline. Operationally, a critical view of alternatives can help evaluators consider, assess, and selectively apply optional evaluation frameworks. The review also provides substance for evaluation training. The main values in studying alternative program evaluation approaches are to discover their strengths and weaknesses, decide which ones merit substantial use, determine when and how they are best applied, and obtain direction for improving these approaches and devising better alternatives.

The Nature of Program Evaluation

The chapter employs a broad view of program evaluation. It encompasses assessments of any coordinated set of activities directed at achieving goals. Examples are assessments of ongoing, cyclical programs, such as school curricula, food stamps, housing for the homeless, and annual influenza inoculations; time-bounded projects, such as development and dissemination of a fire prevention guide; and national, regional, or state systems of services, such as those provided by regional educational service agencies. Such program evaluations both overlap with and yet are distinguishable from other forms of evaluation, especially evaluations of students, personnel, materials, and institutions.

Previous Classifications Of Alternative Evaluation Approaches

In analyzing the 22 evaluation approaches, prior assessments regarding program evaluation's state of the art were consulted. Stake's (1974) analysis of nine program evaluation approaches provided a useful application of advance organizers (the types of variables used to determine information requirements) for ascertaining different types of program evaluations. Hastings' (1976) review of the growth of evaluation theory and practice helped to place the evaluation field in a historical perspective. Guba's (1976) presentation and assessment of six major philosophies in evaluation was provocative. House's (1983) analysis of approaches illuminated important philosophical and theoretical distinctions. Scriven's (1991, 1994a) writings on the transdiscipline of evaluation helped to sort out different evaluation approaches; it was also invaluable in seeing the approaches in the broader context of evaluations focused on various objects other than programs. The book *Evaluation Models* (Madaus, Scriven, & Stufflebeam, 1983) provided a previous inventory and analysis of evaluation models. All of the assessments helped sharpen the issues addressed.

Program Evaluation Defined

In characterizing and assessing evaluation approaches, the various kinds of activities conducted in the name of program evaluation were classified on the basis of their degree of conformity to a particular definition of evaluation. In this chapter, evaluation means *a study designed and conducted to assist some audience to assess an object's merit and worth*. This definition should be widely acceptable as it agrees with common dictionary definitions of evaluation; it is also consistent with the definition that underlies published sets of professional standards for evaluations (Joint Committee on Standards for Educational Evaluation, 1981b, 1994). However, it will become apparent that many studies done in the name of program evaluation either do not conform to this definition or directly oppose it.

Classification and Analysis of the 22 Approaches

Using the above definition of evaluation, program evaluation approaches were classified into four categories. The first category includes approaches that promote invalid or incomplete findings (referred to as pseudoevaluations), while the other three include approaches that agree, more or less, with the definition (i.e., Questions/Methods-Oriented, Improvement/ Accountability, and Social Agenda/Advocacy). Of the 22 program evaluation approaches that are described, two are classified as pseudoevaluations, thirteen as questions/methods-oriented approaches, three as improvement/accountability-oriented approaches, and four as social agenda/ advocacy-directed approaches.

Each approach is analyzed in terms of ten descriptors: (1) advance organizers, that is, the main cues that evaluators use to set up a study; (2) main purpose(s) served; (3) sources of questions addressed; (4) questions that are characteristic of each study type; (5) methods typically employed; (6) persons who pioneered in conceptualizing each study type; (7) other persons who have extended development and use of each study type; (8) key considerations in determining when to use each approach; (9) strengths of the approach; and (10) weaknesses of the approach. Using these descriptors, comments on each of the 22 program evaluation approaches are presented. These assessments are then used to reach conclusions about which approaches should be avoided, which are most meritorious, and under what circumstances the worthy approaches are best applied.

Caveats

I acknowledge, without apology, that the assessments of approaches and the entries in the summary chart in this chapter are based on my best judgments. I have taken no poll, and no definitive research exists, to represent a consensus on the characteristics and strengths and weaknesses of the different approaches. My analyses reflect 35 years of experience in applying and studying different evaluation approaches. Hopefully, these will be useful to evaluators and evaluation students at least in the form of working hypotheses to be tested.

I have mainly looked at the approaches as relatively discrete ways to conduct evaluations. In reality, there are many occasions when it is functional to mix and match different approaches. A careful analysis of such combinatorial applications no doubt would produce several hybrid approaches that might merit examination. That analysis is beyond the scope of this chapter.

PSEUDOEVALUATIONS

Because this chapter is focused on describing and assessing the state of the art in evaluation, it is necessary to discuss bad and questionable practices, as well as the best efforts. Evaluators and their clients are sometimes tempted to shade, selectively release, or even falsify findings. While such efforts might look like sound evaluations, they are aptly termed pseudoevaluations if they fail to produce and report to all right-to-know audiences valid assessments of merit and worth.

Pseudoevaluations often are motivated by political objectives. For example, persons holding or seeking authority may present unwarranted claims about their achievements and/or the faults of their opponents, or hide potentially damaging information. These objectionable approaches are presented because they deceive through evaluation and can be used by those in power to mislead constituents or to gain and maintain an unfair advantage over others, especially persons with little power. If evaluators acquiesce to and support pseudoevaluations, they help promote and support injustice, mislead decision making, lower confidence in evaluation services, and discredit the evaluation profession.

Approach 1: Public Relations-Inspired Studies

The public relations approach begins with an intention to use data to convince constituents that a program is sound and effective. Other labels for the approach are "ideological marketing" (see Ferguson, June 1999), advertising, and infomercial. The public relations approach may meet the standard for addressing all right-to-know audiences but fails as a legitimate evaluation approach, because typically it presents a program's strengths or an exaggerated view of them but not its weaknesses.

The advance organizer is the propagandist's information needs. The study's purpose is to help the program director/public relations official project a convincing, positive public image for a program. The guiding questions are derived from the public relations specialists' and administrators' conceptions of which questions constituents would find most interesting. In general, the public relations study seeks information that would most help an organization confirm its claims of excellence and secure public support. From the start, this type of study seeks not a valid assessment of merit and worth but information to help the program "put its best foot forward." Such studies avoid gathering or releasing negative findings.

Typical methods used in public relations studies are biased surveys; inappropriate use of norms tables; biased selection of testimonials and anecdotes; "massaging" of obtained information; selective release of only the positive findings; reporting central tendency, but not variation; cover-up of embarrassing incidents; and the use of "expert" advocate consultants. In contrast to the "critical friends" employed in Australian evaluations, public relations studies use "friendly critics." A pervasive characteristic of the public relations evaluator's use of dubious methods is a biased attempt to nurture a good picture for a program. The fatal flaw of built-in bias to report only good things offsets any virtues of this approach. If an organization substitutes biased reporting of only positive findings for balanced evaluations of strengths and weaknesses, it soon will demoralize evaluators who are trying to conduct and report valid evaluations and may discredit its overall practice of evaluation.

By disseminating only positive information on a program's performance while withholding information on shortcomings and problems, evaluators and clients may mislead taxpayers, constituents, and other stakeholders concerning the program's true value. The possibility of such positive bias in advocacy evaluations underlies the long-standing policy of Consumers Union not to include advertising by the owners of the products and services being evaluated in its *Consumer Reports* magazine. To maintain credibility with consumers, Consumers Union has, for the most part, maintained an independent perspective and a commitment to identify and report both strengths and weaknesses in the items evaluated and not to supplement this information with biased ads. (An exception is that the magazine advertizes its own supplementary publications and services.)

A contact with an urban school district illustrates the public relations type of study. A superintendent requested a community survey for his district. The superintendent said, straightforwardly, that he wanted a survey that would yield a positive report on the district's performance and his leadership. He said such a positive report was desperately needed at the time to restore the confidence of the community in the school district and in him. The superintendent did not get the survey and positive report, and it soon became clear why he thought one was needed. Several weeks after making the request, he was summarily fired. Another example occurred when a large urban school district used one set of national norms to interpret pretest results and another norms table for the posttest. The result was a spurious portrayal and wrong conclusion that the students' test performance had substantially improved between the first and second test administrations.

Evaluators need to be cautious in how they relate to the public relations activities of their sponsors, clients, and supervisors. Certainly, public relations documents will reference information from sound evaluations. Evaluators should persuade their audiences to make honest use of the evaluation findings. Evaluators should not be party to misuses, especially in cases where erroneous reports are issued that predictably will mislead readers to believe that a seriously flawed program is effective. As one safeguard, evaluators can promote and help their clients arrange to have independent metaevaluators examine the organization's production and use of evaluation findings against professional standards for evaluations.

Approach 2: Politically Controlled Studies

The politically controlled study is an approach that can be either defensible or indefensible. A politically controlled study is illicit if the evaluator and/or client (a) withhold the full set of evaluation findings from audiences who have express, legitimate, and legal rights to see the findings; (b) abrogate their prior agreement to fully disclose the evaluation findings; or (c) bias the evaluation message by releasing only part of the findings. It is not legitimate for a client first to agree to make the findings of a commissioned evaluation publicly available and then, having previewed the results, to release none or only part of the findings. If and when a client or evaluator violates the formal written agreement on disseminating findings or applicable law, then the other party has a right to take appropriate actions and/or seek an administrative or legal remedy.

Clients sometimes can legitimately commission covert studies and keep the findings private, while meeting applicable laws and adhering to an appropriate advance agreement with the evaluator. This can be the case in the U.S. for private organizations not governed by public disclosure laws. Furthermore, an evaluator, under legal contractual agreements, can plan, conduct, and report an evaluation for private purposes, while not disclosing the findings to any outside party. The key to keeping client-controlled studies in legitimate territory is to reach appropriate, legally defensible, advance, written agreements and to adhere to the contractual provisions concerning release of the study's findings. Such studies also have to conform to applicable laws on release of information.

The advance organizers for a politically controlled study include implicit or explicit threats faced by the client for a program evaluation and/or objectives for winning political contests. The client's purpose in commissioning such a study is to secure assistance in acquiring, maintaining, or increasing influence, power, and/or money. The questions addressed are those of interest to the client and special groups that share the client's interests and aims. The main questions of interest to the client are: What is the truth, as best can be determined, surrounding a particular dispute or political situation? What information would be advantageous in a potential conflict situation? What data might be used advantageously in a confrontation? Typical methods of conducting the politically controlled study include covert investigations, simulation studies, private polls, private information files, and selective release of findings. Generally, the client wants information that is as technically sound as possible. However, he or she may also want to withhold findings that do not support his or her position. The strength of the approach is that it stresses the need for accurate information. However, because the client might release information selectively to create or sustain an erroneous picture of a program's merit and worth, might distort or misrepresent the findings, might violate a prior agreement to fully release findings, or might violate a "public's right to know" law, this type of study can degenerate into a pseudoevaluation.

A superintendent of one of the nation's largest public school districts once confided that he possessed an extensive notebook of detailed information about each school building in his district. The information related to student achievement, teacher qualifications, racial mix of teachers and students, average per-pupil expenditure, socioeconomic characteristics of the student body, teachers' average length of tenure in the system, and so forth. The data revealed a highly segregated district with uneven distribution of resources and markedly different achievement levels across schools. When asked why all the notebook's entries were in pencil, the superintendent replied that it was absolutely essential that he be kept informed about the current situation in each school, but that it was also imperative that the community-at-large, the board, and special interest groups in the community, not have access to the information, for any of these groups might point to the district's inequities as a basis for protest and even removing the superintendent. Hence, one special assistant kept the document up-to-date, only one copy existed, and the superintendent kept that locked in his desk. The point of this example is not to negatively judge the superintendent's behavior. However, the superintendent's ongoing covert investigation and selective release of information was decidedly not a case of true evaluation, for what he disclosed to the right-to-know audiences did not fully and honestly inform them about the observed situation in the district. This example may appropriately be termed a pseudoevaluation because it both underinformed and misinformed the school district's stakeholders.

Still another example was seen when an evaluator gave her superintendent a sound program evaluation report, showing both strengths and weaknesses of the targeted program. The evaluator was surprised and dismayed one week later when the superintendent released to the public a revised version showing only the program's strengths.

Cases like these undoubtedly led to the federal and state sunshine laws in the United States. Under current U.S. and state freedom of information provisions, most information obtained through the use of public funds must be made available to interested and potentially affected citizens. Thus, there exist legal deterrents to and remedies for illicit, politically controlled evaluations that use public funds.

While it would be unrealistic to recommend that administrators and other evaluation users not obtain and selectively employ information for political gain, evaluators should not lend their names and endorsements to evaluations presented by their clients that misrepresent the full set of relevant findings, that present falsified reports aimed at winning political contests, or that violate applicable laws and/or prior formal agreements on release of findings. Despite these warnings, it can be legitimate for evaluators to give private evaluative feedback to clients, provided they conform with applicable laws, statutes, and policies, and sound contractual agreements on release of findings are reached and honored.

QUESTIONS/METHODS-ORIENTED EVALUATION APPROACHES (QUASI-EVALUATION STUDIES)

Questions/methods-oriented program evaluation approaches (1) address specified questions, answers to which may or may not be sufficient to assess a program's merit and worth and/or (2) use some preferred method(s). Whether the questions and methodology are appropriate for developing and supporting value claims is a secondary consideration. These approaches may employ as their starting points operational objectives, standardized measurement devices, cost-analysis procedures, expert judgment, a theory or model of a program, case study procedures, management information systems, designs for controlled experiments, and/or an overriding commitment to employ a mixture of qualitative and quantitative methods. Most emphasize technical quality and posit that it is usually better to answer a few pointed questions well than to attempt a broad assessment of something's merit and worth.

These studies can be called quasi-evaluation studies, because sometimes they happen to provide evidence that fully assesses a program's merit and worth, while in other cases, their focus is too narrow or is only tangential to questions of merit and worth. While the approaches are typically labeled as evaluations, they may or may not meet the requirements of a sound evaluation. Quasi-evaluation studies have legitimate uses apart from their relationship to program evaluation, since they can investigate important though narrow questions. The main caution is that these types of studies not be uncritically equated to evaluation.

Approach 3: Objectives-Based Studies

The objectives-based study is the classic example of a questions/methods-oriented evaluation approach. Stufflebeam and Madaus (1988) provided a comprehensive look at this approach by publishing an edited volume of the classical writings of Ralph W. Tyler. In this approach, some statement of objectives provides the advance organizer. The objectives may be mandated by the client, formulated by the evaluator, or specified by the service providers. The usual purpose of an objectives-based study is to determine whether the program's objectives have been achieved. Typical audiences are program developers, sponsors, and managers who want to know the extent to which each stated objective was achieved.

The methods used in objectives-based studies essentially involve specifying operational objectives and collecting and analyzing pertinent information to determine how well each objective was achieved. A wide range of objective and performance assessments may be employed. Criterion-referenced tests are especially relevant to this evaluation approach.

Ralph Tyler is generally acknowledged to be the pioneer in the objectives-based type of study, although Percy Bridgman and E. L. Thorndike should also be credited (Travers, 1977). Many people have furthered Tyler's seminal contribution by developing variations of his evaluation model. These include Bloom et al. (1956), Hammond (1972), Metfessel and Michael (1967), Popham (1969), Provus (1971), and Steinmetz (1983).

The objectives-based approach is especially applicable in assessing tightly focused projects that have clear, supportable objectives. Even then, such studies can be strengthened by judging project objectives against the intended beneficiaries' assessed needs, searching for side effects, and studying the process as well as the outcomes.

The objectives-based study has been the most prevalent approach in program evaluation. It has common-sense appeal; program administrators have had a great amount of experience with it; and it makes use of technologies of behavioral objectives and both norm-referenced and criterion-referenced testing. Common criticisms are that such studies lead to terminal information that is of little use in improving a program or other enterprise; that the information often is far too narrow to constitute a sufficient basis for judging the object's merit and worth; that the studies do not uncover positive and negative side effects; and that they may credit unworthy objectives.

Approach 4: Accountability, Particularly Payment By Results Studies

The accountability study became prominent in the early 1970s. It emerged because of widespread disenchantment with the persistent stream of evaluation reports indicating that almost none of the massive state and federal investments in educational and social programs were making any positive, statistically discernable differences. One proposed solution posited that accountability systems could be initiated to ensure both that service providers would fulfill their responsibilities to improve services and that evaluators would find the programs' effects and determine which persons and groups were succeeding and which were not.

The advance organizers for the accountability study are the persons and groups responsible for producing results, the service providers' work responsibilities, and the expected outcomes. The study's purposes are to provide constituents with an accurate accounting of results; ensure, though something akin to intimidation, that the results are primarily positive; and pinpoint responsibility for good and bad outcomes. Sometimes accountability programs administer sanctions to the responsible service providers, depending on the extent and quality of their services and achievement.

Accountability questions come from the program's constituents and controllers, such as taxpayers; parent groups; school boards; and local, state, and national funding organizations. Their main question concerns whether each involved service provider and organization charged with responsibility for delivering and improving services is carrying out its assignments and achieving all it should, given the resources invested to support the work.

A wide variety of methods have been used to ensure and assess accountability. These include performance contracting; Program Planning and Budgeting Systems (PPBS); Management by Objectives (MBO); Zero Based Budgeting; mandated "program drivers" and indicators; program input, process, output databases; independent goal achievement auditors; procedural compliance audits; peer reviews; merit pay for individuals and/or organizations; collective bargaining agreements; mandated testing programs; institutional report cards/profiles; self-studies; site visits by expert panels; and procedures for auditing the design, process, and results of self-studies. Also included are mandated goals and standards, decentralization and careful definition of responsibility and authority, payment by results, awards and recognition, sanctions, takeover/intervention authority by oversight bodies, and competitive bidding.

Lessinger (1970) is generally acknowledged as a pioneer in the area of accountability. Among those who have extended Lessinger's work are Stenner and Webster (1971), in their development of a handbook for conducting auditing activities, and Kearney, in providing leadership to the Michigan Department of Education in developing the first statewide educational accountability system. Kirst (1990) analyzed the history and diversity of attempts at accountability in education within the following six broad types of accountability: performance reporting, monitoring and compliance with standards or regulations, incentive systems, reliance on the market, changing locus of authority or control of schools, and changing professional roles. A recent major attempt at accountability, involving sanctions, was the Kentucky Instructional Results Information System (Koretz & Barron, 1998). This program's failure was clearly associated with fast pace implementation in advance of validation, reporting and later retraction of flawed results, results that were not comparable to those in other states, payment by results that fostered teaching to tests and other cheating in schools, and heavy expense associated with performance assessments that could not be sustained over time.

Accountability approaches are applicable to organizations and professionals funded and charged to carry out public mandates, deliver public services, and implement specially funded programs. It behooves these program leaders to maintain a dynamic baseline of information needed to demonstrate fulfillment of responsibilities and achievement of positive results. They should focus accountability mechanisms especially on program elements that can be changed with the prospect of improving outcomes. They should also focus accountability to enhance staff cooperation toward achievement of collective goals rather than to intimidate or stimulate counterproductive competition. Moreover, accountability studies that compare programs should fairly consider the programs' contexts, especially beneficiaries' characteristics and needs, local support, available resources, and external forces.

The main advantages of accountability studies are that they are popular among constituent groups and politicians and are aimed at improving public services. They can also provide program personnel with clear expectations against which to plan, execute, and report on their services and contributions. They can be designed to give service providers freedom to innovate on procedures coupled with clear expectations and requirements for producing and reporting on accomplishments. Further, setting up healthy, fair competition between comparable programs can result in better services and products for consumers.

A main disadvantage is that accountability studies often result in invidious comparisons and thereby produce unhealthy competition and much political unrest and acrimony among service providers and between them and their constituents. Also, accountability studies often focus too narrowly on outcome indicators and can undesirably narrow the range of services. Another disadvantage is that politicians tend to force the implementation of accountability efforts before the needed instruments, scoring rubrics, assessor training, etc. can be planned, developed, field-tested, and validated. Furthermore, prospects for rewards and threats of punishment have often led service providers to cheat in order to assure positive evaluation reports. In schools, cheating to obtain rewards and avoid sanctions has frequently generated bad teaching, bad press, turnover in leadership, and abandonment of the accountability system.

Approach 5: Objective Testing Programs

Since the 1930s, American education has been inundated with standardized, multiple choice, norm-referenced testing programs. Probably every school district in the country has some such program. The tests are administered annually by local school districts and/or state education departments to inform students, parents, educators, and the public at large about the achievements of children and youth. The purposes of testing are to assess the achievements of individual students and groups of students compared to norms and/or standards. Typically, tests are administered to all students in selected grade levels. Because the test results focus on student outcomes and are conveniently available, many educators have tried to use the results to evaluate the quality of special projects and specific school programs by inferring that high scores reflect successful efforts and low scores reflect poor efforts. Such inferences can be wrong if the tests were not targeted on particular project or program objectives or the needs of particular target groups of students and if students' background characteristics were not taken into account.

Advance organizers for standardized educational tests include areas of the school curriculum, curricular objectives, and specified norm groups. The testing programs' main purposes are to compare the test performance of individual students and groups of students to those of selected norm groups and/or to diagnose shortfalls related to particular objectives. Standardized test results are also often used to compare the performance of programs and schools and to examine achievement trends across years. Metrics used to make the comparisons typically are standardized individual and mean scores for the total test and subtests. The sources of test questions are usually test publishers and test development/selection committees.

The typical question addressed by testing is whether the test performance of individual students is at or above the average performance of local, state, and national norm groups. Other questions may concern the percentages of students who surpassed one or more cut-score standards, where the group of students ranks compared to other groups, and whether achievement is better than in prior years. The main process is to select, administer, score, interpret, and report the tests.

Lindquist (1951), a major pioneer in this area, was instrumental in developing the Iowa testing programs, the American College Testing Program, the National Merit Scholarship Testing Program, and the General Educational Development Testing Program, as well as the Measurement Research Center at the University of Iowa. Many individuals have contributed substantially to the development of educational testing in America, including Ebel (1965), Flanagan (1939), Lord and Novick (1968), and Thorndike (1971). Innovations to testing in the 1990s include the development of item response theory (Hambleton & Swaminathan, 1985) and value-added measurement (Sanders & Horn, 1994; Webster, 1995).

If a school's personnel carefully select tests and use them appropriately to assess and improve student learning and report to the public, the involved expense and effort is highly justified. Student outcome measures for judging specific projects and programs must be validated in terms of the particular objectives and the characteristics and needs of the students served by the program. However, tests should not be relied on exclusively for evaluating specially targeted projects and programs. Results should be interpreted in light of other information on student characteristics, program implementation, student participation, and other outcome measures.

The main advantages of standardized-testing programs are that they are efficient in producing valid and reliable information on student performance in many areas of the school curriculum and that they are a familiar strategy at every level of the school program in virtually all school districts in the United States. The main limitations are that they provide data only about student outcomes; they reinforce students' multiple-choice test-taking behavior rather than their writing and speaking behaviors; they tend to address only lower-order learning objectives; and, in many cases, they are perhaps a better indicator of the socioeconomic levels of the students in a given program, school, or school district than of the quality of teaching and learning. Stake (1971) and others have argued effectively that standardized tests often are poor approximations of what teachers actually teach. Moreover, as has been patently clear in evaluations of programs for both disadvantaged and gifted students, norm-referenced tests often do not measure achievements well for low and high scoring students. Unfortunately, program evaluators often have made uncritical use of standardized test results to judge a program's outcomes, just because the results were conveniently available and had face validity for the public. Often, the contents of such tests do not match the program's objectives.

Approach 6: Outcomes Evaluation As Value-Added Assessment

Recurrent outcome/value-added assessment is a special case of the use of standardized testing to evaluate the effects of programs and policies. The emphasis is often on annual testing at all or a succession of grade levels to assess trends and partial out effects of the different components of an education system, including groups of schools, individuals and individual teachers. Characteristic of this approach is the annual collection of outcome measures based on standardized indicators, analysis to determine what value is being added to the achievements of students served by particular components of the evaluation system, and reporting of the results for policy, accountability, and improvement purposes. The main interest is in aggregates, not performance of individual students. A state education department may annually collect achievement data from all students (at a succession of grade levels), as is the case in the Tennessee Value-Added Assessment System. The evaluator may analyze the data to look at contrasting results for different schools. Results may be further broken out to make comparisons between curricular areas, teachers, elementary versus middle schools, size and resource classifications of schools, districts, and areas of a state. What differentiates the approach from the typical standardized achievement testing program is the emphasis on sophisticated analysis of data to partial out effects of system components and identify which ones should be improved and which ones should be commended and reinforced. Otherwise, the two approaches have much in common.

Advance organizers in outcome evaluation and employing value-added analysis are indicators of intended outcomes and a scheme for obtaining and classifying gain scores in order to examine policy issues and/or program effects. The purposes of outcome evaluation/value-added assessment systems are to provide direction for policymaking, accountability to constituents, and feedback for improving programs and services. The approach also ensures standardization of data for assessment and improvement throughout a system. The source of questions to be addressed by outcome evaluation originate from governing agencies, funding organizations, policymakers, the system's professionals, and constituents.

One form of outcome evaluation involves value-added assessment, which has been developed by Sanders and Horn (1994); Webster (1995); Webster, Mendro, and Almaguer (1994); and Tymms (1995). Illustrative questions addressed in this form of evaluation are: To what extent are particular programs adding value to students' achievements? What are the cross-year trends in outcomes? In what sectors of the system is the program working best and poorest? What are key, pervasive shortfalls in particular program objectives that require further study and attention? To what extent are program successes and failures associated with the system's groupings of grade levels? Outcome monitoring involving value-added assessment is probably most appropriate in well-endowed state education departments and large school districts where there is strong support from policy groups, administrators, and service providers to make the approach work. It requires systemwide buy-in; politically effective leaders to continually explain and sell the program; annual testing at a succession of grade levels; a smoothly operating, dynamic, computerized baseline of relevant input and output information; highly skilled technicians to make it run efficiently and accurately; a powerful computer system; complicated statistical analysis; and high-level commitment to use the results for purposes of policy development, accountability, program evaluation, and improvement at all levels of the system.

The central advantage of outcomes monitoring involving value-added assessment is in the systematization and institutionalization of a database of outcomes that can be used over time and in a standardized way to study and find means to improve outcomes. This approach makes efficient use of standardized tests; is amenable to analysis of trends at state, district, school, and classroom levels; uses students as their own controls; and emphasizes service to every student. The approach also is conducive to using a standard of continuous progress across years for every student, as opposed to employing static cut scores. The latter, while prevalent in accountability programs, basically fail to take into account meaningful gains by low or high achieving students, since such gains usually are far removed from the static, cut score standards. Sanders and Horn (1994) have shown that use of static cut scores may produce a "shed pattern," in which students who began below the cut score make the greatest gains while those who started above the cut score standard make little progress. Like the downward slope, from left to right, of a tool shed, the gains are greatest for previously low scoring students and progressively lower for the higher achievers. This suggests that teachers are concentrating mainly on getting students to the cut score standard but not beyond it and thus "holding back the high achievers."

A major disadvantage of the value-added approach is that it is politically volatile, since it is used to identify responsibility for successes and failures down to the levels of schools and teachers. It is also heavily reliant on quantitative information such as that coming from standardized, multiple-choice achievement tests. Consequently, the complex and powerful analyses are based on a limited scope of outcome variables. Nevertheless, Sanders (1989) has argued that a strong body of evidence supports the use of well-constructed, standardized, multiple-choice achievement tests. Beyond the issue of outcome measures, the approach does not provide in-depth documentation of program inputs and processes and makes little if any use of qualitative methods. Despite advancements in objective measurement and the employment of hierarchical mixed models to defensibly partial out effects of a system's organizational components and individual staff members, critics of the approach argue that causal factors are so complex that no measurement and analysis system can fairly fix responsibility to the level of teachers for the academic progress of individual and collections of students.

Approach 7: Performance Testing

In the 1990s, major efforts were made to offset the limitations of typical multiple-choice tests by employing performance or authentic measures. These devices require students to demonstrate their achievements by producing authentic responses to evaluation tasks, such as written or spoken answers, musical or psychomotor presentations, portfolios of work products, or group solutions to defined problems. Arguments for performance tests are that they have high face validity and model and reinforce students' needed life skills. After all, students are not being taught so that they will do well in choosing best answers from a list, but so that they will master underlying understandings and skills and effectively apply them in real life situations.

The advance organizers in performance assessments are life-skill objectives and content-related performance tasks, plus ways that their achievement can be demonstrated in practice. The main purpose of performance tasks is to compare the performance of individual students and groups of students to model performance on the tasks. Grades assigned to each respondent's performance, using set rubrics, enables assessment of the quality of achievements represented and comparisons across groups.

The sources of questions addressed by performance tests are analyses of selected life-skill tasks and content specifications in curricular materials. The typical assessment questions concern whether individual students can effectively write, speak, figure, analyze, lead, work cooperatively, and solve given problems up to the level of acceptable standards. The main testing process is to define areas of skills to be assessed; select the type of assessment device; construct the assessment tasks; determine scoring rubrics; define standards for assessing performance; train and calibrate scorers; validate the measures; and administer, score, interpret, and report the results.

In speaking of licensing tests, Flexner (1910) called for tests that ascertain students' practical ability to successfully confront and solve problems in concrete cases. Some of the pioneers in applying performance assessment to state education systems were the state education departments in Vermont and Kentucky (Kentucky Department of Education, 1993; Koretz, 1986, 1996; Koretz & Barron, 1998). Other sources of information about the general approach and issues in performance testing include Baker, O'Neil, and Linn (1993); Herman, Gearhart, and Baker (1993); Linn, Baker, and Dunbar (1991); Mehrens (1972); Messick (1994); Stillman, Haley, Regan, Philbin, Smith, O'Donnell, and Pohl (1991); Swanson, Norman, and Linn (1995); Torrance (1993); and Wiggins (1989).

It is often difficult to establish the necessary conditions to employ the performance testing approach. It requires a huge outlay of time and resources for development and application. Typically, state education departments and school districts should probably use this approach very selectively and only when they can make the investment needed to produce valid results that are worth the large, required investment. On the other hand, students' writing ability is best assessed and nurtured through obtaining, assessing, and providing critical feedback on their writing.

One advantage of performance tests is minimization of guessing. Requiring students to construct responses to assessment tasks also reinforces writing, computation, scientific experimentation, and other life skills.

Major disadvantages of the approach are the heavy time requirements for administration; the high costs of scoring; the difficulty in achieving reliable scores; the narrow scope of skills that can feasibly be assessed; and lack of norms for comparisons, especially at the national level. In general, performance tests are inefficient, costly, and often of dubious reliability. Moreover, compared with multiple-choice tests, performance tests, in the same amount of testing time, cover a much narrower range of questions.

Approach 8: Experimental Studies

In using controlled experiments, program evaluators randomly assign students or groups of students to experimental and control groups and then contrast the outcomes when the experimental group receives a particular intervention and the control group receives no special treatment or some different treatment. This type of study was quite prominent in program evaluation during the late 1960s and early 1970s, when there was a federal requirement to assess the effectiveness of federally funded innovations. However, experimental program evaluations subsequently fell into disfavor and disuse. Apparent reasons for this decline are that educators rarely can meet the required experimental conditions and assumptions.

This approach is labeled a questions-oriented or quasi-evaluation strategy because it starts with questions and methodology that may address only a narrow set of questions needed to assess a program's merit and worth. In the 1960s, Campbell and Stanley (1963) and others hailed the true experiment as the only sound means of evaluating interventions. This piece of evaluation history reminds one of Kaplan's (1964) famous warning against the so-called "law of the instrument," whereby a given method is equated to a field of inquiry. In such a case, the field of inquiry is restricted to the questions that are answerable by the given method. Fisher (1951) specifically warned against equating his experimental methods with science. In general, experimental design is a method that can contribute importantly to program evaluation, as Nave, Miech, and Mosteller (Chapter 8, this volume) have demonstrated, but by itself it is often insufficient to address a client's full range of evaluation questions.

The advance organizers in experimental studies are problem statements, competing treatments, hypotheses, investigatory questions, and randomized treatment and comparison groups. The usual purpose of the controlled experiment is to determine causal relationships between specified independent and dependent variables, such as between a given instructional method and student standardized-test performance. It is particularly noteworthy that the sources of questions investigated in the experimental study are researchers, program developers, and policy figures, and not usually a program's constituents and practitioners.

The frequent question in the experimental study is: What are the effects of a given intervention on specified outcome variables? Typical methods used are experimental and quasi-experimental designs. Pioneers in using experimentation to evaluate programs are Campbell and Stanley (1963), Cronbach and Snow (1969), and Lindquist (1953). Others who have developed the methodology of experimentation substantially for program evaluation are Boruch (1994), Glass and Maguire (1968), Suchman (1967), and Wiley and Bock (1967).

Evaluators should consider conducting a controlled experiment only when its required conditions and assumptions can be met. Often this requires substantial political influence, substantial funding, and widespread agreement—among the involved funders, service providers, and beneficiaries—to submit to the requirements of the experiment. Such requirements typically include, among others, a stable program that will not have to be studied and modified during the evaluation; the ability to establish and sustain comparable program and control groups; the ability to keep the program and control conditions separate and uncontaminated; and the ability to obtain the needed criterion measures from all or at least a representative group of the members of the program and comparison groups. Evaluability assessment was developed as a particular methodology for determining the feasibility of moving ahead with an experiment (Smith, 1989; Wholey, 1995).

Controlled experiments have a number of advantages. They focus on results and not just intentions or judgments. They provide strong methods for establishing relatively unequivocal causal relationships between treatment and outcome variables, something that can be especially significant when program effects are small but important. Moreover, because of the prevalent use and success of experiments in such fields as medicine and agriculture, the approach has widespread credibility.

These advantages, however, are offset by serious objections to experimenting on school students and other human subjects. It is often considered unethical or even illegal to deprive control group members of the benefits of special funds for improving services. Likewise, many parents do not want schools or other organizations to experiment on their children by applying unproven interventions. Typically, schools find it impractical and unreasonable to randomly assign students to treatments and to hold treatments constant throughout the study period. Furthermore, experimental studies provide a much narrower range of information than organizations often need to assess and strengthen their programs. On this point, experimental studies tend to provide terminal information that is not useful for guiding the development and improvement of programs and may in fact thwart ongoing modifications of programs.

Approach 9: Management Information Systems

Management Information Systems are like politically controlled approaches, except that they supply managers with information needed to conduct and report on their programs, as opposed to supplying them with information needed to win a political advantage. The management information approach is also like the decision/accountability-oriented approach, which will be discussed later, except that the decision/accountability-oriented approach provides information needed to both develop and defend a program's merit and worth, which goes beyond providing information that managers need to implement and report on their management responsibilities.

The advance organizers in most management information systems include program objectives, specified activities, and projected program milestones or events. A management information system's purpose is to continuously supply managers with the information they need to plan, direct, control, and report on their programs or spheres of responsibility.

The sources of questions addressed are the management personnel and their superiors. The main questions they typically want answered are: Are program activities being implemented according to schedule, according to budget, and with the expected results? To provide ready access to information for addressing such questions, systems regularly store and make accessible up-to-date information on program goals, planned operations, actual operations, staff, program organization, operations, expenditures, threats, problems, publicity, and achievements.

Methods employed in management information systems include system analysis, Program Evaluation and Review Technique (PERT), Critical Path Method, Program Planning and Budgeting System (PPBS), Management by Objectives (MBO), computer-based information systems, periodic staff progress reports, and regular budgetary reporting.

Cook (1966) introduced the use of PERT to education, and Kaufman (1969) wrote about the use of management information systems in education. Business schools and programs in computer information systems regularly provide courses in management information systems. These focus mainly on how to set up and employ computerized information banks for use in organizational decision making.

W. Edwards Deming (1986) argued that managers should pay close attention to process rather than being preoccupied with outcomes. He advanced a systematic approach for monitoring and continuously improving an enterprise's process, arguing that close attention to the process will result in increasingly better outcomes. It is commonly said that, in paying attention to this and related advice from Deming, Japanese car makers and later Americans greatly increased the quality of automobiles (Aguaro, 1990). Bayless and Massaro (1992) applied Deming's approach to program evaluations in education. Based on this writer's observations, the approach was not well suited to assessing the complexities of educational processes—possibly because, unlike the manufacture of automobiles, educators have no definitive, standardized models for linking exact educational processes to specified outcomes. Nevertheless, given modern database technology, program managers often can and should employ management information systems in multiyear projects and programs. Program databases can provide information, not only for keeping programs on track, but also for assisting in the broader study and improvement of program processes and outcomes.

A major advantage of the use of management information systems is in giving managers information they can use to plan, monitor, control, and report on complex operations. A difficulty with the application of this industry-oriented type of system to education and other social services, however, is that the products of many programs are not amenable to a narrow, precise definition as is the case with a corporation's profit and loss statement. Moreover, processes in educational and social programs often are complex and evolving rather than straightforward and standardized like those of manufacturing and business. The information gathered in management information systems typically lacks the scope of context, input, process, and outcome information required to assess a program's merit and worth.

Approach 10: Benefit-Cost Analysis Approach

Benefit-cost analysis as applied to program evaluation is a set of largely quantitative procedures used to understand the full costs of a program and to determine and judge what investments returned in objectives achieved and broader social benefits. The aim is to determine costs associated with program inputs, determine the monetary value of the program outcomes, compute benefit-cost ratios, compare the computed ratios to those of similar programs, and ultimately judge a program's productivity in economic terms.

The benefit-cost analysis approach to program evaluation may be broken down into three levels of procedure: (1) cost analysis of program inputs, (2) cost-effectiveness analysis, and (3) benefit-cost analysis. These may be looked at as a hierarchy. The first type, cost analysis of program inputs, may be done by itself. Such analyses entail an ongoing accumulation of a program's financial history, which is useful in controlling program delivery and expenditures. The program's financial history can be used to compare its actual and projected costs and how costs relate to the costs of similar programs. Cost analyses can also be extremely valuable to outsiders who might be interested in replicating a program.

Cost-effectiveness analysis necessarily includes cost analysis of program inputs to determine the cost associated with progress toward achieving each objective. For example, two or more programs' costs and successes in achieving the same objectives might be compared. A program could be judged superior on cost-effectiveness grounds if it had the same costs but superior outcomes as similar programs. Or a program could be judged superior on cost-effectiveness grounds if it achieved the same objectives as more expensive programs. Cost-effectiveness analyses do not require conversion of outcomes to monetary terms but must be keyed to clear, measurable program objectives.

Benefit-cost analyses typically build on a cost analysis of program inputs and a cost-effectiveness analysis. But the benefit-cost analysis goes further. It seeks to identify a broader range of outcomes than just those associated with program objectives. It examines the relationship between the investment in a program and the extent of positive and negative impacts on the program's environment. In doing so, it ascertains and places a monetary value on program inputs and each identified outcome. It identifies a program's benefit-cost ratios and compares these to similar ratios for competing programs. Ultimately, benefit-cost studies seek conclusions about the comparative benefits and costs of the examined programs.

Advance organizers for the overall benefit-cost approach are associated with cost breakdowns for both program inputs and outputs. Program input costs may be delineated by line items (e.g., personnel, travel, materials, equipment, communications, facilities, contracted services, overhead), by program components, and by year. In cost-effectiveness analysis, a program's costs are examined in relation to each program objective, and these must be clearly defined and assessed. The more ambitious benefit-cost analyses look at costs associated with main effects and side effects, tangible and intangible outcomes, positive and negative outcomes, and short-term and long-term outcomes—both inside and outside a program. Frequently, they also may break down costs by individuals and groups of beneficiaries. One may also estimate the costs of foregone opportunities and, sometimes, political costs. Even then, the real value of benefits associated with human creativity or self-actualization are nearly impossible to estimate. Consequently, the benefit-cost equation rests on dubious assumptions and uncertain realities.

The purposes of these three levels of benefit-cost analysis are to gain clear knowledge of what resources were invested, how they were invested, and with what effect. In popular vernacular, cost-effectiveness and benefit-cost analyses seek to determine the program's "bang for the buck." There is great interest in answering this type of question. Policy boards, program planners, and taxpayers are especially interested to know whether program investments are paying off in positive results that exceed or are at least as good as those produced by similar programs. Authoritative information on the benefit-cost approach may be obtained by studying the writings of Kee (1995), Levin (1983), and Tsang (Chapter 9, this volume).

Benefit-cost analysis is potentially important in most program evaluations. Evaluators and their clients are advised to discuss this matter thoroughly with their clients, to reach appropriate advance agreements on what should and can be done to obtain the needed cost information, and to do as much cost-effectiveness and benefit-cost analysis as can be done well and within reasonable costs.

Benefit-cost analysis is an important but problematic consideration in program evaluations. Most evaluations are amenable to analyzing the costs of program inputs and maintaining a financial history of expenditures. The main impediment is that program authorities often do not want anyone other than the appropriate accountants and auditors looking into their financial books. If cost analysis, even at only the input levels, is to be done, this must be clearly provided for in the initial contractual agreements covering the evaluation work. Performing cost-effectiveness analysis can be feasible if cost analysis of inputs is agreed to; if there are clear, measurable program objectives; and if comparable cost information can be obtained from competing programs. Unfortunately, it is usually hard to meet all these conditions. Even more unfortunate is the fact that it is usually impractical to conduct a thorough benefit-cost analysis. Not only must it meet all the conditions of the analysis of program inputs and cost-effectiveness analysis, it must also place monetary values on identified outcomes, both anticipated and not expected.

Approach 11: Clarification Hearing

The clarification hearing is one label for the judicial approach to program evaluation. The approach essentially puts a program on trial. Role-playing evaluators competitively implement both a damning prosecution of the program—arguing that it failed—and a defense of the program—arguing that it succeeded. A judge hears arguments within the framework of a jury trial and controls the proceedings according to advance agreements on rules of evidence and trial procedures. The actual proceedings are preceded by the collection of and sharing of evidence by both sides. The prosecuting and defending evaluators may call witnesses and place documents and other exhibits into evidence. A jury hears the proceedings and ultimately makes and issues a ruling on the program's success or failure. Ideally, the jury is composed of persons representative of the program's stakeholders. By videotaping the proceedings, the administering evaluator can, after the trial, compile a condensed videotape as well as printed reports to disseminate what was learned through the process.

The advance organizers for a clarification hearing are criteria of program effectiveness that both the prosecuting and defending sides agree to apply. The main purpose of the judicial approach is to ensure that the evaluation's audience will receive balanced evidence on a program's strengths and weaknesses. The key questions essentially are: Should the program be judged a success or failure? Is it as good or better than alternative programs that address the same objectives?

Robert Wolf (1975) pioneered the judicial approach to program evaluation. Others who applied, tested, and further developed the approach include Levine (1974), Owens (1973), and Popham and Carlson (1983).

Based on the past uses of this approach, it can be judged as only marginally relevant to program evaluation. Because of its adversarial nature, the approach encourages evaluators to present biased arguments in order to win their cases. Thus, truth seeking is subordinated to winning. The most effective debaters are likely to convince the jury of their position even when it is poorly founded. The approach is also politically problematic, since it generates considerable acrimony. Despite the attractiveness of using the law, with its attendant rules of evidence, as a metaphor for program evaluation, its promise has not been fulfilled. There are few occasions in which it makes practical sense for evaluators to apply this approach.

Approach 12: Case Study Evaluations

Program evaluation that is based on a case study is a focused, in-depth description, analysis, and synthesis of a particular program or other object. The investigators do not control the program in any way. Rather, they look at it as it is occurring or as it occurred in the past. The study looks at the program in its geographic, cultural, organizational, and historical contexts, closely examining its internal operations and how it uses inputs and processes to produce outcomes. It examines a wide range of intended and unexpected outcomes. It looks at the program's multiple levels and also holistically at the overall program. It characterizes both central dominant themes and variations and aberrations. It defines and describes the program's intended and actual beneficiaries. It examines beneficiaries' needs and the extent to which the program effectively addressed the needs. It employs multiple methods to obtain and integrate multiple sources of information. While it breaks apart and analyzes a program along various dimensions, it also provides an overall characterization of the program.

The main thrust of the case study approach is to delineate and illuminate a program, not necessarily to guide its development or to assess and judge its merit and worth. Hence, this chapter characterizes the case study approach as a questions/methods-oriented approach rather than an improvement/accountability approach.

Advance organizers in case studies include the definition of the program, characterization of its geographic and organizational environment, the historical period in which it is to be examined, the program's beneficiaries and their assessed needs, the program's underlying logic of operation and productivity, and the key roles involved in the program. A case study program evaluation's main purpose is to provide stakeholders and their audiences with an authoritative, in-depth, well-documented explication of the program.

The case study should be keyed to the questions of most interest to the evaluation's main audiences. The evaluator must therefore identify and interact with the program's stakeholders. Along the way, stakeholders will be engaged to help plan the study and interpret findings. Ideally, the audiences include the program's oversight body, administrators, staff, financial sponsors, beneficiaries, and potential adopters of the program.

Typical questions posed by some or all of the above audiences are: What is the program in concept and practice? How has it evolved over time? How does it actually operate to produce outcomes? What has it produced? What are the shortfalls and negative side effects? What are the positive side effects? In what ways and to what degrees do various stakeholders value the program? To what extent did the program effectively meet beneficiaries' needs? What were the most important reasons for the program's successes and failures? What are the program's most important unresolved issues? How much has it cost? What are the costs per beneficiary, per year, etc.? What parts of the program have been successfully transported to other sites? How does this program compare with what might be called critical competitors? These questions only illustrate the range of questions that a case study might address, since each study will be tempered by the interests of the client and other audiences for the study and the evaluator's interests.

To conduct effective case studies, evaluators need to employ a wide range of qualitative and quantitative methods. These may include analysis of archives; collection of artifacts, such as work samples; content analysis of program documents; both independent and participant observations; interviews; logical analysis of operations; focus groups; tests; questionnaires; rating scales; hearings; forums; and maintenance of a program database. Reports may incorporate in-depth descriptions and accounts of key historical trends; focus on critical incidents, photographs, maps, testimony, relevant news clippings, logic models, and cross-break tables; and summarize main conclusions. The case study report may include a description of key dimensions of the case, as determined with the audience, as well as an overall holistic presentation and assessment. Case study reports may involve audio and visual media as well as printed documents.

Case study methods have existed for many years and have been applied in such areas as anthropology, clinical psychology, law, the medical profession, and social work. Pioneers in applying the method to program evaluation include Campbell (1975), Lincoln and Guba (1985), Platt (1992), Smith and Pohland (1974), Stake (1995), and Yin (1992).

The case study approach is highly appropriate in program evaluation. It requires no controls of treatments and subjects and looks at programs as they naturally occur and evolve. It addresses accuracy issues by employing and triangulating multiple perspectives, methods, and information sources. It employs all relevant methods and information sources. It looks at programs within relevant contexts and describes contextual influences on the program. It looks at programs holistically and in depth. It examines the program's internal workings and how it produces outcomes. It includes clear procedures for analyzing qualitative information. It can be tailored to focus on the audience's most important questions. It can be done retrospectively or in real time. It can be reported to meet given deadlines and subsequently updated based on further developments.

The main limitation of the case study is that some evaluators may mistake its openness and lack of controls as an excuse for approaching it haphazardly and bypassing steps to ensure that findings and interpretations possess rigor as well as relevance. Furthermore, because of a preoccupation with descriptive information, the case study evaluator may not collect sufficient judgmental information to permit a broad-based assessment of a program's merit and worth. Users of the approach might slight quantitative analysis in favor of qualitative analysis. By trying to produce a comprehensive description of a program, the case study evaluator may not produce timely feedback needed to help in program development. To overcome these potential pitfalls, evaluators using the case study approach should fully address the principles of sound evaluation as related to accuracy, utility, feasibility, and propriety.

Approach 13: Criticism and Connoisseurship

The connoisseur-based approach grew out of methods used in art criticism and literary criticism. It assumes that certain experts in a given substantive area are capable of in-depth analysis and evaluation that could not be done in other ways. Just as a national survey of wine drinkers could produce information concerning their overall preferences for types of wines and particular vineyards, it would not provide the detailed, creditable judgments of the qualities of particular wines that might be derived from a single connoisseur who has devoted a professional lifetime to the study and grading of wines and whose judgments are highly and widely respected.

The advance organizer for the connoisseur-based study is the evaluator's special expertise and sensitivities. The study's purpose is to describe, critically appraise, and illuminate a particular program's merits. The evaluation questions addressed by the connoisseur-based evaluation are determined by expert evaluators—the critics and authorities who have undertaken the evaluation. Among the major questions they can be expected to ask are: What are the program's essence and salient characteristics? What merits and demerits distinguish the particular program from others of the same general kind?

The methodology of connoisseurship includes critics' systematic use of their perceptual sensitivities, past experiences, refined insights, and abilities to communicate their assessments. The evaluator's judgments are conveyed in vivid terms to help the audience appreciate and understand all of the program's nuances. Eisner (1975, 1983) has pioneered this strategy in education.[6] A dozen or more of Eisner's students have conducted research and development on the connoisseurship approach, e.g., Vallance (1973) and Flinders and Eisner (Chapter 12, this volume). This approach obviously depends on the chosen expert's qualifications. It also requires an audience that has confidence in, and is willing to accept and use, the connoisseur's report. I would willingly accept and use any evaluation that Dr. Elliott Eisner agreed to present, but there are not many Eisners out there.

The main advantage of the connoisseur-based study is that it exploits the particular expertise and finely developed insights of persons who have devoted much time and effort to the study of a precise area. Such individuals can provide an array of detailed information that an audience can then use to form a more insightful analysis than otherwise might be possible. The approach's disadvantage is that it is dependent on the expertise and qualifications of the particular expert doing the program evaluation, leaving room for much subjectivity.

Approach 14: Program Theory–Based Evaluation

Program evaluations based on program theory begin with either (1) a well-developed and validated theory of how programs of a certain type within similar settings operate to produce outcomes or (2) an initial stage to approximate such a theory within the context of a particular program evaluation. The former condition is much more reflective of the implicit promises in a theory-based program evaluation, since the existence of a sound theory means that a substantial body of theoretical development has produced and tested a coherent set of conceptual, hypothetical, and pragmatic principles, as well as associated instruments to guide inquiry. The theory can then aid a program evaluator to decide what questions, indicators, and assumed linkages between and among program elements should be used to evaluate a program covered by the theory.

Some theories have been used more or less successfully to evaluate programs, which gives this approach some measure of viability. For example, health education/behavior change programs are sometimes founded on theoretical frameworks, such as the Health Belief Model (Becker, 1974; Janz & Becker, 1984; Mullen, Hersey, & Iverson, 1987). Other examples are the PRECEDE-PROCEED Model for health promotion planning and evaluation (Green & Kreuter, 1991), Bandura's (1977) Social Cognitive Theory, the Stages of Change Theory of Prochaska and DiClemente (1992), and Peters and Waterman's (1982) theory of successful organizations. When such frameworks exist, their use probably can enhance a program's effectiveness and provide a credible structure for evaluating its functioning. Unfortunately, few program areas are buttressed by well-articulated and tested theories.

Thus, most theory-based evaluations begin by setting out to develop a theory that appropriately could be used to guide the particular program evaluation. As will be discussed later in this characterization, such ad hoc theory development efforts and their linkage to program evaluations are problematic. In any case, let us look at what the theory-based evaluator attempts to achieve.

The point of the theory development or selection effort is to identify advance organizers to guide the evaluation. Essentially, these are the mechanisms by which program activities are understood to produce or contribute to program outcomes, along with the appropriate description of context, specification of independent and dependent variables, and portrayal of key linkages. The main purposes of the theory-based program evaluation are to determine the extent to which the program of interest is theoretically sound, to understand why it is succeeding or failing, and to provide direction for program improvement.

Questions for the program evaluation are derived from the guiding theory. Example questions include: Is the program grounded in an appropriate, well-articulated, and validated theory? Is the employed theory reflective of recent research? Are the program's targeted beneficiaries, design, operation, and intended outcomes consistent with the guiding theory? How well does the program address and serve the full range of pertinent needs of targeted beneficiaries? If the program is consistent with the guiding theory, are the expected results being achieved? Are program inputs and operations producing outcomes in the ways the theory predicts? What changes in the program's design or implementation might produce better outcomes? What elements of the program are essential for successful replication? Overall, was the program theoretically sound, did it operate in accordance with an appropriate theory, did it produce the expected outcomes, were the hypothesized causal linkages confirmed, what program modifications are needed, is the program worthy of continuation and/or dissemination, and what program features are essential for successful replication?

The nature of these questions suggests that the success of the theory-based approach is dependent on a foundation of sound theory development and validation. This, of course, entails sound conceptualization of at least a context-dependent theory, formulation and rigorous testing of hypotheses derived from the theory, development of guidelines for practical implementation of the theory based on extensive field trials, and independent assessment of the theory. Unfortunately, not many program areas in education and the social sciences are grounded in sound theories. Moreover, evaluators wanting to employ a theory-based evaluation do not often find it feasible to conduct the full range of theory development and validation steps, and still get the evaluation done on time. Thus, in claiming to conduct a theory-based evaluation, evaluators often seem to promise much more than they can deliver.

The main procedure typically used in "theory-based program evaluations" is a model of the program's logic. This may be a detailed flowchart of how inputs are thought to be processed to produce intended outcomes. It may also be a grounded theory, such as those advocated by Glaser and Strauss (1967). The network analysis of the former approach is typically an armchair theorizing process involving evaluators and persons who are supposed to know how the program is expected to operate and produce results. They discuss, scheme, discuss some more, network, discuss further, and finally produce networks in varying degrees of detail of what is involved in making the program work and how the various elements are linked to produce desired outcomes. The more demanding grounded theory requires a systematic, empirical process of observing events or analyzing materials drawn from operating programs, followed by an extensive modeling process.

Pioneers in applying theory development procedures to program evaluation include Glaser and Strauss (1967) and Weiss (1972, 1995). Other developers of the approach are Bickman (1990), Chen (1990), and Rogers (Chapter 13, this volume).

In any program evaluation assignment, it is reasonable for the evaluator to examine the extent to which program plans and operations are grounded in an appropriate theory or model. It can also be useful to engage in a modicum of effort to network the program and thereby seek out key variables and linkages. As noted previously, in the enviable but rare situation where a relevant, validated theory exists, the evaluator can beneficially apply it in structuring the evaluation and in analyzing findings.

However, if a relevant, defensible theory of the program's logic does not exist, evaluators need not develop one. In fact, if they attempt to do so, they will incur many threats to their evaluation's success. Rather than evaluating a program and its underlying logic, evaluators might usurp the program staff's responsibility for program design. They might do a poor job of theory development, given limitations on time and resources to develop and test an appropriate theory. They might incur the conflict of interest associated with having to evaluate the theory they developed. They might pass off an unvalidated model of the program as a theory, when it meets almost none of the requirements of a sound theory. They might bog down the evaluation in too much effort to develop a theory. They might also focus attention on a theory developed early in a program and later discover that the program has evolved to be a quite different enterprise than what was theorized at the outset. In this case, the initial theory could become a "Procrustean bed" for the program evaluation.

Overall, there really is not much to recommend theory-based program evaluation, since doing it right is usually not feasible and since failed or misrepresented attempts can be highly counterproductive. Nevertheless, modest attempts to model programs—labeled as such—can be useful for identifying measurement variables, so long as the evaluator does not spend too much time on this and so long as the model is not considered as fixed or as a validated theory. In the rare case where an appropriate theory already exists, the evaluator can make beneficial use of it to help structure and guide the evaluation and interpret the findings.

Approach 15: Mixed-Methods Studies

In an attempt to resolve the longstanding debate about whether program evaluations should employ quantitative or qualitative methods, some authors have proposed that evaluators should regularly combine these methods in given program evaluations (for example, see the National Science Foundation's 1997 *User-Friendly Handbook for Mixed Method Evaluations*). Such recommendations, along with practical guidelines and illustrations, are no doubt useful to many program staff members and to evaluators. But in the main, the recommendation for a mixed-method approach only highlights a large body of longstanding practice of mixed-methods program evaluation rather than proposing a new approach. All seven approaches discussed in the remainder of this section of the chapter employ both qualitative and quantitative methods. What sets them apart from the mixed-method approach is that their first considerations are not the methods to be employed but either the assessment of value or the social mission to be served. The mixed-methods approach is included in this section on questions/methods approaches, because it is preoccupied with using multiple methods rather than whatever methods are needed to comprehensively assess a program's merit and worth. As with the other approaches in this section, the mixed-methods approach may or may not fully assess a program's value; thus, it is classified as a quasi-evaluation approach.

The advance organizers of the mixed-methods approach are formative and summative evaluations, qualitative and quantitative methods, and intra-case or cross-case analysis. Formative evaluations are employed to examine a program's development and assist in improving its structure and implementation. Summative evaluations basically look at whether objectives were achieved, but may look for a broader array of outcomes. Qualitative and quantitative methods are employed in combination to assure depth, scope, and dependability of findings. This approach also applies to carefully selected single programs or to comparisons of alternative programs.

The basic purposes of the mixed method approach are to provide direction for improving programs as they evolve and to assess their effectiveness after they have had time to produce results. Use of both quantitative and qualitative methods is intended to ensure dependable feedback on a wide range of questions; depth of understanding of particular programs; a holistic perspective; and enhancement of the validity, reliability, and usefulness of the full set of findings. Investigators look to quantitative methods for standardized, replicable findings on large data sets. They look to qualitative methods for elucidation of the program's cultural context, dynamics, meaningful patterns and themes, deviant cases, and diverse impacts on individuals as well as groups. Qualitative reporting methods are applied to bring the findings to life, to make them clear, persuasive, and interesting. By using both quantitative and qualitative methods, the evaluator secures cross-checks on different subsets of findings and thereby instills greater stakeholder confidence in the overall findings.

The sources of evaluation questions are the program's goals, plans, and stakeholders. The stakeholders often include skeptical as well as supportive audiences. Among the important stakeholders are program administrators and staff, policy boards, financial sponsors, beneficiaries, taxpayers, and program area experts.

The approach may pursue a wide range of questions. Examples of formative evaluation questions are: To what extent do program activities follow the program plan, time line, and budget? To what extent is the program achieving its goals? What problems in design or implementation need to be addressed? Examples of summative evaluation questions are: To what extent did the program achieve its goals? Was the program appropriately effective for all beneficiaries? What interesting stories emerged? What are program stakeholders' judgments of program operations, processes, and outcomes? What were the important side effects? Is the program sustainable and transportable?

The approach employs a wide range of methods. Among quantitative methods are surveys using representative samples, both cohort and cross-sectional samples, norm-referenced tests, rating scales, quasi-experiments, significance tests for main effects, and a posteriori statistical tests. The qualitative methods may include ethnography, document analysis, narrative analysis, purposive samples, single cases, participant observers, independent observers, key informants, advisory committees, structured and unstructured interviews, focus groups, case studies, study of outliers, diaries, logic models, grounded theory development, flow charts, decision trees, matrices, and performance assessments. Reports may include abstracts, executive summaries, full reports, oral briefings, conference presentations, and workshops. They should include a balance of narrative and numerical information.

Considering his book on service studies in higher education, Ralph Tyler (Tyler et al., 1932) was certainly a pioneer in the mixed-method approach to program evaluation. Other authors who have written cogently on the approach are Guba and Lincoln (1981), Kidder and Fine (1987), Lincoln and Guba (1985), Miron (1998), Patton (1990), and Schatzman and Strauss (1973).

It is almost always appropriate to consider using a mixed-methods approach. Certainly, the evaluator should take advantage of opportunities to obtain any and all potentially available information that is relevant to assessing a program's merit and worth. Sometimes a study can be mainly or only qualitative or quantitative, but usually such studies would be strengthened by including both types of information. The key point is to choose methods because they can effectively address the study's questions, not because they are either qualitative or quantitative.

Key advantages of using both qualitative and quantitative methods are that they complement each other in ways that are important to the evaluation's audiences. Information from quantitative methods tends to be standardized, efficient, amenable to standard tests of reliability, easily summarized and analyzed, and accepted as "hard" data. Information from qualitative approaches adds depth; can be delivered in interesting, story-like presentations; and provides a means to explore and understand the more superficial quantitative findings. Using both types of method affords important cross-checks on findings.

The main pitfall in pursuing the mixed-methods approach is using multiple methods because this is the popular thing to do rather than because the selected methods best respond to the evaluation questions. Moreover, sometimes evaluators let the combination of methods compensate for a lack of rigor in applying them. Using a mixed methods approach can produce confusing findings if an investigator uncritically mixes positivistic and postmodern paradigms, since quantitative and qualitative methods are derived from different theoretical approaches to inquiry and reflect different conceptions of knowledge. Many evaluators do not possess the requisite foundational knowledge in both the sciences and humanities to effectively combine quantitative and qualitative methods. The approaches in the remainder of this chapter place proper emphasis on mixed methods, making choice of the methods subservient to the approach's dominant philosophy and to the particular evaluation questions to be addressed.

The mixed methods approach to evaluation concludes this chapter's discussion of the questions/methods approaches to evaluation. These 13 approaches tend to concentrate on selected questions and methods and thus may or may not fully address an evaluation's fundamental requirement to assess a program's merit and worth. The array of these approaches suggests that the field has advanced considerably since the 1950s when program evaluations were rare and mainly used approaches grounded in behavioral objectives, standardized tests, and/or accreditation visits.

IMPROVEMENT/ACCOUNTABILITY-ORIENTED EVALUATION APPROACHES

I now turn to three approaches that stress the need to fully assess a program's merit and worth. These approaches are expansive and seek comprehensiveness in considering the full range of questions and criteria needed to assess a program's value. Often they employ the assessed needs of a program's stakeholders as the foundational criteria for assessing the program's merit and worth. They also seek to examine the full range of pertinent technical and economic criteria for judging program plans and operations. They look for all relevant outcomes, not just those keyed to program objectives. Usually, they are objectivist and assume an underlying reality in seeking definitive, unequivocal answers to the evaluation questions. Typically, they must use multiple qualitative and quantitative assessment methods to provide cross-checks on findings. In general, the approaches conform closely to this chapter's definition of evaluation. The approaches are labeled Decisions/Accountability, Consumer-Orientation, and Accreditation. The three approaches emphasize respectively improvement through serving program decisions, providing consumers with assessments of optional programs and services, and helping consumers to gain assurances that given programs are professionally sound and effective.

Approach 16: Decision/Accountability-Oriented Studies

The decision/accountability-oriented approach emphasizes that program evaluation should be used proactively to help improve a program as well as retroactively to judge its merit and worth. The approach is distinguished from management information systems and from politically controlled studies because decision/accountability-oriented studies emphasize questions of merit and worth. The approach's philosophical underpinnings include an objectivist orientation to finding best answers to context-limited questions and subscription to the principles of a well-functioning democratic society, especially human rights, equity, excellence, conservation, and accountability. Practically, the approach engages stakeholders in focusing the evaluation, addressing their most important questions, providing timely, relevant information to assist decision making, and producing an accountability record.

The advance organizers for the approach include decision makers/stakeholders, decision situations, and program accountability requirements. Audiences include not just top managers but stakeholders at all organizational program levels. From the bottom up, such stakeholders may include beneficiaries, parents/guardians, service providers, administrators, program consultants, support personnel, policy makers, funding authorities, and taxpayers. The generic decision situations to be served may include defining goals and priorities, choosing from competing services, planning programs, budgeting, staffing, using services, guiding participation, judging progress, and recycling program operations. Key classes of needed evaluative information are assessments of needs, problems, and opportunities; identification and assessment of competing programs or program approaches; assessment of program plans; assessment of staff qualifications and performance; assessment of program facilities and materials; monitoring and assessment of process; assessment of intended and unintended and short-range and long-range outcomes; and assessment of cost-effectiveness.

The basic purpose of decision/accountability studies is to provide a knowledge and value base for making and being accountable for decisions that result in developing, delivering, and making informed use of cost-effective services. Thus, evaluators must interact with representative members of their audiences, discern their questions, and supply them with relevant, timely, efficient, and accurate information. The approach stresses that an evaluation's most important purpose is not to prove but to improve.

The sources of questions addressed by this approach are the concerned and involved stakeholders. These may include all persons and groups who must make choices related to initiating, planning, implementing, and using a program's services. Main questions addressed are: Has an appropriate beneficiary population been determined? What beneficiary needs should be addressed? What are the available alternative ways to address these needs, and what are their comparative merits and costs? Are plans of services and participation sound? Is there adequate provision for facilities, materials, and equipment? Is the program staff sufficiently qualified and credible? Have appropriate roles been assigned to the different participants? Are the participants effectively carrying out their assignments? Is the program working and should it be revised in any way? Is the program effectively reaching all the targeted beneficiaries? Is the program meeting participants' needs? Did beneficiaries play their part? Is the program better than competing alternatives? Is it affordable? Is it sustainable? Is it transportable? Is the program worth the required initial investment? Answers to these and related questions are to be based on the underlying standard of good programs, i.e., they must effectively reach and serve beneficiaries' targeted needs at a reasonable cost, and do so as well as or better than reasonably available alternatives.

Many methods may be used in decision/accountability-oriented program evaluations. These include, among others, surveys, needs assessments, case studies, advocate teams, observations, interviews, resident evaluators, and quasi-experimental and experimental designs. To make the approach work, the evaluator must regularly interact with a representative body of stakeholders. Typically, the evaluator should establish and engage a representative stakeholder advisory panel to help define evaluation questions, shape evaluation plans, review draft reports, and help disseminate findings. The evaluator's exchanges with this group involve conveyance of evaluation feedback that may be of use in program improvement and use, as well as determining what future evaluation reports would be most helpful to program personnel and other stakeholders. Interim reports may assist beneficiaries, program staff, and others to obtain feedback on the program's merits and worth and on the quality of their own participation. By maintaining a dynamic baseline of evaluation information and applications of the information, the evaluator can use this information to develop a comprehensive summative evaluation report, periodically update the broad group of stakeholders, and supply program personnel with findings for their own accountability reports.

The involvement of stakeholders is consistent with a key principle of the change process. An enterprise—read *evaluation* here—can best help bring about change in a target group's behavior if that group was involved in planning, monitoring, and judging the enterprise. By involving stakeholders throughout the evaluation process, decision-oriented evaluators lay the groundwork for bringing stakeholders to understand and value the evaluation process and apply the findings.

Cronbach (1963) advised educators to reorient their evaluations from an objectives orientation to a concern for making better program decisions. While he did not use the terms *formative* and *summative* evaluation, he essentially defined the underlying concepts. In discussing the distinctions between the constructive, proactive orientation on the one hand and the retrospective, judgmental orientation on the other, he argued for placing more emphasis on the former. He noted the limited functionality of the tradition of stressing retrospective outcomes evaluation. Later, I (Stufflebeam, 1966, 1967) argued that evaluations should help program personnel make and defend decisions keyed to meeting beneficiaries' needs. While I advocated an improvement orientation to evaluation, I also emphasized that evaluators must both inform decisions and provide information for accountability. I also emphasized that the approach should interact with and serve the full range of stakeholders who need to make judgments and choices about a program. Others who have contributed to the development of a decision/accountability orientation to evaluation are Alkin (1969) and Webster (1975).

The decision/accountability-oriented approach is applicable in cases where program staff and other stakeholders want and need both formative and summative evaluation. It can provide the evaluation framework for both internal and external evaluation. When used for internal evaluation, it is usually important to commission an independent metaevaluation of the inside evaluator's work. Beyond program evaluations, this approach has proved useful in evaluating personnel, students, projects, facilities, and products.

A major advantage of the approach is that it encourages program personnel to use evaluation continuously and systematically to plan and implement programs that meet beneficiaries' targeted needs. It aids decision making at all program levels and stresses improvement. It also presents a rationale and framework of information for helping program personnel to be accountable for their program decisions and actions. It involves the full range of stakeholders in the evaluation process to ensure that their evaluation needs are well addressed and to encourage and support them to make effective use of evaluation findings. It is comprehensive in attending to context, inputs, process, and outcomes. It balances the use of quantitative and qualitative methods. It is keyed to professional standards for evaluations. Finally, the approach emphasizes that evaluations must be grounded in the democratic principles of a free society.

A major limitation is that the collaboration required between an evaluator and stakeholders introduces opportunities for impeding the evaluation and/or biasing its results, especially when the evaluative situation is politically charged. Further, when evaluators are actively influencing the course of a program, they may identify so closely with it that they lose some of the independent, detached perspective needed to provide objective, forthright reports. Moreover, the approach may overemphasize formative evaluation and give too little time and resources to summative evaluation. External metaevaluation has been employed to counteract opportunities for bias and to ensure a proper balance of the formative and summative aspects of evaluation. Though the charge is erroneous, this approach carries the connotation that only top decision makers are served.

Approach 17: Consumer-Oriented Studies

In the consumer-oriented approach, the evaluator is the "enlightened surrogate consumer." He or she must draw direct evaluative conclusions about the program being evaluated. Evaluation is viewed as the process of determining something's merit and worth, with evaluations being the products of that process. The approach regards a consumer's welfare as a program's primary justification and accords that welfare the same primacy in program evaluation. Grounded in a deeply reasoned view of ethics and the common good, together with skills in obtaining and synthesizing pertinent, valid, and reliable information, the evaluator should help developers produce and deliver products and services that are of excellent quality and of great use to consumers (for example, students, their parents, teachers, and taxpayers). More importantly, the evaluator should help consumers identify and assess the merit and worth of competing programs, services, and products.

Advance organizers include societal values, consumers' needs, costs, and criteria of goodness in the particular evaluation domain. The purpose of a consumer-oriented program evaluation is to judge the relative merits and worth of the products and services of alternative programs and, thereby, to help taxpayers, practitioners, and potential beneficiaries make wise choices. The approach is objectivist in assuming an underlying reality and positing that it is possible, although often extremely difficult, to find best answers. It looks at a program comprehensively in terms of its quality and costs, functionally regarding the assessed needs of the intended beneficiaries, and comparatively considering reasonably available alternative programs. Evaluators are expected to subject their program evaluations to evaluations, what Scriven has termed *metaevaluation.*

The approach employs a wide range of assessment topics. These include program description, background and context, client, consumers, resources, function, delivery system, values, standards, process, outcomes, costs, critical competitors, generalizability, statistical significance, assessed needs, bottom-line assessment, practical significance, recommendations, reports, and metaevaluation. The evaluation process begins with consideration of a broad range of such topics, continuously compiles information on all of them, and ultimately culminates in a super-compressed judgment of the program's merit and worth.

Questions for the consumer-oriented study are derived from society, from program constituents, and especially from the evaluator's frame of reference. The general question addressed is: Which of several alternative programs is the best choice, given their differential costs, the needs of the consumer group, the values of society at large, and evidence of both positive and negative outcomes?

Methods include checklists, needs assessments, goal-free evaluation, experimental and quasi-experimental designs, modus operandi analysis, applying codes of ethical conduct, and cost analysis (Scriven, 1974a). A preferred method is for an external, independent consumer advocate to conduct and report findings of studies of publicly supported programs. The approach is keyed to employing a sound checklist of the program's key aspects. Scriven (1991) developed a generic "Key Evaluation Checklist" for this purpose. The main evaluative acts in this approach are scoring, grading, ranking, apportioning, and producing the final synthesis (Scriven, 1994a).

Scriven (1967) was a pioneer in applying the consumer-oriented approach to program evaluation, and his work parallels the concurrent work of Ralph Nader and the Consumers Union in the general field of consumerism. Glass (1969) has supported and developed Scriven's approach. Scriven coined the terms *formative* and *summative* evaluation. He allowed that evaluations can be divergent in early quests for critical competitors and explorations related to clarifying goals and making programs function well. However, he also maintained that ultimately evaluations must converge on summative judgments about a program's merit and worth. While accepting the importance of formative evaluation, he also argued against Cronbach's (1963) position that formative evaluation should be given the major emphasis. According to Scriven, the fundamental aim of a sound evaluation is to judge a program's merit, comparative value, and overall worth. He sees evaluation as a trans-discipline encompassing all evaluations of various entities across all applied areas and disciplines and comprised of a common logic, methodology, and theory that transcends specific evaluation domains, which also have their unique characteristics (Scriven, 1991, 1994a).

The consumer-oriented study requires a highly credible and competent expert, together with either sufficient resources to allow the expert to conduct a thorough study or other means to obtain the needed information. Often, a consumer-oriented evaluator is engaged to evaluate a program after its formative stages are over. In these situations, the external consumer-oriented evaluator is often dependent on being able to access a substantial base of information that the program staff had accumulated. If no such base of information exists, the consumer-oriented evaluator will have great difficulty in obtaining enough information to produce a thorough, defensible summative program evaluation.

One of the main advantages of consumer-oriented evaluation is that it is a hard-hitting, independent assessment intended to protect consumers from shoddy programs, services, and products and to guide them to support and use those contributions that best and most cost-effectively address their needs. The approach's stress on independent/objective assessment and its attempt to achieve a comprehensive assessment of merit and worth yield high credibility with consumer groups. This is aided by Michael Scriven's (1991) Key Evaluation Checklist and his *Evaluation Thesaurus* (in which he presents and explains the checklist). The approach provides for a summative evaluation to yield a bottom-line judgment of merit and worth, preceded by a formative evaluation to assist developers to help ensure that their programs will succeed.

One disadvantage of the consumer-oriented evaluation is that it can be so independent from practitioners that it may not assist them to do a better job in serving consumers. If summative evaluation is applied too early, it can intimidate developers and stifle their creativity. However, if summative evaluation is applied only near a program's end, the evaluator may have great difficulty in obtaining sufficient evidence to confidently and credibly judge the program's basic value. This often iconoclastic approach is also heavily dependent on a highly competent, independent, and "bulletproof" evaluator.

Approach 18: Accreditation/Certification Approach

Many educational institutions, hospitals, and other service organizations have periodically been the subject of an accreditation study, and many professionals, at one time or another, have had to meet certification requirements for a given position. Such studies of institutions and personnel are in the realm of accountability-oriented evaluations, as well as having an improvement element. Institutions, institutional programs, and personnel are studied to prove whether they meet requirements of given professions and service areas and whether they are fit to serve designated functions in society; typically, the feedback reports identify areas for improvement.

The advance organizers used in the accreditation/certification study usually are guidelines and criteria that some accrediting or certifying body has adopted. As previously suggested, the evaluation's purpose is to determine whether institutions, institutional programs, and/or personnel should be approved to perform specified functions.

The source of questions for accreditation or certification studies is the accrediting or certifying body. Basically, they address the question: Are institutions and their programs and personnel meeting minimum standards, and how can their performance be improved?

Typical methods used in the accreditation/certification approach are self-study and self-reporting by the individual or institution. In the case of institutions, panels of experts are assigned to visit the institution, verify a self-report, and gather additional information. The basis for the self-studies and the visits by expert panels are usually guidelines and criteria that have been specified by the accrediting agency.

Accreditation of education was pioneered by the College Entrance Examination Board around 1901. Since then, the accreditation function has been implemented and expanded, especially by the Cooperative Study of Secondary School Standards, dating from around 1933. Subsequently, the accreditation approach has been developed, further expanded, and administered by the North Central Association of Secondary Schools and Colleges, along with their associated regional accrediting agencies across the United States, and by many other accrediting and certifying bodies. Similar accreditation practices are found in medicine, law, architecture, and many other professions.

Any area of professional service that potentially could put the public at risk if services are not delivered by highly trained specialists in accordance with standards of good practice and safety should consider subjecting its programs to accreditation reviews and its personnel to certification processes. Such use of evaluation services is very much in the public interest and is also a means of getting feedback which can be of use in strengthening capabilities and practices.

The major advantage of the accreditation or certification study is that it aids lay persons in making informed judgments about the quality of organizations and programs and the qualifications of individual personnel. Major difficulties are that the guidelines of accrediting and certifying bodies often emphasize inputs and processes and not outcomes. Further, the self-study and visitation processes used in accreditation offer many opportunities for corruption and inept performance. As is the case for a number of the evaluation approaches described above, it is prudent to subject accreditation and certification processes themselves to independent metaevaluations.

The three improvement/accountability-oriented approaches emphasize the assessment of merit and worth, which is the thrust of the definition of evaluation used to classify the 22 approaches considered in this chapter. The chapter turns next to the fourth and final set of program evaluation approaches—those concerned with using evaluation to further some social agenda.

SOCIAL AGENDA-DIRECTED/ADVOCACY APPROACHES

Social Agenda/Advocacy approaches are directed to making a difference in society through program evaluation. These approaches seek to ensure that all segments of society have equal access to educational and social opportunities and services. They have an affirmative action bent toward giving preferential treatment through program evaluation to the disadvantaged. If—as many persons have stated—information is power, then these approaches employ program evaluation to empower the disenfranchised.

The four approaches in this set are oriented to employing the perspectives of stakeholders as well as of experts in characterizing, investigating, and judging programs. They favor a constructivist orientation and the use of qualitative methods. For the most part, they eschew the possibility of finding right or best answers and reflect the philosophy of postmodernism, with its attendant stress on cultural pluralism, moral relativity, and multiple realities. They provide for democratic engagement of stakeholders in obtaining and interpreting findings.

There is a concern that these approaches might concentrate so heavily on serving a social mission that they fail to meet the standards of a sound evaluation. By giving stakeholders the authority for key evaluation decisions, related especially to interpretation and release of findings, evaluators empower these persons to use evaluation to their best advantage. Such delegation of authority over important evaluation matters makes the evaluation vulnerable to bias and other misuse. Further, if an evaluator is intent on serving the underprivileged, empowering the disenfranchised, and/or righting educational and/or social injustices, he or she might compromise the independent, impartial perspective needed to produce valid findings, especially if funds allocated to serve these groups would be withdrawn as a consequence of a negative report. In the extreme, an advocacy evaluation could compromise the integrity of the evaluation process to achieve social objectives and thus devolve into a pseudoevaluation.

Nevertheless, there is much to recommend these approaches, since they are strongly oriented to democratic principles of equity and fairness and employ practical procedures for involving the full range of stakeholders. The particular social agenda/advocacy-directed approaches presented in this chapter seem to have sufficient safeguards needed to walk the line between sound evaluation services and politically corrupted evaluations. Worries about bias control in these approaches increase the importance of subjecting advocacy evaluations to metaevaluations grounded in standards for sound evaluations.

Approach 19: Client-Centered Studies (or Responsive Evaluation)

The classic approach in this set is the client-centered study, or what Robert Stake (1983) has termed the responsive evaluation. The label *client-centered* evaluation is used here, because one pervasive theme is that the evaluator must work with and for the support of a diverse client group including, for example, teachers, administrators, developers, taxpayers, legislators, and financial sponsors. They are the clients in the sense that they support, develop, administer, or directly operate the programs under study and seek or need evaluators' counsel and advice in understanding, judging, and improving programs. The approach charges evaluators to interact continuously with, and respond to, the evaluative needs of the various clients.

This approach contrasts sharply with Scriven's consumer-oriented approach. Stake's evaluators are not the independent, objective assessors of Scriven. The client-centered study embraces local autonomy and helps people who are involved in a program to evaluate it and use the evaluation for program improvement. The evaluator in a sense is the client's handmaiden as they strive to make the evaluation serve their needs. Moreover, the client-centered approach rejects objectivist evaluation, subscribing to the postmodernist view, wherein there are no best answers or clearly preferable values and subjective information is preferred. In this approach, the program evaluation may culminate in conflicting findings and conclusions, leaving interpretation to the eyes of the beholders. Client-centered evaluation is perhaps the leading entry in the "relativistic school of evaluation," which calls for a pluralistic, flexible, interactive, holistic, subjective, constructivist, and service-oriented approach. The approach is relativistic because it seeks no final authoritative conclusion, interpreting findings against stakeholders' different and often conflicting values. The approach seeks to examine a program's full countenance and prizes the collection and reporting of multiple, often conflicting perspectives on the value of a program's format, operations, and achievements. Side effects and incidental gains as well as intended outcomes are to be identified and examined.

The advance organizers in client-centered evaluations are stakeholders' concerns and issues in the program itself, as well as the program's rationale, background, transactions, outcomes, standards, and judgments. The client-centered program evaluation may serve many purposes. Some of these are helping people in a local setting gain a perspective on the program's full countenance; understanding the ways that various groups see the program's problems, strengths, and weaknesses; and learning the ways affected people value the program, as well as the ways program experts judge it. The evaluator's process goal is to carry on a continuous search for key questions and to provide clients with useful information as it becomes available.

The client-centered/responsive approach has a strong philosophical base: evaluators should promote equity and fairness, help those with little power, thwart the misuse of power, expose the huckster, unnerve the assured, reassure the insecure, and always help people see things from alternative viewpoints. The approach subscribes to moral relativity and posits that, for any given set of findings, there are potentially multiple, conflicting interpretations that are equally plausible.

Community, practitioner, and beneficiary groups in the local environment, together with external program area experts, provide the questions addressed by the client-centered study. In general, the groups usually want to know what the program achieved, how it operated, and how it was judged by involved persons and experts in the program area. The more specific evaluation questions emerge as the study unfolds based on the evaluator's continuing interactions with stakeholders and their collaborative assessment of the developing evaluative information.

This approach reflects a formalization of the longstanding practice of informal, intuitive evaluation. It requires a relaxed and continuous exchange between evaluator and clients. It is more divergent than convergent. Basically, the approach calls for continuing communication between evaluator and audience for the purposes of discovering, investigating, and addressing a program's issues. Designs for client-centered program evaluations are relatively open-ended and emergent, building to narrative description, rather than aggregating measurements across cases. The evaluator attempts to issue timely responses to clients' concerns and questions by collecting and reporting useful information, even if the needed information was not anticipated at the study's beginning. Concomitant with the ongoing conversation with clients, the evaluator attempts to obtain and present a rich set of information on the program. This includes its philosophical foundation and purposes, history, transactions, and outcomes. Special attention is given to side effects, the standards that various persons hold for the program, and their judgments of the program.

Depending on the evaluation's purpose, the evaluator may legitimately employ a range of different methods. Preferred methods are the case study, expressive objectives, purposive sampling, observation, adversary reports, story telling to convey complexity, sociodrama, and narrative reports. Client-centered evaluators are charged to check for the existence of stable and consistent findings by employing redundancy in their data-collecting activities and replicating their case studies. They are not expected to act as a program's sole or final judges, but should collect, process, and report the opinions and judgments of the full range of the program's stakeholders as well as those of pertinent experts. In the end, the evaluator makes a comprehensive statement of what the program is observed to be and references the satisfaction and dissatisfaction that appropriately selected people feel toward the program. Overall, the client-centered/responsive evaluator uses whatever information sources and techniques seem relevant to portraying the program's complexities and multiple realities, and communicates the complexity even if the result instills doubt and makes decisions more difficult.

Stake (1967) is the pioneer of the client-centered/responsive type of study, and his approach has been supported and developed by Denny (1978), MacDonald (1975), Parlett and Hamilton (1972), Rippey (1973), and Smith and Pohland (1974). Guba's (1978) early development of constructivist evaluation was heavily influenced by Stake's writings on responsive evaluation. Stake has expressed skepticism about scientific inquiry as a dependable guide to developing generalizations about human services, and pessimism about the potential benefits of formal program evaluations.

The main condition for applying the client-centered approach is a receptive client group and a confident, competent, responsive evaluator. The client must be willing to endorse a quite open, flexible evaluation plan as opposed to a well-developed, detailed, preordinate plan and must be receptive to equitable participation by a representative group of stakeholders. The client must find qualitative methods acceptable and usually be willing to forego anything like a tightly controlled experimental study, although in exceptional cases a controlled field experiment might be employed. Clients and other involved stakeholders need tolerance, even appreciation for ambiguity, and should hold out only modest hopes of obtaining definitive answers to evaluation questions. Clients must also be receptive to ambiguous findings, multiple interpretations, the employment of competing value perspectives, and the heavy involvement of stakeholders in interpreting and using findings. Finally, clients must be sufficiently patient to allow the program evaluation to unfold and find its direction based on ongoing interactions between the evaluator and the stakeholders.

A major strength of the responsive/client-centered approach is that it involves action-research, in which people funding, implementing, and using programs are helped to conduct their own evaluations and use the findings to improve their understanding, decisions, and actions. The evaluations look deeply into the stakeholders' main interests and search broadly for relevant information. They also examine the program's rationale, background, process, and outcomes. They make effective use of qualitative methods and triangulate findings from different sources. The approach stresses the importance of searching widely for unintended as well as intended outcomes. It also gives credence to the meaningful participation in the evaluation by the full range of interested stakeholders. Judgments and other inputs from all such persons are respected and incorporated in the evaluations. The approach also provides for effective communication of findings.

A major weakness is the approach's vulnerability regarding external credibility, since people in the local setting, in effect, have considerable control over the evaluation of their work. Similarly, evaluators working so closely with stakeholders may lose their independent perspectives. The approach is not very amenable to reporting clear findings in time to meet decision or accountability deadlines. Moreover, rather than bringing closure, the approach's adversarial aspects and divergent qualities may generate confusion and contentious relations among stakeholders. Sometimes, this cascading, evolving approach may bog down in an unproductive quest for multiple inputs and interpretations.

Approach 20: Constructivist Evaluation

The constructivist approach to program evaluation is heavily philosophical, service oriented, and paradigm-driven. Constructivism rejects the existence of any ultimate reality and employs a subjectivist epistemology. It sees knowledge gained as one or more human constructions, uncertifiable, and constantly problematic and changing. It places the evaluators and program stakeholders at the center of the inquiry process, employing all of them as the evaluation's "human instruments." The approach insists that evaluators be totally ethical in respecting and advocating for all the participants, especially the disenfranchised. Evaluators are authorized, even expected, to maneuver the evaluation to emancipate and empower involved or affected disenfranchised people. Evaluators do this by raising stakeholders' consciousness so that they are energized, informed, and assisted to transform their world. The evaluator must respect participants' free will in all aspects of the inquiry and should empower them to help shape and control the evaluation activities in their preferred ways. The inquiry process must be consistent with effective ways of changing and improving society. Thus, stakeholders must play a key role in determining the evaluation questions and variables. Throughout the study, the evaluator regularly and continuously informs and consults stakeholders in all aspects of the study. The approach rescinds any special privilege of scientific evaluators to work in secret and control/manipulate human subjects. In guiding the program evaluation, the evaluator balances verification with a quest for discovery, balances rigor with relevance and the use of quantitative and qualitative methods. The evaluator also provides rich and deep description in preference to precise measurements and statistics. He or she employs a relativist perspective to obtain and analyze findings, stressing locality and specificity over generalizability. The evaluator posits that there can be no ultimately correct conclusions. He or she exalts openness and the continuing search for more informed and illuminating constructions.

This approach is as much recognizable for what it rejects as for what it proposes. In general, it strongly opposes positivism as a basis for evaluation, with its realist ontology, objectivist epistemology, and experimental method. It rejects any absolutist search for correct answers. It directly opposes the notion of value-free evaluation and attendant efforts to expunge human bias. It rejects positivism's deterministic and reductionist structure and its belief in the possibility of fully explaining studied programs.

Advance organizers of the contructivist approach are basically the philosophical constraints placed on the study, as noted above, including the requirement of collaborative, unfolding inquiry. The main purpose of the approach is to determine and make sense of the variety of constructions that exist or emerge among stakeholders. Inquiry is kept open to ongoing communication and to the gathering, analysis, and synthesis of further constructions. One construction is not considered more "true" than others, but some may be judged as more informed and sophisticated than others. All evaluation conclusions are viewed as indeterminate, with the continuing possibility of finding better answers. All constructions are also context dependent. In this respect, the evaluator does define boundaries on what is being investigated.

The questions addressed in constructivist studies cannot be determined independently of participants' interactions. Evaluator and stakeholders together identify the questions to be addressed. Questions emerge in the process of formulating and discussing the study's rationale, planning the schedule of discussions, and obtaining various initial persons' views of the program to be evaluated. The questions develop further over the course of the approach's hermeneutic and dialectic processes. Questions may or may not cover the full range of issues involved in assessing something's merit and worth. The set of questions to be studied is never considered fixed.

The constructivist methodology is first divergent, then convergent. Through the use of hermeneutics, the evaluator collects and describes alternative individual constructions on an evaluation question or issue, ensuring that each depiction meets with the respondent's approval. Communication channels are kept open throughout the inquiry, and all respondents are encouraged and facilitated to make their inputs and are kept apprised of all aspects of the study. The evaluator then moves to a dialectical process aimed at achieving as much consensus as possible among different constructions. Respondents are provided with opportunities to review the full range of constructions along with other relevant information. The evaluator engages the respondents in a process of studying and contrasting existing constructions, considering relevant contextual and other information, reasoning out the differences among the constructions, and moving as far as they can toward a consensus. The constructivist evaluation is, in a sense, never-ending. There is always more to learn, and finding ultimately correct answers is considered impossible.

Guba and Lincoln (1985, 1989) are pioneers in applying the constructivist approach to program evaluation. Bhola (1998), a disciple of Guba, has extensive experience in applying the constructivist approach to evaluating programs in Africa. In agreement with Guba, he stresses that evaluations are always a function not only of the evaluator's approach and interactions with stakeholders, but also of his or her personal history and outlook. Thomas Schwandt (1984), another disciple of Guba, has written extensively about the philosophical underpinnings of constructivist evaluation. Fetterman's (1994) empowerment evaluation approach is closely aligned with constructivist evaluation, since it seeks to engage and serve all stakeholders, especially those with little influence. However, there is a key difference between the constructivist and empowerment evaluation approaches. While the constructivist evaluator retains control of the evaluation and works with stakeholders to develop a consensus, the empowerment evaluator "gives away" authority for the evaluation to stakeholders, serving in a technical assistance role.

The constructivist approach can be applied usefully when evaluator, client, and stakeholders in a program fully agree that the approach is appropriate and that they will cooperate. They should reach agreement based on an understanding of what the approach can and cannot deliver. They need to accept that questions and issues to be studied will unfold throughout the process. They also should be willing to receive ambiguous, possibly contradictory findings, reflecting stakeholders' diverse perspectives. They should know that the shelf life of the findings is likely to be short (not unlike any other evaluation approach, but clearly acknowledged in the constructivist approach). They also need to value qualitative information that largely reflects the variety of stakeholders' perspectives and judgments. However, they should not expect to receive definitive pre-post measures of outcomes or statistical conclusions about causes and effects. While these persons can hope for achieving a consensus in the findings, they should agree that such a consensus might not emerge and that in any case such a consensus would not generalize to other settings or time periods.

This approach has a number of advantages. It is exemplary in fully disclosing the whole evaluation process and its findings. It is consistent with the principle of effective change that people are more likely to value and use something (read *evaluation* here) if they are consulted and involved in its development. It also seeks to directly involve the full range of stakeholders who might be harmed or helped by the evaluation as important, empowered partners in the evaluation enterprise. It is said to be educative for all the participants, whether or not a consensus is reached. It also lowers expectations for what clients can learn about causes and effects. While it does not promise final answers, it moves from a divergent stage, in which it searches widely for insights and judgments, to a convergent stage in which some unified answers are sought. In addition, it uses participants as instruments in the evaluation, thus taking advantage of their relevant experiences, knowledge, and value perspectives; this greatly reduces the burden of developing, field-testing, and validating information collection instruments before using them. The approach makes effective use of qualitative methods and triangulates findings from different sources.

The approach, however, is limited in its applicability and has some disadvantages. Because of the need for full involvement and ongoing interaction through both the divergent and convergent stages, it is often difficult to produce the timely reports that funding agencies and decision makers demand. Further, if the approach is to work well, it requires the attention and responsible participation of a wide range of stakeholders. The approach seems to be unrealistically utopian in this regard: widespread, grass-roots interest and participation are often hard to obtain and sustain throughout a program evaluation. The situation can be exacerbated by a continuing turnover of stakeholders. While the process emphasizes and promises openness and full disclosure, some participants do not want to tell their private thoughts and judgments to the world. Moreover, stakeholders sometimes are poorly informed about the issues being addressed in an evaluation and thus are poor data sources. It can be unrealistic to expect that the evaluator can and will take the needed time to inform, and then meaningfully involve, those who begin as basically ignorant of the program being assessed. Further, constructivist evaluations can be greatly burdened by itinerant evaluation stakeholders who come and go, and reopen questions previously addressed and question consensus previously reached. There is the further issue that some evaluation clients do not take kindly to evaluators who are prone to report competing, perspectivist answers, and not take a stand regarding a program's merit and worth. Many clients are not attuned to the constructivist philosophy and they may value reports that mainly include hard data on outcomes and assessments of statistical significance. They may expect reports to be based on relatively independent perspectives that are free of program participants' conflicts of interest. Since the constructivist approach is a countermeasure to assigning responsibility for successes and failures in a program to certain individuals or groups, many policy boards, administrators, and financial sponsors might see this rejection of accountability as unworkable and unacceptable. It is easy to say that all persons in a program should share the glory or the disgrace; but try to tell this to an exceptionally hardworking and effective teacher in a school program where virtually no one else tries or succeeds.

Approach 21: Deliberative Democratic Evaluation

Perhaps the newest entry in the program evaluation models enterprise is the deliberative democratic approach advanced by House and Howe (Chapter 22, this volume). The approach functions within an explicit democratic framework and charges evaluators to uphold democratic principles in reaching defensible conclusions. It envisions program evaluation as a principled, influential societal institution, contributing to democratization through the issuing of reliable and valid claims.

The advance organizers of deliberative democratic evaluation are seen in its three main dimensions: democratic participation, dialogue to examine and authenticate stakeholders' inputs, and deliberation to arrive at a defensible assessment of a program's merit and worth. All three dimensions are considered essential in all aspects of a sound program evaluation.

In the democratic dimension, the approach proactively identifies and arranges for the equitable participation of all interested stakeholders throughout the course of the evaluation. Equity is stressed, and power imbalances in which the message of powerful parties would dominate the evaluation message are not tolerated. In the dialogic dimension, the evaluator engages stakeholders and other audiences to assist in compiling preliminary findings. Subsequently, the collaborators seriously discuss and debate the draft findings to ensure that no participant's views are misrepresented. In the culminating deliberative stage, the evaluator(s) honestly considers and discusses with others all inputs obtained but then renders what he or she considers a fully defensible assessment of the program's merit and worth. All interested stakeholders are given voice in the evaluation, and the evaluator acknowledges their views in the final report, but may express disagreement with some of them. The deliberative dimension sees the evaluator(s) reaching a reasoned conclusion by reviewing all inputs; debating them with stakeholders and others; reflecting deeply on all the inputs; then reaching a defensible, well-justified conclusion.

The purpose of the approach is to employ democratic participation in the process of arriving at a defensible assessment of a program. The evaluator(s) determines the evaluation questions to be addressed, but does so through dialogue and deliberation with engaged stakeholders. Presumably, the bottom-line questions concern judgments about the program's merit and its worth to stakeholders.

Methods employed may include discussions with stakeholders, surveys, and debates. Inclusion, dialogue, and deliberation are considered relevant at all stages of an evaluation—inception, design, implementation, analysis, synthesis, write-up, presentation, and discussion. House and Howe present the following ten questions for assessing the adequacy of a democratic deliberative evaluation: Whose interests are represented? Are major stakeholders represented? Are any excluded? Are there serious power imbalances? Are there procedures to control imbalances? How do people participate in the evaluation? How authentic is their participation? How involved is their interaction? Is there reflective deliberation? How considered and extended is the deliberation?

Ernest House originated this approach. He and Kenneth Howe say that many evaluators already implement their proposed principles, and point to an article by Karlsson (1998) to illustrate their approach. They also refer to a number of authors who have proposed practices that at least in part are compatible with the democratic dialogic approach.

The approach is applicable when a client agrees to fund an evaluation that requires democratic participation of at least a representative group of stakeholders. Thus, the funding agent must be willing to give up sufficient power to allow inputs from a wide range of stakeholders, early disclosure of preliminary findings to all interested parties, and opportunities for the stakeholders to play an influential role in reaching the final conclusions. Obviously, a representative group of stakeholders must be willing to engage in open and meaningful dialogue and deliberation at all stages of the study.

The approach has many advantages. It is a direct attempt to make evaluations just. It strives for democratic participation of stakeholders at all stages of the evaluation. It seeks to incorporate the views of all interested parties, including insiders and outsiders, disenfranchised persons and groups, as well as those who control the purse strings. Meaningful democratic involvement should direct the evaluation to the issues that people care about and incline them to respect and use the evaluation findings. The approach employs dialogue to examine and authenticate stakeholders' inputs. A key advantage over some other advocacy approaches is that the democratic deliberative evaluator expressly reserves the right to rule out inputs that are considered incorrect or unethical. The evaluator is open to all stakeholders' views, carefully considers them, but then renders as defensible a judgment of the program as possible. He or she does not leave the responsibility for reaching a defensible final assessment to a majority vote of stakeholders—some of whom are sure to have conflicts of interest and be uninformed. In rendering a final judgment, the evaluator ensures closure.

As House and Howe have acknowledged, the democratic dialogic approach is, at this time, unrealistic and often cannot be fully applied. The approach—in offering and expecting full democratic participation in order to make an evaluation work—reminds me of a colleague who used to despair of ever changing or improving higher education. He would say that changing any aspect of our university would require getting every professor to withhold her or his veto. In view of the very ambitious demands of the democratic dialogic approach, House and Howe have proposed it as an ideal to be kept in mind even though evaluators will seldom, if ever, be able to achieve it.

Approach 22: Utilization–Focused Evaluation

The utilization-focused approach is explicitly geared to ensure that program evaluations make an impact (Patton, Chapter 23, this volume). It is a process for making choices about an evaluation study in collaboration with a targeted group of priority users, selected from a broader set of stakeholders, in order to focus effectively on their intended uses of the evaluation. All aspects of a utilization-focused program evaluation are chosen and applied to help the targeted users obtain and apply evaluation findings to their intended uses, and to maximize the likelihood that they will. Such studies are judged more for the difference they make in improving programs and influencing decisions and actions than for their elegance or technical excellence. No matter how good an evaluation report is, if it only sits on the shelf gathering dust, then it will not contribute positively to the evaluation and possibly should not have been written.

Placement of Patton's evaluation approach within the category system used in this chapter was problematic. His chapter was placed in the Social Agenda section because it requires democratic participation of a representative group of stakeholders, whom it empowers to determine the evaluation questions and information needs. Patton gives away such authority over the evaluation to increase the likelihood that the findings will be used. However, utilization-focused evaluations do not necessarily advocate any social agenda, such as affirmative action to right injustices and better serve the poor. While the approach is in agreement with the improvement/accountability-oriented approaches in guiding decisions, promoting impacts, and invoking the Joint Committee (1994) *Program Evaluation Standards*, it does not quite fit there. It does not, for example, require assessments of merit and worth. In fact, Patton essentially has said that his approach is pragmatic and ubiquitous. In the interest of getting findings used, he will draw upon any legitimate approach to evaluation, leaving out any parts that might impede use. As for the dilemma of categorizing the Utilization-Based Evaluation Model, the reader will note that we placed Patton's chapter in this volume, not in the Social Agenda Evaluation Models section, but in the section on overarching matters (Section V).

The advance organizers of utilization-focused program evaluations are, in the abstract, the possible users and uses to be served. Working from this initial conception, the evaluator moves as directly as possible to identify in concrete terms the actual users to be served. Through careful and thorough analysis of stakeholders, the evaluator identifies the multiple and varied perspectives and interests that should be represented in the study. He or she then selects a group that is willing to pay the price of substantial involvement and that represents the program's stakeholders. The evaluator then engages this client group to clarify why they need the evaluation, how they intend to apply its findings, how they think it should be conducted, and what types of reports (e.g., oral and/or printed) should be provided. He or she facilitates users' choices by supplying a menu of possible uses, information, and reports for the evaluation. This is done not to supply the choices but to help the client group thoughtfully focus and shape the study. The main possible uses of evaluation findings contemplated in this approach are assessment of merit and worth, improvement, and generation of knowledge. The approach also values the evaluation process itself, seeing it as helpful in enhancing shared understandings among stakeholders, bringing support to a program, promoting participation in it, and developing and strengthening organizational capacity. According to Patton, when the evaluation process is sound and functional, a printed final report may not be needed.

In deliberating with intended users, the evaluator emphasizes that the program evaluation's purpose must be to give them the information they need to fulfill their objectives. Such objectives may include socially valuable aims such as combating problems of illiteracy, crime, hunger, homelessness, unemployment, child abuse, spouse abuse, substance abuse, illness, alienation, discrimination, malnourishment, pollution, and bureaucratic waste. However, it is the targeted users who determine the program to be evaluated, what information is required, how and when it must be reported, and how it will be used.

In this approach, the evaluator is no iconoclast, but rather the intended users' servant. Among other roles, he or she is a facilitator. The evaluation should meet the full range of professional standards for program evaluations, not just utility. The evaluator must therefore be an effective negotiator, standing on principles of sound evaluation, but working hard to gear a defensible program evaluation to the targeted users' evolving needs. The utilization-focused evaluation is considered situational and dynamic. Depending on the circumstances, the evaluator may play any of a variety of roles—trainer, measurement expert, internal colleague, external expert, analyst, spokesperson, or mediator.

The evaluator works with the targeted users to determine the evaluation questions. Such questions are to be determined locally, may address any of a wide range of concerns, and probably will change over time. Example foci are processes, outcomes, impacts, costs, and cost benefits. The chosen questions are kept front and center and provide the basis for information collection and reporting plans and activities, so long as users continue to value and pay attention to the questions. Often, however, the evaluator and client group will adapt, change, or refine the questions as the evaluation unfolds.

All evaluation methods are fair game in a utilization-focused program evaluation. The evaluator will creatively employ whatever methods are relevant (e.g., quantitative and qualitative, formative and summative, naturalistic and experimental). As far as possible, the utilization-focused evaluator puts the client group in "the driver's seat" in determining evaluation methods to ensure that the evaluator focuses on their most important questions; collects the right information; applies the relevant values; answers the key action-oriented questions; uses techniques they respect; reports the information in a form and at a time to maximize use; convinces stakeholders of the evaluation's integrity and accuracy; and facilitates the users' study, application, and—as appropriate—dissemination of findings. The bases for interpreting evaluation findings are the users' values, and the evaluator will engage in values clarification to ensure that evaluative information and interpretations serve users' purposes. Users are actively involved in interpreting findings. Throughout the evaluation process, the evaluator balances the concern for utility with provisions for validity and cost-effectiveness.

In general, the method of utilization-focused program evaluation is labeled "active-reactive-adaptive and situationally responsive," emphasizing that the methodology evolves in response to ongoing deliberations between evaluator and client group, and in consideration of contextual dynamics. Patton (1997) says that "Evaluators are active in presenting to intended users their own best judgments about appropriate evaluation focus and methods; they are reactive in listening attentively and respectfully to others' concerns; and they are adaptive in finding ways to design evaluations that incorporate diverse interests . . . while meeting high standards of professional practice (p. 383)."

Patton (1980, 1982, 1994, 1997, Chapter 23, this volume) is the leading proponent of utilization-based evaluation. Other advocates of the approach are Alkin (1995), Cronbach and Associates (1980), Davis and Salasin (1975), and the Joint Committee on Standards for Educational Evaluation (1981b, 1994).

As defined by Patton, the approach has virtually universal applicability. It is situational and can be tailored to meet any program evaluation assignment. It carries with it the integrity of sound evaluation principles. Within these general constraints, the evaluator negotiates all aspects of the evaluation to serve specific individuals who need to have a program evaluation performed and who intend to make concrete use of the findings. The evaluator selects from the entire range of evaluation techniques those that best suit the particular evaluation. And the evaluator plays any of a wide range of evaluation and improvement-related roles that fit the local needs. The approach requires a substantial outlay of time and resources by all participants, both for conducting the evaluation and the needed follow-through.

The approach is geared to maximizing evaluation impacts. It fits well with a key principle of change: Individuals are more likely to understand, value, and use the findings of an evaluation if they were meaningfully involved in the enterprise. As Patton (1997) says, "by actively involving primary intended users, the evaluator is training users in use, preparing the groundwork for use, and reinforcing the intended utility of the evaluation" (p. 22). The approach engages stakeholders to determine the evaluation's purposes and procedures and uses their involvement to promote the use of findings. It takes a more realistic approach to stakeholder involvement than some other advocacy approaches. Rather than trying to reach and work with all stakeholders, Patton's approach works concretely with a select, representative group of users. The approach emphasizes values clarification and attends closely to contextual dynamics. It may selectively use any and all relevant evaluation procedures and triangulates findings from different sources. Finally, the approach stresses the need to meet all relevant standards for evaluations.

Patton sees the main limitation of the approach to be turnover of involved users. Replacement users may require that the program evaluation be renegotiated, which may be necessary to sustain or renew the prospects for evaluation impacts. But it can also derail or greatly delay the process. Further, the approach seems to be vulnerable to corruption by user groups, since they are given so much control over what will be looked at, the questions addressed, the methods employed, and the information obtained. Stakeholders with conflicts of interest may inappropriately influence the evaluation. For example, they may inappropriately limit the evaluation to a subset of the important questions. It may also be almost impossible to get a representative users group to agree on a sufficient commitment of time and safe-guards to ensure an ethical, valid process of data collection, reporting, and use. More-over, effective implementation of this approach requires a highly competent, confident evaluator who can approach any situation flexibly without compromising basic professional standards. Strong skills of negotiation are essential, and the evalu-ator must possess expertise in the full range of quantitative and qualitative evalua-tion methods, strong communication and political skills, and working knowledge of all applicable standards for evaluations. Unfortunately, not many evaluators are suf-ficiently trained and experienced to meet these requirements.

The utilization-based approach to evaluation concludes this chapter's discussion of social agenda/advocacy approaches. The four approaches concentrate on making evaluation an instrument of social justice and modesty and candor in presenting findings that often are ambiguous and contradictory. All four approaches promote utilization of findings through involvement of stakeholders.

BEST APPROACHES FOR 21ST CENTURY EVALUATIONS

Of the variety of evaluation approaches that emerged during the 20th century, nine can be identified as the strongest and most promising for continued use and devel-opment beyond the year 2000. The other 13 approaches also have varying degrees of merit, but I chose in this section to focus on what I judged to be the most promising approaches. The ratings of these approaches appear in Table 1. They are listed in order of merit, within the categories of Improvement/Accountability, Social Mission/Advocacy, and Questions/Methods evaluation approaches. The ratings are based on the Joint Committee *Program Evaluation Standards* and were derived by the author using a special checklist keyed to the *Standards*.

All nine of the approaches earned overall ratings of Very Good, except Accredi-tation, which was judged Good overall.[1] The Utilization-Based and Client-Centered approaches received Excellent ratings in the standards area of Utility, while the Decision/Accountability approach was judged Excellent in provisions for Accuracy. The rating of Good in the Accuracy area for the Outcomes Monitor-ing/Value-Added approach was due not to this approach's low merit in what it does, but to the narrowness of questions addressed and information used; in its narrow sphere of application, the approach provides technically sound information. The comparatively lower ratings given to the Accreditation approach result from its being labor intensive and expensive; its susceptibility to conflict of interest; its overreliance on self-reports and brief site visits; and its insular resistance to independent metaevaluations. Nevertheless, the distinctly American and pervasive accreditation approach is entrenched. All who use it are advised to strengthen it in the areas of weakness identified in this chapter. The Consumer-Oriented approach also deserves its special place, with its emphasis on independent assessment of developed products and services. While the approach is not especially applicable to internal evaluations for improvement, it complements such approaches with an outsider, expert view that becomes important when products and services are put up for dissemination.

The Case Study approach scored surprisingly well, considering that it is focused on use of a particular technique. An added bonus is that it can be employed on its own or as a component of any of the other approaches. As mentioned previously, the Democratic Deliberative approach is new and appears to be promising for testing and further development. Finally, the Constructivist approach is a well-founded, mainly qualitative approach to evaluation that systematically engages interested parties to help conduct both the divergent and convergent stages of evaluation. All in all, the nine approaches summarized in Table 1 bode well for the future application and further development of alternative program evaluation approaches.

SUMMARY AND CONCLUSIONS

The last half of the 20ᵗʰ century saw considerable development of program evaluation approaches. In this chapter, 22 identified approaches were grouped as pseudoevaluations, questions/methods-oriented evaluations, improvement/accountability-oriented evaluations, and social mission/advocacy evaluations. Apart from pseudoevaluations, there is among the approaches an increasingly balanced quest for rigor, relevance, and justice. Clearly, the approaches are showing a strong orientation to stakeholder involvement and the use of multiple methods.

When compared to professional standards for program evaluations, the best approaches are decision/accountability, utilization-based, client-centered, consumer-oriented, case study, democratic deliberative, constructivist, accreditation, and outcomes monitoring. While House and Howe's (Chapter 22, this volume) democratic deliberative approach is new and in their view utopian, it has many elements of a sound, effective evaluation approach and merits study, further development, and trial. The worst bets were found to be the politically controlled, public relations, accountability (especially payment by results), clarification hearings, and program theory-based approaches. The rest fell in the middle. A critical analysis of the approaches has important implications for evaluators, those who train evaluators, theoreticians concerned with devising better concepts and methods, and those engaged in professionalizing program evaluation.

A major consideration for the practitioner is that evaluators may encounter considerable difficulties if their perceptions of the study being undertaken differ from those of their clients and audiences. Frequently, clients want a politically advantageous study performed, while the evaluator wants to conduct questions/methods-oriented studies that allow him or her to exploit the methodologies in which he or she was trained. Moreover, audiences usually want values-oriented studies that will help them determine the relative merits and worth of competing programs, or advocacy evaluations that will give them voice in the issues that affect them. If evaluators ignore the likely conflicts in purposes, the program evaluation is probably doomed to fail. At an evaluation's outset, evaluators must be keenly sensitive to their own agenda for the study, as well as those that are held by the client and the other right-to-know audiences. Further, the evaluator should advise involved parties of possible conflicts in the evaluation's purposes and should, at the beginning, negotiate a common understanding of the evaluation's purpose and the appropriate

Table 1. RATINGS Strongest Program Evaluation Approaches Within types, listed in order of compliance with *The Program Evaluation Standards*

Evaluation Approach	Graph of overall merit	Overall Score & Rating	UTILITY Rating	FEASIBILITY Rating	PROPRIETY Rating	ACCURACY Rating
IMPROVEMENT/ACCOUNTABILITY						
Decision/Accountability		92 (V G)	90 (V G)	92 (V G)	88 (V G)	98 (E)
Consumer Orientation		81 (V G)	81 (V G)	75 (V G)	91 (V G)	81 (V G)
Accreditation		60 (G)	71 (V G)	58 (G)	59 (G)	50 (G)
SOCIAL MISSION/ADVOCACY						
Utilization-Focused		87 (V G)	96 (E)	92 (V G)	81 (V G)	79 (V G)
Client-Centered		87 (V G)	93 (E)	92 (V G)	75 (V G)	88 (V G)
Democratic Deliberative		83 (V G)	96 (E)	92 (V G)	75 (V G)	69 (V G)
Constructivist		80 (V G)	82 (V G)	67 (G)	88 (V G)	83 (V G)
QUESTIONS/METHODS						
Case Study		80 (V G)	68 (V G)	83 (V G)	78 (V G)	92 (V G)
Outcomes Monitoring/Value-Added		72 (V G)	71 (V G)	92 (V G)	69 (V G)	56 (G)

Graph scale: 0 ⟶ 100, with categories P | F | G | VG | E

The procedures behind the ratings: The author rated each evaluation approach on each of the 30 Joint Committee program evaluation standards by judging whether the approach endorses each of 10 key features of the standard. He judged the approach's adequacy on each standard as follows: 9-10 Excellent, 7-8 Very Good, 5-6 Good, 3-4 Fair, 0-2 Poor. The score for the approach on each of the 4 categories of standards (Utility, Feasibility, Propriety, Accuracy) was then determined by summing the following products: 4 x number of Excellent ratings, 3 x number of Very Good ratings, 2 x number of Good ratings, 1 x number of Fair ratings. Judgments of the approach's strength in satisfying each category of standards were then determined according to percentages of the possible quality points for the category of standards as follows: 93%-100% Excellent, 68%-92% Very Good, 50%-67% Good, 25%-49% Fair, 0%-24% Poor. This was done by converting each category score to the percent of the maximum score for the category and multiplying by 100. The 4 equalized scores were then summed, divided by 4, and compared to the total maximum value, 100. The approach's overall merit was then judged as follows: 93-100 Excellent, 68-92 Very Good, 50-67 Good, 25-49 Fair, 0-24 Poor. Regardless of the approach's total score and overall rating, a notation of unacceptable would have been attached to any approach receiving a poor rating on the vital standards of P1 Service Orientation, A5 Valid Information, A10 Justified Conclusions, A11 Impartial Reporting. The author's ratings were based on his knowledge of the Joint Committee Program Evaluation Standards, his many years of studying the various evaluation models and approaches, and his experience in seeing and assessing how some of these models and approaches worked in practice. He chaired the Joint Committee on Standards for Educational Evaluation during its first 13 years and led the development of the first editions of both the program and personnel evaluation standards. Nevertheless, his ratings should be viewed as only his personal set of judgments of these models and approaches. Also, his conflict of interest is acknowledged, since he was one of the developers of the Decision/Accountability approach. The scale ranges in the above graphs are **P** =Poor, **F**=Fair, **G**=Good, **VG**=Very Good, **E**=Excellent.

approach. Evaluators should also regularly inform participants in their evaluations of the selected approach's logic, rationale, process, and pitfalls. This will enhance stakeholders' cooperation and constructive use of findings.

Evaluation training programs should effectively address the ferment over and development of new program evaluation approaches. Trainers should directly teach their students about expanding and increasingly sophisticated program evaluation approaches. When students clearly understand the approaches, and provided they know when and how to apply them they will be in a position to discern which approaches are worth using and which are not.

For the theoretician, a main point is that the approaches all have inherent strengths and weaknesses. In general, the weaknesses of the politically oriented studies are that they are vulnerable to conflicts of interest and may mislead an audience into developing an unfounded, perhaps erroneous, judgment of a program's merit and worth. The main problem with the questions/methods-oriented studies is that they often address questions that are too narrow to support a full assessment of merit and worth. However, it is also noteworthy that these types of studies compete favorably with improvement/accountability-oriented evaluation studies and social agenda/advocacy studies in the efficiency of methodology employed. Improvement/accountability-oriented studies, with their concentration on merit and worth, undertake a very ambitious task, for it is virtually impossible to fully and unequivocally assess any program's ultimate worth. Such an achievement would require omniscience, infallibility, an unchanging environment, and an unquestioned, singular value base. Nevertheless, the continuing attempt to address questions of merit and worth is essential for the advancement of societal programs. Finally, the social mission/advocacy studies are to be applauded for their quest for equity as well as excellence in programs being studied. They model their mission by attempting to make evaluation a participatory, democratic enterprise. Unfortunately, many pitfalls attend such utopian approaches. These approaches are especially susceptible to bias, and they face practical constraints in involving, informing, and empowering targeted stakeholders.

For the evaluation profession itself, the review of program evaluation approaches underscores the importance of standards and metaevaluations. Professional standards are needed to maintain a consistently high level of integrity in uses of the various approaches. All legitimate approaches are enhanced when evaluators key their studies to professional standards for evaluation and obtain independent reviews of their evaluations.

NOTE

1. A test to determine differences between overall ratings of models based on one approach that sums across 30 equally weighted standards and the approach used in Table 1 that provides the average of scores for four equally weighted categories of standards (having different numbers of standards in each category) yielded a Pearson correlation of .968.

II. QUESTIONS/METHODS-ORIENTED EVALUATION MODELS

The book's first group of evaluation models are labeled **Questions/Methods-Oriented Models**. They are oriented to (1) address specified questions whose answers may or may not be sufficient to assess a program's merit and worth and/or (2) use some preferred method(s). Studies following these models employ as their starting points operational objectives, standardized measurement devices, cost analysis procedures, expert judgment, a theory or model of a program, case study procedures, management information systems, designs for controlled experiments, and/or a commitment to employ a mixture of qualitative and quantitative methods. Most of them emphasize technical quality and posit that it is usually better to answer a few pointed questions well than to attempt a broad assessment of something's merit and worth. Since these models tend to concentrate on methodological adequacy in answering given questions rather than determining a program's value, they may be referred to as **quasi-evaluation** models. While studies following these approaches are typically labeled as evaluations, they may or may not meet the requirements of a sound evaluation.

4. A RATIONALE FOR PROGRAM EVALUATION

RALPH W. TYLER

There are two closely related rationales, each of which is often referred to as the *Tyler Rationale*. One was developed specifically for evaluation activities and was first published in 1934 under the title *Constructing Achievement Tests* (Tyler, 1934). The other evolved from my work as director of evaluation for the Eight-Year Study. It was a general rationale for curriculum development and was first published in 1945 as a mimeographed syllabus for my course at the University of Chicago, entitled *Basic Principles of Curriculum and Instruction*. This was later picked up by the University of Chicago Press and published as a book in 1949 (Tyler, 1949). Each of these statements was formulated as an outgrowth of particular circumstances and is intended to furnish a defensible and orderly procedure to deal with such situations.

THE BACKGROUND OF CONSTRUCTING ACHIEVEMENT TESTS

I was brought to the Ohio State University in 1929 by W. W. Charters, director of the university's Bureau of Educational Research, to head the Division of Accomplishment Testing. He believed that one of the major missions of the bureau was to provide assistance to the university in seeking to improve the instruction of undergraduates. At that time, the university administrator and many members of the Ohio legislature expressed great concern over the fact that a large percentage of the students did not continue their university education beyond the freshman year. The faculties were urged to improve their teaching, particularly in first- and second-year classes where the failures and drop-outs were highly concentrated. Charters believed that teaching and learning in the university could be markedly improved with the

D.L. Stufflebeam, G.F. Madaus and T. Kellaghan (eds.). EVALUATION MODELS. Copyright © 2000. Kluwer Academic Publishers. Boston. All rights reserved.

aid of relevant research and the use of tests and measurements. He asked me to focus my initial efforts on research in the undergraduate courses. I began in the biology courses with the cooperation of the instructors.

The instructors told me of their difficulties in trying to help their students to understand biological phenomena so that they could explain the phenomena in terms of basic concepts and principles, and solve some common biological problems by drawing upon observations, making inferences from data, and applying relevant principles. Most of the students would perform well on written tests, but in class and laboratory few of them could explain newly observed phenomena or solve problems not taken up in class. I found that the instructors were using tests that demanded only that students recall specific information. None of the test exercises required the more complex behaviors that the courses were planned to help students learn. This was typical of the tests commonly in use at that time. The most widely used tests in high school and college appraised only recall of information on specific skills in mathematics and reading.

Using tests of this sort, the instructors were unable to assess objectively the progress of their students in learning what the courses were designed to help them learn. Furthermore, the use of tests of recall gave the students the wrong notion of what they were expected to learn. They were being rewarded by their good test performance on memorizing specific information and were given no opportunity in the examinations to demonstrate the behaviors that the instructors believed to be most important. As we discussed this observation, it seemed clear that new tests should be constructed, tests that would appraise the degree to which students were achieving the objectives of the courses.

At that time, the accepted methodology for constructing objective achievement tests was to sample the content of the textbooks and other instructional materials used by teachers, and to write questions requiring the students to reproduce this content. In my own earlier experience in constructing tests, I usually had in mind what I thought the student should be able to do with each category of content, and I believed that most skillful test-item writers had some notion of what the educational objectives should be, but these unexamined ideas were too idiosyncratic to substitute for an explicit statement by those responsible for the curriculum and instructional program. Hence, the first step in constructing tests useful in guiding instruction in these biology courses was to identify the educational objectives of these courses.

As I worked with the instructors, asking them what they expected students to be learning in and from their courses, I found that the first answers were usually very general and often vague. For example, "I am trying to teach them to think," "I am teaching the scientific method," "I want them to develop skill in the laboratory." Since the fundamental purpose of education is to help students acquire new ways of thinking, feeling, and acting, objectives should be defined clearly enough to indicate what the educational program is intended to help students develop—what kinds of behavior; what ways of thinking, feeling, or acting; and with what content.

As instructors recognized the need for clear definition they were able to set aside several afternoons during which we worked out definitions of the objectives they had in mind, expressing them in terms of *behavior* and *content*. For example, the definition they developed for understanding biological phenomena was: to explain common biological phenomena in terms of relevant concepts and principles. Then, they listed some 23 concepts and 93 principles that were dealt with in the course and that could be used to explain most of the common biological phenomena encountered in that geographic region. The objective, making inferences from experimental data, was defined as making logical inferences from data presented in dealing with common biological phenomena and presented in current publications in biology. The objective, skill in the use of laboratory instruments, was defined as using the compound microscope properly and making sections of common plant and animal tissues that can be mounted on slides. These are illustrations of the result of their efforts to clarify their educational goals. Other objectives that they defined were: application of biological principles, interest in biology, and recall of important facts and definitions.

As these objectives were defined, it became evident that the exercises to be constructed to test for them would require much more than multiple-choice test items and that, for some, no paper-and-pencil test would likely be valid. We thought that skillfully constructed multiple-choice tests would serve for appraising the students' recall of information and definitions, and some modifications of such paper-and-pencil tests could be used to assess the students' understanding of biological phenomena, their ability to draw inferences from experimental data, and their ability to apply principles in explaining biological phenomena. However, we saw no valid substitute for a direct test of performance in using laboratory instruments. Furthermore, an appraisal of students' interest in biology would require the development of a new test procedure.

This experience with the biology courses was repeated in work with instructors of courses in chemistry, mathematics, philosophy, accounting, history, and home economics in the period from 1930–34. It led to my writing the article, "A Generalized Technique for Constructing Achievement Tests," which appeared in the volume, *Constructing Achievement Tests*, referred to in the first paragraph of this paper.

As we developed tests for the objectives of the biology course, we used them to gain greater understanding of what the students were leaning and where they seemed to have difficulty. For example, we found that the students were able to draw appropriate inferences from the data that the instructors were interpreting in class and laboratory, but few were able to interpret data that they had not seen before. This finding led naturally to modifying the course procedure so that students could have practice in reading and interpreting experimental data that had not previously been discussed in class. The instructors and I worked closely together in developing tests, studying and discussing the results, and trying to improve the courses where the test results suggested inadequacies. The changes in the courses were tested continuously in order to find out what changes seemed to remedy the faults identified earlier. Program evaluation proved to be a very useful means in assisting course improvements.

GENERALIZING FROM THESE EXPERIENCES

Although this rationale for achievement testing was conceived and developed to serve the particular purpose of furnishing assistance to instructors in under-graduate courses in the Ohio State University, I perceived it as having general usefulness and wrote the article mentioned above, "A Generalized Technique for Constructing Achievement Tests." This procedure involves the following steps:

1. *Identifying the objectives of the educational program.*
2. *Defining each objective in terms of behavior and content.* The definition should not be so specific that it is in conflict with the basic aim of all educational activi-ties, which is to help students generalize, that is, to be guided by principles, modes of approaching situations, cognitive maps, and the like, rather than by rigid rules and habits. The objective should be clearly defined at the level of generality intended by those planning and conducting the course.
3. *Identifying situations where objectives are utilized.* The logic of this step should be obvious. If one has learned something, one has internalized it and can be expected to utilize it wherever it is appropriate. Hence, if we wish to find out whether a student has learned something, we should look at those situations where the learner can use what he has learned. A test, therefore, should sample these situations.
4. *Devising ways to present situations.* For the students to demonstrate what they have learned, the appropriate situations need to be presented in a way that will evoke the reactions that the normal situations would evoke; or, alternatively, practical ways should be devised to observe the students' reactions in the situa-tions that they normally encounter where the attainment of the objectives can be shown. It is often difficult to devise artificial situations in which the simula-tions seem so real as to assure the students' motivation to respond. This is the reason for using the term *evoke* rather than the more passive phrase, *requiring a response.*
5. *Devising ways to obtain a record.* In most written tests the students make the record by writing their response or by checking one or more of the responses presented to them. The popularity of the multiple-response test is due to the case of recording the responses as well as the apparent simplicity of appraising them. When the skill or ability is accurately indicated by a product the students make, such as a composition, a dress, or a work of art, the product itself becomes the record that can be preserved for careful appraisal. Observation checklists, anecdotal records, and photographs can furnish records of reactions that do not furnish their own record.
6. *Deciding on the terms to use in appraisal.* The tradition of scoring or grading tests in terms of the number of correct responses has often prevailed when the sum of correct responses does not furnish a useful or a reasonably accurate appraisal of the students' attainment of the objectives. An important consideration is to use terms or units that properly reflect the desirable characteristics of the students' reactions in contrast to the undesirable or less desirable. For example,

in appraising the reactions of students in attacking a problem of resource allocations, the number of relevant major factors they consider can be the units of desirable characteristics, while the failure to work on their interrelation can be a descriptive term of an undesirable reaction. In some cases, as in diagnosis, the terms used may need to indicate syndromes or types of difficulties the learner is encountering. In appraising products like compositions, two appraisal schemes can be used—one indicating the level of quality of the total product and the other furnishing a report on the number of different desirable or undesirable features, like compound sentences and misspelled words.

7. *Devising means to get a representative sample.* We all know that human behavior may vary under different conditions, even when these conditions are clearly defined. One may read newspaper articles easily and find it hard to read the directions for assembling an appliance. One can use a large vocabulary in speaking of art and still be limited in the words used to discuss social issues. For a test to furnish reliable information about what students have learned, it must be based on a representative and reliable sample of the situations in which this learning can be exhibited. To obtain a representative sample of something, it is necessary to define the universe of this *something* and then to draw random or stratified samples from this universe. For example, to obtain a representative sample of the reading situations for a sixth-grade test in comprehension, it is necessary to define the universe of things the sixth-grader reads, such as kinds of textbooks, stories, newspapers, directions, etc. It is from this universe that samples can be drawn for testing. A sample is likely to be representative if it is drawn from the universe by a random procedure or by being divided into strata, each randomly sampled and then put together with the samples from the other strata by the appropriate weights. The adequacy of the sample—that is, its required size—depends upon both the precision demanded for the purposes that the test is to serve and the variability of the students' reactions to the different situations. The more variable the student reactions are, the larger the sample required for the desired reliability.

THE BACKGROUND FOR THE CURRICULUM RATIONALE

In 1934, I was asked to serve as director of evaluation for the Eight-Year Study. This study grew out of pressures for change in the high school curriculum, which came from several sources. The high schools of 1930 were still very much like those of 1920, particularly in terms of curriculum content and learning activities. High school staffs felt that they were prevented from making improvements because of the rigidity of college entrance requirements and of state accreditation regulations. Pressures for change were mounting, coming in part from the students themselves. Many of the young people entering high school came from elementary schools that had given them greater freedom and more opportunities for self-direction in learning than they were permitted as high school students. Moreover, with the onset of the Great Depression in 1929, new demands for change came with such force that they could no longer be denied. Many young people, unable to find work, enrolled in high school. Most of these new students did not plan to go to college, and most of them found little meaning and interest in their high school tasks. But still they went to school; there was no other place for them to go.

The high school curriculum of 1930 was not designed for these young people. Most teachers and principals recognized this fact, and many favored a move to reconstruct the high school curriculum and the instructional program both to meet the needs of these Depression youth and to respond to the pressures to give greater opportunities for self-direction in learning. At the same time, however, they did not want to jeopardize the chance of college admission for students who wished to go there, or to lose their state accreditation. This was the dilemma.

The Progressive Education Association took the lead in attacking the problem. Its officers appointed the Commission on the Relation of School and College and charged it with the task of devising a way out of the impasse. The commission served as a forum for the presentation of conflicting points-of-view. Finally, a sufficient degree of consensus was reached to enable the commission to recommend a pilot program. A small number of secondary schools—ultimately 30 schools and school systems—were to be selected by the commission and, for eight years, were to be permitted to develop educational programs that each school believed to be appropriate for its students, without regard to the current college entrance requirements or state accreditation regulations. The schools would be responsible for collecting and reporting information about what students were learning—information that would help the colleges in selecting candidates for admission. The commission would make sure that a comprehensive evaluation of the pilot program would be made and the findings reported.

The schools of the Eight-Year Study began their pilot efforts in September 1933. It soon became apparent that they needed assistance, both in curriculum development, and evaluation. The Progressive Education Association established the Commission on the Secondary School Curriculum, which sponsored a series of studies of adolescents. The adolescent studies, under Caroline Zachry's direction, were to provide helpful information about the interests, needs, activities, and learning characteristics of youth. Under the leadership of Harold Alberty, subject-matter committees were formed to draw upon these studies and others, and to publish volumes that would furnish statements, overall objectives, relevant subject-matter, and possible learning activities for these subjects.

To meet the need for assistance in evaluation, the Steering Committee asked me to serve as director of evaluation and to assemble a staff to develop the procedures and the instruments. The curriculum associates and the evaluation staff worked closely with the schools throughout the pilot period. Learning how to develop and operate a new curriculum and instructional program designed to be serviceable to high school students proved to be a highly significant experience.

Most of the schools began their curriculum development efforts with one or two ideas about what needed to be done, but they soon discovered that the problems were more complex than they had earlier conceived. Those who had become very conscious of the large gap between the needs and interests of students and the content of the curriculum soon found that there was also a serious problem of relating the curriculum to the opportunities and demands of the changing situations that students were encountering in life outside the school. Others who began with their focus on developing a curriculum relevant to the social changes so evident in the 1930s were soon faced with the fact that the students' motivation to learn was closely related to their perception of the value of what was being taught in terms of meeting their needs and interests. Further, all the schools were reminded of the fact that much of the current content was considered obsolete by many scholars in the several subject-matter fields. It soon became apparent that the development of the curriculum and instructional program and the plan of evaluation required more time than was available on weekends, when the working committees met during the first year-and-a-half of the program. It was then that we devised the summer workshops, in which representative teachers from all of the schools worked together with the Study staffs and subject-matter consultants for six weeks each summer to develop what was needed.

In 1936, the Curriculum Staff pointed out that the Evaluation Staff had an excellent rationale to guide its work, but there was no such rationale to guide the curriculum efforts. With the encouragement of my associate, Hilda Taba, we developed the rationale that is presented in the syllabus entitled, *Basic Principles of Curriculum and Instruction*. It, like the rationale for testing, evolved from the particular situations of the Eight-Year Study and was designed as a general procedure to guide the development activities in our summer workshops. However, as I participated later in other situations, particularly, in the Cooperative Study in General Education sponsored by the American Council in Education, I found the rationale applicable to those different contexts. This recognition led to my use of it in my courses in curriculum development.

The rationale is simply an orderly way of planning. It identifies four basic questions that should be answered in developing curriculum and plan of instruction. These questions are.

1. *What education objectives are the students to be helped to attain?*   That is, what are they to be helped to learn? What ways of thinking, feeling, and acting are they to be helped to develop in this educational program?
2. *What learning experiences can be provided that will enable the students to attain the objectives?*   That is, how will the students be helped to learn what is proposed?
3. *How will the learning experiences be organized to maximize their cumulative effect?* That is, what sequence of learning and what plan of integration of learning experiences will be worked out to enable students to internalize what they are learning and apply it in appropriate situations that they encounter?
4. *How will the effectiveness of the program be evaluated?*   That is, what procedure will be followed to provide a continuing check on the extent to which the desired learning is taking place?

The efforts to answer these questions are not to be treated in a one-way, linear fashion. As committees worked on learning experiences, developing resources, and trying them out, they often obtained information or thought of new points that caused them to re-examine the objectives and to check on the organization of experiences, as well as to see that the evaluation procedure was appropriate for the learning activities proposed. Similarly, working out a plan for the sequence and integration of learning experiences often gave rise to re-examination of the treatment of the other three questions. Always, of course, evidence obtained from evaluation led to further consideration of objectives, learning experiences, and organization. The basic questions in the rationale were viewed as parts of a cyclical procedure rather than a linear one.

In connection with each question, the rationale suggests the kinds of empirical data that can inform the judgments that are made and the kinds of criteria to guide the judgments. Thus, in selecting educational objectives data regarding the demands and opportunities in contemporary society, information about the needs, interests, activities, habits, knowledge, and skills of the students, and the potential contributions of relevant subject-matters can inform the committees in a more comprehensive way than most curriculum groups have considered. Furthermore, the explicit formulation of the accepted philosophy of education and the state-of-the-art in the psychology of learning can provide criteria that are more thoughtfully considered than the intuitive judgments that committees often make.

In developing learning experiences, teachers were helped by recognizing the conditions commonly identified in conscious, complex, human leaning. At the time the rationale was formulated, I found little empirical research on the effects of various ways of organizing learning experiences. Hence, the rationale suggests criteria for planning and evaluating the organization. The rationale's treatment of evaluation is largely a modification of the generalized procedure for achieving test construction.

PREVIOUS PRACTICE AND THEORY OF EVALUATION

Prior to my use of the term *evaluation* in 1930, the common terms for appraisal of learning were *examining* and *testing*. Assessment of educational achievement has been practiced for several thousand years. The prevailing name for this activity changes from time to time—examining; quizzing; testing; measuring; evaluating; appraising; and, currently, assessing—but the primary function of ascertaining the educational attainment of students has remained constant. The scientific or systematic development of assessment has taken place largely in the twentieth century. During this relatively short period of time, some profound changes have taken place in both the purposes and expectations for testing.

The successful use of psychological and educational tests in World War I led to their wide adoption by schools and other civilian institutions. When America drafted two million men for military service in 1918, the problem of organizing and training this large number of persons who had had no previous military experience was overwhelming. Who were to be selected for officer training, and who for the variety of technical tasks—construction, battalions, signal corps, quartermaster corps, and the like? The psychological advisors developed the Army Alpha Test and other classification tests that provided the basis for selecting and classifying this large assortment of young men. After the war, groups tests, both of intelligence and achievement, were constructed and developed for school use, employing the same methodology that was formulated for the Army Alpha and other military classification tests.

This methodology is designed to arrange those who take the test on a continuum from those who make the highest score to those who make the lowest score. Such an arrangement permits one to identify the position of any individual in terms of his or her standing in the total group. By administering the tests to a representative sample of a defined population, like children in the third grade of U.S. schools, the continuum on which those best scores are arranged is the distribution of the scores of all American third graders. This makes it possible to overcome the limitations in comparisons within an individual classroom, school, city, or state by referring to a national norm. The original purpose was to sort students or to grade them from excellent to poor. Test items were selected that differentiated among students, and items that all or almost all students answered correctly and that few, if any, answered correctly were dropped after tryout. Hence, the resulting test was not a representative sample of what students were expected to learn.

As I began to work with the instructors at the Ohio State University, it was clear that they needed tests that would inform them about what students were learning and where they were having difficulty. Sorting students was not the purpose; instead, their concern was to improve the curriculum and the instructional program. I realized that test theory developed for purposes of sorting and based on measures of individual differences would not produce the kinds of evaluation instruments needed. Hence, I developed a procedure based on theories of instruction and learning.

Similarly, in formulating a rationale for curriculum development, I was guided by the theories of Dewey and Whitehead regarding educational aims and theories of instruction and learning. The prevailing curriculum development procedure was to identify significant content and to design ways of presenting the content. This left in limbo the question of learning objectives, that is, what the student is expected to do with the content. Furthermore, the then-usual procedure for preparing lesson plans was based on a very primitive view of student learning systems, that is, the several conditions necessary or helpful in assuring that the desired learning takes place.

MAJOR APPLICATIONS

At the time the rationales were developed, they were used first in the undergraduate colleges of Ohio State University, then in the Eight-Year Study and in the college chemistry tests of the Cooperative Test Service.

In 1938, the evaluation rationale became the basis for the development of the University of Chicago comprehensive examinations and the instruments constructed by the 22 colleges in the Cooperative Study in General Education. In 1943, I was made director of the Examinations Staff of the U.S. Armed Forces Institute, and the evaluation rationale guided the construction of the hundreds of tests and examinations developed for the Armed Forces.

The curriculum development rationale has been utilized most extensively in the construction and revision of curricula for some of the professions, for example, medicine, nursing, social work, engineering, and agriculture. I do not know how extensively it has been used in elementary and secondary schools.

CHANGES IN CONCEPTUALIZATION

As the rationales began to be utilized in new situations, I made several changes in my own conceptions. Others who have used the rationales have probably made modifications that they found helpful. As evaluation became a term widely used in educational discourse, its meaning was greatly broadened. It is not often used to refer to any and all of the efforts to compare the reality of an educational situation with the conception that has guided the planning and execution. Thus, there is evaluation of a proposed educational program made by comparing the conception of the program with whatever relevant information or generalizations are appropriate to judge the soundness and practicability of the plan. The testing out of curriculum units and their modification in the light of the test results was a larger part of the evaluation in the Ohio State University course and in the Eight-Year Study, but it is now often given a special label of formative evaluation. Then, there is the evaluation of implementation, which was a significant activity in the evaluation of the New York City Activity Schools in the 1940s and was dramatically presented in Goodlad and Klein's "Behind the Classroom Doors." There is evaluation in the continuous monitoring of programs to identify significant changes, either improvements or deterioration. There is evaluation of the unintended outcomes of a program, as well as the effort to identify the extent to which the intended results are being achieved; and, finally, there is "follow-up" evaluation to ascertain the long-term effects as learners live and work in different environments, some of which are supportive and some otherwise.

In the use of evaluation as a means of both understanding an educational program and improving it, I have come to realize the importance of identifying and appraising factors in the environment that have a significant influence on learning in addition to the planned curriculum and the activities of the teacher. The need to evaluate, measure, or describe such matters as the classroom ethic, the learner's expectations, the teacher's concern for the students, and the standards the teacher believes the students can reach are illustrations of some of those environmental factors. In brief, my conception of evaluation has greatly expanded since 1929.

As we learn more about the ways in which persons acquire new kinds of behavior and develop this knowledge, these skills, and the attitudes and interests in various situations and changing environments, I believe our conceptions of the purposes, the procedures, and the appropriate instruments of evaluation will continue to expand as well as to be more sharply focused.

5. OUTCOME EVALUATION

THOMAS KELLAGHAN and GEORGE F. MADAUS

The first edition of *Evaluation Models* did not contain a chapter on outcome evaluation. Why is there one in this edition? After all, the idea of measuring outcomes is not new and, as we shall see, outcome evaluation can hardly be regarded as a unitary approach, given the variety of practices encompassed by the term. Nor can it really be considered a *model*, if by model we mean a more or less elaborate representation of the structure and relationships of a range of phenomena. Some would say it is not even evaluation. However, there is still good reason for including in this volume a description of activities that can be broadly categorized as outcome evaluation, since they now account for a considerable amount of program monitoring activities throughout the world, in some cases displacing more traditional approaches to evaluation and research, both in countries with long-established traditions in these disciplines and ones where formal evaluation activities are only being developed. Outcome evaluation has received the backing and financial support of governments as well as of international organizations, such as the European Union, the Organisation for Economic Co-operation and Development, UNESCO, and the World Bank.

In this chapter, we shall first describe the characteristics of outcome evaluation. Following that, we shall outline reasons for its growth and advantages attributed to its use. We shall then identify a number of traditions and developments to which current practice in outcome evaluation is indebted, followed by examples of outcome evaluation at state, national, and international levels. After that, we shall consider approaches used in outcome evaluation. In our concluding remarks, we

D.L. Stufflebeam, G.F. Madaus and T. Kellaghan (eds.). EVALUATION MODELS. Copyright © 2000. Kluwer Academic Publishers. Boston. All rights reserved.

shall outline a number of issues raised by outcome evaluation, and consider how it fits among traditional approaches. Most of our illustrative material will come from the field of education, where outcome evaluation probably has had its greatest impact. But such evaluation is by no means confined to education.

WHAT IS OUTCOME EVALUATION?

A number of features of outcome evaluation can be identified. Firstly, it is a term that is applied to activities that are designed primarily to measure the (often presumed) effects or results of programs, rather than their inputs or processes. Second, since more than measurement is required if an activity is to be regarded as evaluative, a judgment as to where a product lies with respect to a standard is often made. Thus, outcomes may be related to a target, standard of service, or achievement. Often the idea of "excellence" is used or implied. The widespread use of the nebulous term "world class standards" by those in the standards-based reform movement in the U.S. is typical of this accent on excellence. Sometimes the judgment of merit or worth is implicit rather than explicit. An implicit judgment is involved when information on outcomes (e.g., the mean achievement level of students in a school) is normative (e.g., indicating where a school stands relative to other schools) and it is left to clients and the public to make the evaluative judgment and, perhaps, to take action.

Third, the range of outcomes that have been used in outcome evaluation is considerable. Within the field of education, academic achievement is the outcome most frequently assessed, and a variety of performance and portfolio modes have been employed with mixed success. Most states now employ writing samples and these have been more successful. Other performance and portfolio assessments, however, have proved to be inefficient, costly, and unreliable. Kentucky had to drop its performance assessment, while Vermont had to rethink its reliance on portfolios (Kortez, 1994; Koretz, Barron, Mitchell, & Stecher, 1996). Other outcomes have also been considered relating to building, educational materials, teaching, attitudes to school, learning motivation, and change in use of a service (student retention rates, absenteeism, and students' post-school destinations). Fourth, the effects or results that are the focus of outcome evaluation may be observed at varying points in a program—during its life, at it completion, or later in time to assess long-term effects. Most frequently, the focus is on outcomes at the completion of a program.

Fifth, it is not usual in outcome evaluation to seek to describe or specify what is actually happening in a program, though the kind of information obtained will obviously, in general terms at least, be chosen to reflect program activities. In many circumstances in which outcome evaluation is used, a description of program activities would be very difficult, if at all possible. This is because many programs are extremely complex and can only be considered programs in the broadest sense of the word (e.g., elementary education). Such programs are perhaps more accurately described as complexes of programs, which are implemented in a variety of ways, and for which the term system might be more appropriate.

Sixth, while outcome evaluations may eschew descriptions of program activities, efforts may be made to relate outcomes to contextual factors or to presumed relevant antecedent variables. Evaluations vary greatly in the extent to which they attempt to do this, and, later in the paper, we shall refer to analytical techniques used to address the issue. When such techniques are used, the main purpose is to distinguish in outcome data between the gross and net effects of program activity. It is important to do this if outcome information is to be used, as it frequently is, in the management of resources, in control, for quality assurance, or for accountability purposes (e.g., to recognize and attach sanctions to the performance of institutions or individuals with responsibility for the implementation of a program).

Finally, outcome evaluation may be once-off or may involve monitoring (i.e., comparisons of outcomes over time). When integrated into a performance management system, it is likely to be the latter, since it has to fit into an ongoing activity.

REASONS FOR GROWTH IN OUTCOME EVALUATION

A number of reasons can be identified for growth in outcome evaluation. First, from an historical point of view, the 1966 Equal Educational Opportunity Survey, commonly called the Coleman report, moved the attention of educational policymakers away from a definition of equal educational opportunity in terms of school resources toward a focus on educational outcomes as measured by tests (Coleman et al., 1966). A second reason is the perceived poor record of traditional evaluation approaches in providing direction for policymakers in making decisions about the large number of public programs that have been developed since the 1960s. Short-term readily applicable solutions did not seem to be forthcoming from such evaluation (Radaelli & Dente, 1996), while many evaluations were perceived to be costly, slow, and complex, not paying sufficient attention to outcomes.

A third reason for the growth in outcome evaluation is the development of a corporatist approach to government administration, signaled by a rise in "managerialism." The approach is heavily influenced by ideas from the business world, involving strategic and operational planning, the use of performance indicators, a focus on "deliverables"/results, a growth in incentive and accountability systems based on results (e.g., performance-related pay), and the concept of the citizen as consumer (Davies, 1999). In this situation, "the gentlemanly cult of the amateur administration", as Pollitt (1993) has observed, is being displaced, and its successor is "managerialism, not professional evaluation and analysis" (p. 354). The management consultant is expected to be able to provide the quick, narrow-focused analysis that is needed.

A fourth reason for growth in outcome evaluation is the increasing influence of the accounting and audit community in non-financial areas of public administration. The influence is reflected in "comprehensive audits", "value for money audits", "performance audits", and "environmental audits." In a variety of countries today (e.g., the United States, the United Kingdom, New Zealand, Sweden), audits of performance indicators are carried out, and opinions are issued on the extent to which systems or programs are meeting indicator targets (Davies, 1999).

Fifthly, growth in outcome evaluation reflects increasing use of assessment as a policy tool. In the field of education, this involves a shift from the use of assessment information for localized instructional decision making to centralized high stakes policy making and accountability monitoring (Madaus & Raczek, 1996).

Sixth, the growth of outcome evaluation owes much to a reorganization of the public service in several countries, resulting in the use of relatively autonomous service providers (e.g., National Health Service trusts and grant-maintained schools in Britain). With decentralization of program authority, and the consequent loss of direct control over the implementation of programs, the need arose for new contractual arrangements with service providers and for regulation and compliance monitoring. "Quality" and "standards" are the theme terms, and evaluation arrangements are designed to check that organizations are delivering flexible, cost-effective services to citizen users (Pollitt, 1993).

Finally, a situation in which growth in demand for public services and social program funding (e.g., education, health care, social security) is growing more rapidly than resources can be found for expansion leads to the need for greater efficiency, which in turn calls for selectivity in deciding what programs are to be continued and what new activities are to be launched (Blalock, 1999; Duran, Monnier, & Smith, 1995; Pollitt, 1993).

THE VALUE OF OUTCOME EVALUATION

Several advantages have been attributed to the use of outcome evaluation. One is based on business experience, where well-articulated goals are associated with organizational effectiveness. The situation in schools, which are notorious in lacking such goals, stands in strong contrast to this. It is argued that if schools were to specify outcomes relating to goals, this would identify what is important, and would help focus teachers and students on essential curriculum content (see Schmidt, McKnight, & Raizen, 1996). It is also the position of advocates of outcome evaluation that the specification of outcomes is likely to have a greater impact when aligned with appropriate assessment. This orientation toward specifying outcomes of schooling is at the heart of the standards-based reform movement. Various states have developed curriculum frameworks that mandate, first, academic learning standards by grade and subject area, and second, assessments to measure achievement related to these frameworks. For example, the Massachusetts Comprehensive Assessment System (MCAS), a new assessment program for public schools, "measures the performance of students, schools, and districts on the academic learning standards contained in the Massachusetts Curriculum Frameworks, fulfilling requirements of the Education Reform law of 1993" (Massachusetts Department of Education, 1998, p. 1).

The driving force behind many state reform efforts would appear to be the coupling of rewards or sanctions to performance on the statewide test. Policymakers are aware that testing programs that have the greatest impact on the curriculum, instruction, and learning are ones that students, teachers, administrators, parents, or the general public perceive as having sanctions or high-stakes associated with them

(Madaus & Kellaghan, 1992). In 1999, 33 of the United States had or shortly will have high stakes (e.g., high school graduation, ending social promotion) attached to their tests, while 14 states link moderate stakes (e.g., a special diploma) to their assessment systems. Sanctions may involve financial considerations for districts, schools, or teachers. Sometimes, however, the mere publication of outcome information is considered a sanction. There would appear to be two principles underlying the use of sanctions. First, individuals and institutions that are subject to sanctions will take action to obtain rewards and avoid punishment. Second, if information on outcomes is brought into the public domain, principles of competition will come into operation, and, as in the commercial world, those that do well will thrive, those that do poorly will wither away.

ORIGINS OF OUTCOME EVALUATION

The rationale for, and practice of, outcome evaluation owe a debt to at least six sources: traditional evaluation, traditions of assessment in education, school effectiveness and education production function research, the performance management movement, accountability concerns, and technical developments.

Traditional Evaluation

A consideration of the outcomes of programs is an integral feature of many traditional approaches to evaluation, and, up to the 1970s, educational evaluations focused primarily on assessing program outcomes. The emphasis on outcomes is most obvious in objectives–oriented evaluation approaches. Tyler (1949), for example, focused on educational objectives and their measurement in the context of curriculum evaluation. Other approaches in the Tylerian tradition also accorded prominence to the specification of objectives and judgments of the extent to which they could be said to have been achieved on the basis of program outcome data (e.g., Provus, 1971). However, these approaches differed from many current outcome evaluation efforts in linking program objectives to the goals or objectives of individual schools or teachers rather than to statewide curriculum frameworks, while outcomes were not used for high stakes decisions or for accountability purposes.

Traditions of Assessment in Education

Few people would disagree with the view that the outcomes of education are important. However, agreement would not be as widespread on the relative importance of outcomes, since individuals differ in their perceptions of the prominence that should be given to the variety of goals or objectives that have been posited for schooling. Literacy and numeracy skills are usually accorded particular importance, and the use of information on outcomes to make decisions about the effectiveness of schools and teachers, based on students' acquisitions of these skills, reaches back into the last century. Perhaps the best-known examples of this approach are payment-by-results schemes which were introduced into British schools in 1862 to help improve students' literacy and mathematical skills and teacher efficiency, while at the same time saving money. In these schemes, the allocation of funds to schools was linked to students' achievements as measured by written and oral examinations in reading, writing, and arithmetic. Responsibility for the failure of students was placed on the shoulders of teachers.

Growth in the use of standardized testing in this century, especially in the United States, reflects continuing interest in the outcomes of education. Rice's (1897) work on spelling is an early example of outcome evaluation. Information on outcomes, of course, has been used for a variety of purposes, only some of which related to the evaluation of programs or even of schools. Tests were most frequently used to assess the performance of individual students. On the basis of their value in this context, however, Coleman and Karweit (1972) proposed that they could also be used to provide measures of school performance in evaluating "educational environments."

Over the past three decades, standardized tests have been used increasingly as instruments of national education reform. Their use in diagnosing what is wrong in education, together with the legislative attention which testing has received, reflect a fundamental shift in the official education world, not only in the purpose for which standardized tests are used, but also in perceptions of quality which have moved from a consideration of school facilities, resources, and conditions to the outcomes of schooling (Madaus & Raczek, 1996). A recent illustration of the extent to which outcomes have become a prominent concern of policymakers is to be found in President Bush's America 2000 proposal (US Departments of Education and Labor, 1993) that paved the way for the Educate America Act of 1994. This legislation proposed that new American Achievement Tests should form part of a 15-point accountability package designed to encourage parents, schools, and communities "to measure results, compare results, and insist on change when the results aren't good enough" (Goals 2000: Education America Act, 1994). This legislation was never implemented and the idea of a "voluntary" national test is still on hold. Nonetheless, many states have adopted the central ideas in the legislation in designing their own standards-based reform programs.

School Effectiveness and Education Production Function Research

A large number of studies of school effectiveness and of education production function research has used measures of educational outcomes, usually standardized tests, in their efforts to determine characteristics of effective schools. An input-output representation of schooling was the model most frequently employed: student achievement at a point in time was related to a series of inputs, usually identified as family and background influences, school resources, and school characteristics (e.g., current expenditure, teacher qualifications and experience, pupil-teacher ratio) (see Hanushek, 1997; Madaus, Airasian, & Kellaghan, 1980).

In line with this tradition, several approaches to outcome evaluation collect data on input in an effort to identify factors associated with student achievement. The use of indicators (which might be described as statistics with evaluative relevance) in outcome evaluation fits particularly well with the input-output conceptualization of schooling. Reflecting the input-output model, indicators used by the National Center for Education Statistics of the U.S. Department of Education now include context and outcome data (Stern, 1986). At the international level, OECD (1997) in describing the education systems of member countries has, during the 1990s, used indicators to describe the demographic, social, and economic context of education, financial and human resources invested in education, the learning environment and the organization of schools, and student achievement.

The Performance Management Movement

Sensitivity to the needs of program managers and decision makers is not new in evaluation. Stufflebeam (1983), for example, considered that the decision that had to be made, rather than program objectives, should be the key concern of the evaluator. Current interest in the use of evaluation findings for management decisions has a rather different origin, however: performance management, which has its roots in the 1930s but grew in popularity in the late 1980s and in the 1990s alongside more established evaluation approaches. While the general aims of performance management "to base judgments of the effectiveness of program efforts on more appropriate and trustworthy information, and to improve these efforts" (Blalock, 1999, p. 118) do not differ from the aims of many more traditional evaluation approaches, concepts underlying performance management differ from such approaches in a number of ways.

While traditional evaluation grew out of social science research, adopting its basic concepts and techniques, performance management has its roots in a bureaucratic environment. It is based on planning and management ideas, particularly ones relating to quality assurance, customer satisfaction, and continuous improvement. It involves defining performance in terms of results, setting performance targets, determining the extent to which results are achieved using performance indicators, and basing resource allocation decisions on performance information. Its aim is to provide rapid and continuous feedback on a limited number of outcome measures that are perceived to be of interest to policymakers, administrators, stakeholders, politicians, and customers, and to be of value in making decisions (Blalock, 1999; Davies, 1999). The manager, not the "scientific" policy analyst, is the charismatic figure; efficiency and economy are the main concerns; and the achievement of performance targets is the sign of "administrative health" (Pollitt, 1993).

It was in this context that management information systems (MIS) grew in the 1980s, designed to specify the structures and procedures governing the collection, analysis, presentation, and use of information in organizations. The development was, at least in part, a response to the need to monitor the growth and increasing complexity of systems and to justify decisions about resource allocation. Outcome evaluation fits readily into this picture by providing relatively simple statistical information about a system, program, or activity on a timely basis. While more or less complex analyses may accompany this information in some evaluations, it is not the primary purpose of outcome evaluation to provide them.

Acountability

In recent years, accountability has achieved increasing prominence in government administrations in many countries. Measures to control how stakeholders discharge their obligations have been devised as a mechanism for dealing with issues which arise from a number of phenomena: increasing demand for services coupled with diminishing resources; a multiplication of reform strategies; weak administrative instruments; and competing values and demands in pluralist cultures. These measures, which have been applied to a range of public services, might seem a reasonable way to bring order to complex and poorly understood environments. It is envisaged that information based on the measures would lead to the use of administrative controls over the use of inputs to ensure that specified procedures are complied with. But it might also simply involve the identification of products that meet a specified standard and products that do not. It is regarded as a relatively simple and straightforward task to use data from an outcome evaluation to place the onus for change and adjustment on the person or institution identified as being accountable, and to place one's trust in the operation of a competitive market and the threat or promise of sanctions to bring about the desired effect. In this situation, the onus is not on a manager to identify desirable aspects of implementation or conditions that need to be changed. He or she does not have to try to understand or explain why some individuals or institutions are "effective" and some are not. All that is necessary is to identify the effective and the noneffective, and to have statistical data to support the judgment.

Despite problems associated with outcome evaluation considered below, accountability issues loom large in considerations of school reform today. For example, the Educational Improvement Act adopted in Tennessee in 1991 created the need to specify the means by which teachers, schools, and school systems could be held accountable for meeting objectives set for Tennessee's education systems. Since the focus was on product rather than on process, an outcomes-based assessment system was established and has been embedded in the Tennessee Value Added Assessment System (TVAAS) which forms an integral part of legislation (Sanders & Horn, 1994).

Technical Developments

The availability of relatively low cost technologies with massive computing capabilities has greatly aided the development, not only of large-scale testing programs to obtain outcome data, but also of management information systems in general and logistical planning. Outcome evaluation is greatly facilitated by the capacity to store vast amounts of data, to link data collected at different points in time, and to carry out sophisticated statistical analyses.

THE USE OF OUTCOME EVALUATION

The tendency for governments to take responsibility for quality by setting standards and monitoring scholastic achievement, coupled with an allocation of responsibility for the use of resources/inputs to providers, can be found in a wide range of countries. This is a change from a situation in which, up to recently, monitoring and evaluation systems were more concerned with resources and implementation than with assessing results. In many countries, aspects of performance measures are now underwritten by legislation.

In the United States, the Government Performance and Results Act (GPRA) of 1993 was implemented in October 1997 as a response to reports of waste and inefficiency in government spending. To restore public confidence in government, all federal agencies would be held accountable for achieving program results, service quality, customer satisfaction, and for providing Congress with sufficient information to improve decision making. Performance measurement would be required and the resulting data would be made public. A range of publications providing a rationale for, and description of, performance measurement ("managing for results"), as well as experience in its use has been prepared by the U.S. General Accounting Office and other agencies (http://www.reeusda.gov/part/gpra/gpralist.htm).

Major changes have occurred in government agencies following the legislation. For example, the United States Agency for International Development (USAID) has developed for its funded projects a "results framework" which involves specification of goals, objectives, indicators with periodic targets, intermediate results, and long-term net results (representing the effect of the intervention) (Toffolon-Weiss, Bertrand, & Terrell, 1999).

Evaluation activity outside the United States is not well documented. However, it seems reasonable to say that the extent or range of evaluation activities found in the United States is not found elsewhere, despite a recent surge of evaluation activity, or at least a recognition of its need, in many countries. In Spain, for example, government has responded to legislation requiring evaluation following government action in contracting services, creating conditions for competition, and raising the issue of accountability. The response reflects a preference for evaluation approaches that are compatible with the production of management control indicators and are useful in informing decision making in the policy process. For example, the Catalan Health Services Administrative Office monitors populations served, cost, and outputs (e.g., number of visits per inhabitant per day, number and cost of prescriptions) (Ballart, 1998).

Use of evaluation (through usually of a rather old fashioned variety) has also grown rapidly in other countries during the 1980s and 1990s. In Denmark, traditional empirical methodologies (usually surveys) to provide data for political and organizational development, control, monitoring, and modernization are favored (Hansson, 1997). In France, "widespread infatuation with public policy evaluation" as a means of modernizing public service has been reported (Duran, Monnier, & Smith, 1995, p. 45). In Italy, demands to produce an evaluation framework for recent reforms in health services (*azienda lizzazione della sanita publica*) have resulted in tensions between an approach focused on management and one more oriented to effectiveness and quality assessment. Norway also seems to be showing signs of increasing enthusiasm for evaluation, though issues have not yet developed with the sharpness of focus observable in Anglo-Saxon countries (see News from the Community, *Evaluation*, 1998, *4*, 373–379). In the Russian Federation, the requirement of a uniform curriculum in schools is being replaced by greater autonomy for regional authorities and schools in conjunction with outcome-based curricula (Bakker, 1999). While the evaluation ambitions of many countries seem less than modest, realization is being hampered by lack of data, expertise, instruments, and the infrastructure required for large-scale data collection and analysis. This point has been made regarding the development of evaluation in the People's Republic of China, where evaluation was unknown up to the early 1980s, but is now seen to be important in the context of national development and economic growth. Many steps are being taken to improve the country's evaluation capacity (Hong & Rist, 1997).

We turn now to descriptions of specific outcome evaluation efforts in education at state level (U.S.), national level, and international level.

Outcome Evaluation at State Level

In the United States, state departments of education are the major players in outcome evaluation, collecting data on student achievement, publishing the data, and allowing comparisons to be made between schools and school districts.

In Texas, for example, outcome data are provided at all grade levels for a range of variables including academic achievement, student promotion rate, student attendance, dropout rate, percentage taking the Scholastic Aptitude Tests, and post-school college enrolment rate. Cash rewards to schools and to individual professional staff are given to schools that provide test data for 95 percent of eligible students and in which at least half its cohorts perform better than a norm group (Webster, Mendro, & Almaguer, 1994).

The Tennessee Value-Added Assessment System (TVAAS) is also an outcomes-based system, in which the focus of accountability is on the product of the educational experience, not the process. The TVAAS has been adopted and legislated for in state law. According to *The Master Plan for Tennessee Schools 1993* of the State Board of Education, "State and local education policies will be focused on results; Tennessee will have assessment and management information systems that provide information on students, schools, and school systems to improve learning and assist policy making" (cited in Sanders & Horn, 1994, p. 301). Testing takes place at all grade levels in reading, mathematics, science, language, and social studies. Judgments are made on the basis of the data that are collected on the effects of school systems, individual schools, and individual teachers. Data on the first two are released to the public.

Outcome Evaluation at National Level

The most obvious exemplars of outcome evaluation at national level are "national assessments", which have operated in the United Kingdom in one form or another since 1948, in the United States since 1969, and in France since 1979. The United States National Assessment of Educational Progress (NAEP) is the most widely reported assessment model in the literature. It is an ongoing survey, mandated by the U.S. Congress and implemented by trained field staff, usually school or district personnel. The survey is designed to measure students' educational achievements at specified ages and grades and reports the percentage of students scoring in the three controversial performance categories: "basic", "proficient", and "advanced". It also examines achievements of subpopulations defined by demographic characteristics and by specific background experience. Over the years, details of the administration of NAEP have changed; for example, in the frequency of assessment and in the grade level targeted. At present, assessments are conducted every second year on samples of students in grades 4, 8, and 12. Eleven instructional areas have been assessed periodically. Most recent reports have focused on reading and writing, mathematics and science, history, geography, and civics. Data have been reported by state, gender, ethnicity, type of community, and region.

National assessments are now a feature of many other education systems throughout the world, not only in industrialized countries (e.g., Australia, Canada, Finland, France, Ireland, the Netherlands, Norway, Sweden, New Zealand, United Kingdom) but also in developing countries (see Chinapah, 1997; Greaney & Kellaghan, 1996). An assessment of students' first language and mathematics at the elementary school level is included in all national assessments. Science is included in some, and a second language, art, music, and social studies in a small number. In most countries, data are collected for a sample of students at a particular age or grade level, but in some countries, all students at the relevant age or grade level are assessed (Kellaghan & Grisay, 1995).

Outcome Evaluation at International Level

International assessments differ from national assessments in that they involve measurement of the outcomes of education systems in several countries, usually simultaneously. Representatives from many countries (usually from research organizations) agree on an instrument to assess achievement in a curriculum area, the instrument is administered to a representative sample of students at a particular age or grade level in each country, and comparative analyses of the data are carried out (Kellaghan & Grisay, 1995). The main advantage of international studies over national assessments is the comparative framework they provide in assessing student achievement and curricular provision. International assessments give some indication of where the students in a country stand relative to students in other countries. They also show the extent to which the treatment of common curriculum areas differs across countries, and, in particular, the extent to which the approach in a given country may be idiosyncratic. This information may lead a country to reassess its curriculum policy.

The International Association for the Evaluation of Educational Achievement (IEA) has pioneered international assessment studies and has carried out a series of studies of school achievement, attitudes, and curricula in a variety of countries since 1959. Although one of IEA's primary functions is to conduct research designed to improve understanding of the educational process, studies were also intended to have a more practical and applied purpose: to obtain information relevant to policymaking and educational planning in the interest of improving education systems (Husén, 1967; Postlethwaite, 1987).

To date, the IEA has conducted studies of mathematics achievement, science achievement, reading literacy, written composition, English as a foreign language, French as a foreign language, civic education, computers in education, and preprimary childcare. Levels and patterns of achievement have been described and compared across countries. So also have differences in intended and implemented curricula and in the course-taking patterns of students. A variety of correlates of achievement has been identified, including students' opportunity to learn, the amount of time a subject is studied, the use of computers, and resources in the homes of students.

APPROACHES IN OUTCOME EVALUATION

A variety of approaches, depending on the outcome to be assessed, has been used in outcome evaluation. In evaluations in the field of education, assessments of student achievement usually involve the administration of tests or examinations. The performances of individual students may then be aggregated to the level of the teacher, school, district, state, or even nation to allow judgments to be made about achievement at the desired level.

Judgments may be made on the basis of unadjusted results. In British league tables, the percentages of students in schools awarded varying grades on public examinations ("performance tables") have been published since 1992. In the United States, most state accountability systems in the past compared schools and school districts on the basis of unadjusted outcome measures (Guskey & Kifer, 1990). Similarly, in international comparative studies, countries are ranked on the basis of unadjusted mean scores.

This procedure is perhaps not surprising if outcome evaluation is concerned primarily with description, not explanation, with the product of the educational experience, not the process by which it was achieved. There is, however, concern about the extent to which such comparisons are fair, particularly if evaluation results are used for accountability purposes. The issue at stake is that of distinguishing between the "net" impact of a program which represents outcomes that are directly attributable to the program, and "gross" impact which reflects, in addition to net impact, influences other than the program being monitored. The distinction is readily illustrated in the case of student achievements, which are generally recognized as reflecting a variety of influences, including genetic endowment, achievement on entering school, and the support and assistance that students receive at home and in the community, all of which may be independent of school and teacher influences (Sanders & Horn, 1994; Webster et al., 1994). If students differ from school to school in their levels of achievement when entering a school, measures of absolute levels of student achievement at a later date may not adequately reflect a school's success in moving students from their initial entry levels. However, it seems reasonable to say that schools and institutions should be held accountable only for things that they can be expected to influence, not for the characteristics students bring with them when they come to school (Woodhouse & Goldstein, 1996).

In line with this thinking, several attempts have been made to develop statistical methodologies that will permit an assessment of the contributions of schools to student development in situations in which the nonrandom assignment of students is assumed. These methodologies are based on two concepts. One relates to "normal" academic progression, which is the average progression that students make from a given starting point over a particular period in the school system (described as "expected" progress). The other is related to the extent to which individual students or groups of students (e.g., in a class or school) exceed or fall below that average progress in the specified time period. The difference is regarded as representing the value which a particular class or school has "added" to students' progress.

Statistical procedures are usually based on multiple-regression analysis and involve comparing actual student outcomes with expectations or predictions determined empirically on the basis of relevant inputs (attendance, gender, ethnicity, earlier achievement). The most sophisticated of these approaches use longitudinal student data, in which individual students' earlier achievement scores are matched with their later achievement scores. In the Tennessee Value-Added Assessment System, for example, estimated student gain scores are aggregated to the levels of teacher, school, and system and are compared with national norm gains, which each school is expected to achieve. Schools with scores less than two standard deviations below the norm must show positive progress or risk intervention by the State (Sanders & Horn, 1994).

Problems associated with the use of value-added measures include inadequate coverage of the achievements of schools, which may vary by curriculum area, grade level, and teacher; incomplete data for students arising from absenteeism or student turnover rate; regression to the mean in statistical analyses; problems with reliability of measures when the number of students in a school is small; and how to factor in the contextual effect on achievement created by the ability level of students in a school or class (Sanders & Horn, 1994; School Curriculum and Assessment Authority, 1994; Tymms, 1995; Webster et al., 1994; Woodhouse & Goldstein, 1996).

ISSUES IN OUTCOME EVALUATION

Despite its popularity, the use of outcome evaluation gives rise to a series of issues. First, since outcome evaluation rests primarily on assumptions related to planning, incentives, accountability, and consumerism, it is not likely to lead to greater understanding of what goes on in programs, or to an identification of the factors that affect outcomes (e.g., the relative contributions of teachers, schools, and a variety of other influences, within a program or outside it). However, many would regard progress in understanding "how" and "why" programs have an impact as important for real improvement. Second, and related to the first point, is the issue of identification and specification of the responsibility of providers and clients, particularly in situations in which roles may be ambiguous and not clearly separated. How does one establish that a particular outcome was, even in part, amenable to the influence of a person to whom responsibility for it may have been assigned? For example, while it is reasonable to assume that a school and teachers bear some responsibility for student achievement, do not students and parents also bear responsibility? If this is so, how should responsibility between the parties be apportioned? And should the apportionment be the same for all students, in all circumstances, at all age levels?

Third, performance indicators may be used, recorded, and interpreted in varying ways, thus giving rise to problems of comparability. For example, a core set of measures developed by a Federal Interagency Task Force to monitor market programs in the United States was designed to form the basis of state-level management information systems supporting performance monitoring. However, since no state operates a fully integrated data system serving multiple programs, and since choice of performance measures differ from one program to another, data are not directly comparable (Blalock, 1999).

Fourth, since many outcome evaluations focus on a limited range of outcomes, the data that are obtained may not adequately reflect system or program goals and objectives. The temptation, of course, is to focus on what is easy to measure, but this may be to the detriment of important objectives. Perrin (1998) reminds us that "many activities in the public policy realm, by their very nature, are complex and intangible and cannot be reduced to a numerical figure . . . What is measured, or even measurable, often bears little resemblance to what is relevant" (pp. 373–373). However, focusing on a limited set of outcomes is likely to mean that other outcomes will be neglected in program implementation.

Fifth, when outcome evaluation is associated with high stakes, meeting the requirements of measuring and reporting may become more important than what a program was designed to achieve, resulting in goal displacement. In education, for example, when assessment results become the goal of instruction, the true purpose of the instructional process may be subverted as goals are reoriented to meet or exceed "standards." Further, efforts to improve performance on the measure do not necessarily result in improvement in the areas that programs were designed to achieve. When meeting standards becomes the basis for budgetary decisions, there is the further consequence that programs that meet standards, rather than program goals, may be continued, while programs that meet goals, but not standards, may be discontinued.

Sixth, when evaluations are based on predetermined objectives or standards, it is unlikely that unintended or unanticipated consequences will be detected. Seventh, the interpretation of data in outcome evaluations may not adequately acknowledge diversities in the environment in which programs were implemented. It may well be that a program is "successful" in one context, but not in another. Finally, the cost of outcome evaluation may divert funds from other needs, a not unimportant consideration at a time of resource constraints (Battistich et al., 1999; Blalock, 1999; Davies, 1999; Natriello, 1996; Perrin, 1998).

OUTCOME EVALUATION AND OTHER FORMS OF EVALUATION

In conclusion, we may ask: Where does outcome evaluation fit among traditional approaches to program evaluation? The question may be addressed from three not entirely mutually exclusive points of view: the context in which an evaluation is carried out, its methodology, and its relationship to the policy process and decision making.

Context

As far as context is concerned, outcome evaluation, as it has recently developed, differs from traditional approaches in a number of ways, fitting more comfortably with its managerial antecedents that with any program evaluation approach. First, it tends to be part of a bureaucratic routine, providing knowledge that, in theory at any rate, is relevant to policy. Second, it frequently involves accountability considerations, relating to the scrutinization of programs and reporting of performance indicators. Third, the most common use of such evaluation is in the context of very broad and complex programs (represented in, for example, all the efforts made by a school or school system over a number of years) rather than more discrete and more clearly specified programs. Fourth, outcome evaluation, as most commonly practised, relates to on-going practice rather than to innovative or experimental programs designed to address social or economic problems. Thus, it is not normally associated with trial runs of new programs, as traditional program evaluation is, nor is it normally combined with qualitative approaches to assess program implementation and impact.

Methodology

The methodologies of outcome evaluation have some affinity with early (1960s) evaluation approaches, which were largely based on Popperian logical positivism, employing quantitative measures, deductive chains, and aspirations towards generalization. While outcome indicators in themselves will not provide valid causal knowledge, interest in causality associated with their use is evidenced in efforts to identify correlates of achievement and in the assumptions underlying the use of added value techniques.

While these aspects of outcome evaluation may point to an affinity with traditional views of evaluation and indeed of research, there are also indications that outcome evaluation is perceived as a genre that is distinct from traditional evaluation (see Blalock, 1999; Pollitt, 1993). This conclusion seems warranted when one considers that outcome monitoring (represented in national assessments and international comparative studies) is being promoted by governments and international agencies at the same time as, and independently of, more traditional approaches to evaluation (see, e.g., European Commission, 1997).

Policy and Decision Making

At this stage, there is little documentation available on the use of outcome evaluations in a policy context. The extent to which information derived from such evaluations enters the policy arena will no doubt differ from country to country, depending on a country's traditions of government and of policy and decision making, as well as on the relationships which have already been established between policymakers, decision makers, and evaluators. Insofar as the methodology of outcome evaluations seems close to that involved in empirical quantitative approaches, with their rational view of the policy process, one might expect outcome information to be considered exogenous to the process, providing "objective", "neutral", and apolitical information to be used instrumentally in policy and decision making. In this view, as in early evaluation efforts, the evaluator has a role to play in resolving policy issues, but not as a player in the actual policy process (Radaelli & Dente, 1996). This conclusion is reinforced when we consider the number of outcome evaluation projects in which there often is no identifiable "evaluator." Indeed, the term evaluation often does not have a prominent place in discourses on the activities of what we are calling outcome evaluation.

This should not surprise us, given the limited number of goals of information production that are considered relevant to outcome evaluation. Of the six goals identified by Blalock (1999) that more conventional methods of evaluation strive to meet, outcome evaluation is likely to address only one: determining if a program's outcomes for clients (and perhaps its net impact) are consistent with desired outcomes and to improve these outcomes. Outcome evaluation is not likely to provide information on Blalock's five other goals: whether or not a program's interventions are as intended; whether a program is being delivered to the intended target population; whether a program is being implemented as intended; identification of the major influences shaping a program's outcomes; or the appropriateness, utility, and societal value of policies on which a program is based.

The way in which outcome evaluation information is predicted to work in some systems suggests that the effort to accommodate the information in policy will be slight. If, for example, the prime purpose of providing outcome information on school performance is to attach to it rewards or punishments for school districts, schools, or teachers, then there would seem to be little need to reflect on, or try to understand, how schools function, or what it is about programs that facilitates student growth. Perhaps, the questions raised by these issues are too demanding and challenging for a busy administrator. The easier course is to import market models and leave it to competition and consumer choice to bring about desired reform. However, as long as this approach is followed, many questions that have traditionally occupied evaluators will remain unanswered: does a program contribute to improvement, is it equitable, what are the unintended consequences, and at what cost is change achieved?

6. THE ROLE OF TESTING IN EVALUATIONS

GEORGE F. MADAUS, WALTER HANEY, and AMELIA KREITZER

Testing is closely tied to evaluation. Tests of some sort play a role in virtually all educational program evaluations; indeed, too often an "evaluation" is no more than a hasty analysis of whether test scores rose.

Supervising or conducting evaluations requires an understanding of basic concepts and central issues in testing; such an understanding helps ensure that tests will not be misused as an overly simplistic "bottom line." When tests are chosen carefully and interpreted appropriately in evaluations, test results can help answer the question, "Is this project making a difference?" Because testing is a complex technology, it is easy for program sponsors to assign concerns about how tests work or how they are constructed to the experts. But just as a wise patient would never undergo surgery without asking questions, those who intend to make use of test results need to pose pertinent questions about the costs, alternatives, and consequences of the testing decisions made in evaluations. This chapter will introduce some of the aspects of test use that ought to be looked into by those who commission and employ program evaluations.

The chapter opens with an explanation of what a test is. Subsequently, two types of testing will be considered with respect to evaluation. Traditional forms of testing, such as the multiple choice test, will be discussed first. Other forms of testing, the "alternative" forms of assessment which have received much recent

From G. F. Madaus, W. Haney, & A. Kreitzer (1992). *Testing and evaluation: Learning from the projects we fund.* Washington, D.C.: Council for Aid to Education.

D.L. Stufflebeam, G.F. Madaus and T. Kellaghan (eds.). EVALUATION MODELS. Copyright © 2000. Kluwer Academic Publishers. Boston. All rights reserved.

attention, will also be discussed. The chapter will close with a list of questions to ask and issues to consider when using tests or interpreting test results in an evaluation.

WHAT IS A TEST?

Despite extensive experience with tests, many Americans, including some who regularly administer and use tests, would be lost if asked by that famous extraterrestrial, ET, "What is a test? We don't have these things on my planet." ET's confusion could be cleared up with an explanation of four concepts central to the definition of a test:

- A test focuses on a particular *domain* of interest.
- A test is a *sample* of behavior, products, answers, or performance from that domain.
- A test permits the user to make *inferences* about the larger domain of interest, and then, to use those inferences in *describing, making decisions, or determining consequences* about the test taker.
- The degree to which the specific inferences, descriptions, decisions, or consequences are appropriate is called *validity.*

Test Domain

A test is designed to measure a particular body of knowledge, skills, abilities, or performances which are of interest to the test user. This area of interest is called the test *domain* or test *universe*. The first step in constructing a test is to define the domain, so one can readily decide whether a particular aspect of knowl-edge, or a particular skill, task, ability, or performance clearly falls within the domain.

A straightforward, albeit somewhat simplistic, way to think about the domain for an achievement test is as a textbook, or as part of a textbook. For example, if a test writer wanted to construct a fourth-grade mathematics operations test, she might conceive of the test domain as the operations chapters from a typical fourth-grade mathematics textbook. The test domain could then be divided into four sections, called sub-domains or facets, representing the basic operations of addition, subtraction, multiplication, and division. Any of these four sub-domains could be specified further. For example, we might limit the addition facet to problems involving three or fewer digits. The sub-domains could also each be divided into numerical computational problems and word problems. Once we are satisfied with the domain specification, a test can be constructed to assess either the entire domain of fourth-grade arithmetic, or some facet of it.

The arithmetic example above represents a comparatively simple content or achievement domain in education. Not all test domains can be so easily defined, let alone divided so cleanly into sub-domains or facets. Furthermore, of course, test domains are not limited to academic or curricular areas. A test domain might focus on job-related skills for a particular occupation, for example, or on one of a wide range of more abstract traits such as intelligence, motivation, honesty, teacher competence, musical aptitude, mathematics problem-solving ability, or psychopathic deviation. Defining the test domain for an abstract trait is necessarily a more thorny undertaking than specifying the content of a typical textbook.

The concept of the test domain is relevant to evaluations in two important ways. First, too often people fail to question whether the domain is the correct one for the uses to which the test will be put. For example, imagine a standardized third-grade science test being used to evaluate the success of an innovative hands-on science curriculum. The test domain for the standardized test might, for example, cover facts concerning seeds and plants, matter and changes, rock formation, machines, weather, ecology, the moon, and health. The hands-on curriculum might, instead, emphasize skill development in the areas of observing, classifying, measuring, predicting, making generalizations, hypothesizing, and hypothesis-testing. While nothing is inherently wrong with the facts-related standardized test, it was drawn from a domain of "third-grade basic science" that differs dramatically from the vision of "third-grade science" reflected in the hands-on science curriculum; thus, the standardized test's appropriateness in evaluating a hands-on curriculum should be carefully examined. The question, "Does this test cover the domain I am really interested in?" is central to proper test use.

A second major issue with respect to test domains in evaluation is the connotative power of the name given to a domain, and hence to its related test. Names of tests, such as those that are designed to measure "intelligence" or "functional literacy," can carry powerful cultural and personal meanings. These associative meanings color the way people use, interpret, and understand test performance. Thus, even when the definition of the test domain is appropriate for a given evaluation purpose, the name of the test may shape how test results are interpreted by various evaluation audiences.

A domain's name, for example, may fail to convey the uncertainty or sometimes the incompleteness of our conceptualizations. For example, people often forget, or may never know, that a particular "intelligence" or "teacher competency" test might represent only a small, and sometimes relatively unimportant, facet of a larger domain. Taking the test name too literally may mean that a person's test performance acquires all the generalized semantic, affective, connotative, emotional, and metaphorical baggage associated with the name of the particular domain—be it "honesty," "intelligence," or "readiness"—the test supposedly represents. Naming a test also affects attitudes about test use, sometimes at a profound level. For example, people resist the use of an "intelligence test" to retain children in kindergarten. However, when the same sort of test is labeled a "readiness" test, the practice becomes defensible and ultimately acceptable (Cunningham, 1988).

When a tester builds tests to measure constructs like intelligence, the only hope for some semblance of shared meaning is through clear communication of the specific facets of the domain the test is supposed to reflect. But this is easier said then done! The users of tests often do not reference test performance to the test devel-

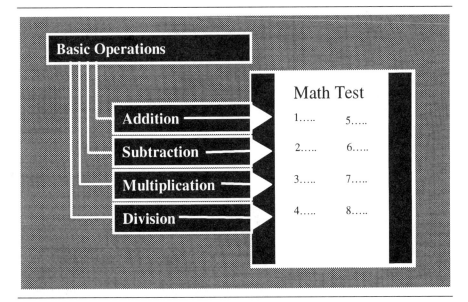

Figure 1. Sampling from the Domain of Fourth-Grade Math Basic Operations

opers' carefully crafted domain definition. Instead, they interpret test performance in terms of the contexts, meanings, purposes, and cultural sensibilities that they associate with a test's name. Thus, when choosing and using tests, we must be sensitive to the potential for misinterpretation based on the name of a test.

Sampling from the Test Domain

A second basic concept that needs to be explained when answering the question, "What is a test?" is that a test is a *sample* of behavior, products, answers, or performance from the larger domain of interest. Even for the comparatively simple domain of fourth-grade arithmetic problems, the number of possible test questions that could be constructed is staggering; we could never hope to ask students to solve all of them. Thus, we select a sample of problems to represent the important parts of the domain. It is this sample that constitutes the test of the domain.

Figure 1 illustrates the concept of sampling from the domain of fourth-grade arithmetic. The domain is represented by the chapter of a textbook, with the four relevant sub-domains represented by chapter sub-headings. The test is made up of questions from the content of the chapter; in our illustration, each chapter part is represented by at least one question on the test. If an entire sub-domain, like "division," was not represented at all, or by only a few items, the representativeness of the sample would be called into question. "Does the sample of test questions adequately represent the domain?" is an important issue to address when using tests in evaluation.

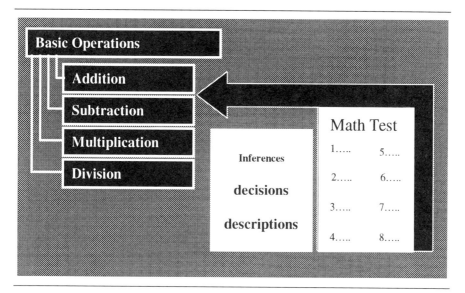

Figure 2. Making Inferences Back to the Domain of Fourth-Grade Basic Operations

The sample of items that forms the test and is meant to represent the domain is generally developed according to plans, called test specifications. Test specifications describe in detail such matters as the type of items to be used, the number of items on the test, the proportion of test items representing each part of the domain, the time allocated to the test, and the statistical characteristics of the item such as item difficulty and readability levels. Test specifications, therefore, are the detailed blueprint for constructing the test. Well written test manuals typically include some of these details for the test user.

Making Inferences from Test Results

Implicit in the above discussion is the concept that it is the domain, not the test per se, which is of interest in any testing situation. Performance on the particular small sample of questions that constitute the test is of interest *only* in so far as it permits us to make *inferences* about the whole test domain. This concept of inferences is the third major component of the definition of a test: A test permits one to make *inferences* about the domain of interest, and then to use those inferences in describing, making decisions about, or determining consequences for the test-taker, the institution, or the program.

To continue with the example of the fourth-grade arithmetic test, a student's performance (or the average performance of a class) on the ten, twenty, or one hundred problems making up the arithmetic test is never the ultimate concern. The ultimate concern is what the performance on the sample of problems, the test, suggests about student or class mastery of basic arithmetic (see Figure 2).

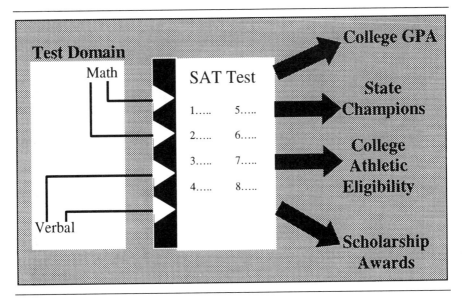

Figure 3. Making Inference from the SAT

Test results can lead to inferences that do not refer back to the original test domain but, instead, to a different domain. The content of aptitude tests, for example, is drawn from one domain, but the chief inference made from a student's score is typically not about how fully he has mastered that domain; instead, the score is usually used to make an inference about the student's future performance. The SAT is a case in point: the items are drawn from mathematics and language arts domains, but the most common inference from the test scores—and the one for which the test was designed—concerns the likelihood of success in college. When SAT scores are used to determine eligibility for college athletics, to award scholarships, or to compare individual states on educational quality, the inferences are made to different domains altogether. The large black arrows in Figure 3 represent inferences made to different domains from the SAT.

Test Validity

The final concept necessary to understanding a test is *validity*. Validity is the appropriateness, correctness, or meaningfulness of the specific inferences, descriptions, decisions, or consequences that are triggered by a test score. When the students in an innovative mathematics program get an average of 20 percent of the problems on the arithmetic test correct, and the project evaluator infers that they do not know very much about basic mathematics operations, the validity question is, "Is it correct to infer that the students have not mastered arithmetic operations?" When the students are then all assigned to the remedial mathematics class for the remainder of the school year, the validity question is, "Is it appropriate to assign all students to remedial math (and hence, potentially, label them as low achievers) based on the program's average test score?"

Validity is a widely misused term. Some of the most common misunderstandings can be clarified by considering the following:

- *There is no such thing as a generically valid test.* In other words, it is incorrect to broadly and simply assert, "This is a valid test." Obviously, an inappropriate inference could be made from even the most well constructed and carefully administered test. Thus, statements about a test's validity must be qualified in terms of the correctness of a *particular* inference and consequent description or decision about *particular* populations of test takers.
- *Validation is an ongoing, indeed, never-ending process* of accumulating evidence about validity. The fundamental characteristic of validation is the search for the *meaning* behind the test score. A true validation study seeks evidence that not only confirms, but also evidence that might cast doubt on the ability of the test to measure what it purports to measure.

The validity of a test is a matter of degree, not a simple dichotomy of "valid" or "not valid." There is no such thing as a perfect test; inferences are always problematic. Validation offers a reasoned defense for an inference, decision, or description, not proof.

USING MULTIPLE-CHOICE TESTS IN EVALUATION

When constructing a test, a test writer must decide how the test takers will demonstrate what they know and can do. She can ask the examinees to select an answer from among several alternatives, as on a multiple-choice test. Or, she could ask them to produce a response, as in answer to an essay question, and then evaluate the resultant product. She could also consider requiring that the students perform something, then assess the performance or observed process as it happens.

When using tests in evaluation, we can choose among these different modes of testing in order to answer our evaluation questions. Our choice of test type must be based on a clear understanding of the advantages and disadvantages of each mode, an awareness of the logistical and contextual constraints of the evaluation, and an understanding of the evaluation issues we want the tests to inform.

Asking examinees to select among alternatives, as in multiple-choice or true/false examinations, has been the predominant mode of school testing in the United States for over four decades. Multiple-choice tests are also the most common way of gathering achievement data in formal educational program evaluations—indeed, multiple-choice standardized tests are mandated for evaluations of many federally-funded projects such as Chapter I.

Multiple-choice tests rose to their position of prominence for reasons that are easy to understand in a historical context. During the first half of the 1800s in the United States, students graduating from high school typically took oral examinations. In Boston, educator Horace Mann found these examinations too time consuming. Further, the questions presented to each examinee had to be different; once an examinee exited the examination room, the questions presented to him could be revealed to the next examinees. Mann replaced the oral exams with essay examinations, which allowed the same questions to be administered to many students at once. The practice of giving essay examinations grew and by the Civil War were the most common testing methodology in American schools.

Large scale immigration and greater access to schooling in the last decades of the nineteenth century dramatically increased the size of the school-going population. Even more efficient means of testing were needed. What's more, studies had revealed that scores on essay tests varied greatly depending on who scored them. The invention of the multiple-choice item, credited to Frederick Kelley in 1914, solved the problems of inefficiency and subjectivity in essay testing. The use of multiple-choice tests grew rapidly, especially after the development of optical scanners in the 1950s. Efficiency and objectivity still head the list of advantages of multiple-choice tests.

Advantages of Using Multiple-Choice Tests in Evaluation

Multiple-choice tests are recommended for use in evaluation for many reasons. Some of the most common are below:

- They are objectively scored: no matter which person, or for that matter, which machine corrects the test, the scores will be the same.
- In addition, multiple-choice tests are extremely efficient; they can be administered to many students at a time and can be scored quickly, accurately, and inexpensively thanks to optical scanners. There is typically no need for trained administrators or subject-area specialists.
- Multiple-choice tests can cover a great deal of the test domain in comparatively little time. For example, students can answer 50 questions in 40 minutes.
- Multiple-choice tests often possess a desirable test characteristic called reliability. Reliability refers to the consistency of test scores across different testing conditions or different forms of a test.
- Multiple-choice tests, in part because they are objectively scored and widely used, are perceived by many evaluation audiences to be good, credible sources of information.
- Multiple-choice tests provide scores in metrics that are familiar to many evaluation audiences. For example, percentiles or grade-equivalent scores are two norm-referenced metrics that are widely reported in evaluations.

A Closer Look

Norm-
Referenced
versus
Criterion-
Referenced
Scores

Norm-referencing and criterion-referencing are two different ways to report test scores. Nothing is inherently better about either method of attaching meaning to test performance; they simply serve different purposes.

Norm-referenced scores compare an examinee's test performance to the performance of other examinees. In routine classroom testing, a student's score would typically be compared to those of her classmates: "Maria performs above the class average in mathematics, but is in the lower third in reading." In standardized educational testing or employment testing, an examinee's performance is compared to the performance of a clearly defined reference group of examinees called a norming group. The scores of the norming group are used to devise test norms—that is, the data about normal, below normal, and above normal performance.

Test users need to know that the norms for a test are appropriate. For example, if the norms were developed over a decade ago, the test user needs to question whether comparing a person's score with that group is reasonable. Norm groups should also be representative; for example, national norms should be derived from a group of examinees who are representative of the United States population with respect to such characteristics as gender, age, race, and region of the country.

Criterion-referenced scores, on the other hand, say something about how the examinee performed relative to an absolute performance standard or a criterion. Ideally, a criterion-referenced score provides a clear answer to the question, "What does this student know?" or "What can this student do?" For example, if a content domain is thoroughly defined, and if the test items sampled from the domain are representative, then a student's score of 80 percent correct should be interpretable in terms of how much of the content domain the student knows. Other criterion-referenced interpretations might indicate what percent or how many of the course objectives were passed. For some professionals, criterion-referencing is synonymous with mastery testing, in which individual test performance is described as "pass" or "fail" relative to a pre-determined cut-off score. Interestingly, such a cut-off score is sometimes norm-referenced at its root, in that it is determined by considering the performance of a norming group.

Continued

Many standardized achievement batteries provide both norm-referenced and criterion-referenced interpretations of student performance. For example, a student's performance on the language mechanics portion of a test could be expressed as a national percentile, which compares his performance to a national norming group. It could also be expressed as a local percentile, which indicates how well he did compared to the other students in the district. At the same time, the score report might provide some criterion-referenced interpretations: "this student demonstrated mastery of sentence-final punctuation, partial mastery of pronoun usage, and non-mastery of capitalization."

Example from classroom testing: A 50-item mathematics operations test is given to a class of 25 fourth-grade students. In this class, Rosalyn got 42 questions right. Twenty of Rosalyn's classmates scored below 42.

Criterion-referenced scorings of Rosalyn's performance:	Norm-referenced scoring of Rosalyn's Performance:
Rosalyn got 42 out of 50 questions right.	Rosalyn scored at the 80th percentile.
Rosalyn got 84%.	Rosalyn ranked 6th in her class.

Disadvantages of Using Multiple-Choice Tests in Evaluation

Despite their many advantages, multiple-choice tests have been criticized for some of the following reasons.

- Multiple-choice test items are often inherently ambiguous. Wording that may appear clear to a test writer may unintentionally confuse the test taker.
- Multiple-choice tests provide little truly diagnostic information about students. They provide no information about *why* pupils get items right or wrong and no data about the process that the students employed in responding.
- In a similar sense, typical multiple-choice-standardized tests provide little information that can be directly used by the teacher to guide or improve instruction.
- Multiple-choice tests often do not tap (hence often do not provide information about) students' higher order thinking skills. It is easier to write multiple-choice items to measure factual knowledge than complex, multi-step mental processes, though the latter can be done.
- If multiple-choice tests are associated with important sanctions and rewards, such as promotion to the next grade or graduation from high school, they can exert

negative influences on the curriculum. Imagine a school that wishes to receive continued project funding for an innovative program they have developed. If continued funding is contingent on test score improvement, we would almost certainly see such an improvement. Unfortunately, the reason for a score increase under such circumstances is often that instruction has been reduced to drilling for the test.

A Closer Look

_____
Reliability

Reliability refers to the accuracy, consistency, or lack of measurement error associated with a set of test scores. If you stepped on your bathroom scale at 6:00 a.m. and got on it again at 7:00 a.m. the same morning and got two very different readings, you would question its reliability. Similarly, the trustworthiness of a test would be called into question if it yielded very different results under slightly different testing conditions. Of course no test, or bathroom scale, or opinion poll, or measuring instrument of any sort is without some error; you just want to be sure that the accuracy is adequate for the decisions you want to make from test results.

Perfect reliability is 1.00; complete lack of reliability is 0.00. Many tests used for important decisions at the individual level, such as the SAT, have reliabilities in the low .90s. One rule of thumb given for tests that are used for decisions about groups, as is usually the case in evaluations, is that they should have reliabilities above .65 (Mehrens & Lehmann, 1987).

USING ALTERNATIVE ASSESSMENTS IN EVALUATION

The well documented problems with multiple-choice tests, such as those highlighted above, have provoked a demand for different kinds of tests. These "different" kinds of tests are generally referred to as "alternative assessments," since they represent an alternative to the dominant multiple-choice standardized tests. Performance assessments, portfolios, and even multiple-choice items that require higher-order thinking, have all been included under this rubric.

What these alternative test and item types have in common are the following characteristics:

• They focus on a whole task, not on discrete bits of information.
• They require that the examinee produce or perform, not select.

A Closer Look

<table>
<tr>
<td>

—————
Examples of
Alternative
Assessment

</td>
<td>

Performance assessment requires students to demonstrate their knowledge of particular subject matter. These types of assessment are commonly encountered in science in the form of experiments and other laboratory work, but they can be used in any subject area. For example, in social studies, a unit on reading and using a compass could culminate in an outdoor orienteering contest to find a "buried treasure." Given a list of directions and a compass, a student would have to follow the directions successfully from start to finish to locate the treasure.

    Portfolios are simply repositories for student work. Ideally, they can showcase and document a student's development in a given subject over time. Typically, the overall format is decided upon by the teacher, but the student has at least some role in selecting which work to include and determining how that work will be evaluated. For example, a writing portfolio might include several drafts of several different papers, as well as an essay in which the student explicitly compares two of the papers. Later in the semester, the student might write a table of contents for the portfolio and an evaluative essay about the contents and the development they reflect.

</td>
</tr>
</table>

QUESTIONS TO ASK WHEN USING TESTS IN PROGRAM EVALUATION

We have to use tests and assessment instruments, but we must not deceive ourselves or others into believing that our test results are infallible. Wise test use involves asking informed questions about every testing decision. None of the disadvantages mentioned above with respect to either traditional or alternative testing presents insurmountable difficulties as long as we know about the potential pitfalls and know what to ask about them.

When making testing decisions in evaluation, or working with an evaluator who is making testing decisions, some of the questions you might ask are:

- What are our purposes for testing? What inferences, decisions, descriptions, or consequences do we hope to produce from test results?
- Is the domain of the test the domain we are interested in? Does the name of the test mask an incomplete conception of the domain?
- Is the norm group for the test appropriate for our testing decisions? Are the norms up-to-date?

- Are we using an appropriate metric and ensuring that those who use our evaluation results understand it?
- Are there other indicators that can support the conclusions drawn from the test results? What other sources of information (such as other tests or teacher opinions) can help us judge the inferences we make from the test?
- Do we have to test every student in every grade to make our decisions? If you are using an expensive or disruptive testing procedure, and you do not need to make decisions at the level of the individual student (that is, "Should Johnny do more work on addition?"), consider testing only a random sample of the students (see box below).
- How can we tap the context-rich knowledge of the teacher?
- What contextual and logistical constraints will affect our choice of testing mode?

A Closer Look

_____

Matrix
Sampling

"Do the fifth graders in our innovative reading program now read better?" This is a common sort of question to ask in an evaluation; the most common way to answer it has been to choose a test, administer it to all fifth graders in the program, and look at the results.

But think about this: When a banana boat arrives in the harbor from a foreign country, does the agricultural inspector open every banana in order to determine if the shipment is up to standards? He or she samples from among the bananas in the boat, and makes inferences about the whole shipment based on the bananas in the sample. We can apply the same principle in educational evaluation. We do not have to test everyone in a group in order to make inferences about that group. If we are using an expensive, time consuming, or disruptive testing procedure, sampling becomes an especially attractive option.

Another variation on sampling is called matrix sampling. In matrix sampling, both students and types of assessment are systematically sampled. For example, of the 100 fifth graders in our innovative reading program, a randomly selected 25 might take a multiple-choice test of reading skills, another randomly selected 25 might provide oral reading samples, 25 might retell a story they had read, and the last 25 might turn in portfolios of book reports. Matrix sampling allows us to use a wide range of assessment techniques and thus increases the scope of information we have about the targeted skill or subject area, in this case, reading.

---

7. THE DISCREPANCY EVALUATION MODEL

ANDRÉS STEINMETZ

The word *evaluation* is used loosely to encompass many different activities and purposes. When educators evaluate a reading program, they may be referring to deciding which of several reading programs their school district should adopt; when evaluating a school-bell schedule, they may mean finding out how popular the schedule is among students and faculty and what the advantages and disadvantages of several other bell schedules may be; when evaluating students, they may mean administering achievement or psychological tests; and so on.

Also, the more educators stress the need for evaluation and the more it is associated with accountability and funding decisions, the more the term appears in their vocabulary. People become willing to call a lot of things evaluation when they need to show that they have done something called evaluation.

While a wide variety of activities is encompassed by the term, there is an apprehensiveness associated with it that seems to remain invariant. Evaluation suggests making judgments of worth, and these judgments are generally accompanied by strong emotional reactions. The term raises apprehension that judgments will be made which will affect the social and/or professional status of people, their career plans, their self esteem, the scope of their authority, and so on.

Steinmetz, Andrés. "The Discrepancy Evaluation Model." *Measurement in Education*, no. 1, 7 (Winter 1976), 1–7. Copyright 1976, National Council on Measurement in Education, Washington, D.C. Reprinted with permission.
    Steinmetz, Andrés. "The Discrepancy Evaluation Model." *Measurement in Education*, no. 2, 7 (Spring 1976), 1–6. Copyright 1977, National Council on Measurement in Education, Washington, D.C. Reprinted with permission.

What all this amounts to is that when one is called upon to do evaluation, it is usually hard to escape first doing battle with a lot of expectations people have about what is going to happen. To work effectively, a practitioner is forced to clarify his/her position relative to all these expectations. The Discrepancy Evaluation Model (DEM)[1] represents an assembly of ideas and procedures arising out of attempts to respond constructively to such expectations. It represents a scheme with which to respond to the challenges presented by the difficult task of evaluating educational programs.

BASIC TENETS OF THE MODEL

The Concepts of Standards, Performance, and Discrepancy

In order to evaluate something, we inevitably make comparisons. More specifically, we say that to evaluate a given object (whether a person, a motorcycle, or a program) it must be compared to a standard. By a standard we mean a list, description, or representation of the qualities or characteristics the object should possess. In other words, a description of how something *should be* is called the Standard (S).

Once we are clear about how things should be, we can proceed to find out whether they *actually are* that way. When we are engaged in finding out the actual characteristics of the object to be evaluated, we are taking Performance measures (P). Thus, evaluation is a matter of comparing S against P.

There is another term involved in the comparison between S and P. We say that the comparison yields Discrepancy (D) information, and thus we can speak of evaluation as being a matter of making judgments about the worth or adequacy of an object based upon D information between S and P.

The concepts of S, P, and D surface quite naturally whenever, under the name of evaluation, one wants to judge the adequacy or worth of something. Suppose, for example, that you want to purchase a motorcycle but are uncertain whether the specific one you are considering is in good mechanical condition, and you, therefore, arrange to have a mechanic examine it. We can use the concepts of S, P, and D to describe what the mechanic will do pursuant to your request to find out whether the motorcycle is in good mechanical condition. Essentially, the mechanic will take certain P measures and compare these to an S. The D information generated in making the comparison will somehow aggregate into a judgment about whether the motorcycle is or is not in good mechanical condition.

The mechanic has some ideas about how the motorcycle *should be* functioning when it functions adequately and he/she will proceed to test these out. For example, he/she may refer to the motorcycle specifications manual to find out what compression the pistons should generate, and that information will become part of the S. Then, as a P measure, he/she can find out whether the pistons do in fact generate the compression specified. He/She may also listen to the way the motorcycle is idling (P) and compare that to his/her experience in order to decide whether the engine sounds the way *it should* sound (S). Or, he/she may refer to both his/her experience and the specifications manual (S) in order to generate D

information about the actual condition (*P*) of the brakes. As another *P* information-collecting strategy, the mechanic is also likely to drive the motorcycle and compare how it feels and sounds with how he/she thinks the motorcycle *should* feel and sound.

Thus, to find out whether the motorcycle is in good mechanical condition, the mechanic will do certain things, like measure compression, test the brakes, examine the spark plugs, etc., all of which represent gathering *P* information. Of course, the mechanic will probably restrict himself/herself to collecting *P* measures on a limited number of dimensions according to time available; the price he/she has agreed on with you; his/her experience about what is important to look at; and, also, the availability of an *S* governing what he/she is looking at. Note also that *S* will vary in specificity and will be a mixture of the mechanic's experience and the operating and engineering specifications of the motorcycle. The *D* information he/she generates by comparing *S* and *P* will become a basis for the conclusions he/she submits to you. In his/her conclusions, he/she is likely to pass a judgment by saying that the motorcycle is or is not in good condition. He/she will probably substantiate his/her conclusion by referring to some of his/her findings. He/She might add things like, "the piston rings are worn," or "it needs a new clutch" and thus roll into one phrase a *P* statement, an *S*, *D* information between the two, and a conclusion indicating what to do about it. Furthermore, knowing that you are trying to decide whether or not to buy the motorcycle, he/she is likely to make a recommendation such as, "it's OK for the price," or "I wouldn't buy it."

In similar fashion, the *S*, *P* and *D* concepts can be shown to underlie the making of any judgment of adequacy or worth. More than that, they seem to underlie any cybernetic process and much of human behavior. Under the DEM, however, the important thing is how these concepts are applied. To discuss how they are applied, I would first like to make some summary observations about the work of the mechanic in the example considered above. Then, I will consider the role of a DEM evaluator by elaborating a bit further on the same motorcycle example. At that point, we will be in a position to understand the application of the DEM and can go on to apply it to something a bit more complex than a motorcycle—an educational program.

Summary Observations

1. The person you consulted to determine whether the motorcycle is in good mechanical condition is considered by you to be an expert in motorcycle mechanics.
2. Both the *S* and the specific characteristics of the motorcycle to be examined (the specific *P* information to be gathered) were selected and determined by the mechanic. In particular, the sources of the *S* were the mechanic's experience and knowledge, and the manufacturer's specifications.
3. Much of the *S* was left implicit. You might ask to have the *S* applied, verbalized or explained to you, but the custom governing the exchange between you, the

client, and the mechanic (as expert and as evaluator) tends to keep that sort of conversation to a minimum and on a relatively superficial level. And, whatever conversations might be held about S are usually jargon-loaded and assume knowledge over the very conditions or phenomena which, as client, you don't have, and which led to your turning to someone else in the first place. Thus, the specific S brought to bear on certain performance information may remain unknown to you and, to some extent because they are not articulated by him/her, less than consciously known to the mechanic. For example, in examining the condition of the spark plugs the mechanic may notice that they are a brand which he/she considers inferior to another brand. That, in itself, may tend to make him/her more willing to consider their life exhausted than he/she might otherwise be. And the influence of that bias in his/her judgment is something the mechanic may not be ready to acknowledge.

4. You are not likely to see the specific performance information obtained. The mechanic is likely to report to you an overall judgment about the mechanical condition of the motorcycle, elaborate a bit on some of his/her findings, and respond to some questions you might have. He/She is unlikely, however, to itemize P and D information for you or to be explicit about how he/she aggregated the D information to arrive at his/her judgment. He/She may also recommend to you a course of action—repair, price negotiation, etc.

The Role of the Evaluator

We have seen how what the mechanic was asked to do can be discussed in terms of S, P and D. Thus, we can say that the mechanic was evaluating the mechanical adequacy of the motorcycle. But we would not say that he/she was applying the DEM, even though we can describe what he/she did in terms of S, P and D, because the critical thing about the DEM is the *manner* in which these concepts are applied. The crucial thing rests in the role relationship that is assumed by the evaluator vis-a-vis the client. In particular, the DEM evaluator would neither set S nor judge the comparisons made between S and P, though he/she would normally collect P. Instead, he/she would assist the client to do these things for himself/herself.

Let's suppose, to explore this role relationship, that you come to me, a DEM evaluator and neither a motorcycle expert nor mechanic, and ask me to help you with your larger problem—namely, to evaluate a specific motorcycle with the aim of deciding whether or not to purchase it. As a DEM evaluator, the first thing I would be concerned about is the existence of an S. I would want to know from you what you are looking for in a motorcycle, what characteristics or qualities you feel that motorcycle *should* possess. If my turning to you for an S seems a little odd at this point, it may be because we have some different ideas about and expectations from an evaluation. Remember that this role characteristic of the evaluator is chosen in order to permit constructive response to technical, political, organizational, and emotional problems encountered in the applied situation.

Table 1. First Attempt at a Standard

Characteristics the motor cycle should possess:
— *Cost:* should not cost over $800
— *Power:* should be able to cruise at 60 mph
— *Stability:* should be large and heavy enough to stay on the road
— *Noise:* should be quiet
— *Appearance:* should have the classic "World War I look"
— *Mechanical Condition:* should be in good condition and not presently need repairs

Table 2. Elements of an Evaluation Workplan

Evaluation Question	Standard	Source of Information	Instrument	Data Collector	Date Info is Needed
1. How much does this motorcycle cost	The motocycle should not cost more than $800	Seller of motorcycle	Interview	Evaluator	Next Friday
2. Does this motorcycle cruise at 60 mph?	Should be able to cruise at 60 mph				

As a DEM evaluator, I would be seeking a model representing the kind of motorcycle you are looking for, which can then be used as the *S* against which to compare any particular motorcycle. This stands in contrast to summary observations (1) and (2) above, which noted how the mechanic (as evaluator) was considered an expert authority and the source of the *S* governing mechanical functioning. I might begin by helping you make a list of the characteristics or qualities you value or find desirable, as shown in Table 1.

While this first attempt at an *S* gives an idea of the kinds of characteristics you feel the desired motorcycle *should* possess, I would still need further guidance from you before I could collect *P* information that would be useful to you. I would ask you to formulate some questions—evaluation questions—which you would want answered relative to each characteristic making up the *S*. These would be questions which ask directly whether the quality, condition, or characteristic desired and specified by the *S* obtains in reality. Let's take cost and power, for example. In the case of cost, an evaluation question might be: What does this specific motorcycle cost? In getting ready to answer this question, I would make a little work plan, something like that shown in Table 2, which I would review with you.

It would be clear that when I get the answer to question one in dollars, it will be easy for you to determine whether or not the *S* is met, since you have said it should not cost over $800. Let's consider power, however. As shown in Table 2, an evaluation question here might be: Does this motorcycle cruise at 60 mph? In thinking through the elements of the evaluation work plan here, however, I would be faced right away with a basic problem, and I would turn to you for clarification of the following points: I can answer the question in many different ways and still meet your Standard. For example, I could ride down a long incline and maintain 60 mph, or drive a straightaway with no passengers or wind and maintain 60 mph for one-half hour, or I could find that the engineering specifications say the motorcycle will cruise at 65 with one passenger, or so on. So, I would think through these difficulties with you and urge you to set an *S* that restricted more severely the number of different conditions and answers that would satisfy it. We might thus end up with a more specific *S* as shown in Table 3.

Let's now turn to another aspect of the *S* mentioned in Table 1, i.e., stability. We can see right away that the same problem with the *S* reappears here. You claim a relationship between size, weight, and stability, but if we don't know what it is, then simply finding out the size and weight of a given motorcycle will not let you know whether your *S* for stability will have been met. Again, I would urge you to decide what you will consider adequate stability and to agree with me on an appropriate way of taking performance measures. If you could reach no conclusion on your own, I would help you think through a number of different options. You could consult motorcycle engineers for constellations of variables and conditions that might define stability; you could launch a research project yourself aimed at defining stability and the factors involved, etc. You could also decide to remove the whole matter of stability from your *S*. While I would facilitate an *S*-setting process and seek to confront you with decisions you would need to make in order to have an *S* available, I would not get involved in the work or decisions involved in creating the *S* itself. Thus, for example, I would not carry out the research project that would build the *S*—unless I completely changed my contract with you, and it was made clear I would no longer be an evaluator. To me, evaluation would presume the existence of the *S* and would entail merely looking at a specific object or event to see whether pertinent characteristics or conditions are present.

Table 3. Elements of an Evaluation Workplan

Evaluation Question	Standard	Source of Information	Instrument	Data Collection	Date Info Needed
1. How much does this motorcycle cost?	The motocycle should not cost more than $800	Seller of Motorcycle	Interview	Evaluator	Next Friday
2. Does this motorcycle cruise at 60 mph?	It should maintain 60 mph with 2 passengers on a straightaway all day.	Engineering specifications	Review of engineering specs	Evaluator	Next Friday
	It should maintain 60 mph with 2 adults up the mile-long hill on Rt. 629	Motorcycle	Road test	Evaluator	Next Friday

Under most circumstances, I would not even collect any data unless the pertinent S was explicitly stated. Otherwise, you, as client, would be left open to the possibility that I, and not you, would make the ultimate judgment of adequacy in the evaluation. Suppose you decide that the research questions concerning stability are too time-consuming and expensive given that you want to reach a decision within a brief time period. Thus, you are in the position of remaining interested in a certain quality (stability) yet find yourself without an S for it. This certainly is a common enough situation in most daily affairs, and there is a popular method for dealing with it: leave the S unexplicated and decide on the adequacy of the P information as you collect it. Applying this method to our example, one could drive the motorcycle and draw some conclusion about how "stable" one feels—which involves conjuring up an S based on the immediate experience. One would be contrasting the immediate experience to an ideal implicit model of stability. One could also make a comparative judgment by riding a number of motorcycles and comparing the feelings of stability involved. Either way, one collects some psycho-motor knowledge about the stability one desires, formulates as S, and generates D information while test driving. However, if this latter route were chosen in order to obtain P measures on stability, then *you*, as client, would have to do the test driving. You are the one, after all, who is primarily interested in knowing whether a specific motorcycle meets your S. If the S is left unobservable and if I, as evaluator, do the test driving, the matter of stability would end up being judged against *my* (implicit) S and not yours.

Review

While the work of both the mechanic and the DEM evaluator can be described in terms of the S, P and D concepts and thus be called evaluation, there are important differences in the way each discharged his/her role. These differences can be summarized in terms of the relationship of the mechanic and the evaluator of S involved. The mechanic was the source of S, selected S, defined the P measures to be made, the procedures involved, and also collected the P information. He/She then compared S and P in each case and formed an overall judgement concerning the mechanical adequacy of the motorcycle based on the D information generated. He/She was also not particularly concerned with making S explicit nor with presenting P in any great detail. At least, he/she did so only as it seemed necessary to make his/her conclusions plausible and convincing to the client, or in answer to specific questions.

In contrast, the DEM evaluator approached the problem by helping the client articulate the dimensions involved in S by making it clear that the responsibility for deciding what S *should be* rests with the client. The evaluator also made it clear that the client had to specify the kind of evidence that would be an acceptable index of the S as well as what would be considered criterion performance. Moreover, the significance attached to all discrepancies found and, thus, the overall judgment of adequacy, was also left to the client. The DEM evaluator was thus the facilitator of a process. The actual evaluator, in the sense of making the judgment of worth, was the client.

To ensure that the client would be in the position of making the judgment of worth, both the S and P information to be collected had to reach a certain level of specificity independent of the personality of the DEM evaluator. This is one thing that makes the role of the evaluator tricky. While the DEM evaluator would generally consider it part of his/her responsibility to collect P information, he/she would not do so in cases where it would evidently compromise the client's ability to compare S and P and thus give D significance. The example involving stability was a case in point. We saw that by leaving S embedded in personal experience, the very definition and collection of P tacitly set S. Therefore, in that instance, the client was asked to collect P himself/herself.

There are two aspects of the posture of the DEM evaluator that require further comment. They have to do with the interest of distinguishing clearly between the acts of setting S and determining whether S has been met. First, as already noted, setting S is the responsibility of the client, but facilitating the process is the responsibility of the evaluator. It the client is unable to formulate a pertinent S, then he/she can undertake whatever activity necessary to create it, which may involve consulting experts or launching research projects. He/She may also engage an expert to do the "evaluation" for him/her. This was the situation in the example above, where a mechanic was engaged to judge the mechanical condition of the motorcycle because the client did not feel he/she had the expertise to do it himself/herself. Yet, because of the way in which this "evaluation" was performed, or, more exactly, because of the client's relation to it, we would not consider it a DEM evaluation. The major reason for this is that the client is not expressly setting S, and this would be considered pre-empting his/her decison making role and responsibility. It may be objected that the client is still free to accept or reject whatever the expert ends up recommending. That is, of course, true, but the point is not so much that the client end up making the final decisions as it is that he/she expand his/her awareness of the raw ingredients that go into making the decision. Choosing to accept or reject a formed judgment is different from being a party to the making of that judgment.

The second matter is a variation of the difficulty often encountered in specifying S. One can say that leaving the definition of something like stability to an unexplicated feeling derived from test driving is not objective, is not scientific, or does not provide the evaluator with an operational or observable definition. And not being objective or scientific in this sense is generally shunned. I prefer, however, not to talk about the issue in this way. I think it is better to discuss the issue in terms of roles and responsibilities. The client is the one who has to live with the choice made. He/She is the one who has to take responsibility for the evaluation and the decisions resulting from it. The specific data or performance information one responds to in comparing P and S is certainly a matter of one's belief structure and one's preferred way of relating to the world. If nothing other than empirical or scientific data will do, then certainly one could proceed to construct an empirical definition of "stability." But I don't think that is automatically the best or most appropriate way to proceed. A client may find his/her own personal judgment based on *feel* or unexplicated criteria satisfactory, and if *he/she* does, I will too. That doesn't mean that I would not try to explore with the client other alternatives or the consequences of doing things in different ways. It also doesn't mean that I would accept any evaluation contract whatsoever. It means that the credibility of evidence is a function of one's beliefs and that quantitative objective data is not necessarily the thing to strive for.

An interesting corollary here is that, in the case of program evaluation, absolutely any program objective is an adequate objective as far as the DEM evaluator is concerned. There is no need to insist on behavioral or other kinds of objectives. The role description already provided emphasizes freedom to set S as seems desirable and pertinent to the client, who carries the responsibility for the program. Rules for expressing criterion performance, in particular, are not necessarily deduced from a certain methodological orientation or logical framework. Acceptable S and P are seen, rather, as a function of the set of agreements and beliefs that make up the world of the client.

These role characteristics may be unwieldly when a layperson wants to evaluate a motorcycle, but they are essential to the comprehensive and useful evaluation of something like an educational or social service program. This is because programs represent organized human activity and, as such, always represent normative states of affairs. For here, S's ultimately are issues in social and moral philosophy, and, immediately, ideological and political matters. The position taken here is that S not be left to experts dissociated from the responsibilities of program operation and management. For program staff to choose and commit themselves to the S pertinent to their clients' contexts and personalities is fully as important as having an S that is rooted in abstract empirical generalizations (i.e., expert knowledge).

Finally, it should be evident that setting the role of the evaluator in this way formalizes the common human evaluative activity that is associated with any deliberate act. When applied to a program, DEM evaluation refers to making explicit the procedures and norms governing the SPD cycles that make up planning, implementation, and review activities. Thus, DEM program evaluation is aimed at program improvement. With the client in control of S and guiding the collection of P, D information can be used to keep action flexible, responsive, and informed. Since D is the result of comparing S and P, we can reduce D by changing S or changing P. Changing S involves program redesign, perhaps changing basic objectives or activities. To change only P in a program requires that management exert greater control over operations.

THE APPLICATION OF THE DEM TO AN EDUCATIONAL PROGRAM

Review of the Model

We have said that evaluation always consists of comparing *Performance (P)* with a *Standard (S)*. This comparison yields *Discrepancy (D)* information, which can be

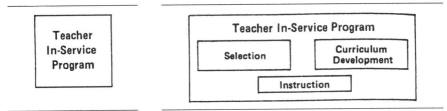

Figure 1. Level I Analysis   **Figure 2.** Level II Component Analysis

used as a basis for making a judgment of value or worth about the object being evaluated.

To evaluate something, we must have a pertinent S available. Obtaining such an S is usually not easy and, in most circumstances, has to be created—a job done by the client, assisted by the evaluator, to clarify and make conscious the S that should govern the activity or object being evaluated. Usually the extent to which S can be made explicit and observable is a matter of degree—important dimensions of it remaining implicit.

The evaluator collects data for which an explicit S is available; but, in order to do so, the evaluator and client must first agree on both the specific P information to be collected and the source of that information. This may involve the client and evaluator working together to continually clarify S.

Basic Steps in the Application of the DEM to a Program

The first thing to do is to understand that the purpose of the evaluation is to improve the program by making SPD cycles explicit and public insofar as is possible. This includes agreeing to the role distinctions between client and evaluator discussed above, and clearing the way for the first task, which is to create S.

Creating S is action-oriented planning. The client must turn both to existing knowledge and to his/her own experiences, values, and purposes in order to construct S. He/She must seek to involve others on his/her staff, those affected by the program, or those for whom the program is designed, in order to end up with an adequate and realistic S. Creating S is thus very much an exercise in applied goal- and value-clarification and may be thought of as creating a concrete model of a program.

A useful way to proceed in order to create S is to do a component analysis: to break the program into its major activities, functions, or components. Each component, in turn, can then be broken into its subcomponents and so on, until a level of detail is reached suitable to the needs of program management. For example, suppose the program we are concerned about is a teacher in-service program. We can represent it as shown in Figure 1. However, upon thinking through the basic organization, we might decide that the program really consists of three major components: selection, curriculum development, and instruction. These can then be represented as subcomponents of the teacher in-service program as shown in Figure 2.

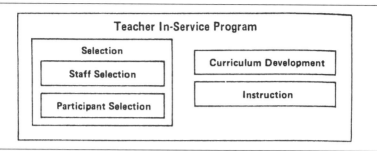

Figure 3. Level III Component Analysis of the Teacher In-Service Program

Each time we break a component into subcomponents, we reach a new level of detail. Thus, we call Figure 1 level I analysis and Figure 2 level II analysis. Figure 3 shows a level III analysis for the selection component. While selection alone has been chosen for the sake of brevity, the other components would be similarly broken down when constructing a program design.

In order to write a practical description of each component and subcomponent, we do an input-process-output analysis for each. This means that we assume program activity is not random, that it is goal-directed and that each activity has one or more objectives. These objectives, which may be conditions, behaviors, tangible products, or any purpose an activity is trying to realize, are *outputs*. The things we do to bring about the outputs are *processes*. Processes indicate what will be done, who will do it, how, when, and where. They describe how resources will be combined or transformed to produce outputs. The resources themselves, the personnel, facilities, materials, prerequisites, etc., that are needed to support the processes, are *inputs*.

Let's assign the entire program the numeral 1.0. We could then call the selection component 1.1, curriculum development 1.2, and instruction 1.3. Similarly, staff selection can be 1.1.1. and participant selection, 1.1.2. (This numbering system offers a convenient way to refer to components and follows the usual outlining form.) An abbreviated input-process-output description for each might look as shown in Table 4.

In the same way, a program design or S would be developed for each of the other subcomponents, breaking these down further into their components (thus going to level IV detail), if that is useful. Notice that the output of 1.1.1, two teacher trainers, is referenced: "to 1.1.2, 1.2, and 1.3." This indicates that the output of 1.1.1 is used as input to 1.1.2, 1.2, and 1.3. In other words, the teacher trainers will be inputs to the participant selection, curriculum development, and in-service instruction activities. The input-process-output description for 1.1.2 shows this relationship between 1.1.1 and 1.1.2 with the entry "teacher trainers (from 1.1.1)" in the input column. We would thus expect to find the contribution of the teacher trainers mentioned in the description of the process for 1.1.2, participant selection. The

Table 4. Input-Process-Output Description for Two Components

Input	Process	Output
	1.1.1 STAFF SELECTION.	
— Program director	The program director meets with	— 2 teacher trainers
— 3 principals	the principals and building	(to 1.1.2, 1.2, 1.3).
	coordinators of each of the 3 schools	
	in order to:	
— 3 building coordinators	— write job descriptions for	
— teacher needs assessment data	2 full-time teacher trainers	
	based on needs assessment data;	
— $30,000 personnel budget	— coordinate with the school	
— Personnel Office procedures	district personnel office and	
	their recruitment procedures;	
	— plan the applicant screening	
	and selection procedures;	
	— carry out the selection procedure.	
	1.1.2 PARTICIPANT SELECTION.	
— Program director	(Describes how the participants	— 10 teachers from
— teacher trainers (from 1.1.1)	for the in-service program	each school (to 1.3).
— teacher needs assessment data	will be selected.)	
— 3 building coordinators		

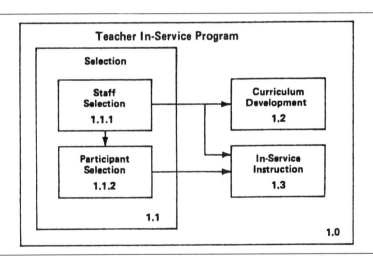

Figure 4. Level III Program Network

design also shows that the ten teachers from each school are inputs to component 1.3, in-service instruction (that makes sense, of course, since they will be the beneficiaries of the program).

These input-to-output relationships are shown in the network in Figure 4, which is the same as Figure 3, except that the component numbers and some arrows between components have been added. An arrow between components means that one component produces at least one output that is an input to the other component. Thus, the fact that teacher trainers selected in 1.1.1 are an input to 1.1.2, as already noted, is shown with an arrow connecting 1.1.1 and 1.1.2. The other (input-output) relationships among components are also shown with arrows. This additional information to the component analysis of Figure 3 leads us to call Figure 4 a network.

This kind of component and relationship analysis eventually produces a detailed program design. It will consist of input-process-output narratives for each component, along with a network showing all components (and subcomponents) and the major relationships among them. This design then acts as S; specifying what *should* be, the intent of the program. As we will see in a moment, P data can then be collected on any aspect of the program to determine whether what should be occurring or resulting (S) is *actually* taking place (P).

It should be evident that this planning procedure stands to surface differences in values, approaches, procedures, philosophical orientations, etc. Properly facilitated by the DEM evaluator, planning promotes resolution or negotiation of these differences and agreement on the S that will govern formal evaluation. As these plans are implemented and periodically reviewed in light of P information, they may be changed or amended; that is, the S may change as conditions change and as continuous assessment of results occurs. Thus, programmatic decisions and actions utilize feedback. The evaluator's job includes gathering that feedback and putting it at the disposal of the evaluator's client(s).

The input-process-output description suggests different kinds of information that may be deliberately or formally gathered in order to assist feedback-guided action. These are summarized in Table 5.

Table 5. Kinds of Evaluation Useful to Program Improvement

Management Action	Kinds of Evaluation	Standards Relative to:
Program Planning	Design Evaluation	— design adequacy; construct validity, comprehensiveness, internal or logical consistency, relationship to need, appropriateness.
Program Implementation	Input Evaluation	— availability of resources; extent to which prerequisites and preconditions are met, extent to which program resources (moneys, people, materials, etc.) are available and deployed as planned.
	Process Evaluation	— extent to which activities are carried out as planned; existence or frequency, intensity, manner, and other qualities and characteristics of the activities.
	Outcome Evaluation	— interim outcomes; outcomes which are prerequisite to other outcomes; terminal outcomes.

Design evaluation in Table 5 refers to judging the adequacy of program intentions. The object being evaluated here is the program plan. Any program is bound to have a basis in social and moral philosophy, as well as empirical research, and the critique of these bases may be referred to as the problem of construct validity. But the program plans may also be examined for their comprehensiveness, appropriateness to the situation, relationship to known interests and needs, and so on. An analysis may also be made to see whether resources, such as the kinds and qualifications of personnel and materials, seem adequate to support the activities that the program intends to undertake. Similarly, one may critique the logical relationship between program objectives and the activities designed to bring them about. Design evaluation, then, refers to the construct and logical or operational validity of a set of intentions. The standards involved in this sort of evaluation are often not entirely explicit in advance and are made explicit incrementally. The method used it that of logical argument and the evaluation itself is readily understood in terms of the S, P, D concepts.

Program plans may themselves serve as S for other evaluation undertaken during the life cycle of the program. Program plans specify and direct program implementation and, as such, may serve as S to input, process, and outcome evaluation. For example, any program utilizes certain kinds and amounts of resources over time. Program plans that specify the number and kind of resources to different activities and purposes can act as an S governing the installation of the program. Thus, P information may be gathered concerning be extent to which the resources planned for are indeed available and are in fact deployed as required (input evaluation). A program whose design has been judged adequate may nevertheless falter if it does not have the proper resources available when they are needed. Input evaluation is aimed at helping management make sure these resources are available when necessary.

Process evaluation involves determining whether planned activities are carried out in the manner called for by the program plans and whether they are of the quality expected. Again, the S here is the program plan, which specifies and describes the program processes to be set into motion. Because of the complex interaction between S and action (which was known first?), thorough process evaluation overlaps with action research.

Outcome evaluation refers to determining the extent to which planned outcomes are achieved. It is useful to distinguish at least two classes of outcomes. Enabling or interim outcomes refer to milestones or sub-objectives essential to the execution of the program from month to month. In contrast, terminal objectives refer to the major purposes or aims of the program.

It should be clear that properly specifying inputs, processes, and outputs for each component and subcomponent and specifying the relationships among all subcomponents, amounts to making available the S essential for input, process, and outcome evaluation. This makes it possible to conduct evaluation on a continuous basis throughout the life of the project, because P data can be gathered relative to a larger class of program characteristics than just terminal objectives. Finally, the D information produced in the course of evaluation may be used to support two broad categories of management action. It may be used, on the one hand, to exert greater control over program operations in order to insure that P meets S. On the other hand, management may decide that the S originally set is inappropriate or unrealistic and may thus change the S involved.

Now it is, of course, impossible to formally collect empirical information on *all* inputs, processes, and outputs. Thus, program management is faced with setting some priorities. Management must identify the P information that would be most useful to it, given its limited resources and its internal and external needs. There will be P information useful primarily to program management in the day-to-day operation of the program, and there will be information that has to be provided to individuals and other organizations in the environment that serves to justify the program. Thus, management must set priorities around its needs for proper internal management and its need to remain accountable to the external environment. The decisions involved are made by management, not the DEM evaluator, although the latter again facilitates the deliberations involved. Having a complete program design available literally points out trouble spots and helps in making the trade-offs involved.

The collection of P information is guided by what the DEM evaluator calls "evaluation questions." Such questions ask whether what *should be* actually *is*; whether inputs are available *as specified*; whether processes are carried out *as planned*; and whether outcomes are being achieved *as intended*.[2] In other words, evaluation questions direct attention to the P information needed in order to determine whether the applicable S has been met. Examples might be: Are there ten participants from each school, and do they meet selection criteria? (outcome evaluation; the S required that there be ten from each school meeting certain criteria); Is the needs assessment data available? (input evaluation; the S required that needs assessment data be available to the people planning the selection of staff); or, Is the personnel committee meeting as planned? (process evaluation; the S specifies who should meet to design and carry out the staff selection). There might also be evaluation questions about the operation of the other components, similarly aimed at ensuring effective program operation. And, no doubt, there would be evaluation questions aimed at determining whether the terminal outcomes have been realized.

It is important to notice the very narrow definition given to evaluation questions. Evaluation questions assume the existence of an S. This is because evaluation is defined as the comparison between what *is* and what *might be* and is impossible unless the S is specified. The DEM evaluator will not let himself/herself get involved in collecting P information to answer questions for which no S exists. But, as already discussed, he/she will work with the client to articulate the S and to define the action that needs to be taken in order to make a pertinent S available.

The connection between the program design, the *intent* or expectations of the program, in short, the program S, and the program as it *actually is*, is provided by the evaluation questions. Dozens of these questions may be asked and many can be answered through informal interviews, meetings, or planning sessions. Some will be

Table 6. Summary of Data Collection Plan

(a) Evaluation Questions	(b) Design Referent	(c) Standard	(d) Data Collection Strategy	(e) Instrument	(f) Date Information Needed
(The specific question about the program and its operation that management wants answered. These questions give feedback important to determining whether standards should be changed or whether greater control over performance should be exerted. The standards applicable to each evaluation question must be known.)	(Names the component, its number, and whether the evaluation question is dealing with an input, process, or output. This refers you to the design where the standards governing the evaluation question are described.)	(Summarizes the standards pertinent to the evaluation question. information is extracted from the program design.)	(Lists sources of information and techniques for obtaining the information Represents the thinking that must lead to the "instrument" in the next column and to table 5–7.)	(A general term standing for the method or procedure to be used in gathering data; i.e., test, questionnaire, interview, observation, etc.)	(Dates are crucial particularly when information is supposed to support program planning and operation.)

Table 7. Summary of Data Collection Plan (continued)

(a) Instrument	(b) Evaluation Question Addressed	(c) Instrument Administration Schedule	(d) Data Collector	(e) Respondents	(f) Sample	(g) Data Analysis Procedure & Analyst	(h) Audience	(i) Report Preparation and Date
(From column (e) in table 5–6.)	(Shows the number of each evaluation question for which the instruments gather data. Often any one instru– is designed to answer more than one question.)	(Shows data collection dates and times.)	(Shows who is responsible for administering the instrument or collecting the data.)	(Shows the direct source of data: people, files, etc.)	(Usually limited resources demand that the respondents be sampled.)	(Who will analyze data and how the analysis will be done must be thought through in advance.)	(All persons or places expecting the information gathered are listed.)	(Names the persons with primary report preparation responsibility and the date by which reports must be ready.)

pursued more formally, depending upon the interests and needs of management and the problems and cost involved in collecting the information. The major steps essential to the collection of P information are summarized in Tables 6 and 7. Thus, a DEM evaluation will consist of an S (a detailed program design showing a network and input-process-output descriptions for all components and subcomponents) and a data collection plan filled out for each evaluation question asked. In this way, an internal feedback cycle can be set up so that the program is managed as much as possible on the basis of D information generated by comparing S and P; that is, on the basis of systematic evaluation.

CONCLUSION

The Discrepancy Evaluation Model offers a pragmatic, systematic approach to a wide variety of evaluation needs. From the daily activities of an individual teacher to educational program evaluation, the DEM can be utilized to structure the gathering of information essential for well-informed decision making. A major feature of the DEM is its emphasis on self-evaluation and systematic program improvement.

NOTES

1. The DEM was first put forth by Malcolm Provus; see *Discrepancy Evaluation*, McCutchan, 1971. It was further developed at the Evaluation Research Center in 1971–1975 by a team of people, including the author, led by Malcolm Provus. Different versions of the DEM have arisen. The views presented here are those of the author.

2. This does not necessarily mean that the DEM evaluator will not be open to unexpected events. How to handle this problem is negotiated between client and evaluator; the important thing, again, is for the evaluator to stay away from setting S and deciding on his/her own what information to collect.

8. THE ROLE OF FIELD TRIALS IN EVALUATING SCHOOL PRACTICES: A RARE DESIGN

BILL NAVE, EDWARD J. MIECH, and FREDERICK MOSTELLER

"It sounds like a good idea, but does it work in practice?" Whenever educators propose reforms in schools—such as reduced class size, cooperative learning, or expanded preschool—this fundamental question about effectiveness needs answering. To find an answer, educators have turned to a repertoire of strategies, most frequently ones based on survey data. They have, however, largely neglected a powerful and persuasive research design to demonstrate program effectiveness: the randomized-controlled field trial. Widely used in other disciplines, such as medicine and public health, this design appears to be rare in U.S. evaluation research of education practices in preschool through 12th grade (pre-K-12). Because of the power of field trials to reflect results rather than intentions in evaluations of school practices and to link interventions to outcomes, this infrequent use of field trials needs to be examined.

In this article, we first define "randomized-controlled field trial" and discuss its strengths in demonstrating program effectiveness. Second, we offer several examples of randomized-controlled field trials in education in the hope that it will increase historical awareness of field trials and show how this design has contributed valuable knowledge about school practices. Third, we describe some steps that might make field trials more relevant in educational research.

DEFINING FIELD TRIALS

When we speak of field trials, we specifically refer to *randomized-controlled field trials*. Because field trials can be confused with various types of "experiments" or

D.L. Stufflebeam, G.F. Madaus and T. Kellaghan (eds.). EVALUATION MODELS. Copyright © 2000. Kluwer Academic Publishers. Boston. All rights reserved.

"comparison studies," we provide a concise definition of the field trial design. In a field trial, researchers assign participants at random to control and experimental groups and then compare the results when the experimental group (or groups) receives some intervention[1] and the control group receives some other treatment. The intervention takes place in a real-world setting of practice, such as a regular classroom, and not in a more artificial setting such as a psychological laboratory. Because participants have been randomly allocated, the difference in performance between experimental and control groups can be reasonably attributed to the differential effect of the experimental treatment.

A brief example from a recent field trial in education can help illustrate its design features. In 1985, researchers in the Tennessee study on class size randomly assigned about 6,400 kindergarten students and 300 experienced teachers to one of three groups formed at each participating school: "small" classes, with 13–17 students; "regular-size" classes with 22–25 students; and regular size classes with a teacher's aide. Students then remained in their small or regular-size classes for the next four years, from kindergarten to the end of third grade.[2] Researchers compared the average reading and math performance of students in the three groups, and, based on these findings, were able to demonstrate that small class size did have a favorable effect on student achievement (Blatchford & Mortimore, 1994; Finn & Achilles, 1999, 1990; Mosteller, 1995; Mosteller, Light, & Sachs, 1996; Nye, Hedges, & Konstantopoulos, 1999; Word et al., 1990).

STRENGTHS OF FIELD TRIALS

Perhaps the greatest strength of field trials is their ability to demonstrate that a specific treatment caused certain effects. Without the random assignment of participants to experimental and control groups,[3] it can prove extremely difficult to convince others—as well as one's self—that differences in results between groups at the end of a program can be ascribed to the treatment rather than to preexisting differences in individuals in the two groups.[4]

The ability to assign effects to treatments can be especially important when dealing with small but valuable effects (or, alternatively, lack of effects or negative effects) of a program under evaluation. If a program has a huge effect on its participants, an evaluation with rigorous design may be unnecessary. For example, if people recover when given a new treatment for a disease, whereas formerly people with the disease all died in short order, then the evidence favoring the new treatment is compelling. For such large effects, the dramatic results speak for themselves and clearly seem to be the result of the intervention.

But relatively few programs produce effects large enough to meet this "slam-bang" criterion. In less dramatic circumstances, other differences between the groups might serve as rival explanations for the results of the intervention. Overwhelming effects are generally rare in social or medical interventions and are similarly rare in education interventions because factors such as family socioeconomic status and level of parental schooling have long been established as major explanatory variables for differences in student achievement.

For example, the Tennessee class size study showed an effect size of about .25 of a standard deviation for the performance of elementary students in small classes on reading and math standardized test scores, when compared with their peers in regular-size classes. This effect size translates into moving the average student, who formerly performed at the 50th percentile level, to the 60th percentile level. If the evaluators had not used a rigorous design, they would have found it difficult to state with confidence that the .25 effect size was due to differences in class size rather than to other factors such as differences between the teachers in the experimental and control groups (perhaps the group of teachers with the smaller class sizes were more talented practitioners, on average, than the teachers with the regular class sizes); differences between the students (perhaps the students in the smaller classes came from families with higher socioeconomic status and more parental education, on average, than students in the regular classes) or differences between the schools.[5]

Another strength of randomized-controlled field trials is the credibility of their findings to those both inside and outside the education community. The overall straightforwardness of field trials—the idea that several comparable groups were formed, and treatment groups received the experimental program whereas the control groups did not—can appeal to a diverse constituency, from teachers and parents to policymakers and the general public. For example, in the aftermath of the Tennessee class size study in 1989, the Tennessee state legislature allocated several million dollars to implement small K-3 classes in the 17 school districts that served communities with the lowest per-capita incomes in the state.[6]

A NOTE ON THE ETHICS OF FIELD TRIALS

Some have objected to designs that deliver new treatments to some but not all students because students assigned to the control group are denied access to the educational program under evaluation. Although we believe this is an important concern, we think some reflection on the usual state of affairs in schools places these objections in a larger context in which they lose much of their strength.

U.S. schools are generally awash in innovation: new educational ideas, programs, and reforms are constantly being implemented in schools and classrooms, often at the same time (Cuban, 1990; Elmore, 1996). Advocates of these innovations bring intelligence and good intentions to this task of improving schools and usually have a theory about how a particular innovation, once implemented, will benefit students and educators. These innovations, however, frequently play out differently in practice than originally predicted.[7] Some students may benefit from the effects of the innovations, while others may not. Further, because the innovations usually occur without systematic evaluation to gauge their relative effectiveness, policymakers have no sound basis for deciding whether to expand, modify, or scrap the new programs.

With field trials, by contrast, researchers can evaluate the effects of education programs and provide compelling evidence either to support the broad-scale implementation of innovations that prove successful, or to avoid false steps and wasted resources that would result from implementing ineffective innovations. In this way, rigorous designs convey serious respect for the teaching and learning process and for the risks students run when participating in new programs, just as Tennessee did.[8]

Furthermore, policymakers can use research findings from field trials to inform large-scale school improvement efforts elsewhere. At least 30 states have initiated class size reduction measures since the Tennessee study, and California alone has invested approximately $3 billion in reducing class sizes in the early grades (Finn & Achilles, 1999, p. 104). Overseas, the Republic of Ireland has implemented its own class size reduction initiative in some of its more economically-depressed regions (Kellaghan, Weir, Ó hUallacháin, & Morgan, 1995).

NOTABLE FIELD TRIALS OF PRE-K-12 EDUCATION

Readers might wish to ask themselves this question: Off the top of your head, if you were asked to name some well-known field trials in U.S. education, what comes to mind? At first, we had a difficult time answering the question ourselves. In subsequent review of the literature, we identified seven such studies that we felt might interest the larger education community, and we describe them in this section. We make no claim for the definitiveness or comprehensiveness of this list, but rather offer it as an effort to present a useful, thought-provoking collection of randomized-controlled field trials in education.

We present the field trials in an order roughly corresponding to the strength and direction of the studies' findings (from strong positive effects to zero effects to results still pending). For each we describe the study, summarize its findings, provide a measure of its influence,[9] note its possible policy implications, and comment on policy decisions it may have influenced.

Tennessee Class Size Study (1985–1989)

The randomized-controlled field trial known as Project STAR (Student-Teacher Achievement Ratio), conducted in Tennessee in the mid-1980s, is probably the largest, most important field trial in public schools ever funded by a state. Project STAR studied the effects of small class size on student achievement in kindergarten and grades one, two, and three, and involved about 80 public elementary schools throughout Tennessee.

The origins of Project STAR date to the early 1980s when Lamar Alexander, then governor of Tennessee, sought to improve public schools in his state. A modest study in neighboring Indiana, Project PrimeTime, suggested that smaller class sizes in kindergarten through third grade enhanced student achievement in school. This two-year study was interrupted after two semesters because Indiana was so impressed by the gains in student performance that they decided to implement smaller classes statewide immediately. Prior to committing large sums of money for the purpose of reducing class sizes, Governor Alexander and the Tennessee Legislature agreed to fund a four-year $12-million randomized-controlled field trial to determine the effects of reduced class size and of teacher's aides on student achievement in the lower grades. The Tennessee legislature required that the study include students from inner-city, suburban, urban, and rural areas; schools across the state were invited to participate in the study (Mosteller, 1995; Word et al., 1990). The introductory sections of this chapter described Project STAR's sample size, its class size intervention, and the study's findings.

A follow-up study to Project STAR, begun in 1989, asked if the differential achievement effects of small classes continued after all students participating in the field trial moved to regular-size classes in the fourth grade. This observational study, known as the "Lasting Benefits Study," found that improved student achievement continued through at least the eighth grade for students who were in the small classes for kindergarten and grades one, two, and three during Project STAR (Achilles et al., 1993; Nye, Hedges, & Konstantopoulos, 1999).

Based on the results of Project STAR, the Tennessee legislature voted in 1989 to allocate millions of dollars to institute small class sizes in kindergarten and grades one, two, and three in the 17 school districts in Tennessee with the lowest per-capita incomes in the state. This initiative, known as "Project Challenge," has also yielded impressive results in follow-up observational studies: the average end-of-year rank of second-grade reading scores for students in the 17 districts rose from 99th in 1990 (out of a total of 138 school districts in Tennessee) to 78th in 1993; the average end-of-year rank of math scores for the same group of students during the same time period rose from 85th rank to 56th (Achilles, Nye & Zaharias, 1995).

A search in the Social Science Citation Index (SSCI) for citations of the primary articles detailing the Tennessee study yielded a total of 80 citations. This relatively modest number of citations in the scholarly literature suggests that the results of the study may not yet be widely known in the educational research community. This state of affairs is apparently changing, however. In a recent special issue on class size findings in *Educational Evaluation and Policy Analysis*, a quarterly journal published by the American Educational Research Association, half of the featured articles were about the Tennessee study (Finn & Achilles, 1999; Hanushek, 1999; Nye, Hedges, & Konstantopoulos, 1999; Ritter & Boruch, 1999). In the introduction to the issue, David Grissmer of the RAND Corporation noted the growing influence of the Tennessee study on the policymaking community:

. . . the Tennessee experiment has had significant influence among policymakers. . . . Although the Tennessee results were known as early as 1990, they did not receive much attention from the research or national policymaking community until years later. Initially, the results seemed to be treated as simply one more set of findings—among scores of studies done on class size. . . . But the results of the Tennessee study are increasingly being interpreted by many as "definitive" evidence that supplants the scores of studies using non-experimental data. (Grissmer, 1999, p. 93)

The High/Scope Perry Preschool Study (1962–1965)

The High/Scope Perry Preschool Project was a randomized-controlled field trial begun in the 1960s. It investigated the short- and long-term effects of an intensive, high-quality preschool program for children from economically disadvantaged backgrounds (Barnett, 1985, 1993, 1995, 1996, 1998; Schweinhart et al., 1993; Schweinhart & Weikart, 1997; Zigler & Styfco, 1994).

Several hypotheses served as the foundation for the study: that a good preschool program could help young children who were at high risk of school failure to develop the cognitive skills needed to succeed in school and thus graduate from high school; that preparation for school could be linked to success in school; "that good preschool programs can help children in poverty make a better start in their transition from home to community and thereby set more of them on paths to becoming economically self-sufficient, socially responsible adults"; and that success in school could be linked to success in the "real world" of jobs, families, and community (Schweinhart et al., 1993, pp. 3–7). Another goal for the High/Scope Perry Preschool Project—"too bold at the time to be framed as a hypothesis"—was that participants would ultimately be less likely to be involved in the criminal justice system because they were more successful in school (Schweinhart et al., 1993, p. 7).

The sample size for the study was modest. From 1962 through 1965, 123 African-American children in Ypsilanti, Michigan participated in five waves, with an average of approximately 25 children per wave.[10] These three-year-olds (except for "Wave Zero," which involved four-year-olds) were identified as living in poverty and assessed to be at high risk of school failure. Children were randomly assigned to a treatment group, which received the Perry Preschool program for two years (except for the four-year-olds in "Wave Zero," which received only one year of preschool) and a control group, which did not receive any preschool program.

The Perry Preschool program consisted of a daily 2 1/2 hour classroom session for children on weekday mornings, and a weekly 1 1/2 hour home visit to each mother and child on weekday afternoons. The curriculum heavily emphasized active learning, in which "children plan, or express their intentions; carry out, or generate, their play experiences; and reflect on their accomplishments" (Schweinhart et al., 1993, p. 227).

A striking and important feature of the Perry Preschool field trial has been its 30-year longitudinal reach with little attrition from the original groups of participants. Researchers collected data on the 123 individuals in the treatment and control groups annually from ages 3 through 11, then at ages 14–15, 19, and 27, and reported the results of their data analyses after each of these phases (Barnett, 1993, 1996; Schweinhart et al., 1993; Schweinhart & Weikart, 1997). A number of assessment instruments and data-gathering techniques were used at various times throughout the study, including interviews; cognitive, performance, and behavior instruments; and analyses of public and private records from sources such as schools, police departments, courts, and social services.[11]

A wide variety of long-term benefits were associated with participation in the Perry Preschool program. In educational benefits, students in the preschool group had significantly higher average IQ scores than students in the control group from the end of the first year of the preschool to the end of the first grade, significantly higher school achievement at age 14, and significantly higher general literacy scores at age 19. They had a significantly higher level of schooling completed, with an average of 71 percent completing 12th grade or higher, as compared to 54 percent of the students in the control group. In addition, students in the preschool group spent significantly fewer years in special education in programs for "educable mental impairment" during their school careers, with 15 percent of the preschool group and 34 percent of the control group spending a year or more in one of these programs (Barnett, 1993; Schweinhart et al., 1993; Schweinhart & Weikart, 1997).

The study also showed lasting economic and social benefits from participation. In the 1990s, adults who had attended Perry Preschool in the 1960s had significantly higher monthly earnings at age 27 than students in the control group, with 29 percent of the former vs. 7 percent of the latter earning $2,000 or more per month (Schweinhart, 1993; Schweinhart & Weikart, 1997).

This economic self-sufficiency also translated into a significantly lower percentage of adults in the preschool group in receipt of social services at some time over the previous decade (59 percent) as compared with adults in the control group (80 percent). Adults in the preschool group also had significantly fewer arrests by age 27, with 7 percent of the program group and 35 percent of the control group having five or more arrests (Barnett, 1993; Schweinhart et al., 1993; Schweinhart & Weikart, 1997).

Based on their overall findings, the researchers had ample evidence to support the basic hypotheses they formulated at the beginning of the study in the areas of educational performance, delinquency and crime, economic status, family formation, childrearing, and health. (Schweinhart et al., 1993, p. xviii; see also Barnett, 1993, 1995, 1996, 1998; Schweinhart & Weikart, 1997). The results of the Perry Preschool randomized-controlled field trial have supported policymakers in their decisions to fund preschool programs for disadvantaged children in the United States. The eight primary High/Scope publications reporting on the results of the Perry Preschool Experiment since 1967 have over 500 citations in the SSCI, making it one of the best-known randomized-controlled field trials in education.

Pygmalion in the Classroom (1964–1966)

The field trial that came to be known as *Pygmalion in the Classroom* examined teacher expectancy effects in an elementary school identified as "Oak Park School" (Rosenthal & Jacobson, 1968). The study involved over 500 students enrolled in kindergarten through fifth grade,[12] and was "designed specifically to test the proposition that within a given classroom those children from whom the teacher expected greater intellectual growth would show such greater growth" (Rosenthal & Jacobson, 1968, p. 61). In other words, the *Pygmalion* study investigated whether teachers' perceptions of student ability could actually lead to changes in a child's cognitive performance. The field trial also examined teacher expectancy effects by grade level, track level, gender, and minority group status.

In the spring of 1964, all students in grades kindergarten through 5 in Oak Park School were given the "Harvard Test of Inflected Acquisition." Teachers were led to believe that the test was in its final stage of validity testing and that it was designed to predict academic "spurting" or "blooming." In reality, the test was Flanagan's 1960 Tests of General Ability (TOGA), a relatively nonverbal test of intelligence available in both Spanish and English (Buros, 1953). The test was chosen for a variety of reasons: it was unlikely that any teachers at "Oak Park School" had seen it; Oak Park School had many bilingual students with poor English skills, and the test did not rely heavily upon school-acquired skills such as reading, writing, and arithmetic; and it was group-administered.

The following school year, Oak Park School teachers were given a list of the students in their class who were likely to bloom academically because these students supposedly had scored among the top 20 percent on the TOGA. In reality, however, the researchers selected these "late bloomers" using a table of random numbers. These students were distributed among 18 of the school's teachers, one in each track (high, middle, low) for each of the grades 1–6. Lists varied from 1 to 9 students in each class, and varied from 33 to 66 percent female (on lists of more than one student).

To measure expectancy effects, posttests were given one semester, one year, and two years after the initial administration of the TOGA. The first two posttests were administered by the teachers, who had been given reason to expect late blooming on the part of some of their students and who had also been told that these additional tests were part of a further attempt by the researchers to predict late-blooming students.

Two different scorers independently scored the TOGA; neither scorer knew whether children were in the treatment group or in the control group. Statistically significant gains in IQ points were found for the treatment group students in grades 1 and 2, and for girls in the middle track.[13] No main effects were found to be associated with any of the three academic tracks at the school.

Pygmalion in the Classroom has proven to be one of the more controversial randomized-controlled field trials in educational research. Several scholarly studies, such as *Pygmalion Reconsidered* by Janet Elashoff and Richard Snow (1971), have critiqued the design and implementation of the study in considerable detail. The controversy and discussion of the merits of the original study, and the many that have followed it, have continued over the last 35 years (see, for example, Rosenthal, 1994 and Spitz, 1999).

Nevertheless, *Pygmalion in the Classroom* has also proven to be one of the more influential field trials in educational research. The original study has been cited more than 1,400 times since its publication in 1968 making it perhaps the most widely-known field trial in U.S. education. In addition, over 400 studies have been carried out to test or extend the findings of expectancy effects.[14] Seven meta-analyses carried out by Robert Rosenthal and others between 1968 and 1990 consistently find that 35 to 40 percent of these studies result in statistically significant effects.

We return to the subject of teacher expectancy later in this chapter when we discuss the study of the effects of standardized testing, in which the researchers performed an extensive analysis of expectancy effects as part of their national randomized-controlled field trial in Ireland. In terms of policy influence in the United States, the importance of "teacher expectation" has become a truism in the 1990s. A widely-held belief is that good teachers have "high expectations" for their students.

The Carolina Abecedarian Study (1972–1985)

Noting that ". . . there are actually few scientifically rigorous studies of the efficacy of early educational programs, with subjects randomly assigned to treatment and control conditions, and periodic long-term assessment of the outcomes" (Campbell & Ramey, 1995, p. 744), the Abecedarian researchers set out in 1972 to determine, among other things, whether an educational intervention to improve education outcomes for children born into poverty was more effective at preschool or during early elementary school.

The researchers selected a set of healthy infants (N = 109) born to poor families living in a small town in the southern U.S. Half the infants (N = 55) were randomly assigned to a specially designed five-year preschool program that extended from the first year of life until the time to enter public kindergarten, whereas the other half (N = 54) were randomly assigned to a control group. At the end of five years, the preschool group and the no-preschool control group were randomly split again. Half of the preschool group, as well as half of the no-preschool group, were randomly assigned to a three-year school-based intervention covering grades K, 1, and 2; the other half of each group received no school-age intervention. Thus, there were a total of four groups in the study: one with eight years of intervention (5-year preschool plus 3-year K-2 school-based intervention, N = 25), one with five years (preschool only, N = 22), one with three years (K-2 only, N = 24), and one with no educational intervention over the eight-year period (N = 22).[15]

Four cohorts, with an average of 28 infants per cohort, entered the study between 1972 and 1977. The researchers assigned each infant a risk score based on a 13-factor risk index, matched them on the basis of the score, then randomly assigned one of each pair to the experimental preschool group and the other to the preschool control group. Upon entry to kindergarten, children within each group were matched on the basis of their 48-month IQ score, then randomly assigned to the school-age intervention or the school-age control group.

The preschool was a full-day, year-round program with a caregiver-to-infant ratio of 1:3. The program's custom-designed curriculum addressed four major domains: cognitive and fine motor development, social and self-help skills, language, and gross motor skills. As children moved into the toddler and preschool stages, the caregiver-to-child ratios increased gradually to 1:6. The preschool included centers for art, housekeeping, blocks, language, literacy, and fine motor manipulatives. The language program was integrated throughout the day's activities, emphasizing pragmatic interactive features of adult-child language.[16]

The school-age intervention focused on increasing parent involvement to enhance their children's academic development. Each family in the experimental group was assigned a home/school resource teacher (HST) for the first three years their child attended public school. The HST served as a liaison, working with both parents and teachers, providing families with learning activities designed specifically for each child to support his/her work on the reading and math being taught at school.[17] Parents were encouraged to do these learning activities with their children for at least 15 minutes a day. The HST also functioned in some ways like a social worker, referring families to various agencies for services as needed.

The study found that children in the preschool treatment group fared better in several ways than students who had been in the preschool control group. The average advantage in IQ for the preschool treatment group was 8.8 points (16.4 points at age 36 months, 4.5 points at age 8, 4.6 points at age 15). Students in the preschool treatment group scored significantly higher at age 15 in reading and math than students in the preschool control group. Finally, "Through 10 years in school, children who had the Abecedarian preschool treatment made better school progress, in terms of fewer retentions in grade and fewer assignments to special education programs, than those in the preschool control groups" (Campbell & Ramey, 1995, p. 761).

The school-age portion of the treatment produced no significant effects by itself, leading the investigators to conclude that

the value of providing only a supplemental program in the primary grades of public school appears doubtful, being, by itself, not associated with greatly enhanced academic outcomes. Even though it is easier to provide supplemental services for children once they are in school, those who plan interventions for poor children should be aware that elementary school programs may have less impact on the children's academic performance than would programs begun earlier in the life span. (Campbell & Ramey, 1995, p. 769)

The Abecedarian researchers continue to collect data as the study participants reach the age of 21, and plan to evaluate outcomes "across the full developmental span from infancy to young adulthood" (p. 769).

Taken together with earlier published reports of the Abecedarian study (Barnett, 1995; Campbell & Ramey, 1994; Ramey & Campbell, 1984, 1991; Ramey & Smith, 1977), the SSCI lists 125 citations. Although this study appears to be less well-known than the Perry study, we believe it is noteworthy because of its longitudinal follow-up (like the Perry study) and because of its attempt to discover the relative efficacy of preschool versus in-school educational interventions for disadvantaged children.

Harvard Project Physics (1967–1968)

Harvard Project Physics (HPP) was a national curriculum development effort designed to reverse the precipitous decline in the percentage of high school students enrolling in physics courses by making the course more engaging to students, especially to those not planning careers in math, science, or technology (Bottoms, 1977). The project was co-sponsored by the Carnegie Corporation, the National

Science Foundation, the Sloan Foundation, Harvard University, and the U.S. Office of Education.

Beginning in 1967, researchers conducted a year-long randomized-controlled field trial to evaluate the results of this curriculum development. Investigators randomly selected a pool of high school physics teachers from a list of most U.S. physics teachers. Teachers from this pool were invited to participate in the study, and 53 were able to do so. These were randomly assigned to the experimental group (N = 34), which received a six-week summer course on how to teach the HPP curriculum, or the control group (N = 19), which attended a two-day session at Harvard hosted by university physicists, who asked control group teachers to teach their regular physics courses and also emphasized to them the importance of their participating in the experiment.[18]

The achievement and attitudes of students in the physics classes of these two groups of teachers were then compared at the end of the academic year. Students in the HPP classrooms reported much greater satisfaction and interest in physics than their counterparts in the control group. No significant differences were found between the students in the HPP sections and the students in the control group in terms of achievement in physics (Welch & Walberg, 1972). It should be noted, however, that the Project's primary stated goal was to increase student enrollment in physics courses, not to increase physics achievement, and by this criterion, evaluators considered the Project a success.

We think the Harvard Project Physics study is notable because it represents an early example of a curriculum project evaluation designed as a national randomized-controlled field trial. Although we found many articles discussing the project itself, the brief article reporting the HPP field trial evaluation has been cited only 21 times in the SSCI. Lee Cronbach (1982) examined the HPP study in some detail as one of three examples used to illustrate field trials as evaluation tools. Using HPP's unpublished final evaluation report, Cronbach analyzed in detail the strengths and weaknesses of the study's design and analysis of results.

The Career Academies Study (1992–2003)

The Manpower Demonstration Research Corporation (MDRC) began this field trial in 1992 to examine the effects of "career academies" on high school students' academic achievement, progress towards graduation, and preparation for postsecondary education and employment. Career academies are specialized public high schools that combine academic and vocational instruction and provide work-based internships as a way to prepare students for college, employment, or both. Each of the nine[19] career academies participating in the MDRC study has a career theme, such as aerospace technology, business, electronics, health, or public service. The nine career academies are scattered throughout the country[20] (Kemple & Rock, 1996; Kemple & Snipes, 2000).

Over a three-year period, beginning with the 1992–93 school year, about 1,700 eighth- and ninth-grade students participated in a lottery in which they were randomly assigned to a "program group" or a "control group." Students in the program group (N = 959) enrolled in a career academy, and students in the control group (N = 805) enrolled in their traditional high school (or participated in another option offered by the school district). Data used in the study included school records on attendance, achievement, course-taking patterns, and progress through high school (Kemple & Rock, 1996; Kemple & Snipes, 2000).

In 2000, MDRC released its first report on the study that included an analysis of student performance data (Kemple & Snipes, 2000). The report, assessing the progress of the student cohort from 8th and 9th grade through the end of 12th grade, found that "high-risk" students in the Career Academies had substantially reduced dropout rates along with improved attendance, increased academic course-taking, and increased likelihood of earning enough credits to graduate on time when compared with their high-risk counterparts in the control group.[21] "Low-risk" students in Career Academies had an increased likelihood of graduating on time compared to the corresponding subgroup in the control group. On average, all students in the Career Academies received more interpersonal support at school and participated more in career awareness and work-based learning activities than students in the control group (Kemple & Snipes, 2000).

However, of the 490 students (out of the study total of 1,764, or 28 percent) who completed standardized math and reading tests[22] at the end of their 12th grade, no significant differences were found in math or reading performance between the students in the Career Academies and their counterparts in the control group. Furthermore, when all students in the study were averaged together, the Career Academies showed only small reductions in dropout rates and slight increases in other measures of school engagement (Kemple & Snipes, 2000).

The Career Academies field trial will continue through 2003 to follow students through postsecondary education and employment to evaluate the impact of career academies on future educational and economic prospects.

The Career Academies study is a notable example of a field trial in educational research for several reasons. First, the scope of the study—with 9 sites, about 1,800 students, and a time span of 10 years—is substantial. Second, the experience of the Manpower Demonstration Research Corporation in carrying out the study may be of considerable value to the education research community. MDRC, based in New York City, has a long-established reputation for designing rigorous investigations to study the economic impact of programs intended to benefit disadvantaged populations, including youth from low-income families. The Career Academies study is MDRC's first major education evaluation in its 25-year history (Kemple & Rock, 1996; Kemple & Snipes, 2000). Third, the Career Academies study is funded by a consortium of seventeen private foundations in addition to the U.S. Department of Education and the U.S. Department of Labor, a private/public funding strategy similar to that which supported the Harvard Project Physics evaluation. Fifth, the Career Academies study continues to look to the future. As a randomized-controlled field trial, it provides an opportunity for the education community to look forward with anticipation to the results of a study that bears directly on an important issue for pre-K-12 practice: the subject of school-to-work transition.

Table 1. Description of control and treatment groups in the standardized test study in Ireland.

First control group	Students not given any standardized tests
Second control group	Students in grades 2–6 were given standardized tests of ability and achievement, but no feedback on test performance was provided
Treatment groups	Students in grades 2–6 took standardized tests and teachers received standardized scores and percentile ranks of all students; in some treatment groups, teachers also received additional diagnostic information on individual students

The Effects of Standardized Testing (1973–1977)

This study, conducted over a four-year period in the mid-1970s, examined the effects of standardized testing and of the use of test data on school organization, teacher attitudes and practices, and student attitudes and achievement. The study took place in elementary schools in the Republic of Ireland, which did not have a prior tradition of using standardized tests.

The researchers stratified the approximately 3,400 elementary schools in the country by pupil composition (all male, all female, or mixed) and location (city, town, or rural); schools were randomly selected within each stratum. For each school selected, four additional schools matched by size (number of teachers) and administration (lay or religious) were randomly selected. Each school within this matched set of five schools was randomly assigned to one of several treatment or control groups (see Table 1). The final sample of 35 sets of 5 matched schools yielded a total sample of 175 schools.

In the treatment groups, there was considerable planned between-group variation in terms of which students took the standardized tests, whether the students took norm-referenced or criterion-referenced tests, and what types of information was given to teachers (Kellaghan, Madaus, & Airasian, 1982).

The study found that standardized testing had little impact on schools. Admission practices and report cards were unchanged, communication practices remained the same, grouping decisions were largely unaffected, and decisions about students with learning difficulties were not altered. The researchers concluded that their findings "provide no evidence to support the position that standardized testing, when based in classrooms under the control of teachers, differs in kind in its effects from any other evaluative procedure available to the teacher" (Kellaghan, Madaus & Airasian, 1982, p. 261).

The researchers were able to use the data generated in this large national study to examine the role of teacher expectancy effects on student achievement, the topic investigated in *Pygmalion in the Classroom*. Rather than changing teacher expectations by identifying so-called late bloomers as was done in the *Pygmalion* study, the study looked for evidence of expectancy effects in natural classroom settings by analyzing changes over time in the relationships between student test scores and teacher expectations or teacher perceptions of students' abilities and achievement potential.

It was argued that if teacher expectancy effects occurred, these effects should be evident both in the control groups of teachers who received no test information about their students and in the treatment groups of teachers who did receive that test information. They found that

> when test information was made available to teachers, their subsequent ratings of the pupils' intelligence and scholastic achievement tended to move into line with that information. . . . If, on the other hand, test information was not available to the teachers, pupils' subsequent test performance tended to move into line with initial teacher perceptions of their intelligence and achievement, in comparison with the group that received test information. . . . Thus, an expectancy process seems to have been operating in classrooms, regardless of whether or not standardized norm-reference test information was provided to teachers. (Kellaghan, Madaus, & Airasian, 1982, p. 199)

This randomized-controlled field trial is notable for its scope. Its random sample of elementary schools is meant to generalize to an entire country, and it tackles one of the largest issues in educational evaluation: the effects of standardized testing. We note that arguably the most ambitious field trial discussed in this chapter is among the least well-known. The study, carried out in the 1970s, has been cited fewer than 25 times in the SSCI, suggesting that it remains largely overlooked by educational researchers.

CONCLUSION

Each school year many new programs and innovations are introduced into U.S. classrooms, affecting the lives of millions of students, teachers, parents, and administrators. Policymakers and the general public need good evaluations of these programs in practice to make informed decisions about the deployment of school resources to benefit children. Field trials afford special advantages in establishing the benefits or shortcomings of educational interventions.

We think that researchers could conduct field trials in education more often if three factors could be aligned: resources, expertise, and leadership. Because constitutional authority for public education in the U.S. is vested in the states, a large portion of state budgets flow to public education. State-level resources made Project STAR possible in Tennessee, and many opportunities exist for individual states and groups of states to use their organizational and fiscal resources to launch field trials. Likewise, consortia of cities, foundations, or universities might find it practical and economical to study classroom practices with field trials. The federal government might also contribute resources to such trials; the Career Academy study, for example, was funded by a group of 17 private foundations in addition to the U.S. Department of Education and the U.S. Department of Labor.

In terms of expertise, we believe that ample capacity exists. In our estimation, there are at least a dozen organizations and centers around the U.S. that have the technical knowledge and experience to assist in the design and execution of a field trial in education. It takes leadership, however, to couple organizational resources with expertise. This leadership on behalf of field trials could come from many different places, from elected officials to public administrators to concerned citizens. In Tennessee, for example, a key actor behind Project STAR was educator Helen Bain. Bain not only carried out a pilot experiment in Tennessee on class size before Project STAR, but also visited and discussed this proposal with every Tennessee state legislator and gained approval from the Tennessee Education Association, the state teachers' union. Bain's leadership was crucial (Ritter & Boruch, 1999, pp. 117, 120–121).

Field trials appear to be tools that are rarely used in the set of evaluation strategies for education. We hope that this chapter will raise awareness of their value, and that members of the education community and general public will consider using this design as part of a research strategy to identify effective educational practices. If leadership can bring together resources and expertise to rework the role of field trials in education, trials could help improve student learning by focusing on results and revealing progress on the ground.

NOTES

The preparation of this paper was supported in part by a grant from the Andrew W. Mellon Foundation to the American Academy of Arts and Sciences project *Initiatives for Children* for its Center for Evaluation.

We wish to thank Charles Abelmann, John D. Emerson, Howard Hiatt, Nathan Keyfitz, Richard Light, George Madaus, Lincoln Moses, Marjorie Olson, Igor Perisic, Jason Sachs, John Tyler, and Cleo Youtz for their thoughtful and helpful comments on earlier drafts of the article. We thank Julius Richmond for historical background on the Perry Preschool Study and the early years of the federal Head Start program and Thomas Kellaghan for information on the class size initiative in Ireland.

1. In education, this experimental treatment is typically a modification of an existing program or a completely new program intended to improve the outcome obtained under usual conditions.

2. Some changes to the original design were made during the four-year course of Project STAR. For a fuller discussion of these modifications, see Mosteller (1995).

3. One way to form the groups of children is to assign them randomly as individuals into two or more different groups. Then the unit of analysis is the child. Sometimes, however, this is not convenient or feasible. Another approach might deal with classrooms or even schools. A collection of classrooms or of schools might be assigned randomly to one or another treatment. In this case, the unit of analysis would be the classroom or the school. For a more detailed look at randomization and the design and use of field trials in evaluation of educational and other social programs, see Boruch (1997), Cook and Campbell (1979), and Cronbach (1982).

4. Not only is it valuable to detect the actual benefits of a particular treatment, but it is also worth knowing that a treatment yields little or no benefit. Otherwise the treatment in question might be continued, giving the mistaken impression that a problem has been solved when it has not. Continuing treatments with little or no benefit can be costly in other ways. For example, after careful appraisal of research results, the medical community no longer considers radical mastectomy the treatment of first choice for breast cancer.

5. Another example of a field trial detecting a small but valuable effect is the 1954 Salk study, a landmark randomized-controlled field trial in medicine that tested the effectiveness of a new vaccine for polio with about 750,000 children in the first through third grades. The Salk study showed a drop in the incidence of cases of polio from 57 per hundred thousand (0.057%) of the non-vaccinated control group to 16 per hundred thousand (0.016%) of the vaccinated group An effect of this size, though tiny (less than 1/10th of 1%), benefited thousands of children by verifying the efficacy of the vaccine (Meier, 1972).

6. Researchers can also use field trials to investigate specific between-group differences. In one field trial on the effects of tracking, for example, a researcher looked at class participation in question-and-answer sessions in non-tracked and tracked classrooms. In non-tracked classrooms, the researcher found that the more skilled students dominated the time, whereas in tracked classes the less skilled students were able to participate equally (Drews, 1963). Replication of this study would be valuable.

7. The field of education does not seem to have an analysis of innovations that succeed versus those that fail. Surgery provides an illustration of such an analysis: in 13 innovations in surgery intended to improve the patients' outcomes to their primary disease, 6 showed improvement over standard treatment and 7 did not. In 24 innovations intended to improve the patients' recovery from the surgery, 15 showed improvement over standard therapy, 8 showed worse performance, and 1 was a tie. In each instance, as in education, the innovator was confident that the innovation would be a success (Bunker, Barnes, & Mosteller, 1977, pp. 132–133).

8. For a detailed discussion of the ethics of conducting field trials, see Boruch (1997).

9. We use the number of citations in the Social Science Citation Index (SSCI) as of February 2000 as a proxy for the study's influence, reasoning that many citations in the scholarly literature suggest a broader influence than fewer citations might.

10. Children entered the study annually in five waves. In 1962, the first year of the study, there was a "Wave Zero" and a "Wave 1." Wave Zero involved only four-year-olds, where children in the treatment group received one year of preschool. In Wave 1, a group of three-year-olds randomly assigned to the treatment group received two years of preschool. The process for Wave 1 was repeated for Wave 2 in 1963, Wave 3 in 1964, and finally with Wave 4 in 1965 (Barnett, 1985).

11. These included initial parent interview, interviews with youths and parents at age 15, interview at age 19, case-study interview at age 21, interview at age 27, the Stanford Binet Intelligence Scale, the Adapted Leiter International Performance Scale, the Illinois Test of Psycholinguistic Abilities, the Peabody Picture Vocabulary test, the Wechsler Intelligence Scale for Children, California Achievement Tests, the Adult APL Survey, the Pupil Behavior Inventory, and the Ypsilanti Rating Scale.

12. Over 500 students initially took the IQ test that was the foundation for the study. Fewer than 400 took the first year's retests, and fewer than 300 took the two-year follow-up test. Reasons for the declining numbers were students moving away, illness at time of testing, and the sixth graders (first retest) and fifth graders (second year retest) having moved into the junior high school.

13. These findings should be interpreted in light of the issue of multiple comparisons. When many comparisons are made, some observed differences will stand out as a result of chance fluctuations. For example, imagine that 20 independent comparisons are made, and that the 5% level is used as a criterion for considering a difference as "significant." In this case, on the average, one of the twenty comparisons will stand out by chance alone. Since grade level, track, gender, and minority status are specified in the *Pygmalion* study, it is likely that several comparisons were made; hence, due to the multiple comparison problem, the findings may not be as "significant" as the 5% level being used suggests.

14. Expectancy effect experiments have been carried out in studies of physical fitness, psychotherapy, nursing homes, the workplace, ordinary social situations, courtrooms, psychosocial judgments, inkblot tests, and reaction time, among others (Rosenthal, 1994).

15. At the beginning of the experiment, 122 families were considered eligible. Attrition for various reasons yielded a base sample of 111, with 93 finally fully eligible to be placed into one of the four cells of the experiment at the time of analysis after the completion of the school-age intervention. The researchers note that the subjects "lost to attrition do not differ from the others on any entry-level demographic characteristics" (Campbell & Ramey, 1995, p. 749).

16. Assessments used during the preschool portion on the study included the Bayley Scales of Infant Development for the infants, and the Stanford-Binet Intelligence Scale, Form LM (at ages 24, 36, and 48 months) and the McCarthy Scales of Children's Abilities (at ages 42 and 54 months) for the preschoolers.

17. Assessments used during the school-age portion of the study included the Wechsler Preschool and Primary Scale of Intelligence (at age 5), the Wechsler Intelligence Scale for Children-Revised (at age 6.5 and again at end of treatment), the Peabody Individual Achievement Test (fall and spring of first

two years of school), the Woodcock-Johnson Psycho-Educational Battery, Part 2: Tests of Academic Achievement (fall and spring third year of school), and the Classroom Behavior Inventory (each of first three years of school).

18. The researchers brought the control group teachers to campus for the two-day meeting in an effort to avoid the so-called Hawthorne Effect that might result if only the treatment group teachers received the special attention of time on a university campus. The researchers didn't comment in the cited report, however, on the potential differential impact of six weeks of classes for the experimental group vs. the two day visit for the control group, quite apart from the impact of the curriculum itself.

19. One of the original ten career academies disbanded after two years.

20. Four of the career academies are in California, two are in Florida, and one each is located in Maryland, Pennsylvania, Texas, and Washington, DC. Each career academy in the MDRC study is a "school-within-a-school," meaning that the specialized school is physically housed in a traditional high school building, though the program is separate from the rest of the high school. The career academies are relatively small, and generally have 30 to 60 students per grade in grades 9–12 or 10–12.

21. There were 474 "high-risk" students in the study out of a total of 1,764 participants (27%). Students were identified as "high-risk" based on baseline risk characteristics including low attendance rates, low number of credits earned by 9th grade, low grade-point averages, age at grade 9, number of schools attended since 1st grade, and having a sibling who dropped out of school.

22. The test consisted of the math and reading sections of the National Educational Longitudinal Survey of 1988 (NELS: 88) Follow-Up Study.

9. COST ANALYSIS FOR IMPROVED EDUCATIONAL POLICYMAKING AND EVALUATION

MUN C. TSANG

Many important policy issues in education in the United States and elsewhere are concerned with resources invested in education. A common issue, for example, is whether the level of resources devoted to education is adequate and feasible. There is a concern among educators in many countries that not enough resources are devoted to education, especially resources targeted at basic educational programs for disadvantaged population groups, and some education programs favored by decision-makers may be too costly and financially infeasible (World Bank, 1995). Another example is the issue of whether education resources are utilized efficiently in achieving desired educational goals. There is often a concern that additional spending on educational administrators or teachers may not lead to higher student learning. This raises interest in the role of incentives, compensation structure, and other potentially more cost-effective strategies for improving education outcomes (Hanushek & Jorgenson, 1996). Some observers argue that, because of a lack of competition, public schools are inefficient and public resources may be more productively spent on other approaches to schooling such as private schools and charter schools. These market approaches to schooling are concerned with issues of resources, efficiency, and the purposes of schooling (Cohn, 1996; Geske, Davis, & Hingle, 1997). One more example is the increased call for monitoring and evaluating how resources are actually utilized and distributed in education. Such a call may be derived from a concern over persistent inequities and disparities in public

From *Educational Evaluation and Policy Analysis*, 1997, *19*, 318–324.

spending on education (World Bank, 1995) and from public demand for increased accountability in education. Analyses of resources utilization in education can contribute to more informed public discussion or debate on this and other important resource-related issues in education.

The costs (or opportunity costs) of education refer to the resources utilized in the production of education; they are measured as the economic value of such inputs in their best alternative use. They consist not only of public spending on education personnel, facilities, supplies, and equipment, but also direct private costs of education (such as household spending on education fees, textbooks, uniforms, transportation, etc.), indirect private costs of education (such as students' forgone earnings), as well as private contributions in cash and in kind to education. Educational cost studies focus on resources utilized in education. There is a large and growing literature on educational cost studies in both developed and developing countries that demonstrate how cost analysis can improve policymaking and evaluation in education. Most educators are unfamiliar with cost analysis because of their lack of exposure to the subject. Many educational administrators and decision makers have to deal with education costs, but their knowledge and attention are more narrowly focused on certain types of costs and analysis. Traditional evaluation studies in education generally deal with assessment of effectiveness and alternative design strategies, without incorporating costs into the overall evaluation framework. There is a need to recognize the importance and usefulness of cost analysis in educational policymaking and evaluation.

Based on a review of previous educational cost studies in the United States and other countries, this article attempts to (1) identify, classify, and describe the broad range of cost studies in education and explain how they may contribute to improved policy analysis and evaluation in education; (2) present three examples to illustrate the applications of cost analysis to some recurrent policy issues in education; and (3) reflect on the key lessons learned in previous applications of cost analysis in educational policymaking and evaluation. The aim is to call for more competent cost studies in policymaking and evaluation in education.

TYPES AND APPLICATIONS

An economic approach to studying education is the educational production framework consisting of educational input, educational process, and educational output (Lau, 1979). According to this framework, inputs to education (such as teachers' and students' time and school facilities) are transformed by an educational process (encompassing, for example, the curriculum, school organization, and pedagogy) into desired educational outputs (such as cognitive and non-cognitive skills), given educational objectives, prices of education inputs, and a known educational technology. This input-process-output framework can be applied to the study of resource-related issues in education. The input component of the framework draws central attention to the amount of resources devoted to educational production; estimation of resource requirements is necessary in addressing policy concerns about financial feasibility and adequacy in level of educational investment. The process component calls for analyses of how educational resources are utilized and distributed in education; such analyses are useful for monitoring trends in resource utilization in education and in identifying and assessing extent of inequality or inequity in education. The input-output components highlight the importance of examining both education resources and outputs at the same time; input-output analyses in education inform the issue of efficiency in educational investment.

Based on this framework, the diverse studies on educational costs can be classified into seven types within three categories (see Table 1). These studies execute a range of tasks, such as estimation of costs, assessment of financial feasibility and sustainability, construction of indicators and indices of costs, survey of resource utilization, determination of enrollment-cost relationship, and comparison of cost-benefit or cost-effectiveness ratios of alternative interventions. They may be undertaken to achieve a number of policy objectives, such as finding out resource requirements, ensuring financial feasibility and sustainability, monitoring resource utilization and promoting accountability, identifying and addressing inequalities/inequities in resource allocation, and promoting efficient utilization of scarce resources.

Cost-estimation studies and feasibility/sustainability studies fall into the first category of cost studies, which deal with education inputs only. Both types of studies estimate the costs of an education program or project, but feasibility/sustainability studies also compare required costs with available resources. (Feasibility studies compare project costs to available resources during the period of implementation, and sustainability studies compare the costs required to sustain the effects of a completed project with available resources after project completion.) Educational costing is the earliest and most common application of cost analysis in education. Its application in traditional education ranges from the costing of education interventions in the classroom or school to the costing of an entire education system or plan (Coombs & Hallak, 1987; Levin, 1983). Cost estimation has been conducted for a large variety of programs at different levels, including early childhood education programs (Barnett, Frede, Cox, & Black, 1994), special education programs (Hartman, 1990), career-oriented high school programs (Chambers, 1994), and vocational education and training (Tsang, 1997). The cost of new technology (including new education media and computers) in traditional education or distance education has been and will continue to be an important area of application (Jamieson, Klees, & Wells, 1978; Klees, 1995; Levin, Glass, & Meister, 1987). Also, with the ongoing world wide effort to promote access to quality basic education for all, more attention has recently been devoted to the costs of the variety of education programs for marginalized or disadvantaged populations in the United States and elsewhere (Inter-Agency Commission for Basic Education for All, 1990; King, 1994; Levin, 1996; Tsang, 1994a) and the estimation of the social costs of school failure (Catterall, 1987).

Cost studies in the second category deal with the relationship among inputs and the utilization of inputs in the educational production process. They are often con-

Table 1. Applications of Cost Studies in Educational Policy Analysis and Evaluation

Type of cost studies	Applications in policy analysis and evaluation (tasks and objectives)	Major lessons learned
I. Costing/feasibility studies; Cost estimation.	Determining total cost; distribution of cost burden among parties involved and equity implications; short-term and long-term cost implications.	Conceptual and methodological advances made in costing. Lack of information and expertise is major technical barrier in application. Importance of private costs. Cost estimation not conducted in order to hide real costs or disparity/inequities in education costs.
Feasibility/sustainability.	Evaluating financial feasibility during program implementation; evaluating financial sustainability after program completion.	Many education programs or plans have failed due to improper assessing of feasibility and sustainability prior to implementation. Intention to hide lack of feasibility/sustainability is a major barrier in application.
II. Behavioral studies of costs; Expenditure/unit costs and other cost indicators and indices.	Cost estimation and projection; monitoring resource utilization over time to promote efficiency and accountability; identifying disparities and inequities in resource allocation.	Lack of information can be a problem. Use of information for capacity building or self-improvement may conflict with use for accountability. Large disparities in unit costs across population groups, areas, and institutions; thus "average" policy may not apply to diverse settings.
Resource utilization surveys.	Assessing how fully existing resources are utilized to relative resource-allocation norms, in order to promote efficiency.	Significant underutilization of facilities, equipment, and personnel can exist. Need to assess appropriateness of existing resource-allocation norms before investing additional resources.
Estimation of cost functions and economies of scale.	Determining how output/enrollment varies with costs; determining optimal institutional size to promote efficiency.	Achieving optimal institution size improves efficiency in resource utilization.
III. Cost-output studies; Cost-benefit studies.	Determining rate of return, choosing among alternative investment options using efficiency as one of the criteria.	Conceptual and methodological difficulties exist in quantifying education benefits. Policymakers need to understand strength and weakness of cost-benefit analysis.
Cost-effectiveness studies.	Determining cost-effectiveness, choosing among alternative interventions in education using efficiency as one of the criteria.	Conventional evaluation studies ignore costs, and cost-effectiveness analysis can have wide application in education. Such studies can inform educational reform and result in substantial cost savings.

ducted to ascertain how education resources are utilized, to uncover the behavioral patterns of education costs, and to assess how efficiently existing resources are utilized. Three types of cost studies can be distinguished in this category. Studies of unit costs (e.g., recurrent costs per student) and other cost indicators/indices (e.g., public expenditure on education as a percentage of GDP and rate of change in teacher salary over time) have been applied in education to monitor the level of government spending on education to ensure an adequate level of spending, to monitor resource utilization over time and improve accountability, as well as to determine disparities in resource allocation within education and address the implied inequalities and inequities (Eicher, 1995; Tsang, 1994b). Studies of rates of utilization of education inputs have been applied to education institutions to compare actual rates of utilization of educational personnel, facilities, and equipment with the respective established norms of utilization so as to improve the overall rate of utilization of scarce resources (Tibi, 1986). Studies of education cost functions have been applied to traditional education institutions, new educational-media projects, and distant education to determine how some proxies of output (enrollment or broadcast hours) vary with costs with the objective of determining the optimal size of an institution or project and improving the efficiency in resource utilization (Brinkman & Leslie, 1987; Jamieson et al., 1978).

Cost-benefit and cost-effectiveness studies fall into the third category. While cost studies in the first two categories deal with input costs and their characteristics only, cost studies in the third category explicitly relate input costs to education outputs. They are conducted to inform decisions regarding the choice among alternatives, based on the criterion of efficiency. Cost-benefit studies compare the benefit of education (such as increased productivity and earnings, expressed in monetary terms) to the costs of education. A large cross-national literature on cost-benefit studies in education exists. Some analysts argue that the findings of these studies can be used to inform decisions regarding choices among education and non-education programs at different levels, between general and vocational programs at the same level, and among population groups by gender and by ethnicity (Psacharopoulos, 1994). Other analysts draw attention to the underlying assumptions and methodological difficulties of such studies (Hough, 1994). Cost-effectiveness studies compare the effects of education (such as student learning) to the costs of education. Applications have been made on teacher selection, educational television and radio, teacher training, choice of a mathematics curriculum, computer-assisted instruction, increasing the length of the school day, reducing class size, and cross-age tutoring (Levin, 1995). If a substantial amount of resources will be invested in educational quality, conducting a cost-effectiveness study to determine the most cost-effective intervention can be a very profitable undertaking.

SOME EXAMPLES

To illustrate the usefulness of cost analysis in education, the following discusses briefly the application of cost analysis to three policy issues in education.

On Access to Quality Basic Education for All

Providing access to quality basic education for all has been a major policy challenge of many governments across the world (Inter-Agency Commission for Basic Education for All, 1990). Obviously, estimating the costs of supplying the necessary education facilities over time and assessing the financial feasibility of the education plan are necessary tasks to ensure that a realistic plan is devised. Previous failure in implementing such a plan has resulted from either an incompetent feasibility study or from intentional neglect of feasibility by policymakers (Jalil & McGinn, 1992). Assuming that there is genuine political commitment from key policymakers, the estimation of the costs of educational supply requires particular attention to programs for marginalized population groups. The costs of educational inclusion for these groups can be very different from those for the average or non-marginalized populations because of differences in input prices, program design, and other factors (Tsang, 1994a, pp. 18–19). Even education programs for similar marginalized groups can differ significantly in their resource requirements. A cost analysis of three comprehensive models aimed at at-risk students in elementary schools in the United States found substantial variations among the three models in terms of additional school expenditures, additional time requirements placed on existing staff, and additional time requirements for parents (King, 1994). Moreover, simply providing education facilities is not sufficient to get and keep children in school. Besides cultural factors, the private costs of schooling can be a heavy burden on poor families and have an adverse impact on their demand for education (Mayoya, 1997; Tsang, 1995). To lessen the economic burden of private costs, it is often not sufficient to have a free-tuition policy as non-tuition private costs can be substantial. Government subsidies to the poor for textbooks and nutrition may be necessary. Some international development organizations have suggested that the financing of education-for-all programs should rely more on community contributions. While community involvement in education is generally beneficial, it does not imply that the government should ignore their financial assistance to poor communities. Also community contributions can be disequalizing (Bray, 1995). Thus the government should encourage all communities to contribute more to education and target more of its resources to poor communities that cannot make it on their own.

On Privatization of Schooling

One important aspect of the recurrent debate on public versus private provision of schooling is the relative efficiency of government schools and private schools. Proponents of privatization often claim that private schools are more efficient than public schools in terms of higher student achievement and/or lower unit costs. Yet most of the discussion of empirical evidence focuses on student achievement, with little analysis of costs. But a comparison of cost-effectiveness of government and private schools is necessary to assess their relative efficiency. Some studies have attempted a cost-effectiveness comparison, but the validity of their findings are undermined by the use of school-revenue data (which are not costs) and by an underestimation of costs (Jimenez, Lockheed, & Wattanawaha, 1988). To date, there are relatively few comparative studies of the costs of government and private costs, partly because of the challenge in obtaining reliable data on private education, private costs of education, and donated inputs. A study of primary schools in Thailand found that private schools had lower per-student recurrent costs and per-student capital costs than their public counterparts; however, private schools also had much higher private costs. The total costs per student for these two types of school were actually quite similar (Tsang & Taoklam, 1992). Thus, the efficiency of private schools relative to public schools in Thailand would be overestimated if private costs were not taken into account. Higher private costs for private schools were also reported in a recent study of secondary schools in Africa (Mayoya, 1997). A proper accounting of the necessary resources devoted to public and private schooling is needed to assess the relative cost and relative efficiency of the two types of schooling.

Comparison of Reform Alternatives

Historically in the United States, there have been recurrent calls for the reform of education, including the demand for better educational quality. Educators are often confronted with alternatives for improving student achievement. A good example of how cost analysis can inform the decision about the choice of alternatives for raising student achievement is the cost-effectiveness study by Levin et al. (1987). This study considered four alternative interventions in elementary school to raise mathematics and reading scores: computer-assisted instruction (CAI), a longer school day, smaller class sizes, and peer tutoring. CAI consisted of daily sessions of 10 minutes of drill and practice on a computer. The school day was lengthened by one hour, which was split equally between mathematics and reading instruction. Various changes in class size were considered, for example, from 35 to 30 students, 30 to 25 students, 25 to 20 students, and 35 to 20 students. Peer tutoring consisted of 15 minutes of tutoring of second-grade students by fifth- and sixth-grade students. The study found peer tutoring to be the most cost-effective alternative. It showed that some popularly discussed alternatives, such as lengthening the school day, might not yield the most learning gains given cost. The cost-effectiveness ranking of alternatives is an important piece of information in the choice of educational intervention to raise student achievement.

KEY LESSONS LEARNED

A lot has been learned in previous applications of cost analysis to educational policymaking and evaluation (see Table 1). Although space limitation does not allow a presentation of detailed findings in various studies, a concise summary of key lessons learned is given in this section. Conceptually, the notion of the opportunity costs of education has been very useful in identifying and measuring all the explicit and implicit costs or inputs used in education. A competent cost analysis can inform decision makers about the full resource requirements of an education program, thus avoiding a significant underestimation in costs that can cause difficulty during program implementation.

While the costs of education to the government have traditionally been the focus of policy analysis and evaluation, recent studies have demonstrated the policy relevance of private costs of education. Private costs can be a substantial part of the total cost of education; they can have an impact on education quality, the demand for education, and inequality and inequity in education: they also affect the relative efficiency of public-versus-private schooling.

Methodologically, a cost-estimation component can be readily integrated into a traditional effectiveness evaluation to yield a cost-effectiveness comparison of alternative interventions for improving education quality. Cost-effectiveness studies can have wide application in education, they can inform educational reform, and may result in substantial cost savings. Cost indicators (such as per-student expenditures, staffing norms, and total public educational expenditure as a percentage of total public spending or total national output) and cost indices (such as educational price indices) can be constructed to monitor resource utilization at a point in time and over time; they are often used in comparative analyses of educational spending. Cost-benefit analysis remains a controversial tool in educational policy-making, partly because of the difficulties in quantifying the benefits of education. While there is increased recognition of the importance of having reliable and timely cost data, the informational base for cost analysis remains inadequate in many countries.

Previous experience has demonstrated that a competent cost analysis can contribute significantly to improved policymaking in education, given genuine interest of the decision maker. Cost analysis can inform the decision maker about the resource requirements of an education project or program and the scope and design of a realistic education plan or intervention. It can be used to improve the efficiency in resource utilization in education and to address inequalities and inequities in resource allocation in education. It can also promote monitoring and accountability in education.

However, there are two sources of difficulty in applying cost analysis in education. The first is technical. The difficulty may be because of a lack of expertise, a lack of reliable information, or a lack of awareness of decision makers about the usefulness of cost analysis. The second is political or ethical in nature. Some decision makers may want to keep the discussion of desired education goals at a rhetorical level and do not want to confront the costs associated with education programs to achieve such goals; thus no cost analysis is initiated. When cost analysis is initiated, its scope and findings may be manipulated in some situations either to support preconceived conclusions or to minimize harmful results. Also, there may be some tension among different stakeholders of education regarding the capacity-building role and accountability role of cost analysis. For example, some educators may want to use cost information to improve the education process, while administrators may want to use the cost information to assess the performance of other education personnel or programs.

A number of factors are likely to contribute to the need for more cost analysis in educational policymaking and evaluation in the near future. They include the demand for more education in the global economy, the further tightening of government budgets for education, and the increased call for accountability and improved efficiency in the utilization of education resources. Most of the technical barriers to the application of cost analysis may be addressed through better communication, increased training, and the development and strengthening of an information base. And the increased use of cost analysis can contribute to improved policymaking in education. However, some of the political barriers will likely persist, and cost analysis can be a contentious tool.

NOTE

The author acknowledges the helpful reviews by Henry Levin and two anonymous referees.

10. THE CLARIFICATION HEARING: A PERSONAL VIEW OF THE PROCESS

GEORGE F. MADAUS

It was early morning of the second day of the Clarification Hearings in Washington, D.C. I was seated in front of the makeup table cluttered with bottles, tins, and brushes of all sorts, my new TV-compatible suit and blue shirt carefully protected by a bib. As the makeup artist was applying a brown fluid to my face (and undoubtedly wishing she had the skills of a plastic surgeon). Bob Ebel happened by the door. Seeing Bob, the incongruity of the situation hit me. How did I and a number of my colleagues in the next room waiting their turn in front of the light-bulb-studded mirror, get involved in this alien world? While I had my doubts from the beginning, Bob's appearance triggered the realization that 11 months earlier, when I agreed to serve as team leader for the negative side in the Clarification Hearings on Minimum Competency Testing (MCT). I really had no idea what I had let myself in for. I was again brought up short about the implications of the whole process and my part in two weeks ago after viewing, along with students and colleagues here at Boston College, the edited version of the hearings on public television. In what follows I have attempted to describe my reactions and feelings, both positive and negative, to various aspects of the process leading up to the hearings, the hearing itself, and the final TV product developed by Maryland Public Broadcasting (MPB).

Madaus, George F. "The Clarification Hearing: A Personal View of the Process." *Educational Barcarcher.* (January 1982), 4–11. Copyright 1982, American Educational Research Association. Washington, D.C. Reprinted with permission.

The following chapter represents the author's perceptions and suggestions about the process—a judicial evaluation model—used in the National Clarification Hearings on Minimum Competency Testing.

I will not get into the specifics of either case except where it might illustrate a more general point about the process itself. This paper does not rehash the pros or cons of MCT. Interested readers can find the outline of both cases in the *Phi Delta Kappan*, October 1981 issue, and the tapes of the full 24 hours of hearings and the three hour edited version are readily available.

Instead of specifics about MCT, I will concentrate on the strengths and weaknesses—as I see them—of the clarification process itself—as I experienced it. Further, in a more general sense, I have set down my reflections about the strengths and weaknesses of using a modified judicial evaluation model at the national level to illuminate and clarify education issues.

THE MODEL

We employed a modified version of the adversary of judicial evaluation model (JEM). The principal modification was the elimination of a jury or panel whose purpose was to hand down a decision or make recommendations about the object being evaluated. There were very good reasons for this deletion. By eliminating a "verdict" or a set of recommendations, NIE avoided the unpleasantness and controversy that would have certainly followed on a federally sponsored panel declaring one side or the other the "winner," or promulgating a set of recommendations on how to structure a MCT program. If the verdict or recommendations favored the negative side, it would have surely unleashed a raft of criticism and complaints about unwarranted federal intervention in state programs. If the pro side was the beneficiary, then NIE would have had to deal with the enmity of those advocacy groups opposed to MCT. By eliminating the panel or jury component from the Clarification Hearing process, NIE avoided this non-win situation. "Winning" or "losing" was left to the eyes of the beholders: *de gustibus non est desputandum*.

This modification, made in August, took on added significance after the November election. The Clarification Hearing mode was viewed as an acceptable, nonintrusive federal presence in education; it provided information to state and local policymakers which they could use or ignore as they saw fit.

From the beginning, NIE insisted that we were engaged in a clarification process; our task was to illuminate the issues surrounding MCT. Winning and competition between the teams were not to be part of the process leading to the hearing. Therefore, one of my main criterion in evaluating the clarification hearing model is the extent to which I feel it effectively and efficiently clarifies and illuminates issues.

THE AUDIENCE AND THE MODEL

From the outset, the plan was to make the videotaped proceedings of the hearing, along with written transcripts, available to interested policymakers at all levels. These products were to help inform their decisions concerning the design or modification of MCT programs. Initially, there were no plans to produce a television program to be aired nationally by the Public Broadcasting System (PBS), but this feature was added to the process in the late fall.

Staying with the original, more limited goal for a moment, one must ask how reasonable it is to expect policymakers, or even their surrogates, to view the full 24 hours of proceedings? I thought then, and nothing has happened to change my mind since, that it was preposterous to expect legislators or board members to find the time to view unexpurgated tapes.

The next question was: How reasonable is it to extract a one or two hour executive summary tape, which policymakers might be more apt to view and which truly reflects the complexity of the issues? I did not know the answer to this question initially. However, after viewing the three hour edited version of the tapes, I feel that altogether too much clarity and illumination is lost through the editing process. These doubts about the validity of the summary tapes are not a reflection on the work done by MPB. Based on material recommended by both teams, producer Frank Batavick did a superb job of putting together the edited version for the series, "Who's Keeping Score?" The difficulty is that you necessarily do violence to a carefully constructed, 12 hour case when you are forced to reduce the testimony and evidence to 75 minutes.

This leads me to my next question: Why go through 24 hours of exhausting hearings if the product that will receive the widest circulation and viewing is a three hour summary tape? If I had been cleverer, perhaps I could have structured each witness' testimony so that a piece could have been lifted intact for the expurgated version. But had I been that shrewd, why bother with the rest? Unlike a real trial, we were not building a record for an appeal.

Here I also must record my pessimism about the possibility of policymakers taking the time to read a more traditional, written evaluation of MCT. In hindsight—and I would caution the reader that mine is not always 20/20—I think that the TV medium has the potential of reaching and affecting more policymakers than does our more traditional evaluation reports. However, I also feel that the clarification hearing mode does not exploit the potential of that medium to reach and educate viewers. I am convinced now that the expertise of the participants, the TV time allocated to the project, and the funds expended for the series, "Who's Keeping Score?" would have been better used to produce a three- or four-part documentary on MCT—not a flashy but shallow, commercial-type documentary, but one of more substance and visual power, perhaps a NOVA or Cosmos-type product.

If such a four hour documentary had been our goal at the outset, the two teams could have worked cooperatively with the TV experts to put together a TV production that could have more effectively exploited the medium in presenting the pros and cons of MCT. Such a series would have been a more effective, efficient, and dramatic way to illuminate the issues than the static question-and-answer format employed in the hearings. Also, more public television outlets might have picked up the product, than have to the date elected to show "Who's Keeping Score?"

When NIE informed us of the decision to involve MPB in producing a series of three one-hour excerpts for each day of the hearing, to be aired on public television and to be preceded by a one hour documentary produced solely by MPB with very little input from the team, the whole enterprise was transformed. We had a new audience, the general public or that segment of it that watched PBS. We were repeatedly admonished not to alter our efforts to continue as before; nonetheless, the spectre of the nationally aired product had considerable psychological impact. We certainly sensed that the process had been changed, but we did not appreciate until after the editing process to what extent the medium had altered the process. The announcement did change the way we chose some of our witnesses. For example we wanted some witnesses who would be recognized as creditable by a more general audience than the education, testing/research communities. We also asked the question: "How will this witness come across on TV?"

Presented with NIE's decision to seek funds for the public broadcasting component, our team requested that part of that budget include a TV expert for each team. This request, like several others, was ignored. However, if a similar process is ever repeated, it is crucial that each team have a TV person working closely with it to help the team utilize the power of the medium in presenting their case. Of course, such an addition adds to the cost.

If I had it to do again—God forbid—and the hearing mode was still the vehicle, then I would want to rehearse witnesses before a TV consultant and a small panel of lay people. The lay panel could provide feedback on whether technical points were properly translated and presented and whether the material and testimony were understood. Some evidence and testimony that I understood because of my background were clear neither to educators without a research background nor to those outside the field. The extent of this problem was not evident to me until the hearing and the editing process. A lay panel watching a rehearsal of the evidence and testimony would have helped us avoid this problem. But again, this would have added to the cost of the project and necessitated cooperation on the part of the witness that might not always be forthcoming from busy public personalities.

A TV consultant could offer advice on how the witness might better come across on TV. For example, two witnesses read a great deal of their testimony. If you read the transcript the testimony is very powerful. However, it does not make for good TV viewing; eye contact was not maintained and the testimony lost spontaneity. Perhaps I should have anticipated this problem, but I did not.

More importantly, the TV consultant would have been invaluable in helping us better utilize the visual medium to present some of our evidence and technical arguments. Technical matters are difficult to present to a general audience through the question-and-answer format of the JEM. While both teams used graphics to illustrate material, these were static renditions of drawings supplied by the teams. Non-static graphics, such as those seen on Wall Street Week, and other visual devices, such as short film clips or animations could have helped to make some of the arguments more understandable to a general audience. Here again, there are budget implications. The TV person could also have helped us to anticipate the editing process in structuring the testimony of each witness. In short, if you are going to reach a large audience to clarify an educational issue by using TV, don't go into the process with one hand tied behind your back. While I knew a fair bit about the issues surrounding MCT, I knew nothing about the medium.

THE ISSUE AND THE MODEL

My perception is that NIE was very happy with the Clarification Hearing. The hearings and NIE's effort were received favorably by the public. The process resulted in a NIE-sponsored product that may be seen by a very large audience of both professional educators and lay people, depending on how many PBS affiliates choose to air it. The hearings were seen as an acceptable federal presence in education—informative but not intrusive. I have heard since that NIE was considering using the model with other issues and this gives me pause. Care needs to be taken in using the clarification hearing model with some issues.

In some respects, NIE was lucky that MCT was the subject of the first national use of the Clarification Hearing model, lucky in the sense that MCT is not a highly divisive issue encompassing deeply felt ideological or value-rooted positions. Moreover, it is not a burning issue in the minds of the public. You do not see bumper stickers that say, "Toot if you're against MCT." You are not accosted in airports by people with signs that say, "A Little MCT Never Hurt Anyone." Further, the possible positive and negative effects of MCT are rather easy to document, and technical issues of testing are fairly straightforward.

I have serious reservations, however, about using the model for highly divisive issues, such as busing or abortion. I also have my doubts whether it should be used for clarifying the issues surrounding bilingual education. I think that a federally sponsored Clarification Hearing on such ideologically based issues, which affect deeply held beliefs on both sides, could cause great mischief. The composition of the two teams and the selection of the hearing officer could touch off protests from groups on the right and left of the issue. Cooperation and data-sharing would be difficult. I would anticipate severe and bitter fights over the admissability of evidence and witness testimony.

Thus, while I feel that the clarification model or some variant on it has the potential to illuminate a number of issues for various stakeholders and publics not reached through more traditional evaluations, I think the issue needs to be chosen with care, particularly if federal funds are involved.

THE TEAM

The first task I faced after agreeing to be the team leader for the con, or negative, team was to build a team. This is a crucial step in the process. In choosing team members, I tried to select peers who could serve an outreach function to the various constituencies concerned about MCT. I was blessed with a superb team. Ours was truly a team effort from beginning to end.[1]

Unfortunately because of budget limitations, we met as a team only twice prior to the hearing. The first occasion was a meeting in Washington to orient both teams. Our second meeting in January was devoted to the development of strategy for case building and identifying potential witnesses and groups to contact. While subsets of the team met from time to time, the whole team never came together again until the hearing. Further, the budget did not cover very much in the way of the team members' time once the days for the two meetings, the hearings, and the editing were deducted. If the model is ever used again, the budget should accommodate at least three or four team meetings prior to the hearing and sufficient funds to cover the team members' work during the case-building process. There was altogether too much "contributed service" on the part of generous team members. Both teams should come together for the two final data-sharing sessions and for both sessions with the hearing officer. Once again, these recommendations would increase the cost of the project. However, it does little good to have an excellent team but not be able to optimally utilize their talent.

There were disagreements on some details of strategy and on a few issues, and there was one that is worth recounting. What part should team members play at the actual hearing? Originally, I was not comfortable with handling all the direct and cross-examination myself. I felt that each team member, if he or she wished, should participate to some extent in both of these functions. Some team members disagreed. They felt that if all eight of us were directly involved in examining witnesses it would be confusing to the TV audience viewing the edited copies (another example of how the spectre of the TV production influenced us). Further, there was some sentiment that the direct and cross-examination should be handled by someone with trial experience. However, most of us felt that if the JEM was to work, non-lawyers should be able to handle those functions. After polling the team, it was agreed that the task of direct and cross-examination would be split between Diana Pullin and myself. Instinctively, I was troubled by the decision. A few weeks before the hearing, I reconsidered, after one team member asked what the team would do during the hearing other than sit and take notes. At the 11th hour I decided that all team members would participate in either the direct examination and/or cross-examination of witnesses. I would recommend this course to anyone using the model. People in the audience and those who viewed the TV version commented on the team participation and involvement. We looked and acted like a team. Those who originally had reservations also agreed that this involvement was beneficial.

BUDGET

One serious reservation about applying the JEM on a national scale is the cost. Each team had a budget of $107,000 with which to work. An additional $100,000 went to a subcontractor for project management and for the hearing. About $250,000 (I do not know the exact amount) went to MPB for the TV component.

One hundred thousand dollars is simply not sufficient to do the job correctly. Travel for the team to meet before, during, and after the hearing, and for data-sharing and meeting with the hearing officer; travel for 30 witnesses to come to Washington, and for case development—all this took a large chunk out of the budget. In keeping a daily log of my activities, I found the job to be nearly a full-time one from December through July, although I was budgeted for one quarter time. As I mentioned earlier, the budget for team members was stingy and only their generosity made some of the work possible.

The budget did not permit us to do research, as originally planned, nor did it permit a first-hand investigation of the sites chosen by the opposing team. On the first point, we had to rely pretty much to what was out there, and much of that was simply testimony or hearsay. There were a number of issues on which we would have liked to have gathered data, but we could not because of the costs. Bob Linn did the analysis of extant data tapes to illustrate points about the cut score, measurement error, and item bias, but that was the extent of our original research. For the rest we collated the data, testimony, and hearsay that we found, primarily by mail and phone.

Not being able to visit the opposing team's sites was a major disadvantage. While we had a very broad outline of what each of their witnesses was going to say, the best we could do was to call them or contact individuals who might help us develop a line of cross-examination. This approach was not very beneficial. Our cross-examination was by far the weakest aspect of our case. However, if we had had the funds to go to each site and could have gotten the necessary cooperation to interview and observe for a week or so, I am confident that we could have turned up rebuttal witnesses or at least better lines of cross-examination. Whether those rebuttal witnesses would have felt free to testify is another matter to which I will return.

A national Clarification Hearing is not cheap, and the funds expended on this project do not reflect what is needed to do the job adequately. I have already made a number of suggestions that would increase the costs. As Jim Popham said to me at one point, it's a matter of a 15-watt bulb for illumination instead of 100 watts. The basic question is whether additional wattage can be justified through a cost-benefit analysis.

TIME

One major difference between the JEM and the actual judicial process is that the JEM has sharp time limits, for practical reasons, related to budget and audience. Direct, cross, redirect, and recross are all constrained by a fixed time limit.

A good deal of witness preparation involved timing. A major decision we had to make was how much of our time should be allocated to direct and how much to cross-examination. At one point, we felt that we would cross-examine only a few witnesses husbanding our time for our case in chief. Eventually I think we cross-examined all but two witnesses. However, in editing the tape for "Who's Keeping Score?" we selected very little cross-examination, using our precious 75 minutes for direct testimony.

We employed two stop watches to keep track of time. The cross-examination of one witness was progressing very well, but we were forced to cut it short because we had gone over our allotted time. Another five to ten minutes and we might have made some very telling points. Whether they would have been included in the edited version is another question. If we had turned up a witness to directly rebut a pro witness, we would have been faced with an interesting time trade-off between rebuttal and direct testimony.

Considerations related to time influenced the kind of case we chose to develop. There were two strategies. The first was to develop only a few points and have all witnesses hammer repeatedly at the same theme. The pro team selected this strategy, and it was very effective. It is easier for the audience to follow the more limited arguments, and repetition hammers the point home.

The second strategy, and the one we followed, was dubbed by Wade Henderson as "the death by a thousand cuts." We felt that in addition to the three issues there were a number of important contentions that also had to be developed—for example, the technical limitation of tests when used for certification—if the issues surrounding MCT were to be truly clarified and illuminated. Further, as far as possible, the views of various concerned groups had to be represented. The involved allocating time across many points and constituencies.

I did not have a good solution to the problem of the time constraints association with the model. However, two teams jointly developing a documentary with a TV crew, I feel, would have been able to clarify the issues and contentions most effectively and efficiently with less time than was needed for the three days of hearing.

THE NEGATIVE OR CON LABEL

The label *con* or negative team was a difficult burden to carry for a number reasons. First, being against competency testing is akin to being against motherhood. The adjective *competency* in front of the noun *test* puts the opposition in difficult position. Second, it is always difficult to argue against the status quo, is to mention trying to prove a negative. Certainly our side was the more threatening one to established programs. This, in turn, made it difficult to gain entry programs or to obtain data we wanted to investigate. Why should an administrate collaborate on a process that might involve dirty linen appearing on national television.

Third, we repeatedly had to emphasize that our team was not anti-testing against standards. Fourth, we felt that we had to spend part of our time a resources presenting an alternative to MCT. In short, I felt our side had to carry heavier burden of proof.

Perhaps the most difficult aspect of the negative label was trying to get school people to testify. Very often we were told of problems endemic to MCT, but the person did not feel free to testify because either district or state administrators were sold on the program. For a while we even wrestled with ways witnesses might remains anonymous. We were very explicit in warning people that there might be backlash associated with their public appearances. Further, we decided not to have students relate their problems with MCT, because they might later be embarrassed by their TV appearance.

If the goal is to clarify and illuminate issues through TV, then using the documentary approach might help to lessen the problem and the difficulties associated with the negative or con label. In fact, using such an approach might involve only one team with different views represented.

PROJECT MANAGEMENT

Future uses of the model should involve one major change. After providing the funds directly to the teams, rather than going through the red tape of month billings to a third-party contractor, the funding agency should withdraw from the management of the project. Day-to-day project management should be in the hands of the hearing officer and his or her staff. Alternately analogous to a court-appointed monitor, an independent group or individual appointed by the hearing officer could manage the mechanics of the project. The funding agency should not be involved in directly telling or even suggesting to a team what it thinks the team should or should not do; nor should the agency intervene with its view of what should be, in debates or arguments between the two teams. Such disagreements should be adjudicated by the hearing officer, or a designate, without either the explicit or implicit intrusion of views on the part of the funding agency staff.

At the very least, the whole issue of the funding agency's role in the process needs more discussion. The JEM is held out as one that presents an opportunity for impartial pursuit of the "truth." When the funding agency or its representatives have an implicit or explicit agenda of their own related either to the substantive area being evaluated or concerns about backlash that might ensue, then it is no longer an impartial party in the process.

THE ISSUES

A key ingredient in the process is the framing of the issues and the definition of key terms. This is a place where I felt we went awry. Both sides thought that they understood the boundaries of the debate and the terms as defined. It turned out that they meant different things to the two teams. For example, we thought we were debating programs where, if a pupil did not pass a test, he or she was not promoted, could not graduate, or was automatically put in a remedial program. After examining them, we felt that the South Carolina and Detroit programs did not fit these parameters. In South Carolina, they do not use the test results as a sole or primary determiner for promotion or graduation. Further, the state's regulations forbid using the test score alone to classify students for remediation. In Detroit, pupils who fail the test still receive a regular diploma, but if they pass they receive an endorsed diploma. There was a heated, even bitter, debate over the inclusion or exclusion of these two sites. In the case of Detroit, the pro team considered the endorsed diploma a form of classification. We were not aware of this variant when we agreed to the definition of classification, and hence we objected. We did not know if we were opposed to endorsed diplomas. In the case of South Carolina, they argued that the test information was part of a classification procedure. We argued that it did not fit the sole or primary determiner criterion. The point is not to revisit these arguments but to recommend that a fuller discussion of the boundaries of the debate and definition of key terms should include specific reference to the actual sites to be used. This type of discussion, moreover, should not be put off but should come very early in the data-sharing process.

DATA SHARING

Data-sharing is a key component in the JEM. Unfortunately, there were weaknesses in this process, part of the problem being related to distance. The training tape showed a project at the University of Indiana, where the two teams were on the same campus and worked closely together. It is very difficult to collaborate when you are 3,000 miles apart, and only a small portion of your time is supposedly covered by the contract. True, we did have meetings in which we were able to share data, but discussions of the TV process ate into the available time, and there were not a lot of data to share until about 10 weeks or so before the hearings. Rather than inundating the other team with all the material and leads we were following, it was agreed that we would wait until the case was more or less firm before sending essential material. This was to keep the reading down to an acceptable level.

I do not know exactly how to overcome these problems except to say that the teams need more, or at least longer, joint meetings in which the actual evidence, testimony and cross-examination of each witness are discussed in detail. Exposing your hand completely at a joint meeting, like a dummy hand in bridge, is a difficult concept psychologically when deep down you often feel you're in a poker game. A joint effort at building a TV documentary might alleviate this problem. Another interesting variant might be to have one team develop and present both sides of the case.

THE HEARING

The hearing itself was both stimulating and exhausting. Eight hours a day of hearings for three days, coupled with nightly preparation, is a fatiguing experience. Before the hearing, some sort of introduction to the TV cameras is needed. Also, during the hearing a TV monitor should be provided for each team to give the team feedback on such basic matters as eye contact, posture, positioning and delivery.

On the hearing mode itself, I think once you eliminate the panel, decide to televise the proceedings, and are not evaluating a particular program with its direct acquiescence and cooperation, then, at least on a national scale, the hearing format is not the most efficient or effective way to clarify or illuminate issues. The hearing mode is probably effective and efficient at the state or local level when you are assured that the stakeholders to the evaluation will be in attendance and when a panel is constituted to make recommendations about a program that has agreed to this form of evaluation. Furthermore, limiting the hearing to the state or local level greatly reduces costs.

An interesting variant in the present model would be to have the two teams come together after the hearings to cooperatively make recommendations to design a MCT program, taking into account evidence and testimony introduced at the hearing.

THE HEARING OFFICER

This project was indeed fortunate to have as its hearing officer Barbara Jordan, who was very ably assisted in her task by Paul Kelley of the University of Texas. There were at least two possible roles for the hearing officer. The first, and the one Professor Jordan chose, was that of neutral arbitrator: She set the stage for the hearings by describing the process, purpose, and procedures; she introduced witnesses, ruled on objections, and acted as a referee. The second option was for the hearing officer to intervene directly by questioning witnesses. A minor problem with this second option was the already tight time constraints built into the process. A more troubling problem would have been that questions put by a nationally respected hearing officer could tip a case in favor of one side or another. The tone of the questioning might implicitly signal to the viewing audience a "decision" by the hearing officer in favor of one side. This would negate the benefits of eliminating the jury or panel from the proceedings. For this reason, I would recommend the first role as the most appropriate one when the model is used in a national context.

THE PRODUCT

After the hearings, each team had the job of editing their four hours of each day's proceedings down to 25 minutes. Several things became apparent immediately. First, the written transcript was not a particularly good guide for editing; material that read well did not necessarily view well. Second, our evaluation of witnesses made at the hearings did not necessarily hold up when we saw the tapes. It was very difficult to edit 15 or 20 minutes of testimony down to two or three. Basically, this involved making sure that all of our arguments were covered by quick snippets. This, in turn, resulted in a final product that lacked depth and clarity. We were forced to ask "Why three days of hearings if the most widely disseminated product is a bastardized version?"

There is a wealth of material in the full 24 hours of tapes, which could be excerpted to develop into short tapes for specific audiences dealing with focused issues. For example, tapes dealing with all of the evidence and testimony concerning MCT and the handicapped would make excellent viewing for concerned groups and for pre- and in-service teachers. Similarly, the testimony on reading or on technical issues could be excerpted for teaching purposes. These potential spin-off tapes for special audiences or for pre- or in-service teaching could be a very desirable side effect associated with the full three days of hearings.

CONCLUSION

The model, with its public television component, has the potential to reach and educate audiences that would not ordinarily be reached through more traditional evaluation reports. Research on the model, or variants of it, should be pursued. Evaluations of the process now in progress should shed additional light on the model's strengths and weaknesses.

At the local and state level, with a specific program that agrees to the process, the model may be very useful, although it might tax the attention span and retention powers of the audience. When the model is used nationally, costs go up substantially, and the issue to which the model is applied must be chosen with care. Further, a panel to hand down a verdict is probably not desirable. More importantly, if the purpose is to clarify and illuminate issues for the general public and for various stakeholders through the television medium, then the question-and-answer, basically aural mode of the model may not be the most effective or efficient use of available time. Going through three days of intensive hearings using the question-and-answer format and then editing out 90 percent of the proceedings makes little sense to me. Rather, it would be better to start out with the final product in mind and utilize the medium and its technology to its best advantage.

My experience with the Clarification Hearing was like my experience in the Army. After it was over and I was out, I was glad I had the experience. I had learned all kinds of new things and met some wonderful people, but no way would I re-up.

NOTE

1. The team members, who helped to develop arguments, located and prepared witnesses, helped with both direct and cross-examination of witnesses during the hearing, and assisted in the editing of the TV tapes, were: James Breeden, Senior Manager, Office of Planning and Policy, Boston Public Schools; Sandra Drew, Chicano Education Project, Denver, CO; Norman Goldman, Director of Instruction, New Jersey Education Association, Trenton; Walter Haney, National Consortium on Testing, Huron Institute, Cambridge, MA; Wade Henderson, Executive Director, Fund for Public Education, Council on Legal Education Opportunities, American Bar Association, Washington, D.C.; Robert Linn, Chairman, Department of Educational Psychology, University of Illinois at Urbana-Champaign; Renee Montoya, Chicano Education Project, Denver; and Diana Pullin, Staff Attorney, Center for Law and Education, Washington, D.C. While not a member of the team, Simon Clyne of Boston College was invaluable as an administrative assistant to the team.

11. CASE STUDY EVALUATIONS: A DECADE OF PROGRESS?

ROBERT K. YIN

The American Evaluation Association's tenth-anniversary theme, "A Decade of Progress," was the inspiration and point of departure for the present article. Leonard Bickman invited me to reflect on the use of case studies in evaluation. In considering the use of case studies, the tenth-anniversary theme quickly became a question rather than an assertion: "Has the case study produced a decade['s worth] of progress?" This article addresses the question first by defining the case study method, then by examining the use of the case study method from a historical perspective, and finally by commenting on the progress (or lack of progress) during the past decade (roughly 1987 to 1997).

DEFINITION OF THE CASE STUDY METHOD

Critical to the discussion is the definition of the case study method. As will be pointed out shortly, two different types of research have been confused within the rubric of the case study method. Selecting one or the other type will yield different interpretations regarding the possible progress over the decade's time. Therefore, for the sake of discussion, the case study method may be briefly profiled as follows (Yin, 1994a, 1997).

A Three-Featured Profile

First, the method depends on the use of—and ability to integrate in converging fashion (some would say "triangulate")—information from multiple sources of evi-

From *New Directions for Evaluation*, 1997, 76, 69–78.

dence. The evidence may include direct observations, interviews, documents, archival files, and actual artifacts. The facts and conclusions for the case study will be built around the consistency of data from these sources, and these facts and conclusions may be expressed in both quantitative and qualitative terms.

Second, the method implicitly assumes a richness of data because a case study is intended to examine a phenomenon in its real-life context. Often, the boundary between the phenomenon and the context is not sharp, and inherent in all case studies is the potentially important influence of contextual conditions. A major investigative concomitant—usually taken for granted—is the need to collect case study data in the field, thereby collecting data about the context, although under unusual circumstances a case study can be conducted from library and secondary sources alone. A major technical concomitant is that case studies will always have more variables of interest than data points, effectively disarming most traditional statistical methods, which demand the reverse situation.

Third and last, the case study method includes research that contains single case studies as well as multiple-case studies. The process of generalizing the results of either type of case study depends on the development, testing, and replication of theoretical propositions (analytic generalization)—rather than any notions based on the selection of numeric samples and extrapolating to a population (statistical generalization). Especially helpful is the specification and testing of rival theories or explanations, which can even take place within a single case study; in a multiple-case study one possible rationale for case selection is that certain cases have been included because they represent rivals.

Methods Falling Within And Outside The Profile

Profiling the case study in this manner provides a broad umbrella for different styles of case study research, including those based on differing philosophies of science. For instance, Bob Stake's recent book characterizes my case study research as "quantitative," appearing to contrast strongly with his own "qualitative" approach (Stake, 1995). However, examination of both approaches reveals similar ingredients. Although the qualitative approach gives less attention to multiple-case situations, it clearly draws on the same multiple sources of evidence and is concerned with the richness of case and context. Stake also agrees that the matter of defining the "case" requires close attention. Further, in discussing case study data collection and analysis, he devotes an entire chapter of his book to triangulation.

At the same time, the profile excludes certain methods that have sometimes been confused with case study research and evaluation. The primary exclusion is the classic ethnographic study—commonly using the participant-observer method (Jorgensen, 1989). Such a study traditionally focused on a preliterate society, resulting in evidence based mainly on observations and discussions but with little opportunity to rely on documentary or archival records. Ethnographic methods have been used in a variety of contemporary settings (Fetterman, 1989), including the study of organizations (such as Leonard-Barton, 1987). For evaluations, two advocates of the ethnographic method note that its strength is maximized where a strong clash in values permeates an organization or project (Lincoln & Guba, 1986). However, because the participant-observer is limited in the ability to cover multiple events occurring at the same time, many ethnographic studies also tend to be studies of small groups within a culture (or organization), rather than systematic coverage of the whole culture (or organization). If more than participant-observation is used in doing an evaluation, the resulting study may begin to resemble and be considered a case study. To this extent, judgments about inclusion or exclusion must, as always, appreciate the actual array of techniques being used, not just broad labels.

The Importance Of The Profile As A Statement About Case Study Design

In her major historical overview of case studies in American methodological thought, Platt (1992) characterized our profile of the case study method as giving greater emphasis to case study *design* rather than *data collection*. The distinctiveness of the design, especially with the number of potentially relevant variables far exceeding the number of data points (often, only a single data point or case), forces investigators to use different strategies for establishing internal, external, and construct validity, compared to experimental or quasi-experimental research. Likewise, the need to pursue analytic and not statistical generalizations means that cross-case strategies must go beyond merely counting the number of cases, as if they were a sample of anything.

At the same time, the basic profile should not be construed as ignoring issues of data collection. Case study investigators must be intensely concerned with collecting data in a reliable and rigorous manner. In doing data collection, case study investigators also must struggle with the problem of divulging identities or maintaining the confidentiality and anonymity of sources and even of the case itself.

THE USE OF THE CASE STUDY METHOD FROM A HISTORICAL PERSPECTIVE

From a historical perspective, Platt (1992) traces the practice of doing case studies back to three strands of research during the early twentieth century: the conduct of life histories, the work of the Chicago school of sociology, and casework in social work. She then shows how participant-observation emerged as a common data collection technique in doing these case studies. However, over time the data collection technique eventually became confused with the entirety of the case study method. The effect of this confusion on social science was dramatic, as traced by Platt. Prior to 1970, she found that 29 out of 31 textbooks covered the topic of case studies, yet from 1970 to 1979, 18 out of 30 textbooks published failed to mention case studies *at all*. Instead, these textbooks usually discussed participant-observation or other forms of "fieldwork" as alternative data collection techniques, reflecting the only coverage given to qualitative research.

In evaluation, this trend was serendipitously reinforced during the same period of time by the classic work of Campbell and Stanley (1963) in describing their variety of "quasi-experimental" designs. Their work—used for many years and by nearly every scholar as the defining text for evaluation research—unfortunately disparaged case studies as a "pre-experimental" form of research (the infamous "one-shot case study"). Thus, Platt notes that, even when mentioned in textbooks, the orthodoxy of the times frequently treated case studies not as a distinct method but as an optional part of the exploratory work that might occur during the early stages of the complete research process. Coverage of the case study method by evaluation textbooks continues to be spotty to this day. As but one example of a complete and consistent oversight, none of Rossi and Freeman's first five editions of their popular evaluation textbook—1979, 1982, 1985, 1989, and 1993—contains the term *case study*, much less a discussion of it as a method.

Platt credits the first edition (1984) of my book on case study research (Yin, 1994a) as having raised fresh consciousness over the method. (Important publications leading up to the first edition were Yin, 1981a and 1981b.) The fact that the significant features of the case study—as profiled in the previous section of this paper—focused on design rather than data collection distinguished the method from participant-observation. Further, according to Platt, the couching of the method within a practical format readily encouraged more people to do case studies. Whether as a result of my work or not, during the late 1980s there appears to have been much more attention given to the case study method, mainly for research but also in evaluation, especially federally-supported evaluations of education programs. The 1990s have now produced whole texts, again, about the case study (such as Feagin, Orum & Sjoberg, 1991; Ragin & Becker, 1992; Stake, 1995). In addition, professions such as public administration (Agranoff & Radin, 1991), business administration and management information systems (Benbasat, Goldstein, & Mead, 1987; Cash & Lawrence, 1989), and social work (Rubin & Babbie, 1993; Gilgun, 1994) have reincorporated case study research into their repertory of research methods, not just using case studies as a teaching tool.

In evaluation, the 1990s also saw a major case study handbook published by no less an authority than the (now defunct) Program Evaluation and Methodology Division of the U.S. General Accounting Office (1990; an earlier version was issued in 1987). The book covers the major topics in applying the case study method to evaluations—design, site selection, data collection, data analysis, and reporting—providing guidance, illustrative examples, and warnings about common pitfalls. The book notes that, at the time, "the history of the case study as an evaluation method is little older than a decade" (p. 10). Key concepts underlying the method continued to be "triangulation" and the "rich, in-depth nature of the information sought."

Again, parallel developments in evaluation methods more generally also occurred and in retrospect may have helped to produce this revived attention. In particular, Campbell now the author and coauthor of two works bearing directly on a revised view of case studies in evaluation. The first was a rather little-known article, "Degrees of Freedom and the Case Study" (Campbell, 1975). In this article, Campbell questioned whether he and others had fully appreciated the power of the case study method in the past. He noted that if a case indeed followed the same numeric mindset of other quasi-experimental designs, every case study should have a "plethora" of explanations—because of the numerousness of variables and the paucity of data points. Instead, he showed how classic case studies arrived at satisfactory explanations only after a long and agonizing analytic process. Something else, besides the mere tallying of variables, was at work.

The second was a widely used textbook, which was a follow-up to the classic Campbell and Stanley (1963) work, and of which Thomas D. Cook was now the first author (Cook & Campbell, 1979). The book disentangled the case study method from the earlier categorization of the case study as a quasi-experimental design with the following unequivocal statement: "Certainly the case study as normally practiced should not be demeaned by identification with the one-group post-test-only design" (the infamous one-shot case study) (p. 96). In addition, the book even contained, as one of the variant quasi-experimental designs, a design that was in fact applicable to case studies (although the book did not refer to such applicability): the non-equivalent, dependent variables design (p. 118). According to this design, an experiment or quasi-experiment may have multiple dependent variables—that is, a variety, of outcomes. If, for each outcome, the initially predicted values have been found, and at the same time alternative patterns of predicted values (including those deriving from methodological artifacts or threats to validity) have not been found, strong causal inferences can be made. Because of this applicability to case studies (which normally have multiple dependent variables), this design then became the basis for using pattern matching as an analytic technique in doing case study research (Yin, 1994a, pp. 106–110). (Campbell's contribution both to case studies and to evaluation is the topic of a much more extensive article: Yin & Bickman, forthcoming).

Whether related to my book (as credited by Platt), to changes in evaluation research more generally (as just discussed), or to yet other reasons, the gains and renewed foothold made by the case study method in appearing as part of the routine range of research and evaluation methods represent a major advance. However, although the new texts and references began to appear in the early 1990s, they were the culmination of forces that began in the late 1970s and the 1980s. As such, they are only the beginning of the story of whether there has been a decade of progress in case studies as an evaluation tool from 1987 to 1997. The rest of the story is told next.

PROGRESS (OR LACK OF IT) DURING THE PAST DECADE

If the legacy of the immediately preceding period was the increased documentation of the case study method, the 1987–1997 decade itself has produced increased use and diversification of case study tools and thus the elaboration of the method. Somewhat equivocal is the effect this diversification has had on actual case study products.

Use and Diversification Of Case Study Tools

The elaboration of the case study method begins with a more refined understanding of the uses of case studies in evaluation. The GAO volume (U.S. Government Accounting Office, 1990, p. 9) explicitly lays out at least six different situations: illustrative, exploratory, critical instance, program implementation, program effects, and cumulative (meta-analysis of multiple-case studies done at different times). Each situation demands slightly different designs. For instance, the design for an illustrative case study may be limited to the point being illustrated, whereas the design for a program implementation or program effects case study requires extensive expression of presumed causal links. At the time of its publication, the GAO volume noted that existing reports tended to use only two of the six applications (illustrative and critical instance); that trend may have since broadened.

A second area of use and diversification has been in preparing for and documenting case study evidence. The use of *case study protocols* to organize the data collection—protocols that are far broader in scope than a simple questionnaire—is now commonly accepted as the most desired prelude to systematic data collection. The need for a case study protocol is especially great and has become frequent practice where multiple investigators are collaborating in doing multiple case studies, but are all still part of the same overall evaluation. Similarly, the understanding that case study evidence may be contained in a separate *case study database*—different from the actual final case study report—has taken greater hold. The database may take both narrative and tabular form, a key feature being that the noted information contains explicit footnotes or references to the specific source of the evidence (thereby helping to preserve the desired *chain of evidence*). Further, the database, though not edited or intended for public presentation, nevertheless needs to be available for independent inspection by other investigators.

However, during the decade, possibly the most important advance in tools has been the use of *logic models* as part of the design in doing case study evaluations (Yin, 1992; Yin, 1993, pp. 65–68). A logic model presents the presumed causal sequence of events expressed in a series of cause-and-effect steps. Developed initially to carry out evaluability assessments (Wholey, 1979), the specification of logic models is a rewarding activity in at least two respects. First, the logic model reveals the underlying theory of a program that is being evaluated, and the specification of the model provides the guidance for the relevant data that need to be sought during the case study. Second, the process of putting a logic model together—especially when shared between program managers and evaluators working together—often yields insights that need not await the completion of all evaluation but that are immediately useful for program development.

At the same time, the proper and complete specification of logic models is still an evolving craft. Potentially worrisome is that the most common logic models still only identify different effects or stages but do not give an actual explanation of how events move from one stage to another. For instance, as shown in the upper part of Figure 5.1, the typical logic model consists of a series of boxes (stages) connected by a series of arrows (causal relations among the stages). The accompanying logical statements take the following form: "By implementing this activity (input), the program will engage the needed number of participants (output) and will eventually have the desired effect on these participants (outcome)." Left unstated is exactly how the activity will indeed engage the participants or how the effect will arise

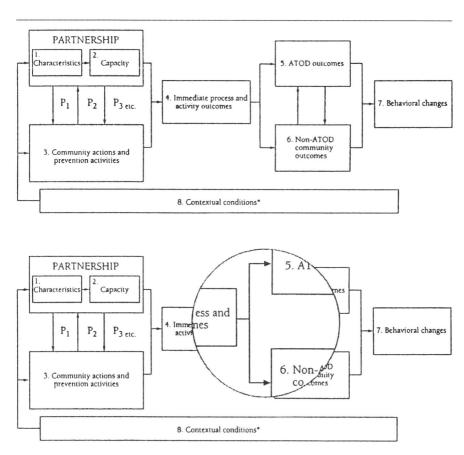

Key

P_1, P_2, P3 = Phase 1, Phase 2, Phase 3
* Other arrows from Contexual Conditions to all other components not shown

Figure 1. Relating Partnership Actions to Prevention Outcomes

from the act of participating. One possible shortcoming in these specifications has therefore been that too much attention has been given to the boxes in a logic model and not enough to the connecting arrows. The lower part of Figure 1 therefore deliberately focuses attention on one set of arrows, and the challenge to the case study investigator is to associate substantive how and why explanations with the arrows.

Case Study Practices During The Past Decade

Examinations of case study evaluations—and discussions with investigators attempting to do case studies—reveals greater use of these various case study tools over the decade. More important, the craft is now explicitly recognized as having tools and rigor, a norm going considerably beyond the earlier and crude notion that doing case studies mainly required an ability "to tell it like it is." With the increased availability of texts referring to and describing the case study method, investigators also have more ways of finding the needed guidance to practice the craft. Overall, the major progress in case study evaluations during the past decade may very well be the fact that investigators are knowingly pursuing practices that are part of a formal craft.

The process of doing case study evaluations also has become a more collaborative activity. Case study evaluators now work more closely with the officials of the program being evaluated to conduct the initial phases of evaluation, including the definition of the questions to be addressed by the evaluation, the evaluation design, and the preferred data collection methods. Similar trends, covered under such rubrics as "action research," "cluster evaluation," and "empowerment evaluation," are increasingly true of all evaluation methods, not just case studies. However, case study evaluations—focusing on concrete and readily understandable issues—lend themselves best to this new participatory type of evaluation.

Case Studies During The Past Decade

Whether all this documentation, awareness, and changes in practice have led to new and better kinds of case studies, however, is yet to be seen. In this sense, the final judgement on a decade of progress remains open. The routine case studies, frequently part of a multi-method evaluation design not limited to the case study method, appear to be better constructed and documented. For instance, 15 communities were the subject of ongoing research on as contemporary a topic as managed care (Ginsburg & Fasciano, 1996). Along the same lines, graduate students, both in this country and abroad, appear to be practicing better and more rigorous case studies, especially as part of their theses or dissertations.

But the decade has not produced any particularly distinctive case studies, such as Graham Allison's *Essence of Decision* (1971), much less any landmark multiple case study evaluation. There has also not emerged any streamlined way of sharing case studies, which still require a burdensome amount of text (and hence space) that probably precludes the creation of any journal devoted to case studies (in turn limiting the amount of professional communication about case studies). Even when a study takes over the whole issue of a 200-page journal ("Tracking Health System Change," 1996), as in the case of the managed care study previously cited (Ginsburg & Fasciano, 1996), the case studies are not presented as part of the publication. In these situations, a frequent problem is that the original case studies are usually too long, but there is great difficulty in preparing a second set of abbreviated texts.

At the same time, also possibly true is that the experience with case study evaluations bears great similarity to the experience with evaluation more generally (Yin, 1994b). For instance, evaluation as a whole may not have produced landmark studies during the past decade, in part because of the difficulty of improving on the exemplars of the past. Thus, interpreting the past decade of progress with case study evaluations shares the inevitable problem of interpreting many evaluation findings: no milestone stands out to any absolute extent; but somehow, conditions appear to be slightly better than before, based on process considerations—in this case, improved case study practices. Overall, and again as with the problem of interpreting many evaluation findings, possibly, the passage of more time is needed to provide a more revealing, if not definitive, perspective.

12. EDUCATIONAL CRITICISM AS A FORM OF QUALITATIVE INQUIRY

DAVID J. FLINDERS and ELLIOT W. EISNER

In this article we focus on the forms and functions of educational criticism, an artistically grounded qualitative approach to classroom research. Our aims are to describe the features of this approach and to identify its underlying theory. What assumptions undergird educational criticism? What roles does it perform? What promise does it have for improving educational practice?

Recent developments in English education have renewed interest in these and other questions concerning the goals of research. As Judith Langer and Richard Allington (1992) have written, "Although it might be easy to conclude that research is on the right track and that more similar work is needed, this is not at all the case" (p. 717). They go on to argue that while past studies have concentrated on the processes of reading and writing in general, future research must focus on the complexities of the classroom and how contextual factors interact with the curriculum that students actually experience. In their view, the field is poised for changes that will increase, not lessen, the need for alternative models of inquiry, particularly approaches that make vivid the vicissitudes and opportunities of classroom life. Can educational criticism contribute to this agenda? And if so, are its contributions in any way unique? We believe that the approach serves a dual purpose, adding to the field's repertoire of research tools, and providing a perspective from which to better understand qualitative modes of inquiry.

From *Research in the Teaching of English*, 1994, *28*, 341–357. Copyright 1994 by the National Council of Teachers of English. Reprinted with permission.

Although many aspects of educational criticism are not "new" to good classroom research, teacher assessment, and program evaluation, the arts-based orientation of criticism brings into focus dimensions of qualitative work that would otherwise be taken for granted. Equally important, educational criticism offers an alternative frame of reference for thinking about the more explicit concerns that interest qualitative researchers, including the role of subjectivity in research, questions of generalizability, and how terms such as "validity" and "rigor" apply to qualitative studies of teaching.

Setting these broader issues aside for a moment, we also want to point out that educational criticism now includes a growing number of studies in all subject areas[1]. Much of this research has been based in universities and graduate schools of education. At Stanford University alone, for example, at least 17 dissertations have used educational criticism as either their primary approach or in conjunction with other methods. In addition, educational criticism has been used to assess curriculum materials and educational software (e.g., Huenecke, 1992) and more generally as a model in designing forms of case study research (e.g., Barone, 1983; Beath, 1991a; Flinders, 1989; Nyberg, 1991; Thornton, 1988; Uhrmacher, 1991). While these studies have pursued a wide variety of open-ended research questions, their strong suit has been to elucidate through description and interpretation what Snyder, Bolin, and Zumwalt (1992) call "the enacted curriculum," those qualities, understandings and patterns of meaning that comprise school experience as it is played out at the day-to-day levels of classroom practice. Broadly stated, educational criticism is centrally concerned with what gives teaching and curriculum its distinctive character, significance, or purpose.

Our aim in this article, however, is neither to review this research nor report a particular study. Instead, we will focus on educational criticism itself as a genre of qualitative research. In order to clarify what educational criticism is and what educational critics do, we have divided this essay into three parts. First, as alluded to earlier, we examine the assumptions and conceptual underpinnings of this approach. Second, we describe its four dimensions: the descriptive, interpretative, normative, and thematic. Finally, we turn to questions of credibility and rigor, identifying three criteria appropriate to the assessment of work carried out within qualitative traditions of inquiry.

RE-EDUCATING OUR PERCEPTIONS OF THE CLASSROOM

The conceptual foundations of educational criticism rest on two basic analogies: the researcher-as-critic and teaching-as-art. The first analogy builds on the similarities between qualitative forms of educational research and the work of critics in such fields as film, literature, drama, music, and the visual arts. The second analogy is based on the set of similarities between classroom teaching and disciplined forms of artistic expression. The teaching-as-art analogy is the more fundamental of the two, and for that reason we consider it first.

Most people are willing to acknowledge that the act of teaching has elements of an aesthetic performance. In ordinary descriptions of teaching, for example, we might refer to a well-orchestrated class discussion or a beautiful lesson. These casual metaphors are significant because they point to the underlying basis on which teaching can be regarded as an art. First, both teaching and art are expressive activities; both involve some type of skilled performance intended to convey meaning. Second, both activities require that their practitioners mediate or transform the qualities of a given experience; hence, they share similar technical challenges with respect to the use of presentational forms. Third, teachers (like painters, actors, and musicians) make judgments based on qualities that unfold during the course of their performance. They seek emergent ends, outcomes that can be anticipated but not fully predicted prior to beginning the work itself.

Our general claim is that aesthetic considerations are relevant and applicable well beyond the four walls of an art classroom, studio, or gallery. It does not denigrate art to remove it from its pedestal or to recognize that art shares some of its most essential features with other sorts of human activity. From carpentry to basketball, any endeavor that exhibits consummate skill and imaginative thought, that is practiced with interest and affection, and that offers satisfaction in a job well done, may be regarded as artistic in the full sense of what art entails (Dewey, 1934). From this perspective, teaching represents one among the range of activities in which the achievement of qualities having aesthetic import is significant in the eyes and minds of those engaged in such work.

This is not to say that all teaching can be regarded as artistic. Teaching can be as mindless, mechanical, and unimaginative as any other activity. Most of us are able to recall examples of such teaching from our past experience in the classroom. However, we can also recall those adept teachers who exploited the artistic possibilities of pedagogy, and who therefore encouraged a climate in which students were able to deliterize perception, explore ideas, and take satisfaction from their own achievements. In other words, the artistic dimensions of teaching enhance its effectiveness and model some of our most valued forms of human intelligence. When such aspects of teaching are present, they deserve recognition.

Criticism, a method used in the arts to illuminate the qualities of a particular performance or work, brings us to our second analogy. What artistry is to teaching, criticism is to the qualitative study of classroom life. Again we want to stress the similarities between these two domains. Critics and researchers share an explicit agenda; both strive to describe and expound upon the meanings and qualities of work within their respective areas of inquiry. This common agenda is systemic; it is rooted in a shared sense of purpose. John Dewey (1934), who wrote on aesthetics as well as educational philosophy, describes this purpose as an extension of artistic ways of knowing. In his words:

The function of criticism is the re-education of perception of works of art; it is an auxiliary in the process, a difficult process, of learning to see and hear. The conception that its business is to appraise, to judge in the legal and moral sense, arrests the perception of those who are influenced by the criticism that assumes this task. . . . The moral function of art itself is to remove prejudice, do away with the scales that keep the eye from seeing, tear away the veils due to wont and custom, perfect the power to perceive. The critic's office is to further this work, performed by the object of art. (pp. 324–25)

What Dewey here defines as the functions of art and art criticism includes the educational as well as the aesthetic. Dewey also suggests that the ability to perceive freshly is not easy. It requires a special effort for several reasons. First, the critic's perception must be informed in ways that disclose differences across individual cases. That is, his or her task is one of discernment, not merely recognition. Second, all of us live and work in a culture that teaches us to ignore the familiar. "The world is too much with us," as Wordsworth wrote. And even if schools were not as familiar as they typically are, the objects of educational criticism are rarely black and white. What distinguishes skilled teaching—its intellectual, social, personal, and political achievements—are no less subtle than what distinguishes a beautiful painting or good literature.

Although the abilities to see and to hear are relevant to all forms of systematic inquiry, they are particularly relevant to criticism because in this approach the effects of a performance are assessed largely on the basis of the critic's own sensibilities and perceptions. Film critics, for example, may be deeply interested in what audiences take away from observing a particular film, and critics often talk with others about how the film is understood. However, critics do not typically administer questionnaires to randomly selected audiences. Instead, they view the film firsthand, and doing so is considered essential to comprehending the achievements and qualities of that work.

DIMENSIONS OF EDUCATIONAL CRITICISM

We turn now to address the dimensions of educational criticism. These dimensions overlap, and we have separated them only to permit a more focused discussion than would otherwise be possible. Taken together, they provide some of the ways that educational critics disclose the significant qualities of a situation, event, or object.

Educational Criticism As Descriptive Inquiry

It took me a while to locate the front of Barb Grant's classroom. Every wall seems important, adorned with bright posters and displays of student handiwork. Two walls boast blackboards as well, filled with flowery cursive. With the teacher's desk shoved into a far corner, no focal point of authority or control is evident. Usually student desks lined up in strict, column formation like an approaching regiment, right arms raised in salute, provide a clue. But Mrs. Grant's unorthodox arrangement of student desks into clusters of four and her strategic placement of those clusters at various angles around the room remind one more of a bridge party than basic training. Students face each other in this classroom. Learning occurs in concert with one's peers. The teacher's job is orchestration.

Orchestration begins with attention to the classroom environment. Barb Grant surrounds her students with the stuff of instruction. A progression of posters on punctuation frame the front blackboard with large black letters against a field of blue and white. . . . Learning centers are sprinkled around the room. To the left of the board is the developmental Reading Skills Center. Piles of colorful books—bright purple and green (*Skimming and Scanning*), rainbow (BFA *Reading Vocabulary Comprehension Skills Lab*), light green (*Read Ability*), vivid yellow and orange (*Success in Reading*), and smart green checks (*Be a Better Reader*)—attract the eye.

Stacked on the table next to them are popular paperbacks: *The Pigman, The Mystery at Long-cliff Inn, The Red Pony*, and *Harriet Tubman*. A tape recorder rests near the stacks under a huge, haunting poster depicting scenes from John Steinbeck's *The Pearl*. Around the poster, Mrs. Grant has stapled up student papers from the reading class—plot diagrams of the short story "Spring Over Brooklyn." Captions written on colorful construction paper in her familiar cursive announce THE PLOT DEVELOPS. . . . (pp. 60–61)

So begins Rebecca Hawthorne's (1992) educational criticism of an eighth-grade language arts classroom. (Barb Grant is Hawthorne's pseudonym for this teacher.) The full text of this criticism runs 30 pages and is published with three additional criticisms that together comprise her book, *Curriculum in the Making*. The two paragraphs quoted here can in no way capture the expanse of Hawthorne's work. They do, however, help us illustrate the idea that direct observations play a leading role in this type of inquiry. Hawthorne was there in Grant's classroom (for more than 90 hours in this particular case); she felt its linoleum floor beneath her feet, listened as the students learned, experienced the classroom firsthand, and observed the daily drama that transpired within its four walls. Like other researchers, Hawthorne fits what Johan Galtung (1990) calls a "collectionist"—someone who, by habit, is attentive to the particular attributes of a representative case.

Critics are also collectionists of a sort. They have no choice but to place themselves in the way of what they seek to understand. A wine critic must examine with an informed eye the color and clarity of wine, taste its blend of flavors, smell its bouquet. A literary critic must read literature; an art critic must visit art galleries and museums. By the same token, educational critics must put themselves in the way of what they seek to understand. Their work is "field-focused" (Eisner, 1991, pp. 32–33). Some educational critics, like Hawthorne, visit classrooms and interview teachers, talk with students, eat lunch in the school cafeteria, and attend faculty meetings or extra-curricular activities. They may also review text materials, curriculum guides, and student work. Other critics shadow students or teachers throughout their school day, going "back to school," as it were, so they may experience for themselves the routines and patterns of classroom life.

The emphasis we are placing here on sense experience is directly related to the arts-based orientation of educational criticism. One need only reflect on the arts—dance, music, poetry, painting, sculpture—to recognize that these processes and products of human invention are resolutely grounded in basic modalities of sensory perception. Yet, it is not only in the arts per se, but also in everyday life, that a person's sensory system serves as his or her primary access to the world. Russell Baker's (1982) "prosaic" memories of growing up in rural Virginia illustrate this point:

On a broiling afternoon when the men were away at work and all the women napped I moved through majestic depths of silences, silences so immense I could hear the corn growing. Under these silences there was an orchestra of natural music playing notes no city child would ever hear. A certain cackle from the henhouse meant we had gained an egg. The creak of a porch swing told of a momentary breeze blowing across my grandmother's yard. Moving past Liz Virts's barn as quietly as an Indian, I could hear the swish of a horse's tail and knew the horseflies were out in strength. As I tiptoed along a mossy bank to surprise a frog, a faint splash told me the quarry had spotted me and slipped into the stream. Wandering among the sleeping houses I learned that tin roofs crackle under the power of the sun, and when I tired and came back to my grandmother's house, I padded into her dark cool living room, lay flat on the floor, and listened to the hypnotic beat of her pendulum clock on the wall ticking the meaningless hours away (p. 58).

Baker's account is one that exemplifies both the foundations and craft of qualitative description. Its foundations, as we have already mentioned, concern the ability to see and listen, to discern through active perceptual construction "an orchestra of natural music" beneath "majestic depths of silences." This type of informed perception is sometimes referred to in the arts as connoisseurship; the term connoisseur is derived from the Latin root *cognoscere*, meaning to know or to understand. An art connoisseur is someone who knows about art, someone who understands what to look for in the way of qualities possessed by works within that particular form of expression. An educational connoisseur is likewise someone who knows what to look for, someone who is able to read the qualities of an educational performance. Connoisseurship is the art of appreciation (Eisner, 1991), the ability to differentiate and discern complexities, nuances, and subtleties in aspects of the world around us.

The craft side of descriptive inquiry is of a more public nature. It involves a *representation* of whatever insights were gained from private acts of perception. In order to make perceptions public, artists and critics turn to forms of representation (language, number, dance, film, photography) that allow them to transform one type of experience into another. In Baker's case, he aims to transform his early memories into language. He seeks an expressive equivalent, a "true" description. We refer to this as craft because it requires close attention to the range of styles in which language is used to convey meaning—what the words themselves denote, but also their cadence, tone, idiomatic meanings, and metaphorical qualities. Dewey (1934) made an important (if not wholly accurate) distinction when he wrote that, "science states meanings; art expresses them." Critics employ expressive modes of description in their work, but not simply for the sake of being artistic. Rather, they do so because the literal and propositional use of language alone is unable to take the full impress of qualitative relationships.

The descriptive aspects of criticism are relevant to English education research in at least three ways. First, we believe they reaffirm the importance of moving research inside English and language arts classrooms at all levels of teaching. Wine connoisseurs should be familiar with viticulture and methods of wine making. Yet, we would be rightly suspicious of a wine connoisseur who, although obsessively interested in wine, refused to drink it. For some, the analogy with research is uncomfortably apt. Earlier we noted Langer and Allington's (1992) concern that compared with the general processes of reading and writing, researchers know much less about the daily classroom experiences of students and teachers. How Ms. Purnell teaches her fourth-graders to write or how Professor Murry teaches *Heart of Darkness* to college freshmen are not idle questions. Their day-to-day lessons speak to broader pedagogical themes, and researchers will find much to see and hear in these classrooms that the teachers and students themselves take for granted.

Second, although the methods of educational criticism share much in common with other forms of qualitative inquiry, the focus of this approach on the qualities of a classroom environment, teaching style, or curriculum text is one that sheds light on what often makes classroom experiences most memorable. Vivid renderings, particularly of exemplary lessons (as judged by researchers or others who have an informed basis for making this determination), put teaching in a form that can be shared and discussed, ensuring that the best of a teacher's work is not lost with each performance.

Third, the descriptive dimension of criticism urges researchers to give special attention to the forms of representation used for depicting classroom life. Exploiting a broad range of representational forms—including the literary uses of language, symbols and images, as well as the use of visual and multi-media formats—will require imagination and skills for which most researchers have not yet been previously trained. Qualitative researchers are only just beginning to explore such alternative modes for describing various aspects of school experience[2]. The rationale for doing so, however, is significant. As in the arts, methods of description shape what researchers are able to describe and, thus, what they are able to understand.

Educational Criticism As Interpretative Inquiry

Implied in our earlier remarks is the assumption that critics not only *sense* the world, they *make sense* of it. Inseparable from their descriptive accounts are points of view and understandings about what things mean or why events happen as they do. This is the case in all forms of disciplined inquiry, qualitative and quantitative alike. No one can, or at least would want to, do research empty-headed. Even researchers initially unsure of what they intend to study are guided by suspicions, hunches, or some notion of how various parts of the world operate. In this broad sense, there is always an interpretative element in practicing research.

However, by labeling criticism as interpretative we mean to stress not only what critics do, but also the focus of the critic's work. This focus is on the meanings of a performance, object, or event. To illustrate, one might say that Melville's novel *Moby Dick* is a book about whaling. Of course this description is "true" in a literal sense, but it hardly begins to satisfy questions about what the novel means or why it was written in a particular way. Literary criticism is intended to disclose such meanings, and educational criticism is intended to disclose the meanings of school and classroom experience. Educational critics may even employ concepts quite similar to those used in literary analysis. A classroom lesson can be viewed as a type of text or narrative, for example, with its own story, grammar, plot, setting, characters, use of imagery, symbols, themes, underlying metaphors, and so forth.

The focus of this approach on interpretative concepts is, nevertheless, only one side of the coin. The other side concerns the schemata and points of view that critics themselves bring to their work. These points of view are not only used to focus a study, but also to explain its findings. In the arts, critics have exercised a good deal of imagination when it comes to constructing or adapting different ways to interpret the objects of their criticism. Literary and art critics are rarely of a single mind (see, for example, Garber, 1988). Structuralist critics, feminist critics, psychoanalytic critics, Marxist critics, and others co-exist in what in political circles is called "loyal opposition." They agree to disagree, recognizing that there are different ways to read a novel or poem, just as there are different ways to look at a Fauvist painting, or different ways to "read" a classroom.

The implications of such diversity concern a field's tolerance for multiple schools of thought. In many forms of quantitative research, disagreement among observers is regarded as a weakness because it threatens the reliability of the research. In qualitative forms of inquiry, including educational criticism, researchers also expect appropriate levels of agreement on those matters that afford consensual validation (Eisner, 1991). When two researcher-critics visit the same schools, as with the accounts published in *Daedalus* by Philip Jackson (1981a; 1981b; 1981c) and Sara Lawrence-Lightfoot (1981a; 1981b; 1981c), readers find some degree of overlap between what each describes. Many aspects of schooling are clearly robust. Yet, consensual validation is not the same as interrater reliability. Even two critics in the same classroom at the same time will usually attend to different aspects of its social life or interpret similar events from different points of view. For this reason, most educational critics (e.g., Barone, 1983; Flinders, 1989; Beath, 1991b; Uhrmacher, 1991) have made an effort to be explicit within the criticism itself about their particular values and perspectives.

Our main point, however, is that differences among critics are not necessarily a failed measure of reliability. Given the hundreds of criticisms that have been made of Shakespeare's *Hamlet*, for example, little would be gained by somehow calculating their mean and standard deviation. Indeed, variation in what critics see and how they understand it is not a weakness but a strength, if those working in the field genuinely value a range of perspectives from which to view education. One reason for promoting multiple perspectives is that they contribute to informed choice and empowerment, topics that are now of particular interest at all levels of educational practice.

Educational Criticism As Normative Inquiry

A third dimension of educational criticism is represented in the values that critics bring to their work. These values play an active role in guiding both the expressive and interpretative dimensions of inquiry. Inevitably, what researchers attend to and the questions they ask are a reflection of what they take to be important. Educational criticism is no different in this respect than any other approach. However, critics do bring to the field a type of normative orientation that sets criticism apart from the conventional methods of school and classroom research.

In particular, textbook accounts tend to describe educational research as a problem-driven process (e.g., Borg & Gall, 1989). A researcher's first task is to select a problem that will serve to motivate and determine the focus of a particular study. The more self-evident this problem is, the better. Educational critics, by comparison, are pulled in a different direction. Their work is informed by artistic traditions that seek to recognize exemplary practice. This is not to say that educational critics are indifferent to social or school-related problems; they are no less interested than artists and critics in other fields are in the problems relevant to their work. Thomas Barone (1989; 1993), for example, has used educational criticism to focus attention on how schools fail to meet the needs of underachieving students. He argues, moreover, that educational criticism should take a form similar to what Jean-Paul Sartre called "socially committed literature." Yet, even Barone's arguments do not negate the abiding interest that critics hold for meritorious work.

Now, what gets priority in terms of research topics and agendas is the result of a highly complicated process, and we do not mean to oversimplify the politics of that process by relying on textbook accounts of research. We only want to stress that normative issues play into educational criticism in a distinctive way. Here the potential of educational criticism is to provide greater balance in recognizing the achievements as well as the shortcomings of classroom teaching. Are we able to recognize good teaching when we see it? And by what criteria is this judgment made? Educational critics must rely to some extent on their own experiences and sensibilities, which again underscores the critical role of connoisseurship as the foundation of this approach. In addition, critics may consider teaching that has previously received public recognition for its successes. Both of these approaches are common in the arts and other realms in which evaluation is considered a regular part of what critics do. People fully expect a wine critic to judge the quality of wine. They expect a film critic to judge how well the actors have performed and generally whether or not a particular film is well made. Critics, in short, are among those responsible for helping people understand what constitutes "goodness" in those domains where goodness counts.

These issues are relevant because education itself is normative in ways that wine and film making are not. R. S. Peters (1970) points out that some notion of moral goodness is either explicit or strongly implied in even our most mundane uses of the term education. This normative bent connects foundational studies with empirical research in a more direct manner than is usually the case. An educational critic might observe a series of lessons on a particular topic, say the thematic development of an assigned novel or a unit on descriptive writing. The normative dimension of a critic's work involves situating these lessons relative to their educational functions. Will the lessons, for example, encourage students to exercise their intelligence and imagination, read more critically, or develop the type of cognitive skills that facilitate continued learning? To raise a different question, will these lessons in some way promote what E. D. Hirsh (1987) calls cultural literacy? That is, are the lessons worth learning from an academic point of view? A critic might also ask whether the students are able to find any personal relevance in what they learn.

And from yet another perspective, are the lessons in any way responsive to social needs? Will they help prepare students for some aspect of life beyond the classroom?

Such questions highlight the diversity of values that inform language arts education. In this and other subject areas, different values compete within a range of intentions, practices, and methods of evaluation. It is not surprising then that critics are often unable to use a common matrix when it comes to assessing the educational worth of a given teaching style or type of educational experience. The qualities that might make one class discussion *good*, for example, may be totally absent in a second, but equally *good* class discussion. To judge both by the same standard is likely to hide more than it reveals. Moreover, even if critics were able to agree on one particular standard or desirable outcome, this agreement would not in and of itself dictate how the outcome is to be achieved. In education, as in the arts, different practitioners are likely to employ different methods in order to accomplish similar ends. Here we could also draw an analogy with sports. A fan of baseball or golf, for example, attends to how well games are played and not just to the final score.

Educational Criticism As Thematic Inquiry

It might seem that the descriptive, interpretative, and normative dimensions of criticism are more than enough to keep an educational critic busy. Yet, a fourth dimension of criticism is also important, particularly with respect to the utility of criticism. That dimension is thematics, the effort to extract some general principles, findings, lessons, and the like from the study of particulars. Every major literary achievement has a thematic message that in some way transcends the particulars of a story or text. Similarly, educational criticism attempts to identify the major thematic notions—the recurring messages and qualities, dominant features, or salient images—that come from the study of individual cases.

Such themes are based on a form of inductive logic. That is, every particular case is a case of something. It displays not only itself, but also the patterns and attributes held in common with other cases of the same type. Consequently, we are able to apply what we have learned to other situations through a process known as "naturalistic generalization" (Donmoyer, 1980; Stake, 1975a). Unlike formal generalizations (those based on random samples and statistical probabilities), naturalistic generalizations are inherent in the ordinary, non-random processes of learning, and in the everyday task of using what one knows to make sense of situations that are both different from and the same as situations previously encountered. This type of generalizing is accomplished by attending to attributes and by matching images of best fit (Eisner, 1991). A few examples will serve to illustrate our point.

Shakespeare's Lear, Cervantes' Quixote, Dostoyevsky's Raskolnikov, and many other fictional characters are of enduring interest, not for their own sake, but because these characters tell us something about human passions, the psyche, conceptions of good and evil, cultural mores, and so forth. Played out on a less grand but still significant scale, analogous figures found in qualitative studies of education include, among others, Ted Sizer's (1984) Horace; Tom Barone's (1989) at-risk student, Billy

Charles Barnett; and Philip Jackson's (1992) former mathematics teacher, Mrs. Theresa Henzi. Like literary characters, Horace, Billy Charles, and Mrs. Henzi are implicated in matters that transcend the particulars of who they are. Horace's workday, vividly described, serves to comment on the demands and waning social status of classroom teaching. Billy Charles' personal history reveals disturbing patterns of home and school life. Mrs. Henzi's commanding pedagogy displays the power and endurance of Mrs. Henzi; not all adolescents are like Billy Charles. Yet, the patterns they exemplify are instructive, nonetheless, and of considerable interest to those who design and evaluate educational programs.

The utility of themes in literature, history, and criticism is that they give a person something to take away from a particular study. The aim for critics and qualitative researchers is to recognize and name a pattern that will help explain what people have experienced and puzzled over in the past. Themes of this sort are not uncommon in the education literature. One theme developed in a study by Powell, Farrar, and Cohen (1985), for example, is the concept of "treaties," those forms of tacit accommodation between students and teachers that ease the demands, but also undermine the opportunities, of classroom life. Does this concept apply in every classroom, and is it always the best way to understand what takes place between teachers and students? Obviously not. The application of themes is never that simple or straightforward. However, while themes do not offer rules or formulas for understanding a given classroom, they still serve a vital heuristic function. They provide a premise for framing expectations, and perhaps most helpful in the long run, themes offer ways of discussing education at a more incisive level than would otherwise be possible.

QUESTIONS OF RIGOR

Having described the structure of educational criticism—its descriptive, interpretative, normative, and thematic dimensions—we now turn to questions of credibility and rigor. How does one judge the believability of a critic's account? In our eyes, it is never possible for researchers to view the world from God's knee, to know with certainty that one's perceptions and understandings mirror a pristine version of reality. What researchers see and tell is always a transactional outcome, mediated first by conceptual frameworks and methods of observation, and second by the forms of representation through which a study is reported (Eisner, 1992; Schwandt, 1993). For this reason, we do not seek in educational criticism some form of ontological objectivity. Instead, we look for reasonable claims and warranted plausibilities. Our search, to paraphrase Stephen Toulmin (1982), is for sound beliefs rather than certain truths.

Rigor in this context is a matter of being able to adequately assess what educational critics report. Are there good reasons to be confident in the way a critic describes a particular classroom? What forms of support lend credibility to the account? We have already mentioned *consensual validation* as a criterion relevant to the credibility of educational criticism. This form of validation is established by critics sharing their work with others knowledgeable within a given area. In her study of home schooling, for example, Lesley Talyor (1993) asked a group of home schoolers (who were not research participants) to read and comment on her educational criticisms of three families. Those who reviewed her work agreed that Taylor's accounts concurred with their own experiences, not in the details of her description, but in its typification of home schooling practices. Such feedback lends support to this particular study consensual validation, however, is not the only basis on which to assess the warrant of educational criticism. Two additional criteria include *structural corroboration* and *referential adequacy*.

Structural corroboration refers to the weight and consistency of cumulative data. Is a critic's description sufficiently "thick" to provide a compelling image of what was observed? Or to use a legal metaphor, is there a preponderance of evidence? Does the critic provide details and examples drawn from multiple sources such as direct observations, interviews, sample curriculum materials, or other documents? And are these details reasonably consistent across different sources and settings? Moreover, is the weight of evidence consistent with the critic's interpretation of its meaning? Do recurrent examples and details point in the direction the critic says? Readers may reject an interpretation on ideological grounds, but they still should be able to trace the lines of evidence and reasoning that have led a critic to his or her conclusions.

While structural corroboration gauges the degree to which the criticism is well informed, referential adequacy gauges the degree to which the criticism enables the reader to experience qualities within the situation that the critic claims to be there. Earlier we noted that the primary function of criticism is what Dewey called the re-education of perception. Simply put, critics write so that others may learn. Referential adequacy is based on this service; that is, the educational function of illuminating aspects of classroom meaning that would otherwise remain hidden.

Referentially adequate criticism tells its readers something about a particular work, its nuances, its style, its genre. The criticism acts as a set of cues that allows others to locate these and other qualities within the subject matter described. These cues work by foregrounding specific aspects of classroom life in ways that reframe what readers may already know at a tacit level. When criticism is informative in this sense, it not only enlarges understanding, but serves to guide future observations as well. Referential adequacy, thus, has a prospective element, that being the degree to which criticism aids in perception by helping others know what to look for.

CONCLUSION

We have described educational criticism by focusing on its assumptions and four of its dimensions. The descriptive dimension is rooted first in discernment—the critic's ability to notice what is subtle yet significant—and second in the forms of representation through which private acts of perception are made public. The interpretative dimension is represented in the conceptual frameworks that critics use to account for the meanings and qualitative attributes that others instill in their work. The normative dimension of criticism looks to assessment, not in any absolute sense of the term, but as a way to articulate those values that inform conceptions of goodness within a given domain. Finally, the thematic dimension involves the critic's effort to extract general understandings, images, or lessons from the study of what is always, to some degree, context specific.

To summarize our main points, educational criticism seeks to create compelling and richly textured accounts of classroom practice. In doing so, the critic's aim is to enhance the perceptions and understandings of the qualities that constitute an educational performance or product. The achievements of skilled teachers are made most visible through informed accounts of their work. Criticism aspires to this end; it ventures to transfix in a stable form what the critic has observed.

We have also discussed ways of evaluating the credibility of educational criticism, specifically in terms of consensual validation, structural corroboration, and referential adequacy. On the issue of standards, we agree with Aristotle that it is equally mistaken to accept probable reasoning from a mathematician as to demand scientific proofs from a rhetorician. Today the question is no longer whether science or art will guide educational research, but rather what to expect from each. In arts-based forms of inquiry, criticism provides a model for understanding how the research itself is defined. Like the contributions of literature and art, educational criticism has the potential to make vivid those features of schools and classrooms that matter. It can help us grasp much of what needs to be known about how such places work, giving us new windows through which to see and understand the educational world.

NOTES

1. For examples of educational criticisms and their use, see Eisner (1985).

2. The use of unconventional forms of representation in qualitative research and education is addressed in Beath (1991b), Epstein (1989), Flinders (1991), Singer (1991), Thornton (1991), and Uhrmacher and Greene (1991).

13. PROGRAM THEORY: NOT WHETHER PROGRAMS WORK BUT HOW THEY WORK

PATRICIA J. ROGERS

Evaluations which are based on program theory have two essential elements: an explicit model of the program (in particular, the mechanisms by which program activities are understood to contribute to the intended outcomes) and an evaluation which is guided by this model. While the first suggestions for evaluating programs in this way date from the 1960s and 70s (Argyris & Schoen, 1978; Suchman, 1967; Weiss, 1972), interest in the approach has grown through the 1980s and 90s (Bennett, 1982; Funnell, 1990; Lenne & Cleland, 1987; Patton, 1986). This is reflected in special journal issues (Bickman, 1987, 1990a; Chen, 1980), special conference sessions, a special interest group (a Topical Interest Group of the American Evaluation Association), endorsement by various government agencies (e.g., Australian Commonwealth Department of Finance, 1998), and proliferating examples of evaluations based on this approach (although not in all program fields).

Like any attractive idea, the devil is in the details. At their best, program theory evaluations can be analytically and empirically powerful and can lead to better evaluation questions, better evaluation answers, and better programs. At their worst, they can be self-serving and uncritical, excessively narrowing attention to intended outcomes. Program theory evaluation can even be a time-consuming way to avoid doing evaluation at all. Some accounts of evaluations suggest that sometimes so much time and energy is spent on developing the model that it is not really used to guide the evaluation, and only cursory data are collected and analyzed. Like any other approach to program evaluation, it needs to be used in appropriate circumstances and in appropriate ways. It may be that evaluations based on program theory also

D.L. Stufflebeam, G.F. Madaus and T. Kellaghan (eds.). EVALUATION MODELS. Copyright © 2000. Kluwer Academic Publishers. Boston. All rights reserved.

need to include processes for explicitly addressing the unintended outcomes of the program (both positive and negative) and for reviewing intended outcomes in terms of their congruence with the assessed needs of the intended beneficiaries. Such processes might include frameworks associated with goal-free evaluation (Scriven, 1991) or some participatory process for gathering different perspectives about what the program is doing and ought to be doing (Wadsworth, 1991).

This chapter begins by comparing some of the different types of models of a program we might develop, showing how increasingly complex models provide more detail about the mechanisms which are understood to cause the intended outcomes. We then review three examples of program theory evaluation: summative evaluations of an adolescent mental health program and of a prison education program and a formative evaluation of a preadolescent resiliency program. The chapter concludes by addressing the questions most commonly asked in workshops and classes on program theory, including when program theory evaluation is most appropriate.

USES OF PROGRAM THEORY FOR EVALUATION

Accumulated experience in using program theory for evaluation has shown it to be remarkably versatile. Evaluators have used it for three quite different purposes: certain types of summative evaluation which focus on answering the question "Does the program cause the intended outcomes?" (e.g., Bickman, 1996); formative evaluations which are intended to suggest how the program can be improved (e.g., Clarke, 1995; Finnan & Davis, 1995; Milne, 1993; Wadsworth, 1991); and ongoing program monitoring which provides continuous indicators of program performance (e.g., Funnel, 1997; Funnell & Lenne, 1990).

When program theory has been used for the first of these purposes, the focus has been on building and testing the validity of the program model—the articulated model of the mechanisms by which the program is understood to reach its intended outcomes. This test can provide information to guide summative decisions about whether to continue, terminate, or replicate the program. Such an evaluation is not usually comprehensive. As discussed later, evaluations based on program theory rarely consider unintended outcomes, nor the cost-effectiveness of alternative programs.

If a program achieves its intended outcomes, program theory can help to identify the elements of a program which are understood to be essential for its widespread replication and can then analyze whether these elements are plausibly and empirically associated with success. It should also be able to identify whether program success has been achieved despite (or perhaps because of) failure to implement the program as designed.

If a program does not achieve its intended outcomes, a program theory evaluation may be able to identify whether this is due to implementation failure (the program wasn't implemented as intended, which might, in itself, explain the lack of outcomes); unsuitable context (the program was implemented in a context in which the necessary mechanisms did not operate); and theory failure (the program was implemented as intended, in a suitable context and evaluated with a powerful design and measures which would probably have detected important effects if they had been present).

A metaevaluation (an evaluation of the evaluation) will also be necessary to investigate whether the apparent lack of results is due to evaluation failure. It may be that the evaluation was not powerful enough or appropriately focused to detect differences in outcomes. For example, sample sizes may have been too small for observed differences to be statistically significant, or outcome measures might not have been entirely appropriate.

The second purpose of evaluations based on program theory has been for formative program evaluation designed to guide program improvement. In evaluations where program theory has been used for this purpose, program staff have usually been involved in articulating how the program is meant to achieve its intended outcomes and in gathering evidence about how the program is going. Formative program theory evaluation helps improve programs in three ways. Firstly, when staff make explicit their implicit program models, they often identify gaps or inconsistencies, and make immediate changes to program implementation to address these. Secondly, staff often find that having a common explicit model helps them to keep focused on the most important aspects of their work and co-operate with other staff. Finally, the data gathered provides feedback about effectiveness which can point to required adjustments to the program, a feature that is particularly important for programs in which the ultimate outcomes are long-term. Program theory often helps to identify intermediate outcomes and to provide feedback about these outcomes. Program theory evaluation has also been used for a third purpose: to help programs respond to increasing demands for monitoring and performance measurement. Program models can suggest the sorts of information that are most important and relevant to monitor and report and can also assist in the interpretation of these data.

What Should We Call It?

At this point, it may be helpful to deal with the problem of what to call this type of evaluation. At present it is plagued by a variety of labels, none of them very apt. The term most commonly used is "program theory evaluation" or "theory-based evaluation" (e.g., Conner et al., 1990); sometimes the term "theory-driven evaluation" is used (e.g., Chen, 1990; Heflinger, Bickman, Northrup & Sonnichsen, 1997). These labels, however, have often led to confusion. The first problem is that the word "theory" suggests a complex system of empirical, hypothetical and explanatory propositions (such as atomic theory, evolutionary theory, or the theory of relativity). But the theory at the heart of this sort of evaluation is usually much more modest—one describing how programs of a particular type will lead to particular intended outcomes. Sometimes, particularly in evaluations described as being "theory-driven", the program theory is explicitly related to a more general theory such as a particular social theory or psychological theory, but this is not always the case. The other problem with using a "theory" label is that it might be taken to imply that other types of program evaluation are atheoretical. This is clearly not so. Approaches to program evaluation, implicitly at least, are based on a variety of theories relating to knowledge construction and evaluation practice. But in evaluation based on program theory, the theory explicitly states how the program is expected to lead to its intended outcomes.

Other labels used for this type of evaluation have their own problems. The terms "program logic" and "logical framework" have often been used instead, the latter referring to a particular way of representing a program's theory-of-action that has been extensively used by international aid agencies (Sartorius, 1996). These terms can convey the idea that program outcomes flow logically and effortlessly from program activities, while the term "outcomes hierarchies," which is also sometimes used, encourages people to think in single linear causal chains, which may not be appropriate.

Since program theory evaluation is based on a model of the program, perhaps the term "program model evaluation" might be a better label to communicate what this type of evaluation is all about. Even this is not perfect, however, since the term is interpreted in different ways. In this chapter we use the label "program theory", which is less likely to be confusing; at least it signals that we are referring to a theory about the program.

BUILDING A PROGRAM MODEL

Components Of A Program Model

Program theory evaluation most commonly begins with the development of a program model, which is then used to guide the evaluation. Sometimes, however, program theory evaluation follows an iterative process—cycling from collecting and analyzing data to building and revising the program model.

Program models have at least three components: the program activities, the intended outcomes, and the mechanisms by which program activities are understood to lead to the intended outcomes. They may also have a fourth component: the contexts in which these mechanisms operate. The distinguishing characteristic of a program model is that it includes mechanisms.

The following examples are intended to show the difference between models with and without mechanisms. We begin with two types of models which do not include mechanisms—"black box" evaluation and "process-outcome evaluation"—and then move to increasingly complex program models which do include mechanisms.

Each example refers to the evaluation of a program designed to improve elementary student learning through teacher home visits, the same program chosen to illustrate one of the earliest discussions of program theory (Weiss, 1972). Such a program might operate through several different mechanisms, including its impact on the attitudes, knowledge, and behavior of children, teachers and parents (Johnston & Mermin, 1994; Moll et al., 1992) and on the collaboration between families and the school (Heleen, 1992; Davies, 1990; Klass et al., 1993).

Black Box Evaluation

Black box evaluation refers to evaluation which focuses on the actual outcomes of a program, without investigating the processes within the program which led to those outcomes. If we used a black box evaluation of a teacher home visiting program, we would measure the improvements to student learning among children who received home visits.

Black box evaluations are quite appropriate if we are evaluating a product or an intervention which is standardized, because we can be fairly confident the outcomes observed in the evaluation will be repeated when the product is used again in the future or when the intervention is repeated. When interventions are not tightly prescribed and standardized, however, it is difficult to generalize the findings from an evaluation to subsequent implementation because we cannot be confident that the program will be the same, even if it is given the same label.

If the home visiting program appeared to have succeeded (that is, if student learning has increased compared to students who didn't receive home visits), we would need to know what it was about the home visits that was important in making them work to ensure that these elements were incorporated in subsequent replications. Was it the mere fact of the teacher visits that made it work? Or was it something they did during the visit? Conversely, if the program appeared to have failed, it may not be because home visits are ineffective but because these particular home visits were ineffective—that is, they lacked essential elements.

Process-Outcome Evaluation

One response to the concerns raised about the black-box evaluation is to include some detail about the program, as well as its outcomes. Process-outcome evaluations analyze the association between various program characteristics or activities and intended outcomes. For example, an evaluation of teacher home visits could collect data about the numbers of visits made, the length of time spent in each visit, and how much of the visit the teacher spent listening to the child, and then examine the relationship between these characteristics and *improvements* in student learning.

Such an evaluation might find, for example, that the length of the visit was not correlated with improved student learning, that the number of visits was positively correlated with outcomes (so that students who received more visits showed bigger improvement), and that improved student learning was associated with visits where teachers spent a moderate percentage time listening to students (not extremely high or extremely low).

We would now have some predictors, but not a model of *how* the program contributes to the observed outcomes. Even though we have some detail about how the home visiting program has been implemented, we don't yet have any suggested mechanisms which link the activities with the outcomes. We might try to replicate the program by specifying the length of visits and percentage of time spent listening to the student, but still fail to replicate the essential mechanisms. More importantly, we would not know w' er we had gathered data about the important process variables. Maybe we should gather data about time of year that visits were conducted, or how parents were involved during the visit.

We move on, then, to increasingly complex models of the program which all include some mechanisms, and which therefore suggest which process variables are more likely to be important.

Two-Step Program Model With A Mediator

The simplest program model adds a single mediating variable between program activities and outcomes. The program is understood to lead to the intended outcomes by first affecting this variable, which then leads to the ultimate outcome. For example, we might suspect that the key ingredient in the success of a home visiting program is that the children subsequently believe that their teacher is interested in them.

If this program model were valid, the child's belief would be a necessary intermediate outcome for the program in order to achieve its untended outcome. We might think of the two-step model as the simplest type of program model which includes mechanisms. It is on the one hand, a considerable simplification of the program. While the child's belief in the teacher's interest might be a necessary intermediate outcome, there may be other intermediate outcomes that are also required in to achieve the ultimate intended outcome. Even this level of detail is comparatively rare in program evaluation. As Lipsey (1993) has observed, if all evaluations were required to report on at least one mediator in this way, they would all contribute something to the cumulative knowledge about how programs do or do not work.

Program Model With A Chain Of Mechanisms

More complex program models explore a chain of mechanisms which link program activities with intermediate outcomes and ultimate outcomes. Yin (1997) has described this as being interested not in the "boxes" in a causal diagram but in the arrows. A more complex program model specifies what it is about the program activities that leads to the intermediate outcome, and how this intermediate outcome leads to the ultimate outcome. Perhaps a moderate amount of listening by the teacher means that teachers and students are sharing information, rather than either being cast in the role of interviewer, and this is the mechanism which leads to the child believing that the teacher is genuinely interested in them. Perhaps, in turn, this belief leads to an increased willingness to co-operate with the teacher in class, and this is the basis of the improvement in student learning (Figure 1).

Program model diagrams rarely represent programs in this way, however. They are more likely to show these mechanisms as a series of intermediate outcomes, as in Figure 2. An evaluation based on this model might be particularly interested in students who fail to make improvements in student learning after the introduction of home visits. Did the home visits with these particular students fail to achieve mutual sharing? Or were these students already fully co-operating with teachers in class before the introduction of home visits? These instances of program failure can

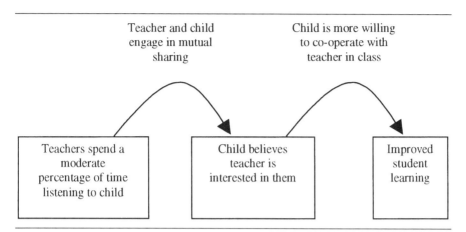

Figure 1. Program model with a chain of mechanisms

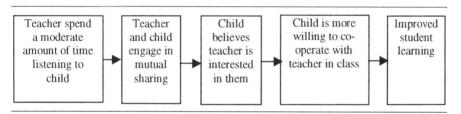

Figure 2. Program model with a chain of mechanisms shown as a series of intermediate outcomes

provide more evidence that the program theory is sound, as well as suggest ways to improve implementation (for example, by ensuring that all students have an opportunity to engage in mutual sharing with the teacher, even if the home-visits did not achieve this).

Program Model With Parallel Chains Of Mechanisms

So far we have concentrated on the effect that home visits have on students. But the outcome of home visits may be due to other mechanisms involving effects on parents or teachers. These other mechanisms may be complementary to the main mechanisms, or they may provide an alternative explanation for the untended outcomes. It is often important to identify these other mechanisms and to collect data about them.

Figure 3 adds a complementary chain of mechanisms which refers to effects of home visits on parents and teachers. Teachers may be able to use knowledge about the child's interests, which they gained through mutual sharing, to adapt their lessons to make them more engaging and relevant. At the same time, teachers may have learned more about the barriers to learning that the child faces and be able to provide additional resources. Parents' responses may also be important;

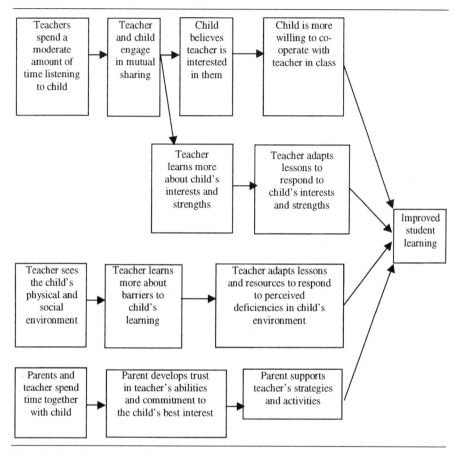

Figure 3. Complementary mechanisms in a program model

perhaps they are better able to provide support at home for teachers' activities and strategies. These may be alternative mechanisms; that is, the program can lead to increased learning through any one of these mechanisms. Or they may be complementary mechanisms; that is, a successful program will require the operation of all of them.

Differentiated Program Model

All the models presented so far describe mechanisms that are understood to be universal. While many evaluators argue that program theory should try to discover universal mechanisms, others (particularly Pawson & Tilley, 1997) have argued that mechanisms operate within particular contexts, and that program models ought to articulate both the mechanisms that are understood to cause the intended outcomes and the contexts within which these mechanisms are effective. Before we leave the example of home visiting, we will look briefly at how such a program might be described by a differentiated program model which shows different mechanisms operating in different contexts.

Three examples in Figure 4 show how the complementary mechanisms shown in Figure 3 might act as alternative mechanisms which operate in particular contexts. For example, in a context where the teacher is unfamiliar with the resources available to the child (especially access to books, and a workspace for homework) and where the school does not adequately respond to gaps in the availability of resources, home visits may lead to improved student learning primarily because the teacher is better informed about barriers to the children's learning and addresses those barriers.

USING THE MODEL TO GUIDE THE EVALUATION

Developing a program model that summarizes the available knowledge about how a program is understood to work is only the start of an evaluation that uses program theory. The next step is to design an evaluation guided by this model. The models of the home visiting program described above would each suggest a different type of data collection and analysis.

The examples which follow have been drawn from published examples of evaluations using program theory. Two were summative evaluations designed to test the program model. In one, a single model was developed for the program; in the other, several models were developed for different contexts. In one case, data about program participants were compared to data about a comparison group; in the other, data were compared to a predictive model. The third example was a formative evaluation, designed to describe and improve an existing innovative program, and to lay a foundation for a subsequent summative evaluation.

Testing A Single Program Model

One of the largest reported implementations of a program theory evaluation was the Fort Bragg adolescent mental health managed care demonstration program (Bickman, 1996). This $80 million demonstration program was designed to test the program theory that "a comprehensive, integrated and co-ordinated continuum of care is more cost-effective than a fragmented service system with a limited variety of services" (Bickman, 1996, p. 112). The detailed program model was developed in two iterations: a preliminary model was developed before the program began; a more detailed version was then developed through interviews with staff, a review of program documentation, and focus groups.

Outcomes for participants (in terms of clinical outcomes and patient and family satisfaction) were compared to outcomes from two sites which treated similar children in a similar environment but without the continuum of care. The results did not support the theory that this type of program would lead to more effective treatment and hence cost-effective outcomes. Children did not achieve significantly better outcomes and the cost of services was much higher due to longer time spent

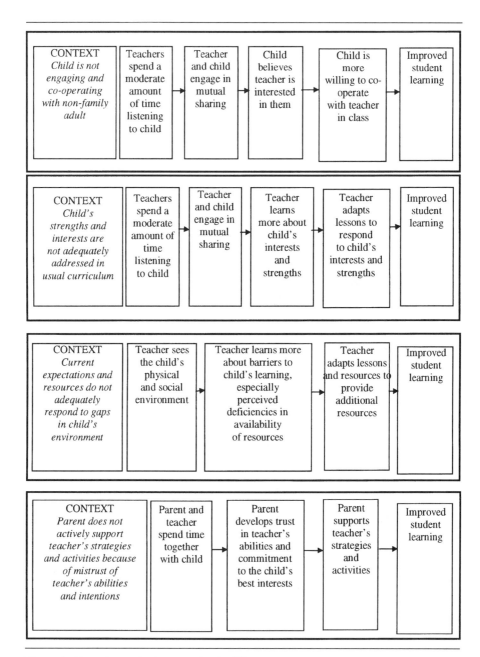

Figure 4. Alternative mechanisms operating in different contexts

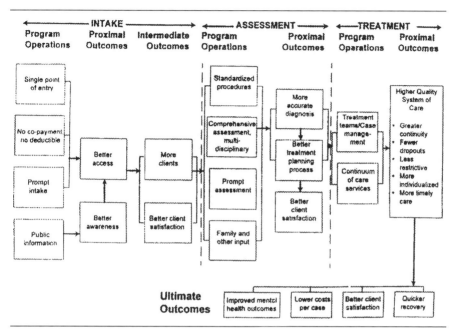

Figure 5. Final model of the Fort Bragg program theory. Reprinted from Bickman et al. (1995)

in treatment, greater volume of traditional services, heavy use of intermediate services, and higher per unit costs (Bickman, 1996, p. 117).

By using program theory, the evaluators were able to more carefully select or develop appropriate measures for program implementation and program quality (see Bickman, 1990b; Bryant & Bickman, 1996) and were able to rule out implementation failure. This allowed the evaluators to point to theory failure as the reason for the observed lack of outcomes.

Developing and Testing Different Program Models in Different Contexts

A quite different use of program theory was Pawson's evaluation of the impact of the Simon Fraser University Prison Education Program on the rehabilitation of inmates in British Columbian penitentiaries. (The study is reported more fully in Pawson & Tilley, 1997, pp. 103–114.) This program worked through centers in federal men's prisons where inmates could take college (undergraduate university) courses over a number of semesters and gradually earn credits towards a college degree. Over 20 years of this program, more than 1,000 prisoners had enrolled in at least one course. The evaluation was conducted in three stages: developing theories of why and for whom the program might work, analyzing outcome data to check the predictions of the theories, and comparing this program theory with the prisoners' interpretations of why the program works.

Possible theories were developed from reviews of academic literature and through discussions with program co-ordinators who were asked "to search their memory for cases, illustrations and commonalities in respect of 'what was it about the course which seemed to have the most impact in changing the men' and 'what type of inmate is most likely to turn away from crime as a result of being in the program'" (Pawson & Tilley, 1997, p. 107). Two of the hypotheses developed in this first stage were labeled the "mediocrity" theory and the "high engagement" theory. The mediocrity theory grew out of the observation that many of the prisoners for whom the program seemed to have the most impact had had poor school records, mediocre crime records of gradual escalation, and initially poor but gradually improving marks in the university courses (although never getting As). The high engagement theory arose out of a belief that high levels of engagement in the program were generally likely to be associated with greater success and, on the basis of informal observations, that this mechanism only seemed to hold for hardened criminals with previous convictions for serious crimes. The program theory that was developed was differentiated by context as set out in Table 1.

In the second phase, data were collected on the 700 men who had completed at least two semesters in the program. Data on 50 variables were gathered from prisoner files and program files over 20 years, including educational status on entry, previous criminal record, involvement in the program (including a judgment of their classroom performance based on their educational records), and any convictions after release. The rate of reconviction for each group was compared to the rate predicted by the statistical information on recidivism (SIR) scale based on of various predictor variables.

The outcomes for prisoners participating in the program compared favorably with those predicted by the SIR. SIR predicted that 58 percent of participants would remain out of prison for three years after release; in fact 75 percent did. Analysis of

Table 1. Differentiated program theories (context-mechanism-outcome) adapted from Pawson & Tilley (1997)

Context	+ New mechanism	= Outcome
Prisoners with little or no previous education with a growing string of convictions—representing a "disadvantaged" background	Modest levels of engagement and success with the program trigger 'habilitation' process in which the inmate experiences self-realization and social acceptability (for the first time)	Lower rates of reconviction
Prisoners serving majority of sentence in maximum security penitentiaries—representing a "criminal" background	High levels of engagement and success with the program trigger "rehabilitation" process in which the inmate experiences changes in powers of self-reflection and reasoning.	Lower rates of reconviction

results for sub-groups tended to support the differentiated program models. For group 1 (prisoners with three or more convictions who entered prison with a school education of grade 10 or below), the intensity of their classroom experiences did not appear to make much difference to their outcomes, once they had achieved the threshold of average intensity. Prisoners in this group who had had average classroom intensity or higher all had about a 50 percent relative improvement. For group 2 (prisoners who had served most or all of their sentences in maximum security), the intensity of their classroom experience appeared to be extremely important, with the greatest improvements in recidivism among prisoners who had the most intensity in their classroom performance. Prisoners in this group who had the most intense classroom experience had an 87 percent relative improvement in their outcomes. While these results supported the differentiated models, they raised more questions about the details of the processes involved. These questions were addressed in the next phase of the evaluation which gathered more data to elaborate the program theories, particularly the processes which led to the observed patterns.

Using The Model To Guide Formative Evaluation And Program Monitoring

The third example used program theory evaluation for formative evaluation of a resiliency program (Rogers & Huebner, 1998). The program worked directly with preadolescent children to prevent school failure, exclusionary education and risk-taking behavior through a mixture of mentoring, advocacy and developing links between school, family, and community.

The program had been seen by students and teachers as generally successful and plans were underway to replicate it in another state. The purpose of the evaluation was to develop a better understanding of for whom, in what ways, and how the program was effective. The evaluation was aimed at developing better information about how the program worked, including the identification of areas where it did not work as well, to guide current and future practitioners.

The focus of the evaluation was decided partly in response to local needs and partly in response to the state of knowledge about prevention programs where there is a need for "clearer specification of intervention procedures and program goals, assessment of program implementation, more follow-up studies, and determining how characteristics of the intervention and participants relate to different outcomes" (Durlak & Wells, 1997, p. 115).

In the first stage of the evaluation, the evaluator worked with program stakeholders (administrators and program staff) to develop a program model which represented links between various program activities and intermediate and ultimate intended outcomes for the program. In the second stage, stakeholders responded to a series of questions about each intended outcome in the program model based on Funnell's (1997) program logic matrix.

Describing "what would it look like if it was successful" is a useful first step before developing measures of program performance. Participants were encouraged to explore the different dimensions of success for each identified outcome and to use language and images that captured the essence of what the program was about. This step captured tacit knowledge about the program which was then used to guide the development and selection of outcome measures.

The process of identifying the factors which influence success offers an opportunity to reflect on and discuss the difficult issues of whether the program might need to change to be more effective. This might involve adding additional program activities to bring about favorable conditions or perhaps targeting the program to operate only in favorable conditions such as with program consumers who are likely to benefit from the program. Such decisions require information about the accuracy of the analysis, the cost and feasibility of expanding program activities, and whether the policy imperative is to work with the most needy program consumers or those who are most likely to benefit. These discussions and decisions are very often reported as being the more important outcomes of a program theory evaluation, and they parallel the positive impacts of evaluability assessment. The matrix of questions about each intended outcome also assisted the evaluation team to identify and address gaps in available information. For example, little information was available about students' engagement with school and their homework patterns, which were two of the outcomes the program addressed.

The final question, about comparisons, focused discussion about what comparisons were appropriate to make, including comparisons with other children, and whether significant change on certain outcomes was likely within the period of a single school year.

The third stage of the evaluation involved gathering data to fill the gaps which had been identified (such as developing a questionnaire about school engagement and homework activity) and reporting it to program staff to assist their work with particular children.

In a subsequent stage, different program models were developed to describe the way the program worked with particular types of children, and these were tested using a range of data about the characteristics of children, program activities, and various outcomes, including individual assessments of children using clinical scales; student survey on homework, after-school behavior, and school attachment; interviews with students, teachers, parents and program staff; student grades and disciplinary records.

In this evaluation, as in others where program theory evaluation has been used for formative evaluation (see Owen, 1998), the reported benefits were an increased clarity about the main priorities of the program, and data collection and analysis which were more focused on providing important and timely information to improve program implementation. The iterative and collaborative process of developing the program model (and subsequent different models for different types of children) enabled program stakeholders to reach a common understanding about the program's intended outcomes and intended ways of reaching these outcomes, and to address uncomfortable questions about program implementation.

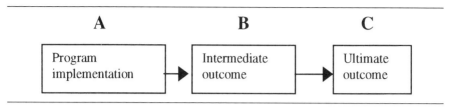

Figure 6. Simple causation model

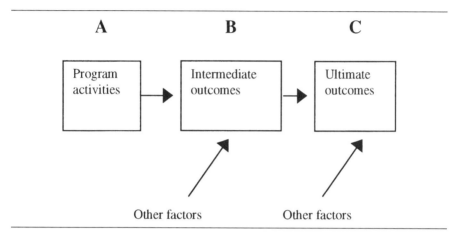

Figure 7. "Other Factors" affecting the achievement of intended outcomes

QUESTIONS AND ANSWERS

A brief introduction such as this to program theory evaluation inevitably raises questions. The more common questions which arise are addressed in this section.

Does Program Theory Oversimplify Causal Relationships?

Program theory diagrams tend to be a collection of boxes and arrows, and it is tempting to consider these to be like wiring diagrams where, if we flick a switch at Point A, it will cause the lights at Points B and C to light. The complex human service programs most commonly evaluated are like this. They tend to have three important additional complexities: the enormous importance of factors external to the program in determining whether or not intended outcomes are achieved, the non-linearity of causal relationships, and the role of program clients in making programs work or not. External factors can be fairly easily incorporated within existing diagrams as in Figure 7. Funnell's (1997) technique of the program logic matrix deals with external factors in just this way.

The non-linearity of many causal relationships, which includes such relationships as vicious circles and virtuous circles where an initial outcome is reinforced through its impact on the system, has been less frequently represented by program theory diagrams. A common educational example of a vicious circle is where a student who is performing poorly loses motivation and stops trying, leading to even poorer performance. A virtuous circle also has a cycle of increasingly strong outcomes but of a desirable sort. These sorts of relationships are important when deciding at which point of a program to measure outcomes. It may be that such outcomes will become even stronger over time. Other types of non-linear causal relationships have been described in organizational learning literature (e.g., Senge, 1992) but few evaluators have used these for program models. A rare example was developed by Owen and Lambert (1994) who used nonlinear models drawn from organizational learning to examine the broader impacts of the introduction of notebook computers across all subjects in a school.

The third issue, representing the role of program clients in making programs work, has been even less frequently addressed in evaluations using program theory. Most program theory diagrams show program clients as passive recipients of treatments which change their lives. Now if the treatment involves swallowing a pill, we might expect certain physiological effects, regardless of the active involvement of the patient, but even in this example we know that the patient's expectations about the treatment can influence its reported impacts. It is even less realistic to describe program clients as passive recipients when the program is endeavoring to bring about permanent change in, for example, students' school behavior or communication strategies of the hearing-impaired—change which requires program clients to learn, apply, and maintain new ways of operating.

In most programs, it is more accurate to say that we understand that A contributes to B which contributes to C. Rather than flicking a switch, A contributes to B and hence C by changing the range of choices available to participants and their capacity to enact these choices. A program is (usually) intended to contribute to changed or maintained behavior through changing the options available to participants and their capacities to choose and enact these choices. Usually programs seek to increase options and capacities; some, such as burglary prevention, seek to reduce them. Pawson & Tilley (1997) have argued that we need to shake off those conceptual habits which allow us to speak of a program "producing outcomes" and to replace them with an imagery which sees the program offering chances which may (or may not) be triggered into action via the subject's capacity to make choices. Social programs involve a continual round of interactions and opportunities and decisions. Regardless of whether they are born of inspiration or ignorance, the subject's choices at each of these junctures will frame the extent and the nature of change. . . . Potential subjects will consider a program (or not), volunteer for it (or not), co-operate closely (or not), stay the course (or not), learn lessons (or not), retain the lessons (or not), apply the lessons (or not). (p. 38)

This understanding of causality in program theory is important because it helps us to look beneath apparent similarity in program implementation to find differences in participants' reactions to the program and in the processes of change within the participants. It is these internal changes that we refer to as "mechanisms" in program theory, although, as we can see, there is nothing mechanistic about them.

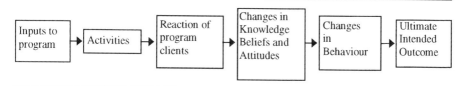

Figure 8. Bennett's Hierarchy: An example of a generic program model

It is important to note that even a complex program model which addressed these three issues would remain a simplification of the causal relationships in a program. We should remember that the program models we create are simply models. If we remember this, they can be useful, despite their simplification.

Who Should Develop A Program Model?

Many evaluators report developing a program model collaboratively with a stake-holder group of program developers and staff. It is also possible for evaluators to develop a model based on reviews of similar programs or relevant social science research. Evaluators can also use a grounded theory approach to identify and describe the implicit model which appears to guide the actual implementation of the program. Patton (1996) has discussed the advantages and disadvantages of these different ways of developing program theory.

Some evaluators have reported success in using generic program models as the basis for a program model, and adapting it to suit a particular program. For example, Bennett's (1982) hierarchy of intended outcomes (see Figure 8) has found many uses beyond the agricultural extension programs for which it was originally developed. Funnell and Lenne (1990) and Funnell (1998) have developed a series of generic program models for particular types of human service programs: advisory, regulatory, case management, direct service provision.

How Complex Should the Program Model Be?

When we look at the program theory diagrams (or narratives) used in different evaluations, it is obvious that they vary from a very simple two-step model to a very complex model. Level of complexity needs to be determined by the purpose of the evaluation. If the evaluation is intended to investigate and document a program which is complex and poorly understood, a complex model will probably be best and can be used to guide decisions about whether it is better to get some information about all mechanisms or to focus on some key mechanisms, and which ones.

For monitoring purposes, the desired level of complexity of the model depends a great deal on the audience for the information. For those with an awareness of the broad scope of a program and the factors affecting it, it may be reasonable to base reporting on a simple model, because the audience will be able to draw on a more detailed implicit model of the program which includes the other factors. But if the information is being reported to an audience which lacks detailed knowledge about the program, but is expected to make decisions about it on the basis of monitoring information (an increasingly common phenomenon), a program model which is too simple risks being misleading. If we only show one of the mechanisms which is necessary for program success, there is a danger that management will encourage program activities which optimize that mechanism at the expense of other mechanisms. This can lead to staff being directed to achieve targets on certain indicators by changing the program in ways which diminish its overall success, a common phenomenon called "goal displacement."

A simple, real-life example demonstrates this problem. An organization that provided telephone advice had a problem with customer satisfaction. Customers were happy with the attention and advice they received once they spoke to an advisor, but had trouble getting through on the phone. Staff were directed to ensure that all telephones were to be answered within three rings. This direction was, at least implicitly, based on a simple program model that involved three stages: telephone answered promptly; accurate, appropriate advice given; followed by customer satisfaction. Since there was no trouble with the quality of the advice being given, it seemed entirely appropriate to seek to optimize the first process. Unfortunately, after this new policy was implemented, customer satisfaction declined even further. Answering calls quickly didn't actually help clients, as their call was then redirected repeatedly or queued for an advisor. And once they got to speak to an advisor, the consultation was constantly interrupted as the advisor broke off to answer telephones.

A more complex program model, such as the one illustrated in Figure 9, would have made it clear that timely pick-up and uninterrupted consultation were both necessary elements for program success, and that optimizing one would have a negative impact on the other if the same people were responsible for both activities. In hindsight, a more complex model such as this was needed which showed that prompt attention and uninterrupted attention were both necessary for the program to work and that it was not possible for the same staff to do both. It also points to the benefit of responsive, retrospective modeling. While it may be usual to create the program model before the program and the evaluation begins, it will often be beneficial to change the model in order to improve both the program and the evaluation.

Can There Be More Than One Program Model?

Different program models may represent alternative plausible explanations for observed outcomes; different mechanisms which operate in certain contexts, such as for particular types of program clients; and different ways of viewing the program which illuminate particular aspects. A single evaluation may or may not be able to investigate each of these different models.

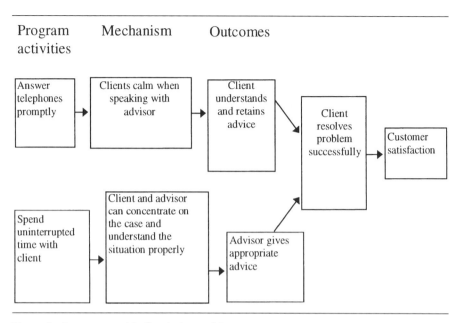

Figure 9. A program model of a telephone advice program

What's the Difference Between A Program Model and a Flowchart of Program Tasks?

A common error is to draw a flowchart of program activities and tasks which finish at the program goal, rather than a program model. For example, consider what we would include in a model for a program which provided delivered meals to elderly people to allow them to remain living in their home. Beginners will sometimes construct a program model of the type illustrated in Figure 10. There are several problems with this diagram, in terms of representing the program theory. To begin with, the "boxes" are sequential, in that they follow in time, but they are not consequential. For example, developing delivery schedules does not help get meals cooked. More importantly, the diagram does not communicate how program activities are understood to lead to intended outcomes. It is fine as a checklist of tasks, but it does not convey what it is about the program activities that seems to help bring about the goal. It would be possible for someone to complete all of these tasks and yet not make the program work.

The model needs to communicate what it is about program activities that are expected to contribute to the desired outcomes. In this program, there are generally understood to be three components which are important for achieving its intended outcomes: the provision of nutritious food, social contact, and informal health monitoring. These components should be represented in the model, as illustrated in Figure 11. Two hints may help create program models which focus on

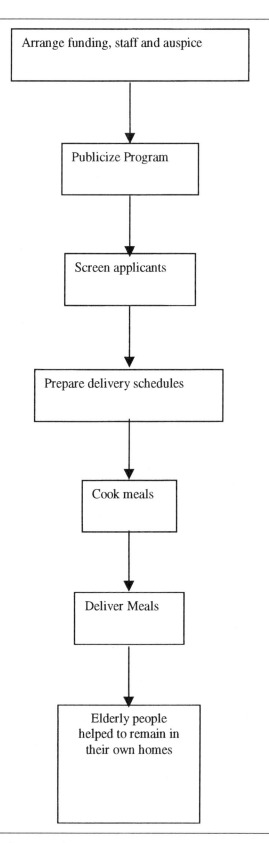

Figure 10. Diagram of program tasks

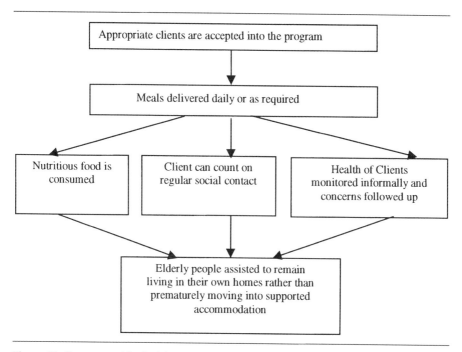

Figure 11. Program model of a delivered meals program showing the program's mechanisms

mechanisms rather than tasks: begin at the ultimate intended outcome and work backwards and focus on the intended changes among program clients. Of course, there is often value in articulating the tasks involved in implementing a program and in checking that these incorporate the important mechanisms. Weiss (1997) has suggested showing separately a model of program implementation and a model of the mechanisms which lead to the intended outcomes.

What Other Types Of Program Models Are There?

The models we described earlier show how a program's activities can contribute to a series of consequential outcomes. At least two other types of model are sometimes used in program theory evaluation. One focuses on modeling an undesirable process (such as committing crime or dropping out of school) where the program is understood as a way of interrupting this process (for example, Harmon, 1992). This type of model seems to be particularly common in criminal justice evaluations, which focus on developing a model of the development of a social problem such as an individual crime (e.g., a burglary) or criminal behavior in an individual (e.g., use of illegal drugs). Previous research is used to identify the factors that contribute to the development of the problem. A program is intended to disrupt this sequence of events. Another type of model focuses on the change process which program participants follow and shows how different activities are understood to help people change from one stage to the next. It is often used in the evaluation of rehabilitation programs (e.g., Batterham, Dunt, & Disler, 1996).

How Should A Program Model Be Represented (and Can A Computer Help)?

Although program theory is sometimes represented through a narrative, it is more common to use a diagram to represent models. Since models are used for different purposes, it is hardly surprising that they have been drawn in different ways, both in terms of the process of drawing them and the shape they take.

The usual shape is some variation on linear—from left to right, from top to bottom, or from bottom to top. Whichever of these is chosen, there is an opportunity to position the boxes purposefully. For example, if two program activities need to occur in order to contribute to a subsequent outcome, the diagram should show this clearly, especially if the activities will potentially make conflicting demands on program staff. The diagram can incorporate parallel boxes which then converge on a consequential outcome. This reminds staff and managers that optimizing just one of these will be counter-productive (e.g., answering phones promptly and being attentive and helpful when taking telephone enquiries). Some evaluators have used circular diagrams, but these tend to obscure the connections between program activities and subsequent outcomes.

When drawing program models, large sheets of blank paper or white boards work well for collaborative development of program models, especially if different colors are used for the different stages. The drawing packages available on computers (either stand-alone or as part of a word processing package) can easily create boxes with text and straight arrows between them. It is harder to make feedback arrows or wavy, less mechanistic-looking arrows with these packages but not impossible. Even more useful would be a layered diagram which, through a system of highlighting, would display the information on the program logic. Specialized computer packages have been developed for particular versions of program theory, including the program logic matrix (Milne and Brooks, 1996) and the logical framework approach (Sartorius, 1996).

Is This Really An Evaluation Model Or A Planning Tool?

Common ways in which program theory is seen to be useful is in helping program developers and staff to improve program design before or during implementation, helping them to identify gaps in their logic and additional program activities that are required, and providing program staff with a mental map for reflecting on their work and prioritizing activities. While such outcomes are very satisfying for evaluators, they raise the very real danger that the activity will end there. Developing program models is hard and time-consuming work and once they have been developed there is often considerable pressure to stop and allow the program staff to get back to work. But to get the most benefit from program theory we cannot afford to stop here. The evaluation work remains to be done.

How Can A Program Model Evaluation Investigate Unintended Outcomes?

The choice of a program theory evaluation approach is no guarantee that the evaluation will support organizational learning. As Turner (1998) has pointed out, there is a very real danger that such an evaluation will "overlook unanticipated program consequences through excessively narrow reliance on a priori theories of program interventions." Weiss' (1997) technique of negative program theory addresses this particular concern and would be a useful addition to the repertoire of techniques. It involves working with program stakeholders to develop a model of how the program might be implemented as intended but produce undesirable outcomes. For example, increases in teacher salaries, intended to attract a better pool of applicants, may instead lead to fewer vacancies as existing teachers choose to remain in their positions (which may be a negative outcome if these teachers are less competent than those who would take their places).

Can Program Theory Evaluation Be Used With Other Evaluation Models?

The choice of program theory evaluation does not define the type of data which will be collected and analyzed nor the type of design. It can therefore be combined with evaluation models which focus on a particular type of design or data collection, such as an experimental or naturalistic design. It is not compatible with models which are not concerned with causal questions, such as goal-free or cost-benefit evaluations.

Why Is Program Theory Evaluation Not More Widely Used?

Given the paucity of research into evaluation practice, we can only speculate why program theory is not more widely or successfully used. Three reasons in particular should be addressed. One common reason is that so many programs lack a program model which has either been articulated or can readily be articulated (e.g., Weiss, 1996). This appears to be more common for policies such as providing Internet access to schools which are often introduced by policymakers with little understanding of how they will work. Evaluators who work with practitioners to articulate the program theory of their project are less likely to report this as a problem (e.g., Milne, 1993). A more intransigent problem might be the quality of the program models. When exposed in a diagram, program models can seem overly simplistic and deterministic. With increasing use, we might expect models to be more carefully constructed.

The second problem is that as program models become more complex, the prospect of basing an evaluation on them becomes more daunting in terms of design and data collection and analysis. Unless exceptionally well resourced, a single evaluation is unlikely to be able to test all the mechanisms identified in a model. The solution to this problem is for individual evaluations to examine a few pieces of a program jigsaw in ways that can be aggregated or synthesized across many evaluations. Pawson and Tilley (1997) have suggested that evaluations report the particular configuration of context-mechanism-outcome which they are investigating so that evaluations of similar programs or similar mechanisms can be readily identified, retrieved, and cumulated.

The third barrier, the apparent disinterest of many evaluation audiences in questions about causes, and particularly about mitigated success, is more intransigent. Program theory evaluations are more likely to provide some information about hard questions than definitive answers about narrow questions. For some, this is not attractive.

When Is Program Theory Evaluation Most Appropriate?

All programs are based on a theory of how the program activities will lead to particular outcomes, although the theory is sometimes implicit rather than explicit, and incomplete or contradictory. But we don't always need to articulate a theory and use it to guide the evaluation, as we do in program theory evaluation.

Given the additional effort required to develop a model of how the program works, the question arises "Why not just look at whether or not the program works?" Certainly, there are times when it is perfectly reasonable to "just" look at the outcomes for people who have participated in a program and to compare these to the outcomes of a similar group who didn't receive the program. But for those who work in complex human service programs, there are many times when measuring outcomes is not enough. The following considerations indicate when program theory evaluation is likely to be appropriate.

- When a program is very complex, we need to know what "it" is before we can tell whether "it" works and in order to get "it" to work next time. And a long detailed description is not what we need for replication; we need some way of establishing which aspects are essential features and which can be varied while still achieving intended outcomes.
- When a program's effectiveness depends on characteristics of the participants or the context in which it is implemented, we need to have some way of predicting its likely appropriateness in a new situation.
- When a program's outcomes are long-term, we need interim measures which give accurate indications of whether we are on track.
- And when we are trying to improve a program, it is helpful to have something other than blind trial-and-error to guide our efforts.

CONCLUSION

Program theory evaluation is not an easy type of evaluation to do successfully. Skills in conceptualization are required, as well as, skills in measurement and in helping people articulate tacit knowledge. It often raises harder and more threatening questions than can be satisfactorily answered in any one evaluation. But it can lead to better information about programs that is important for replication or for improvement, and which is unlikely to be produced through other types of program evaluation. In many cases, these advantages are worth the extra trouble.

III. IMPROVEMENT/ACCOUNTABILITY-ORIENTED EVALUATION MODELS

The second set of evaluation models are labeled **Improvement/Accountability-Oriented Evaluation Models**. Studies following these models are designed primarily to assess and/or improve a program's merit and worth. Such studies are expansive and seek comprehensiveness in considering the full range of questions and criteria needed to assess a program's value. Often they employ the assessed needs of a program's stakeholders as the foundational criteria for assessing the program's merit and worth. They seek to examine the full range of appropriate technical and economic criteria for judging program plans and operations. They also look for all relevant outcomes, not just those keyed to program objectives. Such studies sometimes are overly ambitious in trying to provide broad-based assessments leading to definitive, documented, and unimpeachable judgments of merit and worth. Typically, they must use multiple qualitative and quantitative assessment methods to provide cross-checks on findings. In general, the Improvement/Accountability-Oriented Evaluation Models conform closely to this book's definition of evaluation.

14. COURSE IMPROVEMENT THROUGH EVALUATION

LEE J. CRONBACH

The national interest in improving education has generated several highly important projects attempting to improve curricula, particularly at the secondary-school level. In conferences of directors of course content improvement programs sponsored by the National Science Foundation, questions about evaluation are frequently raised.[1] Those who inquire about evaluation have various motives, ranging from sheer scientific curiosity about classroom events to a desire to assure a sponsor that money has been well spent. While the curriculum developers sincerely wish to use the skills of evaluation specialists, I am not certain that they have a clear picture of what evaluation can do and should try to do. And, on the other hand, I am becoming convinced that some techniques and habits of thought of the evaluation specialist are ill-suited to current curriculum studies. To serve these studies, what philosophy and methods of evaluation are required? And, particularly, how must we depart from the familiar doctrines and rituals of the testing game?

DECISIONS SERVED BY EVALUATION

To draw attention to its full range of functions, we may define evaluation broadly as the *collection and use of information to make decisions about an educational program*. This program may be a set of instructional materials distributed nationally, the instruc-

From *Teachers College Record*, 64 (1963), 672–83. Copyright 1963, Teachers College, Columbia University, New York. Reprinted with permission of the author and publisher using an edited version found in R. W. Heath, *New Curricula*. Harper & Row, 1964, at Professor Cronbach's request.

tional activities of a single school, or the educational experiences of a single pupil. Many types of decision are to be made, and many varieties of information are useful. It becomes immediately apparent that evaluation is a diversified activity and that no one set of principles will suffice for all situations. But measurement specialists have so concentrated upon one process—the preparation of pencil-and-paper achievement tests for assigning scores to individual pupils—that the principles pertinent to that process have somehow become enshrined as *the* principles of evaluation. "Tests," we are told, "should fit the content of the curriculum." Also, "only those evaluation procedures should be used that yield reliable scores." These and other hallowed principles are not entirely appropriate to evaluation for course improvement. Before proceeding to support this contention, I wish to distinguish among purposes of evaluation and relate them to historical developments in testing and curriculum making.

We may separate three types of decisions for which evaluation is used:

1. Course improvement: deciding what instructional materials and methods are satisfactory and where change is needed.
2. Decisions about individuals: identifying the needs of the pupil for the sake of planning his instruction, judging pupil merit for purposes of selection and grouping, acquainting the pupil with his own progress and deficiencies.
3. Administrative regulation: judging how good the school system is, how good individual teachers are, etc.

Course improvement is set apart by its broad temporal and geographical reference; it involves the modification of recurrently used materials and methods. Developing a standard exercise to overcome a misunderstanding would be course improvement, but deciding whether a certain pupil should work through that exercise would be an individual decision. Administrative regulation likewise is local in effect, whereas an improvement in a course is likely to be pertinent wherever the course is offered.

It was for the sake of course improvement that systematic evaluation was first introduced. When that famous muckraker Joseph Rice gave the same spelling test in a number of American schools and so gave the first impetus to the educational testing movement, he was interested in evaluating a curriculum. Crusading against the extended spelling drills that then loomed large in the school schedule—"the spelling grind"—Rice collected evidence of their worthlessness so as to provoke curriculum revision. As the testing movement developed, however, it took on a different function.

The greatest expansion of systematic achievement testing occurred in the 1920s. At that time, the content of any course was taken pretty much as established and beyond criticism, save for small shifts of topical emphasis. At the administrator's direction, standard tests covering this curriculum were given to assess the efficiency of the teacher or the school system. Such administrative testing fell into disfavor when used injudiciously and heavy-handedly in the 1920s and 1930s. Administrators and accrediting agencies fell back upon descriptive features of the school program in judging adequacy. Instead of collecting direct evidence of educational impact, they judged schools in terms of size of budget, student-staff ratio, square feet of laboratory space, and the number of advanced credits accumulated by the teacher. This tide, it appears, is about to turn. On many university campuses, administrators wanting to know more about their product are installing "operations research offices." Testing directed toward quality control seems likely to increase in the lower schools as well, as is most forcefully indicated by the statewide testing just ordered by the California legislature.

After 1930 or thereabouts, tests were given almost exclusively for judgments about individuals: to select students for advanced training, to assign marks within a class, and to diagnose individual competences and deficiencies. For any such decisions, one wants precise and valid comparisons of one individual with other individuals or with a standard. Much of test theory and test technology has been concerned with making measurements precise. Important though precision is for most decisions about individuals, I shall argue that in evaluating courses we need not struggle to obtain precise scores for individuals.

While measurers have been well content with the devices used to make scores precise, they have been less complacent about validity. Prior to 1935, the pupil was examined mostly on factual knowledge and mastery of fundamental skills. Tyler's research and writings of that period developed awareness that higher mental processes are not evoked by simple factual tests and that instruction that promotes factual knowledge may not promote—indeed, may interfere with—other more important educational outcomes. Tyler, Lindquist, and their students demonstrated that tests can be designed to measure general educational outcomes, such as ability to comprehend scientific method. Whereas a student can prepare for a factual test only through a course of study that includes the facts tested, many different courses of study may promote the same *general* understandings and attitudes. In evaluating today's new curricula, it will clearly be important to appraise the student's general educational growth, which curriculum developers say is more important than mastery of the specific lessons presented. Note, for example, that the Biological Sciences Curriculum Study offers three courses with substantially different "subject matter" as alternative routes to much the same educational ends.

Although some instruments capable of measuring general outcomes were prepared during the 1930s, they were never very widely employed. The prevailing philosophy of the curriculum, particularly among progressives, called for developing a program to fit local requirements, capitalizing on the capacities and experiences of local pupils. The faith of the 1920s in a "standard" curriculum was replaced by a faith that the best learning experience would result from teacher-pupil planning in each classroom. Since each teacher or each class could choose different content and even different objectives, this philosophy left little place for standard testing.

Many evaluation specialists came to see test development as a strategy for training the teacher in service, so that the process of test making came to be valued more than the test—or the test data—that resulted. The following remarks by Bloom (1961) are representative of a whole school of thought:[2]

The criterion for determining the quality of a school and its educational functions would be the extent to which it achieves the objectives it has set for itself. . . . (Our experiences suggest that unless the school has translated the objectives into specific and operational definitions, little is likely to be done about the objectives. They remain pious hopes and platitudes.) . . . Participation of the teaching staff in selecting as well as constructing evaluation instruments has resulted in improved instruments on one hand, and, on the other hand, it has resulted in clarifying the objectives of instruction and in making them real and meaningful to teachers. . . . When teachers have actively participated in defining objectives and in selecting or constructing evaluation instruments, they return to the learning problems with great vigor and remarkable creativity. . . . Teachers who have become committed to a set of educational objectives which they thoroughly understand respond by developing a variety of learning experiences which are as diverse and as complex as the situation requires.

Thus "evaluation" becomes a local, and beneficial, teacher-training activity. The benefit is attributed to thinking about the data to collect. Little is said about the actual use of test results; one has the impression that when test-making ends, the test itself is forgotten. Certainly there is little enthusiasm for refining tests so that they can be used in other schools, for to do so would be to rob those teachers of the benefits of working out their own objectives and instruments.

Bloom and Tyler describe both curriculum making and evaluation as integral parts of classroom instruction, which is necessarily decentralized. This outlook is far from that of course improvement. The current national curriculum studies assume that curriculum making can be centralized. They prepare materials to be used in much the same way by teachers everywhere. It is assumed that having experts draft materials and revising these after tryout produces better instructional activities than the local teacher would be likely to devise. In this context, it seems wholly appropriate to have most tests prepared by a central staff and to have results returned to that staff to guide further course improvement.

When evaluation is carried out in the service of course improvement, the chief aim is to ascertain what effects the course has—that is, what changes it produces in pupils. This is not to inquire merely whether the course is effective or ineffective. Outcomes of instruction are multidimensional, and a satisfactory investigation will map out the effects of the course along these dimensions separately. To agglomerate many types of post-course performance into a single score is a mistake, since failure to achieve one objective is masked by access in another direction. Moreover, since a composite score embodies (and usually conceals) judgments about the importance of the various outcomes, only a report that treats the outcomes separately can be useful to educators who have different value hierarchies.

The greatest service evaluation can perform is to identify aspects of the course where revision is desirable. Those responsible for developing a course would like to present evidence that their course is effective. They are intrigued by the idea of having an "independent testing agency" render a judgment on their product, but to call in the evaluator only upon the completion of course development, to confirm what has been done, is to offer him a menial role and make meager use of his services. To be influential in course improvement, evidence must become available midway in curriculum development, not in the home stretch when the developer is naturally reluctant to tear open a supposedly finished body of materials and techniques. Evaluation, used to improve the course while it is still fluid, contributes more to improvement of education than evaluation used to appraise a product already placed on the market.

Insofar as possible, evaluation should be used to understand how the course produces its effects and what parameters influence its effectiveness. It is important to learn, for example, that the outcome of programed instruction depends very much upon the attitude of the teacher; indeed, this may be more important than to learn that on the average such instruction produces slightly better or worse results than conventional instruction.

Hopefully, evaluation studies will go beyond reporting on this or that course and help us to understand educational learning. Such insight will in the end contribute to the development of all courses rather than just of the course under test. In certain of the new curricula, there are data to suggest that aptitude measures correlate much less with end-of-course achievement than they do with achievement on early units (Ferris, 1962). This finding is not well-confirmed, but is highly significant if true. If it is true for the new curricula and only for them it has one implication; if the same effect appears in traditional courses, it means something else. Either way, it provides food-for-thought for teachers, counselors, and theorists. Evaluation studies should generate knowledge about the nature of the abilities that constitute educational goals. Twenty years after the Eight-Year Study of the Progressive Education Association, its testing techniques are in good repute, but we still know very little about what these instruments measure. Consider "Applications of Principles in Science." Is this in any sense a unitary ability? Or has the able student only mastered certain principles one-by-one? Is the ability demonstrated on a test of this sort more prognostic of any later achievement than is factual knowledge? Such questions ought to receive substantial attention, though to the makers of any one course they are of only peripheral interest.

The aim of comparing one course with another should not dominate plans for evaluation. To be sure, decisionmakers have to choose between courses, and any evaluation report will be interpreted in part comparatively. But formally designed experiments pitting one course against another are rarely definitive enough to justify their cost. Differences between average test scores resulting from different courses are usually small, relative to the wide differences among and within classes taking the same course. At best, an experiment never does more than compare the present version of one course with the present version of another. A major effort to bring the losing contender nearer to perfection would be very likely to reverse the verdict of the experiment.

Any failure to equate the classes taking the competing courses will jeopardize the interpretation of an experiment, and such failures are almost inevitable. In testing a drug, we know that valid results cannot be obtained without a double-blind control, in which the doses for half the subjects are inert placebos; the placebo and the drug look alike, so that neither doctor nor patient knows who is receiving medication.

Without this control, the results are useless even when the state of the patient is checked by completely objective indices. In an educational experiment, it is difficult to keep pupils unaware that they are an experimental group, and it is quite impossible to neutralize the biases of the teacher as those of the doctor are neutralized in the double-blind design. It is thus never certain whether any observed advantage is attributable to the educational innovation, as such, or to the greater energy that teachers and students put forth when a method is fresh and experimental. Some have contended that any course, even the most excellent, loses much of its potency as soon as success enthrones it as the traditional method.[3]

Since group comparisons give equivocal results, I believe that a formal study should be designed primarily to determine the post-course performance of a well-described group, with respect to many important objectives and side effects. Ours is a problem like that of the engineer examining a new automobile. He can set himself the task of defining its performance characteristics and its dependability. It would be merely distracting to put his question in the form: "Is this car better or worse than the competing brand?" Moreover, in an experiment where the treatments compared differ in a dozen respects, no understanding is gained from the fact that the experiment shows a numerical advantage in favor of the new course. No one knows which of the ingredients is responsible for the advantage. More analytic experiments are much more useful than field trials applying markedly dissimilar treatments to different groups. Small-scale, well-controlled studies can profitably be used to compare alternative versions of the same course; in such a study the differences between treatments are few enough and well-enough defined that the results have explanatory value.

The three purposes—course improvement, decisions about individuals, and administrative regulation—call for measurement procedures having somewhat different qualities. When a test will be used to make an administrative judgment on the individual teacher, it is necessary to measure thoroughly and with conspicuous fairness; such testing, if it is to cover more than one outcome, becomes extremely time-consuming. In judging a course, however, one can make satisfactory interpretations from data collected on a sampling basis, with no pretense of measuring thoroughly the accomplishments of any one class. A similar point is to be made about testing for decisions about individuals. A test of individuals must be conspicuously fair and extensive enough to provide a dependable score for each person. But if the performance will not influence the fate of the individual, we can ask him to perform tasks for which the course has not directly prepared him, and we can use techniques that would be prohibitively expensive if applied in a manner thorough enough to measure each person reliably.

METHODS OF EVALUATION

Range of Methods

Evaluation is too often visualized as the administration of a formal test, an hour or so in duration, at the close of a course. But there are many other methods for examining pupil performance, and pupil attainment is not the only basis for appraising a course.

It is quite appropriate to ask scholars whether the statements made in the course are consistent with the best contemporary knowledge. This is a sound, even a necessary, procedure. One might go on to evaluate the pedagogy of the new course by soliciting opinions, but here there is considerable hazard. If the opinions are based on some preconception about teaching method, the findings will be control versial and very probably misleading. There are no theories of pedagogy so well established that one can say, without tryout, what will prove educative.

One can accept the need for a pragmatic test of the curriculum and still employ opinions as a source of evidence. During the tryout stages of curriculum making one relies heavily on the teachers' reports of pupil accomplishment—"Here they had trouble"; "This they found dull"; "Here they needed only half as many exercises as were provided"; etc. This is behavior observation, even though unsystematic, and it is of great value. The reason for shifting to systematic observation is that this is more impartial, more public, and sometimes more penetrating. While I bow to the historian or mathematician as a judge of the technical soundness of course content, I do not agree that the experienced history or mathematics teacher who tries out a course gives the best possible judgment of its effectiveness. Scholars have too often deluded themselves about their effectiveness as teachers— in particular, they have too often accepted parroting of words as evidence of insight—for their unaided judgment to be trusted. Systematic observation is costly and introduces some delay between the moment of teaching and the feedback of results. Hence, systematic observation will never be the curriculum developer's sole source of evidence. Systematic data collection becomes profitable in the intermediate stages of curriculum development, after the more obvious bugs in early drafts have been dealt with.

The approaches to evaluation include process studies, proficiency measures, attitude measures, and follow-up studies. A process study is concerned with events taking place in the classroom, proficiency and attitude measures with changes observed in pupils, and follow-up studies with the later careers of those who participated in the course.

The follow-up study comes closest to observing ultimate educational contributions, but the completion of such a study is so far removed in time from the initial instruction that it is of minor value in improving the course or explaining its effects. The follow-up study differs strikingly from the other types of evaluation study in one respect. I have already expressed the view that evaluation should be primarily concerned with the effects of the course under study rather than with comparisons of courses. That is to say, I would emphasize departures of attained results from the ideal, differences in apparent effectiveness of different parts of the course, and differences from item to item. All these suggest places where the course could be strengthened; but this view cannot be applied to the follow-up study, which appraises effects of the course as a whole and which has very little meaning unless outcomes can be compared with some sort of base rate. Suppose we find that 65 percent of the boys graduating from an experimental curriculum enroll in scientific and technical majors in college. We cannot judge whether this is a high or low figure save by comparing it with the rate among boys who have not had this course. In a follow-up study, it is necessary to obtain data on a control group equated at least crudely to the experimental cases on the obvious demographic variables.

Despite the fact that such groups are hard to equate and that follow-up data do not tell much about how to improve the course, such studies should have a place in research on the new curricula, whose national samples provide unusual opportunity for follow-up that can shed light on important questions. One obvious type of follow-up study traces the student's success in a college course founded upon the high school course. One may examine the student's grades or ask him what topics in the college course he found himself poorly prepared for. It is hoped that some of the new science and mathematics courses will arouse greater interest than usual among girls; whether this hope is well-founded can be checked by finding out what majors and what electives these ex-students pursue in college. Career choices likewise merit attention. Some proponents of the new curricula would like to see a greater flow of talent into basic science as distinct from technology, while others would regard this as potentially disastrous; but no one would regard facts about this flow as lacking significance.

Attitudes are prominent among the outcomes that course developers are concerned with. Attitudes are meanings or beliefs, not mere expressions of approval or disapproval. One's attitude toward science includes ideas about the matters on which a scientist can be an authority—about the benefits to be obtained from moon shots and studies of monkey mothers, and about depletion of natural resources. Equally important is the match between self-concept and concept of the field: what roles does science offer a person like me? Would I want to marry a scientist? and so on. Each learning activity also contributes to attitudes that reach far beyond any one subject, such as the pupil's sense of his own competence and desire to learn.

Attitudes can be measured in many ways; the choices revealed in follow-up studies, for example, are pertinent evidence. But measurement usually takes the form of direct or indirect questioning. Interviews, questionnaires, and the like are quite valuable when not trusted blindly. Certainly, we should take seriously any undesirable opinion expressed by a substantial proportion of graduates of a course (e.g., the belief that the scientist speaks with peculiar authority on political and ethical questions, or the belief that mathematics is a finished subject rather than a field for current investigation).

Attitude questionnaires have been much criticized because they are subject to distortion, especially where the student hopes to gain by being less than frank. Particularly if the questions are asked in a context far removed from the experimental course, the returns are likely to be trustworthy. Thus, a general questionnaire administered through homerooms (or required English courses) may include questions about liking for various subjects and activities; these same questions administered by the mathematics teacher would give much less trustworthy data on attitudes toward mathematics. While students may give reports more favorable than their true beliefs, this distortion is not likely to be greater one year than another or greater among students who take an experimental course than among those who do not. In group averages, many distortions balance out. But questionnaires insufficiently valid for individual testing can be used in evaluating curricula, both because the student has little motive to distort and because the evaluator is comparing averages rather than individuals.

For measuring proficiency, techniques are likewise varied. Standardized tests are useful, but for course evaluation it makes sense to assign *different* questions to different students. Giving each student in a population of 500 the same test of 50 questions will provide far less information to the course developer than drawing for each student 50 questions from a pool of, say, 700. The latter plan determines the mean success of about 75 representative students on every one of the 700 items; the former reports on only 50 items (See Lord, 1962). Essay tests and open-ended questions, generally too expensive to use for routine evaluation, can profitably be employed to appraise certain abilities. One can go further and observe individuals or groups as they attack a research problem in the laboratory or work through some other complex problem. Since it is necessary to test only a representative sample of pupils, costs are not as serious a consideration as in routine testing. Additional aspects of proficiency testing will be considered below.

Process measures have especial value in showing how a course can be improved, because they examine what happens during instruction. In the development of programed instructional materials, for example, records are collected showing how many pupils miss each item presented; any piling up of errors implies a need for better explanation or a more gradual approach to a difficult topic. Immediately after showing a teaching film, one can interview students, perhaps asking them to describe a still photograph taken from the film. Misleading presentations, ideas given insufficient emphasis, and matters left unclear will be identified by such methods. Similar interviews can disclose what pupils take away from a laboratory activity or a discussion. A process study might turn attention to what the teacher does in the classroom. In those curricula that allow choice of topics, for example, it is worthwhile to find out which topics are chosen and how much time is allotted to each. A log of class activities (preferably recorded by a pupil rather than the teacher) will show which of the techniques suggested in a summer institute are actually adopted, and which form part of the new course only in the developer's fantasies.

Measurement of Proficiency

I have indicated that I consider item data to be more important than test scores. The total score may give confidence in a curriculum or give rise to discouragement, but it tells very little about how to produce further improvement. And, as Ferris (1962) has noted, such scores are quite likely to be mis- or overinterpreted. The score on a single item or on a problem that demands several responses in succession is more likely than the test score to suggest how to alter the presentation. When we accept item scores as useful, we need no longer think of evaluation as a one-shot, end-of-year operation. Proficiency can be measured at any moment, with particular interest attaching to those items most related to the recent lessons. Other items calling for general abilities can profitably be administered repeatedly during the course (perhaps to different random samples of pupils) so that we can begin to learn when and from what experiences change in these abilities comes.

In course evaluation, we need not be much concerned about making measuring instruments fit the curriculum. However startling this declaration may seem and however contrary to the principles of evaluation for other purposes, this must be our position if we want to know what changes a course produces in the pupil. An ideal evaluation would include measures of all the types of proficiency that might reasonably be desired in the area in question, not just the selected outcomes to which this curriculum directs substantial attention. If you wish only to know how well a curriculum is achieving *its* objectives, you fit the test to the curriculum; but if you wish to know how well the curriculum is serving the national interest, you measure all outcomes that might be worth striving for. One of the new mathematics courses might disavow any attempt to teach numerical trigonometry and, indeed might discard nearly all computational work. It is still perfectly reasonable to as how well graduates of the course can compute and can solve right triangles. Even the course developers went so far as to contend that computational skill is not proper objective of secondary instruction, they will encounter educators and laymen who do not share their view. If it can be shown that students who come through the new course are fairly proficient in computation despite the lack of direct teaching, the doubters will be reassured. If not, the evidence makes clear how much is being sacrificed. Similarly, when the biologists offer alternative courses emphasizing microbiology and ecology, it is fair to ask how well the graduate of one course can understand issues treated in the other. Ideal evaluation in mathematics will collect evidence on all the abilities toward which a mathemation course might reasonably aim, likewise in biology, English, or any other subject.

Ferris states that the ACS Chemistry Test, however well constructed, inadequate for evaluating the new CBA and CHEM programs, because it does not cover their objectives. One can agree with this without regarding the ACS test inappropriate to use with these courses. It is important that this test not stand aline as the sole evaluation device. It will tell us something worth knowing, namely, just how much "conventional" knowledge the new curriculum does or does not provide. The curriculum developers deliberately planned to sacrifice some of the conventional attainments and have nothing to fear from this measurment, if it competently interpreted (particularly if data are examined item-by-item).

The demand that tests be closely matched to the aims of a course reflect awareness that examinations of the usual sort "determine what is taught." questions are known in advance, students give more attention to learning the answers than to learning other aspects of the course. This is not necessarily detrimental. Wherever it is critically important to master certain content, the knowledge that it will be tested produces a desirable concentration of effort. On the other hand, learning the answer to a set question is by no means the same acquiring understanding of whatever topic that question represents. There is therefore, a possible advantage in using "secure" tests for course evaluation. Security is achieved only at a price: one must prepare new tests each year a cannot make before-and-after comparisons with the same items. One would how that the use of different items with different students and the fact that there is low incentive to coach when no judgment is to be passed on the pupils and the teacher would make security a less critical problem.

The distinction between factual tests and tests of higher mental processes, is elaborated for example in the *Taxonomy of Educational Objectives*, is of some value in planning tests, although classifying items as measures of knowledge, application, original problem solving, etc., is difficult and often impossible. Whether a given response represents rote recall of reasoning depends upon how the pupil has been taught, not solely upon the question asked. One might, for example, describe a biological environment and ask for predictions regarding the effect of a certain intervention. Students who had never dealt with ecological data would succeed or fail according to their general ability to reason about complex events; those who had studied ecological biology would be more likely to succeed, reasoning from specific principles; and those who had lived in such an ecology or read about it might answer successfully on the basis of memory. We rarely, therefore, will want to test whether a student *knows* or *does not know* certain material. Knowledge is a matter of degree. Two persons may be acquainted with the same facts or principles, but one will be more expert in his understanding, better able to cope with inconsistent data, irrelevant sources of confusion, and apparent exceptions to the principle. To measure intellectual competence is to measure depth, connectedness, and applicability of knowledge.

Too often, test questions are course-specific, stated in such a way that only the person who has been specifically taught to understand what is being asked for can answer the question. Such questions can usually be identified by their use of conventions. Some conventions are commonplace, and we can assume that all the pupils we test will know them. But a biology test that describes a metabolic process with the aid of the symbol presents difficulties for students who can think through the scientific question about equilibrium but are unfamiliar with the symbol. A trigonometry problem that requires use of a trigonometric table is unreasonable, unless we want to test familiarity with the conventional names of functions. The same problem in numerical trigonometry can be cast in a form clear to the average pupil *entering* high school; if necessary, the tables of functions can be presented along with a comprehensible explanation. So stated, the problem becomes course-independent. It is fair to ask whether graduates of the experimental course can solve such problems, not previously encountered, whereas it is pointless to ask whether they can answer questions whose language is strange to them. To be sure, knowledge of a certain terminology is a significant objective of instruction; but, for course evaluation, testing of terminology should very likely be separated from testing of other understandings. To appraise understanding of processes and relations, the fair question is one comprehensible to a pupil who has not taken the course. This is not to say that he should know the answer or the procedure to follow in attaining the answer, but he should understand what he is being asked. Such course-independent questions can be used as standard instruments to investigate any instructional program.

Pupils who have not studied a topic usually will be less facile than those who have studied it. Graduates of my hypothetical mathematics course will take longer to solve trigonometry problems than will those who have studied trigonometry. But speed and power should not be confused; in intellectual studies, power, is almost always of greatest importance. If the course equips the pupil to deal correctly, even though haltingly, with a topic not studied, we can expect him to develop facility later when that topic comes before him frequently.

The chief objective in many of the new curricula seems to be to develop aptitude for mastering new materials in the field. A biology course cannot cover all valuable biological content, but it may reasonably aspire to equip the pupil to understand descriptions of unfamiliar organisms, to comprehend a new theory and the reasoning behind it, and to plan an experiment to test a new hypothesis. This is transfer of learning. It has been insufficiently recognized that there are two types of transfer. The two types shade into one another, being arranged on a continuum of immediacy of effect; we can label the more immediate pole *applicational transfer*, and speak of slower-acting effects as *gains in aptitude* (Ferguson, 1954).

Nearly all educational research on transfer has tested immediate performance on a partly new task. We teach pupils to solve equations in x and include in the test equations stated in a or z. We teach the principles of ecological balance by refer-ring to forests and, as a transfer test, ask what effect pollution will have on the pop-ulation of a lake. We describe an experiment not presented in the text and ask the student to discuss possible interpretations and needed controls. Any of these tests can be administered in short time. But the more significant type of transfer may be the increased ability to learn in a particular field. There is very likely a considerable difference between the ability to draw conclusions from a neatly finished experi-ment and the ability to tease insight out of the disordered and inconsistent obser-vations that come with continuous laboratory work on a problem. The student who masters a good biology course may become better able to comprehend certain types of theory and data, so that he gains more from a subsequent year of study in eth-nology; we do not measure this gain by testing his understanding of short passages in ethnology. There has rarely been an appraisal of ability to work through a problem situation or a complex body of knowledge over a period of days or months. Despite the practical difficulties that attend an attempt to measure the effect of a course on a person's subsequent learning, such *learning to learn* is so important that a serious effort should be made to detect such effects and to understand how they may be fostered.

The technique of programed instruction may be adopted to appraise learning ability. One might, for example, test the student's rate of mastery of a self-contained, programed unit on heat or some other topic not studied. If the program is truly self-contained, every student can master it, but the one with greater scientific comprehension hopefully will make fewer errors and progress faster. The program might be prepared in several logically complete versions, ranging from one with very small steps to one with minimal internal redundancy, on the hypothesis that the better-educated student could cope with the less redundant program. Moreover, he might prefer its greater elegance.

CONCLUSION

Old habits of thought and long-established techniques are poor guides to the evaluation required for course improvement. Traditionally, educational measurement has been chiefly concerned with producing fair and precise scores for comparing individuals; educational experimentation has been concerned with comparing score averages of competing courses; but course evaluation calls for description of outcomes. This description should be made on the broadest possible scale, even at the sacrifice of superficial fairness and precision.

Course evaluation should ascertain what changes a course produces and should identify aspects of the course that need revision. The outcomes observed should include general outcomes ranging far beyond the content of the curriculum itself: attitudes, careers choices, general understandings and intellectual powers, and aptitude for further learning in the field. Analysis of performance on single items or types of problems is more informative than analysis of composite scores. It is not necessary or desirable to give the same test to all pupils; rather, as many questions as possible should be given, each to a different moderate-sized sample of pupils. Costly techniques, such as interviews and essay tests, can be applied profitably to samples of pupils, whereas testing everyone would be out of the question.

Asking the right questions about educational outcomes can do much to improve educational effectiveness. Even if the right data are collected, evaluation will have contributed too little if it only places a seal of approval on certain courses and casts others into disfavor. Evaluation is a fundamental part of curriculum development, not an appendage. Its job is to collect facts the course developer can and will use to do a better job and facts from which a deeper understanding of the educational process will emerge.

NOTES

1. My comments on these questions and on certain more significant questions that *should* have been raised, have been greatly clarified by the reactions of several of these directors and colleagues in evaluation to a draft of this paper. J. Thomas Hastings and Robert Heath have been especially helpful. What I voice, however, are my personal views, deliberately more provocative than *authoritative*.

2. Elsewhere, Bloom's paper discusses evaluation for the new curricula. Attention may also be drawn to Tyler's highly pertinent paper (1951).

3. The interested reader can find further striking parallels between curriculum studies and drug research (see Modell, 1963).

15. EVALUATION IDEOLOGIES

MICHAEL SCRIVEN

New disciplines are often wracked by ideological disputes. In this respect, evaluation is no different from some of the other new entries in the disciplinary sweepstakes—in recent decades these include sociobiology, computer science, feminist theory, non-formal logic, serious parapsychology, ethnic and policy studies, ecobiology, molecular biology, structural linguistics, computerized mathematics, physiological and cognitive psychology, psychohistory, and others. There is nothing new about this, as some reflection on the history of evolutionary theory and astronomy will remind us. But it is hard to achieve perspective on any revolution of which we are part. The proliferation of evaluation models is a sign of the ferment of the field and the seriousness of the methodological problems which evaluation encounters. In this sense, it is a hopeful sign. But it makes a balanced overview very hard to achieve; one might as well try to describe the "typical animal" or the "ideal animal" in a zoo.

Evaluation is a peculiarly self-referent subject. In this respect, it is like the sociology of science; that is, the sociology of science includes the sociology of the sociology of science and, hence, is self-referent. Similarly, systematic objective evaluation—the kind with which the discipline is concerned—is not restricted to the evaluation of microscopes. If it were, it would not include itself. But evaluation applies to the process and products of all serious human endeavor and hence to evaluation. The application of evaluation to itself is sometimes called meta evaluation, and it has generated the standards for educational program evaluation that are summarized and discussed elsewhere in this book.

D.L. Stufflebeam, G.F. Madaus and T. Kellaghan (eds.). EVALUATION MODELS. Copyright © 2000. Kluwer Academic Publishers. Boston. All rights reserved.

Just as it is especially disappointing that the sociology of science—a subject older than this century and dedicated to a self-referent activity—was almost blind to the sexist bias in science, no doubt because that bias pervaded sociology of science as well as other branches of science, so it is depressing to notice the extent to which certain prejudices continue to shape the practice of evaluation. I have no doubt that many more apply than I shall mention here—Ernest House (1980) has warned us about some others in *Evaluating With Validity*—but the ones discussed here may constitute a useful start for creating the kind of anxiety and self-scrutiny that will uncover the rest. Later in the paper, I critique standard evaluation processes in the light of these biases, and I also talk about methods and models which avoid them.

FOUR IDEOLOGIES

Four ideologies or fundamental biases that have pervaded much of evaluation are described in this section.

The Separatist Ideology

"I am an evaluator, you are a subject, she is an object"—i.e., the denial or rejection of self-reference, less kindly described as a kind of criticism. This is most clearly seen in the failure of evaluators to turn their attention to the procedures by which they are themselves evaluated as—and which they use to evaluate others—members of the scientific community. The most scandalous of these procedures include peer review—for research funding or personnel dicisions—by uncalibrated, unvalidated, and un-followed-up review panels. It was easy to get away with this as long as evaluation was treated as meaning first of all the evaluation of students (when the word *evaluation* occurs in the title of a book published before 1960, it almost invariably refers to the practices of student performance assessment), and then program evaluation. Program evaluation is not self-referent, since evaluating a program does not itself constitute a programmatic activity. This may have been one of the reasons for the almost phobic intensity of the focus on program evaluation, though undoubtedly another reason was that the funding lay in that direction. In any case, we see here an unhealthy example of parasitism; the constricted notion of what evaluation was all about fed on the improper practices in everyday scholarly operations, from the allocation of funds to the selection of personnel. I postulate as the psychological dynamics behind this kind of error, which would be hard to explain unless there was a deep motivation for it, the existence of something which I will call *value-phobia*, a pervasive fear of being evaluated, which I take to be a part of the general human condition—with rare exceptions—and to apply to scientists very generally, evaluators amongst them. We have frequently seen examples of "going native," the phenomenon of field evaluators posted at program sites who are unable to withstand the social tensions of that role and succumb to the pressure of need-affiliation, joining the staff in point of view and commitment. Often one finds that within a year, staff evaluators begin to develop significant blindnesses to obvious weaknesses in the program which they are supposed to be evaluating—weaknesses that they would never have overlooked when they first came in. Going native may be an empathic response to valuephobia of the staff under one's evaluative eye, or it may be motivated by the anti-evaluative backlash from that staff.

Thus, the phenomenon of the unscientific scientist, psychologically comprehensible in terms of epidemic valuephobia, represents a simple distortion of scientific inquiry—separatism—which misrepresents it as requiring a permanent role separation between the observer and the observed. In fact, though objectivity is hardest to achieve in self-reference, it is an ideal towards which we must strive, and which we do commonly recognize as part of the obligation of professionalism. Moreover, though claims to achieve it should be viewed with suspicion, there are many ways to approach it. So the first ideology that affects evaluation, driven by valuephobia, is the ideology of the separation of subject and object in an inappropriate way.

The Positivist Ideology

The various phases in the development of evaluation proceeded against a most important backdrop of a great ideological battle in the philosophy of science, indeed in philosophy as a whole. This was the battle between the positivists and their opponents, originally the idealists and later many others. Right though the positivists were to attempt a drastic reduction in the cant and circumstance of much then-current philosophy, they over-corrected heavily, and we are still a long way from recovering our equilibrium along with a sense of the possibility of objectivity in ethics and other domains of value inquiry such as evaluation.

Since it is obvious from a cursory review of the contents of scientific works that they are frequently highly evaluative and that the evaluations in them are frequently and carefully rendered highly objective by analysis and documentation (I particularly have in mind evaluations of experimental designs, scientific instruments, the contributions of other scientists, and alternative explanations of the data), it is somewhat bizarre that science of the twentieth century represented itself as value-free. Again, one must consider the possibility that this was an ideology generated to reduce valuephobic anxieties. Surely it is necessary to reach for psychological explanations of such glaring discrepancies as that between the assertion that no evaluative judgments can be made with scientific objectivity and the ease with which evaluative judgments about the performance of students were produced by the very instructors who had just banned them from the domain of objectivity. Thus, both in their pedagogical practice and their professional publications, scientists acted as evaluators who were prepared to back up their evaluations as objective and appropriate, yet who denied the possibility of any such process within the field of their expertise. Since the field of expertise of an educational psychologist includes the practice of grading educational efforts, those academics were guilty of the most direct inconsistency.

Thus, while the separatist ideology or bias rejects the self-referent nature of science or evaluation, the positivist ideology rejects the evaluative nature of science. Both involve inconsistencies between professed philosophy and professional practice, and both have constricted the growth of evaluation severely, since it violates both taboos. One has only to observe the vehemence with which many scientists attack the idea of student evaluation of their teaching on *a priori* grounds without the faintest consideration of whether there is scientific evidence for its validity (see the January 1983 correspondent columns of the *Chronicle of Higher Education*) to see the separatist ideology at work; and the rejection slips which accompanied submissions of articles about evaluation to social science journals prior to the mid-1960s amply demonstrate the power of the positivist ideology, the value-free component of which was often and misleadingly called "empiricism." The wolfdog of evaluation is acceptable as a method of controlling the peasants, but it must not be allowed into the castle—that is the message which each of these ideologies represents, in its own way.

The Managerial Ideology

When program evaluation began to emerge, who commissioned it? Program instigators and managers, legislators and program directors. And whose programs were being evaluated? Programs initiated by the same legislators and managers. It is hardly surprising that a bias emerged from this situation. In the baldest economic terms, the situation could often be represented in the following way: someone looking for work as an evaluator (e.g., bidding on an evaluation contract) knew that they could not in the long run survive from the income from one contract. It followed that it was in their long-term self interest to be doing work that would be attractive to the agency letting the contract. Since that agency was typically also the agency responsible for the program, it also followed the evaluators understood that favorable reports were more likely to be viewed as good news than unfavorable ones. Absent extreme precautions, such as radical separation of the evaluation office from the program offices and direct reporting/promotion, etc. of the evaluators by the chief-of-staff, on a highly professional basis, there was a strong predisposition towards favorable evaluations. It is extremely noticeable that when the General Accounting Office or the Congressional Budget Office or the Audit Agency or the Inspector General's Office—all of which are well-insulated evaluation shops—do evaluations of federal programs, the results are very much more critical than those done by allegedly independent contractors, when the contract is let by the agency itself. Even these "internal-external" evaluation shops—the General Accounting Office for example—are not immune to the bias of ultimate shared self interest, since all are agents of a government that wants to look good; but there is a great difference in degree. When we move further down the spectrum, to the usual situation in a school district where the Title I evaluator may be on the staff of the Title I project manager, the pressures toward a favorable report become extreme. Everyone knows of cases where the project manager simply removes the critical paragraphs from the evaluator's report and sends it on upstairs as a co-authored evaluation.

The managerial ideology went far beyond a simple conflict-of-interest bias, though that reaches so far that perhaps only the appointment of lifetime evaluators, following the standard legislative model of the appointment of superior court justices, could be taken seriously as a countermeasure that showed the society to be fully aware of the problem. The managerial ideology generated a major conceptual scheme, which pervasively contaminates almost all contemporary program evaluations. This is the achievement or success model for evaluation, translated to the view that program evaluation consists of identifying the goals of programs and determining whether they have been met. Relevant though that is to the concerns of the manager, it is of no interest at all to the consumer. The road to hell is paved with good intentions, and the road to environmental desolation is paved with successful programs of pest eradication. The distinction between intended effects and side effects is of no possible concern to the consumer, who is benefitted or damaged by them alike, and consumer-oriented evaluation is, on the whole, considerably more important than manager-oriented evaluation. Although goals and objectives are considerably overrated as aids to good management, resulting in the absurdities of detailed daily lesson plans which may inhibit good teaching more than they facilitate it, there is at least some argument for them in a planning context. There is no argument for them in the evaluation context, *except* for providing managerial feedback and for providing meta-managers with some index of the success of their subordinates in projecting reasonable goals.

Once again, we can find here the cavalier disregard of one's own behavior so characteristic of the separatist syndrome. The very program manager who thinks that goal-free evaluation is either absurd or obscene or illegal, walks straight into the local automobile dealership and proceeds to evaluate the products there without the slightest inclination to request a statement of objectives from the General Motors design team that labored long and hard to produce them. Nor will any reference to such goals be found in *Consumer Reports*, widely read by scientists who loudly proclaim the impossibility of objective empirical evaluation and by managers who proclaim the impossibility of goal-free evaluation.

Consumer Reports is an irrefutable counter-example to the paradigm of goal-achievement program evaluation. The coterie of program managers and their consultants work up many rationalizations to keep program evaluation separate from product evaluation ("people aren't products," etc.), lest the obvious incongruity between the goal-based paradigm they espouse and the needs-based paradigm they employ in their own affairs should become too apparent. It is a phenomenon of some significance that for 15 years all books about the "new discipline of program evaluation" were entitled *evaluation*, talked about evaluation, and turned out to only deal with program evaluation. Not only did they thereby ignore product evaluation, the one kind of evaluation for which we had many decades of thoroughly reliable development; but they also ignored personnel evaluation, an extraordinary achievement since no serious program evaluation can be done without looking at the treatment of personnel in the program, i.e., at personnel evaluation. Now the treatment of personnel involves considerations of justice—that is, ethics—as well as some other quite sophisticated methodological issues, and it comes perilously close to home since it involves the evaluation of people—and even program managers are people.

So we find valuephobia once more leading to extraordinary global and logistical maneuvers designed—unconsciously, no doubt—to screen off the ethics and the personnel evaluation as if somehow they could be avoided in the course of program evaluation. If they were brought in, of course, then we would have to face the possibility that managers had to be evaluated, that the goals of programs were just as evaluable as their impacts, and that even ethics itself had to be faced as a legitimate part of serious comprehensive program evaluation. In particular, affirmative action issues could not be treated as merely part of the legal background of program evaluation. They would have to be dealt with as serious issues with respect to which correct answers have to be discovered—or else most programs could not be given a clean bill of health.

The managerial ideology dovetailed very nicely with the positivist ideology, because treating a program as equivalent to its success in achieving its goals was a wonderful way of avoiding having to make any value judgments. It merely passed the value judgment buck along to the program managers, accepting their determination of goals as the presupposition of the investigation. "You tell us what counts as a good outcome, and we (scientists) will tell you whether you got it" was the posture, and it was a very attractive one for the valuephobe. The manager, in turn, could often pass the buck back to a legislature, and they—if they so desired—could always blame the public. Goal-achievement evaluation was thus a smokescreen under which it was possible for adherents of value-free dogma to come out of the woodwork and start working on some rather well-financed evaluation contracts. They were not, they said, violating the taboo on making scientific value judgments; they were just investigating the success of a means to a given end. They were also, thereby, committed to connivance-without-cavil in some pretty unattractive programs, including the efforts of the CIA in Central and South America as well as Southeast Asia. When the radical left of the sixties turned up these activities, it concluded that such behavior showed that science was not in fact value-free. All it showed was that scientists were not value-free, a conclusion which no one had ever denied. Although badly bitten over the politics of these exposés, establishment social scientists rightly regarded them as irrelevant to the fundamental logical propriety of the value-free position. For that position maintained only that scientific evidence could not substantiate evaluative judgments, and it never involved the claim that science could not be used for good or ill, by scientists or others. I have mentioned above, and argued in greater detail elsewhere, that the fundamental logical position—that science cannot substantiate value judgments—was completely wrong, and indeed obviously wrong; it is for this error that the social scientists must be condemned, and it was this positivist error that led to the managerial error. For only if one believed oneself incapable of disciplined and scientific investigation of value claims could one so readily adopt, without careful scrutiny, the shoddy value premises of the counterinsurgency programs.

Substantial branches of the federal government are in fact concerned with product evaluation—perhaps the Federal Drug Administration is the most conspicuous example. The very methodology that they employed was one which placed an absolutely minimal emphasis upon the achievement of the goals or objectives of the manufacturers or vendors of the product; there was never much doubt that if something came through the doors of the FDA labeled "post-anesthetic analgesic," it would reduce post-operative pain. The problem was always focussed on the side effects. Now one can hardly evaluate side effects by asking whether they represent the achievement of the intended effects, to which they are by definition irrelevant. So what does one use in evaluating side effects? One uses the needs of the patient—or client, or consumer, or user, or student. Thus, in order to evaluate side effects, which one cannot avoid doing if one is to do responsible program or product evaluation, one must have some kind of needs assessment in hand. But if one has some kind of needs assessment in hand, then one can use it to evaluate all effects, whether intended or not. Indeed, it is exactly the appropriate device for doing so. Consequently, one can completely by-pass the reference to goals. Programs, like products should be evaluated by matching their effects against the needs of those whom they affect. And that is what the doctrine of "goal-free evaluation" recommends.

What happens in the managerial ideology is of course that one presupposes the goals of the program were based upon an infallible and eternally valid needs assessment, so that one can use the goals as a surrogate for needs. Unfortunately, that leaves the side effects out of consideration; and it is of course ludicrous to assume either that managers (or those who employ them) always do needs assessment, or always do valid needs assessments, or that any such needs assessments, even if done and valid, will *still* be valid years later when the time has come to evaluate the program. Needs change, not only because we come to recognize new ones, but because programs come and go, population demographics change, the state of the economy varies, and the extent to which needs have been already met varies. Hence up-to-date needs assessment—or something equivalent to this, such as the functional analysis that is often a surrogate for needs assessment in the case of product evaluation—is an essential part of any serious evaluation.

The managerial ideology has another extremely unfortunate error built into it. Not only does it ignore the consumer's point of view, disregard side effects and the justice of the delivery process, but it also pays little attention to a special concern of the taxpayer. One often hears managers arguing that their programs should only be evaluated on the basis of whether the program goals were achieved, "because that is all that they undertook to do." The evaluation point of view is not concerned solely with—and frequently not at all concerned with—the narrow legal obligations of managers, but also with their ethical obligations, and—transcending the managers altogether—the true merit or worth or value of the program itself. Now *that* raises such questions as whether the same results could have been achieved for less money via another approach, or even for considerably less money using this approach, despite the fact that the contract was completed within the allowed budget.

It is of great significance that the whole question of serious cost analysis was virtually unknown to academic circles until quite recently and that even now it is not part of the standard training of social scientists within the applied fields. Those of us in evaluation who have pushed hard for cost analysis as an equal partner in the team of evaluation methodologies, recall vividly that the notion of cost effectiveness originated not in the academy, but with the Army Corps of Engineers. And cost analysis is by no means conceptually clear to this day; the standard references contradict each other even on the definition of cost.

The effective use of the money available on the project for which it was allocated is one dimension of cost effectiveness; another dimension involves opportunity costs, that is, the comparison of this particular way of expending the resources with other ways that would have achieved similar or better results. This second dimension in cost analysis raises the awkward spectres of a series of "ghosts at the banquet," the ghosts of all the alternative possibilities that were not realized. Should the evaluator have to evaluate not just the program under evaluation, but all the alternatives to it? The cost of such evaluations would be unrealistically great. But if no evaluation is done of the critical competitors—the most important alternatives—then one can never say that the expenditure on the present project was justified. And that conclusion, that the project represented the best or even a justifiable expenditure, is precisely the type of conclusion that many clients for evaluations request, or need even if they do not request it. In particular, it is part of the evaluation imperative to address that question unless there are specific reasons for avoiding it, since it is the question that directly concerns society as a whole rather than special interests of the funding agency and the managers and staff of the program.

So, it is clear that the managerial bias furthered an ideology that omitted a number of important dimensions of the most important kind of evaluation—the systematic and objective determination of worth or value. It is also clear that there are procedures available to reverse this bias and move towards needs-based rather than goal-based evaluation, to what we might call consumer-oriented rather than manager-oriented evaluation. These methodologies include a full range of techniques of cost analysis, including techniques for the analysis of opportunity costs and non-money costs; the provision of opportunities for those who are evaluated to respond to the drafts of the evaluation before it is given to the client officially; and the procedures of goal-free evaluation.

The latter approach not only represents a counterveiling methodology, but a useful methodological simplification, because the practical task of identifying the true "goals of the program" is often completely beyond reasonable solution. One may dig into the historical transcripts—the General Accounting Office goes back to the discussions in committee hearings prior to the formation of legislation—but one then faces the fact that the working goals of the program change with the experience of program delivery. Should one then use the goals of the senior staff members; of the firing-line staff; of the responsible individuals in the funding agencies; or all of the above at the beginning of the evaluation, or during the evaluation, etc., etc.? The problems of converting these goals, expressed informally or rhetorically, into behavioral objectives; of avoiding or resolving inconsistencies in them; of handling the prioritizing of them; of dealing with clear cases of mistaken empirical assumptions in them; and so on, still remain to be solved. Goals are often best seen as inspirational devices—they make poor foundations for analysis.

It is also important to note that for the evaluators to be aware of the goals of the program is for them to be given a strong perceptual bias in a particular direction, which, in conjunction with whatever positive or negative effect they possess for the program, unleashes the possibility of a distorted perception of the results. It is entirely typical for evaluators to look mainly in the direction of the intended results, because they know that the client is particularly interested in that direction; they know that not doing a thorough job in that direction will count against them for future contracts or employment, and they know that they typically will be completely off the hook as far as the client is concerned if they report only on results in that general area. The possibility of this kind of "lazy evaluation" thus opens up, and it is all too often enough to keep one busy without a serious search for side effects. When the field staff do not know the goals of the program, except in the most obvious and general sense, and are only allowed to talk to the program's clients rather than program staff, then they are much more likely to pick up other effects. For one thing, they are on their mettle with no clues; for another, they begin to identify with the recipients and that is a much more appropriate identification—if one has to be made—than with the program staff, not only methodologically (since it generates a new set of biases that can offset the managerial ones), but also ethically. After all, the program staff existed only to serve the recipients, not the other way around. It is therefore extremely unfortunate if evaluators spend most of their time talking to program staff and relatively less of their time talking to program clientele. Social linkages created by these contacts are another source of bias in addition to the perceptual bias in knowing the goals.

There is no need for program evaluation to be done on a wholly goal-free or wholly goal-based commitment. A mixture of the two—with some staff aware of goals and others, isolated from the first group, not aware of them—often works very well. A mode reversal is also possible, with the staff beginning their work in ignorance of the goals and proceeding as far as the preliminary report in writing; then being informed about the goals, and proceeding through such further work as may appear necessary at that point. So one can often eat one's cake and have it, if one does it in the right order. Goal-free evaluation roughly corresponds to double-blind design in the medical field, and for those same reasons is to be deemed advantageous where possible. It is not, in general, more expensive, though it will certainly be so in some cases, and it will be less expensive in other cases—especially since the cost of disruption of staff and services (so often not counted into the cost of evaluation) is largely eliminated.

Given that evaluation is an essential part of quality control, one learns something extremely important from the discovery that the very term *evaluation* is such anathema in many quarters—for example, in large parts of the federal government system—that people go to great lengths to use other language such as *assessment* or *policy analysis* to cover precisely an evaluation process. It is clear that valuephobia, given the educational background and professional commitment of most people working in the human services area, is far more powerful than their commitment to quality. While it may well be true that evaluation is often performed extremely badly, that it may be a damaging activity for worthwhile programs and involve a risk of unfair treatment for worthy people, that hardly justifies the extraordinary defensive maneuvering that goes on in order to avoid it or its impact. The interest in quality control that the Japanese have shown with the institution of Quality Circles has been widely remarked, but a much deeper and more serious deficiency underlies the fact that Quality Circles, invented here, were disregarded until Japan took them up. Valuephobia runs deep.

Another example: there is no such thing as professionalism without a commitment to evaluation of whatever it is that one supervises or produces—and to self-evaluation as well. Yet few professional schools have even the most superficial curriculum commitment to evaluation training of any kind, let alone of professionals.

At the very least, one would expect to find some willingness among managers to treat investment in evaluation on a straight investment basis; since it is clear that it makes claims to pay off in much the same way as any kind of management consulting pays off, or indeed in the way in which computerization pays off, managers who were seriously oriented towards quality consideration would certainly run up some experimental evidence as to the extent to which evaluation by certain evaluators, done in certain ways, etc., pays off or does not pay off. While most program evaluation may be too biased and superficial to be worth following up, it is patently obvious that good product evaluation and good personnel evaluation can pay off very many times over. There are also a number of clear cases where large-scale program evaluation has paid off by factors between 10 and 100. (The doctrine that evaluation should more than pay for itself, on the average, is a meta evaluation criterion of merit and has been referred to as the doctrine of cost-free evaluation.) Thus, the managerial bias is carried to the extreme of a very self-serving indulgence in valuephobia.

The Relativist Ideology

Whereas the positivists were committed to the view that there was some kind of definite external world about which we learned through our senses and through experiments, more recent philosophy of science has tended to move away from this "realistic" or "external world" commitment towards the view that everyone has his or her own reality, all equally legitimate. And evaluation has been very much influenced by this movement in the philosophy of science. Throughout this book, in articles by the most distinguished workers in evaluation, one finds not only a shying away from the notion of objective determination of worth—as in Cronbach's aversion to summative evaluation—but also a shying away from even the notion of objectively correct descriptions of programs. Multiple perspectives, yes; multiple realities, no. While it is in my view perfectly appropriate to respond to the obvious need for multiple perspectives and multiple levels of description by abandoning any naive assumption about the existence of a single correct description of objects in the external world (including programs), it is equally mistaken to overreact in the direction of solipsism or relativism. The relativist ideology or bias is, in my view, a case of such overreaction; it is often to be recognized by the emphasis placed by its supporters upon the impossibility of establishing "the truth," or "the existence of a correct view of the world," and so on. If it were really the case that there is no objective superiority of some descriptions above others, then there could be no discipline of physics any more than evaluation. The concept of relativism is self-refuting; if everything is relative, then the assertion that everything is relative cannot itself be known to be true. So, although we may reject the existence of a single correct description, we should not abandon the idea that there is an objective reality, though it may be a very rich one that cannot be *exhaustively* described. It may even be one which can only be described in a non-misleading way by giving descriptions which are relativised to each audience; we may concede all this, and yet insist that in many cases there is such a thing as a correct—though not a unique—description (given a certain audience and level) by contrast with a number of incorrect descriptions. Indeed, these descriptions may involve descriptions of the merit, worth, or value of parts or aspects of the entity being investigated.

It has been argued above that the very core of science, as of other disciplines, is committed to the objectivity of evaluation—in fact, if one could not distinguish good from bad scientific explanations, one could not be said to be a scientist at all—and there is thus no shame or indeed any further commitment involved in treating evaluation as an objective discipline. The fact that ethical issues must also be handled raises the question of the status of objectivity in that subfield of evaluation; but whatever decision one comes to there, one cannot weaken the resolve with which one must address the search for the best and the better and the ideal when evaluating all aspects of a program other than the ethical. Programs are simply very complicated institutions, but they are no more complicated than theories or even experimental designs, which we have no hesitation in evaluating by strictly scientific criteria. It is a modest enough—and surely a scientific—suggestion that we should evaluate programs in terms of their latent rather than their alleged function.

Thus, I see the re-emergence of relativism as the latest and most serious bias in evaluation methodology, because it comes from the evaluators themselves. It is quite easy to show that those who support it officially actually disregard it in their common practice. Just as managers act as goal-free evaluators of consumer goods, so relativists act as objectivists in their grading of their students or of the interpretations by their colleagues of certain experimental results. This inconsistency between practice and philosophy is a sure sign of the immaturity of this field at the present moment. There are many other such signs, and in the ensuing paragraphs we will call attention to a few standard evaluation practices that violate some of the most obvious criteria for systematic evaluation—and yet have not been universally condemned by professional associations of evaluators and often are not even seen as particularly relevant to the narrowly conceived business of program evaluation. In the course of discussing these examples, albeit very briefly, we will also take the opportunity to introduce one or two conceptual distinctions that clarify practices and malpractices as well as referring to the four fallacious ideologies that we have outlined above.

THE SOCIAL SCIENCE MODEL

This set of four fallacious ideologies often seems to congeal into something that could be called the traditional social science model of evaluation. Since we are here proposing a set of alternative positions or ideologies, which we will elaborate in modest detail below, it can be argued that we are proposing an alternative and more appropriate model for the social sciences. Thus, if this argument is correct, evaluation should lead us to a considerable sophistication of the rather primitive philosophy of science that has been associated with the social sciences, and one might sum this up by saying that evaluation turns out to be a better model for the social sciences than they have proved to be for it. Taking this view seriously, one looks more carefully at the publications in the traditional social science journals and sees many ways in which these could be increased in their value, to science and to society, if a range of further questions were to be addressed about them, both at the design level and the meta level. So there is a second goal for this paper, the commitment to substantial reform of the ideology and hence the practice of the social sciences and not just of evaluation.

The examples that follow come from educational experience, not just because we are all familiar with such cases, but because it may be that the largest payoff from improvement in evaluation can be achieved if reforms in educational evaluation take place—by contrast with reforms in the administration of criminal justice or other human services. The examples chosen scarcely exhaust the area; we could have focussed solely on the kind of evaluation that underlies the current mania about computers, e.g., the absence of serious needs assessment behind the push for teaching BASIC as "computer literacy." But we focus on older sins.

THE EVALUATION OF STUDENT WORK

In this most common of all educational experiences, we find example after example of methodological misconceptions and misdirections, which clearly show how well segregated our intellectual efforts were from our pedagogical practices. It is only as the discipline of evaluation has grown to some degree of autonomy and as external social pressures have forced us to re-examine the evaluation of students that we have come to raise our eyebrows over practices which many of our most intelligent and best-trained social scientists had set up and nurtured for decades.

We will not here rehearse the whole sorry story of the abuses of norm-referenced testing and the gradually improving mix with criterion-referenced testing that is emerging. As the fights over minimum competency achievement tests for graduation or promotion, over the definition of test bias, over the concept of instructional validity, and about other issues are reaching a more mature level of discussion, assisted by the courts and public opinion as well as the scholars, we are seeing the development of evaluation by contrast with mere testing. We will here simply comment on a basic logical point that has not been treated with appropriate respect in the literature on measurement, but which becomes crucial as we attempt to develop the logic of evaluation in any consistent and comprehensive way. The basic logical relations in evaluation seem to be four in number: grading, ranking, scoring, and apportioning. The following definitions are partly stipulative, but involve very little straightening out, being mainly a reflection of the implicit logic of the common terms. *Grading* is the allocation of objects to a set of classes that are ordered by merit or worth; the number of classes usually being small compared to the number of entities graded, and the description of each class being given in terms that refer to some external standards of merit or worth, i.e., not simply to relative position. *Ranking* is the allocation of individuals to some position in an ordering, usually one where the number of positions is equal to or almost equal to the number of individuals; the order being by merit or worth. *Scoring* is the most elaborate standard mensurable approach associated with evaluation; it involves the ascription of a quantitative measure of merit or worth to each individual in the group being evaluated. And *apportioning* is the process of allocating a finite valuable resource in varying amounts to each individual as a means of expressing an assessment of merit or worth. Certain obvious connections and lack of connection can be quickly stated. Ranking does not imply grading nor vice versa; scoring will entail a ranking but not a grading (in general); neither grading nor ranking will entail an apportioning, although apportioning can be defined in terms of a very complicated set of gradings and rankings of parts of whatever is being evaluated, whenever such parts can be identified. Both criterion-referenced and norm referenced tests require cutting scores in order to define a grading; normed tests always, and criterion referenced tests sometimes, define a ranking. The body of basic training in tests and measurement is weak on these distinctions, because of the valuephobic exclusion of explicit discussion of merit. As a result, elementary mistakes are to be found in almost every text and in many published tests, where confusions between these types of evaluation are rampant. A typical example occurs when the translation of the ratings on a five point rating scale is given as excellent; very good; average; below average; very poor. The first two of these refer to grading; the next two refer to a norm-referenced or ranking approach, and the last reverts back to a grading approach. The scale is logically unsound since the average performance of the group being rated may be very good, or poor, or anywhere else, so there are often two correct responses. The "anchors" given presuppose a more or less normal distribution *and* a coincidence of the upper reaches of the distribution with excellent performance (and correspondingly with the lower reaches), both of them are extremely implausible assumptions in most contexts of student evaluation.

The concept of grading on the curve, another symptom of valuephobia, exhibits the same distortion of the difference between grading and ranking. With typical managerial bias, it assumes that the difficulty level of the test has been set at precisely the right point so that the top ten percent (or 15 percent) which are automatically given an *A* will in fact deserve to be regarded as having performed not merely superior work (which is tautologically correct) but excellent work, and similarly for the other grades. If it is argued that psychologists ascribe no more significance to the A than top decile performance, then we must focus on the bottom end of the class and inquire why it should be assumed that there must always be ten percent who fail. Obviously, such an assumption is completely false in many circumstances, and, if false at that end of the distribution, the converse must be in question at the other end. And in the middle.

Of course, built into the very conception of scoring that leads to the normal distribution used in grading on the curve is precisely that identification of merit with a point in the scoring system, the commitment to an independent assessment of worth or value, that is supposedly rejected by going to grading on the curve. If one is prepared to commit oneself to the view that any point, however earned on whatever question in the test, is of equal value—the assumption without which one cannot justify scoring at all as a basis even for ranking—then one might as well commit oneself to the rather more modest assumption that one can identify a truly excellent or hopeless performance not just by its salience.

Another example of logical confusion occurs in funding decisions, where the review panel is instructed to rank or grade programs, whereas apportioning is the question at issue. (Using the wrong instructions may, however, make managerial manipulation of the results much easier.)

TEACHER EVALUATION

The evaluation of research has always been thought to be relatively straightforward by comparison with the evaluation of teaching; close examination of the implicit assumptions in the way research evaluation has been done has led to increasing disquiet with this in recent years, and a great deal more needs to be done towards developing reasonably objective standards for the valuation. But the evaluation of teaching and teachers is much more scandal (see Scriven, 1981c). A great deal has been written about this recently, and we will simply mention two points here. First, it has rarely been remarked that there is a complete difference between an evaluation of merit and an evaluation of worth in teaching, and that these two considerations have quite different relevance to different kinds of personnel decisions. The evaluation of worth (to the institution) is an evaluation which brings in questions of the salaries in the marketplace, of the extent to which the subject matter is popular or essential to mission, of payoffs from fame (in the media sense) of the instructor and so on. None of these is involved in the evaluation of professional merit, a property of the individual and his or her performance against the standards of merit in that profession. Thus, a teacher at the college level may have the greatest merit and be of so little worth to the institution that it does not make sense to grant tenure, simply because the subject matter in which this instructor specializes no longer draws any students at all; the reverse may also be true of the great showman or grantsman who attracts income and/or students but does so without a foundation of true professional merit. Roughly speaking, initial and tenure appointments should be made on the basis of worth as well as merit, but promotions and awards should be made solely on the basis of merit.

A second interesting point that can be made about the evaluation of teachers concerns the fact that the universal procedure employed in the evaluation of primary and secondary school teachers is invalid for every possible reason (see Centra, 1979; Scriven, 1981c). That procedure consists of visiting a very few classes, often with advance notice and using checklists or subjective judgment to determine whether appropriate practices are occurring during the visit. The sample size is too small to be of any use, even if the sample is random; the sample is not random, since the measurement process may affect the treatment; the judge is not free of significant social biases from non-classroom relationships with the teacher; the checklists are invalid; and finally the judge is completely invalidated as a detector of learning gains, which must be regarded as at least a major part of what teaching is all about. The continuance of this practice in the light of these obvious invalidities is a reflection upon the state-of-the-art of (or interest in) evaluation amongst professional administrators and teachers. It should, of course, be noted that neither unions nor management would benefit from switching to an alternative approach since neither is rewarded for the replacement of bad teachers by good ones, and indeed would be heavily punished by the emotions, costs, and struggles that would be involved in a changeover. Only the children and the taxpayer are cheated and their representatives are not yet sufficiently sophisticated to speak up about the impropriety of this process.

Apart from this generally dismal situation, there is an extremely interesting and more sophisticated point involved. Supposing that we *had* established a very reliable list of indicators of good teaching, and that we *were* able to observe teachers at work without affecting the way they teach, in a *large enough* sample of lessons. It seems that then our problems would all be solved. (In fact, we do have one such indicator, not the dozens which are widely touted; it appears that "interactive time on task" is a good indicator of amount of learning.) We now come to see one of the more radical differences between formative and summative evaluation. For purposes of summative evaluation—that is, in this context, the making of personnel decisions—we cannot use statistical indicators of merit that refer to only one or some aspects of the performance. This claim of course directly contradicts the standard operating procedure in the evaluation of teachers. We cannot use such an indicator any more than we can use skin color, even when we are in possession of job-related, valid generalizations about skin color, e.g., that the crime rate is higher among blacks, and the oppression rate higher among whites. We cannot use such generalizations in the evaluation of individual cases, because, in the first place, they apply only to randomly chosen samples from the population to which they refer, and the individual in a personnel evaluation situation is by no means a random sample— we know much too much about such individuals for them to be "representative" or "typical" or "random" samples of that population. In the second place, if we do *not* know more than this about the individual in a personnel decision case, then we can and should go out and get some more evidence, evidence directly related to track record performance in this or the most similar work situation we can identify in their case history. This is scientific common sense. The ethical imperative, in addition, requires that we not use membership in a very general class as the basis for judgment about the individual; we have various terms for the associated error, for example, "guilt by association," or "stereotyping." Since there are always feasible and superior alternatives to these generalizations in personnel work, there is no justification for using them. In the case of summative teacher evaluation, the clearly superior alternative is the use of direct evidence of learning, plus appropriate standards obtained from suitable comparisons with other teachers of similar children. (Even *holistic* ratings by judges present *most of the time*, who lack the chance to acquire *social bias*, will be superior; which is to say, student evaluations of teaching.)

The various absurdly primitive attempts to use pupil performance as an indicator of teacher merit have produced an understandable backlash against this kind of approach; but when the comparisons are made with other teachers of children in the same school, where allocation to classroom is almost entirely random—or to children in similar schools serving essentially similar populations—then the difference in final achievement on a sound common test must be due to the differences in teaching ability. Minor differences are of no interest since the matching is not perfect and circumstantial variables will have some minor effectsh (e.g., classroom architecture, the presence of a single highly disruptive student, etc.) However, if multiple measurements of student gains are made (e.g., in an elementary school, three successive measurements across three successive terms) there is not going to be much doubt that teachers who are always two standard deviations off the mean are either genuine super-teachers or genuine failures. The courts having upheld this kind of evidence as grounds for dismissal; we should now be using it. (Where it is not available, student evaluations are the best alternative.)

Of course, even though the courts have upheld the use of comparative gain score evidence alone, it is not all that we should be gathering. We also need evidence of the quality of the content taught and not covered in the test. This is readily obtainable by inspection of materials (especially student products) by a curriculum specialist or even by a principal with experience in this area. We also need evidence about the ethicality and professionality of the teaching process. (Where student ratings are used instead of gain scores, the evaluation of all content becomes crucial.) The ethicality of the teaching process is not a matter of whether one uses negative reinforcement rather than positive reinforcement—often inappropriately regarded as cruel and unusual punishment by supervisors and principals. It is rather a matter of whether there is flagrant disregard of due process and considerations of justice, e.g., by the use of sexist or racist remarks or practices; by unfair grading practices; and by inappropriate test construction. This will best be picked up by a review of the test materials and anonymous student responses. Finally, although it is not absolutely essential, it is highly desirable to use evidence of professionality, usually best based upon a dossier submitted by the instructor. Professionalism requires self development, so evidence of advanced courses in both subject matter and method would be relevant. It requires self-evaluation; so it requires evidence that testing of one's teaching success, including (usually) the use of student evaluations, has been obtained. Both of these considerations require a steady process of experimentation, with new materials and approaches. Even a program of critical reading of new and promising literature or current research literature would be relevant to these considerations and could be documented in such a dossier.

The preceding will generate a highly satisfactory model for summative evaluation. But does it not, in one version, involve a violation of the very principles which it was set up to support? In using student evaluations, especially as our only indicator of learning, are we not using an indicator that has only a statistical correlation with merit in teaching? This is true, but this is one of the cases where a statistical indicator may be justifiable. To see why, consider an even more extreme example. Test scores by students on well-constructed scholastic achievement tests are used in order to select the entering class for colleges and graduate schools. But it is well known that such tests are not infallible indicators of what we may take to be the criterion variable—success at those colleges. If they are "merely statistical indicators," then surely we are not entitled to use them since they violate the principle of judging the individual on the basis of his or her own work rather than on the performance of people who are related by some statistical generalization to the individual being evaluated? The reader will no doubt notice two crucial differences about this case. In the first place, we *are* using the individual's own work, a comprehensive and relevant work sample, in fact. In the second place, we do not have a feasible and better alternative available, (cf., also the validity of an end-of-term course exam).

People sometimes propose that the use of the high school teachers' evaluations of the college-bound student—based, as they are, upon very extensive observation—would be superior to the use of test scores. Investigation shows that this is not usually the case, essentially because of the problem of inter-judge unreliability. In short, it is not a *systematic* alternative because there is no feasible *system* of having the same set of judges look at all candidates, so the test—which is administered in the same form to all candidates—wins on the swings of reliability what it loses on the roundabouts of inadequate work sampling. And so it is with student evaluations of teachers. Especially when the questionnaire is appropriately constructed and administered, a high score has a good positive correlation with the learning outcome. Of course we could always directly measure the learning outcomes—that is not the problem; the problem is identifying the extent to which the gains are due to teaching merit (as opposed to the textbooks, peer interaction, and intellectual or familial background), and deciding on the cutting scores that will separate good teaching performance from bad. Absent the comparative situation described earlier, our only alternative is the use of student evaluations. Now these evaluations are holistic evaluations of the particular work of the particular individual, not evaluations of part or one aspect of what the teacher does (cf., brief visits or time-on-task measures); they are probably related to learning, *and* they include allowances for other causes and for what could have been done, by contrast with what *was* done. The method is imperfect of course, but based on considerable exposure to other teachers, in the consumer's role. In short, they provide us with the comparative dimensions that we lack if we just collect gain scores. (It does not follow, by the way, that we should use a comparative *question*: "Rate this teacher against others you have had. . . ." That will get you a ranking—but few personnel decisions can be based on a ranking, certainly not a promotion or tenure decision. That's grading on the curve. You must ask for a grading: "Rate this teacher A–F, where A means excellent . . . F means extremely bad." The student's experience with other teachers will create the range of the *feasible*; the top of that range is the locus of excellence.)

While time-on-task measurements *are* empirically related to the performance of the individual, as is skin color, the relationship is of a weaker kind, one that does not survive an increased specification of the individual's characteristics. Student evaluations are holistic of both individual and performance and, though by no means perfect, are—as far as we know and as we'd expect—superior to ratings by any other general category of judges (e.g., principals or supervisors or process experts) though we certainly need more sampling of the matrix of subject matter by age, by school environment, etc., to support this claim more substantially. Hence, we should be using them in the high school and college situation, where there are usually no comparative norms available. When comparisons *are* possible, as with multi-section freshman courses in college, it is preferable though sometimes politically impossible to set up random allocation, common tests and blind grading, and revert to the use of comparative norms.

The preceding discussion will make clear the way in which ethical considerations interact with scientific ones in personnel evaluation. It should also make clear the important distinction between holistic and what can be called analytic evaluation—one might use the terms macro evaluation and micro evaluation instead. The holistic evaluation is an evaluation of the total relevant performance, whereas the analytic evaluation evaluates some component or dimension of that performance. The evaluation of components is in some ways more useful for formative evaluation than the evaluation of dimensions, because it is likely to be easier to manipulate components than dimensions. But either may provide an adequate basis for assembling *or justifying* an overall evaluation. Counterintuitively, however, it transpires that we have clear evidence showing holistic evaluation is sometimes considerably more valid—as well as far more economical—than syntheses of micro evaluations. The problem with the analytic approach to overall evaluations is that the assembly of component scores or grades involves a weighting and combining arrangement of typically unknown validity. (See Davis, Scriven, & Thomas, 1981). The evaluation of teaching also illustrates clearly the differences among evaluation, explanation, and remediation, so often confused in program evaluation, where the client frequently *demands* that the evaluator submit remedial recommendations as well as an overall evaluation. Attractive though that is to the client, and important though it is to do it when possible, there is often an urgent necessity to choose between sound summative evaluation and relatively unreliable and more expensive formative evaluation. It is fairly easy to evaluate teachers on the basis of their success, where one can get appropriate comparison groups set up; but it is not a consequence of the validity of this evaluation that one can give any advice whatsoever to the teachers who perform less well as to how to improve their performance. The reason for this is not only that the best approach to summative evaluation is often holistic; it is also that we lack the grounded theory to provide the appropriate explanations, since all efforts to find components of a winning style (apart from interactive time-on-task which is only marginally describable as "style") have so far failed. Absent a diagnosis of the causes of failure, whence comes a prescription?

Although the traditional approach to remediation is through explanation, the occasional success of "folk-medicine" demonstrates the *possibility* of finding remedies whose success is not inferred from a general explanatory theory, but discovered directly. And so it is with teaching; we might find that a certain kind of in-service training package is highly successful, although it does not proceed from an analysis of the causes of failure. It is thus triply wrong for a client to demand micro explanations as part of an evaluation as a route to remediation or justification. They will not necessarily lead to remediation; there are other ways to get to remediation to provide evidence for the validity of the evaluation. The latter is provided on a holistic basis, e.g., by correlational data relating evaluations by this method (or these judges) with the subsequent performance of the criterion variable. Of course, remedial suggestions are often obvious or easily uncovered from an analytic summative evaluation; but not always and the analytic approach is often not the best one.

I have already mentioned that if one approaches the evaluation of something by evaluating components or dimensions of it, which are then assembled into an overall evaluation, serious problems of validation arise about the formula used for assembly. I have discussed elsewhere the use of some traditional approaches, e.g., weighted-sum with overrides, and we have of course the well known model of cost-benefit analysis, in which we reduce costs and benefits to a single dimension and thereby convert evaluation into measurement. Much more needs to be done about the synthesis step in program evaluation; the present trends, partly because of the difficulty of this step and partly because of the influence of the relativist ideology, is towards mere "exhibiting" of performance on the multiple dimensions involved. This is simply passing the buck to the non-professional, and represents far less than the appropriate response by a professional evaluator.

Review

What is emerging from our discussion of these common evaluation practices? Two points. On the one hand, we are seeing gross errors of practice emerge under critical study, and it is not hard to see how these reflect—directly or indirectly—the ideologies or biases we have discussed. By far, the greatest influence of those ideologies is indirect in that they have discouraged recognition of the essential self-reference and evaluative nature of science; discouraged emphasis on the client's perspective; and discouraged any sustained commitment to the existence of correct versus incorrect conclusions.

THE CONSUMERIST IDEOLOGY

For many people, committed to the relativist ideology, it follows from the fact that one is attacking some ideologies that one must be supporting another. This is in error as a general conclusion, but it would be fair to say that the sum total of all the criticisms so far does add up to a point-of-view that needs to be made explicit at this point. I'll use a label for it that has been contaminated with largely irrelevant opprobium, but still retains enough common meaning and a connotation of an ethically appropriate position; I'll say that we have been presenting a *consumerist ideology*. Consumerism is like unionism; both came into existence to represent a movement which, even from the beginning, involved some wrong activities, while representing a long overdue balancing of power and involving an essentially moral concern with people who had been left out of the reckoning. By and large, consumerism has done well by us, from the first day that Ralph Nader provided an over-simplified and in many ways unjustified analysis of the General Motors Corvair automobile, although it has brought with it some overkill pseudo-safety and pseudo-consumer protection legislation. The essential point of the consumerist ideology in evaluation is that all parties affected by something that is being evaluated should be taken into account and given at least their appropriate moral weighting—and in many cases, an appropriate opportunity for explicit participation and/or response to the evaluation process or outcome.

   We can proceed quite briefly with a few more examples of bad practice still tolerated because of acceptance of the fallacious ideologies, and then conclude with a brief description of a model of evaluation methodology that can be said to unpack the consumerist ideology, just as the goal-based evaluation model unpacks the managerial ideology.

THE EVALUATION OF EDUCATIONAL INSTITUTIONS BY ACCREDITATION

Just as there is a completely standard model for primary or secondary teacher evaluation, so there is one for the evaluation of primary, secondary and professional schools. This model, accreditation, has a number of distinctive features, some virtues, and a number of serious weaknesses that cannot be dismissed as due to constraints on resources available for accreditation.

   The distinctive features of accreditation, nearly all present in all applications of this approach, are:

1. The use of a handbook of standards, involved in several other components, beginning with
2. A self study by the institution, resulting in a report on how well they are achieving what they see as their mission; which is read by
3. A team of external assessors, usually volunteer members of the same general professional enterprise, who not only read the self-study, but also make

4. A site visit, usually for one to three days, which involves direct inspection of facilities, interviews with staff, clients, and students, plus review of prior reports, and which results in

5. A report on the institution, which usually makes various recommendations for change and for/or against accreditation (possibly with various conditions); this report is subject to

6. A review by some august panel, at which the right to appeal against the recommendations is sometimes granted to the institution being evaluated and at which some censoring of the recommendations sometimes occurs; after which

7. A final report and decision is issued.

Some of the desirable features here include: some use of external evaluators, self-scrutiny as a method of preparing the ground for the external suggestions and for providing a linkage group with the external assessors, a review process which gives some chance to address injustices, and a rather modest cost. Within this general framework, good evaluation could indeed be done. But it is rare to see it done.

We'll pick up only a few of the problems, more to illustrate than to provide a thorough analysis. We can conveniently group the problems under the same heading as the components.

1. The handbook of standards is usually a mishmash ranging from the trivial to the really important, and there is usually no weighting suggested. (Sometimes there isn't even a handbook of standards.) Consequently, the bits and pieces can be assembled in more or less any way that the panel feels like assembling them, without any focus on the justification of the implicit weighting of such a synthesis. It is common for the handbook of standards to begin with some piece of rhetoric about how institutions should only be judged against their own goals, but yet we will find buried in the handbook a number of categorical standards that must be met by all institutions. This inconsistency reflects a failure to resolve the ideological tension between managerial and consumerist approaches. Managers do not want to be blamed for not doing what they did not undertake to do; on the other hand, consumers do not like to be treated badly and don't much care whether the maltreatment was unintentional or not. Ethics obviously requires that the rights of consumers be protected at least in certain respects, so that minimum standards of justice should be met by all educational institutions. It might also be argued that public institutions have some obligations to provide a service that is reasonably well-tailored to public needs, and that even private institutions—who may select more or less whomever they wish to enroll—must nevertheless provide services that are related to the needs of those whom they do enroll. (Note that the absolute standards one does encounter in these typical standards checklists are usually considerably less ethics-related than the ones just mentioned, indeed are often highly debatable; e.g., the requirement of vast libraries for graduate programs.)

2. The self-study is frequently devoted towards a review of goals in the light of mission, and of achievements in the light of goals. This tends to involve the usual

managerial biases, because of the failure to give due weight to the consumer; in particular, there is poor attention to the need to search for side effects, there is little concern with comparisons or cost-effectiveness, and usually little concern with the ethics of the process. (This of course varies considerably across the huge range of accredited institutions, but of the many that I have seen from the medical and legal area as well as from many college and high school reports, the above seems to be a fair generalization.) Another type of weakness emerges at this point; there is rarely a professional evaluator on the internal self-study review team, and consequently many of the usual traps are fallen into, including careless ascriptions of casual effi-cacy to programs, misinterpretations of data about learning gains, and alleged success of graduates and so on. It is impossible to expect that there will not be some adjust-ment of goals to achievement—and this may sometimes be healthy—but it does provide an opportunity to duck behind goal-relativism, which is allegedly the stan-dard by which the accrediting association will make the final judgment. Thus the managerial bias is supported by the relativist one.

3. The team of external assessors is usually picked from volunteers, and, conse-quently, professional evaluators and the busiest administrative analysts and consul-tants are more or less automatically excluded. Professional evaluators are by no means automatically an advantage on these panels; it would be absurd for a professional evaluator to assume that they are. The only imperative is that they should some-times be present and that careful meta-studies should be done to see if this does lead to any improvement. The idea that one can dismiss the supposed experts entirely seems naive, given the low quality of the usual reports. It must be expected that professional evaluators will have to be paid for this activity, so the price goes up; that price could be offset by reducing the size of the panel, since the indirect costs per diem and travel are quite substantial. We should find out whether some profes-sionalism would offset some loss of numbers. There could also be systematic studies with funds from foundations, to see whether the addition of the best management consultants and evaluators will yield cost-saving suggestions that would compensate for increasing the fees to cover their costs. There would then be problems about equity as far as the still-unpaid members of the panel are concerned and serious problems about total cost. However, the quality of the evaluation reports, judged against professional evaluation standards, is so spotty that the entire process should be subject to serious scrutiny; it hardly constitutes an acceptable way in which to evaluate most of our important educational institutions.

Professionals and other busy people are not the only ones left off by the process of volunteering and subsequent selection, usually by central staff personnel. There is a strong tendency to leave radicals and other "extremists" off the panel. No doubt there are accreditation units here and there—I know of one—where this is not true; but it is certainly the general pattern, and it is a typical sign of managerial bias. If we were searching for truth, we would realize that radical perspectives often uncover the truth and can demonstrate it to the satisfaction of all panelists. And we would realize that establishment-selected judges are likely to be blind to some of the more deep-seated biases of the institution; one can see how serious this is by tracking back through old accreditation reports given during pre-feminist days. Not a sign can be seen of sensitivity to radical sexist exploitation and inappropriate passing over of women for positions which they should have received; but there were plenty of feminists around in those days, if anyone had been looking for them.

This managerial bias is of course one that will favor the institution by not uncovering the skeletons in its closet; and it is not accidental that the whole accreditation process is run by a system of fees levied on the very institutions that are accredited and which provide the personnel for the accreditation. The system is thus in a fairly straightforward way incestuous; the question is whether one can conclude that it is corrupt. To the extent it is not, we must thank the innate professional competence and commitment and integrity of the panelists, which does not entirely evaporate under the background pressure towards promanagement, pro-establishment reports. However, to jump a few steps, it is important to notice that the report by the site team will sometimes be radically censored by the review board, which has of course not been to the site, in the direction of excising many or all of its most serious criticisms or conditions. This is an unattractive situation, and one which is not widely recognized. It suggests inappropriate bias, and when we look at the procedure whereby the review boards themselves are selected, we find in many cases an even more unattractive situation. For the review panels—for example, the governing board of the regional accreditation associations in the case of schools and colleges—are often entirely self-selected and often consist almost entirely of active or retired administrators.

4. The site visit is also not designed to capture the input of the most severe critics. Such obvious devices as setting up a suggestion box on the campus during the site visit, providing an answering machine to record comments by those who wish to call them in anonymously, or careful selection of the most severe critics of the institution from among those who are interviewed are practices that one rarely if ever encounters. Failure to adopt these practices simply shows a failure to distinguish between the need for a balanced overall final view and the need for input from the whole spectrum of consumers; both are imperative, the former does not exclude the latter, and the two are quite distinct.

So, from the use of inappropriate standards, such as the requirement of large research libraries for graduate programs instead of *access* to such libraries *or* to online databases, to the failure to enforce serious standards for the self-study (to the point where the great post-secondary institutions go through this stage without most of their faculty ever hearing that it is going on), we are dealing with grossly unprofessional evaluation. Nervousness about the incestuousness of the process is not lessened when one sees the defensive nature of the accreditation agencies' reactions to the proposal that federal or state governments should have some input to accreditation. Undesirable though this may be in various ways, a hybrid system would at least provide minimal insurance against the more outrageous examples of "National Tobacco Research Institute" whitewashes. The extremely lax enforcement of professional standards by the medical and legal professions is a well known scandal and, although there are some professions—the psychologists and a pretty good example— which rise above this kind of managerial/separatist bias it must be realized that the society and its legitimate government have extremely strong rights to be represented in a process which deals with the key service provided to its relatively unprotected citizenry. When we do get an occasional glimpse at the actual standards of compe- tence in a profession—as when we see the results of competency exams on teach- ers, or the analysis of drug prescription written in a certain region—we have every right to suspect that the self regulation process is not being done any better than one would expect, given the biases built into it. Accreditation is an excellent example of what one might with only slight cynicism call a pseudo evaluative process, set up to give the appearance of self-regulation without having to suffer the inconve- nience.

If one had to sum the whole matter up, one might call attention to the fact that in virtually no system of accreditation is there a truly serious focus on judging the institution by the performance of its graduates, which one might well argue is the only true standard. Not to look at the performance seriously, not even to do phone interviews of a random sample of graduates, not even to talk to a few employer and/or employment agencies who deal with graduates from this and others insti- tutions; *this* is absurd.

It is scarcely surprising that in large areas of accreditation, the track record on enforcement is a farce. Among all state accreditation boards reviewing teacher prepa- ration programs, for example, it is essentially unknown for any credential to be removed. Nor is it surprising that at one point the state of California was threat- ening to close down all unaccredited law schools, although some of these had a much higher success rate in getting their graduates past the bar exam than many prominent law schools in the state. And passing the bar exam is presumably one of the most important things that a law school is supposed to do for you—as far as I know, it is the only one for which we obtain a measurement. Crude measurements are not as good as refined measurements, but they beat the hell out of the judge- ments of those with vested interests.

Another example of crude measurement that turns out to be quite revealing is one that can be applied to the evaluation of proposals and the allocation of funds for research in the sciences, as well to the accreditation process, and it is such an obvious suggestion that the failure to implement it must be taken as a serious sign of the operation of the separatist ideology in the service of elitism. This modest pro- posal concerns checking the reliability of team ratings. When a review panel of peers judges that a particular proposal should be funded and another rejected, just as when a review panel judges that a particular institution should be accredited and another disaccredited (or warned, or not accredited), it seems reasonable for those affected to raise the question whether another panel drawn from the same pool of profes- sionals would have made the same recommendation. This is of course the question of inter-judge (in this case inter-panel of judges) reliability, and until very recently no such test had ever been made (although it is the simplest and most obvious recommendation that a freshman student of one of the social sciences would make about a judgmental process of any kind that was officially regarded as subject to scientific investigation). Only separatism insulates the scientist (or other professional) from this scrutiny; and in the couple of cases where a study of inter-panel consistency has been performed, the results have not been encouraging. The North Central Association sent in two teams to have a look at the school—Colorado Springs High School—and the results demontrated not so much a lack of agreement but some important disagreements coupled with the possibility that most of the agreements were due to shared bias. A small National Science Foundation study of the results when more than one panel, drawn from the same pool of professionals, was assigned the task of rating proposals, showed striking and substantial differences. When these relatively crude measures are the only measures we have, the only appropriate conclusion from these results much be an extremely skeptical view of the validity of the accreditation approach to program evaluation.

IDEOLOGIES AND MODELS

Ideologies are intermediate between philosophies and models, just as models are intermediate between ideologies and methodologies. Thus more than one ideology may support a particular model; just as the relativist ideology supports Elliot Eisner's connoisseurship model, so the empiricist ideology as well as the managerial and relativist ones support goal-based evaluation models. Some subtler relations can be plausibly inferred. Recently, for example, we have seen Cronbach's group coming out strongly in favor of formative evaluation as the only legitimate kind of evaluation, by contrast with summative. In this respect, their position matches that of some staff members of the American Federation of Teachers, who are willing to support the idea of evaluation of teachers for improvement, but not the idea of quality review. Apart from logical problems with the artificial nature of this separation, it is certainly an emphasis attractive to both the positivist and the relativist ideology, because each is much more willing to tolerate the idea of improvement—with its connotations of goals and local values as the criteria—than categorical assertions about merit and worth. Few people are valuephobic about the suggestion they are less than perfect, need some improvement; but to be told they are incompetent or even far worse than others, is less palatable.

In remediating (formative evaluation), as in ranking or grading, the fundamental task is that of determining the direction of improvement of superiority, and the mere avoidance of the "cutting scores" problem that is required before you can establish grades does not avoid the logical task of establishing, i.e., justifying and evaluative assertion. Thus I see the preference for formative over summative as—from one perspective—an attempt to limit the amount of evaluative logic that one has to get into, but it does not eliminate the first and crucial step, the step that refutes both relativism and empiricism.

Relatedly, the recent tremendous emphasis on implementation and implementability as meta-evaluative criteria for the merit of evaluations can be seen as another attempt to duck the head-on confrontation with the necessity for demonstrating the *validity* of categorical value judgments, especially those involved in grading. The validity of value judgments, whether they are gratings or rankings, is what the empiricist and relativist deny; but it is a problem that must be faced, and it cannot be converted into the problem of whether the program achieves the goals of its instigators or whether an evaluation is implemented by its clients. Goal achievement and evaluation-implementation are perfectly compatible with a categorical denial of all merit in the program or evaluation; their absence is perfectly compatible with a categorical assertion of flawless merit. In short, these proposed substitutes are not even universal correlates of the concept they seek to replace, let alone definitional components. (Perspectivism accommodates the need for multiple accounts of reality as perspectives from which we build up a true picture, not as a set of true pictures of different and inconsistent realities. The ethicist believes that objective moral evaluations are possible.)

So far we have talked very favorably about the consumerist ideology. Other strands in the position advocated here must also be recognized as implicitly supported by our criticism of the alternatives to them. These include the perspectivist and ethicist strands that stand opposed relativism and empiricism, the holistic orientation that is the alternative to reductionism (the other half of positivism), and the self-referent ideology that contrasts with separatism. We should add a word about what may seem to be the most obvious of all models for a consumerist ideologue, namely *Consumer Reports* product evaluations. While these serve as a good enough model to demonstrate failures in most of the alternatives more widely accepted in program evaluation, especially educational program evaluation, it must not be thought that the present author regards them as flawless. I have elsewhere said something about factual and logical errors and separatist bias in *Consumer Reports* (Scriven, 1981b). Although *Consumer Reports* is not as good as it was and it has now accumulated even more years across which the separatist/managerial crime of refusal to discuss its methodologies and errors in an explicit and non-defensive way has been exacerbated many times, and although there are now other consumer magazines which do considerably better work than *Consumer Reports* in particular fields, *Consumer Reports* is still a very good model for most types of product evaluation.

The Multimodel

Evaluation is a very peculiar breed of cat. The considerable charm of each of a dozen radically different models for it, well represented in this book, can only be explained by the fact that it is a chimerical, Janus-faced and volatile being. Even at the level of aphorism, one is constantly attracted by radical variations in such claims as "evaluation is one-third education and one-third art—including the arts of composition, graphics, and politics" or "evaluation should be driven one-third by the professional obligation to improvement, one-third by the society's need for quality, and one-third by the need to economize." The "Ninety-Five Theses" of the Cronbach (1983) group carry this further. Analogies with other subjects keep springing into life: architecture is one that seems particularly appealing, with its powerful combination of aesthetic component with the engineering necessities, and with the economics and needs assessment that must be taken into account before a structure can be successful. A dozen others have been advocated as paradigms, from anthropology to operations research.

But during these last few years, it is not accidental that two rather similar approaches to clarification of the practice of evaluation have emerged and gained a certain amount of support. They both represent an attempt at distilling solid principles from the models, but they also represent a kind of model in their own right. These two approaches are the *Evaluation Standards* approach, and the *Evaluation Checklist* approach, to which we will turn in a moment. It is not accidental that both are consumer-oriented; we all know the kinds of checklists that we get out of consumer magazines and which facilitate our evaluation of alternatives for purchase, and we all know the way in which professional standards are used as checklists when supposedly questionable behavior by professionals is under scrutiny. More than this practical and value-orientation is involved here, however. I think that the checklist approach—if I may use the term to cover both instantiations of what I see as essentially a similar point of view—represents a kind of model in its own right. It is not like one of the relatively simple and relatively monolithic models with which we normally associate the term. But the emergence says something about the subject of evaluation, something about its complexity and its relation to other subjects; I shall call it the Multimodel, an ungainly minotaur among models. The complex CIPP model is an important intermediate case (see Chapter 16, this volume).

The Multimodel is multiple in a number of ways. In the first place, it commits evaluation to being *multi-field*—that is, applicable to products, proposals, personnel, plans and potentials, not just programs. Then it is *multi-disciplinary* (rather than inter-disciplinary); this means that solid economic analysis, solid ethical analysis, solid ethnographics and statistical analysis, and several other types of analysis are often required in doing a particular evaluation, and not just some standard blend of small parts of these. (Consequently, teams and consultants are often better than any soloist.) The investigations along each of these and other dimensions, some of which are devoted to entirely different disciplines, constitute a set of dimensions for an evaluation, which must eventually be integrated, since the overall type of conclusion for an evaluation (a grading, a ranking, and apportioning) is often pre-determined by the client's needs and resources. In many respects, the *multi-dimensionality* is the most crucial logical element in evaluation, because specific evaluative conclusions are only attainable through the synthesis of a number of dimensions; some involving needs assessments or other sources of value; others referring to various types of performance.

Another aspect of the multiple nature of evaluation concerns what can be called its need for *multiple perspectives* on something, even in the final report. It is often absolutely essential that different points of view on the same program or product be taken into account before any attempt at synthesis is begun, and some must be preserved to the end. The necessity here is sometimes an ethical one as well as a scientific one.

Relatedly, evaluation is a *multi-level* enterprise. When one gets a call over the phone to ask if one could possibly evaluate a certain program in an unrealistically short time-frame, it is entirely appropriate to respond that one most certainly can indeed that one can evaluate it there and then, over the phone and without charge. One does have, after all, a considerable background of common sense and evidence about related programs which make it possible to produce an evaluation at this superficial level. We do not associate such evaluations with professionality or with high validity, but that may be a little too severe depending upon the extend of the evaluator's professional background, the similarity of the present example to other well-documented cases and the nature of the evaluative conclusion that is being requested. But if we move down from that superficial level, it is clear that there is a wide range of levels of validity/cost/credibility among which a choice must be made in order to remain within the resources of time and budget. Given certain demands for credibility, comprehensiveness, validity, and so on, there may not be a solution within the constrains of professionality, time, and budget. But more commonly there are many, and it is this that must lead one to recognize the importance of the notion of multiple levels (of analysis, evidential support documentation) in coming to understand the nature of evaluation. One could go on; *multiple methodologies, multiple functions, multiple impacts, multiple reporting formats*—evaluation is a multiplicity of multiples.

To conclude, then, let me simply list the dimensions that must be taken into account in doing most evaluations, whether of product or program, personnel on proposals. There are certainly special features of the evaluation of—for example— teachers that do not jump out from this listing. But even the four-part checklist that I have suggested above for the evaluation of teachers can be seen to be buried in the following checklist, and indeed it can be enriched in a worthwhile way by paying more attention to some of the steps in this longer effort.

Checklists can function in different ways—there are checklists that list desiderata, and there are checklists that list necessitata. This checklist comes from the latter end of the spectrum, and it is relatively rarely that one can afford to dispense with at least a quick professional check on each of the checkpoints mentioned here. Checklists are also sometimes of a one-pass nature, and sometimes of a multiple pass, or iterative nature. Again, this is of the latter kind; one can't answer all the questions that come up under each of the early headings in adequate detail until one has studied some of the later dimensions; and, having studied them, one must come back and rewrite an earlier treatment, which will in turn force one to refine the later analysis that depends on the former. In designing and in critiquing evaluations, as well as in carrying one out, one is never quite done with this checklist.

The simple terms that I use for the title of each dimension need much unpacking, and they are there just as labels to remind the reader of a string of associated questions. More details will be found in the current edition of *Evaluation Thesaurus* (Scriven, 1983), but I think enough is implied by the mere titles and the word or two that I attach to some of them to convey a sense of the case for the Multimodel. The traditional social science approach deals at most with half of these check-

points and deals with those, in most cases, extremely superficially, as far as evaluation needs are concerned.

THE KEY EVALUATION CHECKLIST

1. *Description.*   An infinity of descriptions is possible, of which a sub-infinity
   would be false, another sub-infinity irrelevant, another overlong, another over-
   short, and so on. Whereas relativisim infers from the fact that a large number
   would be perfectly satisfactory to the conclusion that there are no absolute standards here, perspectivism draws the more modest conclusion that there are a
   number of right answers, several of which need to be added together to give
   an answer that is both true and comprehensive, a fact which in no way alters
   the falsehood or irrelevance or redundancy of many other compound descriptions and hence the difference between right and wrong. The description with
   which we begin the iterative cycles through the checklist is the client's description; but what we finish up with must be the evaluator's description, and it
   must be based, if possible, on discussions with consumers, staff, audiences, and
   other stakeholders.
2. *Client.*   Who is commissioning the evaluation, and in what role are they acting?
   (Distinguish from inventors, consumers, initiators, and so on.)
3. *Background and Context.*   Of the evaluation and of whatever is being evaluated:
   the hopes and fears. (This checkpoint will be set aside in the early stages of an
   evaluation that is to have a goal-free phase.)
4. *Resources (or strengths assessment).*   For the evaluation and for whatever is being
   evaluated.
5. *Consumer.*   Distinguish the targeted population from the impacted population
   (in a goal-based approach), and the directly impacted from the indirectly
   impacted.
6. *Values.*   The needs assessment, the ideals review, the relevant professional standards, expert survey, functional or conceptual analysis, and so on. The source of
   values for the evaluation. To be sharply distinguished from a wants assessment
   ("market research") unless *no relevant needs* exist.
7. *Process.*   Here we have to consider the legal, political, aesthetic, and scientific
   standards, some of which will have emerged from the values review, and apply
   them to the intrinsic nature of whatever is being evaluated.
8. *Outcomes.*   Here the traditional social, scientific, engineering, medical, etc.,
   methodologies come into their own, except that we must treat discovering
   unintended outcomes as of equal importance with the search along the intended
   dimensions of impact.
9. *Generalizability, Exportability, Saleability.*   Across sites, staff, clients, and
   consumers.
10. *Costs.*   Money and non-money, direct and indirect.
11. *Comparisons.*   The selection of the "critical competitors" is often the most
    important act of the evaluator, since the winner may be one the client had not
    considered (but which is perfectly feasible).

12. *Significance.*   A synthesis of all the above.
13. *Remediation.*   There may or may not be some of these recommendations—they do not follow automatically from the conclusions of all evaluations.
14. *Report.*   As complicated as the description, with concern for timing, media, format, and presenters, to a degree quite unlike the preparation for publication of scientific results in a scientific journal.
15. *Meta evaluation.*   The reminder that evaluation is self-referent—the requirement that one cycle the evaluation itself—its design and final form—through the above checklist.

CONCLUSION

Evaluation practice is still the victim of fallacious ideologies, because we have not applied the essential insight that evaluation is a self-referent discipline. The plethora of evaluation models provides a fascinating perspective on the complexity of this new subject, perhaps the keystone in the arch of disciplined intellectual endeavor. We can only build that arch strong enough to support the huge load of educational and social enterprises that it must bear if we come to understand its architecture and thus the function of its keystone considerably better, and in so doing, come to understand better everything else that we know.

16. THE CIPP MODEL FOR EVALUATION

DANIEL L. STUFFLEBEAM

This chapter presents a description of the CIPP Evaluation Model, a comprehensive framework for conducting and reporting evaluations. The model is intended for the use of service providers, such as policy boards, program and project staffs, directors of a variety of services, accreditation officials, school district superintendents, school principals, teachers, college and university administrators, physicians, military leaders, and evaluation specialists. The model is configured for use in internal evaluations conducted by organizations, self-evaluations conducted by individual service providers, and contracted external evaluations.

Corresponding to the letters in the acronym CIPP, the model's core concepts are context, input, process, and product evaluation. Context evaluations assess needs, problems, and opportunities as bases for defining goals and priorities and judging the significance of outcomes. Input evaluations assess alternative approaches to meeting needs as a means of planning programs and allocating resources. Process evaluations assess the implementation of plans to guide activities and later to help explain outcomes. Product evaluations identify intended and unintended outcomes both to help keep the process on track and determine effectiveness. By employing these four interrelated types of evaluation, policymakers, program and project staffs, and individual service providers can conduct or contract for evaluations to help initiate, develop, and install sound programs, projects, or other services; to strengthen existing programs or services; to meet the accountability requirements of oversight groups, sponsors, and constituents; to disseminate effective practices; and to contribute to knowledge in the area of service. Evaluations following the CIPP Model

D.L. Stufflebeam, G.F. Madaus and T. Kellaghan (eds.). EVALUATION MODELS. Copyright © 2000. Kluwer Academic Publishers. Boston. All rights reserved.

also help external groups—funding organizations, persons receiving or considering using the sponsored services, policy groups and program specialists outside the program being evaluated, and other audiences—to understand and assess the merit and worth of the program, project, or other service.

Two key definitions undergird this chapter: evaluation and standards. An *evaluation* is a systematic investigation of the merit and/or worth of a program, project, service, or other object of interest. Operationally, evaluation is the process of delineating, obtaining, reporting, and applying descriptive and judgmental information about some object's merit and worth in order to guide decision making, support accountability, disseminate effective practices, and increase understanding of the involved phenomena. Professional *standards* for evaluations are principles commonly agreed to by specialists in the conduct and use of evaluations for the measure of an evaluation's value or quality.

The remainder of the chapter presents the CIPP Model's philosophical stance; identifies objects of CIPP evaluations; delineates context, input, process, and product evaluations; presents techniques that are particularly useful in each of these types of evaluation; identifies values and criteria appropriate to democratically-oriented CIPP evaluations; provides structures for designing and contracting for CIPP evaluations; and presents illustrations of applying the model.

THE CODE OF ETHICS UNDERGIRDING THE CIPP MODEL

The CIPP Model has a strong orientation to service and the principles of a free society. It calls for evaluators and clients to identify and involve rightful beneficiaries, clarify their needs for services, obtain information of use in designing responsive programs and other services, assess and help guide effective implementation of services, and ultimately assess the services' merit and worth. The thrust of CIPP evaluations is to provide sound information that will help service providers regularly assess and improve services and make effective and efficient use of resources, time, and technology in order to appropriately and equitably serve the well-being of rightful beneficiaries.

CIPP evaluations must be grounded in the democratic principles of equity and fairness. A key concept used in the model is that of *stakeholders*. They are those persons who are intended to use the findings, persons who may otherwise be affected by the evaluation, and those expected to contribute to the evaluation. Consistent with the Joint Committee's (1994) *Program Evaluation Standards* and writings of House and Howe (chapter 22, this volume), Bhola (chapter 20, this volume), Alkin (1979), Guba and Lincoln (1989), and Patton (chapter 23, this volume), evaluators should search out all relevant stakeholder groups and engage them in hermeneutic and consensus-building processes to help define evaluation questions, clarify criteria of merit and worth, contribute needed information, and help interpret findings. Such rich, sustained, consequential involvement positions stakeholders to understand, value, and act upon evaluation findings and conclusions.

Since information empowers whoever holds the information, the CIPP Model emphasizes the importance of even-handedness in involving and informing all of a program's stakeholders. Moreover, evaluators should make special efforts to reach and involve those most in need and with little access to and influence over services. Involving all levels of stakeholders is the right thing to do, because it equitably empowers the disadvantaged as well as the advantaged to help define the appropriate evaluation questions and criteria, provide evaluative input, and receive and use evaluation findings. Involving all stakeholder groups is also the intelligent thing to do, because involvement of stakeholders in a change process (*read evaluation*) increases the likelihood that they will accept and act upon the change process's products (e.g., evaluation reports).

The CIPP Model reflects an objectivist orientation. Objectivist evaluations are based on the theory that moral good is objective and independent of personal or merely human feelings. Such evaluations are firmly grounded in ethical principles; strive to control bias, prejudice, and conflicts of interest in seeking determinations of merit and worth; invoke and justify appropriate and (where they exist) established standards of merit; obtain and validate findings from multiple sources; search for best answers, although they may be hard or nearly impossible to find; set forth and justify best available conclusions about the evaluand's merit and/or worth; report findings honestly, fairly, and as circumspectly as necessary to all right-to-know audiences; subject the evaluation process and findings to independent assessments against the evaluation field's standards; and project the need for future investigations to gain further insights into the pertinent evaluative questions. Fundamentally, objectivist evaluations are intended, over time, to lead to conclusions that are correct—not correct or incorrect relative to an evaluator's or other party's predilections, position, preferences, standing, or point of view. When different objectivist evaluations are focused on the same object in a given setting, when they are keyed to fundamental principles of a free society and to agreed-upon criteria of merit, when they meaningfully engage all stakeholder groups in the quest for answers, and when they are carried out in accordance with the professional standards of the evaluation field, different evaluators should arrive at fundamentally equivalent conclusions.

According to the objectivist position, those who conduct evaluations—whether an independent evaluator or those in charge of the evaluand—should carefully select, clarify, validate, and apply appropriate criteria for assessing evaluands. In American society, the fundamental criteria for evaluating public services are found in the U.S. Constitution and the Bill of Rights. For example, public schools should be evaluated for their effectiveness in producing an enlightened citizenry, fully meeting the requirements of equal opportunity, protecting citizens' freedoms, and, in general, upholding human rights. Such basic criteria are not negotiable; they are ingrained in a free society.

In addition, sound objectivist evaluations incorporate criteria of merit established by learned societies. These include, for example, the standards for mathematics education established by the National Council on the Teaching of Mathematics. Also, the American National Standards Institute (ANSI) has approved more than 10,000 national standards that span a wide range of services and products. Among the ANSI standards is *The Program Evaluation Standards.*

This ANSI standard encompasses the 30 standards for program evaluations developed by the North American Joint Committee on Standards for Educational Evaluation (Joint Committee, 1994). This chapter posits that evaluations of U.S. educational programs should be conducted in accordance with these *Standards*. In general, they require evaluations to meet conditions of utility, feasibility, propriety, and accuracy. Additionally, it is recommended that evaluators outside education and/or outside North America determine and report standards for judging their evaluations that are defensible within their fields and cultures.

It is also the position of this chapter and a requirement of the CIPP Model that evaluations be subjected to metaevaluations. A metaevaluation is an evaluation of an evaluation against an appropriate set of professional standards for evaluation. Service providers can apply the selected standards to assess the evaluation's various components—stakeholder identification and engagement, evaluator qualifications, questions and criteria, information sources, data collection methods and tools, analysis procedures, information storage and retrieval system, reports, etc. This will help them evolve and improve the evaluation process through a means of *internal metaevaluation*. In addition, service providers should consider contracting for an *outside metaevaluation*. They should consider doing so whether or not they are conducting their own internal evaluation or have contracted for an outside evaluation. Applying an outside metaevaluation in either case provides an important check on whether the evaluation design, process, and reports meet pertinent evaluation standards.

OBJECTS OF CIPP EVALUATIONS

The CIPP Model is adaptable and widely applicable. This model has been applied to evaluate materials, personnel, students, programs, and projects in a range of disciplines. This chapter applies the model to program and project evaluations and to personnel evaluations. Referenced applications include elementary and secondary education, continuing medical education, community and economic development, and community programs for children and youth.

Sometimes programs or projects have subcomponents. In the case of programs, the subparts might be called projects. The subparts of projects might be called tasks. The CIPP Model calls for identifying the multiple, often hierarchical program or project components and audiences and addressing them both individually and holistically. Almost invariably, the information needed at one level will differ from information required at a higher or lower level. For example, teachers need specific information about individual students, whereas school principals or school board members usually need only aggregate information about groups of students. Evaluators must attend closely to this *levels* issue in order to collect and aggregate findings so that the information needs of different audiences are well met.

CIPP AS A STRATEGY FOR IMPROVING SYSTEMS

The CIPP Model is in line with a systems view of education and human services. It concentrates not only on guiding individual studies, but also on providing ongoing evaluation services to institutional decision makers and other stakeholders. Fundamentally, the model is designed to promote growth. Applied correctly, it helps an institution's leaders and staff obtain and use feedback systematically to meet important needs and to pass accountability examinations.

Especially, the model is based on the view that *the most important purpose of evaluation is not to prove, but to improve.* It is a move against the views that evaluations should be inquisitions, one-shot investigations, activities solely conducted by evaluators, or only instruments of accountability for externally funded projects. Instead, it treats evaluation as a tool by which evaluators in concert with stakeholders help programs, projects, and other services work better for the beneficiaries. As already mentioned, it emphasizes the importance of stakeholder involvement in the evaluation process and advocates cumulative studies keyed to continuous improvement.

However, the CIPP orientation does not exclude or discount the likelihood that some programs or other services are unworthy of efforts to improve them and instead should be canceled. By helping stop unneeded or hopelessly flawed programs, projects, or other services, evaluations also serve an improvement function by assisting organizations to free resources for allocation to more worthy efforts.

The flowchart in Figure 1 displays the CIPP Model's orientation to assist institutions maintain and improve operations. Starting in the left-hand corner, it acknowledges that the operations of a school, college, or another institution include various and perhaps uncoordinated evaluation efforts. It also shows that periodically the institution needs to conduct a special context evaluation.

Such a context evaluation would examine the needs of the institution's clients (e.g., as reflected in prior assessments and analyses of the academic progress of a school's students), uncover assets and opportunities (such as skilled persons who would volunteer services if asked, funding programs, advanced educational technologies, and/or industries with a willingness and capacity to aid the institution), collect and examine perceptions about shortcomings and problems in the institution that warrant change, and assess the clarity and appropriateness of institutional goals and priorities.

The institution might initiate such a context evaluation. For example, the chief executive officer might deliver an annual "state of the institution" assessment. Also, the institution might conduct a context evaluation to address questions from outside groups. For instance, the institution might conduct a self-study to meet an accrediting organization's requirements. Or it might conduct a needs assessment to justify a funding request to taxpayers, a foundation, or a government agency. The institution might target specified areas of concern or focus such context evaluations on a wider range of institutional functions.

Such studies focus system renewal efforts and promote better and more efficient services. They help decision makers diagnose particular problems and write improvement goals. They help the institution assess its strengths, weaknesses, and needs. Institutions use context evaluations to convince stakeholders of the need for change and

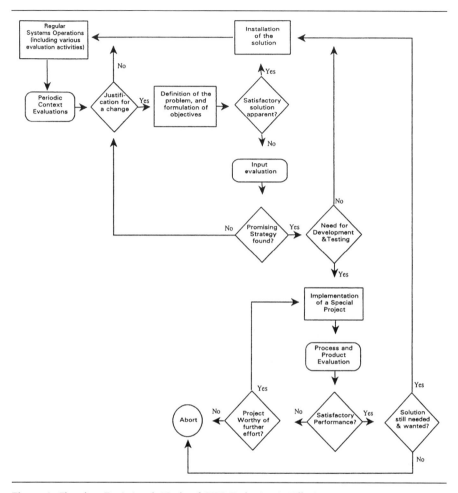

Figure 1. Flowchart Depicting the Role of CIPP Evaluation in Effecting System Improvement

to motivate their participation. Context evaluations also provide evidence-based standards against which to later assess outcomes.

Ideally, the context evaluation results would lead to a decision about whether to change the system. If institutional authorities decided they needed no change, then the staff would sustain usual program operations. Typically, however, service institutions should be committed to a continuous process of institutional learning and improvement. If the authorities decided to improve the institution in some way, then the staff would clarify the problem(s) to be solved and write appropriate goals. For example, school district officials might decide to improve the district's approach to teaching reading, especially for students from disadvantaged backgrounds.

Next, they would consider whether some appropriate solution strategy is apparent and readily adaptable to their situation. They might, for example, decide to install Reading Recovery, especially if the state has sanctioned, advocated, and/or funded it. If so, the district would install it and start evaluating it on a regular basis.

If no satisfactory solution were apparent, then according to the flowchart, the staff would conduct an input evaluation. Such an evaluation includes a review of the relevant literature. It would question personnel in other institutions that had dealt successfully with a similar problem. It would draw on the ingenuity and creativity of staff and constituent groups. Possibly it would obtain information from outside experts. Ultimately, the input evaluation would screen and array the potential alternatives. In reading, these might include Hooked on Phonics, Waterford Integrated Systems approach, Writing to Read, Reading Recovery, a locally generated hybrid proposal, etc.

Subsequently, one or more teams would write up one or more of the screened solution strategies for use in the local setting. The school district would then assess the competing proposal(s) against pertinent criteria. This is the essential input evaluation step. The criteria might include responsiveness to the defined needs, problems, and goals; theoretical soundness; evidence of successful use elsewhere; compatibility with the existing system; cost; affordability; acceptability to teachers and parents; and administrative feasibility.

The decision makers (e.g., teachers, pertinent committees, and administrators) would use the input evaluation results to decide whether they had found a promising strategy. If not, they would reconsider whether the change was sufficiently important to warrant a further search. If so, they would recycle the input evaluation process. Once the school district had found an acceptable strategy, its authorities would decide whether they could justifiably install it without further testing. If they knew much about the strategy and were confident they could make it work in the district, then they would directly incorporate the change into district activities. They would do so without further specialized evaluation support.

However, if they decided to examine it further, they might well conduct a pilot test. The test could occur in a limited setting, e.g., one or a few schools. It would entail a process evaluation and a product evaluation. The district would carry out these studies over whatever period they required to validate the intervention and prepare it for installation. At some point, however, if the project has not succeeded or authorities decide it is too costly, the district's leadership might abort the effort.

Institutions have frequently stopped projects when federal funding ended. In such cases they have to decide whether to allocate local funds to continue the project. As shown in the bottom right-hand corner of the flowchart, even if a project had succeeded, the institution's leadership might determine that conditions in the institution had changed sufficiently that they no longer need the previously desired change. Accordingly, they would terminate the effort. This point further illustrates the importance of ongoing context evaluation to maintain an up-to-date perspective on institutional needs and capacity.

Under the assumption that the project succeeded and was still needed, the institution would fund and install the proven project. It would integrate it into regular operations, including evaluation of the ongoing program and its new elements.

The preceding analysis of evaluation in an institution's change process points up several important features of a systems approach to evaluation:

1. Evaluation can be an integral part of an institution's regular operations and not merely a specialized activity involved in innovative projects, and the use of the CIPP Model or any other specialized approach is only a part of the institution's mosaic of informal and formal evaluation activities.
2. Evaluations have a vital role in stimulating and planning changes.
3. Program staffs, individual service providers, and/or evaluators, in a formal or informal sense, regularly make judgments that could be categorized as context, input, process, and product evaluations in carrying out their responsibilities; and sometimes they can use existing information to conduct one or more of these types of evaluation.
4. Evaluators should collect new information for each type of evaluation in the CIPP Model only if they need information beyond what already exists. In other words, context, input, process, and product evaluations are part of the institution's general evaluation activities. The most important reasons to collect new information are to serve marginal needs for new evaluative information and to corroborate the existing information.
5. After installing a new program, an institution should regularly evaluate it. Regarding curricula, a school or college might employ curriculum-embedded evaluation. Using this approach, the institution builds evaluation into the curriculum process and materials. In carrying out the curriculum, instructors and students receive information they can use to check progress, diagnose learning problems, formulate solutions, and document outcomes.
6. Institutions can use information obtained through CIPP evaluations to solve institutional problems and meet accountability requirements. If they store the information they can retrieve it and report it to interested audiences. This helps the institution show stakeholders that decisions to abort or institutionalize a special project were based on sound information.
7. Decisions to commence, sustain, install, or abort programs and program improvement efforts usually reflect dynamic forces—irrational and rational—that extend far beyond the evaluator's sphere of study and influence.

**A DETAILED LOOK AT THE CIPP CATEGORIES,
INCLUDING RELEVANT PROCEDURES**

Building on the preceding characterization of the CIPP Model as a systems approach, this section provides a more specific discussion of the essential elements of each type of evaluation. This section also presents certain techniques that evaluators have found especially useful for conducting each type of evaluation.

Context Evaluation

Context evaluation assesses needs, problems, assets, and opportunities within a defined environment. *Needs* include those things that are necessary or useful for fulfilling a defensible purpose. *Problems* are impediments to overcome in meeting and continuing to meet targeted needs. *Assets* include accessible expertise and services—usually in the local area—that could be used to help fulfill the targeted purpose. *Opportunities* include, especially, funding programs that might be tapped to support efforts to meet needs and solve associated problems. *Defensible purposes* define what is to be achieved related to the institution's mission while adhering to ethical and legal standards.

While context evaluation is often referred to as needs assessment, the latter term is too narrow since it focuses on needs and omits concerns about problems, assets, and opportunities. All four elements are critically important in designing sound programs, projects, and individual services and should be considered in context evaluations. A context evaluation's main objectives are to

- describe the context for the intended service
- identify intended beneficiaries and assess their needs
- identify problems or barriers to meeting the needs
- identify area assets and funding opportunities that could be used to address the targeted needs
- assess the clarity and appropriateness of program, instructional, or other service goals

Context evaluations may be initiated before, during, or even after a project, program, or other improvement effort. In the before case, institutions may carry out context evaluations as narrowly bounded studies to help set goals and priorities in a particular area. When started during or after a project or other special improvement effort, institutions will often conduct and report context evaluations in combination with input, process, and product evaluations. Here context evaluations are useful for judging already established goals and for helping the audience assess the effort's significance in meeting beneficiaries' needs.

A context evaluation's methodology may involve collecting a variety of information about members of the target population and their surrounding environment and conducting various types of analysis. A usual starting point is to ask the evaluation's clients and other stakeholders to help define the study's boundaries. Subsequently, evaluators may employ a variety of techniques to generate and test hypotheses about needed services or changes in existing services. These might include reviewing documents, analyzing demographic and performance data, conducting hearings and community forums, and interviewing beneficiaries and other stakeholders.

The evaluators might construct a survey instrument to investigate identified hypotheses. Then they could administer it to a carefully defined sample of stakeholders. The evaluators could also make the survey instrument available more generally to anyone who wishes to provide input. They would separately analyze the two sets of responses.

Evaluators should also examine existing records to identify performance patterns and background information on the target population. In educational programs, these might include immunization records; enrollment in different levels of courses; attendance; school grades; test scores; honors; graduation rates; participation in extracurricular activities; participation in special education; home situations; health histories; and/or feedback from teachers, parents, former students, counselors, coaches, health personnel, librarians, custodians, and administrators.

The evaluators might administer special diagnostic tests to members of the target population. They might engage an expert review panel to visit, closely observe, and identify needs, problems, assets, and opportunities in the targeted environment. The evaluators might conduct focus group meetings to review the gathered information. These procedures contribute to an in-depth perspective on the system's functioning and highest priority needs.

Throughout the context evaluation, the evaluators might involve a representative advisory committee to help clarify the evaluative questions and interpret the findings. The evaluators might use a consensus-building technique, such as Delphi, to solidify agreements about priority needs and goals. In statewide or other large-scale efforts, they might conduct a meeting—such as the many White House conferences on societal problems—to engage experts and constituents in studying and interpreting the findings and making recommendations.

After the initial context evaluation, the institution needs to continue collecting, organizing, filing, and reporting context evaluation data, since needs, problems, and opportunities are subject to change. The institution's evaluators should draw selectively from the same set of methods recommended above. They should help stakeholders maintain current information on beneficiaries' characteristics and achievements. In addition, institutions should set up a functional input-process-output information system. They should employ it to receive, code, clean, store, retrieve, and use the information. After setting up this system, it may be feasible and useful to convert it to a computerized database.

During or after a project or program, the evaluators might issue updated context evaluation reports. They would also incorporate context evaluation information in more holistic reports. These reports should help the client group see the intervention's guiding design, operations, and outcomes in relationship to pertinent needs of the intended beneficiaries.

Often audiences need to view the effort within both its present setting and its historical context. Considering the relevant history helps the decision makers avoid past mistakes. Thus, the methodology of context evaluation includes historical analysis and literature review as well as methods aimed at characterizing and understanding current environmental conditions.

A context evaluation may have many constructive uses. It might provide a means by which school district officials communicate with the public to gain a shared conception of the district's strengths and weaknesses, needs, assets, opportunities, and priority problems. An institution might use it to convince a funding agency that it directed a proposed project at an urgent need or to convince an electorate to pass a tax issue. A social service organization might use a context evaluation to formulate objectives for staff development or to identify target populations for priority or emergency assistance.

Institutions should employ context evaluations to launch needed improvement efforts. For example, a school could use a context evaluation to help students and their parents or advisers focus their attention on developmental areas requiring more progress—such as socio-psychological development or moral development. An institution could use it to help decide how to make the institution stronger by cutting marginal or ineffective programs. At the national level a government agency or professional society might issue an attention-getting report to mobilize the public to support a program of reform. A famous example of this is *A Nation at Risk* (National Commission on Excellence in Education, 1983), which spawned new national education reform programs in the U.S., including Goals 2000.

Another use of context evaluation comes later when an institution or individual service provider needs to assess the significance of what an improvement effort accomplished. Here the institution or individual assesses whether the investment in improvement effectively addressed the targeted needs and goals. The inquirer also refers to context evaluation findings to assess the relevance of operating plans. Similarly, the inquirer uses context evaluation findings to examine how the project's process is affecting the project's environment. Considering such uses, an institution or other group of service providers can benefit greatly by establishing, keeping up-to-date, and using information from a context evaluation database.

The Program Profile Technique, As Applied In Context Evaluations

As noted above, many methods are useful in conducting context evaluations, including analysis of demographic records, site visits, examination of relevant documents, and issue-oriented workshops or conferences. Evaluators at the Western Michigan University Evaluation Center have combined data from such methods into an overall approach labeled The *Program Profile Technique*. This technique includes:

- a checklist to collect data from a variety of sources about relevant history; current environment; constituent needs; system problems; assets and opportunities; and program structure, operations, and achievements
- a database
- periodic reports that characterize the program's background, environmental circumstances, and present status
- feedback workshops to the client and designated stakeholders

The following is an abbreviated outline of a program profile used to report periodically on a longitudinal study of a community development program in Hawaii:

I.   Program Background and Current Context
     A. Program Vision and Mission
     B. Establishment and Evolution of the Program
     C. The Homeless in Hawaii
     D. Serving the Homeless
     E. Selected Demographic Characteristics of Program Participants Compared
        With Other Relevant Population Segments
     F. Program Area Market Factors
II. Governance and Management of the Program
     A. Mission, Goals, and Planning
     B. Program Organization
     C. Financial Management and Resource Development
III. Program Characteristics
     A. The Program Site
     B. Selection of Builders/Homeowners
     C. Construction of Homes
     D. Community Center
     E. Legal Aspects
     F. Other Services
IV. Community Relations
     A. Local Community Relations
     B. Relations with City and County Government
     C. Relations with Other Groups, Stakeholders, and Power Brokers
V.   Stakeholder Impressions of the Program
     A. Builders
     B. Program Staff
     C. Project Consultants
VI. Concluding Assessment
     A. Overall Assessment of the Program in Context
     B. Recommendations
VII. Exhibits

Analysis Of Patient Records, As A Procedure For Context Evaluation In Individual Medical Practice

Institutions need context evaluation to guide and assess the performance of individual professionals as well as programs. A technique of use in conducting context evaluations related to improvement needs of individual physicians is the *Compilation and Analysis of Patient Records* (see Manning & DeBakey, 1987). Many such records are routinely completed and stored as a part of the doctor-patient process, including patient files, hospital charts, and insurance forms. In addition, a doctor might maintain a card file on unusual, little understood, or otherwise interesting patient problems. This helps the doctor gain historical perspective on such cases. Patient records are a valuable source of evaluative information. Context evaluation questions that physicians might answer by analyzing patient records include the following: What illnesses and types of accidents are most prevalent among the doctor's patients? What are the important systematic variations in illnesses and accidents, aligned with seasons and with age, gender, and occupation of the patients? To what extent do the doctor's patients evidence chronic problems that treatments only temporarily help? What diagnostic tests and procedures does the doctor use most frequently? What are relative levels of usefulness and cost-effectiveness of the diagnostic tests frequently ordered by the doctor? What types of problems does the doctor typically treat without referral? What types of problems does the doctor typically refer to other professionals? What are the success rates, at least relative absence of complaints, of referrals to the different referral services? To what extent are patient records complete, clear, and up-to-date? To what extent are patients' immunizations up-to-date and inclusive of what they need? To what extent have patients been taking physical examinations and other needed tests on an appropriate schedule? To what extent do the patient records reflect success in managing weight, blood pressure, and cholesterol? To what extent do the doctor's patients take flu shots and with what outcomes? What are the numbers and types of complaints from patients and/or other health professionals about the doctor's practice? To what extent do the patients pay their bills on time? To what extent are the doctor's charges within rates set by third-party payers?

The *Analysis Of Patient Records* procedure is a valuable means of answering such questions. As illustrated, individual doctors can use this technique to look for weaknesses and strengths in all aspects of their practice, then formulate improvement goals. Medical educators can also usefully employ the technique in cooperation with doctors to set appropriate goals for individualized continuing medical education services and later to assess the outcomes of the medical education experiences.

Input Evaluation

An input evaluation's main orientation is to help prescribe a program, project, or other intervention by which to improve services to intended beneficiaries. An input evaluation assesses the proposed program, project, or service strategy and the associated work plan and budget for carrying out the effort. It does this by searching out and critically examining potentially relevant approaches, including the one(s) already being used. The key criteria for assessing competing strategies are potential success in achieving program goals and attending effectively to assessed needs, problems, area assets, and opportunities. Input evaluation is a precursor of the success or failure and efficiency of a change effort. Initial decisions to allocate resources constrain improvement efforts. A potentially effective solution to a problem will have no possibility of impact if a planning group does not at least identify it and assess its merits.

Essentially, an input evaluation should identify and rate relevant approaches and assist decision makers to prepare the chosen approach for execution. It should also search the clients' environment for political barriers, financial or legal constraints, and potential resources. An important function of input evaluation is to help clients avoid the wasteful practice of pursuing proposed innovations that predictably would fail or at least waste resources.

Evaluators conduct input evaluations in several stages. These occur in no set sequence. An evaluator might first review the state of practice in meeting the specified needs and goals. This could include reviewing relevant literature; visiting exemplary programs; consulting experts and government representatives; querying pertinent information services (e.g., those on the World Wide Web); referencing a pertinent article in *Consumer Reports* or similar publications that critically review available products and services; and inviting proposals from involved staff.

Evaluators might organize this information in a special planning room. They might engage a special study group to participate in a special planning seminar to analyze the material. The evaluators would use the information to assess whether potentially acceptable solution strategies exist. They would rate promising approaches on relevant criteria, such as responsiveness to beneficiaries' priority needs, potential effectiveness, cost, political viability, compatibility to existing institutional operations, and administrative feasibility.

Next the evaluators could advise the decision makers about whether they should seek a novel solution. In seeking an innovation, the client and evaluators might document criteria the innovation should meet, structure a request for proposals, obtain competing proposals, and rate them on the chosen criteria. Subsequently, the evaluators might rank the potentially acceptable proposals and suggest how the institution could combine their best features. They might conduct a hearing, focused on the critical competitors, to obtain additional information. They could ask staff and administrators to express concerns. They would also appraise resources and barriers that the institution should consider when installing the intervention. The planning group could then use the accumulated information to design what they see as the best combination strategy and action plan.

Input evaluations have several applications. A chief one is in preparing a proposal for submission to a policy board and/or funding agency. Another is to assess one's existing practice, whether or not it seems satisfactory, against what is being done elsewhere and proposed in the literature. Subsequent to selecting and explicating a service strategy, planners may request a follow-on, detailed input evaluation to closely assess the viability and potential effectiveness of the work plan and budget. At the end of the project, program year, or service period, funding authorities or other stakeholders may reference the initial input evaluation to consider whether the adopted service plan was justified. Such an application is especially important when activities were carried out according to the plan but failed to produce valuable outcomes. The key question then is whether a previous input evaluation showed the adopted strategy, work plan, and/or budget to be flawed and/or inferior to other possibilities.

Input evaluation has been used in the Dallas Independent School District; the Des Moines, Iowa, Public Schools; and the Shaker Heights, Ohio, School District to decide whether locally-generated proposals for innovation would likely be cost-effective. Detroit, Michigan's public school district also used input evaluation to generate and assess alternative architectural designs for new school buildings. The Southwest Regional Educational Laboratory used input evaluation to help historically antagonistic groups agree on how to use ten million dollars to serve the education needs of migrant children. The U.S. Office of Education (now the U.S. Department of Education) used input evaluation to develop and assess two competing plans for evaluating all of the federally-funded regional educational laboratories and research and development centers. The United States Marine Corps contracted an input evaluation to identify and assess 10 alternative personnel systems that might provide an acceptable replacement for the Corps' system. In addition to informing and facilitating decisions, input evaluation records help authorities defend their choice of one course of action above other possibilities. School district superintendents, school boards, social service administrators, chief executive officers of companies, military leaders, and government authorities would find input evaluation records useful when they must defend sizable expenditures for new programs.

The Advocacy Teams Technique As Used In Input Evaluations

The Advocacy Teams Technique is a procedure designed specifically for conducting input evaluations. This technique is especially applicable in situations where institutions lack effective means to meet specified needs and where stakeholders hold opposing views on what strategy the institution should adopt. The evaluators convene two or more teams of experts and stakeholders. They give the teams the goals, background data on needs, specifications for a solution strategy, and criteria for evaluating the teams' proposed strategies. They may staff these teams to match members' preferences and expertise regarding the nature of leading candidate approaches. Evaluators should do so, especially if stakeholders severely disagree about what type of approach they would accept. The advocacy teams then compete, preferably in isolation from each other, to develop a "winning solution strategy." A panel of experts and stakeholders rates the advocacy team reports on pre-specified criteria. The institution might also field test the teams' proposed strategies. Subsequently, the institution would operationalize the winning strategy. Alternatively, it might combine and operationalize the best features of the two or more competing strategies.

The advocacy team technique's advantages are that it provides a systematic approach for designing interventions to meet assessed needs; generating and assessing competing strategies; exploiting bias and competition in a constructive search for alternatives; addressing controversy and breaking down stalemates that stand in the way of progress; involving personnel from the adopting system in devising, assessing, and operationalizing improvement programs; and documenting why a particular solution strategy was selected.

Additional information, including a technical manual and the results of five field tests of the technique, is available in a doctoral dissertation by Diane Reinhard (1972).

Process Evaluation

In essence, a process evaluation is an ongoing check on a plan's implementation plus documentation of the process, including changes in the plan as well as key omissions and/or poor execution of certain procedures. One goal is to provide staff and managers feedback about the extent to which staff are carrying out planned activities on schedule, as planned, and efficiently. Another is to help staff identify implementation problems and to make needed corrections in the activities or the plan. Typically, staffs cannot determine all aspects of a plan when a project starts. Also, they must alter the plan if some initial decisions are unsound or become inapplicable. Still another objective of process evaluation is to periodically assess the extent to which participants accept and can carry out their roles. A process evaluation should contrast activities with the plan, describe implementation problems, and assess how well the staff addressed them. It should document and analyze the effort's costs. Finally, it should report how observers and participants judged the quality of the process.

The linchpin of a sound process evaluation is the process evaluator. More often than not, a staff's failure to obtain guidance for implementation and to document their activities is due to a failure to assign anyone to do this work. Sponsors and institutions too often assume erroneously that the managers and staff will adequately evaluate process as a normal part of their assignments. They can routinely do some review and documentation through activities such as staff meetings and minutes of the meetings. However, these do not fulfill the requirements of a sound process evaluation. Experience has shown that staffs can usually meet these requirements well only by assigning an evaluator to provide ongoing review, feedback, and documentation.

A process evaluator has much work to do in monitoring and documenting an intervention. The following scenario illustrates what the process evaluator might do. Initially, he/she could review the relevant strategy and work plans and any prior background evaluation to identify what planned activities they should monitor. Possible examples in education are staff training, materials development, management of the project library, counseling students, meetings between teachers and parents, tutoring students, project planning, skill or interest grouping of students, classroom instruction, classroom assessment, field trips, homework assignments, analysis and use of standardized test results, use of diagnostic tests, and reporting progress. Examples extending beyond education are orientation and training of workers, securing and maintaining equipment, ordering and distributing materials, monitoring and inspecting work flow, and communication. Beyond looking at the elements of work plans, the process evaluator might also periodically consult a broadly representative advisory group. The evaluator could ask the group to identify what important concerns and questions the effort should address. Other questions will occur to the evaluator in observing activities, providing feedback, and interacting with participants.

With questions and concerns such as those mentioned above in mind, the process evaluator could develop a general schedule of data collection activities and begin carrying them out. Initially, these probably should be as unobtrusive as possible so as not to threaten staff and beneficiaries, get in their way, constrain their exploration and creativity, or interfere with the process. Subsequently, as rapport develops, the process evaluator can use a more structured, visible approach.

At the outset, the process evaluator should get an overview of how the work is going. This can be achieved by visiting and observing centers of activity, reviewing pertinent documents (especially the work plans, budgets, and minutes of meetings), attending staff meetings, and interviewing key participants. A process evaluator could also maintain a photographic record showing, for example, attendance and activities at project or program events.

The process evaluator then could prepare a brief report that summarizes the data collection plan, findings, and observed issues, highlighting existing or impending process problems that the staff should address. The evaluator should provide drafts of the report to appropriate stakeholders so they can review it prior to discussing it with their colleagues and the evaluator. The evaluator would next meet with the stakeholders to go over the report and discuss it. In this context, the project team could use the report for decision making as they see best.

The process evaluator could also review with the staff plans for further data collection and the subsequent report and ask them to react to the plan. They could say what information they would find most useful at the next meeting. They could also suggest how the evaluator could best collect certain items of information. These might include observations, staff-kept diaries, interviews, or questionnaires. The evaluator should also ask the staff to say when they need the next evaluation report.

Using this feedback, the evaluator would schedule future feedback sessions, modify the data collection plan as appropriate, and proceed accordingly. The evaluator should continually show that process evaluation helps staff carry out its work through a kind of quality assurance and ongoing problem-solving process. He or she should also sustain the effort to document the actual process and lessons learned.

Following the preceding example, the process evaluator should periodically report on how well the staff carried out the work plan and integrated the project into the surrounding environment. The evaluator should describe main deviations from the plan; note variations concerning how different persons, groups, and/or sites are carrying out the plan; and characterize and assess the ongoing planning activity. In addition, the evaluator should maintain and periodically analyze the effort's pattern and categories of expenditure.

Staffs use process evaluation to guide activities, correct faulty plans, and maintain accountability records. Some managers use regularly scheduled process evaluation feedback sessions to keep staff "on their toes" and abreast of their responsibilities. Process evaluation records are useful for accountability, since funding agencies, policy boards, and constituents typically want objective and substantive confirmation of whether grantees did what they had proposed. Such information is also useful to new staff, as a part of their orientation to what has gone before. Moreover, process evaluation information is vital for interpreting product evaluation results. One needs to learn what was done in a program, project, or other service effort before deciding why the outcomes turned out as they did. Process evaluations can also help external audiences—who might want to conduct a similar effort—to learn problems were encountered, how they were addressed, how much the effort cost, and how the funds were allocated.

Traveling Observer Technique For Use In Process Evaluations

Over the years, The Evaluation Center has developed and employed a procedure labeled the *Traveling Observer Technique* (Evers, 1980; Reed, 1991; Thompson, 1986). This technique most heavily addresses process evaluation data requirements but, like other techniques, also provides data of use in context, input, and product evaluations. The technique involves sending a specially trained investigator into a program's field sites. This Traveling Observer (TO) investigates and characterizes how staff members are carrying out the project at the different sites and reports the findings to the other evaluation team members. The TO also participates in feedback sessions to the client group.

The TO follows a set schedule of data collection and writes and delivers reports according to predetermined formats and reporting specifications. Before entering the field, the TO develops a traveling observer handbook under the principal evaluator's supervision (Alexander, 1974; Nowakowski, 1974; Reed, 1989; Sandberg, 1986; Sumida, 1994). This handbook serves as an evaluation tool and should be tailored to the particular evaluation's questions. The handbook includes information and specifications such as the following:

- Traveling Observer's credentials
- Evaluation questions
- Description of the study sites and program or project activities
- Contact personnel and phone numbers
- Maps showing program or project locations
- Data sources suggested, including interviewees and pertinent documents
- Protocols for contacting field personnel and obtaining needed permissions and cooperation
- Rules concerning professional behavior expected of the TO
- Guidelines to help the TO avoid cooptation by program staff
- Recommended data collection procedures
- Sampling plans, including both preset samples and exploratory grapevine sampling
- Data collection instruments
- Data collection schedule
- Daily log/diary format
- Rules for processing information and keeping it secure
- Audience for TO feedback
- Reporting specifications and schedule, including interim progress reports, briefing sessions, and expense reports
- Criteria for judging TO reports

- Rules about communicating/disseminating findings, including provisions for reporting to those who supplied data for the TO's study
- Responsibilities for scheduling and facilitating follow-up investigations, e.g., by a site visit team of experts
- Issues that may arise and what to do about them
- Summary of the standards being used to judge the overall evaluation effort
- Form for the TO's periodic self-assessment
- Budget to support the TO's work, including spending limitations

In an early application of this technique, The Evaluation Center sent out Traveling Observers as "advance persons" to do initial investigation on two $5 million statewide National Science Foundation programs. The Center assigned the TOs to prepare the way for follow-up site visits by high level teams. These teams included national experts in science, mathematics, technology, evaluation, and education. Each program included many projects at several sites across the state. The evaluation budget was insufficient to send the five-member teams of "high priced" experts to all the potentially important sites.

Instead, the Center trained and sent a TO to study the program in each state. Each TO spent two weeks investigating the program and prepared a report, which included a tentative site visit agenda for the follow-up teams of experts. The TO also contacted program personnel to prepare them for the follow-up visits and gain their understanding and support for the evaluation.

On the first day of the team site visits, each TO distributed her/his TO report and related materials and explained the results. The TO also oriented the team to the geography, politics, personalities, etc., in the program. He or she presented the team with a tentative site visit agenda and answered questions. The TO's recommended plans for the site visit team included sending different members of the site team to different project sites and some total team meetings with key program personnel. During the week-long team visit, the TO remained accessible by phone so that he or she could help the site team members.

At the end of this study, the Center engaged Michael Scriven to evaluate the evaluation. He reported that the TO reports were so informative that, except for the credibility added by the national experts, the TOs could have successfully evaluated the programs without the experts. Overall, The Evaluation Center has found that the Traveling Observer Technique is a powerful evaluation tool; it is systematic, flexible, efficient, and inexpensive. Its focal use is to conduct process evaluation, but it sets the process in context of assessed needs, program structure, and outcomes. It also is useful in preparing for follow-up, in-depth site visits.

Product Evaluation

The purpose of a product evaluation is to measure, interpret, and judge an enterprise's achievements. Its main goal is to ascertain the extent to which the evaluand met the needs of all the rightful beneficiaries. Feedback about achievements is important both during an activity cycle and at its conclusion. A product evaluation should assess intended and unintended outcomes and positive and negative outcomes. Moreover, evaluators should often extend a product evaluation to assess long-term outcomes.

A product evaluation should gather and analyze stakeholders' judgments of the enterprise. Sometimes it should compare the effort's outcomes with those of similar enterprises. Frequently, the client wants to know whether the enterprise achieved its goals, what it cost, and whether the outcomes were worth the investment. Usually, evaluators should interpret whether poor implementation of the work plan caused poor outcomes or whether such inadequate outcomes resulted for execution of an unsound plan. Generally, it is useful to ground interpretations of product evaluation findings in the findings of previous context, input, and process evaluations. A product evaluation should usually view outcomes from several vantage points: in the aggregate, for subgroups, and sometimes for individuals.

Evaluators may classify an individual's achievement as a success or failure depending on whether the program, project, or other service met his or her diagnosed and targeted needs. Such individualized product evaluations also allow aggregation across individuals to get an overall index of success. Still, evaluators can do this only if they tailor the measures to individual assessed needs, yet make them comparable.

For example, no single standardized instrument would suffice in assessing a program's success in meeting special education students' very different needs. However, evaluators must achieve some level of standardization if they are to aggregate the different measures. They would have to search for outcomes related to each student's diagnosed needs. These data could and probably would vary widely for the different students. To aggregate these measures, the evaluators would need to employ special procedures. For example, they might code the outcomes for individuals from very different measures on a common scale, such as the following: fully successful, partially successful, no effect, partially damaging, very damaging. Then the evaluators could aggregate the findings for each category of the evaluation scale. This would permit them to assess the extent to which the program was successful in meeting the differential needs of all the involved students.

Product evaluations follow no set algorithm, but many methods are applicable. Evaluators should use a combination of techniques. This aids them to make a comprehensive search for outcomes. It also helps them cross-check the various findings. The following discussion illustrates the range of techniques that evaluators might employ.

Evaluators might assess students' test scores compared with a specified standard. The standard might be a profile of previously assessed needs, pretest scores, selected norms, program goals, or a comparison group's performance. Product evaluators might assess achievements related to some previously stated principle. Sanders and Horn (1994) advocate a general principle of sustained academic growth for each student, across three or more years. Webster, Mendro, and Almaguer (1994) propose comparing schools on one-year, schoolwide gains, when they have partialed out student background variances. Product evaluators might use published objective tests or specially made criterion-referenced tests. They might also employ performance assessments or applied performance tests (see Sanders & Sachse, 1977). Experts might compare program recipients' work products to specified standards.

To assess performance beyond goals, evaluators need to search for unanticipated outcomes, both positive and negative. They might conduct hearings or group interviews to generate hypotheses about the full range of outcomes and follow these up with efforts to confirm or disconfirm the hypotheses. They might conduct case studies of the experiences of a carefully selected sample of participants to obtain an in-depth view of the program's effects. They might survey, via telephone or mail, a sample of participants to obtain their judgments of the service and their views of both positive and negative findings. They might ask the participants to submit concrete examples of how the project or other service influenced their work or well-being. These could be written pieces, other work products, or new job status. They might engage observers to identify program and comparison groups' achievements. They can then use the reported achievements to develop tests that reflect the hypothesized outcomes. By administering the test to program recipients and a comparison group, the evaluators can estimate the intervention's unique contributions (see Brickell, 1976). Evaluators might conduct a "jury trial" of the project. The adversaries and advocates would introduce evidence both supporting and attacking the intervention. The jury would then judge the intervention as either successful or unsuccessful (see Chapter 10, this volume; Wolf, 1974). Evaluators might also compare program achievements with a comprehensive checklist of outcomes of similar programs or services.

Product evaluators might also conduct a "goal-free evaluation" (Scriven, 1991). Accordingly, the evaluator engages an investigator to find whatever effects an intervention produced. The evaluator purposely does not inform the goal-free investigator about the intervention's goals. The point is to prevent the investigator from developing tunnel vision focused on stated goals. The evaluator then contrasts identified effects with the program beneficiaries' assessed needs. This provides a unique approach to assessing the intervention's merit and worth, whatever its goals. This approach to product evaluation is consistent with the Total Quality Management movement's stress on producing quality products that meet customer requirements.

Reporting of product evaluation findings may occur at different stages. Evaluators may submit interim reports during a project or during different program cycles. These reports should show the extent the intervention is addressing and meeting targeted needs. End-of-project/program cycle reports may sum up the results achieved. Such reports should interpret the results in the light of assessed needs, costs incurred, and execution of the plan. Evaluators may also submit follow-up reports to assess long-term outcomes.

On the latter point, The Evaluation Center has in certain evaluations adapted the CIPP Model to add emphasis to the later stages in the change/institutionalization process. Three such stages are assessing *impact* (to what extent did the program reach and serve the rightful or targeted beneficiaries?), assessing *effectiveness* (how profound were the effects on the persons served?), and assessing *viability* (to what extent is the project/program *sustainable* and *transportable?*).

People use product evaluations to decide whether a given program, project, service, or other enterprise is worth using, continuing, repeating, and/or extending to other settings. A product evaluation also should provide direction for modifying the enterprise or replacing it so that the institution will more cost-effectively serve the needs of all members of the target audience. Of course, it should help potential adopters decide whether the approach merits their serious consideration.

Product evaluation information is an essential component of an accountability report. When authorities document significant achievements, they can better convince community and funding organizations to provide additional financial and political support. When authorities learn that the intervention made no important gains they can justifiably cancel the investment. This frees funds for more worthy interventions. Moreover, other developers can use a product evaluation report to help decide whether to pursue a similar course of action.

Continuous Progress Matrix Sampling Testing Technique as Used in Product Evaluations

The *Continuous Progress Matrix Sampling Testing Technique* is a product evaluation technique, developed by the author, for use in his classroom teaching. This technique provides a periodic look at a course's evolving gross learning product and students' progress and retention of each course unit. The technique is designed to help teachers and students overcome their frequent dissatisfaction with pretest-posttest gains data. These indicate only what students gained over several months; they do not show what learning trends occurred between the two tests. Instructors express frustration when the gains are small; they do not know why, and they learned this too late to do anything about it. Probably most instructors and students would be interested to see and examine learning trends between a pretest and posttest. Then they could decide to revisit important content that the students either did not learn or did not retain.

The *Continuous Progress Matrix Sampling Testing Technique* is based on matrix sample testing (Cook & Stufflebeam, 1967; Owens & Stufflebeam, 1964). About weekly, an instructor administers a parallel form of the final course examination. Different students respond to different random samples of items from this test. The instructor aggregates the responses for each content area of the course and maintains week-by-week trend lines for the total test and each course unit. During selected class sessions the instructor devotes a few minutes to administering the test and then discussing the most recent results. Starting with the second such session (and continuing thereafter on a regular basis), the instructor distributes and explains the latest update on trends in tested achievement.

Each week, the instructor and students can see how well the class as a whole is progressing toward a high total score on the final exam. By looking at the trend line for the unit taught last, the students can see whether they, as a group, mastered the recently taught material. They can also assess whether they retained or regressed in what they learned in units taught earlier. Instructors are encouraged when they see that test scores for untaught units remain, week after week, at the chance level, then dramatically improve following instruction. They should be concerned when test score trends show that students regressed on previously mastered material. Such feedback can motivate and guide instructors and students to revisit and regain the prior learning. It can lead instructors to search for a better way to teach the material. Students and the instructor can discuss the results weekly to detect where past instruction and learning activities may have been weak and for what reasons. They can collaborate in deciding what material they should review and how the instructor could best get it across.

Advantages of this approach are that it helps students see that testing in the course is instrumental to improving teaching and learning; they are partners in producing a good outcome for the entire class; they and the instructor can use relevant empirical data to assess progress and recycle instructional and learning activities; the time involved in taking weekly tests can be small; weekly testing is not threatening since students receive no individual scores; validity of the results for the class as a whole is enhanced, since test items are randomly selected from the course's item pool, then randomly divided into subtests, and since the subtests are randomly assigned to students.

Limitations of the technique are that it provides no feedback on performance of individual students; it is based exclusively on multiple choice test questions; and it obtains feedback on each item from only one or a few students. Overall, the technique is decidedly better than a pretest-posttest or posttest only approach. Like these approaches, it assesses course effectiveness. Equally or more important, it also guides instruction and learning activities.

The matrix in Table 1 is provided as a convenient overview of the preceding explanation of the CIPP categories.

THE POINT-OF-ENTRY PROBLEM AND GUIDELINES FOR ADDRESSING IT

At first glance, the CIPP Model provides for an orderly succession of four different types of studies that help in planning and conducting successful projects and programs and other services. However, evaluation and change efforts are seldom neat, orderly, linear activities. It would be a mistake to assume that evaluators should always formally conduct context, input, process, and product evaluations in that order. Sometimes clients legitimately may request a different order of evaluation studies. They might even appropriately request only one, two, or three of the study types or none at all.

This contradiction between the real world and the apparent logical ordering of the CIPP constructs is evident in the so-called point-of-entry problem. It concerns when to initiate an evaluation, what evaluative questions to pursue, and what new data to collect to address the questions. Scriven (1969b) identified this problem many years ago, but it has received little analytical attention. On the other hand, evaluators frequently encounter this problem. A discussion of the issue is appropriate because the failure to deal effectively with it can render evaluations superfluous,

Table 1. Four Types of Evaluation

	Context Evaluation	Input Evaluation	Process Evaluation	Product Evaluation
Objective	• To define the institutional/ service context • To identify the target population and assess its *needs* • To identify pertinent area *assets* and *resource opportunities* for addressing the needs • To diagnose *problems* underlying the needs • To judge whether *goals* are sufficiently responsive to the assessed needs	• To identify and assess system *capabilities* and alternative *service strategies* • To closely examine planned *procedures, budgets,* and *schedules* for implementing the chosen strategy	• To identify or predict *defects* in the procedural design or its implementation • To provide information for the programmed decisions • To record procedural events and activities for later analysis and judgment	• To collect descriptions and judgments of *outcomes* • To relate outcomes to *goals* and to *context, input,* and *process* information • To interpret the effort's *merit* and *worth*
Method	• By using such methods as survey, document review, secondary data analysis, hearings, interviews, diagnostic tests, system analysis, and the Delphi technique	• By *inventorying and analyzing* available human and material resources • By using such methods as *literature search, visits to exemplary programs, advocate teams,* and *pilot trials* to identify and examine promising solution strategies • By *critiquing* procedural designs for relevance, feasibility, cost, and economy	• By *monitoring* the activity's potential procedural barriers and remaining alert to unanticipated ones • By obtaining specified information for programmed decisions • By interviewing beneficiaries, *describing* the actual process, maintaining a *photographic record,* and continually interacting with and observing the activities of staff and beneficiaries	• By operationally defining and *measuring* outcomes • By *collecting judgments* of outcomes from stakeholders • By performing both *qualitative* and *quantitative* analyses • By *comparing* outcomes to assessed needs, goals, and other pertinent standards
Relation to decision making in the change process	• For deciding on the *setting* to be served • For defining *goals* and setting *priorities* • For surfacing and addressing potential *barriers* to success • For providing a *basis for judging assessed needs* as a basis for judging outcomes	• For selecting *sources of support* and solution *strategies* • For explicating a sound procedural *design,* including a budget, schedule, and staffing plan • For providing a *basis for monitoring and judging implementation*	• For *implementing and refining the program design and procedures,* i.e., for effecting *process control* • For logging the actual process to provide a *basis for judging implementation and interpreting outcomes*	• For deciding to *continue, terminate, modify,* or *refocus* a change activity • For presenting a clear *record of effects* (intended and unintended, positive and negative) • For *judging* the effort's merit and worth

ineffective, too expensive, and/or counterproductive. The problem may appear different from the perspective of a client of evaluation services than from that of an evaluator.

From the client's perspective, the problem often concerns whether and when to perform a certain kind of study (e.g., a context, input, process, or product evaluation). From this perspective, the point-of-entry problem may entail several common mistakes. Sometimes clients mistakenly request the wrong type of study—for example, a product evaluation—when they more urgently need a context evaluation. Clients make this mistake when they incorrectly assume that project goals reflect underlying needs and problems. Clients also err by waiting until a program is over or nearly over before starting any formal evaluation. Too often, they procrastinate in fulfilling evaluation requirements in the funding agreement or resist evaluation until it becomes a condition for continued funding. Conversely, clients sometimes call too early for structured evaluations of process and products. Often clients should support staff to exercise creativity and trial and error—absent scrutiny—in their search for better tools and strategies. Starting the process and product evaluation too early can intimidate staff, constrain their exploratory work, and stifle their creativity. Clients also might request too much evaluation given the project's nature and the availability of relevant information and/or funds for evaluation. They may try to collect too much new information instead of using existing information. Instead, they should concentrate on collecting new information on the most important data gaps and on what they can reasonably afford. Obviously, clients need proficiency in dealing with the point-of-entry problem. Timely launching of the right type of study and gathering of the most important new information frequently depends on the foresight, initiative, and support of pertinent authorities.

Evaluators may see the point-of-entry problem differently. Often clients do not ask evaluators what type of study would be best in a given situation. Or they make their request too late. Evaluation clients too seldom plan early and jointly with evaluation specialists. Therefore, an evaluator must often decide how to catch up in gathering data that someone should have obtained earlier. Sometimes the evaluator also must assess past decisions. In such cases, evaluators must decide whether to second-guess clients' past decisions. They should especially scrutinize decisions related to the program's goals, procedural plan, theoretical rationale, and budget. By accepting a client's program decisions that assessment may not have informed, evaluators may become accomplices in the pursuit of flawed goals and plans. However, insisting on assessing past decisions may threaten a client's authority enough that they will reject evaluators' services completely. Even if the client agrees to an evaluation of past program decisions, evaluators may have trouble learning the relevant history.

To address the point-of-entry problem best, clients and evaluators should keep in mind that evaluation's most important purpose is to improve services. That is, an institution should commission an evaluation only if it potentially would benefit clients. It might do so either through strengthening services or terminating harmful or ineffective programs. Evaluations serve the improvement function, not only by giving input to guide future decisions, but also by assessing past decisions that may need to be corrected. As Scriven (1969b) recommends, an evaluator should ask the client to consider evaluating the still reversible decisions about a program. Evaluators should consider declining an evaluation contract if they find that past decisions, considered fixed, are indefensible. Again, evaluators should help clients develop and strengthen worthwhile services. They should not help clients sustain poor programs. They should not obtain or continue an evaluation contract at any cost.

In pursuing evaluations designed to improve services, the evaluator should consider two questions: (1) What type(s) of evaluation is(are) needed to guide future decisions or examine the appropriateness of past decisions? (2) Can the needed evaluation(s) be based on already available evidence, or must new information be obtained? The first of these questions is the more important one. It helps evaluators decide what evaluative questions are presently most important and what priorities should be assigned to other evaluative questions. Once these decisions are made, the evaluator next considers whether to collect new information. Sometimes the evaluator might complete an evaluation basing it mainly or solely on available information. The evaluator should collect new information only if it does not duplicate the available information or if he or she needs it to corroborate that information.

Table 2 is designed to help evaluators decide which types of evaluation to conduct and what new information to collect in given situations. It presents considerations for and against undertaking each of the CIPP Model's four evaluation types. It also provides guidelines for determining whether or not to gather new information.

Evaluators should first decide the potential usefulness of each type of evaluation as described in the first row of the table. If they see potential uses, they should check the table's second row to decide whether that type of study might be premature, superfluous, diversionary, or counter-productive. They should not pursue study types that they judge to be inappropriate or have no potential utility. If the evaluators judge that the study type is appropriate, then they can confidently pursue it as an important service, not an expensive but useless exercise. The evaluators would next check the third and fourth rows of the table to decide whether and to what extent they need new information.

Depending on circumstances, a study can justifiably be retrospective, prospective, or both. For example, if a program is under way but not yet evaluated, the client and evaluator might agree to first conduct retrospective context and input evaluations. Subsequently, they could conduct process and product evaluations. On the other hand, they may conclude that past planning efforts were sufficiently data based and justified and, therefore, that retrospective analysis is unnecessary. Stake (1967), in his development of the Countenance approach, assumed that clients typically would call in evaluators midway in a program. Accordingly, he advised evaluators to begin their work by examining the program's antecedents, then to look at transactions and outcomes. The CIPP Model allows for entry at any point in a program, project, or other intervention but, as suggested by Stake, the entry will often be midway in a project.

VALUES AND CRITERIA

The root term in evaluation is value, meaning an ideal held by a society, group, or individual, or an attribute of the relative merit, worth, or usefulness of an object. At the basic level, evaluators assess the services of an institution, program, or person against a pertinent set of societal, institutional, program, and professional values. The values provide the foundation for deriving the particular evaluative criteria. The criteria, along with questions of stakeholders, dictate information needs. These, in turn, provide the direction for selecting/constructing the evaluation instruments and interpretation standards. Thus, evaluators and their clients must regularly employ values clarification as the foundation stone of their evaluation activities.

Values clarification is no easy task. It provides a constant challenge in evaluation work. Different stakeholders in an organization and the larger society may hold conflicting values about many matters. These may include legalized abortion; school choice; sex education; prayer in the public schools; outcomes-based education; welfare; socialized medicine; collective bargaining; environmental conservation; centralized government; gun control; and other political, educational, social, religious, economic, and philosophical matters. In addition, a society usually emphasizes certain values at the expense of others, periodically changing the emphasis.

The history of the U.S., during the latter half of the twentieth century, shows how a society can shift from emphasizing one set of values to another. The shift may be illustrated by the following observations. In the late 1950s, Americans reacted strongly to the USSR's launching of Sputnik 1. Congress channeled huge amounts of money to science, technology, and education to overtake the Soviets in space technology. The overriding value was *national security*—a dominant value in the U.S. Constitution. In the early and middle 1960s, lobbyists for persons with special needs and disabilities became a powerful political force at the federal, state, and local levels. A new, heavy emphasis on *equal access for the disabled* emerged. In the middle 1960s, the attention of U.S. society was drawn to the plight of minorities, and the government launched multibillion-dollar programs aimed at providing *equal opportunities* for all Americans. Equality of opportunity is now an entrenched value and legal requirement in the U.S. In the 1960s and 1970s, the federal government began requiring grantees to be accountable for using federal moneys. These requirements spawned the *age of accountability* and brought prominence to the basic value of *effectively addressing the needs of constituents*. In the late 1970s, the nation faced a major economic recession. It de-emphasized costly, innovative programs for minorities and shifted to cutting costs. Programs had to prove they were cost-effective. In the 1980s, W. Edwards Deming (1982) and others made a convincing argument that America's economic downturn was largely due to a decline in international competitiveness. Deming said this was due to the poor quality of American products and called for concerted, continuing efforts to improve quality in all aspects of society, especially

Table 2. Guidelines for Deciding When to Do Context, Input, Process, or Product Evaluation and What New Information to Collect

	Context Evaluation	Input Evaluation	Process Evaluation	Product Evaluation
Indicators of appropriateness	• Clients require a needs assessment to prepare a funding proposal. • The CEO must report on the state of the institution. • An accrediting body will review the institution. • The institution must update its mission and goals. • Services and/or staffing may be inequitable. • Institutional performance is under attack. • Resource allocation patterns need to be changed. • The institution has not justified a proposed intervention. • The institution needs to confirm the wisdom of institutionalizing a project. • The needs of intended beneficiaries are poorly understood.	• The institution has defined needs and problems but has not found an appropriate solution. • Institutional decision makers are not aware of how other institutions have addressed similar areas of need. • The institution has found a promising solution but must engineer it for use in the given setting. • The relative merits of two or more promising strategies for given goals are unclear. • Choice of a solution strategy will be controversial.	• A selected strategy needs to be field tested and modified for use in the institution. • The institution must submit progress reports to the sponsor on implementation of a funded plan. • Staff and oversight groups will require regular feedback on the implementation of a plan. • The evaluation audience will require in-depth information on the implementation of a program or project to help explain assessed outcomes.	• The institution needs to validate a selected strategy before institutionalizing it. • An institution must account to its funding agency for a funded program's results. • There is a need to identify and assess the full range of outcomes. • The staff and oversight group require regular feedback on results.

Indicators of inappropriateness	• A project or other intervention is already operational and needs to run a full cycle before returning to questions about need.	• The institution has not established the need for a proposed intervention.	• Implementation of the intervention plan presents no special information requirements. • The institution needs to learn what the intervention can produce, lacking evaluative feedback.	• The effectiveness of the intervention is clear.
Indications that existing information is sufficient	• The institution already has sufficient background information about beneficiaries' needs, associated problems, area assets, and/or funding or other pertinent opportunities.	• Extensive field test reports are available on the approaches being considered.	• Staff regularly document, share, and discuss the progress of the effort.	• The needed information about results will be routinely available from other sources.
Indications that new information is needed	• Some pertinent information is available but out of date or suspect. • The institution has not recently engaged in a relevant context evaluation.	• Some needed information on alternatives is available but out-of-date or otherwise insufficient. • The institution must invent and assess new solution strategies.	• The coordinator needs but does not have independent, objective information on how well the staff members are carrying out their assignments. • Without a process evaluation the institution will have no dependable record on how well the staff carried out the intervention.	• Existing product evaluation efforts include no information on side effects and/or whether the observed outcomes responded to assessed needs.

the processes used in production. Thus, the value of *excellence* gained priority in American society. Tom Peters (1982) gave this value prominence in his book *In Search of Excellence*.

These observations illustrate the difficulty of equitably addressing the values-selection problem in evaluation work. Many institutions and programs are supposed to serve multiple interests. Political considerations often determine which values will receive priority. Evaluators must strive to bring equity and rationality to the consideration of multiple values. Otherwise, as in any suboptimization, some areas will gain (e.g., equity) and others lose (e.g., excellence). Realistically, decision groups must make trade-offs in allocating attention and resources among competing objectives. However, such decisions will be more just if evaluators help their clients consider the values of all legitimate interest groups, the foundation values of the society, and the trade-offs implicit in decision alternatives.

The CIPP Model advises evaluators to address seven levels of values and criteria: basic societal values; criteria inherent in the definition of evaluation; criteria in the definitions of context, input, process, and product evaluation; institutional values; pertinent technical standards; duties of professionals; and idiosyncratic criteria. Evaluators should consider all seven levels of criteria to assure comprehensiveness in their evaluations.

Basic Societal Values

Four sets of basic values are fundamental to preserving, protecting, and advancing the common welfare of the U.S. society. These are *equality of opportunity*, which is legally mandated and an ethical imperative; *effectiveness* in serving the needs of constituents and protecting their safety, which is a fundamental requirement of any service; *conservation*, i.e., prudence in consuming the natural and economic resources so citizens do not waste them, so cities and the countryside can continue to be fit for future generations, and so institutions/programs can operate cost-effectively; and striving for *excellence* in all endeavors, a basic obligation of all professionals. Programs that violate or fail to serve these values are counterproductive to the common good of America and/or particular organizations/programs. Evaluators should promote and assess these basic societal values.

Merit and Worth

The second set of criteria derive from the meaning of evaluation. Evaluations must assess *merit* and *worth*. Merit denotes an object's intrinsic value or quality. Merit assessments address the issue of whether a program, product, or service is sound in concept, design, delivery, material, and outcomes. Evaluators gauge the evaluand's merit by comparing it with the state of the art and critical competitors against established technical criteria. Worth involves an object's extrinsic value or how useful it is in meeting the assessed needs of a defined group of beneficiaries. All institutions must strive to offer meritorious services. Sometimes, however, institutions must terminate even good programs or excellent staff members, because the institution's constituents no longer need their services or cannot afford them. Overall, institutions should develop and maintain programs, products, and services that have both merit and worth. They should discontinue those that fail to meet either or both of these standards.

CIPP Criteria

Context, Input, Process, and Product categories of information contribute the third set of evaluative criteria. The most important of these are *assessed needs* of beneficiaries; *quality and feasibility of plans*; *responsiveness of plans* to assessed needs; *congruence between activities and plans*; and *quality, significance, safety, and cost-effectiveness of outcomes*. The CIPP Model provides a general framework within which to generate locally relevant criteria, while keeping in mind basic societal and institutional values.

Institutional Values

All institutions have their particular *missions*, *goals*, and *priorities*. This applies both to the development/service organizations and to their client organizations. Evaluators should inform themselves about the values of the development organization so they can assess, for example, whether a project or other intervention is or would be consistent with the organization's mission. The evaluator should also examine the full range of possible beneficiaries to learn whether the offered product or service is responsive to their assessed needs. By attending carefully to institutional values, the evaluator can help the development or service organization to pursue interventions that fit both its values and those of clients.

Technical Standards

Standards have been developed and continue to be refined for many technical and professional areas. These include state *codes* and *licensing standards* and *professional and technical society standards*. Among the many involved areas are electrical and plumbing installations, water quality, teaching competence, medical specialties, elementary and secondary schools, and various university programs. As previously mentioned, the magnitude of the applicable codes and standards is evident in the fact that the American National Standards Institute (ANSI) has registered more than 10,000 American national standards. To earn ANSI's accreditation of a set of standards, a group must carefully define its standards through an extensive consensus process. To retain ANSI accreditation, the group must subject its standards to review every five years and update them as needed. When planning an evaluation, the evaluator should search out and employ relevant published standards and codes.

Duties of Personnel

A sixth area of values and criteria is especially important in evaluating the performance of personnel. These are the individual's duties, i.e., *professional obligations* and *organizational responsibilities*. The employing organization determines performance evaluation criteria by examining each staff member's obligations as a member of a particular profession and her or his assigned responsibilities in the organization. For example, a teacher's duties might include knowledge of content, effective classroom management, effective communication of content to students, sound assessment of student needs and achievement, fostering parent involvement, counseling and referring students, and cooperating in school improvement efforts.

School districts and many other organizations invest substantial resources in personnel. Therefore, personnel evaluation is crucially important in improving organizational operations. The organization should clarify each member's duties. These duties provide the most relevant criteria for assessing and strengthening performance by the organization's personnel and assuring that they fulfill the highest ideals of their professions.

Idiosyncratic Criteria

Evaluators must consider yet a seventh level of values and criteria. Michael Scriven calls these the *ground-level criteria*. Evaluators *cannot define them in advance*; they *must negotiate them* in consideration of the particular program being evaluated; and they *must define them in considerable operational detail*. These criteria are idiosyncratic to particular evaluations. An organization's staff must conceptualize and negotiate these specific criteria when planning a particular study. One can do this by studying relevant background information, holding a discussion with the client, and conducting focus group meetings with other stakeholders to help clarify the key issues. One might also study reports from past evaluations of similar programs. Moreover, some of these criteria may not be clear until the evaluation is well under way. Again, organizations should be flexible in designing and conducting evaluations, so they can continually improve the evaluation criteria and data collection plan. The main point here is that one can never predetermine all the values and criteria needed in a given evaluation. One must work hard and thoughtfully throughout the evaluation process to derive, negotiate, explicate, and apply the appropriate criteria.

DESIGNING EVALUATIONS

Once the evaluator and client have decided to conduct an evaluation, the evaluator needs to design the work to be done. This involves preparing the preliminary plans and subsequently modifying and explicating them as the evaluation proceeds. These plans must deal with a wide range of choices concerning the evaluation. For example, these could include

- key users, other audiences, and questions
- the object to be assessed
- pertinent values and criteria
- the needed information
- the evaluation's timing and location
- the extent and nature of study controls
- the contrasts to be made
- the sources of needed information
- the data collection instruments and methods to be employed

- the methods of analysis and interpretation
- provisions for communicating findings
- evaluation standards and arrangements for assessing the evaluation results

Decisions about such evaluation activities form the basis for contracting and financing the evaluation, working out protocols with the involved institutions, staffing the evaluation, scheduling and guiding staff activities, and assessing the evaluation plans.

Evaluators might wish they could finalize design decisions at the outset and follow them precisely. However, many evaluations' dynamic and interactive qualities and service orientation make difficult, if not impossible or undesirable, the accurate, long-range projection of specific information needs. Consequently, evaluators often find that initial data collection and analysis plans are based on incorrect assumptions or are incomplete. Rigid adherence to the original evaluation design—especially if it were very specific—can detract greatly from the evaluation's utility and credibility. Particularly, it might be unresponsive to emergent evaluation needs and to the varying needs of different members of the target audience, sustain incorrect guiding assumptions, and/or convince the audience that the evaluator has little common sense.

Evaluators face a dilemma. On the one hand, they need to plan their evaluation activities carefully. This is necessary to make the evaluation budget, conduct the work efficiently and rigorously, and demonstrate competence and confidence. On the other hand, they need to approach the design of evaluation studies flexibly. They should also provide for the design's periodic review and modification so that the evaluation remains responsive to the needs of targeted users and the broader audience.

This dilemma is especially troublesome to evaluators when negotiating evaluation plans and modifications with clients. Clients often require up-front technical designs. Later they may become disenchanted when adherence to the original design yields information they no longer perceive to be useful. Clients often perceive that somehow evaluators should have been smarter in projecting information needs, more skilled in planning the data collection activities, and more responsible in fulfilling their original commitments. Also, when clients or other users of the evaluation do not like negative evaluation findings, they might try to discredit the evaluation because it did not completely follow the original design.

To address this dilemma evaluators should help their clients and other key users to view design as a process, not a product. Evaluators should sketch evaluation goals and procedures in advance. Periodically, they should review, revise, expand, and operationalize the evaluation plan. Fundamentally, evaluators should guide this process by a defensible view of what constitutes sound evaluation and a sensitivity to factors that often complicate evaluation work. These include changing information needs of users and even changes in the user group. The evaluators should regularly communicate with their audiences, especially the program's various stakeholders, about the design's pertinence and the adequacy of the obtained information.

At the outset of the process, the evaluator should query stakeholders and listen carefully but critically to what they say. Who are the primary clients? What do they want from the evaluation (e.g., guidance for program development, accountability to program sponsors, solid information on which to ground adoption/dissemination decisions, new insights into cause and effect relationships in the program)? Why do they consider these purposes important? What type(s) of evaluation (evaluations of needs, plans, implementation, costs, outcomes, sustainability, transportability, etc.) would be most responsive? How do the client and other key users think the evaluation should be conducted? How do they think it should not be conducted? Does the client and/or other users want the evaluator to conduct evaluation training and other capacity development within the context of the program evaluation? What time line do they have in mind? Whom does the client see as the main users of evaluation findings? Whom might the evaluation "hurt" or alienate? Why? Whose cooperation will be essential? What information already exists? To what extent should and could the evaluation assess the program's personnel? What is the program's relevant history? Realistically, what could clients and other users expect as positive benefits from the evaluation? What deleterious effects are real possibilities, and how could the evaluators avoid these? What qualifications must the evaluators have to do the job? And so on. Whenever evaluators have a choice, they should pursue such questions with the client and other right-to-know audiences before agreeing that an evaluation should be done or that they are the right persons to do it. They should investigate such questions primarily with the client but also with the targeted users of the evaluation.

In his 1969 AERA audiotape on evaluation, Scriven strongly advised evaluators not to accept an evaluation job until they learn a great deal about the involved politics. He also warned evaluators not to accept the assignment if they would become the client's political tool. Evaluators can use the questions in the preceding paragraph to guide preliminary investigations of stakeholder interests and concerns before accepting an evaluation assignment.

Assuming a positive decision to go ahead with an evaluation, the evaluator should sketch an overall plan. This plan should reflect what the evaluator learned about the setting and the evaluative needs of the evaluation's client and broader audience. It should conform to generally accepted standards of sound evaluation. In addition, it should speak, at least in a general way, to the full range of indicated tasks. The evaluator should seek the client's and other stakeholders' reactions to the draft evaluation design. Such exchanges often help evaluators strengthen evaluation designs, solidify agreements with the client, and reach common understandings with the other targeted users on the evaluation procedures and projected evaluation process.

Table 3 outlines points to be considered in designing an evaluation. These points are applicable when developing the initial design or later when revising or explicating it. They serve only as general indications of the detailed information that the evaluator eventually must provide to flesh out and operationalize the design.

Table 3. Outline for Documenting Evaluation Designs

Review of the Charge
  Definition of the object of the evaluation
  Identification of the client, intended users, and other right-to-know audiences
  Purpose(s) of the evaluation (i.e., program improvement, accountability, dissemination, and/or understanding)
  Type of evaluation (e.g., context, input, process, or product)
  Values and criteria (i.e., basic societal values, merit and worth, CIPP criteria, institutional values, technical standards, duties of personnel, and ground-level criteria)

Plan for Obtaining Information
  The general strategy (e.g., survey, case study, advocacy teams, or field experiment)
  Working assumptions to guide measurement, analysis, and interpretation
  Collection of information (i.e., sampling, instrumentation, data collection procedures and instruments, and permissions from data sources)
  Organization of information (i.e., coding, filing, and retrieving)
  Analysis of information (both qualitative and quantitative)
  Interpretation of findings (i.e., interpretive standards, processing judgments, developing conclusions)

Plan for Reporting the Results
  Drafting of reports
  Prerelease reviews and finalization of reports
  Dissemination of reports
  Provision for follow-up activities to promote the evaluation's impact

Plan for Administering the Study
  Summary of the evaluation schedule
  Plan for meeting staff and resource requirements
  Provision for metaevaluation
  Provision for periodic updates of the evaluation design
  Budget
  Memorandum of agreement or contract

The formulation of the design requires that the client and evaluators collaborate, from the outset, when they must agree on a charge. The client needs to define the object to be evaluated and is a prime source for identifying the various groups who should be served by the study. The evaluator should help the client define clear and realistic boundaries for the study. The evaluator also needs to touch base with the potential audiences, including some that may not have been mentioned by the client. He or she should think about the evaluation within the relevant social context to identify the full range of legitimate audiences.

The evaluator should engage the client and other audiences to help clarify the study's purpose and pertinent evaluative criteria. He or she should ask these parties to describe the information they need and how they would use it. The evaluator should ask clarifying questions to sort out different (perhaps conflicting) purposes. He or she should also obtain the assistance of the client and other targeted users in identifying the most important questions. The evaluator should recommend the most appropriate general type(s) of study (evaluations of needs, program plans, implementation, delivery of services, costs, outcomes, program follow-through, etc.). The client should confirm the general choice(s) or help to modify it. In rounding out the charge, the evaluator should emphasize that the evaluation must meet professional standards for sound evaluations, i.e., utility, feasibility, propriety, and accuracy.

The evaluator should provide an overview of the general evaluation strategies. These could include surveys, case studies, site visits, advocacy teams, goal-free searches for effects, adversary hearings, and field experiments. The evaluator should expect stakeholder reactions to influence substantially how he or she will interpret the findings. For example, the evaluator might interpret findings according to guiding values, goals, or prior needs assessments' findings. He or she might base interpretations on her or his professional judgment and/or stakeholder judgments.

The evaluator should also write technical plans for collecting, organizing, and analyzing the needed information. The evaluator, client, and other targeted users should come to an understanding that the data collection plan will likely change and expand during the evaluation. This will happen as they identify new audiences and as information requirements evolve.

Evaluators should gear reporting plans to promote use of findings. They should involve clients and other audiences (especially targeted users) in deciding the contents, nature, and timing of needed reports. The evaluators should engage the client and other intended users to help in planning how the evaluator will disseminate findings. The reporting plan should consider report formats and contents, audiovisual supports, review and revision, means of presentation, occasions for give-and-take exchanges, and right-to-know audiences. This reporting plan should promote impact through appropriate dissemination procedures. These might include oral reports, hearings, community forums, focus groups to examine and respond to findings, multiple reports targeted to specified audiences, press releases, sociodramas to portray and explore the findings, and feedback workshops aimed at applying the findings. Moreover, the client and evaluator should seriously consider whether the evaluator might play an important role beyond delivering the final report. For example, the client might engage the evaluator to conduct follow-up workshops on applying the findings.

The final part of the design is the plan for administering the study. It details the plans for controlling, facilitating, supporting, and assessing the evaluation. The evaluator should identify and schedule the evaluation tasks consistent with the needs of the client and other targeted audiences and in consideration of the relevant practical constraints. The evaluator should define staff assignments and needed special resources, such as office space or special software, and should also make sure the proposed evaluation personnel are credible to the client and other audiences. The evaluator and client need to agree on who will assess the evaluation plans, processes, and reports against appropriate standards. They also should agree on a mechanism by which to review, update, and document the evolving evaluation design periodically. They need to lay out a realistic budget. They also should formalize their general agreements about the evaluation's form and function. The discussion of Table 3 has been necessarily general, but it shows that designing an evaluation is a complex and ongoing task.

CONTRACTING FOR EVALUATIONS

The *Memorandum of Agreement* or *Formal Contract* is one of an evaluation's most important components and always has been a key component of the CIPP Model. According to the Joint Committee on Standards for Educational Evaluation (1994), evaluators should write evaluation agreements that contain ". . . mutual understandings of the specified expectations and responsibilities of both the client and the evaluator" (p. 87). Such an agreement clarifies understandings and helps prevent misunderstandings between the client and evaluators and provides a basis for resolving any future disputes about the evaluation. As the Committee further states, "Having entered into such an agreement, both parties have an obligation to carry it out in a forthright manner or to renegotiate it. Neither party is obligated to honor decisions made unilaterally by the other" (p. 87). Written agreements for evaluations should be explicit but should also allow for appropriate, mutually agreeable adjustments during the evaluation.

Table 4 contains a checklist designed to help evaluators and clients to identify key contractual issues and make and record their agreements for conducting an evaluation. Advance agreements on these matters can mean the difference between an evaluation's success and failure. Without such agreements the evaluation process is constantly subject to misunderstanding, disputes, efforts to compromise the findings, attack, and/or withdrawal—by the client—of cooperation and funds. In one high-stakes study, reference to the advance agreements on editorial authority and release of findings helped prevent the client from burying the report or rewriting it. It helped the evaluators assure skeptical stakeholders that the study had provided for and maintained its independence and objectivity. Clients can also reference sound contracts to convince their policy boards and/or constituents that the institution contracted for sound, clearly defined evaluation services and can hold the evaluators to the agreements.

CONCLUSION

This chapter has stressed the improvement function of evaluation but has also emphasized the importance of summative evaluations. It has updated the CIPP Model, explained its main concepts, and shown how evaluators can use it to guide improvement efforts and serve accountability needs. It has cited applications of the model in a wide range of fields. It has provided general guidelines for designing and contracting for evaluation studies and described applicable techniques. The chapter has also emphasized that evaluators must interact with the client and the other right-to-know audiences throughout, even after an evaluation, in order to learn the audience's information needs and promote and support their effective use of findings. The chapter emphasizes that evaluations should be useful, feasible, proper, and accurate.

The CIPP Model treats evaluation as a necessary concomitant of improvement and professional responsibility. Society and its agents cannot make their programs, services, and products better unless they know where they are weak and strong.

Table 4. Evaluation Contracts Checklist[1]

Basic Considerations	*Reporting Safeguards*
_____Object of the evaluation	_____Anonymity/confidentiality
_____Purpose of the evaluation	_____Prerelease review of reports
_____Client	_____Rebuttal by evaluatees
_____Other Right-to-know audiences	_____Editorial authority
_____Authorized evaluator(s)	_____Final authority to release reports
_____Guiding values and criteria	*Protocol*
_____Standards for judging the evaluation	_____Contact persons
_____Contractual questions	_____Rules for contacting program personnel
Information	_____Communication channels and assistance
_____Required information	*Evaluation Management*
_____Data collection procedures	_____Time line for evaluation work of both
_____Data collection instruments and protocols	clients and evaluators
_____Information sources	_____Assignment of evaluation responsibilities
_____Participant selection	*Client Responsibilities*
_____Provisions to obtain needed permissions to	_____Access to information
collect data	_____Services
_____Follow up procedures to assure adequate	_____Personnel
information	_____Information
_____Provisions for assuring the quality of	_____Facilities
obtained information	_____Equipment
_____Provisions to store and maintain security	_____Materials
of collected information	_____Transportation assistance
Analysis	_____Work space
_____Procedures for analyzing quantitative	*Evaluation Budget*
information	_____Payment amounts and dates
_____Procedures for analyzing qualitative	_____Conditions for payment, including delivery
information	of required reports
Reports	_____Budget limits/restrictions
_____Deliverables and due dates	_____Agreed-upon indirect/overhead rates
_____Interim report formats, contents, lengths,	_____Contracts for budgetary matters
audiences, and methods of delivery	*Review and Control of the Evaluation*
_____Final report format, contents, length,	_____Contract amendment and cancellation
audiences, and methods of delivery	provisions
_____Restrictions/permissions to report via	_____Provisions for periodic review, modification,
diskettes, web site, etc.	and renegotiation of the evaluation design
_____Restrictions/permissions to publish	as needed
information from or based on the	_____Provision for evaluating the evaluation against
evaluation	professional standards of sound evaluation

Preparer _____ Date _____

[1] Mark each item as *important and incorporated* __✓___or *not applicable* na or leave it blank_____, indicating *not agreed to* though important.

They cannot be sure that their goals are worthy unless they can match them to beneficiaries' needs. They cannot plan effectively and invest their time and resources wisely if they are unaware of options and their relative merits. Service providers cannot earn continued support unless they can present evidence that they have fulfilled their commitments and produced beneficial results. For these and other reasons, professionals must subject their work to competent evaluation. It must help them sort out good from bad, point the way to needed improvements, be accountable to sponsors and clients, inform institutionalization/dissemination decisions, and better understand their field. Finally, evaluation is an indispensable tool for helping to realize the ideals of a democratic society. The CIPP Model is presented as a general framework supported by a theory of use and many practical guidelines, but also grounded in the principles of a free society and professional standards for evaluations. The model is designed to help evaluators and their audiences design, conduct, and use sound evaluations and thereby continually improve services and outcomes.

17. ACCOUNTABILITY: IMPLICATIONS FOR STATE AND LOCAL POLICYMAKERS

MICHAEL W. KIRST

During the 1980s, 40 states put new testing provisions into effect; local school districts across the country began revamping their teacher evaluation procedures; and the federal government, in cooperation with the states, embarked on a process to formulate and assess national goals. These developments mean that most education policymakers will, sooner or later, be confronted with decisions about evaluating or implementing some type of accountability system.

This paper is designed to help policymakers understand and select various options for holding schools accountable for their performance. It does *not* recommend one system over another, however, because a given accountability option must be compatible with, and adapted to, particular state and local contexts. The paper begins with a review of the lessons policymakers can learn from more than a century of experience with accountability. It examines failures and false starts, as well as promising practices. The key organizing device for the paper is six broad approaches to accountability, each entailing several specific alternatives. These six approaches are: accountability through performance reporting; accountability through monitoring and compliance with standards or regulations; accountability through incentive systems; accountability through reliance on the market; accountability through changing the locus of authority or control of schools; and accountability through changing professional roles.

From Accountability: Implications for state and local policymakers. Washington D.C.: Office of Educational Research and Improvement, U.S. Department of Education, 1990, pp. 1–33. The writer acknowledges the assistance of Lorraine McDonnell (The RAND Corporation) and Henry Levin (Stanford University) in devising some of the typologies.

These six general strategies are *not* mutually exclusive alternatives, and state or local governments usually employ several of these approaches simultaneously. The appropriate emphasis to place on each is, however, one of the most important policy decisions to be made, and this paper provides research findings that will help policymakers devise a multistrategy accountability system. Finally, because knowledge about accountability mechanisms is increasing constantly—several promising practices were undergoing development as of late 1989; for example the paper concludes with some current developments, both positive and negative, that policymakers should watch closely.

While reading this paper, however, one caveat should be kept in mind: accountability is but one of several strategies to improve and restructure U.S. education. Therefore, particular attention should be paid to analyses within the paper of potential conflicts between specific accountability systems and other reforms. For example, a centralized accountability system that promotes uniform school-level instructional emphasis on low-level skills is in direct conflict with a restructuring strategy that emphasizes flexible teaching strategies for higher order skills, using decentralized school-site decision making. Thus, in reading about various accountability alternatives, policymakers should think about the appropriate emphasis, consistency, and effectiveness within a particular state and local context.

HISTORICAL OVERVIEW

A major theme of this paper is that throughout history education policy has advanced through incremental or trial and error stages, sometimes called "disjointed incrementalism." Accountability is an excellent example of this process, as can readily be seen by examining several specific advances of the past 100 years.

While accountability has recently been "rediscovered" and has gone through yet another transformation and refinement, it actually has a long history of use, misuse, and controversy. For example, in mid-19th century England, schooling was administered under an incentive system known as "payment by results." State school inspectors gave a standard exam to each child and then paid the schools according to students' exam scores (Martin et al., 1976). Almost immediately, this sparked debate over whether accountability excessively narrowed the curriculum, because administrators dropped geography and history in order to spend more time on the 3 Rs measured by the inspectors.

Across the Atlantic, in 1879, New York state initiated the Regents exams with the view that many academic subjects needed to be part of an accountability system. With the arrival of the 20th century, scientific measurement and appropriate grade placement were featured from 1915 to 1930, and this movement overlapped with the 1920s "cult of efficiency," which applied business cost-accounting techniques to the solution of many education problems (Callahan, 1962). It would be another half-century, however, before educators witnessed the advent of the U.S. accountability movement's bible, Leon Lessinger's (1970) book, *Every Kid a Winner*, which stressed the same kind of cost-accounting strategies that had been popular decades earlier.

Like his predecessors, Lessinger wanted learning stated in quantifiable terms that could be related to cost statements. However, his thinking was also in tune with that of his own era, since the 1960s and early 1970s featured Program Planning Budgeting Systems (PPBS) and Management by Objectives (MBO) as favored strategies for accountability. These were followed in 1977 by President Carter's Zero Based Budgeting (ZBB). All of these budget techniques were resisted by school boards and local educators and have disappeared with barely any residue (see Kirst, 1975).

In sum, both the early 20th century and the recent accountability movements highlighted (1) business as the model for educators to emulate; (2) objective measures as the primary criterion for educational evaluation; and (3) sophisticated accounting procedures and cost control as crucial for improving education.

Not surprisingly, an abundance of literature exists on accountability. Indeed, the period from 1969 to 1976 produced a veritable blizzard of information on the topic, including an estimated 4,000 articles and books. At the same time, 35 states passed legislation based on the rubric of accountability (Browder, 1975), and two major federal projects chronicled the activity: the Cooperative Accountability Project, a federally funded consortium of seven state education departments, and the State Education Accountability Repository (SEAR), managed by the Wisconsin State Education Department. Furthermore, model legislation spread through states, while many local education agencies (LEAs) adopted accountability techniques without state legislation. But while most of the state legislation is still on the books, implementation of the 1970s versions such as PPBS and teacher evaluation based on behavioral objectives has been curtailed or watered down (Kirst & Meister, 1985).

Beginning in 1983, however, school reforms brought with them still another wave of accountability legislation, focusing this time on such concepts as school report cards, merit schools, outcome-based accreditations, and interstate achievement comparisons. While the names have changed, these concepts are offshoots of the historical evolution. Therefore, while history demonstrates that effective and long-lasting accountability programs are possible, it also shows that maintaining them requires both a sophisticated understanding of past experience and a committed political constituency. In addition, even well-designed accountability techniques must be implemented through a loosely coupled administrative system that includes a complex web of state and local school control. That makes it difficult to predict the impact of a specific accountability policy upon classroom practice and provides numerous political constituencies as potential roadblocks. The remainder of this paper will expand on the reasons why some accountability techniques have become a long-run part of school operations, while others—like merit pay—have disappeared into a Bermuda triangle, probably to reappear in a subsequent era.

THE ORIGINS OF ACCOUNTABILITY CONCEPTS

Accountability has roots in many areas of management, including economic theories about incentives and business concepts about control. Before educators borrowed the term and imbued it with their own additional meanings, accountability expressed a relationship between those who controlled institutions and those who possessed the formal power to displace them.

The heart of the process is for the party "standing to account," the steward, to explain as rationally as possible the results of efforts to achieve the specified tasks or objectives of his stewardship. (Browder, 1975)

When Lessinger, then an associate commissioner with the U.S. Office of Education, began to publicize accountability in education during the late 1960s, he did so by drawing analogies to business:

Instead of certifying that a student has spent so much time in school or taken so many courses, the schools should be certifying that he is able to perform specific tasks. Just as a warranty certifies the quality performance of a car, a diploma should certify a youngster's performance as a reader, a writer, a driver, and so on. (Lessinger, 1969)

He also urged state and local educators to adopt a new objective:

. . . "zero reject" through basic competence for all. In order to measure how these actual results compare to the detailed objectives of the plan, it makes sense to call for an outside educational audit, much like the outside fiscal audit required of every school system today. The education "redevelopment plan" that is audited should be based on "market research," that is, an investigation of the needs of students in each particular school. The plan would stress "performance specifications" that the school considers essential. (Lessinger, 1969)

There was, of course, nothing particularly new in this rhetoric. Indeed, the same concepts were actively considered in education at the turn of the 20th century (James, 1968). But Lessinger's ideas caught on in media and educational leadership circles, and President Nixon, at the urging of Department of Health, Education, and Welfare officials, endorsed accountability in his 1970 message on education. Some, such as Henry Levin, were skeptical, however.

Find a significant shortcoming of the educational system, and it is certain that someone will marshal a word to fight the problem. . . . Just as was the case with individualization of instruction and compensatory education, the concept of accountability is vague and rhetorical, and if history again prevails, the word should be supplanted by new terminology within a few years, while our schools remain stubbornly steadfast in their reluctance to change. (Levin, 1974)

Levin's 1972 assessment of accountability as a "vague and rhetorical" concept received support in 1975 when a review of the 4,000 pieces of accountability literature reached the following conclusions:

1. There are no commonly agreed-upon definitions. The range is from simply holding someone responsible for doing something to highly detailed technical specifications.

2. As a concept, accountability needs refinement. Confusion abounds among such terms as "general accountability," "institutional accountability," "technological accountability," and so on. There is no common framework to organize the vast array of techniques.
3. Accountability has become highly politicized. Various groups who can be held accountable attack the concept and pounce on malfunctions in order to discredit it. (Browder, 1975)

Despite these problems, however, the notion of accountability survives, and in 1989 it emerged as a major theme at the Education Summit convened by President Bush who recommended measures such as annual report cards and national goals at the federal, state, and local levels.

SIX APPROACHES TO ACCOUNTABILITY

Given the tremendous and continuing interest in accountability, it is important to know that over the years there have been several attempts to build typologies of accountability techniques (Darling-Hammond, 1988). In this vein, Levin has provided some useful rubrics that this writer has extended and adapted (Levin, 1974). Although each will be explored in depth, it is essential to bear in mind that these are broad strategy options that must be tailored to specific state and local contexts. These options must also be combined and interrelated in a sensible way. While policymakers can choose to emphasize one or another of these strategies, they should be careful to recognize concerns about appropriate balance among them.

Accountability As Performance Reporting

Performance reporting includes such measurement techniques as statewide assessment, National Assessment of Educational Progress (NAEP), school report cards, and performance indicators, and it has some similarities to the audit report in business. In essence, performance reports assume that information per se will stimulate actions to improve education. An aroused parent group, for example, will follow up on the results of a negative school report card by lobbying the school board for a new principal. Also, state performance reporting can be used to monitor regulatory compliance for such state requirements as minimum graduation requirements. The state performance reporting system, however, would have to include grade enrollments in specific academic courses.

Performance reporting in the 1980s was often linked to policies that triggered state takeovers or intervention in schools, such as occurred in New Jersey and California. However, this technique can be used to provide rewards as well as sanctions, and one recent version used in South Carolina shows that positive school-site academic performance indicators can actually stimulate state deregulation and waivers for qualifying schools.

Since all the other categories described below rely to some extent on the process and outcome of performance reports, it is not surprising that during the past decade, performance reporting was the area receiving the most widespread developmental effort related to accountability. Still, it is questionable whether performance reports alone lead to much change in either citizen or professional educator behavior. For example, Florida has mandated school report cards since 1973, but with little impact on local policy (Bass & Kirst, 1976). Moreover, serious flaws remain in most existing education information programs. For example, most state information systems do not include data on course enrollment patterns and overemphasize basic-skills testing at the expense of higher order concepts.

Accountability Through Monitoring And Compliance With Standards Or Regulations

Approaching accountability through monitoring and compliance with standards and regulations includes not only such legal issues as the due process rights of handicapped students, but also encompasses auditing approaches, such as budget reviews. Obviously, these techniques also rely on performance reporting, but the key accountability criterion concerns procedural compliance. Prominent examples include individualized education plans (IEPs) for handicapped children and targeting funds under programs of Chapter I of the Elementary and Secondary Education Act (the federal government's primary compensatory education assistance program).

As accountability techniques, mandates and monitoring can be supplemented by other strategies like capacity building and technical assistance that rely less on compliance reviews (McDonnell & Elmore, 1987). For example, some education organizations can be in compliance with regulations but need help to enhance instructional capacity before they can improve educational attainment.

Accountability Through Incentive Systems

The key concept of incentive systems is reward for results, and incentives are designed to provide inducements for specific actions by educators. By using systematic processes that relate and stimulate changes among education input, processes, and outputs, these approaches link performance information with specific policy outcomes that educators presumably can manipulate. Early incentive systems include the English payment-by-results plan, PPBS, and performance contracting. More recent approaches include merit schools, performance-based accreditation, and teacher merit pay. These incentive systems, however, have been plagued with technical problems and have been resisted by education professionals, a problem discussed in the next section.

Accountability Through Reliance On The Market

This approach runs the gamut from such comparatively extreme versions as vouchers or tuition tax credits for public and private schools to the more limited strategy of open enrollment within a public school district. Accountability occurs when consumers choose between schools, with the "bad schools" presumably closing if enough pupils leave. Free market systems, however, have never been tested in the

United States because of various obstacles to vouchers, including political resistance and concerns about equity. Consequently, American school districts have only implemented limited market forces, and rarely have market changes resulted in lost jobs for educators. The Minnesota open enrollment plan is a highly publicized version of a limited market approach. Other examples include magnet schools and tuition tax credits.

Accountability Through Changing The Locus Of Authority Or Control Of Schools

Changing the locus of authority posits that the key to making schools more accountable lies in changing those who control education policy. That may be accomplished by such devices as the creation of parent advisory councils, implementation of school-site decentralization or community-controlled schools, and initiation of state takeovers of local school districts. Whatever the vehicle, however, the assumption is that schools are accountable to some groups but not to others, and that educational improvement lies in changing the political process so that different groups are favored. The radical decentralization of the Chicago schools, for example, relies heavily on a redistribution of influence from the central office to school-site governing bodies with a parent majority. The 1989 Education Summit implied, meanwhile, that the governors wished to be held accountable for overall state education results rather than merely holding educators responsible for outcomes.

Accountability Through Changing Professional Roles

Recently, more attention has been paid to using such professional accountability mechanisms as teachers reviewing each other for tenure and dismissal-the essence of accountability at universities. In Toledo, Ohio, for instance, experienced teachers are asked to review and help colleagues who are judged to be very ineffective by their peers. Another example is the National Board of Professional Teaching Standards, which will begin certifying outstanding teachers in 1993. Two-thirds of the Board is composed of teachers. Other types of professional accountability include school accreditation and teacher-controlled boards for initial licensing of graduates from university teacher education programs. In addition, various plans to devolve policy decisions to the school site call for teacher majorities on school-site councils; this provides teachers with a new role beyond collective bargaining in site-based policymaking.

Interrelating Strategies

Several general points can be made about this typology. First, all accountability mechanisms have their strengths and weaknesses, and each is more or less appropriate for certain types of educational interventions and contexts. For example, legal monitoring and compliance mechanisms are more effective when rights and procedures are clearly definable and when bottom-line outcomes are not crucial. Second, as stated above, the six categories are not mutually exclusive and should be combined in creative and effective ways. Unfortunately, however, it is often difficult for policymakers to think systematically about the interrelationships and balance among the six. Instead, they mostly opt to emphasize one or the other as the key to enhanced school or pupil performance. Few recognize, for example, that enhanced political control at the school site requires a sophisticated school-based reporting system that focuses on broadly defined educational attainment goals.

Overall, elements of all six strategies will be present in a good accountability system, but it is unlikely that every element can or should be implemented at once. Several states have numerous accountability policies, but often they are not complete or interrelated. Some states have major gaps in their accountability systems, such as new curricular goals for teachers but no attention to initial teacher preparation. Others have curricular frameworks stressing higher order concepts like synthesis, analysis, inference, and expository writing, but continue to use a state assessment system that focuses solely on basic and minimum skills.

Inherent Limitations Of Current Accountability Systems

Over the past 20 years, major improvements have been made in accountability systems and procedures. Before turning to these, however, it is useful to review some of the major roadblocks that current accountability techniques must still over-come and that make it difficult to transplant business accountability schemes to education.

Ideally, accountability would be a closed loop reflecting a chain of responses to perceived needs, demands, or objectives. What follows is an outline both of the ingredients needed for an ideal system and of the impediments to its realization.

1. Accountability suggests that there are explicit education objectives for the school or educational system or at least some operational consensus on the results schools will be held accountable for. But as experience with California PPBS and Michigan State Assessment reveals, it is difficult to agree on state goals or even a process to reach them (Kirst, 1975; Murphy & Cohen, 1974). High schools, for example, stress different objectives, with some featuring traditional academics and others emphasizing vocational education or alternatives that permit a lot of student course choice and independent study. Problems of this sort are compounded by ideological objections to even trying to establish precise pupil objectives.

   The behavioral objectives approach is a closed system of thinking. It demands that ends be defined in advance. This tends to place a straitjacket on teachers and students alike and make the learning situation a search for "right" answers. . . . The resulting distortion is further compounded by the fact that behavioral objectives are likely to be determined by the nature of the measuring devices available. (Coombs, 1972)

   Furthermore, many of education's objectives, such as citizenship, are ambiguous and their relationship to curricular development unclear. And finally, multiple forms of intelligence, including creative, artistic, and interpersonal attributes, are not easily reduced to measurable objectives (Gardner, 1983, 1989). And while new tests devised by Connecticut and California do a better job of assessing higher order skills than most nationally standardized tests, they do not encompass all forms of intelligence. Clearly, a broader range of tests must be developed before accountability systems can become first rate.

2. Because of a lack of stated objectives and because many teacher and administrator incentive systems reward longevity rather than educational outcomes, there is a limit to the number and type of accountability incentives that can be imposed on the educational sector (see Wynne, 1972). Indeed, a study by the National Academy of Education concluded:

> The production of educational services takes place in an organizational climate which contradicts in almost every respect the notion of educational units attempting to maximize stated objectives for a given budget. (Levin, 1972)

For example, state education codes and negotiated agreements with educational professionals seriously curtail managerial discretion. As Jesse Burkhead observed:

> But in elementary and secondary education there is no reason to assume that a school principal, or district superintendent, or board of education has knowledge of or interest in marginal productivity of resource inputs. Even if these were known, it could not be assumed that it would be possible to secure least cost-combinations, given the institutional rigidities of mandates and conventional practice. Neither is there a reasonable substitute for the objective function of profits maximization. Thus the optimization rationale that underlies production functions in the private sector is inapplicable for elementary and secondary educational. (Burkhead, 1973)

Merit school programs in Florida and South Carolina have tried to overcome these barriers by providing financial rewards for growth in a number of state and local indicators, including attendance and physical fitness. Both states have modified their merit school programs to a point where results appear promising.

3. A particularly difficult problem exists in ascertaining the unique contribution, or "value added," of a school or classroom to particular students' proficiencies and behaviors. Achievement studies rarely calculate the impact of socioeconomic status and environmental factors upon pupil attainment, and, consequently, we cannot hold teachers accountable for factors they are unable to influence. Moreover, the link between schools and "social benefits" such as citizenship, productivity, and economic growth is far removed in time and space from where schooling actually takes place. And a dynamic social, political, and economic structure is likely to alter relationships so that new jobs do not always match current vocational training programs. Consequently, it is difficult to relate short-run educational outcomes to longer run social outcomes (Gintis, 1971).

Finally, teacher organizations' resistance to many forms of accountability has been strong since the movement's inception. We are, moreover, still in a trial and error stage, and some accountability "comprehensive systems" and slogans raised expectations to unrealistic levels, while some concepts were simply naive or could not be implemented.

Given the constraints outlined above, it is apparent that many of the claims made for accountability mechanisms such as merit pay and PPBS were oversimplified, oversold, and mandated before they were field tested.

Of course, it is easy to recite prior failures and then downplay the whole movement, but that is premature, especially in view of the insistent public demand for the general concepts. Indeed, reports by the National Governors' Association, the National Conference of State Legislators, and the Education Summit all contend that accountability is crucial for the 1990s.

PROMISING DEVELOPMENTS IN ACCOUNTABILITY

Since the late 1960s, much of the initial naivete about accountability has been overcome and more effective techniques discovered. For example, a number of promising combinations of approaches—such as school-site performance reporting and parent choice—have evolved. Still, in reviewing that progress under the six major accountability categories, it is important to remember that areas of controversy remain.

Recently, much of the struggle in accountability has focused on a single conflict: that between political accountability which requires, on the one hand, that schools be answerable to citizens and their elected representatives for educational results, and the professionalism of educators that implies, on the other hand, that they possess sufficient discretion to make judgments about adapting instructional strategies to particular student characteristics (McDonnell, 1987). These competing values can be balanced, but some accountability systems emphasize one to the virtual exclusion of the other. At one extreme, for example, tests can force teachers to cover certain content items or skills at a particular time or even to move pupils from one grade to another against teachers' better judgment. At the other extreme, some teacher contracts insulate teachers from dismissal or even a stringent tenure review despite the desire of school boards to have specific policies in the content or skills areas. Throughout this review of promising practices, this tension must be kept in mind.

Improved Performance Reporting

In the 1980s, accountability has been undergirded with better information systems than in prior eras. Ideally, these information systems perform six key functions (McDonnell, 1987):

1. **Measuring the central features of schooling.** In the 1960s, accountability systems included inputs (resources) and outputs (test scores), but still they were unable to help policymakers understand why trends were getting better or worse, or how to improve performance. More recent state and local information systems,

however, contain information on teachers, access to curriculum, and other processes that provide a more robust set of indicators.

2. **Measuring what should be taught.** Often there has not been much overlap between content that states desire and content covered by teachers. Many state tests focus only on basic or minimum skills, while state curricular frameworks encourage a much wider range of content and topics. That has been a particular problem with older state assessments, although the match is now better in several states. Alignment of curricular frameworks, tests, and texts is providing more overlap with classroom instruction, but this alignment has the potential to excessively centralize policy and to undermine teacher professionalism by requiring teachers to cover specific items at a specific pace.

3. **Providing information that is policy relevant.** Accountability systems should highlight variables, such as teacher preparation or textbooks, that can be changed by education policymakers. Some early accountability techniques stressed unalterable variables like the pupil's socioeconomic status (SES), while failing to focus on items that policymakers could change—such as the number of years of science courses required.

4. **Focusing on the school.** Improvements must be made at the school level where pupils and teachers are directly involved. Consequently, data concentrating solely on entire districts do not provide a specific focus for school-site improvement.

5. **Encouraging fair comparisons.** Not all schools or students start out at the same level in such areas as resources, pupil attainment, or teacher experience. Various techniques, such as comparing schools solely within comparison bands of similar schools or predicting schoolwide pupil test scores based on family SES, have been explored as ways to adjust for these initial differences without rationalizing lower expectations for some schools and students. However, none of these techniques has met both objectives simultaneously.

6. **Minimizing burden and maximizing use.** Most states have at least two different testing programs—one for state assessment and another selected by the LEA for its particular needs. Not surprisingly, that increases costs and lessens student learning time. It also leads us to ask what the relative balance between state and local systems should be. Unfortunately, the question is rarely thought through in terms of a comprehensive accountability system. California, a notable exception, is now experimenting with an integrated system that allows LEAs to choose from a generic set of items are "anchored" to the statewide test. One California school report card meets criteria 1-5 in large part, but has a very high local response burden.)

Policymakers should be careful not to use the same accountability measures for schoolwide indicators as they use to gauge the individual performance of pupils and teachers. There is a fundamental conceptual difference between performance accountability as it applies to school systems and performance accountability as it applies to individuals who work for these systems. Thus, items collected in surveys that are designed to obtain schoolwide scores should not be used for holding individual teachers accountable. Classroom observations are a more reliable device for individual teacher evaluation.

Gaps in Many State Education Data Systems

While states and localities have made improvements in their performance indicators, these systems are no better than their database. The following are some of the crucial gaps that unfortunately remain in many states and localities.

* In almost all states, little data exist on middle schools. Not much is known, for example, about how tracks and courses in the middle grades determine academic choices in senior high schools.
* Typically, no integration exists between colleges and elementary/secondary schools. Most states, for example, have no way of knowing how students from specific high schools perform in colleges or what their freshman grade point averages are. And rarely is there any analysis or publicity about how graduates of specific high schools score on college academic placement tests. Since many colleges are designing new data systems, integration with secondary school needs is a particularly appropriate area for attention.
* In most states, high school performance data focus primarily on those students bound for four-year colleges or on those in the bottom quartile. Many states gather specific data on academic course-taking patterns, but not on "life in the general or middle tracks" where fewer academic courses are taken. And while categorical program data provide insight on the lowest achievers, these findings are oriented to program compliance rather than to curriculum improvement.
* There are serious shortcomings in existing data on the new policy dimensions regarding teacher quality. States need annual surveys of teachers working in subjects for which they have no credentials, as well as supply-and-demand projections by subfield, and assessments of the probability that teachers in the reserve pool will return to the schools. Most states have not been gathering these data because of the teacher surplus that occurred from 1970 to 1982.
* All states need to make a major effort to improve data on dropouts. Currently, many states calculate attrition data but not data on dropouts. (The U.S. Department of Education, in collaboration with the states, has provided nationwide, standard definitions.)

States seeking to bridge these data gaps and, at the same time, comply with reform laws requiring collection of some new types of data should closely scrutinize existing data streams. For example, new data demands on localities to evaluate state reform can frequently be eased by coupling them with reductions in other data requests. Thus, states should look carefully to see if certain kinds of little-used financial data might be eliminated or whether reductions in federal regulations governing Chapter I may have decreased the need for certain compliance-related data.

At the same time, however, states must be aware that assessment programs now used to test reading and math cannot be turned into freight trains used to carry vitally needed data to assess the impact of new state reforms. Any appreciable increase in data requirements attached to state testing programs probably will lead to increased resistance by LEAs and lower data reliability. In California, for example, the statewide California Assessment Program became loaded down with many new items related to categorical program evaluation and school climate and course-taking patterns, because it was the only data vehicle reaching students. California has now restricted the use of the state testing program for ancillary data. States need to consider development of a student information data sheet that would become part of their basic data system along with finance and teacher characteristics.

Despite the need for improvements in database quality, state indicator systems are becoming increasingly sophisticated and are being based on improved information systems. Still, a recent national study argued that we still have a way to go (Kaagan & Coley, 1989). It concluded:

- There is an understandable but often premature drive to report results so as to hold local school officials accountable. Consequently, the use of indicators for local policymaking is not optimal. Localities feel the state indicators are not very relevant to their local context.
- There is a reluctance at the state level to assume responsibility for the quality of the indicator system.
- There is a tentativeness with regard to the exploration of critical relationships among school processes, system outcomes such as student performance, and background or contextual variables.
- There is slow and uneven formation of the necessary building blocks to support an indicator system. States are building an analytical infrastructure to support indicator systems but are hardly finished.

Accountability Through Incentive Systems

As discussed earlier, the use of incentive systems has historically been the most difficult method of approaching accountability, including the failure of performance contracting and merit pay to achieve widespread acceptance. School budgets remain input oriented in categories such as administration and instruction, and cost-effectiveness analysis is rare, even though low-cost programs like peer tutoring and computer-assisted instruction are effective in some circumstances (Levin, 1988).

In the early 1970s, performance contracts used outside business firms to provide intensive remedial programs for disadvantaged children, and contractors were paid according to test score increases. However, the experiment collapsed when a contractor in Texarkana, Texas, falsified test data in order to make more money (Wynne, 1972). Merit pay, meanwhile, has been plagued by measurement problems that have galvanized strong union resistance (Cohen & Murnane, 1985). One obstacle is that while it is possible to identify incompetent teachers, sorting out the top 10 or

20 percent of teachers from their colleagues who perform at above average or adequate levels appears futile.

These difficulties have resulted in a new focus on the school site as the unit for performance pay through such schemes as merit schools, an approach that avoids competition among teachers and that can build school morale. Again, however, problems arise in devising outcome measures that are precise and legitimate enough to stimulate widespread acceptance. States like Florida and South Carolina base their payments in part on increases in state assessment scores. These assessments, in turn, are criticized because they do not stress higher order skills and may omit subject areas like social science and foreign languages. Consequently, they run afoul of the old objections of being too narrow and causing year-to-year random variations in school-site achievement patterns.

However, Florida has been able to overcome these complaints somewhat by permitting LEAs to use some locally established performance objectives as well as state basic skills tests. For example, some Florida localities establish increases in areas such as attendance, physical fitness, and history achievement as their objectives. If the LEA meets these objectives and state test scores increase, the merit school payment is allocated. Florida appropriates $10 million for this program and permits school districts to spend the money on anything they choose, including teacher salaries. Not surprisingly, this provision has brought in teacher union support, particularly in American Federation of Teachers (AFT) locals.

Craig Richards (1989) in a study of state merit school programs for the Center for Policy Research in Education found that 13 states had implemented or were formulating school incentive plans. He reports that states use both "fixed performance plans," where schools compete against a standard for awards, and "competitive performance plans," where they vie with each other. In South Carolina, for example, schools in the top 25 percent compete in one of five groupings, according to LEA socioeconomic status.

Richards stresses that states have not reached a consensus about the best indicators of school performance. States have used test scores, attendance, and local goals—including even physical fitness—but the overall concept of school incentive plans has yet to reach maturity. Unresolved issues include:

- Accommodating the high correlation between test scores and pupils' socioeconomic backgrounds
- Assessing implications for finance equalization if wealthy districts are frequent winners
- Establishing an optimal balance between monetary vs. nonmonetary rewards as incentives for educators
- Determining whether state deregulation is a significant enough incentive to change local educators' behavior
- Developing the process needed to effect a high degree of *perceived* fairness and broad political support for any incentive plan and method of calculating school performance

Despite the lack of consensus on these still unresolved issues, school site goals/objectives can be a useful accountability device even if no specific payment is attached. In his accelerated schools program, Henry Levin uses school system goals on curriculum as a starting point, and then asks each school to set the specific goals it wants to accomplish over a three-year period. These goals are "bottom line" and include test and other outcomes such as increased parent involvement. At the end of the three years he describes the process this way:

There should be at least a preliminary attempt to determine why some goals were exceeded and others were not met. . . . Some questions include: 1) Were some goals too ambitious or easy to reach? 2) What did the school learn about its capabilities and improvements? 3) What changes need to be made in both school and district capacities? (Levin, 1989)

In sum, school site accountability goals need to include a mixture of quantitative and qualitative outcomes and process indicators. Site goals should be precise enough that they can be used for summary evaluations after 3 years or more. The goal-setting process needs to result in frequent reviews of school performance.

Accountability Through Changing The Locus Of Control

American schools have always operated under the motto that "education is too important to be left to educators." Traditionally, the prime accountability mechanism has been the local school board, often elected from a very small geographic region. Indeed, the United States still has more than 15,000 school districts that hold elections for some members at least every other year. Recently, however, the public has begun to lose confidence in school boards, and satisfaction with this crucial accountability device has declined. But despite this phenomenon, Americans still support local school boards—rather than state or federal government—as the preferred locus of control. Indeed, a 1986 Gallup Poll reported that, when asked their views about who should control schools, 57 percent of the public said that local school boards should have more influence. By comparison, 45 percent favored increased state influence and 26 percent supported a larger federal role. Therefore, one strategy for improved accountability is to strengthen school board policy-making capacity and performance, as recommended by the Institute for Educational Leadership (Danzberger et al., 1986).

There are, however, no accepted theories or data to determine whether the school board or some other institution should be the decision maker. Clune puts it this way:

Since no decision maker is perfect, the distrust directed at one decision maker must be carefully weighed against the advantages of that decision maker and both the advantages and disadvantages of alternative decision makers. In other words, although the logic of institutional choice typically begins with distrust, distrust itself proves nothing in the absence of a superior alternative. . . . The logic of comparative institutional advantage also implies the futility of seeking perfect or ideal implementation of a policy. . . . The real world offers a "least worst choice" of imperfect institutions. (Clune, 1987)

Recently, the restructuring movement has promoted more discretion at the school-site level. But who should control flexible school-site resources? Four viewpoints have been advanced:

- First, under the concept of principal as site manager, the principal should control resources and be held accountable for the success of the school. Success can be measured through school-site performance reports that include pupil attainment measures, as well as the impact of budget allocations made by the principal upon specific measurable school-site goals. This view of the principal as site manager was reinforced by the school effectiveness literature's focus on strong school leadership.
- Second, parents should control site policy because they are the consumers and care most deeply about policies at schools their children attend. Parents are less interested in central district policies that have no easily discernible impact on their children, so specific school-site accountability systems should be designed with parents as the primary audience. The American philosophy of lay control implies that parent school-site councils should deliberate and decide on school-level policy. Consequently, decisions on budget, personnel, and curriculum should be made by parent-majority site councils.
- Third, teachers should form a school-site senate to allocate funds and personnel as well as decide instructional issues. Teachers cannot be held accountable for pupil performance if they do not control resource allocations but must instead follow standardized instructional procedures. School-site policymaking by teachers would also enhance their professional image and self-concept.
- Fourth, none of these rationales is sufficiently compelling that it should be the norm. Instead, all factions deserve a place at the table, and the best arguments should prevail. Consequently, a school-site council should have "parity" of membership among teachers, administrators, and parents who would then reach agreements through bargaining and coalitions. At the high school level, students might also be included. (The recently implemented Chicago decentralization embodies the second viewpoint, while in Rochester, New York, the teachers' contract provides for their participation in school-site councils with membership "parity.")

There are, of course, other concepts for changes in governance that do not rely on school sites. State takeover of local schools, for example, reverses the state's historic practice of delegating accountability to the local school board. Accountability accomplished through a state-appointed trustee is another indication that public confidence in some school boards is eroding. At the systemwide level, meanwhile, local businesses are also gaining strong influence over site accountability. For example, the Boston Compact guarantees students local jobs if high schools produce graduates possessing a particular level of competence.

Accountability Through The Market

The rising interest in choice has focused on the market and the parent as crucial accountability devices. However, attempts to legislate vouchers or tuition tax credits for use in private schools have failed politically and continue to face difficult legal obstacles. Meanwhile, choice restricted totally to the public sector may not be a powerful accountability device. For example, experience in Minnesota, which implemented an ambitious statewide choice plan, is still too limited to evaluate, but appears to involve less than 3 percent of the total students. For policymakers contemplating choice programs in their states or districts, analysts highlight several crucial points for ensuring effective programs (Education Commission of the States, 1989).

- **Choice is not a panacea.** It must be linked with other school improvement strategies to achieve the long-run goal of restructuring schools. Choice plans should include a clear statement of goals that schools are expected to meet.
- **Choice is not low-cost school improvement.** When choice is done carefully and when it is linked to other school improvement strategies (e.g., restructuring), it will involve new investments in education. Transportation should be provided for all students within a reasonable geographic area.
- **Choice must offer diversity and quality.** If families are offered a choice among uniform and mediocre schools, choice will have done nothing but stir the fires of discontent. Programs should include help for many schools to develop distinctive features, rather than simply concentrating resources on a few schools.
- **Choice must be well planned.** When choice policies are carefully designed and attention is paid not only to family freedom, but also to school improvement and educational equity, the positive outcomes may outweigh any negative ones. Oversight and modification of the program should be included at the planning stage.
- **Choice must be carefully implemented.** When a change of this magnitude is contemplated, a phased-in process of implementation will do much to avoid potential pitfalls and to assuage political opposition. Implementation should include information and counseling for parents in selecting among the various programs available to their children, and admissions procedures that are fair and equitable-not based on "first come, first served" or on the past achievement or behavior of students.
- **Choice is also for students who do not move.** The success of choice is not measured by the number of children who change schools, but by the improvements that schools make in order to be attractive so that they may retain the students they currently serve (Nathan, 1984).
- **Choice should include procedures for ensuring racial balance and promoting racial integration.** State dollars for special programs should follow the students.

Overall, choice remains complex and costly to design and implement, but does provide a distinctive market-oriented approach to accountability.

Accountability Through Changing Professional Roles

The history of accountability features attempts by higher level authorities to control the behavior of classroom teachers. Professionalism, however, stresses the desirability of accountability coming from *within* the teaching force rather than being imposed by external authorities. The key is for teachers to help each other improve and to take responsibility for assessing quality. This concept is spreading slowly and is most prominent in urban districts and among state licensing boards. In order for this approach to work, however, policymakers must trust teachers to provide sufficient accountability, and they must permit sufficient flexibility in classroom practice for professional discretion to be exercised. That involves a change in attitudes for both administration and teachers.

In Dade County, Florida, professional accountability has been combined with changes in the locus of control through the introduction of school-site management (Timar, 1989). Teachers represent a majority of the school-site council which allocates resources and designs curriculum. Moreover, responsibility for hiring and firing of teachers has shifted substantially toward the council. Teachers in Dade County decentralized schools describe the principal as more of a coach than a foreman, and teacher evaluation is primarily conducted by the department chairs and by other teachers. This decentralized decision making is strongly supported by the AFT union local and is evaluated in part by the elaborate school-site indicators and report card system that has existed in the county for many years. However, the system is still evolving, and a key issue is the role of the teacher-dominated school council in evaluating the school's performance.

TRENDS AND IMPLICATIONS

Over the past 25 years, accountability concepts have constantly been created, discarded, adapted, and improved. The early disillusionment with PPBS and performance contracting has been replaced by an incremental refinement of techniques. At the same time, public demand for accountability has intensified, and that demand is reflected in the national goals and objectives set forth at the Education Summit. Still, the word accountability continues to span a very wide variety of concepts and policies, making it an elusive concept to grasp. The movement, however, has left a large repository of published studies that encompass theory and practical advice.

This paper has used a specific typology that policymakers may find useful in organizing the multifaceted accountability literature. Some important trends that are highlighted in this literature and have important implications for policymakers are:

1. Data systems and performance indicators have improved to the point where we now have a vast array of potential input, process, and outcome variables that are useful for accountability. The big problem is developing and funding the database to include adequately the full range of educational endeavor. We now know

what data are useful to collect, but the expense of funding databases is yet to be faced (Shavelson et al., 1989). Federal goals, for example, will require a revamped and expanded National Assessment of Educational Progress (NAEP) and necessitate close coordination with such national curriculum movements as Science 2061 and the national mathematics frameworks recommended by the National Council of Teachers of Mathematics. Both of these curriculum redesigns envision interdisciplinary work and problem-solving concepts that are not included in current tests like NAEP.

Furthermore, many state education agencies (SEAS) and LEAs have only begun to phase in indicators and report cards. Often these indicators are too narrow to capture the complexity of education, although an awareness is developing of the desirability of more complex and comprehensive indicators. Indeed, some policymakers are now scrutinizing whether existing state and local tests overemphasize minimum competency and low-level general skills at the expense of analysis, synthesis, inference, and expository writing. Subject matter tests in such areas as history and science are being added, as well as assessments that include synthesis, analysis, statistical inference and other higher order skills.

Performance indicators can either help increase academic standards through better assessments or be a straitjacket embodying only low-level skills. Policymakers should be aware that new assessment concepts, being developed by the Educational Testing Service (ETS) and by states like Connecticut and California, will provide more effective performance-driven accountability systems.

2. Policymakers are rethinking their heavy reliance on legal and bureaucratic accountability. The National Governors' Association, for example, is pushing for a "horse trade" offering less regulation if performance indicators demonstrate positive outcomes. And some states, in an effort to spur innovation, are conducting experiments with wholesale waivers of their codes.

Thus, while regulations remain an important part of categorical programs and are essential for auditing, more attention is now being paid to implementation research that stresses the need to allow several models of practice to develop within categorical programs and the value of letting local practitioners experiment with these models to see which one works best in a local context (Elmore & McLaughlin, 1988). Put another way, a new balance within regulatory accountability is being sought that includes the redistribution of discretion from central offices to school sites and the loosening of categorical restrictions. We probably have seen the high point of state-mandated procedural accountability techniques such as standardized checklists for principals to use in assessing teachers. The trade-off among accountability techniques is highlighted by the use of more precise performance output indicators as a rationale for less procedural or bureaucratic accountability. A crucial unknown, however, is how far education can move from rule-driven to performance-driven accountability emphases.

3. Incentive system approaches that use incentive pay as an accountability strategy to promote better input-output relationships remain problematic. Merit pay seems to have lost whatever slight political momentum it had in the early 1980s, and merit schools are spreading very slowly throughout the states—although new federal funds may provide added stimulus.

   Incentive systems that are part of the normal school budget process are also not gaining ground. PPBS and MBO budget procedures that expand specific programs demonstrating high cost-effectiveness ratios are rarely used by LEAs. We need more experimentation in these areas. For example, current input budgeting relies on enrollment-driven formulas and is not very useful for assessing program effectiveness. School budgets still rely on general categories like "instruction" and "administration" that cannot be related to goals or even input categories like English or math services offered.

4. Political accountability is a major topic with dramatic new policies being implemented in Chicago, Illinois; Santa Fe, New Mexico; and other districts. Decentralization is a popular concept, and it can be combined with such strategies as restructuring, professionalism, and community control. While Chicago features community control of each school site, Santa Fe emphasizes professional control at the school site by teachers. Since the central office surrenders some of its procedural accountability under all these schemes, rethinking how the central office can better help school sites has assumed new importance. Industrial restructuring that permits more flexibility at lower levels is a model which has helped create momentum for decentralization in education. Educators are examining industrial restructuring concepts that stress more worker decision making and control of assembly line production.

5. Market accountability advocates currently focus on the public sector, with declining political interest in providing public aid to private schools. While more open enrollment within and between public school districts is likely, how many pupils will use it is unclear. For example, school choice can be based on proximity to the parents' workplace or on the attraction of a particular school or education program. Will parents' knowledge that they have choice (even if they do not exercise it) be an important accountability technique? No one knows at this time. An even more fundamental open question centers on how much market accountability will improve the quality of school performance or pupil attainment. And still another unknown is whether schools that lose pupils will improve their educational performance or continue to deteriorate.

In sum, educational accountability is a very old concept that continues to grow and diversify. It has not yet reached maturity nor achieved an integration of strategies that reinforce each other. Still, substantial progress has been made, and we have learned from the false starts of the 1960s and 1970s.

Thus, while accountability policies still reflect a trial-and-error approach whereby new schemes are proposed and some "work" better than others, refinements have been made in such areas as performance indicators and professional accountability. But while these improvements provide reason for optimism, caution is needed as policymakers rush into accountability without a clear understanding of obstacles and unintended consequences. Indeed, one major concern is that accountability approaches will inhibit restructuring of education and broader concepts of assessment that go beyond basic skills. The potential for accountability systems to conflict with one another is highlighted in an analysis of school restructuring cases (Timar, 1989). The Dade County school-site council—dominated by teachers—is a new form of accountability, but, in order to be effective, one school had to request over 100 waivers from the older system of standards and regulations. Meanwhile, in Jefferson County, Kentucky, new forms of site and professional accountability were inhibited by state-mandated evaluation criteria and by Kentucky's statewide use of the California Test of Basic Skills to evaluate student and school performance. In addition, state accreditation requirements conflicted with Jefferson County's efforts to make curriculum revisions that changed the length of time students were in class.

The difficulties encountered in these districts effectively illustrate the policy issues identified at the beginning of this paper: accountability options are difficult to blend, and policymakers need to consider local contexts when determining the emphasis and balance among alternatives. It is essential to keep those thoughts in mind, since there is one certainty—the political pressure for increased accountability is unremitting and rising, due to public concern about the relative performance of U.S. students on international assessments and the recognition that too many students lack the skills needed to improve America's economic productivity.

IV. SOCIAL AGENDA-DIRECTED (ADVOCACY) MODELS

The third category of evaluation models are labeled **Social Agenda-Directed (Advocacy) Models**. The models in this group are quite heavily oriented to employing the perspectives of stakeholders as well as experts in characterizing, investigating, and judging programs. Mainly, they eschew the possibility of finding right or best answers and reflect the philosophy of postmodernism, with its attendant stress on cultural pluralism, moral relativity, and multiple realities. Typically, these evaluation models favor a constructivist orientation and the use of qualitative methods. These evaluation approaches emphasize the importance of democratically engaging stakeholders in obtaining and interpreting findings. They also stress serving the interests of underprivileged groups. Worries about studies following these models are that they might concentrate so heavily on serving a social mission that they fail to meet the standards of a sound evaluation. For example, if an evaluator is so intent on serving the underprivileged, empowering the disenfranchised, and/or righting educational and/or social injustices, he or she might compromise the independent, impartial perspective needed to produce valid findings. In the extreme, an advocacy evaluation could compromise the integrity of the evaluation process in order to achieve social objectives and thus devolve into a misleading study. The particular social agenda/advocacy-directed models presented in this book seem to have sufficient safeguards needed to walk the fine line between sound evaluation services and politically corrupted evaluations. Worries about bias control in these approaches increase the importance of subjecting advocacy evaluations to metaevaluations grounded in standards for sound evaluations.

18. PROGRAM EVALUATION, PARTICULARLY RESPONSIVE EVALUATION

ROBERT E. STAKE

A program may be strictly or loosely defined. It might be as large as all the teacher training in the United States or it might be as small as a field trip for the pupils of one classroom. The evaluation circumstances will be these: that someone is commissioned in some way to evaluate a program, probably an ongoing program; that he has some clients or audiences to be of assistance to—usually including the educators responsible for the program; and that he has the responsibility for preparing communications with these audiences.

In 1965, Lee Cronbach, then president of the American Educational Research Association (AERA), asked me to chair a committee to prepare a set of standards for evaluation studies, perhaps like the *Standards for Educational and Psychological Tests and Manuals*, compiled by John French and Bill Michael and published in 1966 by the American Psychological Association. Lee Cronbach, Bob Heath, Tom Hastings, Hulda Grobman, and other educational researchers have worked with many of the U.S. curriculum-reform projects in the 1950s and early 1960s, and have recognized the difficulty of evaluating curricula and the great need for guidance on the design of evaluation studies.

Our committee reported that it was too early to decide upon a particular method or set of criteria for evaluating educational programs, that what educational researchers needed was a period of field work and discussion to gain more experience in how evaluative studies could be done. Ben Bloom, successor to Lee Cronbach in the

Stake, Robert E. "Program Evaluation, Particularly Responsive Evaluation." Paper presented at conference on *New Trends in Evaluation*, Göteborg, Sweden, October 1973. Reprinted with permission.

D.L. Stufflebeam, G.F. Madaus and T. Kellaghan (eds.). *EVALUATION MODELS. Copyright © 2000. Kluwer Academic Publishers. Boston. All rights reserved.*

presidency of the AERA, got the AERA to sponsor a monograph series on curriculum evaluation for the purpose we recommended. The seven volumes completed under AERA sponsorship are shown in the Reference section. The series in effect will continue under sponsorship of the University of California-Los Angeles (UCLA) Center for the Study of Evaluation, whose director, Marv Alkin, was a guest professor here at this Institute for Educational Research two years ago. I think this monograph series can take a good share of the credit, or blame, for the fact that, by count, over 200 sessions at the 1973 AERA annual meeting programs were directly related to the methods and results of program-evaluation studies.

There were two primary models for program evaluation in 1965, and there are two today. One is the informal study, perhaps a self-study, usually using information already available, relying on the insights of professional persons and respected authorities. It is the approach of regional accrediting associations for secondary schools and colleges in the United States and is exemplified by the Flexner report (1916) of medical education in the USA and by the Coleman report (1966) of equality of educational opportunity. In *Nine Approaches to Educational Evaluation* (see Appendix A), I have ever so briefly described this and other models; this one is referred to there as the *Institutional Self-Study by Staff Approach*. Most educators are partial to this evaluation model, more so if they can specify who the panel members or examiners are. Researchers do not like it because it relies so much on second-hand information. But there is much good about the model.

Most researchers have preferred the other model, the pretest/post-test model, what I have referred to on the *Nine Approaches* sheet at *Student Gain by Testing Approach*. It often uses prespecified statements of behavioral objectives—such as are available from Jim Popham's Instructional Objectives Exchange—and is nicely represented by Tyler's (1942a) "Eight-Year Study," Husen's (1967) *International Study of Achievement in Mathematics*, and the National Assessment of Educational Progress. The focus of attention with this model is primarily on student performance.

Several of us have proposed other models. In a 1963 article, Cronbach (Chapter 14, this volume) advocates having evaluation studies considered applied research on instruction, to learn what could be learned in general about curriculum development, as was done in Hilda Taba's Social Studies Curriculum Project. Mike Scriven (1967) strongly criticized Cronbach's choice in AERA Monograph no. 1, stating that it was time to give consumers (purchasing agents, taxpayers, and parents) information on how good each existing curriculum is. To this end, Kenneth Komoski established in New York City an Educational Products Information Exchange, which has reviewed equipment, books, and teaching aids but has to this day still not caught the buyer's eye.

Dan Stufflebeam was one who recognized that the designs preferred by researchers did not focus on the variables that educational administrators have control over. With support from Egon Guba, Dave Clark, Bill Gephart, and others (1971), he proposed a model for evaluation that emphasized the particular decisions that a program manager will face. Data-gathering would include data on context, input, process, and product; but analyses would relate those things to the immediate management of the program. Though Mike Scriven criticized this design, too,

saying that it had too much bias toward the concerns and the values of the educational establishment, this Stufflebeam CIPP model was popular in the U.S.
Office of Education for several years. Gradually, it fell into disfavor not because
it was a bad model, but partly because managers were unable or unwilling to *examine
their own* operations as part of the evaluation. Actually, no evaluation model could
have succeeded. A major obstacle was a federal directive, which said that no federal
office could spend its funds to evaluate its own work; that that could only be done
by an office higher up. Perhaps the best examples of evaluation reports following
this approach are those done in the Pittsburgh schools by Mal Provus and Esther
Kresh.

Before I describe the approach that I have been working on—which I hope will
someday challenge the two major models—I will mention several relatively recent
developments in the evaluation business.

It is recognized, particularly by Mike Scriven and Ernie House, that co-option is
a problem, that the rewards to an evaluator for producing a favorable evaluation
report often greatly outweigh the rewards for producing an unfavorable report. I do
not know of any evaluators who falsify their reports, but I do know many who
consciously or unconsciously choose to emphasize the objectives of the program
staff and to concentrate on the issues and variables most likely to show where the
program is successful. I often do this myself. Thus, the matter of *meta evaluation*, providing a quality control for the evaluation activities, has become an increasing
concern.

Early in his first term of office, President Nixon created a modest Experimental
Schools Program, a program of five-year funding for three carefully selected high
schools (from all those in the whole country) and the elementary schools that feed
students into them. Three more have been chosen each year, according to their proposal to take advantage of a broad array of knowledge and technical developments
and to show how good a school can be. The evaluation responsibility was designed
to be allocated at three separate levels, one *internal* at the local-school level; one
external at the local-school level (i.e., in the community attending to the working
of the local school but not controlled by it); and a third at the national level, synthesizing results from the local projects and evaluating the organization and effects
of the Experimental Schools Program as a whole. Many obstacles and hostilities
hampered the work of the first two evaluation teams, and work at the third level—
according to Egon Guba, who did a feasibility study—was seen to be so likely to
fail that it probably should be carried no further.

Mike Scriven has made several suggestions for meta evaluation, one most widely
circulated based on abstinence, called *goal-free evaluation*. Sixten Marklund has jok-
ingly called it "aimless evaluation." But it is a serious notion, not to ignore all idea
of goals with the program sponsors or staff. The evaluator, perhaps with the help of
colleagues and consultants, then is expected to recognize manifest goals and accomplishments of the program as he works it in the field. Again, with the concern for
the consumer of education, Scriven has argued that what is intended is not important, that the program is a failure if its results are so subtle that they do not pene-

trate the awareness of an alert evaluator. Personally, I fault Scriven for expecting us evaluators to be as sensitive, rational, and alert as his designs for evaluation require. I sometimes think that Mike Scriven designs evaluation studies that perhaps only Mike Scriven is capable of carrying out.

Another interesting development is the use of adversarial procedures in obtaining evidence of program quality and, especially, in presenting it to decision-makers. Tom Owens, Murray Levine, and Marilyn Kourilsky have taken the initiative here. They have drawn up the work of legal theorists who claim that truth emerges when opposing forces submit their evidence to cross-examination directly before the eyes of judges and juries. Craig Gjerde, Terry Denny, and I tried something like this in our TCITY report (Stake & Gjerde, 1975) (see Appendix B for a summary of the most positive claims that might reasonably be made for the Institute we were evaluating and a summary of the most damaging charges that might reasonably be made). It was important to us to leave the issue unresolved, to let the reader decide which claim to accept, if any. But we would have served the reader better if we had each written a follow-up statement to challenge the other's claims. At any rate, this is an example of using an adversary technique in an evaluation study.

Now, in the next 45 minutes or so, I want to concentrate on the approach for evaluating educational programs presently advocated by Malcolm Parlett of the University of Edinburgh, Barry MacDonald of the University of East Anglia, Lou Smith of Washington University of St. Louis, Bob Rippey of the University of Connecticut, and myself. You have had an opportunity to read an excellent statement by Malcolm Parlett and David Hamilton (1972). Like they did, I want to emphasize the settings where learning occurs, teaching transactions, judgment data, holistic reporting, and giving assistance to educators. I should not suggest that they endorse all I will say today, but their writings for the most part are harmonious with mine.

Let me start with a basic definition, one that I got from Mike Scriven. Evaluation is an *observed value* compared to some *standard*. It is a simple ratio, but this numerator is not simple. In program evaluation, it pertains to the whole constellation of values held for the program. And the denominator is not simple, for it pertains to the complex of expectations and criteria that different people have for such a program.

The basic task for an evaluator is made barely tolerable by the fact that he or she does not have to solve this equation in some numerical way nor to obtain a descriptive summary grade, but merely needs to make a comprehensive statement of what the program is observed to be, with useful references to the satisfaction and dissatisfaction that appropriately selected people feel toward it. Any particular client may want more than this; but this satisfies the minimum concept, I think, of an evaluation study.

If you look carefully at the TCITY report, you will find no direct expression of this formula, but it is in fact the initial idea that guided us. The form of presentation was chosen to convey a message about the Twin City Institute to our readers in Minneapolis and St. Paul, rather than to be a literal manifestation of our theory of evaluation.

Our theory of evaluation emphasizes the distinction between a *preordinate* approach and a *responsive* approach. In the recent past, the major distinction being made by methodologists is that between what Scriven called *formative* and *summative* evaluation. He gave attention to the difference between developing and already-developed programs and, implicitly, to evaluation for a local audience of a program in a specific setting, as contrasted to evaluation for many audiences of a potentially generalizable program. These are important distinctions, but I find it even more important to distinguish between preordinate evaluation studies and responsive evaluation studies.

I have made the point that there are many different ways to evaluate educational programs. No one way is the right way. Some highly recommended evaluation procedures do not yield a full description nor a view of the merit and shortcoming of the program being evaluated. Some procedures ignore the pervasive questions that should be raised whenever educational programs are evaluated: Do all students benefit or only a special few? Does the program adapt to instructors with unusual qualifications? Are opportunities for aesthetic experience realized?

Some evaluation procedures are insensitive to the uniqueness of the local conditions. Some are insensitive to the quality of the learning climate provided. Each way of evaluating leaves some things de-emphasized.

I prefer to work with evaluation designs that perform a service. I expect the evaluation study to be useful to specific persons. An evaluation probably will not be useful if the evaluator does not know the interests of his audiences. During an evaluation study, a substantial amount of time may be spent learning about the information needs of the persons for whom the evaluation is being done. The evaluator should have a good sense of whom he is working for and their concerns.

To be of service and to emphasize evaluation issues that are important for each particular program, I recommend the *responsive evaluation* approach. It is an approach that sacrifices some precision in measurement, hopefully to increase the usefulness of the findings to person in and around the program. Many evaluation plans are more *preordinate*, emphasizing statement of goals, use of objective tests, standards held by program personnel, and research-type reports. Responsive evaluation is less reliant on formal communication, more reliant on natural communication.

Responsive evaluation is an alternative, an old alternative. It is evaluation based on what people do naturally to evaluate things: they observe and react. The approach is not new; but it has been avoided in planning documents and institutional regulations because, I believe, it is subjective, poorly suited to formal contracts, and a little too likely to raise the more embarrassing questions. I think we can overcome the worst aspects of subjectivity, at least. Subjectivity can be reduced by replication and operational definition of ambiguous terms even while we are relying heavily on the insights of personal observation.

An educational evaluation is responsive evaluation if it orients more directly to program activities than to program intents, if it responds to audience requirements for information, and if the different value perspectives of the people at hand are referred to in reporting the success and failure of the program. In these three separate ways, an evaluation plan can be responsive.

To do a responsive evaluation, the evaluator, of course, does many things. He or she makes a plan of observations and negotiations and arranges for various persons to observe the program. With their help, the evaluator prepares for brief narratives, portrayals, product displays, graphs, etc. He or she finds out what is of value to the audience and gathers expressions of worth from various individuals whose points of view differ. Of course, the evaluator checks the quality of his or her records and gets program personnel to react to the accuracy of the portrayals. He or she gets authority figures to react to the importance of various findings and audience members to react to the relevance of the findings. The evaluator does much of this informally, iterating, and keeping a record of action and reaction. He or she chooses media accessible to his or her audiences to increase the likelihood and fidelity of communication. The evaluator might prepare a final written report, or he or she might not—depending on what the evaluator and the clients have agreed on.

PURPOSE AND CRITERIA

Many of you will agree that the book edited by E. F. Lindquist, *Educational Measurement*, has been the bible for us who have specialized in educational measurement. Published in 1950, it contained no materials on program evaluation. The second edition, edited by Bob Thorndike (1971), has a chapter on program evaluation. Unfortunately, the authors of this chapter, Alex Astin and Bob Panos, chose to emphasize but one of the many purposes of evaluation studies. They said that the principal purpose of evaluation is to produce information that can guide decisions concerning the adoption or modification of an educational program.

People expect evaluation to accomplish many different purposes:

to document events,
to record student change,
to detect institutional vitality,
to place the blame for trouble,
to aid administrative decision making,
to facilitate corrective action,
to increase our understanding of teaching and learning.

Each of these purposes is related directly or indirectly to the values of a program and may be a legitimate purpose for a particular evaluation study. It is very important to realize that each purpose needs separate data; all the purposes cannot be served with a single collection of data. Only a few questions can be given prime attention. We should not let Astin and Panos decide what questions to attend to, or Tyler, or Stake. Each evaluator, in each situation, has to decide what to attend to. The evaluator has to decide.

On what basis will he choose the prime questions? Will he rely on his preconceptions? Or on the formal plans and objectives of the program? Or on actual program activities? Or on the reactions of participants? It is at this choosing that an evaluator himself is tested.

Most evaluators can be faulted for over-reliance on preconceived notions of success. I advise the evaluator to give careful attention to the reasons the evaluation was commissioned, then to pay attention to what is happening in the program, then to choose the value questions and criteria. He should not fail to discover the best and worst of program happenings. He should not let a list of objectives or an early choice of data-gathering instruments draw attention away from the things that most concern the people involved.

Many of my fellow evaluators are committed to the idea that good education results in measurable outcomes: student performance, mastery, ability, attitude. But I believe it is not always best to think of the *instrumental* value of education as a basis for evaluating it. The "payoff" may be diffuse, long-delayed; or it may be ever beyond the scrutiny of evaluators. In art education, for example, it is sometimes the purpose of the program staff or parent to provide artistic experiences—and training—for the *intrinsic* value alone. "We do these things because they are good things to do," says a ballet teacher. Some science professors speak similarly about the experimental value of reconstructing certain classical experiments. The evaluator or his observers should note whether or not those learning experiences were well-arranged. They should find out what appropriately selected people think are the costs and benefits of these experiences in the dance studio or biology laboratory. The evaluator should not presume that only measurable outcomes testify to the worth of the program.

Sometimes it will be important for the evaluator to do his best to measure student outcomes, other times not. I believe that there are few critical data in any study, just as there are few critical components in any learning experience. The learner is capable of using many pathways, many tasks, to gain his measure of skill and aesthetic benefit. The evaluator can take different pathways to reveal program benefit. Tests and other data-gathering should not be seen as essential; neither should they be automatically ruled out. The choice of these instruments in responsive evaluation should be made as a result of observing the program in action and of discovering the purposes important to the various groups having an interest in the program.

Responsive evaluations require planning and structure; but they rely little on formal statements and abstract representations, e.g., flow charts, test scores. Statements of objectives, hypotheses, test batteries, and teaching syllabi are, of course, given primary attention if they are primary components of the instructional program. Then they are treated not as the basis for the evaluation plan but as components of the instructional plan. These components are to be evaluated just as other components are. The proper amount of structure for responsive evaluation depends on the program and persons involved.

SUBSTANTIVE STRUCTURE

Instead of objectives or hypotheses as *advanced organizers* for an evaluation study, I prefer issues. I think the word *issues* better reflects a sense of complexity, immediacy, and valuing. After getting acquainted with a program, partly by talking with students, parents, taxpayers, program sponsors, and program staff, the evaluator acknowledges certain issues or problems or potential problems. These issues are a structure for continuing discussions with clients, staff, and audiences, and for the data-gathering plan. The systematic observations to be made, the interviews and tests to be given, if any, should be those that contribute to understanding or resolving the issues identified.

In evaluating TCITY, Craig Gjerde and I became aware of such issue-questions as:

Is the admissions policy satisfactory?
Are some teachers too permissive?
Why do so few students stay for the afternoon?
Is opportunity for training younger teachers well used?
Is this Institute a "lighthouse" for regular school curriculum innovation?

The importance of such questions varies during the evaluation period. Issues that are identified early as being important tend to be given too much attention in a preordinate data plan, and issues identified toward the end are likely to be ignored. Responsive-evaluation procedures allow the evaluator to respond to emerging issues as well as to preconceived issues.

The evaluator usually needs more structure than a set of questions to help him decide what data to gather. To help the evaluator conceptualize his "shopping list," I once wrote a paper entitled "The Countenance of Educational Evaluation" (Stake, 1967). It contained the matrix, the thirteen information categories, shown in Figure 1. You may notice that my categories are not very different from those called for in the models of Dan Stufflebeam and Mal Provus.

For different evaluation purposes, there will be different emphases on one side of the matrix or the other: descriptive data and judgmental data. And, similarly, there will be different emphases on antecedent, transaction, and outcome information. The "Countenance" article also emphasized the use of multiple, and even contradicting, sources of information.

The article also pointed out the often-ignored question about the match-up between intended instruction and observed instruction and the even more elusive question about the strength of the contingency of observed outcomes upon observed transactions under the particular conditions observed. I think these "Countenance" ideas continue to be good ones for planning the content of the evaluation study.

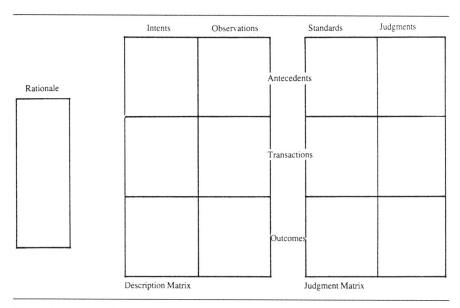

Figure 1. A Layout of Statements and Data to Be Collected by the Evaluator of an Educational Program

I like to think of all of these data as observations: intents, standards, judgments, and statements of rationale. Maybe it was a mistake to label just the second column *observations*. Thoreau said: "Could a greater miracle take place than for us to look through each other's eyes for an instant?"

Human observers are the best instruments we have for many evaluation issues. Performance data and preference data can be psychometrically scaled when objectively quantified data are called for. The important matter for the evaluator is to get his information in sufficient amount from numerous independent and credible sources so that it effectively represents the perceived status of the program, however complex.

FUNCTIONAL STRUCTURE

"Which data" is one thing, but "how to do the evaluation" is another. My responsive-evaluation plan allocates a large expenditure of evaluation resources to observing the program. The plan is not divided into phases because observation and feedback continue to be the important functions from the first week through the last. I have identified 12 recurring events (see Figure 2), which I show as if on the face of a clock. I know some of you would remind me that a clock moves clockwise, so I hurry to say that this clock moves clockwise and counter-clockwise *and* cross-clockwise. In other words, any event can follow any event. Furthermore, many events occur simultaneously, and the evaluator returns to each event many times before the evaluation ends.

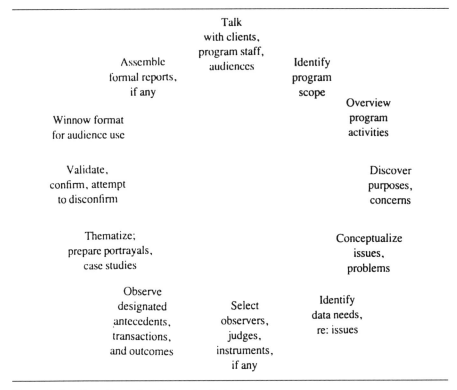

Figure 2. Prominent Events in a Responsive Evaluation

For example, take twelve o'clock. The evaluator will discuss many things on many occasions with the program staff and with people who are representative of his audiences. He will want to check his ideas of program scope, activities, purposes, and issues against theirs. He will want to show them his representations (e.g., sketches, displays, portrayals, photographs, tapes) of value questions, activities, curricular content, and student products. Reactions to these representations will help him learn how to communicate in this setting. He should provide useful information. He should not pander to desires for only favorable (or only unfavorable) information, nor should he suppose that only the concerns of evaluators and external authorities are worthy of discussion. (Of course, these admonitions are appropriate for responsive evaluation and preordinate evaluation alike.)

This behavior of the responsive evaluator is very different from the behavior of the preordinate evaluator. Table 1 illustrates my estimate as to how the two evaluators would typically spend their time.

I believe the preordinate evaluator conceptualizes himself as a stimulus, seldom as a response. He does his best to generate standardized stimuli, such as behavioral objective statements, test items, or questionnaire items. The responses that he evokes are what he collects as the substance of his evaluation report.

Table 1. Comparison of Preordinate and Responsive Evaluators

	Preordinate	Responsive
Indentifying issues, goals	10%	10%
Preparing instruments	30%	15%
Observing the program	5%	30%
Administering tests, etc.	10%	—
Gathering judgments	—	15%
Learning client needs, etc.	—	5%
Processing formal data	25%	5%
Preparing informal reports	—	10%
Preparing formal reports	20%	10%

The responsive evaluator considers the principal stimuli to be those naturally occurring in the program, including responses of students and the subsequent dialogues. At first, his job is to record these, learning both of happenings and values. For additional information, he assumes a more interventionalist role. And, with his clients and audience he assumes a still more active role, stimulating their thought (we hope) and adding to their experience with his reports.

Philosopher David Hawkins (personal communication, 1973) responded to the idea of reversing S–R roles in this way:

. . . I like the observation that one is reversing the S and R of it. In an experiment one puts the system in a prepared state, and then observes the behavior of it. Preparation is what psychologists call "stimulus," . . . In naturalistic investigation one does not prepare the system, but looks for patterns, structures, significant events, as they appear under conditions not controlled or modified by the investigator, who is himself now a system of interest. He is a resonator, a respondent. He must be in such an initial state that (a) his responses contain important information about the complex of stimuli he is responding to, and (b) they must be maximally decodable by his intended audience.

In the next section of this paper, I will talk about maximally decodable reports. Let me conclude these two sections on structure by saying that the evaluator should not rely only on his own powers of observation, judgment, and responding. He should enlist a platoon of students, teachers, community leaders, curriculum specialists, etc.—his choice depending on the issues to be studied and the audiences to be served. The importance of their information and its reliability will increase as the number and variety of observers increase.

PORTRAYAL AND HOLISTIC COMMUNICATION

Maximally decodable reports require a technology of reporting that we educational measurements people have lacked. We have tried to be impersonal, theoretical, generalizable. We have sought the parsimonious explanation. We have not accepted the responsibility for writing in a way that is maximally comprehensible to practicing educators and others concerned about education. According to R. F. Rhyne (1972):

There is a great and growing need for the kind of powers of communication that helps a person gain, vicariously, a feeling for the natures of fields too extensive and diverse to be directly experienced.

Prose and its archetype, the mathematical equation, do not suffice. They offer more specificity within a sharply limited region of discourse than is safe, since the clearly explicit can be so easily mistaken for truth, and the difference can be large when context is slighted (pp. 93–104).

We need this power of communication, this opportunity for vicarious experience, in our attempts to solve educational problems.

One of the principal reasons for backing away from the preordinate approach to evaluation is to improve communication with audiences. The conventional style of research-reporting is a "clearly explicit" way of communicating. In a typical research project, the report is limited by the project design. A small number of variables are identified and relationships among them are sought. Individuals are observed, found to differ, and distributions of scores are displayed. Covariations of various kinds are analyzed and interpreted. From a report of such analytic inquiry, it is very hard, often impossible, for a reader to know what the program was like. If he is supposed to learn what the program was like, the evaluation report should be different from the conventional research report.

As a part of my advocacy of the responsive approach, I have urged my fellow evaluators to respond to what I believe are the natural ways in which people assimilate information and arrive at understanding. *Direct* personal experience is an efficient, comprehensive, and satisfying way of creating understanding, but is a way not usually available to our evaluation report audiences. The best substitute for direct experience probably is *vicarious experience*—increasingly better when the evaluator uses "attending" and "conceptualizing" styles similar to those that members of the audience use. Such styles are not likely to be those of the specialist in measurement or the theoretically minded social scientist. Vicarious experience often will be conceptualized in terms of persons, places, and events.

We need a reporting procedure for facilitating vicarious experience, and it is available. Among the better evangelists, anthropologists, and dramatists are those who have developed the art of storytelling. We need to portray complexity. We need to convey the holistic impression, the mood, even the mystery of the experience. The program staff or people in the community may be uncertain. The audiences should feel that uncertainty. More ambiguity rather than less may be needed in our reports. Oversimplification obfuscates. Ionesco said (Esslin, 1966):

As our knowledge becomes separated from life, our culture no longer contains ourselves (or only an insignificant part of ourselves) for it forms a *social* context into which we are not integrated.

So the problem becomes that of bringing our life back into contact with our culture, making it a living culture once again. To achieve this, we shall first have to kill "the respect for what is written down in black and white . . ." to break up our language so that it can be put together again in order to re-establish contact with "the absolute," or as I should prefer to say, with "multiple reality"; it is imperative to "push human beings again towards seeing themselves as they really are" (p. 298).

Some evaluation reports should reveal the "multiple reality" of an educational experience.

The responsive evaluator will often use portrayals. Some will be short, featuring perhaps a five-minute script, a log, or scrapbook. A longer portrayal may require several media: narratives, maps and graphs, exhibits, taped conversations, photographs, even audience role-playing. Which ingredients best convey the sense of the program to a particular audience? The ingredients are determined by the structure chosen by the evaluator.

Suppose that a junior-high-school art program is to be evaluated. For portrayal of at least one issue, "how the program affects *every* student," the students might be thought of as being in two groups: those taking at least one fine-arts course and those taking none. (The purpose here is description, not comparison.)

A random sample of ten students from each group might be selected and twenty small case studies developed. The prose description of what each does in classes of various kinds (including involvement with the arts in school) might be supplemented with such things as (1) excerpts from taped interviews with the youngster, his friends, his teachers, and his parents; (2) art products (or photographs, news clippings, etc., of same) made by him in or out of class; (3) charts of his use of leisure time; and (4) test scores of his attitudes toward the arts. A display (for each student) might be set up in the gymnasium which could be examined reasonably thoroughly in 10–20 minutes.

Other materials, including the plan, program, and staffing for the school, could be provided. Careful attention would be directed toward finding out how the description of these individual youngsters reveals what the school and other sources of art experience are providing in the way of art education.

It will sometimes be the case that reporting on the quality of education will require a "two-stage" communication. Some audiences will not be able to take part in such a vicarious experience as that arranged in the example above. A surrogate audience may be selected. The evaluator will present his portrayals to them; then he will question them about the apparent activity, accomplishments, issues, strengths, and shortcomings of the program. He will report their reactions, along with a more conventional description of the program, to the true audiences.

These twenty displays could be examined by people specially invited to review and respond to them. The reviewers might be students, teachers, art curriculum specialists, and patrons of the arts. They might also visit regular school activities, but most attention would be to the displays. These reviewers should be asked to answer such questions as: "Based on these case studies, is the school doing its share of providing good quality art experience for all the young people?" and "Is there too much emphasis on disciplined creative performance and not enough on sharing the arts in ways that suit each student's own tastes?" Their response to these portrayals and questions would be a major part of the evaluation report.

The portrayal will usually feature descriptions of persons. The evaluator will find that case studies of several students may represent the educational program more interestingly and faithfully than a few measurements on all of the students. The promise of gain is two-fold: the readers will comprehend the total program, and some of the important complexity of the program will be preserved. The several students selected usually cannot be considered a satisfactory representation of the many—a sampling error is present. The protests about the sampling error will be loud; but the size of the error may be small, and it will often be a satisfactory price to pay for the improvement in communication.

There will continue to be many research inquiries needing social survey technology and exact specification of objectives. The work of John Tukey, Torsten Husen, Ralph Tyler, Ben Bloom, and James Popham will continue to serve as models for such studies.

Often the best strategy will be to select achievement tests, performance tests, or observation checklists to provide evidence that prespecified goals were or were not achieved. The investigator should remember that such a preordinate approach depends on a capability to discern the accomplishment of those purposes, and those capabilities sometimes are not at our command. The preordinate approach usually is not sensitive to ongoing changes in program purpose, nor to unique ways in which students benefit from contact with teachers and other learners, nor to dissimilar viewpoints as to what is good and bad.

Elliot Eisner (1969) nicely summarized these insensitivities in AERA monograph no. 3. He advocated consideration of *expressive objectives*—toward outcomes that are idiosyncratic for each learner and that are conceptualized and evaluated *after* the instructional experience; after a product, an awareness, or a feeling has become manifest, at a time when the teacher and learner can reflect upon what has occurred. Eisner implied that sometimes it would be preferable to evaluate the quality of the *opportunity* to learn—the *intrinsic* merit of the experience rather than the more elusive *payoff*, to use Scriven's terms.

In my own writing on evaluation, I have been influenced by Eisner and Scriven and others who have been dissatisfied with contemporary testing. We see too little good measurement of complex achievements, development of personal styles and sensitivities. I have argued that few, if any, specific learning steps are truly essential for subsequent success in any life's endeavors; I have argued that students, teachers, and other purpose selected observers exercise the most relevant critical judgments, whether or not their criteria are in any way explicit. I have argued, also, that the alleviation of instructional problems is most likely to be accomplished by the people most directly experiencing the problem, with aid and comfort perhaps (but not with specific solutions or replacement programs) from consultants or external authorities. I use these arguments as assumptions for what I call the *responsive evaluation* approach.

UTILITY AND LEGITIMACY

The task of evaluating an educational program might be said to be impossible if it were necessary to express verbally its purposes or accomplishments. Fortunately, it is not necessary to be explicit about aim, scope, or probable cause in order to indicate worth. Explication will usually make the evaluation more useful; but also increases the danger of misstatement of aim, scope, and probable cause.

To layman and professional alike, evaluation means that someone will report on the program's merits and shortcomings. The evaluator reports that a program is coherent, stimulating, parochial, and costly. These descriptive terms are always value-judgment terms. An evaluation has occurred. The validity of these judgements may be strong or weak; their utility may be great or little. But the evaluation was not at all dependent on a careful specification of the program's goals, activities, or accomplishments. In planning and carrying out an evaluation study the evaluator must decide how far to go beyond the bare bones ingredients: values and standards. Many times, he will want to examine goals; many times, he will want to provide a portrayal from which audiences may form their own value judgments.

The purposes of the audiences are all-important. What would they like to be able to do with the evaluation of the program? Chances are they do not have any plans for using it. They may doubt that the evaluation study will be of use to them. But charts and products and narratives and portrayals do not affect people. With these devices, persons become better aware of the program, develop a feeling for its vital forces, and develop a sense of its disappointments and potential trouble. They may be better prepared to act on issues, such as a change of enrollment on the reallocation of resources. They may be better able to protect the program.

Different styles of evaluation will serve different purposes. A highly subjective evaluation may be useful but not be seen as legitimate. Highly specific language, behavioral tasks, and performance scores are considered by some to be more legitimate. In America, however, there is seldom a greater legitimacy than that endorsement of large numbers of audience-significant people. The evaluator may need to discover what legitimacies his audiences (and their audiences) honor. Responsive evaluation includes such inquiry.

Responsive evaluation will be particularly useful during formative evaluation when the staff needs help in monitoring the program, when no one is sure which problems will arise. It will be particularly useful in summative evaluation, where audiences want an understanding of a program's activities, its strengths and shortcomings, and when the evaluator feels that is his responsibility to provide a vicarious experience.

Preordinate evaluation should be preferred to responsive evaluation when it is important to know if certain goals have been reached, if certain promises have been kept, and when predetermined hypotheses or issues are to be investigated. With greater focus and opportunity for preparation, preordinate measurement made can be expected to be more objective and reliable.

It is wrong to suppose that either a strict preordinate design or responsive design can be fixed upon an educational program to evaluate it. As the program moves in unique and unexpected ways, the evaluation efforts should be adapted to them, drawing from stability and prior experience where possible, stretching to new issues and challenges as needed.

APPENDIX A

Table 2. Nine Approaches to Evaluation

Approach	Purpose	Key Elements	Purview Emphasized	Protagonists (see references)	Cases Examples	Risks	Payoffs
Student Gain By Testing	to measure student performance and progress	goal statements; test score analysis; discrepancy between goal and actuality	Educational Psychologists	Ralph Tyler Ben Bloom Jim Popham Mal Provus	Steele Womer Lindvall-Cox Husen	oversimplify, educational aims; ignore processes	emphasize. ascertain student progress
Institutional Self-Study By Staff	to review and increase staff effectiveness	committee work standards set by staff; discussion; professionalism	Professors, teachers	National Study of School Evaluation, Dressel	Boersma-Plawecki Knoll-Brown Carpenter	alienate some staff; ignore values of outsiders	increase staff awareness, sense of responsibility
Blue-Ribbon Panel	to resolve crises and preserve the institution	prestigious panel; the visit; review of existing program and documents	Leading Citizens	James Conant Clark Kerr David Henry	Flexner Havighurst House et al. Plowden	postpone action; over-rely on intuition	gather best insights judgment
Transaction Observation	to provide understanding of activities and values	educational issues; classroom observation; case studies; pluralism	Client, Audience	Lou Smith Parlett-Hamilton Rob Rippey Bob Stake	MacDonald Smith-Pohland Parlett Lundgren	over-rely on subjective perceptions; ignore causes	produce broad picture of program; see conflict in values

Approach	Purpose	Elements	Orientation	Protagonists		Risk	Payoff
Management Analysis	to increase rationality in day-to-day decisions	lists of options; estimates; feedback loops; costs; efficiency	Managers, Economists	Leon Lessinger Dan Stufflebeam Mary Alkin	Kraft Doughty-Stakenas Hemphill	over-value efficiency; undervalue implicits	feedback for decision making
Instructional Research	to generate explanations and tactics of instruction	controlled conditions, multivariate analysis; bases for generalization	Experimentalists	Lee Cronbach Julian Stanley Don Campbell	Anderson, R. Pella Zdep-Joyce Taba	artificial conditions ignore the humanistic	new principles of teaching and materials development
Social Policy Analysis	to aid development of institutional policies	measures of social conditions and administrative implementation	Sociologists	James Coleman David Cohen Carol Weiss Mosteller-Moynihan	Coleman Jencks Levitan Trankell	neglect of educational issues, details	social choices, constraints clarified
Goal-Free Evaluation	to assess effects of program	ignore proponent claims, follow checklist	Consumers	Michael Scriven	House-Hogben	over-value documents & record keeping	data on effect with little co-option
Adversary Evaluation	to resolve a two-option choice	opposing advocates, crossexamination, the jury	Expert: Juristic	Tom Owens Murray Levine Bob Wolfe	Owens Stake-Gjerde Reinhard	personalistic superficial, time-bound	information impact good; claims put to test

Of course these descriptive tags are a great over-simplification. The approaches overlap. Different proponents and different users have different styles. Each protagonist recognizes one approach is not ideal for all purposes. Any one study may include several approaches. The grid is an over-simplification, intended to show some typical, gross differences between contemporary evaluation activities.

APPENDIX B

TCITY–1971 Evaluation Report: An Advocate's Statement[1]

No visitor who took a long, hard look at TCITY-71 kept his skepticism. A young visitor knows how precious it is to discover, to be heard, to belong. An older visitor knows the rarity of a classroom where teachers and students perceive each other as real people. To the non-visitor, it doesn't seem possible that a summer school program can deliver on all these promises to over 800 kids, but TCITY-71 did.

Every curriculum specialist fears that by relaxing conduct rules and encouraging student independence they may be saying good-bye to the hard work and hard thinking that education requires. TCITY-71 teachers and students made learning so attractive, so purposive, that free-ranging thought returned again and again to curricular themes: awareness of the human condition, obstacles to communication, ecological interactions, etc.

TCITY excels because of its staff. Its students give it movement. Its directors give it nurture. Its teachers give it movement, nurture, and direction. It would be incorrect to say that Mr. Caruson, Mr. Rose, and the teachers think alike as to the prime goals and methods of education, but collectively, they create a dynamic, humanistically-bent, academically-based curriculum.

The quality of teaching this summer was consistently high, from day-to-day, from class to class. Some of the teachers chose to be casual, to offer "opportunities," to share a meaningful experience. Others were more intense, more intent upon sharing information and problem-solving methods. Both kinds were there, doing it well.

The quality of the learning also was high. The students were tuned in. They were busy. They responded to the moves of their teachers. They improvised; they carried ideas and arguments, indignations and admirations, to the volleyball court, to the Commons, to the shade of campus elms and Cannon River oaks. The youngsters took a long step towards maturity.

True, it was a costly step. Thousands of hours, thousands of dollars, and at least a few hundred aggravations. But fit to a scale of public schools budgets—and budgets for parks, interstate highways, and weapons of war—TCITY-71 rates as a *best buy*. Eight hundred kids, give or take a few, took home a new talent, a new line of thinking, a new awareness—a good purchase.

It cannot be denied that other youngsters in Minneapolis and St. Paul deserve an experience like this. They should have it. Some say, "TCITY is bad because it caters to the elite." But a greater wisdom says, "Any effort fixated on giving an equal share of good things to all groups is destined to share nothing of value." For less advantaged youth, a more equitable share of educational opportunities should be guaranteed. But even in times of economic recession, opportunities for the talented should be protected.

TCITY-71 has succeeded. It is even a best buy. It satisfies a social obligation to specially educate some of those who will lead—in the arts, in business, in government, in life. The teachers of TCITY-71 have blended a summer of caring, caprice, openness, and intellectual struggle to give potential leaders a summer of challenge.

TCITY–1971 Evaluation Report: An Adversary's Statement[2]

TCITY is not a *scandalum magnatum*. But it is both less than it pretends to be and more than it wishes to be. There is enough evidence at least to question certain facets of the Institute—if not to return a true bill against it. Costly, enlarging, innovative, exemplary: these Institute attributes are worthy of critical examination.

How costly is this Institute? Dollar costs are sufficient to give each group of six students $1,000 to design and conduct their own summer experience. Over 100 Upward Bound students could be readied for their college careers at Macalester. About 25 expert curriculum specialists could be supported for half a year to design and develop new curricula for the high school.

What is the cost of removing 800 talented leaders from the local youth culture? What is the cost of widening the experience gap between Institute students and their parents? . . . and their teachers in "regular" high school? . . . and their non-Institute friends? Not enough here to charge neo-fascist elitism. Enough to warrant discussion.

The Institute abounds with self-named innovators and innovations, with alternatives to the business-as-usual education of high schoolers. Note that the Institute is not promoted as an exemplary alternative *to* schooling. It seeks to promote the development of alternative forms of education *for* schools. And it is failing to do even that job. What is TCITY doing to demonstrate that TCITY style of life could be lived in schools as we know them? Where in the regular school is the staff so crucial to the life of the Institute? . . . the money? . . . the administrative leadership? Where are the opportunities for the teachers, principals, superintendents to come and live that life that they might come to share in the vision? . . . and where are the parents? TCITY should be getting poor grades on affecting the regular school program.

There are other dimensions of TCITY that puzzle the non-believer:

How long can in-class "rapping" continue and still qualify as educative self-exploration? Are there quality control procedures in effect during the summer program: For example: when one-third to one-half of a class is absent from a scheduled meeting, should not that be seen as an educational crisis by the instructor?

What does TCITY do to help students realize that the Institute standards are necessarily high; that the regular schools norms and expectations do not count; that a heretofore "best" becomes just a "so-so"? There are unnecessarily disheartened students in TCITY.

Is it unreasonable to expect that more than 2 of 22 teachers or associate teachers would have some clear idea or plan for utilizing TCITY approaches or curricula in their regular classrooms next fall?

Few students—or faculty—understand the selection procedures employed to staff the teaching cadre and to fill the student corps. Why should it be a mystery?

The worst has been saved for last. This report concludes with an assertion: the absence of crucial dimension in the instructional life of TCITY, that of constructive self-criticism, is a near-fatal flaw. The observation and interview notes taken by the adversary evaluator over four days contain but five instances of students engaging in, or faculty helping students to become skillful in, or desirous of, the cultivation of self-criticism. The instances of missed opportunities were excessive in my judgment. Worse: when queried by the writer, faculty and students alike showed little enthusiasm for such fare. Is it too much to expect from Institute participants after but four weeks? Seven may be insufficient. The staff post-mortem, "Gleanings," are a start—but it seems odd to start at the end.

The paucity of occurrence is less damning than the absence of manifest, widespread intent. Certain classes accounted for all the instances observed. They did not appear to be accidental. The intent was there. An Institute for talented high school youth cannot justifiably fail to feature individual and group self-criticism.

NOTES

1. Prepared by R. Stake, not to indicate his opinion of the Institute, but as a summary of the most positive claims that might reasonably be made.

2. Prepared by T. Denny, not to indicate his opinion of TCITY-1971, but as a summary of the most damaging charges that might reasonably be made.

19. EPISTEMOLOGICAL AND METHODOLOGICAL BASES OF NATURALISTIC INQUIRY

EGON G. GUBA and YVONNA S. LINCOLN

INTRODUCTION

It is important, at the outset, to recognize what naturalistic inquiry is and what it is not. Naturalistic inquiry is a *paradigm of inquiry*; that is, a pattern or model for how inquiry may be conducted. While it is frequently asserted that its distinguishing features are: that it is carried out in a natural setting (and hence the term *naturalistic*), that it utilizes a case-study format, and that it relies heavily on qualitative rather than quantitative methods, none of these features define naturalistic inquiry. While all of these assertions are essentially correct, no one of them, nor indeed all of them together, capture the full significance of the term *paradigm*. Paradigms differ from one another on matters much more fundamental than the locale in which the inquiry is conducted, the format of the inquiry report, or the nature of the methods used. Paradigms are axiomatic systems characterized by their differing sets of assumptions about the phenomena into which they are designed to inquire.

There are many different paradigms of inquiry. We are all intimately familiar with most paradigms, which we use on virtually a daily basis. So, for example, our system of jurisprudence is based on an adversarial paradigm; religious faiths on theological paradigms; and peer reviews of research proposals on a judgmental paradigm. Those persons concered with *disciplined* inquiry, however, in the sense that term is defined by Cronbach and Suppes (1969), have used almost exclusively what is commonly called the scientific paradigm, which we will here term the *rationalistic* paradigm.[1] A second paradigm, which is also aimed at disciplined inquiry and which is currently receiving a great deal of attention, we term the *naturalistic*; it is this paradigm that this paper explicates.

One may well ask why anyone would contemplate the use of a competing paradigm when the rationalistic one has gained such widespread legitimacy and achieved such conspicuous successes. How could one doubt the efficacy of the scientific mode for all inquiry? John Stuart Mill urged social science investigators to adopt the scientific methods as long ago as 1843; can there be any question, a century and a half later, that his advice was well-founded?

It seems to us that a variety of evidence may be cited in counter-argument. First, we believe that the judgment that the rationalistic paradigm has enabled conspicuous successes in social and behavioral inquiry is mistaken. Data collected in these arenas has not proved to be aggregatable; where, for example, is the useful residue of the more than 100 years of psychological and educational research? Investigators have, moreover, repeatedly found it impossible to apply the paradigm according to its own basic principles; random sampling, for example, is virtually impossible for both political and ethical reasons. The impact of research on practice is conspicuous by its absence; for example, evaluation data remain unused and the practice of most social institutions, such as schools, hospitals, and prisons, is still based primarily on experience.

Second, we question the utility of the rationalistic paradigm as typically practiced (and as it will be described here) on the ground that it reflects a discredited epistemology of science—positivism. It is apparent that sophisticated scientists can no longer accept positivism; even a casual acquaintance with the field of particle physics provides ample evidence of its inadequacies, as for example, the Heisenberg Uncertainty Principle (Tranel, 1981). Yet practitioners of scientific inquiry, in the hard but especially in the soft sciences, continue to act as if positivism were valid, thereby accepting a position that is essentially analytic, reductionist, empiricist, associationist, reactivist, nomological, and monistic. As we shall see, this posture is inconsistent with the characteristics of many social/behavioral phenomena.

Finally, we suggest that the rationalistic paradigm, like all paradigms, rests upon certain fundamental axioms or assumptions and that the particular axioms of rationalism can be but poorly fulfilled in social/behavioral inquiry. It is our intention to devote a major segment of this paper to a discussion of the rationalistic axioms and their naturalistic counterparts, and to deal with the question of which set of axioms is better fulfilled in the phenomenological field customarily designated as *social/behavioral*.

But, as we shall demonstrate, the motivation for considering naturalistic inquiry as an alternative paradigm is not founded simply on the desire to avoid the shortfalls of rationalism. Naturalistic inquiry has many characteristics to recommend it on other grounds. So, for example, it offers a contextual relevance and richness that is unmatched; it displays a sensitivity to process virtually excluded in paradigms stressing control and experimentation; it is driven by theory grounded in the data—the naturalist does not search for data that fit a theory but develops a theory to explain the data. Finally, naturalistic approaches take full advantage of the not inconsiderable power of the human-as-instrument, providing a more than adequate trade-off for the presumably more objective approach that characterizes rationalistic inquiry.

Even without depending on these claims for the advantages of naturalistic inquiry, however, it seems clear that the examination of an alternative paradigm has utility, since such examination forces out otherwise hidden assumptions and meanings. If it is true that the examined life is "better" than the unexamined, it is surely the case that the examined paradigm is better than the unexamined.

This paper has two major purposes:

1. To distinguish the rationalistic and naturalistic paradigms on five basic axioms, and to describe, in addition, six postures on which practitioners of these paradigms have traditionally differed.
2. To suggest some methods for responding to four basic criteria for trustworthiness (analogues to the traditional rationalistic criteria of internal and external validity, reliability, and objectivity) that might be used by naturalists to counter charges of lack of discipline (sloppiness).

THE BASIC AXIOMS THAT DISTINGUISH THE NATURALISTIC FROM THE RATIONALISTIC INQUIRY PARADIGM

Axioms may be defined as the set of undemonstrated (and undemonstrable) propositions accepted by convention or established by practice as the basic building blocks of some conceptual or theoretical structure or system. Before undertaking an examination of the axioms that underlie the two paradigms of interest to us here, it may be useful to undertake a small digression to clarify the nature of axiomatic systems.

Probably the best known and most widely experienced system of axioms is that undergirding Euclidean geometry. Euclid set himself the task of formalizing everything known about geometry at his time—essentially, that meant systematizing the rules-of-thumb used by land surveyors, who could not provide any proof of their validity other than experience. It was Euclid's powerful insight that these rules could be *proved* by showing them to be logical derivatives from some simple set of *self-evident truths*. Euclid began with four such axioms (Hofstadter, 1979):

1. A straight line segment can be drawn joining any two points.
2. Any straight line segment can be extended indefinitely in a straight line.
3. Given any straight line segment, a circle can be drawn having the segment as radius and one end-point as center.
4. All right angles are congruent.

With these four axioms, Euclid was able to derive the first 28 of the eventually much larger set of theorems. But the 29th proof he attempted was intractable; Euclid had to assume it instead as a fifth axiom:

5. If two lines are drawn which intersect a third in such a way that the sum of the inner angles on one side is less than two right angles, then the two lines inevitably must intersect each other on that side if extended far enough.

The modern way to state this axiom is as follows: Given a line and a point not on that line, it is possible to construct only one line through the point parallel to the given line.

As compared to the first four axioms, the fifth seems strained and inelegant; Euclid was sure that eventually he would be able to find a way of proving it in terms of the first four. But his hope was not to be realized within his lifetime, or indeed, ever; two millenia of effort by mathematicians have failed to provide a proof.

Early attempts to prove this axiom/theorem were of what mathematicians would call the direct variety; later, mathematicians fell back on indirect proofs, one variant of which is to assume the direct opposite of what one wishes to show and then to demonstrate that this opposite assumption leads to absurd conclusions (theorems). It was exactly this approach, however, that culminated in so-called non-Euclidean geometries. Not only were the consequences of non-Euclidean assumptions not absurd, they were in fact of great utility. One such geometry is called Lobachevskian; this form takes as its fifth axiom: "Given a line and a point not on that line, it is possible to draw a bundle of lines through the point *all of which* are parallel to the given line." Now this axiom flies in the face of all human experience; yet it yields results of great interest, for example, to astronomers. One of the theorems provable from the Euclidean fifth axiom is that the sum of angles in a triangle is 180°, but the sum of angles in Lobachevskian triangles *approaches* 180° as triangles become "small." Earth-size triangles must all be small, since no such triangle has every yielded a sum of angles less than 180°. But astronomically sized triangles are very much larger, and astronomers find that Lobachevskian geometry provides a better "fit" to the phenomena that they investigate than does Euclidean.

From this digression, we may deduce several crucial points:

1. Axioms are arbitrary and may be assumed for any reason, even if only for the sake of the game.
2. Axioms are not self-evidently true, nor need they appear so; indeed, some axioms appear very bizarre on first exposure.
3. Different axiom systems have different utilities depending upon the phenomenon to which they are applied. These utilities are *not* determined by the nature of the axiom system itself but by the interaction between these axioms and the characteristics of the area in which they are applied. Thus, Euclidean geometry is fine for terrestrial spaces but Lobachevskian geometry is better for interstellar spaces.
4. A decision about which of several alternative axiom systems to use in a given case is made by testing the fit between each system and the case, a process analogous to testing data for fit to assumptions before deciding on which statistic to use in analyzing them.

Thus, the axioms to be described below should not be judged on the grounds of their self-evident truth, their common sense qualities, or their familiarity to the inquirer, but *in terms of their fit to the phenomena into which one proposes to inquire.* When the rationalistic axioms fit, the rationalistic paradigm should be used; when the naturalistic axioms fit, the naturalistic paradigm should be used.

Five axioms differentiate the rationalistic and naturalistic paradigms; these five axioms are summarized in Table 1. Immediately following is a formal statement of the five axioms in both their rationalistic and naturalistic versions. We attend to the question of which set provides a better fit to social/behavioral phenomena in a following section.

Axiom 1: The Nature of Reality

- *Rationalistic version:* There is a single, tangible reality fragmentable into independent variables and processes, any of which can be studied independently of the others; inquiry can converge onto this reality until, finally, it can be predicted and controlled.
- *Naturalistic version:* There are multiple, intangible realities which can be studied only holistically; inquiry into these multiple realities will inevitably diverge (each inquiry raises more questions than it answers) so that prediction and control are unlikely outcomes although some level of understanding (*verstehen*) can be achieved.

Axiom 2: The Inquirer-Objective Relationship

- *Rationalistic version:* The inquirer is able to maintain a discrete distance between himself and the object of inquiry.

Table 1. Axiomatic Differences Between the Rationalistic and Naturalistic Paradigms

Axioms About	Rationalistic Paradigm	Naturalistic Paradigm
Reality	Single, tangible, convergent, fragmentable	Multiple, intangible divergent, holistic
Inquirer/respondent relationship	Independent	Inter-related
Nature of truth statements	Context-free generalizations—nomothetic statements—focus on similarities	Context-bound working hypotheses—idiographic statements—focus on differences
Attribution/explanation of action	Real causes; temporally precedent or simultaneous; manipulable; probabilistic.	Attributional shapers; interactive (feed-forward and feed-back): non-manipulable; plausible.
Relation to Values to Inquiry	Value-free	Value-bound

Note: In certain of our previous writing (Guba, 1978, 1981; Guba & Lincoln, 1981) we have focussed on only the first three of these five axioms. However, the latter two now seem to us as equally if not more important.

- *Naturalistic version:* The inquirer and the object interact to influence one another; this mutual interaction is especially present when the object of inquiry is another human being (respondent).

Axiom 3: The Nature of Truth Statements

- *Rationalistic version:* The aim of inquiry is to develop a nomothetic body of knowledge; this knowledge is best encapsulated in generalizations which are truth statements of enduring value that are context-free; the stuff of which generalizations are made is similarities among units.
- *Naturalistic version:* The aim of inquiry is to develop an ideographic body of knowledge; this knowledge is best encapsulated in a series of working hypotheses that describe the individual case; differences are as inherently interest as (and at times more so than) similarities.

Axiom 4: Attribution/Explanation of Action

- *Rationalistic version:* Every action can be explained as the result (effect) of real cause that precedes the effect temporally (or is at least simultaneous with).
- *Naturalistic version:* An action *may* be explainable in terms of multiple interacting factors, events, and processes that shape it and are part of it; inquirers can, at best, establish plausible inferences about the patterns and webs of such shaping in any given case.

Axiom 5: The Role of Values in Inquiry

- *Rationalistic version:* Inquiry is value-free and can be guaranteed to be so by virtue of the objective methodology which is employed.
- *Naturalistic version:* Inquiry is value-bound in at least five ways, captured in the corollaries which follow:

Corollary 1: Inquiries are influenced by *inquirer* values as expressed in the choice of a problem, and in the framing, bounding, and focussing of that problem.

Corollary 2: Inquiry is influenced by the choice of *paradigm* which guides the investigation into the problem.

Corollary 3: Inquiry is influenced by the choice of *substantive theory* utilized guide to the collection and analysis of data and in the interpretation of findings.

Corollary 4: Inquiry is influenced by the values which inhere in the *context*.

Corollary 5: With respect to Corollaries *1* through *4* above, inquiry is either *value-resonant* (reinforcing or congruent) or *value-dissonant* (conflicting). Problem, paradigm, theory, and context must exhibit congruence (value resonance) in order to produce meaningful results.

The decision about which paradigm to use depends, we again assert, on an assessment of the area to be studied to determine the degree of fit between the axioms of each paradigm and the area. If we *limit ourselves to consideration solely of the area commonly designated as social/behavioral inquiry,*[2] we make the following observations about fit:

AXIOM 1: THE NATURE OF REALITY. In the hard and life sciences there can be little doubt that there exists a tangible reality, which is the focus of inquiry: actual events, objects, and processes found in nature that can be observed and often measured. The utility of breaking this physical world into variables is well demonstrated by such terms as time, mass, velocity, acceleration, distance, charge, and the like. Such variables can all be studied independently and related to one another in functional expressions.

In the social/behavioral sciences, however, the class of phenomena typically addressed in inquiry *has no reality* in the physical sense. That is not to say that tangible objects, events, and processes do not enter into human behavior. However, it is not these tangibles that we care about but the meaning and interpretation people ascribe to them, for it is these *constructions* that mediate their behavior. These constructions do not have reality but exist only in the minds of people. As Filstead (1979) suggests, "There are multiple realities. . . . Individuals are conceptualized as active agents in constructing and making sense of the realities they encounter." (p. 36) There are as many constructions as there are people to make them.

Nor are these constructions equivalent to perceptions. We are not belaboring here the well-known fable of the blind men and the elephant. If that fable *were* to provide a useful metaphor, it would do so *only if there were no elephant*. We mean to suggest precisely that there is no tangible reality that can be touched as the blind men touched the elephant. The fable deals with their perceptions of the elephant; we deal with constructions that are developed from whole cloth in the mind of the constructor.

Since these constructions reside wholly in the minds of people, they are substantially inaccessible and must be dealt with in holistic fashion; they cannot be divided into parts or variables. Further, since the realities are multiple, it is futile to expect inquiry to converge. One cannot converge on a common or typical reality since each is idiosyncratic. The more people one explores, the more realities one emcounters; inquiry diverges as a result. Every inquiry finally raises more questions than it answers.

AXIOM 2: THE INQUIRER–OBJECT RELATIONSHIP. In the hard and life sciences, it is not unreasonable to posit the ability of the inquirer to maintain a discrete distance from the phenomenon under study. Balls rolling down inclined planes, chemicals interacting in a test tube, or cells subdividing under a microscope are unlikely to be influenced by the fact that someone is watching, nor is the watcher likely to be influenced (in any way adverse to the investigatory outcome) by what he observes. In the social/behavioral sciences, however, the *reactivity* of subjects (Campbell & Stanley, 1963; Webb et al., 1966) is well recognized. It is commonly understood that objects of inquiry,[3] when they are human, may react to inquirers of their inquiry methods. Less appreciated is the fact that the inquirer is *also* subject to interaction. Just as the inquirer may shape the respondent's behavior, so may the respondent shape the inquirer's behavior. Nor should it be supposed that the interpolation of a layer of objective instrumentation between the inquirer and the respondent(s) is sufficient to overcome or offset this interaction. Images of what the respondent may be like or how he or she might respond guide the inquirer in devising his or her instruments. Images of what the inquirer wants, or what he or she will do with the responses, guide the respondent in dealing with the instruments. Images of what the respondent meant by a response guide the inquirer in coding, interpreting, and even in accepting the respondent's return, and so on.

Far from deploring inquirer-respondent interactivity, the naturalist exploits it. If interactivity could be eliminated by some magical process, the naturalist would not think the trade-off worthwhile, because it is precisely this interactivity that makes it possible for the inquirer to be a *smart* instrument, honing in on relevant facts and ideas by virtue of his sensitivity, responsiveness, and adaptability. More of this will be said below.

AXIOM 3: THE NATURE OF TRUTH STATEMENTS. The development of generalizations is said by many to be the ultimate aim of inquiry. Why would anyone want to invest time and effort in a study that can yield no more insight than the single occurrence has to offer? Context-free statements of enduring truth value are clearly prized. The question that confronts us is whether they are achieveable.

In the hard and life sciences, that question must be answered with a resounding *Yes*. Statements like $F = ma$ and $e = mc^2$ are derivable in physics, for example, and they hold, whether tested in the eighteenth or twentieth centuries, on earth, Mars, the moon, or anywhere else in the universe. Such statement form the cornerstones of most disciplines, indeed, the phrase *nomothetic science* implies exactly the development of law-like generalizations which provide dependable bases for prediction and control.

There is a real question, however, whether generalizations can be made that will be true forever. Cronbach (1975) utilizes an interesting metaphor to make the counterpoint. Generalizations, he asserts, are like radioactive substances; they decay and have half-lives. He gives numerous examples from the hard as well as the social/behavioral sciences, for instance: the failure of DDT to control pests as genetic transformations make them resistant to the insecticide; the shifting of stars in their courses so as to render star maps obsolete; the suggestion by Ghiselli that the superiority of distributed, over massed, practice may not remain valid from one generation to another; and Bronfenbrenner's conclusion that class differences in parenting observed in the 1950s were just the reverse of those observed in 1930. Thus, it is dubious whether generalizations can be made about human behavior with impunity. Time is an enormously important factor, and who can offer an example of human behavior that is context-free?

Now this argument should not be interpreted to mean that there can *never* be any transfer from one situation to another. What we mean to say is that statements cannot be made about human phenomena that are likely to be true for even a substantial number of years (not to mention forever) or for any substantial number of contexts (not to mention any and all contexts). Conditionals, contingencies, and disjunctions must all be taken into account (Wiles, 1981). Moreover, differences in times or contexts are as important to know about in making the judgment of transferability as are similarities. The naturalist, then, is concerned with developing an adequate ideographic statement—thick description—about the situation he is studying, in order to make judgments about transferability possible, should anyone care to ask that question.

AXIOM 4: ATTRIBUTION/EXPLANATION OF ACTION. The search for causality is the mainspring that drives conventional research. Even such authors as Cook and Campbell (1979) who recognize that causality is a slippery concept nevertheless define designs as serving "to probe causal hypotheses" (p. ix), see causal connections as "real," even if "imperfectly perceived" (p. ix), and address their book to those "who have already decided that they want a causal question answered" (p. 2). For them, the question is not whether to entertain a concept of causality but *which* concept to accept.

The meaning to be imputed to the term *causality* has been under discussion for centuries, despite which, as Cook and Campbell note, "the epistemology of causation . . . is at present in a productive state of near chaos" (p. 10). Causality was originally conceived in a common sense way in *if-then* terms, probably because of the tendency of early scientists to view the world as a huge machine. In the early eighteenth century, David Hume noted that causality was never directly observed but merely *imputed* by the observer when two events were physically contiguous and temporally adjacent. He espoused a *regularity* or *constant conjunction* theory of causality that denied the need for the concept of causality at all. Later, an *essentialist* view emerged, based on the idea of necessary and sufficient conditions; essentialists sought functional laws expressing inevitable cause-effect relationships (Weir, 1980). Currently an activity theory of causation placing heavy emphasis on manipulation as the test for inferring cause-effect relationships has wide currency, lending legitimation to the notion that the best test for cause-effect relationships is the experiment (Cook & Campbell, 1979). Cook and Campbell (1979) themselves opt for the *critical-realist* position:

The perspective is realist because it assumes that causal relationships exist *outside of the human mind*, and it is critical-realist because it assumes that these valid causal relationships cannot be perceived with total accuracy by our imperfect sensory and intellective capacities. (pp. 28–29; emphasis added).

Formulations such as these have meaning (to some degree) within the rationalist paradigm insofar as it is applied to the hard and life sciences. There seems to be little question about the appropriateness of seeking cause-effect relationships when one is talking about gas laws, electric circuits, or the impact that mashes the fender of an automobile. But these ideas are highly suspect when applied to the arena of social/behavioral inquiry. The realities that we are dealing with an constructed and exist *only* in the minds of people; if the realities are constructed why not the attributions or explanations of causality? And if that is reasonable emergent attributional and/or semantic theories of causation (if that is now the proper term) are more likely to be meaningful than any of the formulations that have developed in relation to the other inquiry areas. In these views, causality is not merely empirical or contingent but depends heavily on meaning. Questions such as, "Is the treatment applied via a particular instructional program effective in increasing student learning?" imply a cause/effect relation between treatment and student learning, but the nature of that relationship surely depends on what is meant by treatment and student learning and what the criteria of effectiveness are taken to be. In other words, *causality* is a construction less traceable by empirical linkages than by plausible semantic/attributional linkages. The concepts of constructed reality and attributed causality are congenial to and supportive of one another.

Thus, the naturalist argues, there can be no certain way of determining cause-effect; indeed, the very concept of causality seems to have outlived its usefulness. Positivists, such as Hume, believed the concept of causation to be unnecessary; naturalists believe it to be archaic. Instead, the naturalist prefers to think of multiple factors and conditions, all of which *interact*, with feed-back *and* feed-forward, to *shape one another*. Actions can be understood not as having been *caused* but as having *emerged* from the constant interplay of its shapers, all of which are themselves part of the action, indistinguishable from it, shaping and being shaped simultaneously. While rationalists seem to have given up certainty in specifying causal relationships and have fallen back on probabilistic statements, the naturalist is satisfied to tease out *plausible* connections between phenomena.

AXIOM 5: THE ROLE OF VALUES IN INQUIRY. The customary presupposition of rationalists is that inquiry is *value-free*, that is, that the outcomes of the inquiry are guaranteed by the methodology employed by rationalists to be purely empirical. The data, it is often said, "speak for themselves"; that is, they transcend the values of both inquirers and respondents. Naturalists, on the other hand, presuppose that inquiry is inevitably grounded in the value systems that characterize the inquirer, the respondent, the paradigm chosen, the substantive theory selected, and the social and conceptual contexts. Values cannot be set aside, methodologically controlled, or eliminated. It is more reasonable to acknowledge and take account of values, insofar as one can, than to delude oneself about their importance or to hope that methodological hedges will compensate for their intrusion.

Values, naturalists insist, may enter into and influence the course of inquiry in five ways, all of which are *by definition* excluded in the strict rationalist construction:

1. Values influence decisions about what to study, how to study it, and what interpretations to make of the resulting data. The evidence for such influences is overwhelming (Bahm, 1981; Homans, 1978; Kelman, 1979; Krathwohl, 1980; Scriven, 1971), and most rationalists are willing to concede at least this form of value intrusion.
2. Inquiry is influenced by the paradigm selected to guide the investigation. The rationalist, for instance, who believes that reality is singular and convergent, will impose that construction on the findings, even when hearing respondents assert

again and again that *their* constructions of the problem, or of their lives, are at variance with both those of the investigator as well as those of other respondents. Thus, the rationalist proceeds much as does a court of law, constructing and reconstructing into a singular reality that which represents *truth* to him or her.

3. Inquiry is influenced by the choice of substantive theory, which dictates the methods chosen to collect and analyze the data, and ways of interpreting the findings. The substantive theory (like the methodological paradigm) is a construction, having roots in assumptions and values. Freudian constructions of personality are very different from Skinnerian; bureaucratic organization theory from loosely-coupled theory. If seeing is believing, it is also true that believing is seeing.

4. Inquiry is influenced by the multiple value and belief systems which inhere in the context in which the inquiry is carried out. Contextual values include those stemming from individuals and those which inhere in social/behavioral, human, and organizational phenomena. A study of school curricula in a fundamentalist community is very different from a similar study in an upper-middle class suburb.

5. Finally, inquiry may be characterized as being either *value-resonant* (reinforcing or congruent) or *value-dissonant* (conflicting). So, for instance, an inquirer could bound a problem to be studied, choose the paradigm within which he or she will operate, choose a substantive theory to guide the inquiry, and still have to determine whether the inquiry is value-resonant or value-dissonant with the context in which he or she will take the inquiry. When making this decision, problem, paradigm, theory, and context must exhibit internal coherence, value-fit, and congruence (value-resonance)[4] in order for the inquiry to be deemed appropriate and fitting, and in order to produce meaningful findings.

The naturalist admits the role that values play in shaping an inquiry *and* appreciates the possibility of difficulties arising if there is value-dissonance. While he cannot eliminate value effects (any more than can the rationalist), he endeavors to set up whatever safeguards he can, to expose and explicate the values whenever possible, and to test insofar as he can for value-resonance. In this latter regard, we may note that the naturalist's propensity for grounding his inquiry (see below) provides a virtual guarantee of value resonance, since the subjects' constructions and the substantive theory are both extracted from the data rather than laid on them.[5]

SOME CHARACTERISTIC POSTURES

While the axioms represent basic distinctions in premises between the rationalistic and naturalistic paradigms, certain postures typically assumed by practitioners following these two orientations also provide important insights into the differences between them. These postures are not compelled by the axioms, in the sense that they are necessary, logical derivatives (like the theorems of a geometry); yet they are relatively congenial or reinforcing to the practice of the paradigms and probably would be insisted on by each paradigm's adherents.

Six of the most common postures are described below. It should be noted that, unlike the case of axioms where either-or decisions must be made, postures could often be compromised. Yet compromises are infrequently found. The reason for this apparent intransigence cannot be laid to the obduracy of the proponents, however; rather, it stems from the fact that the collectivity of postures support and reinforce one another in extremely synergistic ways. Each is, in a sense, a raison d'etre for the others, and to compromise on any one of them is to considerably weaken the collective power of all.

PREFERRED METHODS. We have already noted that the rationalistic and naturalistic paradigms are often treated as though the major differentiating characteristic is their relative preference for quantitative or qualitative methods. It is likely that, among the six postures that will be briefly described here, the quantitative-qualitative distinction is the one that can be most easily and sensibly compromised. Cook and Reichardt (1979) have referred to the distinction as "unhelpful," and have called for more widespread utilization of both types of methods, a call with which we can agree. Each approach has advantages: quantitative methods have greater precision and are mathematically manipulable, while qualitative methods are richer and can deal with phenomena not easily translatable into numbers. For the naturalist, the propensity toward the use of qualitative methods is less accounted for by these advantages, however, than by the fact that qualitative methods are normally preferred by a human using himself or herself as a prime data collection instrument. Techniques such as interview, observation, use of non-verbal cues and unobtrusive measures, and documentary and records analysis seem more appropriate in that case.

SOURCE OF THEORY. Rationalists prefer *a priori* theory; indeed, they are likely to insist that inquiry without *a priori* theory is impossible. Theories always exist, they say, even if only at the implicit level. It is better to make them explicit than to be uncertain about what is guiding one's inquiry. The naturalist suggests that it is not theory but the inquiry problem that guides and bounds an inquiry. *A priori* theory constrains the inquiry and introduces biases (believing is seeing). In all events, theory is more powerful when it *arises from* the data rather than being imposed *on* them. It is better to find a theory to explain the facts than to look for facts that accord with a theory. Again, there is something to be said for each point of view. Surely rationalists would not wish to devise theory that was never shown to have any relation to facts, nor would the naturalist insist that each inquiry had to establish its own theory de novo. Yet the naturalist, using himself as instrument, building on his or her tacit as well as propositional knowledge and unrolling the inquiry design as the study proceeds, would find *a priori* theory uncongenial, preferring to develop the theory as his or her collection of facts grew and his or her insights into their possible meanings matured.

KNOWLEDGE TYPES USED. Rationalists confine the types of knowledge admissible in any inquiry to *propositional* knowledge (Polanyi, 1966), that is, knowledge that can be cast into language forms (sentences). In view of their insistence on *a priori* theory and their interest in shaping inquiry preordinately around certain questions and hypotheses derived from it, such a tendency is not surprising. Naturalists, intent upon the use of the human as the prime data collection instrument and wishing to utilize the capabilities of that instrument to the fullest, also admit and build upon *tacit* knowledge: intuitions, apprehensions, "vibes," which, while not expressible at any given moment, nevertheless occur to the inquirer by virtue of his or her training and experience.[6] Of course, the naturalist seeks to recast his tacit knowledge into propositional form as soon as possible, since without so doing he cannot communicate with others—and probably not even with himself—about his findings. Yet to confine the inquiry itself only to those things that can be stated propositionally is unduly limiting from the naturalist's viewpoint, since it eliminates to a large extent the characteristic that is the major warrant for the use of the human-as-instrument.

INSTRUMENTS. The rationalist prefers non-human data collection instruments, because they appear to be more cost-efficient, have a patina of objectivity, and produce information that can be systematically aggregated. The naturalist prefers humans-as-instruments because of their greater insightfulness, their flexibility, their responsiveness, the holistic emphasis they can provide, their ability to utilize tacit knowledge, and their ability to process and ascribe meaning to data simultaneously with their acquisition. Just as a "smart" bomb need not be dropped accurately on target to find its way unerringly to it, so the *smart* human instrument need not begin with a precise problem statement, theory, hypothesis, or method in order to find its way unerringly to what is most salient in a situation. As Hofstadter (1979) points out, there is an exact trade-off between perfection and adaptability; the more perfect an instrument is for some use, the less adaptable to others. The human instrument, while admittedly imperfect, is nevertheless exquisitely adaptable. For the naturalist, with his or her propensity for grounded theory and emerging design, the human instrument is the ideal choice.

DESIGN. The rationalist insists on a preordinate design; indeed, it is sometimes asserted that a good design specifies in dummy form the very tables that will ultimately be found in the report. The naturalist, entering the field without *a priori* theory or hypotheses (mostly), is literally unable to specify a design (except in the broadest process sense) in advance. Instead, he or she anticipates that the design will emerge as the inquiry proceeds, with each day's work being heavily dependent on what has gone before. Given his or her other postures, the naturalist has no choice but to opt for an emergent (rolling, cascading, unfolding) design. Of course there is no reason why the naturalist should not be as specific as he or she can, without constraining his or her options.

SETTING. Finally, the rationalist prefers to conduct studies under laboratory (contrived, controlled, manipulable) conditions in order to exclude from the inquiry any influences other than those at which the inquiry is aimed; that is to exclude all confounding variables. The naturalist, on the other hand, prefers natural settings, arguing that only in such settings can one arrive at reasonable formulations and interpretations. If theory is to be properly grounded, the inquirer must observe the facts as they normally occur, not as they are contrived in an artificial context.

It should now be clear why we asserted earlier that these six postures constitute a synergistic set. Compromises are, of course, possible on each posture, but each supports the others; one cannot argue for the naturalist's preference on any one posture without invoking his preferences on other postures as well. It is difficult to imagine a naturalist at work who could be content with a mix-and match strategy, however desirable that might be from the point of view of achieving a rapprochement.

THE TRUSTWORTHINESS OF NATURALISTIC INQUIRY

After some two centuries of experience with rationalistic inquiry, several criteria of importance have been identified for judging the trustworthiness of its finding. It is not unreasonable to ask whether naturalistic inquiry can also meet those criteria; or, in the event that the criteria are deemed inappropriate, meet some new criteria that are more appropriate and of approximately equal power in differentiating good from bad, inadequate, or untrustworthy research. Such criteria have importance for designing, monitoring, and judging an inquiry, whether from the perspective of the inquirer, a monitor (for example, a sponsor, an administrator, or a dissertation committee), or an editor who might be asked to publish the results of such research.

Guba and Lincoln (1981) have summarized the four major traditional criteria into four questions, to which they suggest the naturalist has an equal obligation to attend:

1. *Truth Value:* How can one establish confidence in the truth of the findings of a particular inquiry for the respondents with which and the context in which the inquiry was carried out?
2. *Applicability:* How can one determine the degree to which the findings of a particular inquiry may have applicability in other contexts or with other respondents?
3. *Consistency:* How can one determine whether the findings of an inquiry would be consistently repeated if the inquiry were replicated with the same (or similar) respondents in the same (or a similar) context:?
4. *Neutrality:* How can one establish the degree to which the findings of an inquiry are a function solely of the conditions of the inquiry and not of the biases, motivations, interests, or perspectives of the inquirer?

The terms typically utilized within the rationalistic paradigm in relation to the four questions are, respectively, *internal validity, external validity, reliability*, and *objectivity*. Guba (1981a) and Guba and Lincoln (1981) propose four analogous terms within the naturalistic paradigm to supplant these rationalistic terms: *credibility, transferability, dependability*, and *confirmability*, respectively.

The translation of the conventional terms into the these four naturalistic terms requires some justification (Guba, 1981; Guba & Lincoln, 1981):

CREDIBILITY. Internal validity is best demonstrated through an isomorphism between the data of an inquiry and the phenomena those data represent. While such isomorphism cannot be directly represented in either paradigm, the naturalist does have at least indirect access to the multiple realities he deals with; since they are constructions in the minds of people, he can *ask* those people whether he has represented *their* realities appropriately. Thus, the crucial question for the naturalist becomes, "Do the data sources find the inquirer's analysis, formulation, and inter-pretations to be credible (believable)?"

TRANSFERABILITY. In the rationalistic paradigm, generalizability (external validity) is demonstrated by showing that the data have been collected from a sample that is in some way representative of the population to which generalization is sought. The naturalist, while discounting generalizability, nevertheless believes that some degree of transferability is possible if enough "thick description" is available about both sending and receiving contexts to make a reasoned judgment possible.

DEPENDABILITY. In the rationalist paradigm, reliability is a matter of replicability; a study ought to be *repeatable* under the same circumstances in another place and time. If there are discrepancies or deviations between two repetitions of the same study, the difference is charged to unreliability (error). The naturalist cannot be so cavalier, however, because, first, designs are emergent so that changes are built in with conscious intent, and second, emergent design prevents an exact replication of a study in any event (since a second inquirer might choose a different path from the same data). The naturalist defines the concept of dependability to mean *stability* after discounting such conscious and unpredictable (but logical) changes.

CONFIRMABILITY. As Scriven (1971) has noted, the rationalistic concept of objectivity is based on a quantitative notion of inter-subjective agreement. But clearly, 50 million Frenchmen can be and have been wrong; what is important is not that there be quantitative agreement but qualitative confirmability. The onus of objectivity ought, therefore, to be removed from the inquirer and placed on the data; it is not inquirer certifiability in which we are interested, but in data con-firmability.

It is premature to expect that naturalists would have evolved as sophisticated a methodology for dealing with trustworthiness as have rationalists, especially since the latter have had literally centuries to work on refinements. However, Guba (1981a) has attempted what he himself characterized as a primitive effort. His for-mulations will be summarized here. They are treated in greater detail else where (Lincoln & Guba, 1985).

With respect to *credibility*, Guba suggests the following as means either to safe-guard against loss of credibility or to continually test for it:

Prolonged engagement at a site: to overcome distortions introduced by the inquirer's presence, to test for ethnocentrism (Lincoln & Guba, 1981), to test biases and per-ceptions of both inquirer and respondents, and to provide time to identify salient characteristics of both the context and the problem.

Persistent observation: to gain a high degree of acquaintance with and *verstehen* of pervasive qualities and salient characteristics, to come to appreciate atypical but critical characteristics, and to eliminate those which are irrelevant.

Peers debriefing: to keep the inquirer honest, to provide him or her with the oppor-tunity to test his or her growing insights against those of uninvolved peers, to receive advice about important methodological steps in the emergent design, to leave an audit trail (see below), and to discharge personal feelings, anxieties, and stresses which might otherwise affect the inquiry adversely.

Triangulation: whereby a variety of data sources, different perspectives or theories, different methods, and even different investigators are pitted against one another in order to cross-check data and interpretation (Denzin, 1978).

Referential adequacy materials: that is, documents films, videotapes, audio recordings, pictures, and other raw or slice-of-life materials are collected during the study and archived without analysis; these materials can later be utilized by the inquirer or others, especially an auditor (see below), to test interpretations made from other analyzed data.

Member checks: whereby data and interpretations are continually checked with members of various groups from which data are solicited; done on a continuous basis throughout the study and again at the end when the full report is assembled, using the same members from whom the data were originally collected or other surrogates from the same groups, or both.

With respect to *transferability*, Guba has suggested that the inquirer engage in, or provide:

Theoretical/purposive sampling: that is, sampling intended to maximize the range of information which is collected and to provide most stringent conditions for theory grounding.

Thick description: by which is meant providing enough information about a context, first, to impart a vicarious experience of it and second, to facilitate judgments about the extent to which working hypotheses from that context might be transferable to a second and similar context.

With respect to *dependability*, Guba has suggested:

Use of overlap methods: one kind of triangulation process, which, while usually advocated in support of validity, also undergirds claims of reliability to the extent that they produce complementary results.

Stepwise replication: a kind of split-halves approach in which inquirers and data sources are split into two roughly equal halves to be investigated independently, provided, however, that there is frequent exchange between the two teams to allow for the common development and unfolding of an emergent design.

The dependability audit: modelled on the fiscal audit, but limited to that part of the auditor's role which deals with *process*. In a fiscal audit, the first concern of an auditor is whether the accounts were kept in one of the several modes that constitute acceptable professional practice; to reach that judgment the auditor must, of course, be supplied with an "audit trail," which delineates all methodological steps and decision points and which provides access to all data in their several raw and processed stages.

With respect to *confirmability*, Guba has proffered:

Triangulation: as described above.

Practicing reflexivity: that is, attempting to uncover one's underlying epistemological assumptions, reasons for formulating the study in a particular way, and heretofore implicit assumptions, biases or prejudices about the context or problem. The most appropriate means for this exploration and presentation takes the form of a reflexive journal, kept in the field.

The confirmability audit: a counterpart to the dependability audit, in which the auditor takes the additional step of verifying that each finding can be traced back through the several analysis steps to the original data and that interpretations of data clusters are reasonable and meaningful, in much the same way that a fiscal auditor would verify at least a sample of entries in a bookkeeping journal to be certain that each represented a *real* transaction and that the *bottom line* accurately represented the current fiscal situation (Lincoln & Guba, 1982).

The criteria posed, while not theoretically elegant formulations, do have utility at several stages of the inquiry process; they aid reviewers in making *a priori* judgments about the quality of proposed research; they aid the inquirer in monitoring himself or herself and in guiding activities in the field; and, finally, they may be used to render ex post facto judgments on the products of research, including reports, case studies, or proposed publications. The final reports ought at the very least to include—as do rationalistic paradigm reports—statements about what the inquirer actually did to satisfy each of the four sets of criteria, and reports from dependability and confirmability auditors (if used) concerning their verification of his or her processes and conclusions.

Carrying out even all of these steps (usually not logistically or fiscally possible in an actual inquiry) will not guarantee the trustworthiness of a naturalistic study, but will contribute greatly toward persuading a reader and consumer of the data's meaningfulness.

SUMMARY

We have tried to argue here that we are in the midst of a paradigmatic revolution (Kuhn, 1970), centered about the growing concern that the paradigm which has typically been utilized for scientific (hard and life sciences) inquiry has served poorly when applied to the social and behavioral sciences. It is time for a new paradigm, which takes account of the nature of social experience. We believe that paradigm to be the naturalistic.

The naturalistic paradigm has emerged, in part, from intense scrutiny of the assumptions and epistemological axioms which undergird rationalistic inquiry. We have tried to make explicit the nature of the epistemological assumptions essential to the two paradigms and have addressed persistent criticism that the latter is soft, non-rigorous, and attentive to relevance over rigor.

While it is true that rationalistic inquirers do not accept the axioms we have imputed to them here without reservation, we have tried to deal with them in their purest form, as they can be traced through the philosophy of science and scientific writers. By doing so, we believe, the reader is able to see the sharpest of contrasts and to understand better why it is maintained that there can be no compromise on axiomatic assumptions (just as one cannot accept a compromise between Euclidean and Lobachevskian geometry), although there may be compromises on various postures that are typically ascribed to the two paradigms.

Thus, we have accounted for five major axiomatic differences: the nature of reality, the nature of the inquirer-object (or respondent) relationship, the nature of truth statements, assumptions about causal relationships, and the role of values within disciplined inquiry. Along those assumptions, we have argued, there can be no compromise. The inquirer must choose one set of assumptions (axioms) or another to undergird his inquiry. The choice is an empirical issue, determined by fit.

Along certain other dimensions, called *postures*, however, compromise may be possible, although we would argue that, like dominoes, one choice may impel the inquirer to make other choices which traditionally have characterized naturalistic inquiry.

Finally, we have argued that, while several centuries of rationalistic inquiry has allowed the development of rather strict and inviolable canons of rigor, the naturalistic school is only beginning to develop an arsenal of weapons against the charge of non-rigor or untrustworthiness. We have demonstrated that it is possible to consider the questions of internal validity, external validity, reliability, and objectivity within the framework of naturalism, but argued for concepts which are more germane—credibility, transferability, dependability and confirmability. We proposed criteria by which external reviewers of naturalistic research might judge the trustworthiness of those studies. While these criteria do not provide unassailable defenses against charges of untrustworthiness, they nevertheless assure the consumer of such research that appropriate steps have been taken to produce data from human sources and contexts that are meaningful, trackable, verifiable, and grounded in the real-life situations from which they were derived.

The naturalistic paradigm seems to us to have much to recommend it. We urge that it be given a fair trial.

NOTES

1. In previous writing (Guba, 1978, 1981; Guba & Lincoln, 1981), we have referred to what we here call the rationalistic paradigm as the *scientistic* or the *scientific* paradigm. The use of even the less pejorative of these latter two terms now seems to us inappropriate on two counts. First, readers have tended to view the naturalistic paradigm as *less* scientific (or even as nonscientific), and have, therefore, denigrated it as less valid. Second, several critics have accused us of setting up a straw man, on the grounds

that vanguard scientific thinkers have moved beyond the nineteenth century logical positivism of which our descriptions are at times reminiscent. It is undoubtedly true that many scientists now think differently, but that change does *not* characterize, in our opinion, the large majority of scientists who engage in inquiries in either the hard or soft sciences. It is to that level of practice that our criticisms are directed, and it is of that moribund culture that are descriptions are apt. However, to avoid the unintended meanings that some readers have drawn from our work, we have shifted to the term *rationalistic* to describe the paradigm that guides so much conventional inquiry.

2. An appreciation of the constraints which this limitation places on the subsequent discussion is crucial to an understanding of the points we will make. We are not dealing with tangible objects, events, or processes as would the physicist, chemist, or biologist. Nor do we mean to include those aspects of human studies that can be labeled as genetically or developmentally mediated. Study of such matters is undoubtedly better guided by the rationalistic paradigm than by the naturalistic. We *are* dealing, however, with the large majority of studies undertaken by psychologists, sociologists, anthropologists, educational researchers, and evaluators—including evaluations of other social-process fields such as social work, law enforcement, or health services delivery.

3. We find the use of the term *object* of inquiry, when applied to a human, pejorative; we prefer the term *respondent*, which carries the connotations of interaction and equality.

4. For two instances of value-resonance problems, see Guba (1982) in the field of reading and Lincoln (1982) in the field of special education.

5. It is ironic that the naturalist does permit the data to "speak for themselves" in the sense of grounding theory in them, a use never contemplated by the rationalists who are fond of using that phrase as an assertion of their objectivity.

6. The distinction made here is similar to that between a connoisseur and a critic of art. The connoisseur need only "feel" a painting to appreciate it; the critic must cast his feelings into language in order to convey his critique. Connoisseurship is a private art, but criticism is a public art (Eisner, 1979).

20. DEVELOPING DISCOURSES ON EVALUATION

H. S. BHOLA

I got my first introduction to planned change and evaluation in 1963 from Professor Egon G. Guba, who was a member of my doctoral dissertation committee at The Ohio State University. The Soviet Sputnik had generated considerable interest in the theory and research of planned change and evaluation in America. Professor Guba and Professor Virgil E. Blanke had been awarded a U.S. government grant to develop a model of innovation diffusion for use particularly in education. I was appointed a research associate on the project, which gave me the opportunity to do a theoretical dissertation on the topic of innovation diffusion and planned change (Bhola, 1965, 1988; Tiffany & Lutjens, 1998).

Positivism was deeply entrenched in the American academy in the early 1960s. However, questions were being raised about its indiscriminate adoption in social science research. From my experience in the United States and India, and in a variety of disciplines and careers, I was convinced that planned change was not amenable to formulas, but depended on a whole contexture of variables. In my understanding, it was certainly not an arena for certainties. All one could hope for as a change agent was to increase the probabilities of occurrence of an event. Obviously, I was uncomfortable with the linear and behaviorist models of innovation diffusion being proposed at the time, and I was both inclined and prepared for developing more organic and holistic approaches.

The CLER Model (Bhola, 1965) that I developed as part of my dissertation research said simply that planned change was a function of four categories of variables: Configurational relationships between and within innovators and adopters;

D.L. Stufflebeam, G.F. Madaus and T. Kellaghan (eds.). EVALUATION MODELS. Copyright © 2000. Kluwer Academic Publishers. Boston. All rights reserved.

Linkages, formal and volitional, within and between the configurations involved; Environments surrounding the promoters and adopters of change; and Resources available both to promoters and to potential adopters of change. To increase the probabilities of a change event to occur, these four components had to be synergetically optimized in combinations determined by the change agenda, the context of planned change, and the resources available for implementation at that time (Bhola, 1988; Tiffany & Lutjens, 1998).

According to Egon G. Guba, change and evaluation are two sides of the same coin. To be able to claim success for a change intervention, one would have to have done a baseline survey before introducing the intervention following a study of impact. Both are evaluative tasks. If that is so, then the CLER Model is not only a model of change, it is also a model of evaluation.

The following figure translates the CLER model from a model of change into a model of evaluation:

The CLER Ensemble of $\{P\} \times \{O\} \times \{A\}$ at Time (X)	The Change Intervention and Sinking-in Period	The CLER Ensemble of $\{P\} \times \{O\} \times \{A\}$ at Time (Z)

where $\{P\}$ stands for the system engaged in promoting change, $\{O\}$ for the set of objectives of change, and $\{A\}$ for the adopter system.

An evaluative discourse could be developed by capturing descriptions and dynamics of a change episode in a social setting at Time (X) and at Time (Z) as changes are accounted for and evaluated in relation to expectations and norms.

Back in India during 1966–68, I had the opportunity to apply the CLER Model as an evaluation model to study changes in the institutional life of a nonformal education project in India. The four categories of the model were used in capturing descriptions and dynamics of the project's institutional system at various points in time against the background of the larger canvas of social and political changes in the country. The final report on the evaluation took the form of a case study of institution building and organizational change (Bhola, 1975).

DOUBLE DIALECTICS: BETWEEN TEACHING AND LEARNING AND THEORY AND PRACTICE

During 1968–70, I was appointed a senior field adviser on the UNESCO/UNDP Work-Oriented Adult Literacy Pilot Project in the Lake Region of Tanzania, East Africa. This project was part of a larger program: The Experimental World Literacy Program with pilot projects in 11 different countries. Evaluation was considered the raison d'être of the program, which was planned to test the concept of functional literacy and to evaluate the effectiveness of the functional literacy approach against the so-called traditional literacy approach in generating socioeconomic development in underdeveloped areas of the world (UNESCO, 1976). It was here that I discovered that evaluation had come to be a central concern for multilateral and bilateral institutions within the international foreign aid and technical assistance culture. Evaluation was to form a necessary part of all proposals for projects, programs, and campaigns negotiated between donors and recipient countries.

Beginning in 1976, I was involved in a series of workshops on evaluation in Africa under the sponsorship of the German Foundation for International Development (DSE). At first, the focus was on adult literacy and adult education, but it was later expanded to other sectors of social development including formal education, distance education, nutrition, health, family education, and cooperatives. In the initial stages, the International Institute for Adult Literacy in Teheran, Iran, had collaborated with the DSE in the delivery of workshops on literacy evaluation. The Iranian revolution of 1978–79 put an end to this collaboration.

The workshops were delivered using an approach later formalized as an Action Training Model (Bhola, 1989), which combined participatory planning of, and learning within, evaluation workshops with a particular pattern of time-use before and after the workshops. Participants identified evaluation questions that needed to be answered in their actual work settings, wrote evaluation proposals on these selected questions, and returned home to collect data. Three to four months later they came back for a short time to collate data and begin the process of formulation, interpretation, and validation. Participants came to another workshop to present written reports on their evaluations and to discuss experiences and understandings with their colleagues.

Several national workshops in this mode were conducted in several African countries. An international evaluation workshop was held in November 1994 in Chiang Rai, Thailand, for training and orientation of three-member teams from eight South Asian Countries. Several quick appraisals and more systematic evaluations of projects and programs were conducted in Africa and China.

The first important lesson that I learned from my involvement in these workshops and evaluations was that evaluation models and methods are not sacrosanct and were negotiable in a world of scarcities of human and materials resources. Satisficing was a virtue in a world where we were dealing with evaluation by "barefoot" evaluators. There were not many people around who could write simple items for a quick little quiz or be trained easily to conduct an interview. There were no calculators, and not everybody felt sure of their ability to count and work out averages of a page full of scores. Processing qualitative data was beyond the capacity of most local faculties assisting in the workshops. Communication among evaluators and translating responses from learners and community leaders had to be less than perfect. Copiers (such as stencil duplicators and ditto machines) were not always available. In a world of paper famine, duplicating paper was not always available either, and when available had to be used most economically. These realities also dictated how tests and instruments were to be administered and data collated and stored.

To sum, in Africa then (and in most developing countries, even today) one has to learn "to get rich data through poor means." Most of the time this requires patient field observation and long conversations going back and forth on important issues and details to make sure that you were understood and that you understood what you were told.

I was taught the important lesson that good description came *before* evaluation. Quantities do indeed have qualities, and the first need inevitably was for a numerical description of the program giving us its scope, its size, and its spread. I was convinced that evaluation must be built on the foundation of good old recordkeeping. A properly maintained attendance register and an imaginatively written teacher's logbook, in the classroom or the community center, could work wonders for a program and its evaluability. If we could add to these data the scores from periodical tests of some sort on reading, writing, and numeracy, we could get away by doing nothing much else. Thus, these records form the essential MIS (Management Information System), which does not have to be computer-based and might easily be a pencil-and-paper system.

The MIS, I also learned, was not of much use unless it was accompanied by an SIM (Set of Integrated Materials), such as copies of the tests actually used and the curricular materials on which those tests had been based, as well as policy documents guiding the overall program. Without such information, it was impossible to make sense of test data and other descriptions kept in the MIS. Once again, it should be noted that the SIM is another example of good recordkeeping—hardcopy materials properly organized and kept in a file cabinet. There is nothing fancy about it.

Finally, evaluation required understanding of the program itself. What was the calculus of its means and ends? What would we want to know for delivering the program with effectiveness? Since there is never enough time and money for everything, what evaluation questions must be answered first? In other words, there had to be some evaluation planning leading to an evaluation agenda with priorities clearly set.

LEARNING FROM TEACHING AND DOING

Instructional materials for use in the evaluation workshops in Africa had to be tailor-made for participants to be able to relate to their interests, work experiences, and qualifications. The materials were first developed in the form of instructional sheets and brief notes on definitions and methods. Also included were sample questionnaires and survey instruments, specimens of grids and tables for data collection and collation, etc. After test-in-use of these materials, they were collected into handbooks and monographs. The practice and theory dialectic produced a range of materials over the years.

During 1970–71, I worked with UNESCO to prepare a document entitled, *Reporting Data on the Impact of Functional Literacy: A Standardized Data Reporting Systems* (SDRS). It was to be used in UNESCO's comprehensive evaluation of the implementation of the UNESCO/UNDP Experimental World Functional Literacy Program (UNESCO, 1976). The SDRS was pilot-tested by the author in Ethiopia during July 1971. The necessity of integrating an MIS (and an SIM) within evaluation models was fully affirmed for me by this experience.

The first theoretic statement on how evaluation should be conducted was formulated in a paper: *Making Evaluation Operational in Functional Literacy Programs* (Bhola, 1973). The paper, widely used in the UNESCO literacy sector, argued for in-built evaluation and emphasized the necessity of systemic analysis of a program to determine what information needs existed, what priorities could be developed, and what indicators should be used for data collection. The debts to systems thinking in general and to Stufflebeam's CIPP model (Stufflebeam, 1971) in particular were both abundant and clear in this paper.

The book *Evaluating Functional Literacy* (Bhola, 1979) reflected a distillation of knowledge of theory and of firsthand experience in conducting workshops in Anglophone Africa. Topics addressed included the link between ideology and technology in the choice of evaluation models and methods, some competing models of evaluation in the field at that time, and their synthesis in a Situation-Specific-Strategy (3-S) Model of evaluation. Other topics included how to make evaluation operational within a functional literacy program by systemic analysis, establishing agenda, and developing indicators; simple protocols for the measurement of change; gathering implementation data for management; design of evaluation; and writing reports.

My 1979 book on evaluation had focused almost exclusively on adult literacy. In the meantime, the clientele of DSE evaluation workshops had expanded, and the naturalistic (or the constructive) approach to evaluation was gaining ground (Guba & Lincoln, 1989; Lincoln & Guba, 1985). There was a need to expand my perspective on evaluation, to deal with new methods and approaches, and to take exemplars from development sectors other than literacy. There also was a need to integrate the new constructivist approach into my conceptualization of evaluation.

In 1989, an invitation to return to the theme of evaluation of literacy projects, programs, and campaigns provided the opportunity of integrating my experiences in a model of evaluation. This resulted in the book *Evaluating "Literacy for Development": Projects, Programs and Campaigns* (Bhola, 1990). I decided to stay within the technical assistance culture of developing countries as I reviewed the definitional and theoretical work relating to evaluation models in the United States (Madaus, Scriven, & Stufflebeam, 1983). The new model assumed built-in evaluation. It suggested that institutions or organizations that conduct literacy for development programs should engage in systemic analysis of their programs and develop profiles of information needs and sets of indicators to be used in data collection before launching evaluation studies. A Management Information System was to be central to any built-in evaluation system within a program's organization. Data in the MIS had to be complemented by tests, curriculum materials, and policy documents. Qualitative narratives had to be obtained through naturalistic (constructivist) evaluation studies. In some cases, more fine-tuned comparisons between groups or before-and-after comparisons for the same groups would be necessary, which would require empirical data.

In the context of a capacity building workshop in South Africa (Bhola, 1998a), a "Stream of Information Model" was constructed that shows the continuous flow

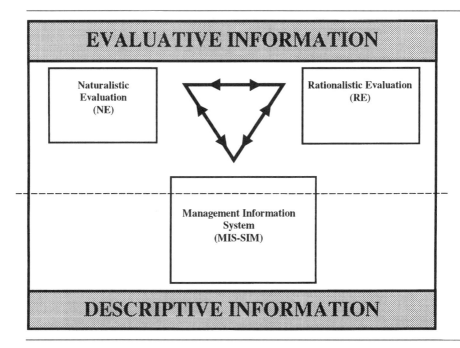

Figure 1. An Integrated Model of Information Development and Evaluation. Source: Bhola (1996)

of the MIS/SIM data in a stream of information, assuming a never-ending making and updating of the MIS/SIM system (Figure 1). The two components of NE and RE are shown to be iterative. Evaluation studies in the NE or the RE mode can be undertaken as and when necessary to illuminate and enrich various aspects of the program. Numbers and narrations together continue to create meanings for program providers. By using this stream of information model, organizations conducting projects, programs, and campaigns for implementing literacy projects (or other projects of education or extension) become cultures of information and, in the process, "intelligent" organizations (Bhola, 1995a).

RETURNING TO ROOTS IN PARADIGMS: THE EPISTEMIC TRIANGLE

On arrival at Indiana University in 1970, I quickly became aware of the epistemological discussions and the paradigm debates that would be raging around us for decades: positivism vs. postpositivism (Phillips, 1990), limits of rationality (Elster, 1983), judgment under uncertainty (Kahneman, Slovic, & Tversky, 1982), use of argument (Toulmin, 1958), systemic vs. systematic (Checkland, 1981), critical thinking (Ingram, 1990), feminist critique (Armstrong, 1995), postmodernity (Harvey, 1990; Lyotard, 1984), and discourse (Lemke, 1995).

On reading and reflecting on the various epistemological positions being contested, I began to realize that each had validity in some particular content and context of reality and that to understand reality in all its richness, all the epistemological positions had to be made coherent. I was encouraged in a search for coherence by Cronbach's distinction between contexts of command and contexts of accommodation (Cronbach et al., 1980) and by Firestone's idea of paradigm-praxis dialectic (1990).

Following formal study of systems theory, I began to observe coherences among paradigms. It soon became clear that systems, both material and social, do not exist out there in nature. They are human constructions, and their boundaries can be construed in multiple ways for reasons of practicality, theory, or ideology. Further, while systems thinking assumes constructivist thinking, constructivist thinking assumes systems and schemata. Human constructions are not just carried in the human head as discrete images and strings of meanings. They are stored as schemata and conceptual systems (Bertalanffy, 1968; Berger & Luckmann, 1967; Checkland, 1981; Delago, 1988; Rickey, 1995).

The concept of "emergence" in systems theory provides the point of intersection with dialectical thinking (in the meaning of mutual shaping of entities in dialectical relationships). The emergences of unanticipated and irreversible structures and functions across systems hierarchies are not amenable to understanding by linear logic and can be explained only by dialectical thinking (Basseches, 1980; Rychlak, 1976; Mitroff & Mason, 1981).

These considerations led me to suggest, by way of coherence among epistemologies, an epistemic triangle formed by systems thinking, constructivist thinking, and dialectical thinking (Bhola, 1991, 1996) (See Figure 2). The epistemic space of the triangle can accommodate positivism, which can be viewed as one particular construction of reality—reality defined by prediction and control. It may not be

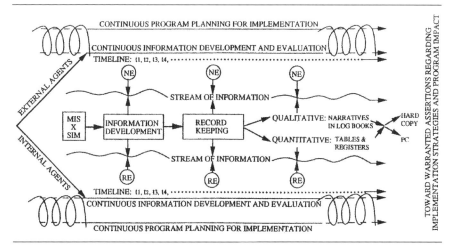

Figure 2. A "Stream of Information" Model for Continuous and Concurrent Program Planning, and Information Development and Evaluation. Source: Bhola (1995a)

possible, or even necessary, to dissolve positivism into constructivism; but a dialectical rather than an oppositional relationship between the two should be assumed. The epistemic triangle can also accommodate the uncertainty debate and discussion about the limits of reality that could be overcome by social praxis for social validation. Further work to discover and develop coherences among epistemologies should continue. The epistemic triangle could perhaps be discussed in relation to postmodernity (Harvey, 1990), critical theory (Ingram, 1990), and the feminist critique (Armstrong, 1995) as special ideological discourses (Lemke, 1995; Salkie, 1995; Van Dijk, 1995).

There was another coherence I discovered as I was working with analysis of epistemologies and methodologies. I realized that planning, implementation, and evaluation as purposive actions (actions with purpose) have a shared calculus of means and ends as purposive actions. In a sense, planning is a script for implementation, and implementation anticipates evaluation. This being the case, a general discourse can be developed on a particular purposive action grounded at the intersection of "means and ends" and "objectives and actual results." From such a discourse, different specialized discourses, or scripts, could be developed: planning discourses, implementation discourses, and evaluation discourses.

The use of the epistemic triangle itself is not deductive or inferential, but intuitive, resonant, and heuristic. In the elaboration of the purposive action taking place within the triangle, it rejects linearity because of its systemic angle. With its other angle of dialectical thinking, it accepts multiple causality and mutual shaping. With constructivism as its third angle, the triangle requires methods of making meanings, even as it does not exclude numbers—numerical assertions being one specific type of construction.

It does not demand naive objectivity. It accepts the individual as the instrument that registers all reality and demands that it be a sharpened instrument: a person with keen perceptions, clear logic(s), and ethical sensibilities. With these qualities, the evaluator should go forth to collect data and evidence, make interpretations, look for impact (by intervention, interaction, and emergence), and seek social validations to be able to make warranted assertions. These assertions need not be universally generalizable; plausibility in context is fine (Dewey, 1936; Toulmin, 1958).

Depending on the time of evaluation in relation to the manifested progress of a purposive action, participants in the evaluation, and their professional capacities and ideological predispositions, institutionalization of the program system and the system of evaluation itself and, finally, the political contexts, different arrowheads of the epistemic triangle may be used as shown in Figure 2(II), (III), and (IV).

The question can be asked: Is the epistemic triangle a completely new beginning? Or is it continuous with earlier conceptual work represented in the CLER model of evaluation (Bhola, 1965, 1988) and the integrated model of information development and evaluation with its extensions and refinements (Bhola, 1990, 1995a)?

It is easy to assert continuity between the CLER model and the epistemic triangle. The CLER model, though it did not use the language of the epistemic triangle, is right at home in the epistemological space of the epistemic triangle. Configurations as arrangements of social formations—large and small, horizontal and vertical—are systems. The boundaries of innovator systems and adopter systems are constructed by stakeholders. The ensemble of innovators, the innovation, and the adopter are in constant dialectical relations.

The continuity between the model of integrated information development and evaluation and the epistemic triangle should also be obvious. The MIS is a numerical description of the program system (complemented with a set of relevant written materials). The naturalistic evaluation is another name for constructivist evaluation. Rationalistic (or positivistic) evaluation is a special construction that holds in contexts of control and prediction. Underlying it all is a dialectic between numbers and meanings.

In an Indian riddle, the child (smoke) is born before the parent (fire). So in theory, it is possible to have the parent born when the child is already tooting the horn on the roof. It is possible to make operational models of evaluation first and only later to discover and connect with their philosophic and epistemological roots.

EVALUATIVE DISCOURSES: APPLICATIONS OF THE EPISTEMIC TRIANGLE

Study I: Evaluating a Literacy System in Namibia

Systems thinking was used by the author as the arrowhead in developing an evaluative discourse on the National Literacy Program in Namibia (NLPN) during 1994–95 (Bhola, 1995b). The reason was that in the Namibian setting, program evaluation was to be joined with a policy analysis. Policy required analyses of the system of delivery as well as of communities (as social systems) where the beneficiaries lived and worked.

To begin with, the NLPN was described in systems categories using 11 subsystems (or components) in the NLPN: ideology, policy and planning, mobilization, institution building and organization, curriculum development, methods and materials, training and orientation, teaching-learning, professional-technical support, education-to-work transition, and built-in evaluation and monitoring.

A three-part description of each of the 11 subsystems and components was developed: (i) the ideal-normative description of such a subsystem, (ii) a description of the subsystem as promised and/or expected in policy statements and planning documents, and (iii) a description of the subsystem as actually manifested based on performance and results.

While the evaluation discourse was arrowheaded by systems thinking and systems categories, it did not stop being constructivist and dialectical. The evaluation was participatively conducted. Realities of the program as constructed by different stakeholders were brought together to build a coherent picture. The dialectics of the history of the blacks and the whites in Namibia and the contradiction in the processes of development of some and underdevelopment of others were all captured.

In the spirit of Dewey, the general methodology sought evidence in order to make warranted assertions. The descriptions were constructed using both qualitative and quantitative information that came from (1) a thorough analysis of policy documents, periodic progress reports and evaluations, statistics from their MIS, and curriculum plans and instructional materials from the SIM; and (2) field visits to most of the educational regions of Namibia for interviews with regional officers, district literacy officers, and teachers, and from observations of classes to conversations with community leaders and learners. The style of evaluation was participative throughout to encourage dialog and dialectic. Constructions and interpretations were validated.

Two studies were conducted in South Africa. The first was in two parts and included constructivist capacity building and a systemic evaluation (Bhola, 1998a); the second was conceptualized and implemented as a constructivist evaluation (Bhola, 1998b).

Study II: Constructivist Capacity Building, Systemic Evaluation

In this study, a general discourse was developed on a purposive action encompassing an adult basic education and training initiative proclaimed in South Africa to begin on February 11, 1996. The initiative had hopes of bringing together the state's *Ithuteng* (Ready to Learn) program and the Thousand Learner Unit (TLU) project of the National Literacy Co-operation, an important civil society institution of South Africa since terminated.

During May-June 1996, a nationwide capacity building exercise called TOFA (Training and Orientation for Field Action) was launched. It was to provide the knowledge and skills that the middle-level professional leaders in the nine provinces thought they needed for field-level implementation of the national initiative in their special contexts.

The general discourse that developed in this exercise was first formulated in a "specialized" discourse for designing and delivering training in all the aspects of implementation of the *Ithuteng* and TLU systems: from ideological clarification to understanding issues of policy and planning, mobilization, institution building, curriculum development, choice of methods and materials, training and orientations, teaching and learning encounters, networking with professional support systems, organizing learning center to workplace transition, and evaluation and monitoring.

Later, the same discourse was specially scripted as an evaluation using the same 11 subsystems. The program had been on the ground for no more than four months, and in several cases for much less. A serious discrepancy analysis comparing the expected with the actual was not possible. Yet, the evaluation served as a useful baseline for future comparisons and uncovered both problems and possibilities in the near future.

Study III: They are Learning and Discerning

In May-June 1997, the National Literacy Cooperation of South Africa wanted a status review of their TLU program for planning the second phase of the program. They also wanted to do another round of TOFA (Training and Orientation for

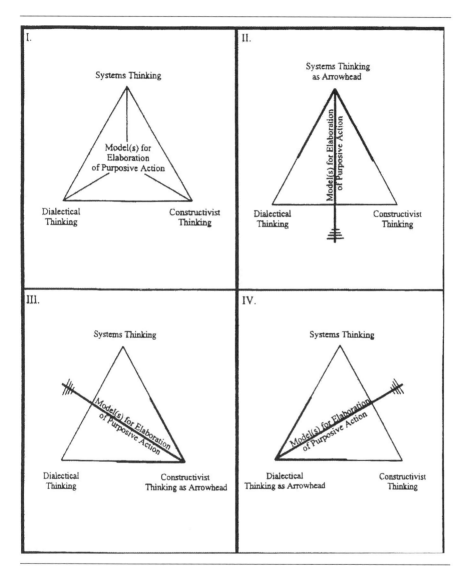

Figure 3. Models of Purposive Action

Field Action) (Bhola, 1998a, 1998b). This was the exact reverse condition to the one described in Study II above.

In this case, the study was arrowheaded by constructivist thinking. The questions to be answered were: What was happening on the ground? How were the various stakeholders in the TLU project relating with the project? Since a systems description had been built only recently, it was not considered useful to build another so soon. The resources of the evaluation effort were put into the study of impact as experienced by the stakeholders themselves. The impact of the program on the lives of people was captured through thick descriptions at learner centers and through group discussions among providers at various levels. They were our eyes and ears, since too much independent collection of empirical data was not possible in the short period of time available.

The evaluative discourse was developed from a multiplicity of constructions of policymakers, provincial directors, teachers, community leaders, and learners. These conversations were placed within appropriately articulated statistical and policy frames.

Data for situation review and for responsive design of training workshops were collected as part of the same overall discourse. This time, the clients did not want a written script on capacity building. They were satisfied that what was learned from the discourse was used in the design and delivery of training desired by participants from all the nine provinces.

It is not impossible to conceptualize an evaluation study where dialectical thinking is the arrowhead of an evaluation. In evaluation as well as in social design, a dialectic is inevitably involved between the conceptual system and its existent or future social manifestation. In other cases, dialectical—that is, mutually shaping relationships between collaborative and competitive systems—are involved, covering donors and beneficiaries, policy systems and performance systems, innovators and adopters, and so on. An evaluation of the adult education project in India referred to earlier (Bhola, 1975) comes close to being an evaluation in the dialectical mode.

CONCLUSION

The description and discussion presented in this paper can be summarized graphically, as in Figure 3. A situated discourse on evaluation of a purposive action must enable evaluators to make warranted assertions about efficiency, effectiveness, and ethicality of a purposive action. This expectation is more likely to be met if evaluators (and others participating in the evaluation process) can face their own identities and ideologies and are able to take clear and coherent epistemological positions. Having done that, they should be able to bound the evaluand as a social system located in a particular social domain and context. They should then understand the means and ends calculus of the purposive action being evaluated: choosing appropriate models for mapping, plotting, and scaffolding, and using appropriate modes, methods, and tactics of data collection and analysis to make warranted assertions.

21. STEPS OF EMPOWERMENT EVALUATION: FROM CALIFORNIA TO CAPE TOWN

DAVID M. FETTERMAN

Empowerment evaluation is the use of evaluation to help others help themselves. It is designed to foster self-determination, rather than dependency. Empowerment evaluation focuses on improvement, is collaborative, and requires both qualitative and quantitative methodologies. As an alternative to traditional external evaluations, it offers program participant buy-in, program focused goals and strategies, an insider's perspective of program operations, a tailored approach to program development, a generalizable skill that can last a lifetime, and the promise of a learning community.

BACKGROUND

Empowerment evaluation has many reinforcing facets, including training, facilitation, advocacy, illumination, and liberation. Training program participants to evaluate their own programs and coaching them in an evaluation that they design themselves is a powerful and popular form of empowerment evaluation. Fundamentally, in this facet of empowerment evaluation, evaluators teach people to conduct their own evaluations and thus become more self-sufficient. This approach desensitizes and demystifies evaluation and ideally helps organizations internalize evaluation principles and practices, making evaluation an integral part of program planning. Program participants learn to establish their own goals and strategies in a collaborative and participatory environment, often with the assistance of a facilitator.

In other forms, the evaluator serves as a coach or facilitator to help others conduct their evaluations. Advocate empowerment evaluators allow participants to shape the

D.L. Stufflebeam, G.F. Madaus and T. Kellaghan (eds.). EVALUATION MODELS. Copyright © 2000. Kluwer Academic Publishers. Boston. All rights reserved.

direction of the evaluation, suggest ideal solutions to their problems, and then take an active role in making social change happen. Empowerment evaluators can also serve as illuminating and liberating facilitators, assisting program participants free themselves from traditional roles and expectations. (See Fetterman, 1994, for a more detailed discussion about the various facets of empowerment evaluation.)

Empowerment evaluation has roots in community psychology and action anthropology. (See Rappaport, 1987; Tax, 1958; Zimmerman & Rappaport, 1988.) Another major influence includes the Accelerated School Project which emphasizes the empowerment of parents, teachers, and administrators to improve educational settings. (See Hopfenberg, Levin, & Associates, 1993.) In addition, work in the area of self-determination and individuals with disabilities has had a profound influence on the development of empowerment evaluation. (See Mithaug, 1991.)

Empowerment evaluation is adaptable to almost every environment, including health, education, business, agriculture, microcomputers, nonprofits and foundations, government, and technology. However, certain conditions should be in place. For example, the group must request assistance in this area. Management can make the request but cannot impose this approach from the top down. In addition, management must support this process and the risk-taking activity associated with it. A climate of trust and a desire for shared responsibility are also essential. Conditions need not be perfect to initiate the process, however; in fact, they rarely are.

This discussion highlights several pragmatic steps that can be used to help others learn how to evaluate their programs: (a) taking stock or determining where you stand as a program, including strengths and weaknesses; (b) focusing on establishing goals, determining where you want to go in the future with an explicit emphasis on program improvement; (c) developing strategies and helping participants determine their own strategies to accomplish program goals and objectives; and (d) helping program participants determine the type of evidence required to document progress credibly toward their goals. This discussion illustrates these steps by drawing heavily on empowerment evaluation activity in three arenas: the School for Transformative Learning at the California Institute of Integral Studies in San Francisco, the Oakland California Public School System, and townships around Cape Town in South Africa.

As research director in San Francisco's School for Transformative Learning, I am serving as an empowerment evaluation facilitator and coach. Each program in the school is using this approach to design their own self-evaluations. The aim is to use the evaluation data in a formative manner and improve program practice and facilitate the academic mission.

In Oakland, I was invited by the superintendent of the public school system to serve as a mentor for their empowerment evaluation/action research facilitators. We are working with members of the entire system, ranging from assistant superintendents to nurses. The aim of the effort is to respond to community and board of education concerns about their five-year plan and to revitalize existing programs.

Colleagues at the Human Sciences Research Council, University of Cape Town, University of Natal, University of the Western Cape, and members of a black impoverished community outside Cape Town invited me to introduce empowerment evaluation to them. Empowerment evaluation workshops for the Human Sciences Research Council were conducted under the auspices of its new Directorate, Research Capacity Building, which focuses primarily on building research capacity among black scholars in the country.

STEP ONE: TAKING STOCK

One of the first steps in empowerment evaluation is taking stock. Program participants are asked to rate their program on a 1 to 10 scale, with 10 being the highest level. They are asked to make the rating as accurate as possible. Beginning with an overall program rating often makes it easier for participants to rate specific parts of a program, such as recruitment, admissions, pedagogy, curriculum, graduation, and alumni tracking in a school setting. The potential list of components to rate is endless, and each participant must prioritize the list of items. Program participants are also asked to document their ratings (both the overall program rating and the ratings of specific program components). Typically, some participants give their programs an unrealistically high rating. However, the absence of appropriate documentation, peer ratings, and a reminder about the realities of their environment— such as a high dropout rate, students bringing guns to school, and racial violence in a high school—helps participants recalibrate their rating. In some cases, ratings stay higher than peers consider appropriate. However, the significance of this process is not the actual rating but the creation of a baseline from which future progress can be measured. In addition, it sensitizes program participants to the necessity of collecting data to support assessments or appraisals.

School for Transformative Learning

Faculty, students, and staff members in the School for Transformative Learning at the California Institute of Integral Studies are using empowerment evaluation among other tools to chart their course for the future. We have embarked on a historic journey in higher education, in many respects. The focus of the program is on collaborative learning and social change. Ideally students learn how to create environments that facilitate transformative learning in various settings, ranging from academe to industry (see Cell, 1984; Elias, 1993; Mezirow, 1991 for detailed discussion about transformative learning).

Empowerment evaluation has been a useful tool to help establish a baseline of performance. Faculty and staff are using this process to evaluate how their individual academic programs are doing, including the Ph.D. in Integral Studies; the Masters of Arts in Business, Organizational Development and Transformation, Traditional Knowledge, and Women's Spirituality; and the Bachelors of Arts Completion Program. Each group of program members clustered together during a faculty/staff retreat and rated individual components of their program, such as recruitment, curriculum planning, teaching, research, administrative procedures, faculty teamwork, and community building.

These ratings were uplifting to some and depressing to others. There was a tendency for some to internalize the ratings as individual personal assessments rather than assessments of the program (or program components). This was an understandable reaction: After all of the work that goes into making new programs work in a short period of time, low ratings in certain areas could be personally discouraging. It is a question of the cup being half empty or half full. Others were elated to see the same scores because they viewed them from the perspective of where they had started only six months before.

Some members of the school generated different ratings for the same program components. The process of sharing scores and then explaining the basis for the scores was generative. It helped to make explicit many implicit assumptions about people's perceptions of progress and how ratings were made. It also helped to establish norms about what certain figures (and words) meant. For example, in an administrative group, two of the staff members rated communication at a 3 and the senior administrator rated it as a 6. They all agreed about the level of miscommunication that had occurred in the school, including the details of specific incidents. However, the senior administrator was viewing communication from a broader perspective, explaining that "as far as I know people feel free to speak their minds in an open and supportive environment." They agreed with his assessment of the overall climate of communication, better understood the discrepancy in their ratings (instead of thinking he was not in touch with specific communication problems in the school), and reframed their own thinking to assume this larger perspective without invalidating their own interpretation of daily interaction and communication. The entire group also agreed that this reframing did not preclude them from taking steps to improve communication.

This exercise helped some individuals recalibrate their ratings—either in terms of actual scores or adjectives used to describe the status of program operations. Good, bad, or indifferent—these were the first formal ratings of critical components of our various programs throughout the school. This provided a useful baseline from which to plan for the future. One of the most difficult elements of this process was to resist the temptation to rush into solutions and to focus on describing strengths and weaknesses in terms of these ratings (as well as providing documentation for high or low ratings).

Students have also been engaged in this process. Students in the Masters of Arts in Business program gravitated toward this self-evaluation approach earlier than other members of the school. One student provided an excellent example of how the recalibration process can work in an unexpected manner. Typically this approach focuses on how a program (not an individual) is doing; however, some students have used it to monitor their own individual performance within the contexts of the program and of their lives in general. One student gave herself a 3 rating in terms of her ability to plan. I asked her to explain why she gave herself that rating—in other words, what evidence did she have to document *even* a 3 rating and what evidence did she have to document *only* a 3 rating. She explained that she was not satisfied with her decision to eliminate a number of extraneous activities in her life so that she could focus on setting up a business, keep a tight schedule on required activities, enroll in this business program to learn about the nuts and bolts of business operations, prepare to raise capital for her business, and begin initial market analyses concerning the products she wanted to sell. The rest of the group laughed, suggesting that she might have been a little hard on herself and that the low rating in planning may have been inappropriate. A higher rating in personal planning was warranted, while a low rating in implementation may have been more appropriate. By exploring the basis for the rating in a supportive group setting, she was able to make a more informed, intelligent, and appropriate assessment. In addition, this process enables people to learn about each other and construct worlds of meaning together—a fundamental step in building a future with a common vision.

Students and faculty of the School for Transformative Learning's on-line Ph.D. program have also used empowerment evaluation to evaluate a program in which students take courses from their homes and offices through a computer network system. In this "virtual classroom," faculty post assignments on the computer, and students respond to the assignments and comment on each other's work. Faculty and students engage in a dialogue about fundamental concepts and concerns related to their course work but rarely meet face-to-face. A strong sense of community is created as faculty and students share thousands of pages of information and insight through computer links. This asynchronous approach to education enables everyone to work and manage their educational and personal lives on their own schedules. A continuous dialogue about course topics and issues is generated and documented on-line, even though students post assignments at different times and in different time zones throughout the United States and Canada.

During one of the face-to-face week-long seminars (at the Headlands Institute located on the Pacific Ocean on the other side of the Golden Gate Bridge), empowerment evaluation provided a useful tool to shape the evaluative component of this experience. Students rated the program on a 1 to 10 point scale, with a resulting range of 7 to 9, a mode of 8 and 9, and a mean of 8.09. This exercise demonstrated how important the norming process is—as people define what they mean by their ratings. For example, one on-line student explained her moderately low assessment of the program (a 7) by explaining that it was based on her Australian background, where 50 percent (or a 5) was a passing grade. This made her implicit evaluative meaning scheme explicit and helped others understand why she came up with that rating and how to interpret it. As we went around the circle, we found that while ratings were comparable, the documentation and basis for the ratings were significantly different. For example, one student gave the program a very high rating because it met personal needs of community building; another rated it highly because it exceeded his expectations about what ethnography could do and because he was impressed by how quickly it could be applied to real-world situations (see Fetterman, 1989, 1993). This facilitated a discussion about the different levels and components of the program and the students' experiences. This type of inquiry into the assessment process—looking at the quality of the quantified rating system—places fundamental assumptions on the table, helps individuals establish group norms, and provides a more solid foundation from which to build for the future.

Oakland Public School System

Cabinet members from the superintendent's office in the Oakland Public School System used an empowerment evaluation approach to determine how well the district was achieving the goals of its five-year education plan. They devoted three full work days to this task and generated a status report on over 600 activities listed in the original educational plan. In the process of conducting this exercise, they realized that much had changed since the plan was first initiated. Some tasks were no longer relevant; others were subsumed by other activities. Taking stock helped to focus on the critical current concerns—and to remove much of the clutter. Another byproduct of this exercise was a thoughtful session focusing on redistributing the remaining relevant tasks. Comments from cabinet members included "I think this task belongs in your department now that you oversee the newly merged departments" and "I hate to say it but I guess I should take that one (task) because it currently falls under my department." They were cooperating in a forthright manner as they tried to make sense of all of these tasks and responsibilities. According to one cabinet member, "this is a marked change from our normal routine of passing the buck and dodging assignments and responsibilities." Once this step was completed, they were able to prioritize significant district goals.

Members then rated the concerns, which ranged from school climate to ethical standards and values, and from leadership to student academic outcomes. After much heated discussion, school climate was rated between a 4 and a 5. A few administrators thought it was in the 8 or 9 category. This was modified by an administrator who mentioned an article in the morning paper highlighting a racially-motivated act of violence in one of his schools. This group norming process was effective and efficient, as each member learned how to use data to validate a comment or rating.

Ethical standards received the lowest rating because of a well publicized scandal. Ironically, the scandal had occurred some time before the session. Few of the administrators thought there was an ethical problem at the time of the rating, but they thought the district's reputation in the community was still suffering from a breach of confidence. The highest rating was for community and parent involvement; administrators quickly provided documentation for that rating, ranging from specific programs to actual attendance figures.

Student academic outcomes received one of the lowest ratings. Surprisingly, there was little argument or discussion about it. Everyone knew and was concerned about the problem of student outcomes. However, once the ratings were shared with everyone the salience of this issue re-emerged. The impact of seeing their own low rating validated by group consensus helped to "shake them up," as one Cabinet member phrased it, and revitalized their commitment to action—to setting new and higher goals for student outcomes.

STEP TWO: SETTING GOALS

After program participants have rated their program's performance and provided documentation to support that rating, they are asked how highly they would like to rate their program in the future. Then they are asked what goals they would like to set to warrant the future rating.

These goals should be established in conjunction with supervisors and clients to ensure relevance from both perspectives. In addition, goals should be realistic, taking into consideration such factors as initial conditions, motivation, resources, and program dynamics.

It is important that goals be related to the program's activities, talents, resources, and scope of capability. One problem with traditional external evaluation is that programs have been given grandiose goals or long-term goals that participants could only contribute to in some indirect manner. There was no link between their daily activities and ultimate long-term program outcomes in terms of these goals. In empowerment evaluation, program participants are encouraged to select intermediate goals that are directly linked to their daily activities. These activities can then be linked to larger more diffuse goals, creating a clear chain of outcomes.

Program participants are encouraged to be creative in establishing their goals. A brainstorming approach is often used to generate a new set of goals. Individuals are asked to state what they think the program should be doing. The list generated from this activity is refined, reduced, and made realistic after the brainstorming phase, through a critical review and consensual agreement process.

Just as the list of program components that can be identified and rated is endless, so there are an equally bewildering number of goals to strive for at any given time. A group begins to establish goals based on this initial review of their program, and they realize quickly that a consensus is required to determine the most significant issues on which to focus. These are chosen according to significance to the operation of the program, such as teaching; timing or urgency, such as recruitment or budget issues; and vision, including community building and learning processes.

Goal setting can be a slow process when program participants have a heavy work schedule. Sensitivity to the pacing of this effort is essential. Additional tasks of any kind and for any purpose may be perceived as simply another burden when everyone is fighting to keep their heads above water.

School for Transformative Learning

At the School for Transformative Learning, after faculty and staff completed a rating of their programs, each program group focused on their own plan or proposal for the future. The Integral Studies Doctoral Program identified four areas to focus on immediately: admissions and recruitment, curriculum, faculty resources, and research. There were many other categories identified during the brainstorming period; however, these topics emerged as the most pressing and significant items that required immediate attention. The group decided to return to the remaining issues at a later date, after steps are initiated in these areas and the workload is more routinized.

Instead of stating that we wanted to move from a 5 to an 8 rating in a certain category, we stated certain goals we wanted to achieve in some of these categories, such as a more streamlined administrative system to handle recruitment and admissions. (Numbers were a useful shorthand for communicating our initial impressions, but words—particularly operationalized terms or phrases—are equally powerful and appropriate measuring tools.) We quickly moved from that stage into specific objectives and strategies that were under our control to improve our performance in the areas of greatest concern at that time.

Oakland Public School System

In the Oakland Public School System, nurses generated extremely positive but omnibus goals, such as helping children. During our discussions, facilitators promptly suggested that everyone wanted to help children; the issue was how do we want to help children given our expertise. These discussions clarified and crystallized specific goals, such as identifying the life circumstances and health of the children in their district, as well as more focused action-oriented goals, such as improving dental hygiene and reducing teenage pregnancy. Once again the greatest difficulty at this stage (aside from focusing on specific goals) was trying to focus on goals rather than prematurely jumping into solutions. Educators and administrators wanted to reduce the dropout rate. However, the goals seemed insurmountable and complex since it was a function of so many variables and conditions. Time was required to sort out the appropriate goals and intermediate objectives of various groups that might be reinforcing and interwoven to reduce the dropout rate. Individual programs identified what they might be able to do to contribute to this effort given their resources, areas of expertise, and type of interaction with students and the school system—as compared with a top-down division and set of tasks that are imposed on individual programs. This led to creative discussions about integrated services, ranging from health to academic counseling, and provided a more integrated picture of each problem and ways to respond to it that contrasted with the traditional piecemeal approaches of the past. Drafting a picture of intermediate objectives, as well as multiple goals and multiple levels of goals, made the effort more rational, comprehensible, and conceivable.

STEP THREE: DEVELOPING STRATEGIES

Program participants are also responsible for selecting and developing strategies to accomplish program objectives. The same process of brainstorming, critical review, and consensual agreement is used to establish a set of strategies. These strategies are reviewed on a routine basis to determine their effectiveness and appropriateness. Determining appropriate strategies, in consultation with sponsors and clients, is an essential part of the empowering process. Program participants are typically the most knowledgeable about their own jobs, and this approach acknowledges and utilizes that expertise, in the process putting them back in the "drivers seat."

Oakland Public School System

The Oakland Public School System had a five-year plan, but its goals and strategies were so general and positive that is was difficult for anyone to argue with them or respond to them. Using the empowerment evaluation approach, program staff members were able to construct goals and strategies that were tailored to their programs and still remain in conformity with the overarching five-year plan. For example, the five-year plan was concerned with addressing the "life circumstances" of all children to facilitate their educational experience. Nurses generated specific goals (discussed above) that fit within that framework. In addition, they generated specific strategies to approximate those goals, including conducting schoolwide surveys of the health conditions at each school in the district to determine, for example, the percentage of students with asthma at each school. Administrators were favorably disposed toward this strategy because it would help them use district funds more effectively. Instead of providing a general health education program for everyone, they could provide specific educational programs tailored to specific populations with specific needs within the district—based on this knowledge.

School for Transformative Learning

The faculty in the Integral Studies Doctorate Program of the School for Transformative Learning have mapped out specific strategies and prioritized tasks to address specific problems and aim toward specific goals. This may seem a normal process for an academic institution, but in this case faculty and staff are developing a new series of programs while implementing them—which is like building a track while you are running on it. This added degree of difficulty makes it critical that evaluation be a part of planning and operations because there is virtually no time for it as an add-on to operations. For example, in planning for faculty resources, the sequential flow of the idealized curriculum through three years was mapped out to determine what faculty resources would be required to support this intellectually engaging (and labor intensive) program. Similarly, appropriate student and faculty evaluations are being integrated into the curriculum so that it is a normal part of the feedback loop—to enable us to improve the program as we develop. This formative evaluation mode is an explicit strategy to help us become a learning organization, as well as meeting accreditation requirements to self-evaluate.

South Africa

Strategy setting can be a highly creative process. For example, in an impoverished black community in South Africa, one of the health prevention program specialists with whom I worked (who was recruited literally from the streets in the community) developed an ingenious strategy to reach a community-based health program goal. He was in charge of a smoking cessation program in the community. It was not particularly successful; recruiting participants and retaining them was extremely difficult. He interviewed participants who dropped out of the program and heard the usual excuses: sickness, conflict with work schedule, too busy looking for work, and not an important problem. (It is important to keep in mind that murder, theft, disease, and pestilence are a normal part of the backdrop of this community.)

He realized that he might be able to recruit more community members (particularly the ones who dropped out of the program) by letting them know who completed the program. He borrowed a camcorder from the local university and videotaped graduates of the program. Many people did not have electricity in their homes, so he invited them to a social in a community building and showed them the videotape. Former dropouts recognized the graduates and said, "if they can do it, I can too." This strategy was extremely successful in recruiting, admitting, and maintaining participants in the program. This was an ingenious strategy to reach his goal concerning the program, which in turn-contributed to community health goals. His smoking cessation program, along with many other programs including desalination and various sanitation programs, contributed to the larger goal of improving the community health overall[1]. Each program worked within their sphere of control. Communication and trust between rival groups in the community led to cooperation and a form of integrated services for community members. Communication and trust between rival groups in the community led to cooperation and a form of integrated services for community members.

STEP FOUR: DOCUMENTING PROGRESS TOWARD GOALS

In Step Four, program participants are asked what type of documentation is required to monitor progress toward their goals. This is a critical step. Each form of documentation is scrutinized for relevance to avoid devoting time to collecting information that will not be useful or relevant. Program participants are asked to explain how a given form of documentation is related to specific program goals. This review process is difficult and time consuming but prevents wasted time and disillusionment at the end of the process. In addition, documentation must be credible and rigorous if it is to withstand the criticisms that this evaluation is self-serving.

South Africa

Members of the community outside Cape Town established the same goal of reducing teenage pregnancy as the Oakland Public School System. This community had impressive statistics about teenage pregnancy in the community; they also had a teenage pregnancy prevention program. However, they were disheartened that the teenage pregnancy figures had remained constant. After much discussion on this topic, it became apparent that they were judging the effectiveness of the program on community-wide figures and patterns. It was necessary to readjust and reframe the evaluative process so that it focused on intermediate objectives and outcomes more directly related to the program, such as the behavior of participating teenagers. Once they described and evaluated the behavior of teenagers who participated in the program, the effectiveness of the program (and the willingness to continue it) became more compelling. In this case, they were using the wrong kind of documentation (figures too far removed from the program treatment or the participants who participated in the program) to evaluate the effectiveness of their program. Over time a comparison of program outcomes with the impact on the entire community would be useful.

One of the most common concerns raised about documenting self-evaluations in South Africa is the issue of illiteracy. How can people conduct an evaluation if they are illiterate (numerically and otherwise)? Pictures and symbols speak volumes. Drawings of toilets and outhouses juxtaposed against drawings of people going to the bathroom on the ground are used in surveys to determine the number of people who use toilets. Drawings of women with their breasts exposed (to nurse children) are used to determine the frequency of breast feeding. Community health workers use ticks and scratch marks to tally up numbers. Community health workers also use actual chocolate cakes to communicate how many interviewees know how to use simple anti-diarrhea medications—they simply cut the cakes in half to indicate 50 percent (see van der Walt & Hoogendoorn, 1993.)

School for Transformative Learning

In the School for Transformative Learning, faculty, staff members, and students are making a concerted effort to identify existing forms of documentation to avoid adding to the existing workload. A new school cannot afford the luxury of a complex, labor-intensive, evaluation project; evaluation must be part of the normal routine. In addition, data that are already collected concerning recruitment, admissions, and teacher evaluations are useful measures to establish baselines and monitor progress. There is no point in reinventing the wheel—and there are no time or resources to do so. Most programs have useful documentation that is often overlooked in terms of its utility for evaluative purposes, ranging from archival material (budget and admissions records) to student and teacher evaluations.

THE POWER AND SIMPLICITY OF SELF-EVALUATION

Program participants determine the type of evaluation they desire and their own goals and strategies for accomplishing those goals. They also determine the type of information needed to document progress toward their goals. They are encouraged to think of this process in the same light as a self-evaluation in their own performance appraisal. They need to select relevant and realistic goals—setting unrealistic expectations can doom a program evaluation to failure. However, the goals should not be unrealistically deflated, or they will not appear credible to a discerning and critical public. A program sponsor, like a supervisor, can distinguish between fluff and substance, and a poor impression is difficult to overcome in the future. However, a rigorous self-evaluation from the onset sets the tone of high expectations and high standards for individuals and the program.

Some of the most powerful community health projects in squatter townships near Cape Town are designed to prevent illness and empower community members. Participatory evaluation places the evaluation process in the hands of the people it is designed to help. They learn a skill that is generalizable and essential as they face the process of reconstructing an entire nation. Evaluation becomes a part of their daily lives, feeding back information into their programs and helping them improve program practice. (See Linney and Wandersman [1991] for an excellent self-evaluation manual focusing on alcohol and other drug prevention programs.)

This is a valuable process for any program. The nurses and administrators in the Oakland School System have also learned how to make evaluation a part of their daily routine—instead of a parasitic add—on to their daily activities. Similarly, both out of necessity and personal commitment, the faculty, staff members, and students in the School for Transformative Learning are becoming engaged in an unending process of self-reflection to improve program practice and facilitate the academic mission, which in this case is transformative learning.

MECHANICAL CONCERNS

Meetings

People need to be given time or must make time to meet with each other to discuss goals, strategies, and documentation. Meetings lose meaning when they are held for the sake of meeting. However, when there is a common focus—to improve current practice—and a specific agenda, meetings can build on strengths, resolve problems, and create a dynamic learning community. The overall group or division should have periodic meetings, and smaller groups or subgroups should hold more frequent meetings focused on addressing very specific common concerns.

These meetings can be conducted face-to-face, on electronic bulletin boards or through e-mail messages, through interactive video, or other creative means appropriate to the group or culture. Meetings will have stages of development, from embryonic stages characterized by confusion, uncertainty, mistrust, ineffectiveness (from a goal or task-oriented perspective), and miscommunication to a mid-range as people get to know each other and begin to share common understandings and objectives, to a more mature state of effective communication and collaboration in which independent threads of a group are woven together to create a tapestry of communication and culture.

Facilitation teams of program participants are needed to help guide the process, keep things on track, and maintain the momentum of the effort. "Outsiders" can help to guide specific components and provide technical expertise, but program participants have to own the entire effort if it is to be meaningful, sustainable, and successful. You cannot empower someone; to attempt to do so is disempowering—fostering dependency instead of self-determination. Program participants must want to control their own destiny and take charge of the specific steps required to do so. Facilitation teams of program participants should have both facilitation and analytical skills. An individual with expertise in group dynamics is instrumental in assuring that all voices are heard. This individual (or set of individuals) can also enhance clarity in communication by serving as a mirror—reflecting comments back to participants to ensure that they are accurately understood by the group. However, there is more to the process than group facilitation. Analytical skills are also required to ensure that the tough questions are raised, such as "how do you define that" and "how else can we interpret that?" In addition, some expertise is needed initially to turn projects into researchable tasks. Some individuals possess equal amounts of both skills. However, there is some benefit to finding individuals that complement each other in this area. Two or more individuals are more likely to be effective than one, especially with a diverse population. Gender or ethnicity may play a significant role in building rapport, facilitation of the group, credibility, and cultural awareness. However, these are characteristics that are "in addition to" not instead of the underlying facilitation and analytical skills required to help stimulate discussion and assist a group in the development of its own self-evaluation. Teams can also debrief each other after particularly difficult or unsuccessful program meetings.

Consensual Validation

Empowerment evaluation is a social event. It relies on a group dynamic from beginning to end, including the difficulties, power plays, personalities, and inertia associated with group interactions. The human bonds created in this process are powerful and can be emotionally rewarding and intellectually intoxicating. The highs and lows associated with empowerment evaluation or any participatory evaluation are not permanent or static states. Empowerment evaluation is a continual challenge to negotiate and validate understandings. Sharing ratings in a group, for example, is a process requiring negotiation. Attempts to reach a consensus, although initially time-consuming and laborious, help to establish a shared understanding of what is or is not valid or meaningful to the group. For example, participants who rate their program success at a moderately high level, such as a 7, may aspire to a self rating of 9 or 10. Individuals who have a slightly inflated rating (even after self-corrective measures discussed above) such as an 8 out of 10, learn to stretch the points in the scale and may aspire to a 9.4 or 9.2 rating in the future. The process of defining what their scores mean and how they arrived at them (and what type of documentation they use to support those ratings) provides a common basis for communication and interaction. During this process, people are negotiating meaning, creating meaning, and sharing reference points together.

Common values are established over time in the process of taking stock, setting goals, collecting relevant and credible data, developing strategies, documenting progress toward program goals—according to an agreed upon measuring stick and evaluation. This common bond builds communities.

CONCLUSION

These basic steps are designed to help program participants internalize evaluation as part of their program planning and management. Each step is illustrated by case examples drawn from work conducted in the School for Transformative Learning at the California Institute of Integral Studies in San Francisco, the Oakland Public School System in California, and townships around Cape Town in South Africa. In addition, relevant mechanical concerns have been discussed including the role of meetings, facilitation teams, and consensual validation. Ideally, this approach is both liberating—freeing participants from the status quo of evaluation and operation—and illuminating, as participants expand their awareness of what is possible in their own universe.

NOTE

1. This example highlights the direct physical health benefits of empowerment evaluation strategies. Wallerstein (1992) presents an excellent health rationale for empowerment strategies in general which apply to this situation on a meta- or socio-political level. According to Wallerstein, "Empowerment becomes a strategy that directly addresses lack of control over destiny. Through challenging social and physical risk factors in a collective setting, people gain a belief that they can control their worlds, a sense of their community, an ability to work together to acquire resources, and an actual transformation of socio-political conditions."

22. DELIBERATIVE DEMOCRATIC EVALUATION IN PRACTICE

ERNEST R. HOUSE and KENNETH R. HOWE

We begin this chapter with a brief sketch of the deliberative democratic approach to evaluation (elaborated in House and Howe, forthcoming). We then turn to several illustrations of how such a view might be incorporated in evaluation studies. Many evaluators have conducted studies based on their own intuitions and approaches which are consistent with the principles we advocate here. There are many ways to implement such democratic guidelines.

A SKETCH OF THE DELIBERATIVE DEMOCRATIC VIEW

The position we advance is one of inclusive, dialogical deliberation in evaluation. By inclusive, we mean that all relevant interests are represented in the evaluation and given full expression. Representation of views and interests should not be dominated or distorted by power imbalances, such as powerful interests curtailing the less powerful in the evaluation.

The approach is also dialogical. Stakeholders and evaluators, and sometimes audiences, engage in dialogues of various types in the evaluation process, anything from surveys to face-to-face meetings. The purpose is to make certain that stakeholder interests, opinions, and ideas are not misrepresented. The stakeholders' authentic interests and views are represented; stakeholders have "voice."

Third, the evaluation conclusions should emerge from deliberation, from careful reasoning, reflection, and debate. By deliberation we mean the way evaluators reason reflectively about relevant issues in order to draw conclusions. Deliberation is used broadly to mean either one person reasoning alone or a group deliberating jointly.

D.L. Stufflebeam, G.F. Madaus and T. Kellaghan (eds.). EVALUATION MODELS. Copyright © 2000. Kluwer Academic Publishers. Boston. All rights reserved.

The evaluation should not be marred by inadequate reflection. Deliberation ensures good judgment.

When are inclusion, dialogical, and deliberative considerations relevant? The answer is: at all stages of the study—in the inception, design, conduct, analysis, synthesis, write-up, presentation, and discussion of findings. There are many different ways in which these three dimensions of evaluation can be achieved. At the same time, it should be recognised that these considerations may conflict with one another occasionally. Sometimes certain types of inclusion may interfere with deliberation, or inclusion may make dialogue more difficult. But all three dimensions are necessary. If the democratic and dialogical dimensions are adequate but the deliberative is deficient, we might have all relevant interests represented, but have inadequate consideration resulting in erroneous conclusions. If the democratic and deliberative dimensions are adequate but the dialogical is missing, we might misrepresent some interests and positions, resulting in an inauthentic evaluation based on false interests and issues. If the dialogical and deliberative dimensions are adequate, but not all relevant interests are included, the evaluation might neglect important stakeholder groups.

The deliberative democratic view conducts evaluation from an explicit democratic framework and places a responsibility on evaluators to uphold democratic values. Evaluators should use procedures that incorporate the views of insiders and outsiders, give voice to the marginal and excluded, employ reasoned criteria in extended deliberation, and engage in dialogical interactions with significant audiences and stakeholders.

It is obvious that stakeholder groups in fact do not have equal power in evaluations and that dialogue among them is not fully democratic in the sense of being undistorted by power relationships, hidden or overt. Evaluators should strive to remedy this problem by ensuring that free and unobstructed deliberations are carried out in the conduct of evaluations, including planning, design, and interpretation. Evaluators should not assume that equal status is given to every group opinion. In fact, some stakeholder views may be ruled out on the grounds they are undemocratic, e.g., racist or sexist.

Of course, evaluators conduct their work in concrete social circumstances, and we recognize that the deliberative democratic view is too idealized to be implemented straightforwardly in the world as it exists. An uncompromising commitment to such an ideal would be impractical. However, because the ideal cannot be fully attained does not mean that it cannot be a guide.

Evaluators should not ignore imbalances of power or pretend dialogue about evaluation is open when it is not. To do so is to endorse the existing social and power arrangements implicitly and evade professional responsibility. It may be that the existing power arrangements are acceptable, but the evaluator should consider this issue explicitly. The solution is to face the issues as best we can and adopt a position of democratic deliberation as an ideal for handling value claims. In this conception, the evaluator is not a passive bystander, an innocent facilitator, or a philosopher king who makes decisions for others, but rather a conscientious professional who adheres to a set of defensible, carefully considered principles for enhancing inclusion, dialogue, and deliberation.

The deliberative democratic view is not an evaluation model which prescribes explicitly how to conduct an evaluation. It is more a middle-range theory which suggests that studies should be unbiased (that is, objective and impartial regarding facts and values). Bias itself can never be fully eliminated, but there are many specific ways of reducing biases. Any number of approaches or models of evaluation or individual studies could fit our middle-range deliberative democratic requirements. In fact, several evaluators have advocated practices which are consistent in important ways with the principles we embrace here, though they might differ in other respects; e.g., Stake's responsive evaluation (Chapter 18, this volume), MacDonald's (1977) democratic evaluation, Proppe's (1979) dialectical evaluation, Scriven's (1980b) objective value judgements, Greene's (1997) advocacy evaluation, as well as Fischer (1980), Weiss (1983), Bryk (1983), Mark and Shotland (1987), Nevo (1994), Garraway (1995), Karlsson (1996), Fetterman (1996), Alkin (1997), Schwandt (1997), and Cousins and Whitmore (1998).

Karlsson (1996) has conducted an evaluation which illustrates many of our concerns about dialogue. He evaluated a five-year program, which provided care and leisure services for children aged 9–12 in Eskilstuna, Sweden, which aimed for more efficient organization of such services and the introduction of new pedagogical content, to be implemented through new School Age Care Centers. Politicians wanted to know how services could be organized, with what pedagogical content, what the centers would cost, and what children and parents wanted the centers to be, in essence a formative evaluation.

A first step was to identify stakeholder groups and choose representatives from them, including politicians, managers, professionals, parents, and children. Karlsson then surveyed parents and interviewed other stakeholder groups on these issues:

Politicians—What is the aim of the program?
Parents—What do parents want the program to be?
Management—What is required to manage such a program?
Staff union—What do the staff unions require?
Cooperating professionals—What expectations are there from others who work in this field?
Children—What expectations do the children have?

The collected data were summarized and communicated to the stakeholder groups in the condensed form of four different metaphors of ideal types of school age care centers. The metaphors for the centers were "the work shop," "the classroom," "the coffee bar," and "the living room."

In the second stage of the evaluation the focus was on the implementation of the centers, twenty-five altogether, serving five hundred students. In contrast to the "top-down" approach of the first stage, this part of the evaluation employed a "bottom-up" approach by first asking children how they experienced the centers.

Next, parents and cooperating professionals were interviewed, then managers and politicians. Dialogue was achieved by presenting to later groups what the previously interviewed groups had said.

In the first two stages the dialogue admitted distance and space among participants. In the third stage the goal was face-to-face interaction and the establishment of a more mutual and reciprocal relationship. The aim was to develop genuine and critical dialogue that could stimulate new thoughts among different stakeholder groups and bring conflicts into open discussion. Four meetings were arranged with representatives from stakeholder groups. To ensure that everyone could have a say, four professional actors played short scenes illustrating critical questions and conflicts to be discussed. The actors involved the audiences in dialogues through scenarios showing the essence of problems (identified from the collected data), and enlisted audiences to help the actors solve or develop new ways to see the problems. About 250 representatives participated in four performances, which were documented by video camera and edited to 20-minute videos. These videos were used in later meetings with parents, politicians, and staff.

In Karlsson's view, the aim of such critical evaluation dialogues should be to develop deeper understandings of program limitations and possibilities, especially for disadvantaged groups. In this process, the important thing is to enable the powerless and unjustly treated stakeholders to have influence. The evaluator has two responsibilities in making critical dialogue possible: developing a theoretical perspective on the program and cultivating critical inquiry. "Theoretical perspective" means not a complete model or explanation, but a framework that puts the evaluation in historical and political context for participants (Haug, 1996). With such a perspective, the evaluation becomes not only a matter of putting together and presenting the opinions and the standpoints of the interest groups but also developing a better theoretical understanding of the context and the problems of the program. In this, the evaluator brings a critical perspective to bear. In Karlsson's view, the difficulty with dialogue as a strategy is that it demands that every interest group have enough resources for participation. There is a risk of achieving participation only by those who are resource-powerful.

ELEMENTS OF A DELIBERATIVE DEMOCRATIC VIEW

We operationalize our deliberative democratic view as ten questions to be asked of evaluations: Whose interests are represented? Are major stakeholders represented? Are any excluded? Are there serious power imbalances? Are there procedures to control the imbalances? How do people participate in the evaluation? How authentic is their participation? How involved is their interaction? Is there reflective deliberation? How considered and extended is the deliberation? We discuss our basic questions one at a time and point to examples of evaluations that exemplify our criteria.

Whose Interests Are Represented?

Ordinarily the evaluation is shaped between the evaluator and the client, the sponsor of the evaluation. The evaluator must take cognizance of whose interests are being represented. It goes without saying that poor people and those without power—the presumed beneficiaries of the programs—rarely sponsor evaluations. Those who are ill do not typically sponsor evaluations of medical services (though philanthropic organizations might), nor do the homeless shape evaluations of welfare.

Typically, the evaluation is sponsored by a government agency and shaped by medical or welfare or education professionals. These participants all affect the design of the study, and evaluators must be aware of whose interests are shaping the evaluation. The concerns and interests of all groups are not necessarily the same.

For example, in Karlsson's evaluation, he identified the major stakeholders and their concerns through extensive dialogue. Politicians, the sponsors, were concerned most with the economic efficiency of the program, managers with how the program could be directed, professionals with how the goals could be realized, parents with the care and security their children received, and the youths themselves about maintaining contact with their peers. All these concerns were legitimate issues for shaping the evaluation, and the evaluator must consider them in the design. Clearly, not all can be met fully. Choices must be made.

Are Major Stakeholders Represented?

It is a requirement of deliberative democratic evaluation that all major stakeholders should be included somehow. Democracies gain legitimacy by including the interests of all. Of course, in evaluation studies we cannot include the interests of every single individual stakeholder who might be affected. Such inclusion is impractical; studies always have financial and time limitations. One compromise is to include the interests of only major stakeholders in the program, that is, those whose interests are most at issue. Such selection requires judgments by evaluators as to who this might be, just as professional judgments are required in other aspects of the study.

Often we can use representation rather than the direct involvement of every single stakeholder. For example, Alkin et al. (1984) evaluated agricultural extension in eight Caribbean countries. The key stakeholders were the sponsor, the US Agency for International Development; the University of West Indies Project staff; agricultural extension officials in participating countries; farmers and their representatives; and American academics involved in the project. The evaluation team was chosen to represent stakeholders by including an American agricultural economist, a West Indies academic, an Ohio State academic, and a UCLA evaluation expert. The West Indies participant assured one important stakeholder group of the trustworthiness of the evaluation, and the economist assured the U.S. Agency for International Development that important technical issues would be addressed. Including stakeholders in the evaluation team is one way of addressing the issue, though by no means the only way.

Are Any Major Stakeholders Excluded?

Another important question is whether major stakeholder groups are not included that should have been. There have been many studies conducted in which not even the interests of the presumed beneficiaries of the program are included. Such an omission biases the study, or else there must be good reasons why these interests are not included. (Perhaps the program is in its early trials and is too rudimentary to see how it affects beneficiaries.)

If major stakeholders are not included, it is incumbent on evaluators to rectify this. For example, Hahn, Greene, and Waterman (1994) evaluated eleven public policy education projects funded by the Kellogg Foundation. They held semi-annual working conferences for project personnel in which discussions about the projects were encouraged (Greene, 1997). The evaluators deliberately represented the interests of citizens who were to be informed by these activities and who were not present at the meetings, thus raising questions with the program staff about the direction of their efforts as it affected the public. Sometimes evaluators must represent the views of missing stakeholders, if necessary, even though it is better to have these groups represent their own interests where possible.

Are There Serious Power Imbalances?

Evaluators must recognize when there may be strong power imbalances that bias the design and findings of the study, just as they must recognize when other forms of bias affect the findings improperly. Improper selection of criteria, improper weighting of criteria, and slanting conclusions and recommendations in certain directions are ways in which these power imbalances are likely to be manifested.

Of course, there are power imbalances in every human activity, and it is not the evaluator's duty to correct all these. Rather it is the evaluator's duty to make sure strong power imbalances do not distort the study's findings, not an easy task. We must identify where these imbalances threaten the integrity of the study. For example, in Karlsson's study, to facilitate dialogue and deliberation, he arranged a critical dialogue among all stakeholder groups in face to face meetings in which participants considered the findings. Here he had to be concerned about how power imbalances affected the dialogue and deliberation. In this case we might expect that the politicians would dominate the discussions and that the children would be least able to represent their own interests. We can have major stakeholders represented and still not achieve proper deliberation. His solution was to hire actors who actively involved the less powerful and more reticent stakeholders in dialogue.

Are There Procedures To Control The Imbalances?

Imagine a class in which one student does all the talking. Ideally, teachers want all students to have a chance to participate. It is incumbent on teachers to find ways to control such imbalances, and good teachers know how to do this through various mechanisms. Likewise, power imbalances need to be redressed by the evaluator. This is particularly true in qualitative studies in which some individuals or groups provide most of the information. The information itself can be seriously out of kilter if some dominate. Evaluators need ways of controlling power imbalances to achieve proper deliberation.

In their review of participatory evaluation, Cousins and Whitmore (1998) say, "In our experience it has been those participants or stakeholders with power who have tended to resist evaluation findings which might be viewed as critical and significant. They hold the power to quash the report or to reshape it in ways that meet their own needs" (1998, p. 20). Cousins and Whitmore raise ethical questions as to who owns the findings, who dictates use, how much misuse the evaluator can stand, and how the evaluator draws the line.

How Do People Participate In The Evaluation?

The mode of participation is critical. The difficulties of communicating with stakeholders is explored in Stake's (1986) analysis of the Cities-in-Schools evaluation. The evaluators of this program simply could not conceive how to deal with the many stakeholders, and the evaluation suffered accordingly. How participation is organized is nearly as important as who is selected to participate.

For primary goods such as food and shelter, perhaps extensive dialogue with beneficiaries is not as necessary as in other cases. Most groups want their share of primary goods. However, even in the case of primary goods, it may make quite a difference to participants how the service is delivered and what it consists of. Dialogue may be important for understanding the issues. And for complex social services like education or welfare, dialogue is usually necessary since programs and policies can be defined and delivered in so many different ways and affect groups differentially.

There can also be improper participation. In evaluating a pilot program to reduce the dropout rate in Ontario, Cousins (Cousins & Earl, 1995) met with the program steering committee, mostly school administrators, to design the study (and recommended they add teachers to the steering group). Stakeholders were given interview training, conducted interviews, and coded the data. The evaluator drafted the report, which was revised by teachers before it went to the steering committee. From this experience Cousins concluded that it is better *not* to involve participants in highly quantitative data analysis (Alkin, 1998). It may be that participants simply can't handle some kinds of analysis and it is improper to expect them to. Democratic deliberation allows for the fact that in a complex, specialized society, expertise may be critical. Specialists may have to perform certain tasks in order to have proper deliberation.

How Authentic Is Their Participation?

Whether participation is through mailed surveys, focus groups, or personal interviews makes a huge difference as to its authenticity. Who is present, who sees the results, and who asks questions are critical. MacDonald and Sanger (1982) used to ask government officials: "What causes you to lie awake at night and worry?" Having just provided the information that their occupational role required, which typically meant protecting their organization, government officials were able to step out of role and give quite different assessments of the situation as individuals speaking personally.

In an ethnographic study, Dougherty (1993) evaluated a welfare-to-work training program in which she established close, long-term contacts with welfare participants on an intensive personal level, thus providing a more authentic interpretation as to how beneficiaries of the program reacted to their training. Participants had far more complex reactions to the program than authorities anticipated and faced different problems than the program addressed. Of course, such intensive work is not called for in every study, but evaluators must be concerned about the authenticity of the data they are considering.

How Involved Is Their Interaction?

Typically, we would want stakeholders to be extensively involved in the study at different stages, depending on the kind of study. This means plenty of opportunity to engage in critical dialogues, to fully express views and reveal important information. In one of the authors' first evaluations, he mailed questionnaires to all Chicago high schools inquiring about the extent of their services for gifted students. The survey forms came back from the Chicago central office all completed exactly the same way and all bound up together. The evaluator decided it was necessary to involve participants in a different manner in order to get an authentic response.

Participation can be very extensive. Pursley (1996) evaluated a network of four family support centers in New York in which program participants and paraprofessional staff were included as partners in the evaluation. They helped develop the evaluation questions and instruments and helped collect and analyze the data. In particular, the evaluation sought to include the contributions of lower-level staff (Greene, 1997). Involving stakeholders in the technical aspects of the evaluation risks a compromise between representation of views and managing the technical procedures properly. There are trade-offs. We want all interests properly represented in the evaluation and we want proper methodology to produce unbiased findings.

Is There Reflective Deliberation?

It is easy enough to see that evaluators must consider all aspects of the data, various types of data, and how the analyses play out. Evaluation findings should be well considered and deliberated on. Unfortunately, sufficient deliberation about findings is often lacking in the hurried final phase of producing an overdue report. Perhaps misfits between the data and the findings are the most common errors in studies generally. The problem is compounded when many stakeholder groups are involved in an active manner. There is seldom enough time. More satisfactory forms of participation have yet to be invented.

For example, Morris and Stronach (1993) constructed a set of findings in summary narrative form and sent it to participants in the study. After each statement of the findings an open box enabled respondents to agree, disagree, or abstain from commenting on that particular finding. And participants were encouraged to make extensive comments as to how they interpreted events. In this way participants had some say in the findings, even though the findings were constructed initially by the evaluators (Stronach & MacLure, 1997). And the evaluators had some sense of the degree to which the stakeholders agreed with their conclusions, in effect, putting the two together established a confidence band around the findings.

How Considered And Extended Is The Deliberation?

Of course, in general, the more extensive the deliberation, the better findings we would expect to emerge. On the other hand, which academic has not sat through hours of faculty meetings exhausted by the endless perambulations of colleagues to no productive end? No point is too small to be raised, no issue too tiny to ponder. For the most part though, in evaluations there is not enough deliberation rather than too much.

We should try to build deliberation into the design of a study rather than hope for it. In the evaluation of an employment program for youths aged 14 to 19 by Greene (1988) initial discussions included the coordinator of the program, the head of the youth department, and the agency director. This was followed by discussions with fifteen stakeholders to develop an evaluation design. The stakeholders included funders, other youth professionals, employers, board members, administrators, program staff, and the youths themselves. There was considerable dialogue with stakeholders to shape the design.

Data were collected from questionnaires, interviews, and group meetings with stakeholders. A subgroup of stakeholders was involved in more intensive interactions about questionnaire development. When data were available, non-technical narratives were shared with stakeholders. Stakeholders reacted to interim reports, and these insights were included in the final report (Alkin, 1998). This study incorporated an extensive deliberation process at all stages, most likely beyond what most studies could manage. How much deliberation is enough is a good question, but so is the question about how sophisticated the data analysis should be.

In all these studies, concern is evident about how and which stakeholder interests were included, what kind of dialogue was encouraged, and how deliberation leading to findings was achieved. The evaluations used different procedures to increase inclusion of stakeholder interests and the authenticity of stakeholder views and interests. No single procedure is clearly superior to others for achieving these goals. A whole range of new procedures to accomplish these tasks has yet to be invented and tested.

No doubt, there are also trade-offs involved, and currently no clear rules for making them. Involving stakeholders at one stage may foster a power imbalance in the findings later on. Including stakeholders in the data analysis may decrease the technical quality of the study. Data collection, analysis, and findings can be biased, just as representation of stakeholder interests can be. There is considerable room for professional judgement as to how to design and manage these activities.

Nonetheless, these evaluations do attempt to include major stakeholder interests, ascertain authentic stakeholder views, and facilitate joint deliberation leading to valid (objective, impartial) findings. Let us admit that these new procedures are more raw and untested than the technical data collection and analysis procedures developed over past decades. Much more work needs to be done, and many evaluators will be less than comfortable blazing new trails. Perhaps gradual testing of new ideas by pioneers is the prudent path.

A HYPOTHETICAL EXAMPLE

Let us pursue a hypothetical example, one which is particularly contentious in American society—ability grouping in schools. Suppose that the Centennial school board has just been taken over by an educationally conservative faction who see the pursuit of the current school administration and former school board as being too concerned with minorities in the school district. The new board would like to reinstitute ability grouping in the schools, which was eliminated under the old regime. Ability grouping is popular with the upwardly mobile professionals who work in the burgeoning local high tech industry and with the academics who teach in the local university.

The new school board orders the superintendent to install ability grouping in the middle schools in language arts, math, and science, by a vote of 6 to 3. The largest minority groups are recently arrived Hispanics from Central and South America and Hmong from southeast Asia. Hispanic activists in the community are vocally opposed to the new policy while the Hmong are silent. The Anglo middle-class professionals and academics are vocally in favor. The school superintendent, under fire himself from the new school board, believes that an evaluation of the new policy on ability grouping is called for. He asks the local university to conduct the evaluation. The university evaluators take on the study, knowing it is politically loaded. How should they proceed, understanding the context of the program and the evaluation?

In general, evaluators are responsible for investigating the pertinent body of social research against which programs may be understood and compared. Evaluators are also responsible for interpreting such research and judging its merits. In doing this, they are required to be *objective* or *unbiased*, not in the sense of refusing to offer judgements of their own, but in the sense of grounding such judgements in defensible methodological and moral principles.

Rarely will programs or policies be so innovative that no pertinent research exists, and this is certainly true of ability grouping. Although contested, much of the research is critical of ability grouping on the moral and political grounds that it denies equal educational opportunity to students placed in low ability groups (e.g., Oakes, 1985; Wheelock, 1992). On the other hand, this research has its own methodological weaknesses.

This information might create a problem for the evaluation. If an evaluator steadfastly believes that ability grouping is wrong and an unmitigated evil, evaluating the Centennial program would be a waste of time. The same is true should an evaluator steadfastly support ability grouping in whatever circumstance. In both cases the conclusions would be a *fait accompli*. This is not to say that whether to practice ability grouping is radically undecidable, but rather that an evaluation in either of the above circumstances would be inappropriate. However, it is asking too much of evaluators to have no opinions about programs or policies going into the evaluation. After all, often evaluators are experts in the areas being investigated. In the case of the Centennial program, so long as evaluators are able to suspend judgement, they might have an initial tilt toward or against the practice of ability grouping and still perform a good evaluation. The key to avoiding bias is insuring that competing claims and evidence are portrayed even-handedly. In the deliberative democratic view, competing claims and evidence must be assessed against the requirements of inclusive representation, dialogue, and deliberation, paying special attention to groups that lack power. For example it would be important to alert stakeholders, especially the Hispanics and Hmong minorities, to research that indicates minorities are often disproportionately represented in low ability groups and that being in a low ability group is associated with low self-esteem as well as diminished opportunities for higher education and desirable employment.

Clearly, the interests of the new school board, those of the minorities, those of the opposition on the school board, those of the administrators, those of the teachers, those of the parents, and those of the children themselves should be included. Is there a more general public interest at issue? Does the society or the state have an interest at issue? It is not clear at this point.

There are several ways we can represent these stakeholders in the evaluation, anything from surveying them individually to involving them in the data collection, and still maintain proper balance. Surely, minority views are important in this case, and the minorities are unlikely to volunteer to work on the evaluation, especially the Hmong. If we open the evaluation to those who can work on data collection, it will be the Anglo professional class that dominates. Certainly, the professional class interests are important but should they be allowed to have a role in conducting the evaluation too, thus increasing their already powerful influence? The evaluators must make some judgments about how much influence to allow each group in the evaluation. It is not as if the evaluators can evade this issue.

On the other hand, we cannot presume to know the minority opinions without talking to the people themselves. Can we talk to them and get an authentic representation of their views and interests? They may be shy of public authorities for the most part. We might decide to involve the leaders of the minority groups, fully aware that they might not represent the real interests of their constituencies, any more than politicians represent the real interests of the public. Yet this is the compromise we might settle for under the circumstances. There are practical limitations we must face in any evaluation.

We arrange interviews with all members of the school board, the leaders of minority groups, the superintendent and his key staff, and the leaders of the parent groups. Clearly, the children's interest is most critical here, but can they express informed opinions about ability grouping? At this age we think not. We think we have covered the major stakeholders. There is the business community, of course, but we cannot see how their interests are affected to the same degree in this particular issue.

There is also the public interest at large. Does ability grouping affect them in a significant way? Does it increase inequality more generally in the society in a way that affects the public interest or is it critically important that future scientists are necessary for the national welfare? If this were consideration of a policy for the entire nation, we might be more concerned about these issues. But we doubt that the national interest can be addressed simply in Centennial alone. These are tough professional decisions.

Some care must be taken to interview and record these various interests and to ensure that the views represented are authentic. It would also be advisable to survey the parents of the students in some way, and not assume that the factions on the school board represent all the interests of the parents at large. Of course, this is difficult and expensive to do. Perhaps the evaluators settle for meeting with local groups of parents in different parts of the school district. This risks misrepresentation but a full-scale survey of the entire district would be too costly.

From all this information the evaluators arrive at criteria for the evaluation: educational achievement, composition of the ability groups, social consequences, and educational opportunities gained or foreclosed in the future. It is advisable to check out these criteria with the various stakeholder groups to ascertain whether something important is missing. The point is not to obtain agreement among the groups but to inform the evaluation itself. We presume there is a right or wrong set of conclusions here and obtaining consensus is not the aim of the evaluation. We could obtain agreement and be wrong.

How should the various groups participate in the evaluation? There are many possibilities, as indicated by the earlier examples, but we might deliberately choose to do the data collection and analysis with a professional evaluation staff to avoid complaints further down the line that the results are contaminated somehow. We anticipate that the findings will emerge in a highly politicized situation. They must be defensible from a methodological point of view. If we let some groups participate in certain aspects of the study, it may call the entire study into question.

After the findings are in will be a critical time to deliberate about them. If they are presented to the school board simply, there is a good chance they will be accepted or rejected by a 6 to 3 vote without sufficient consideration. Perhaps a better procedure is to arrange neighborhood meetings in the local schools and present the findings to small groups of parents and civic groups prior to media presentation. These groups can have time and guidance to consider at some length what they are gaining and losing with ability grouping. Finally, there might be a formal presentation to the entire school board with appropriate media coverage.

From that point, it is up to the school board, the school administration, the parents, and the media as to what decisions are made about ability grouping. The evaluators will have done their job of conducting an evaluation as to the worth of ability grouping, and it is not their job to make decisions for the school district. They may have a further informational role, maybe not. In any case, they have scouted out the relevant issues, conducted the evaluation, and arrived at conclusions by including the appropriate views and interests, engaging in authentic dialogue, and arranging for sufficient deliberation on everyone's part.

Of course, all this is imperfect from a theoretical point of view. We have not included every major group or allowed sufficient time for deliberation, or secured the authentic views of some minorities perhaps. Such is the imperfect world of evaluation practice. No study has ever been done that cannot be criticized. What we can say is that we have made strenuous efforts to live up to our deliberative democratic principles and that the resulting information provides a much better basis for public understanding and decision than without the evaluation.

CONCLUSION

Many evaluators already implement the principles we explicate here without any urging from us. They have developed their own approaches, their own intuitions, and their own robust senses of justice. Nonetheless, such principles are too important to leave to chance or intuition all the time. It may help to have a justification and checklist to remind evaluators caught in the complexities of difficult evaluations what evaluation in democratic societies should aim for: deliberative democracy.

If we look beyond the conduct of individual studies by individual evaluators, we can see the outlines of evaluation as an influential societal institution, one which can be vital to the development of democratic societies. Amidst claims and counterclaims of the mass media, amidst public relations and advertising, evaluation can be an institution that stands apart, reliable for the accuracy and integrity of its claims. And it needs a set of explicit principles to guide its own practice and test its intuitions.

V. OVERARCHING MATTERS

This concluding section of *Evaluation Models* presents material that cuts across the various evaluation models. In this section's initial chapter, Michael Quinn Patton presents the utilization-focused approach to evaluation. Utilization-focused evaluation is pragmatic and ubiquitous and, in the interest of getting findings used, draws upon any legitimate approach to evaluation, leaving out any parts that might impede use. Since the form and content of a utilization-focused evaluation is determined by the preferences and needs of a defined group of users, the approach doesn't fit consistently in the Questions/Methods, Improvement/Accountability, or Social Agenda/Advocacy categories of evaluation approaches. The second chapter in this final section summarizes work in developing professional standards for guiding and judging program evaluations. Of historical interest are the standards produced by the Evaluation Research Society (1982), which were the first set of standards for judging program evaluations across disciplines. The chapter next describes the AEA *Evaluation Principles*, which also apply to program evaluations across disciplines. Finally, the chapter summarizes the Joint Committee *Program Evaluation Standards*, which were first published in 1981 and updated in 1994. Targeted on educational program evaluations, these standards present detailed requirements and guidelines for making evaluations useful, feasible, proper, and accurate. The last chapter is on meta-evaluation, an approach for applying professional standards to assess and strengthen evaluations.

23. UTILIZATION-FOCUSED EVALUATION

MICHAEL QUINN PATTON

How evaluations are used affects the spending of billions of dollars to fight the problems of poverty, disease, ignorance, joblessness, mental anguish, crime, hunger, and inequality. How are programs that combat these societal ills to be judged? How does one distinguish effective from ineffective programs? And how can evaluations be conducted in ways that lead to use? How do we avoid producing reports that gather dust on bookshelves, unread and unused? Those are the questions this chapter addresses, not just in general, but within a particular framework: utilization-focused evaluation.

WHAT IS UTILIZATION-FOCUSED EVALUATION?

Utilization-focused evaluation begins with the premise that evaluations should be judged by their utility and actual use; therefore, evaluators should facilitate the evaluation process and design any evaluation with careful consideration of how everything that is done, *from beginning to end*, will affect use. Nor is use an abstraction. Use concerns how real people in the real world apply evaluation findings and experience the evaluation process. Therefore, the *focus* in utilization-focused evaluation is on *intended use by intended users*.

In any evaluation there are many potential stakeholders and an array of possible uses. Utilization-focused evaluation requires moving from the general and abstract, i.e., possible audiences and potential uses, to the real and specific, i.e., actual primary intended users and their explicit commitments to concrete, specific uses. The evaluator facilitates judgment and decision making by intended users rather than acting

D.L. Stufflebeam, G.F. Madaus and T. Kellaghan (eds.). EVALUATION MODELS. Copyright © 2000. Kluwer Academic Publishers. Boston. All rights reserved.

as a distant, independent judge. Since no evaluation can be value-free, utilization-focused evaluation answers the question of whose values will frame the evaluation by working with clearly identified, primary intended users who have responsibility to apply evaluation findings and implement recommendations. In essence, I argue, evaluation use is too important to be left to evaluators.

Utilization-focused evaluation is highly personal and situational. The evaluation facilitator develops a working relationship with intended users to help them determine what kind of evaluation they need. This requires negotiation in which the evaluator offers a menu of possibilities within the framework of established evaluation standards and principles. While concern about utility drives a utilization-focused evaluation, the evaluator must also attend to the evaluation's accuracy, feasibility, and propriety (Joint Committee on Standards, 1994). Moreover, as a professional, the evaluator has a responsibility to act in accordance with the profession's adopted principles of conducting systematic, data-based inquiries; performing competently; ensuring the honesty and integrity of the entire evaluation process; respecting the people involved in and affected by the evaluation; and being sensitive to the diversity of interests and values that may be related to the general and public welfare (AEA Task Force, 1995).

Utilization-focused evaluation does not advocate any particular evaluation content, model, method, theory, or even use. Rather, it is a process for helping primary intended users select the most appropriate content, model, methods, theory, and uses for their particular situation. Situational responsiveness guides the interactive process between evaluator and primary intended users. Many options are now available in the feast that has become the field of evaluation. In considering the rich and varied menu of evaluation, utilization-focused evaluation can include any evaluative purpose (formative, summative, developmental), any kind of data (quantitative, qualitative, mixed), any kind of design (e.g., naturalistic, experimental), and any kind of focus (processes, outcomes, impacts, costs, and cost-benefit, among many possibilities). It is a process for making decisions about these issues in collaboration with an identified group of primary users focusing on their intended uses of evaluation.

A psychology of use undergirds and informs utilization-focused evaluation. In essence, research and my own experience indicate that intended users are more likely to use evaluations if they understand and feel ownership of the evaluation process and findings; they are more likely to understand and feel ownership if they have been actively involved; and by actively involving primary intended users, the evaluator is training users in use, preparing the groundwork for use, and reinforcing the intended utility of the evaluation every step along the way.

What is program evaluation? I offer the clients with whom I work the following definition:

Program evaluation is the systematic collection of information about the activities, characteristics, and outcomes of programs to make judgments about the program, improve program effectiveness and/or inform decisions about future programming. *Utilization-focused program evaluation* (as opposed to program evaluation in general) is evaluation done for and with specific intended primary users for specific, intended uses.

The general definition above has three interrelated components: (1) the systematic collection of information about (2) a potentially broad range of topics (3) for a variety of possible judgments and uses. The definition of utilization-focused evaluation adds the requirement to specify intended use by intended users. This matter of defining evaluation is of considerable import because different evaluation approaches rest on different definitions. The use-oriented definition offered above contrasts in significant ways with other approaches (see Patton, 1997, p. 23–25).

FOSTERING INTENDED USE BY INTENDED USERS: THE PERSONAL FACTOR

The First Step in Utilization-Focused Evaluation

Many decisions must be made in any evaluation. The purpose of the evaluation must be determined. Concrete evaluative criteria for judging program success will usually have to be established. Methods will have to be selected and timelines agreed on. All of these are important issues in any evaluation. The question is, Who will decide these issues? The utilization-focused answer is *primary intended users of the evaluation*.

Clearly and explicitly identifying people who can benefit from an evaluation is so important that evaluators have adopted a special term for potential evaluation users: *stakeholders*. Evaluation stakeholders are people who have a stake—a vested interest—in evaluation findings. For any evaluation there are multiple possible stakeholders: program funders, staff, administrators, and clients or program participants. Others with a direct, or even indirect, interest in program effectiveness may be considered stakeholders, including journalists and members of the general public, or, more specifically, taxpayers, in the case of public programs. Stakeholders include anyone who makes decisions or desires information about a program. However, stakeholders typically have diverse and often competing interests. No evaluation can answer all potential questions equally well. This means that some process is necessary for narrowing the range of possible questions to focus the evaluation. In utilization-focused evaluation this process begins by narrowing the list of potential stakeholders to a much shorter, more specific group of primary intended users. Their information needs, i.e., their *intended uses*, focus the evaluation.

Beyond Audience to the Personal Factor

Different people see things differently and have varying interests and needs. I take that to be on the order of a truism. The point is that this truism is regularly and consistently ignored in the design of evaluation studies. To target an evaluation at the information needs of a specific person or a group of identifiable and interacting persons is quite different from what has been traditionally recommended as "identifying the audience" for an evaluation. Audiences are amorphous, anonymous entities. Nor is it sufficient to identify an agency or organization as a recipient of the evaluation report. Organizations are an impersonal collection of hierarchical positions. People, not organizations, use evaluation information—thus the importance of the personal factor.

The personal factor is the presence of an identifiable individual or group of people who personally care about the evaluation and the findings it generates. The personal factor represents the leadership, interest, enthusiasm, determination, commitment, assertiveness, and caring of specific, individual people. These are people who actively seek information to make judgments and reduce decision uncertainties. They want to increase their ability to predict the outcomes of programmatic activity and thereby enhance their own discretion as decision makers, policy makers, consumers, program participants, funders, or whatever roles they play. These are the primary users of evaluation.

Though the specifics vary from case to case, the pattern is markedly clear: Where the personal factor emerges, where some individuals take direct, personal responsibility for getting findings to the right people, evaluations have an impact. Where the personal factor is absent, there is a marked absence of impact. Use is not simply determined by some configuration of abstract factors; it is determined in large part by real, live, caring human beings.

Support for the importance of the personal factor is evident in the work of the Stanford Evaluation Consortium, one of the leading places of ferment and reform in evaluation during the late 1970s and early 1980s. Cronbach and associates in the Consortium identified major reforms needed in evaluation by publishing a provocative set of 95 theses. Among their theses was this observation on the personal factor: "Nothing makes a larger difference in the use of evaluations than *the personal factor—* the interest of officials in learning from the evaluation and the desire of the evaluator to get attention for what he knows" (Cronbach and Associates, 1980, p. 6; emphasis added).

The importance of the personal factor in explaining and predicting evaluation use leads directly to the emphasis in utilization-focused evaluation on working with intended users to specify intended uses. The personal factor directs us to attend to specific people who understand, value, and care about evaluation, and further directs us to attend to their interests. This is the primary lesson the profession has learned about enhancing use, and it is wisdom now widely acknowledged by practicing evaluators (see Cousins & Earl, 1995).

Utilization-focused evaluation is often confused with or associated with decision-oriented approaches to evaluation, in part, I presume, because both approaches are very concrete and focused, and both are considered "utilitarian." Ernest House (1980) wrote an important book categorizing various approaches to evaluation in which he included utilization-focused evaluation among the "decision-making models" he reviewed. The primary characteristic of a decision-making model is that "the evaluation be structured by the actual decisions to be made" (p. 28). I believe he incorrectly categorized utilization-focused evaluation because he failed to appreciate the distinct and critical nature of the personal factor. While utilization-focused evaluation includes the option of focusing on decisions, it can also serve a variety of other purposes depending on the information needs of primary intended users.

That is, possible intended uses include a large menu of options. For example, the evaluation process can be important in directing and focusing how people *think about* the basic policies involved in a program, what has come to be called conceptual use; evaluations can help in fine-tuning program implementation; the process of designing an evaluation may lead to clearer, more specific, and more meaningful program goals; and evaluations can provide information on client needs and assets that will help inform general public discussions about public policy. These and other outcomes of evaluation are entirely compatible with utilization-focused evaluation, but do not make a formal decision the driving force behind the evaluation.

What was omitted from the House classification scheme was an approach to evaluation that focuses on and is driven by the information needs of specific people who will use the evaluation processes and findings. The point is that the evaluation is *user-focused*. Utilization-focused evaluation, then, in my judgment, falls within a category of evaluations that I would call, following Marvin Alkin (1995), user-oriented. This is a distinct alternative to the other models identified by House. In the other models the content of the evaluation is determined by the *evaluator's* presuppositions about what constitutes an evaluation: a look at the relationship between inputs and outcomes; the measurement of goal attainment; advice about a specific programmatic decision; description of program processes; a decision about future or continued funding; or judgment according to some set of expert or professional standards. In contrast to these models, user-focused evaluation describes an evaluation process for making decisions about the content of an evaluation—but the content itself is not specified or implied in advance. Thus, any of the eight House models, or adaptations and combinations of those models, might emerge as the guiding direction in user-focused evaluation, depending on the information needs of the people for whom the evaluation information is being collected.

Attending to primary intended users is not just an academic exercise performed for its own sake. Involving specific people who can and will use information enables them to establish direction for, commitment to, and ownership of the evaluation every step along the way, from initiation of the study through the design and data collection stages right through to the final report and dissemination process. If decision makers have shown little interest in the study in its earlier stages, they are not likely to suddenly show an interest in using the findings at the end. They won't be sufficiently *prepared* for use.

No evaluation can serve all potential stakeholders' interests equally well. Utilization-focused evaluation makes explicit whose interests are served—those of explicitly identified primary intended users.

FOCUSING EVALUATIONS: CHOICES, OPTIONS AND DECISIONS

Variable Evaluator Roles

Different types of and purposes for evaluation call for varying evaluator roles. Gerald Barkdoll (1980), as associate commissioner for planning and evaluation of the U.S.

Food and Drug Administration, identified three contrasting evaluator roles. His first type, "evaluator as scientist," he found was best fulfilled by aloof academics who focus on acquiring technically impeccable data while studiously staying above the fray of program politics and utilization relationships. His second type he called "consultative" in orientation; these evaluators were comfortable operating in a collaborative style with policymakers and program analysts to develop consensus about their information needs and decide jointly the evaluation's design and uses. His third type he called the "surveillance and compliance" evaluator, a style characterized by aggressively independent and highly critical auditors committed to protecting the public interest and assuring accountability (e.g., Walters, 1996). These three types reflect evaluation's historical development from three different traditions: (1) social science research, (2) pragmatic field practice, especially by internal evaluators and consultants, and (3) program and financial auditing.

When evaluation research aims to generate generalizable knowledge about causal linkages between a program intervention and outcomes, rigorous application of social science methods is called for and the evaluator's role as methodological expert will be primary. When the emphasis is on determining a program's overall merit or worth, the evaluator's role as judge takes center stage. If an evaluation has been commissioned because of and is driven by public accountability concerns, the evaluator's role as independent auditor, inspector, or investigator will be spotlighted for policymakers and the general public. When program improvement is the primary purpose, the evaluator plays an advisory and facilitative role with program staff. As a member of a design team, a developmental evaluator will play a consultative role. If an evaluation has a social justice agenda, the evaluator becomes a change agent.

In utilization-focused evaluation, the evaluator is always a negotiator—negotiating with primary intended users what other roles he or she will play. Beyond that, all roles are on the table, just as all methods are options. Role selection follows from and is dependent on intended use by intended users.

Consider, for example, a national evaluation of Food Stamps to feed low income families. For purposes of accountability and policy review, the primary intended users are members of the program's oversight committees in Congress (including staff to those committees). The program is highly visible, costly, and controversial, especially because special interest groups differ about its intended outcomes and who should be eligible. Under such conditions, the evaluation's credibility and utility will depend heavily on the evaluator's independence, ideological neutrality, methodological expertise, and political savvy.

Contrast such a national accountability evaluation with an evaluator's role in helping a small, rural leadership program of the Cooperative Extension Service increase its impact. The program operates in a few local communities. The primary intended users are the county extension agents, elected county commissioners, and farmer representatives who have designed the program. Program improvement to increase participant satisfaction and behavior change is the intended purpose. Under these conditions, the evaluation's use will depend heavily on the evaluator's relationship with design team members. The evaluator will need to build a close, trusting, and mutually respectful relationship to effectively facilitate the team's decisions about evaluation priorities and methods of data collection, and then take them through a consensus-building process as results are interpreted and changes agreed on.

These contrasting case examples illustrate the range of contexts in which program evaluations occur. The evaluator's role in any particular study will depend on matching her or his role with the context and purposes of the evaluation as negotiated with primary intended users.

Situational Evaluation

There is no one best way to conduct an evaluation. This insight is critical. The design of a particular evaluation depends on the people involved and their situation. *Situational evaluation* is like situation ethics (Fletcher, 1966), situational leadership (Blanchard, 1986; Hersey, 1985), or situated learning: "Action is grounded in the concrete situation in which it occurs" (Anderson, Reder & Simon, 1996, p. 5). The standards and principles of evaluation provide overall direction, a foundation of ethical guidance, and a commitment to professional competence and integrity, but there are no absolute rules an evaluator can follow to know exactly what to do with specific users in a particular situation. That is why Newcomer and Wholey (1989) concluded in their synthesis of knowledge about evaluation strategies for building high-performance programs: "Prior to an evaluation, evaluators and program managers should work together to define the ideal final product" (p. 202). This means *negotiating* the evaluation's intended and expected uses.

Every evaluation situation is unique. A successful evaluation (one that is useful, practical, ethical, and accurate) emerges from the special characteristics and conditions of a particular situation—a mixture of people, politics, history, context, resources, constraints, values, needs, interests, and chance. Despite the rather obvious, almost trite, and basically commonsense nature of this observation, it is not at all obvious to most stakeholders who worry a great deal about whether an evaluation is being done "right." Indeed, one common objection stakeholders make to getting actively involved in designing an evaluation is that they lack the knowledge to do it "right." The notion that there is one right way to do things dies hard. The right way, from a utilization-focused perspective, is the way that will be meaningful and useful to the specific evaluators and intended users involved, and finding that way requires interaction, negotiation, and situational analysis.

Utilization-focused evaluation is a problem-solving approach that calls for creative adaptation to changed and changing conditions, as opposed to a technical approach, which attempts to mold and define conditions to fit preconceived models of how things should be done. Utilization-focused evaluation involves overcoming what Brightman and Noble (1979) have identified as "the ineffective education of decision scientists." They portray the typical decision scientist (a generic term for evaluators, policy analysts, planners, and so on) as hopelessly naive and intellectually arrogant. Naive because they believe that problem solving begins and ends with analysis, and arrogant because they opt for mathematical rigor over results. They are products of their training. Decision science departments appear to have been more effective at training technocrats to deal with structured problems than problem solvers to deal with ill-structured ones. (p. 150)

Narrow technocratic approaches emphasize following rules and standard operating procedures. Creative problem-solving approaches, in contrast, focus on what works and what makes sense in the situation. Standard methods recipe books are not ignored. They are just not taken as the final word. New ingredients are added to fit particular tastes. Home-grown or locally available ingredients replace the processed foods of the national supermarket chains, with the attendant risks of both greater failure and greater achievement.

Being Active-Reactive-Adaptive

I use the phrase "active-reactive-adaptive" to suggest the nature of the consultative interactions that go on between evaluators and intended users. The phrase is meant to be both descriptive and prescriptive. It describes how real-world decision making actually unfolds. Yet, it is prescriptive in alerting evaluators to consciously and deliberately act, react, and adapt in order to increase their effectiveness in working with stakeholders.

Utilization-focused evaluators are, first of all, active in deliberately and calculatedly identifying intended users and focusing useful questions. They are reactive in listening to intended users and responding to what they learn about the particular situation in which the evaluation unfolds. They are adaptive in altering evaluation questions and designs in light of their increased understanding of the situation and changing conditions. Active-reactive-adaptive evaluators do not impose cookbook designs. They do not do the same thing time after time. They are genuinely immersed in the challenges of each new setting and authentically responsive to the intended users of each new evaluation.

This active-reactive-adaptive stance characterizes all phases of evaluator-user interactions from initially identifying primary intended users, to focusing relevant questions, choosing methods, and analyzing results. All phases involve collaborative processes of action-reaction-adaption as evaluators and intended users consider their options. The menu of choices includes a broad range of methods, evaluation ingredients from bland to spicy, and a variety of evaluator roles: collaborator, trainer, group facilitator, technician, politician, organizational analyst, internal colleague, external expert, methodologist, information broker, communicator, change agent, diplomat, problem solver, and creative consultant. The roles played by an evaluator in any given situation will depend on the evaluation's purpose, the unique constellation of conditions with which the evaluator is faced, *and the evaluator's own personal knowledge, skills, style, values, and ethics.*

Being active-reactive-adaptive explicitly recognizes the importance of the individual evaluator's experience, orientation, and contribution by placing the mandate to be "active" first in this consulting triangle. Situational responsiveness does not mean rolling over and playing dead (or passive) in the face of stakeholder interests or perceived needs. Just as the evaluator in utilization-focused evaluation does not unilaterally impose a focus and set of methods on a program, so too the stakeholders are not set up to impose their initial predilections unilaterally or dogmatically. Arriving at the final evaluation design is a negotiated process that allows the values and capabilities of the evaluator to intermingle with those of intended users.

The utilization-focused evaluator, in being active-reactive-adaptive, is one among many at the negotiating table. At times there may be discord in the negotiating process, at other times harmony. Whatever the sounds, and whatever the themes, the utilization-focused evaluator does not sing alone.

One central value that should undergird the evaluator's active-reactive-adaptive role is respect for all those with a stake in a program or evaluation. In their seminal article on evaluation use, Davis and Salasin (1975) asserted that evaluators were involved inevitably in facilitating change and "any change model should . . . generally *accommodate* rather than *manipulate* the view of the persons involved" (p. 652). Respectful utilization-focused evaluators do not use their expertise to intimidate or manipulate intended users.

User Responsiveness and Technical Quality

User responsiveness should not mean a sacrifice of technical quality. A beginning point is to recognize that standards of technical quality vary for different users and varying situations. The issue is not meeting some absolute research standards of technical quality but, rather, making sure that methods and measures are *appropriate* to the validity and credibility needs of a particular evaluation purpose and specific intended users.

Jennifer Greene (1990) examined in depth the debate about "technical quality versus user responsiveness." She found general agreement that both are important, but disagreements about the relative priority of each. She concluded that the debate is really about how much to recognize and deal with evaluation's political inherency: "Evaluators should recognize that tension and conflict in evaluation practice are virtually inevitable, that the demands imposed by most if not all definitions of responsiveness and technical quality (not to mention feasibility and propriety) will characteristically reflect the competing politics and values of the setting" (p. 273). She then recommended that evaluators "explicate the politics and values" that undergird decisions about purpose, audience, design, and methods. Her recommendation is consistent with utilization-focused evaluation.

PROCESS AND PREMISES OF UTILIZATION-FOCUSED EVALUATION

The Flow of a Utilization-Focused Evaluation Process

Exhibit 1 presents a flowchart of utilization-focused evaluation. First, intended users of the evaluation are identified. These intended users are brought together or organized in some fashion (e.g., an evaluation task force of primary stakeholders), if possible, to work with the evaluator and share in making major decisions about the evaluation.

Second, the evaluator and intended users commit to the intended uses of the evaluation and determine the focus of the evaluation. This can include considering the relative importance of focusing on attainment of goals, program implementation, and/or the program's theory of action. The menu of evaluation possibilities is vast, so many different types of evaluations may need to be discussed. The evaluator works with intended users to determine priority uses with attention to political and ethical considerations. In a style that is active-reactive-adaptive and situationally responsive, the evaluator helps intended users answer these questions: Given expected uses, is the evaluation worth doing? To what extent and in what ways are intended users committed to intended use?

The third part of the process as depicted in the flowchart involves methods, measurement, and design decisions. A variety of options are considered: qualitative and quantitative data; naturalistic, experimental, and quasi-experimental designs; purposeful and probabilistic sampling approaches; greater and lesser emphasis on generalizations; and alternative ways of dealing with potential threats to validity, reliability, and utility. More specifically, the discussion at this stage will include attention to issues of methodological appropriateness, believability of the data, understandability, accuracy, balance, practicality, propriety, and cost. As always, the overriding concern will be utility: Will results obtained from these methods be useful—and actually used?

Once data have been collected and organized for analysis, the fourth stage of the utilization-focused process begins. Intended users are actively and directly involved in interpreting findings and making judgments based on the data and generating recommendations. Specific strategies for use can then be formalized in light of actual findings and the evaluator can facilitate following through on actual use.

Finally, decisions about dissemination of the evaluation report can be made beyond whatever initial commitments were made earlier in planning for intended use. This reinforces the distinction between intended use by intended users (planned utilization) versus more general dissemination for broad public accountability (where both hoped for and unintended uses may occur).

While the flowchart in Exhibit 1 depicts a seemingly straightforward, one-step-at-a-time logic to the unfolding of a utilization-focused evaluation, in reality the process is seldom simple or linear. The flowchart attempts to capture the sometimes circular and iterative nature of the process by depicting loops at the points where intended users are identified and again where evaluation questions are focused. For the sake of diagrammatic simplicity, however, many potential loops are missing. The active-reactive-adaptive evaluator who is situationally responsive and politically sensitive may find that new stakeholders become important or new questions emerge in the midst of methods decisions. Nor is there a clear and clean distinction between the processes of focusing evaluation questions and making methods decisions.

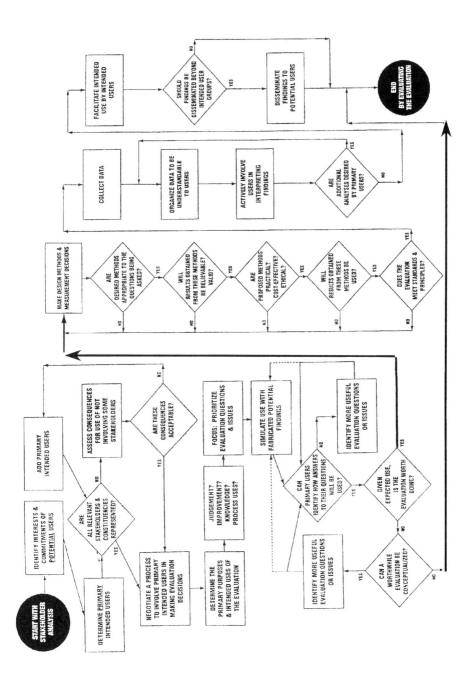

The real world of utilization-focused evaluation manifests considerably more complexity than a flowchart can possibly capture. The flowchart strives to outline the basic logic of the process, but applying that logic in any given situation requires flexibility and creativity.

The Achilles' Heel of Utilization-Focused Evaluation

Achilles' fame stemmed from his role as hero in Homer's classic, the *Iliad*. He was the Greeks' most illustrious warrior during the Trojan War, invulnerable because his mother had dipped him in the Styx, the river of the underworld across which Charon ferried the dead. His heel, where she held him in the river, was his sole point of vulnerability and it was there that he was fatally wounded by an arrow shot by Paris.

The Achilles' heel of utilization-focused evaluation, its point of greatest vulnerability, is turnover of primary intended users. The process so depends on the active engagement of intended users that to lose users along the way to job transitions, reorganizations, reassignments and elections can undermine eventual use. Replacement users who join the evaluation late in the process seldom come with the same agenda as those who were present at the beginning. The best antidote involves working with a task force of multiple intended users so that the departure of one or two is less critical. Still, when substantial turnover of primary intended users occurs, it may be necessary to reignite the process by renegotiating the design and use commitments with the new arrivals on the scene.

Many challenges exist in selecting the right stakeholders, getting them to commit time and attention to the evaluation, dealing with political dynamics, building credibility, and conducting the evaluation in an ethical manner. All of these challenges revolve around the relationship between the evaluator and intended users. When new intended users replace those who depart, new relationships must be built. That may mean delays in original timelines, but such delays pay off in eventual use by attending to the foundation of understandings and relationships upon which utilization-focused evaluation is built.

Fourteen Fundamental Premises of Utilization-Focused Evaluation

The premises of utilization-focused evaluation will seem obvious to some, of dubious merit to others. To some extent, the rationales for and evidence supporting these various premises have been articulated throughout this paper. Here, however, I offer 14 fundamental premises of utilization-focused evaluation.

1. Commitment to intended use by intended users should be the driving force in an evaluation. At every decision point—whether the decision concerns purpose, focus, design, methods, measurement, analysis, or reporting—the evaluator asks intended users, "How would that affect your use of this evaluation?"

2. Strategizing about use is ongoing and continuous from the very beginning of the evaluation. Use is not something one becomes interested in at the end of an evaluation. By the end of the evaluation, the potential for use has been largely deter-

mined. From the moment stakeholders and evaluators begin interacting and conceptualizing the evaluation, decisions are being made that will affect use in major ways.

3. The personal factor contributes significantly to use. The personal factor refers to the research finding that the personal interests and commitments of those involved in an evaluation undergird use. Thus, evaluations should be *specifically* user-oriented—aimed at the interests and information needs of specific, identifiable people, not vague, passive audiences.

4. Careful and thoughtful stakeholder analysis should inform identification of primary intended users, taking into account the varied and multiple interests that surround any program, and therefore, any evaluation. Staff, program participants, directors, public officials, funders, and community leaders all have an interest in evaluation, but the degree and nature of their interests will vary. Political sensitivity and ethical judgments are involved in identifying primary intended users and uses.

5. Evaluations must be focused in some way; focusing on intended use by intended users is the most useful way. Resource and time constraints will make it impossible for any single evaluation to answer everyone's questions or to give full attention to all possible issues. Because no evaluation can serve all potential stakeholders' interests equally well, stakeholders representing various constituencies should come together to negotiate what issues and questions deserve priority.

6. Focusing on intended use requires making deliberate and thoughtful choices. There are three primary uses of evaluation findings: judging merit or worth (summative evaluation), improving programs (instrumental use), and generating knowledge (conceptual use). In addition, there are four primary uses of evaluation *processes*: enhancing shared understandings, reinforcing interventions, supporting participant engagement, and developing programs and organizations. Uses can change and evolve over time as a program matures.

7. Useful evaluations must be designed and adapted situationally. Standardized recipe approaches will not work. The relative value of a particular utilization focus (premise 9) can only be judged in the context of a specific program and the interests of intended users. Situational factors affect use. These factors include community variables, organizational characteristics, the nature of the evaluation, evaluator credibility, political considerations, and resource constraints. In conducting a utilization-focused evaluation, the active-reactive-adaptive evaluator works with intended users to assess how various factors and conditions may affect the potential for use.

8. Intended users' commitment to use can be nurtured and enhanced by actively involving them in making significant decisions about the evaluation. Involvement increases relevance, understanding, and ownership of the evaluation—all of which facilitate informed and appropriate use.

9. High quality participation is the goal, not high quantity participation. The quantity of group interaction time can be inversely related to the quality of the process. Evaluators conducting utilization-focused evaluations must be skilled group facilitators.

10. High quality involvement of intended users will result in high quality, useful evaluations. Many researchers worry that methodological rigor may be sacrificed if nonscientists collaborate in making methods decisions. But, decision makers want data that are useful *and* accurate. Validity and utility are interdependent. Threats to utility are as important to counter as threats to validity. Skilled evaluation facilitators can help nonscientists understand methodological issues so that they can judge for themselves the trade-offs involved in choosing among the strengths and weaknesses of design options and methods alternatives.

11. Evaluators have a rightful stake in an evaluation in that their credibility and integrity are always at risk, thus the mandate for evaluators to be active-reactive-adaptive. Evaluators are active in presenting to intended users their own best judgments about appropriate evaluation focus and methods; they are reactive in listening attentively and respectful to others' concerns; and they are adaptive in finding ways to design evaluations that incorporate diverse interests, including their own, while meeting high standards of professional practice. Evaluators' credibility and integrity are factors affecting use as well as the foundation of the profession. In this regard, evaluators should be guided by the profession's standards and principles.

12. Evaluators committed to enhancing use have a responsibility *to train users* in evaluation processes and the uses of information. Training stakeholders in evaluation methods and processes attends to both short-term and long-term evaluation uses. Making decision makers more sophisticated about evaluation can contribute to greater use of evaluation over time.

13. Use is different from reporting and dissemination. Reporting and dissemination may be means to facilitate use, but they should not be confused with such intended uses as making decisions, improving programs, changing thinking, empowering participants, and generating knowledge (see premise 6).

14. Serious attention to use involves financial and time costs that are far from trivial. The benefits of these costs are manifested in greater use. These costs should be made explicit in evaluation proposals and budgets so that utilization follow through is not neglected for lack of resources.

CONCLUSION

The results of any particular effort cannot be guaranteed. Each evaluation being a blend of unique ingredients, no standardized recipe can assure the outcome. We have only principles, premises, and utilization-focused processes to guide us, and we have much yet to learn. But, the potential benefits merit the efforts and risks involved. At stake is improving the effectiveness of programs that express and embody the highest ideals of humankind.

24. PROFESSIONAL STANDARDS AND PRINCIPLES FOR EVALUATIONS

DANIEL L. STUFFLEBEAM

Members of most professions and many other public service fields must comply with given standards or codes of performance and service. Such standards and codes aim to protect consumers and society from harmful practices, provide a basis for accountability by the service providers, provide an authoritative basis for assessing professional services, provide a basis for adjudicating claims of malpractice, help assure that service providers will employ their field's currently best available practices, identify needs for improved technologies, provide a conceptual framework and working definitions to guide research and development in the service area, provide general principles for addressing a variety of practical issues in the service area, present service providers and their constituents with a common language to facilitate communication and collaboration, and earn and maintain the public's confidence in the field of practice. Such standards and codes typically are defined by distinguished members of the service area, in some cases by government licensing bodies, and occasionally with full participation of users groups. Familiar examples are the standards of practice employed by the fields of law, medicine, clinical psychology, educational testing, auditing, and accounting. Other examples are the codes established for the construction, engineering, electrical, plumbing, and food service areas.

Historically, program evaluators did not have to be concerned about explicit professional standards for program evaluations, because until relatively recently there was not any semblance of an evaluation profession and there were not any standards for evaluations. However, such standards have come into prominence during the 1980s

D.L. Stufflebeam, G.F. Madaus and T. Kellaghan (eds.). EVALUATION MODELS. Copyright © 2000. Kluwer Academic Publishers. Boston. All rights reserved.

and 1990s. Their appearance signifies both the field's historic immaturity and its comparatively recent movement toward professionalization.

In the early 1980s two programs for setting evaluation standards emerged and have survived. The Joint Committee on Standards for Educational Evaluation was established in 1975. Through the years, this standing committee has been sponsored by 12 to 15 professional societies with a combined membership totaling over 2 million. The committee's charge is to perform ongoing development, review, and revision of standards for educational evaluations. This committee issued the *Standards for Evaluations of Educational Programs, Projects, and Materials* in 1981 and an updated version in 1994 called *The Program Evaluation Standards*. The Joint Committee also published standards for evaluating educational personnel in 1988, and in the late 1990s has been working on a set of standards for evaluations of students. The Joint Committee is accredited by the American National Standards Institute (ANSI) as the only body recognized to set standards for educational evaluations in the U.S.

The Evaluation Research Society was established in 1976 and was focused on professionalizing program evaluation as practiced across a wide range of disciplines and service areas. This society published a set of 55 standards labeled the *Evaluation Research Society Standards for Program Evaluations* (ERS Standards Committee, 1982). In 1986, ERS amalgamated with the Evaluation Network (E NET) to form the American Evaluation Association (AEA), which has a membership of about 2,000. AEA subsequently produced the 1995 *AEA Principles for Program Evaluations*.

The purpose of this chapter is to describe and discuss standards and principles that have been posited for program evaluation. The ERS/AEA standards and principles cut across many areas of program evaluation, while the Joint Committee standards concentrate on evaluations of education and training programs and services. Both provide authoritative direction for assessing program evaluation studies. However, the Joint Committee standards are considerably more detailed than the ERS/AEA standards and principles and address practical and technical concerns of importance to the general practice of professional evaluation. The chapter is organized to look first at each program of evaluation standards/principles and second to consider how they are interrelated and complementary.

THE ERS STANDARDS FOR PROGRAM EVALUATIONS

The original *ERS Standards for Program Evaluations* (ERS Standards Committee, 1982) were developed to address program evaluations across a broad spectrum, e.g., community development, control and treatment of substance abuse, education, health, labor, law enforcement, licensing and certification, museums, nutrition, public media, public policy, public safety, social welfare, and transportation. In July of 1977, the ERS president appointed a seven-member committee to develop the ERS standards. All committee members were evaluation specialists, with Scarvia B. Anderson serving as chair. This committee collected and studied pertinent materials, such as the draft standards then being developed by the Joint Committee on Standards for Educational Evaluation. Since the ERS's focus was considerably wider than educational evaluations, the ERS Standards Committee decided to prepare a set of general standards that the Committee deemed to be broader in applicability than those being devised by the Joint Committee on Standards for Educational Evaluation. The ERS Standards Committee then produced a draft set of standards and circulated it mainly to ERS evaluation specialists. Using the obtained reactions, the committee finalized and published the standards in September of 1982.

The ERS standards are 55 admonitory, brief statements presented in about nine pages of text. An example is "1. The purposes and characteristics of the program or activity to be addressed in the evaluation should be specified as precisely as possible." The 55 standards are divided into the following six categories.

Formulation and Negotiation

The 12 standards in this group concretely advise evaluators that before proceeding with an evaluation they should clarify with their client as much as possible and in writing the evaluation work to be done, how it should be done, who will do it, who is to be served, protections against conflicts of interest, protections for participants and human subjects, the evaluation budget, and constraints on the evaluation. A general caveat for this subset of standards warns that initial evaluation planning decisions often must be revisited and revised as the evaluation evolves and circumstances change.

Structure and Design

The six standards concerned with structure and design note that evaluation plans must both prescribe a systematic, defensible inquiry process and take into account the relevant context. The key requirement here is to design the evaluation to produce defensible inferences about the value of the program being studied. The plan should clearly present and justify the basic study design, sampling procedures, data collection instruments, and arrangements for the needed cooperation of program personnel and other participants in the evaluation.

Data Collection and Preparation

The 12 standards here call for advance planning of the data collection process. The plan should provide for selecting and training data collectors; protecting the rights of data sources and human subjects; monitoring, controlling, and documenting data collection; controlling bias; assessing validity and reliability of procedures and instruments; minimizing interference and disruption to the program under study; and controlling access to data.

Data Analysis and Interpretation

Nine standards essentially call for tempering the data analysis and interpretation within the constraints of the evaluation design and data actually collected. These standards require evaluators to match the analysis procedures to the evaluation purposes; describe and justify use of the particular analysis procedures; employ appropriate units of analysis; investigate both practical and statistical significance of quantitative findings; bolster cause-and-effect interpretations by reference to the design and by eliminating plausible rival explanations; and clearly distinguish among objective findings, opinions, judgments, and speculation.

Communication and Disclosure

Ten standards emphasize that evaluators must employ effective communication throughout the evaluation process. Particular requirements are to determine authority for releasing findings; organize data in accordance with the accessibility policies and procedures; present findings clearly, completely, fairly, and accurately; denote the relative importance of different findings; make clear the evaluation's underlying assumptions and limitations; be ready to explain the evaluation procedures; and disseminate pertinent findings to each right-to-know audience in accordance with appropriate, advance disclosure agreements.

Use of Results

The concluding "Use of Results" section includes six standards. These emphasize that evaluators should carefully attend to the information needs of potential users throughout all phases of the evaluation. Accordingly, evaluators should issue reports before pertinent decisions have to be made; anticipate and thwart, as much as possible, misunderstandings and misuses of findings; point up suspected side effects of the evaluation process; distinguish sharply between evaluation findings and recommendations; be cautious and circumspect in making recommendations; and carefully distinguish between their evaluative role and any advocacy role they might be playing.

The ERS standards are not the official standards of any group at this time. Their inclusion reflects their historical significance. Also, like the AEA guiding principles, they address a wide range of evaluations outside as well as inside education. Furthermore, the ERS standards are judged to be still valuable, since they apply to the full range of evaluation tasks, whereas the AEA guiding principles propose mainly a code of ethics for the behavior of evaluators.

THE AEA EVALUATION PRINCIPLES

Following the 1986 merger of E Net and ERS to create AEA, the amalgamated organization revisited the issue of professional standards for evaluators. After considerable discussion at both board and membership levels, the AEA leaders decided to supplement the ERS standards summarized above with an updated statement of evaluation principles. In November 1992, AEA created a task force and charged it to develop general guiding principles rather than standards for evaluation practice. The task force, chaired by William R. Shadish, subsequently drafted the *Guiding Principles for Evaluators*. Following a review process made available to the entire AEA membership, the task force finalized the principles document. After an affirmative vote by the AEA membership, the AEA board adopted the task force's recommended principles as the official AEA evaluation principles. AEA then published the principles in a special issue of AEA's *New Directions for Program Evaluation* periodical (Task

Force on Guiding Principles for Evaluators, 1995). The "Guiding Principles" are presented as a 6-page chapter in this special issue. The AEA guiding principles are consistent with the prior ERS Standards but shorter in the number of presented statements. Essentially, the AEA principles comprise 5 principles and 23 underlying normative statements to guide evaluation practice. The principles, with a summary of the associated normative statements, are as follows.

"A. *Systematic Inquiry*: Evaluators conduct systematic, data-based inquiries about whatever is being evaluated." This principle is supported by three normative statements. These charge evaluators to meet the highest available technical standards pertaining to both quantitative and qualitative inquiry. Evaluators are also charged to work with their clients to ensure that the evaluation employs appropriate procedures to address clear, important questions. The evaluators are charged further to communicate effectively, candidly, and in sufficient detail throughout the evaluation process, so that audiences will understand and be able to critique the evaluation's procedures, strengths, weaknesses, limitations, and underlying value and theoretical assumptions and also make defensible interpretations of findings.

"B. *Competence*: Evaluators provide competent performance to stakeholders." Three normative statements charge evaluators to develop and appropriately apply their expertise. Evaluator(s) must be qualified by education, abilities, skills, and experience to competently carry out proposed evaluations, or they should decline to do them. They should practice within the limits of their capabilities. Throughout their careers, evaluators should constantly use pertinent opportunities to upgrade their evaluation capabilities, including professional development and subjecting their evaluations to metaevaluations.

"C. *Integrity/Honesty*: Evaluators ensure the honesty and integrity of the entire evaluation process." Five normative statements are provided to assure that evaluations are ethical. Evaluators are charged to be honest and candid with their clients and other users in negotiating all aspects of an evaluation. These include costs, tasks, limitations of methodology, scope of likely results, and uses of data. Modifications in the planned evaluation activities should be recorded, and clients should be consulted as appropriate. Possible conflicts of interest should be forthrightly reported and appropriately addressed. Any misrepresentation of findings is strictly forbidden, and evaluators are charged to do what they can to prevent or even redress misuses of findings by others.

"D. *Respect for People*: Evaluators respect the security, dignity, and self-worth of the respondents, program participants, clients, and other stakeholders with whom they interact." The five normative statements associated with this standard require evaluators to show proper consideration to all parties to the evaluation. In focusing the evaluation, collecting information, and reporting findings, the evaluator should identify and respect differences among participants, e.g., age, disability, ethnicity, gender, religion, and sexual orientation. Pertinent codes of ethics and standards are to be observed in all aspects of the evaluation. The evaluator should maximize benefits to stakeholders and avoid unnecessary harms; observe informed consent policies; deal proactively, consistently, and fairly with issues of anonymity and confidentiality; and do whatever is appropriate and possible to help stakeholders benefit from the evaluation.

"E. *Responsibilities for General and Public Welfare*: Evaluators articulate and take into account the diversity of interests and values that may be related to the general and public welfare." Five normative statements are given to support this principle. Evaluators are charged not to be myopic but to show broad concern for the evaluation's social relevance. Evaluators have professional obligations to serve the public interest and good as well as the local need for evaluative feedback. They should consider the program's long-range as well as short-term effects, should search out side effects, and should present and assess the program's broad assumptions about social significance. They should balance their obligation to serve the client with services to the broader group of stakeholders. They should involve and inform the full range of right-to-know audiences and, within the confines of contractual agreements, give them access to the information that may serve their needs. In interpreting findings evaluators should take into account all relevant value perspectives or explain why one or some of these were excluded. Keeping in mind the interests and technical capabilities of their audiences, evaluators should report findings clearly and accurately.

THE JOINT COMMITTEE PROGRAM EVALUATION STANDARDS

The Joint Committee on Standards for Educational Evaluation developed the *Standards for Evaluations of Educational Programs, Projects, and Materials* between 1975 and 1980. This is a 161-page book that essentially includes detailed presentations of each of 30 standards. Each standard includes a statement of the standard, an explanation of its requirements, a rationale, guidelines for carrying it out, pitfalls to be anticipated and avoided, warnings against overzealous application, and an illustrative case.

The 30 standards are grouped according to four essential attributes of a sound evaluation: utility, feasibility, propriety, and accuracy. The Joint Committee advises both evaluators and clients to apply the 30 standards so that their evaluations satisfy all four essential attributes of a sound evaluation.

1. An evaluation should be **useful**. It should be addressed to those persons and groups that are involved in or responsible for implementing the program being evaluated. The evaluation should ascertain the users' information needs and report to them the relevant evaluative feedback clearly, concisely, and on time. It should help them to identify and attend to the program's problems and be aware of important strengths. It should address the users' most important questions while also obtaining the full range of information needed to assess the program's merit and worth. The evaluation should not only report feedback about strengths and weaknesses, but also should assist users to study and apply the findings.

The utility standards reflect the general consensus found in the evaluation literature that program evaluations should effectively address the information needs of clients and other right-to-know audiences and should inform program improvement processes.

2. An evaluation should be **feasible**. It should employ evaluation procedures that are parsimonious and operable in the program's environment. It should avoid disrupting or otherwise impairing the program. It should control as much as possible the political forces that might otherwise impede and/or corrupt the evaluation. And it should be conducted as efficiently and cost-effectively as possible. This set of standards emphasize that evaluation procedures must be workable in real world settings, not only in experimental laboratories. Overall, the feasibility standards require evaluations to be realistic, prudent, diplomatic, politically viable, frugal, and cost-effective.

3. An evaluation should meet conditions of **propriety**. It should be grounded in clear, written agreements defining the obligations of the evaluator and client for supporting and executing the evaluation. The evaluation should protect all involved parties' rights and dignity. Findings must be honest and not distorted in any way. Reports must be released in accordance with advance disclosure agreements. Moreover, reports should convey balanced accounts of strengths and weaknesses. These standards reflect the fact that evaluations can affect many people in negative as well as positive ways. The propriety standards are designed to protect the rights of all parties to an evaluation. In general, the propriety standards require that evaluations be conducted legally, ethically, and with due regard for the welfare of those involved in the evaluation as well as those affected by the results.

4. An evaluation should be **accurate**. It should clearly describe the program as it was planned and as it was actually executed. It should describe the program's background and setting. It should report valid and reliable findings. It should identify the evaluation's information sources, measurement methods and devices, analytic procedures, and provisions for bias control. It should present the strengths, weaknesses, and limitations of the evaluation's plan, procedures, information, and conclusions. It should describe and assess the extent to which the evaluation provides an independent assessment rather than a self-assessment. In general, this final group of standards require evaluators to obtain technically sound information, analyze it correctly, and report justifiable conclusions. The overall rating of an evaluation against the 12 accuracy standards is an index of the evaluation's overall validity.

The 17 members of the original Joint Committee were appointed by 12 professional organizations. The organizations and their appointed members represented a wide range of specialties—school accreditation, counseling and guidance, curriculum, educational administration, educational measurement, educational research, educational governance, program evaluation, psychology, statistics, and teaching. A fundamental requirement of the Committee is that it include about equal numbers of members who represent evaluation users groups and evaluation methodologists. Over the years the Joint Committee's sponsoring organizations have slightly increased. (At the publication of the 1994 *The Program Evaluation Standards*, the committee was sponsored by 15 organizations, including AEA.[1]) Daniel L. Stufflebeam chaired the Joint Committee during its first 13 years, James R. Sanders served as chair during the next 10 years, and Arlen Gullickson has been the chair since the end of 1998. All three are members of the Western Michigan University Evaluation Center, which has housed and supported the Joint Committee's work since its inception in 1975.

In each of its standards-setting projects, the Joint Committee engaged about 200 persons concerned with the professional practice of evaluation in a systematic process of generating, testing, and clarifying widely shared principles by which to guide, assess, and govern evaluation work in education. In each project, the Committee sought widely divergent views on what standards should be adopted. The Committee subsequently worked through consensus development processes to converge on the final set of standards.

Each set of Joint Committee *Standards* is a living document. The Joint Committee is a standing committee. The Committee encourages users of each set of standards to provide feedback on applications of the standards along with criticisms and suggestions. From the outset of its work, the Joint Committee has provided for periodic reviews and improvement of the standards. This feature of its work is consistent with requirements for maintaining the Committee's accreditation by the American National Standards Institute (ANSI).

The Committee's review of its 1981 program evaluation standards led to the development of a second edition, *The Program Evaluation Standards* published in 1994. Like the first edition, 30 standards are presented within the 4 categories of utility, feasibility, propriety, and accuracy. The Committee merged some of the original standards and added some new ones. New illustrative cases were included that pertain to more diverse areas of application than did the illustrations in the 1981 version. The 1994 version covers education and training in such settings as business, government, law, medicine, the military, nursing, professional development, schools, social service agencies, and universities.

The Program Evaluation Standards (Joint Committee, 1994) are summarized in Table 1[2]. ANSI approved these *Standards* as an American National Standard on March 15, 1994. Readers are advised to study the full text of *The Program Evaluation Standards,* so that they can internalize them and apply them judiciously at each stage of an evaluation. The summary presented in Table 1 is only a starting point and convenient memory aid.

The Joint Committee offered advice on which of the above 30 standards are most applicable to each of 10 tasks in the evaluation process: deciding whether to evaluate, defining the evaluation problem, designing the evaluation, collecting information, analyzing information, reporting the evaluation, budgeting the evaluation, contracting for evaluation, managing the evaluation, and staffing the evaluation. The Committee's judgments of the different standards' applicability to each evaluation

Table 1. Summary of the Program Evaluation Standards

UTILITY

The utility standards are intended to ensure that an evaluation will serve the information needs of intended users.

U1 Stakeholder Identification. Persons involved in or affected by the evaluation should be identified, so that their needs can be addressed.

U2 Evaluator Credibility. The persons conducting the evaluation should be both trustworthy and competent to perform the evaluation, so that the evaluation findings achieve maximum credibility and acceptance.

U3 Information Scope and Selection. Information collected should be broadly selected to address pertinent questions about the program and be responsive to the needs and interests of clients and other specified stakeholders.

U4 Values Identification. The perspectives, procedures, and rationale used to interpret the findings should be carefully described, so that the bases for value judgments are clear.

U5 Report Clarity. The evaluation reports should clearly describe the program being evaluated, including its context, and the purposes, procedures, and findings of the evaluation, so that essential information is provided and easily understood.

U6 Report Timeliness and Dissemination. Significant interim findings and evaluation reports should be disseminated to intended users, so that they can be used in a timely fashion.

U7 Evaluation Impact. Evaluations should be planned, conducted, and reported in ways that encourage follow-through by stakeholders, so that the likelihood that the evaluation will be used is increased.

FEASIBILITY

The feasibility standards are intended to ensure that an evaluation will be realistic, prudent, diplomatic, and frugal.

F1 Practical Procedures. The evaluation procedures should be practical, to keep disruption to a minimum while needed information is obtained.

F2 Political Viability. The evaluation should be planned and conducted with anticipation of the different positions of various interest groups, so that their cooperation may be obtained and so that possible attempts by any of these groups to curtail evaluation operations or to bias or misapply the results can be averted or counteracted.

F3 Cost Effectiveness. The evaluation should be efficient and produce information of sufficient value, so that the resources expended can be justified.

PROPRIETY

The propriety standards are intended to ensure that an evaluation will be conducted legally, ethically, and with due regard for the welfare of those involved in the evaluation, as well as those affected by its results.

P1 Service Orientation. Evaluations should be designed to assist organizations to address and effectively serve the needs of the full range of targeted participants.

P2 Formal Obligations. Obligations of the formal parties to an evaluation (what is to be done, how, by whom, when) should be agreed to in writing, so that these parties are obliged to adhere to all conditions of the agreement or formally to renegotiate it.

P3 Rights of Human Subjects. Evaluations should be designed and conducted to respect and to protect the rights and welfare of human subjects.

P4 Human Interactions. Evaluators should respect human dignity and worth in their interactions with other persons associated with an evaluation, so that participants are not threatened or harmed.

P5 Complete and Fair Assessment. The evaluation should be complete and fair in its examination and recording of strengths and weaknesses of the program being evaluated, so that strengths can be built upon and problem areas addressed.

Table 1 (continued)

PROPRIETY

P6 Disclosure of Findings. The formal parties to an evaluation should ensure that the full set of evaluation findings along with pertinent limitations are made accessible to the persons affected by the evaluation and any others with expressed legal rights to receive the results.

P7 Conflict of Interest. Conflict of interest should be dealt with openly and honestly, so that it does not compromise the evaluation processes and results.

P8 Fiscal Responsibility. The evaluator's allocation and expenditure of resources should reflect sound accountability procedures and otherwise be prudent and ethically responsible, so that expenditures are accounted for and appropriate.

ACCURACY

The accuracy standards are intended to ensure that an evaluation will reveal and convey technically adequate information about the features that determine worth or merit of the program being evaluated.

A1 Program Documentation. The program being evaluated should be described and documented clearly and accurately, so that the program is clearly identified.

A2 Context Analysis. The context in which the program exists should be examined in enough detail, so that its likely influences on the program can be identified.

A3 Described Purposes and Procedures. The purposes and procedures of the evaluation should be monitored and described in enough detail, so that they can be identified and assessed.

A4 Defensible Information Sources. The sources of information used in program evaluation should be described in enough detail, so that the adequacy of the information can be assessed.

A5 Valid Information. The information-gathering procedures should be chosen or developed and then implemented, so that they will ensure that the interpretation arrived at is valid for the intended use.

A6 Reliable Information. The information-gathering procedures should be chosen or developed and then implemented, so that they will ensure that the information obtained is sufficiently reliable for the intended use.

A7 Systematic Information. The information collected, processed, and reported in an evaluation should be systematically reviewed, and any errors found should be corrected.

A8 Analysis of Quantitative Information. Quantitative information in an evaluation should be appropriately and systematically analyzed, so that evaluation questions are effectively answered.

A9 Analysis of Qualitative Information. Qualitative information in an evaluation should be appropriately and systematically analyzed, so that evaluation questions are effectively answered.

A10 Justified Conclusions. The conclusions reached in an evaluation should be explicitly justified, so that stakeholders can assess them.

A11 Impartial Reporting. Reporting procedures should guard against distortion caused by personal feelings and biases of any party to the evaluation, so that evaluation reports fairly reflect the evaluation findings.

A12 Metaevaluation. The evaluation itself should be formatively and summatively evaluated against these and other pertinent standards, so that its conduct is appropriately guided and, on completion, stakeholders can closely examine its strengths and weaknesses.

Source: Joint Committee on Standards for Educational Evaluation (1994).

task are summarized in Table 2. The 30 standards are listed down the side of the matrix, while the 10 evaluation tasks are presented across the top. The Xs in the various cells indicate that the Committee judged the standard was particularly applicable to the given task. While the Joint Committee concluded that all of the standards are applicable in all educational program evaluations, the functional analysis is intended to help evaluators quickly identify those standards that are likely to be most relevant to given tasks.

The Committee also presented and illustrated five general steps for applying the standards. These are (1) become acquainted with *The Program Evaluation Standards,* (2) clarify the purposes of the program evaluation, (3) clarify the context of the program evaluation, (4) apply each standard in light of the purposes and context, and (5) decide what to do with the results. The Committee also suggested ways to employ the standards in designing an evaluation training program.

The Program Evaluation Standards are particularly applicable in evaluations of evaluations, i.e., metaevaluations. In such studies, the metaevaluator collects information and judgments about the extent to which a program evaluation complied with the requirements for meeting each standard. Then the evaluator judges whether each standard was "addressed," "partially addressed," "not addressed," or "not applicable." A profile of these judgments provides bases for judging the evaluation against the considerations of utility, feasibility, propriety, and accuracy, and in relation to each standard. When such metaevaluations are carried out early in an evaluation, they provide diagnostic feedback of use in strengthening the evaluation. When completed after a program evaluation, the metaevaluation helps users to assess and make prudent use of the evaluation's findings and recommendations.

PERSONNEL EVALUATION STANDARDS

As mentioned earlier, the Joint Committee also developed *The Personnel Evaluation Standards* (1988). This document includes 21 standards organized according to the four basic concepts of propriety, utility, feasibility, and accuracy. These standards reflect the fact that personnel qualifications and performance are critically important concerns for evaluating programs and that personnel evaluation is important in its own right for helping to assure the delivery of sound, ethical professional services. *The Personnel Evaluation Standards* are designed to give educators and board members a widely shared view of general principles for developing and assessing sound, respectable, and acceptable personnel evaluation systems, plus practical advice for fulfilling the principles.

Institutions need effective personnel evaluation systems to help select, retain, and develop qualified personnel and to supervise and facilitate their work and development. Individual professionals need valid assessments of their performance to provide direction for improvement and be accountable for the responsiveness and quality of their services. The state of personnel evaluation in educational institutions has been poor (Joint Committee, 1988). The Joint Committee's sponsoring organizations charged the Committee to devise personnel evaluation standards that institutions

Table 2. Analysis of the Relative Importance of 30 Standards in Performing 10 Tasks in an Evaluation

	1. Deciding Whether to Evaluate	2. Defining the Evaluation Problem	3. Designing the Evaluation	4. Collecting Information	5. Analyzing Information	6. Reporting the Evaluation	7. Budgeting the Evaluation	8. Contracting for the Evaluation	9. Managing the Evaluation	10. Staffing the Evaluation
U1 Stakeholder Identification	×	×	×			×		×	×	
U2 Evaluator Credibility	×								×	×
U3 Information Scope & Selection			×	×		×	×	×		
U4 Values Identification			×	×	×	×				
U5 Report Clarity						×				
U6 Report Timeliness & Dissemination						×		×	×	
U7 Evaluation Impact	×					×				
F1 Practical Procedures			×	×					×	
F2 Political Viability	×								×	×
F3 Cost Effectiveness	×				×		×		×	
P1 Service Orientation	×					×		×	×	
P2 Formal Agreements	×	×	×	×			×	×	×	
P3 Rights of Human Subjects	×			×		×		×	×	

P4   Human Interactions
P5   Complete & Fair Assessment
P6   Disclosure of Findings
P7   Conflict of Interest
P8   Fiscal Responsibility
A1   Program Documentation
A2   Context Analysis
A3   Described Purposes & Procedures
A4   Defensible Information Sources
A5   Valid Information
A6   Reliable Information
A7   Systematic Information
A8   Analysis of Quantitative Information
A9   Analysis of Qualitative Information
A10 Justified Conclusions
A11 Impartial Reporting
A12 Metaevaluation

could use to correct weaknesses in their personnel evaluation practices and/or develop new, sound personnel evaluation systems.

The 1988 *Personnel Evaluation Standards* are focused on assessing and improving the systems that educational organizations use to evaluate instructors, administrators, support staff, and other educational personnel. This book is intended to be used by board members and educators in school districts, community colleges, four-year colleges, universities, professional development organizations, and other educational institutions.

The utility standards were placed first in *The Program Evaluation Standards*, because program evaluations often are ad hoc. A program evaluation would be done not as a matter of course, but because it is needed and could make an important difference in delivering and improving services. Evaluators and their clients should first make sure that findings from a program evaluation under consideration would be used before taking the trouble to address concerns for feasibility, propriety, and accuracy. For example, it makes no sense to develop a sound data collection and analysis plan, a contract, and a budget if no one is likely to read and act on the projected report. In such a case it is better to abort the evaluation as soon as it is known that carrying it out would make no difference. For these reasons, evaluators should first apply the utility standards to assure that an evaluation could impact on program quality and delivery. If there is no prospect for use, then the evaluator and client should stop the process. In that event they need not look at the standards of feasibility, propriety, and accuracy. But if there is a good prospect for utility, the evaluator should systematically turn to consideration of the full set of standards.

The situation in personnel evaluation is different. Mainly, personnel evaluations are not ad hoc. They are basically inevitable, no matter how badly they will be done. Thus, the Joint Committee said the personnel evaluator should deal first with the contemplated evaluation's propriety. A key reason for this decision is that the first propriety standard addresses the issue of service orientation. This standard emphasizes that the fundamental purpose of personnel evaluation must be to provide effective, safe, and ethical services to students and society. Personnel evaluations especially must help protect the interests of students by uncovering harmful practices of teachers, administrators, etc., as well as providing feedback to help such persons improve their services to the students. The bottom line thrust of *The Personnel Evaluation Standards* is to help assure that students are served well, that services constantly improve, and that harmful practices are quickly uncovered and promptly addressed.

To balance this emphasis on service orientation, *The Personnel Evaluation Standards* also stress that personnel evaluation practices should be constructive and free of unnecessarily threatening or demoralizing characteristics. In this positive vein, personnel evaluations can and should be employed to help plan sound professional development experiences and help each professional assess and strengthen her or his performance. Such evaluations should identify the educator's deficiencies and strengths.

COMPARISON OF THE JOINT COMMITTEE STANDARDS
AND THE ERS/AEA STANDARDS AND PRINCIPLES

Comparisons of the substance of the ERS/AEA and Joint Committee standards and principles documents reveal key differences and similarities in the standards and principles (Cordray, 1982; Covert, 1995; Sanders, 1995; Stufflebeam, 1982). While the Joint Committee's standards focused on evaluations in education, the ERS standards and principles addressed evaluations across a variety of government and social service sectors. Essentially everything covered by the ERS standards is also covered by the Joint Committee's standards, but the latter's coverage is much more detailed and goes deeper into evaluation issues. The Joint Committee's presentations of standards have averaged more than 100 pages, while the ERS/AEA presentations of standards and principles each numbered less than 10 pages. Further, the Joint Committee standards were developed by a joint committee whose 17 members were appointed by 12 professional organizations with a total membership of over 2 million. The ERS standards and the AEA principles were developed by single organizations with memberships of about 1,000 and 2,000, respectively. The standards and principles-development task forces of these organizations respectively had 6 and 4 evaluation specialists respectively, whereas the Joint Committee had 17 members. Another key difference is that the Joint Committee standards were developed by a combination of evaluation users and evaluation specialists, while the ERS standards and AEA principles were developed almost exclusively by evaluation specialists. Finally, the AEA principles were formally adopted by AEA, whereas the Joint Committee's 1994 *Program Evaluation Standards* were accredited by ANSI, but have not been formally adopted by any of the Committee's sponsoring organizations.

The differences in lengths of the documents reflect perhaps somewhat different purposes. The ERS/AEA efforts have focused almost exclusively at the level of general principles to be observed by evaluators. The Joint Committee also stresses general principles—as seen in its requirements for utility, feasibility, propriety, and accuracy—but also attempts to provide specific and detailed standards of good practice along with guidelines for meeting the standards. In this sense, the Joint Committee's standards include both general requirements of sound evaluations and rather specific advice for meeting these requirements. Nevertheless, both standards/principles-setting programs emphasize that the standards and principles must be seen as general guides and that evaluators and their clients must consult and employ much more specific material when dealing with the details of design, measurement, case studies, statistics, reporting, etc.

Both sets of documents are in substantial agreement as to what constitutes sound evaluation practices. Evaluators should seek out and involve their intended audiences in clarifying evaluation questions and in reporting evaluation findings. Evaluations should be beyond reproach, with evaluators adhering to all relevant ethical codes. Moreover, evaluators should strive to produce valid findings and should be careful not to present unsupportable conclusions and recommendations. In addition, evaluators should carefully sort out their roles as independent inquirers from their social advocacy roles and make sure that their evaluations are not corrupted by conflicts of interest. Also, the Joint Committee standards, the ERS standards, and the AEA principles concur that evaluations occur in politically charged, dynamic social settings and call on evaluators to be realistic, diplomatic, and socially sensitive, while maintaining their integrity as evaluators. Both standards/principles-setting movements stress that sound evaluation is vital to the functioning of a healthy society. Service providers must regularly subject their services to evaluation, and evaluators must deliver responsive, dependable evaluation services. Professional standards are a powerful force for bringing about the needed sound evaluation services.

CLOSING COMMENTS

This chapter has provided an overview of the state of standards setting in the field of evaluation as practiced in the U.S. Professional standards and principles are seen as important for assessing and strengthening evaluation practices. It is a mark of American evaluators' move toward professionalism that two separate but complementary standards/principles-development movements are now more than two decades old and continuing. It is fortunate that two sets of standards/principles have been developed. They provide cross-checks on each other, even though they are appropriately aimed at different constituencies. The two sets of presentations have proved to be complementary rather than competitive. The ERS/AEA standards and principles address evaluations across a wide range of disciplines and service areas, while the Joint Committee standards have honed in on education. It should be reassuring to educational evaluators that all the important points in the ERS/AEA standards and principles are also covered in the Joint Committee standards. There seem to be no conflicts about what principles evaluators should follow in the two sets of materials. Moreover, evaluators outside education can find that the details in the Joint Committee standards can help to buttress the general principles in the ERS/AEA standards and principles. (For example, see Patton's chapter in this book.)

For the future the two groups should continue to work at reviewing and updating the standards and principles as needed. They should also promote effective use of the standards and principles. Especially, they should encourage evaluation educators to build the standards and principles into every evaluation degree program and into special training sessions for evaluation users as well as specialists. Evaluators should also employ the evaluation standards and principles to conduct and report metaevaluations. If the standards and principles become well established and if they are regularly applied, then both evaluation consumers and producers will benefit. Adherence to the evaluation standards and principles will improve the quality of evaluations and should increase their value for improving programs and services. These points seem to provide an ample rationale for evaluators to obtain, study, apply, and help to improve the ERS/AEA standards and principles and the Joint Committee standards for program and personnel evaluations. The fact that these efforts developed independently gives added credibility to the consensus reflected in their reports about what constitutes good and acceptable evaluation practice. Now it is time for collaboration as the Joint Committee and AEA move ahead to advance the professional practice of evaluation through adherence to high standards and principles of practice.

NOTES

1. The membership of the Joint Committee on Standards for Educational Evaluation, as of publication of the 1994 *The Program Evaluation Standards,* included the American Association of School Administrators, American Educational Research Association, American Evaluation Association, American Federation of Teachers, American Psychological Association, Association for Assessment in Counseling, Association for Supervision and Curriculum Development, Canadian Society for the Study of Education, Council of Chief State School Officers, Council on Postsecondary Accreditation, National Association of Elementary School Principals, National Association of Secondary School Principals, National Council on Measurement in Education, National Education Association, and National School Boards Association.

2. The summary statements of the 30 program evaluation standards are printed here with the permission of the Joint Committee for Educational Evaluation.

25. THE METHODOLOGY OF METAEVALUATION

DANIEL L. STUFFLEBEAM

This article addresses the professional imperative that evaluations must themselves be evaluated. This type of evaluation activity is labeled **metaevaluation** and is formally defined as the process of delineating, obtaining, and applying descriptive information and judgmental information about the utility, feasibility, propriety, and accuracy of an evaluation in order to guide the evaluation and publicly report its strengths and weaknesses.

Michael Scriven (1969a) introduced the term metaevaluation in the *Educational Products Report* to refer to his evaluation of a plan for evaluating educational products. Essentially, Dr Scriven defined a metaevaluation as any evaluation of an evaluation, evaluation system, or evaluation device. He argued that, by issuing inaccurate and/or biased reports, evaluators could seriously mislead consumers to purchase unworthy or inferior educational products and then use them to the detriment of children and youth. Thus, he stressed that the evaluations of such products must themselves be evaluated.

In general, ensuring that evaluations are rigorously evaluated is in both the professional and public interest. Professional evaluators need feedback to assure the quality of their evaluations and to provide direction for improving individual studies. Consumers of evaluation reports need metaevaluations that will help them decide

A longer version of this paper was written to help the Consortium for Research on Educational Accountability and Teacher Evaluation (CREATE) commemorate the research and evaluation contributions of the late Dr. Jason Millman.

D.L. Stufflebeam, G.F. Madaus and T. Kellaghan (eds.). EVALUATION MODELS. Copyright © 2000. Kluwer Academic Publishers. Boston. All rights reserved.

whether or not to accept and act on evaluative conclusions about products, programs, and services they are using or considering for use.

As with other societal endeavors, an evaluation can be good, bad, or somewhere in between. Many things can and do go wrong in evaluations. Evaluations might be flawed by inappropriate focus, inappropriate criteria, biased findings, technical errors, unjustified conclusions, ambiguous findings, unwarranted recommendations, excessive costs, inadequate interpretation to users, or counterproductive interference in the programs being evaluated. If such problems are not detected and addressed in the evaluation process, evaluators will deliver faulty findings and/or deliver ineffective services. If faulty reports are issued without being exposed by sound metaevaluations, evaluation audiences may make bad decisions based on the erroneous findings. As Scriven (1994b) pointed out, even the highly respected and widely used *Consumer Reports* magazine should be independently evaluated to help readers see the limitations as well as the strengths of the many evaluations published in it.

During the last 30 years, there have been many instructive applications of metaevaluation. The Western Michigan University Evaluation Center, where I work, has conducted or participated in a wide range of such studies. These span evaluations of personnel, programs, and student assessment systems. The aim of this article is to synthesize from those metaevaluation experiences a general methodology for planning and conducting metaevaluations. In pursuing this aim, the remainder of this presentation is divided into three parts. The first gives a general idea of what metaevaluation involves by describing a metaevaluation of a teacher evaluation system. The second part dissembles that experience to identify the main steps in a metaevaluation. The third part identifies illustrative arrangements and procedures for carrying out each metaevaluation step by drawing upon a broad range of metaevaluation experiences.

A METAEVALUATION OF THE TEACH FOR AMERICA PERFORMANCE ASSESSMENT SYSTEM

The TEACH FOR AMERICA (TFA) organization recruits, trains, and certifies graduates of various baccalaureate programs for service as teachers in inner-city schools. These teacher trainees have four-year degrees grounded in an arts and sciences discipline, but most have no university-based teacher education. TFA's role is to recruit able students desiring to serve inner-city students; provide them a year of on-the-job, supervised teacher training in inner-city schools; rigorously evaluate their performance and potential during and immediately following this probationary period; and subsequently recommend only satisfactory performers for certification as effective teachers.

In 1995, TFA commissioned a metaevaluation of its Performance Assessment System (PAS) for evaluating the probationary teachers. The metaevaluation's purpose was to determine whether the PAS–in design and execution—fairly, reliably, and accurately evaluated beginning teachers.

This metaevaluation was important to a range of stakeholders. Many future inner city students needed and deserved to be served by competent teachers. The certifying bodies—be they state education departments or city school districts—needed assurances that they would be making sound certification decisions. The teaching candidates themselves needed assurances that they would be functioning in a profession for which they were well suited and appropriately prepared. They also deserved to be credentialed or screened-out based only on fair, valid, impartial assessments. Politically, TFA needed to demonstrate the TFA program's quality and integrity, since TFA's teaching candidates had no university-based teacher education and some members of the teacher education establishment considered TFA's program to be inferior to traditional college and university teacher education programs. If TFA could expect trainees to enroll and schools to employ the graduates, it needed to achieve and maintain credibility for the soundness of its alternative teacher preparation and certification process.

TFA's evaluation of the teacher trainees was a crucial step in awarding certification and getting only qualified teachers into the schools. The metaevaluation was clearly important to help TFA base its judgments and recommendations on sound evaluations of the beginning teachers and to establish and maintain credibility for the program.

The five main components of TFA's teacher evaluation system were a teacher-compiled portfolio, portfolio assessors, a system of training and calibration for the assessors, actual assessment of portfolios, and certification recommendations derived from the assessments. The evidence in each teacher's portfolio included students' work, videotaped teaching, teaching plans, the teacher's assessment devices, and an analysis of the students' academic growth. The portfolio also contained survey results from the teacher's principal, other supervisors, teacher colleagues, parents, and students. Two assessors evaluated each portfolio according to preestablished rubrics and produced subscores for the specified certification criteria and a total score. A third assessor resolved any unacceptable discrepancies between the first two sets of ratings.

TFA's main metaevaluation questions asked whether each of the following was adequate: the performance assessment design, assessments of teachers' impacts on students' learning, assessors' selection and training, implementation of the portfolio review process, quantitative analysis of the assessors' ratings of probationary teachers, legal defensibility of the PAS, and implications for PAS's wider use. The metaevaluation also assessed the PAS against the requirements of the 21 Joint Committee (1988) *Personnel Evaluation Standards* to determine the PAS's utility, feasibility, propriety, and accuracy.

The metaevaluators obtained and studied documents from TFA relating to the targeted metaevaluation questions and the 21 Joint Committee standards. These documents included the teacher trainees' academic records; the credentials of the assessors who would evaluate the evidence on each probationary teacher; and the TFA plan and associated recruitment, training, and assessment materials. The metaevaluators also observed and prepared field notes on the training of the assessors and examined the beginning teachers' portfolios. Subsequently, they observed the assessors' actual assessments of the teachers' materials and analyzed the ratings and resulting certification recommendations, especially for reliability of subscores and agreements on final recommendations. Examination of this evidence was used to judge whether TFA's performance assessment system met, partially met, or failed to meet each of the 21 Joint Committee standards. The metaevaluators also referenced pertinent policies, statutes, and laws to assess the legal viability of TFA's assessment structure and process. Finally, they produced an executive summary, a full-length report, and a technical appendix for the completed metaevaluation. In accordance with the metaevaluation contract, these reports were delivered to TFA for its discretionary use.

The basic findings were that TFA's evaluation team did a creditable and legally viable job in conducting and reporting summative evaluations of the TFA probationary teachers. TFA was also judged to have performed professionally in informing their state department and school district clients about the evaluation findings and engaging them in making appropriate decisions based on the findings. On the other hand, the metaevaluation identified areas where TFA needed to improve the PAS, especially in providing less hurried training for the assessors and strengthening the assessments of the teacher trainees' effects on student learning, and better matching assessors and trainees on areas and grade levels taught.

THE STEPS IN THE METAEVALUATION PROCESS

While the preceding example is abbreviated, it nevertheless points up the main steps in a metaevaluation process. Of course, up front the metaevaluator must **identify the client and appropriate audiences** for the metaevaluation reports. In this case, the client group included TFA's leaders and staff. The metaevaluation had many other stakeholders, including the participating state education departments, school districts, teachers, and the students in the involved school districts.

The client had to **commission qualified metaevaluators**. Beyond having previous similar experiences in evaluating teacher evaluation systems, the team collectively needed competence in personnel measurement, legal requirements of teacher evaluation systems, and working knowledge of the Joint Committee *Personnel Evaluation Standards*. Other evaluator qualifications—not present in this metaevaluation but often important—are gender and racial diversity.

Another early step in the metaevaluation process is to **negotiate the metaevaluation contract**. Among the important agreements to be reached were clarification of the metaevaluation issues and questions, the professional standards for judging the evaluation system, guaranteed access to the needed information, substance and timing of reports, designated authority to edit and release the metaevaluation reports, and provision of the required resources.

The next metaevaluation task was to **compile and analyze the available, relevant information**. The initial information collection process typically culminates in a desk review. Following this "stay-at-home" work, the metaevaluator often must **collect additionally needed information**. For example, this metaevaluation included on-site interviews and observations and study of portfolios. In order to reach valid conclusions, metaevaluators must have access to all the relevant available information and be able to collect any further needed information. Basically, the metaevaluator should obtain the full range of information required to apply all the applicable standards and address the additional metaevaluation questions.

Next the metaevaluators must **analyze the obtained information** and **write up the metaevaluation findings**. This metaevaluation presented tables showing both quantitative and qualitative analyses and provided judgments on TFA's adherence to each of the Joint Committee's 21 personnel evaluation standards.

The team prepared a semifinal report and submitted it to the client for review. After considering critiques from the client and other stakeholders, the **metaevaluation report was finalized** and presented to the client.

Subsequently, the metaevaluation team stood ready, if required, to **help the client and other stakeholders interpret the findings**. This step can be crucially important both for improving the evaluation system being assessed and helping the interested stakeholders to use the metaevaluation findings appropriately and productively.

The above analysis shows that a metaevaluation may be divided into the following 10 steps:

1. Determine and arrange to interact with the metaevaluation's stakeholders.
2. Establish a qualified metaevaluation team.
3. Define the metaevaluation questions.
4. Agree on standards to judge the evaluation system or particular evaluation.
5. Negotiate the metaevaluation contract.
6. Collect and review pertinent available information.
7. Collect new information as needed, including, for example, on-site interviews, observations, and surveys.
8. Analyze the qualitative and quantitative information and judge the evaluation's adherence to the selected evaluation standards.
9. Prepare and submit the needed reports.
10. Help the client and other stakeholders interpret and apply the findings.

PROCEDURES FOR IMPLEMENTING METAEVALUATION STEPS

Using the preceding 10 metaevaluation steps, we next look at some of the specific procedures that proved useful in six particular metaevaluations—two of personnel evaluation systems, three of program evaluations, and one of a large-scale student assessment system. The referenced evaluations of personnel evaluation involved the system that the United States Marine Corps had previously used to evaluate the performance of officers and enlisted personnel and the system that the Hawaii Department of Education uses to evaluate Hawaii's public school teachers. The example evaluations of program evaluations involved the New York City school district's testing of the Waterford Integrated Learning System—a computer-based basic skills program for elementary school students (Finn, Stevens, Stufflebeam, & Walberg, 1997); evaluations of programs of the Appalachia Regional Educational Laboratory;

and an evaluation of Australia's national distance baccalaureate program called Open Learning Australia. The metaevaluation of a large scale assessment system focused on an attempt to set achievement levels on the National Assessment of Educational Progress (Stufflebeam, Jaeger, & Scriven, 1992; Vinovskis, 1999). Time and space do not permit in-depth discussion of any of these cases. However, they are cited because the procedures employed proved useful in terms of the 10 metaevaluation steps identified above.

1. Determine and Arrange to Interact With the Metaevaluation Stakeholders

The metaevaluation for the Marine Corps was especially instructive regarding the identification and involvement of stakeholders. From the beginning, the Corps established two stakeholder panels and arranged for systematic interaction between them and the metaevaluators. The executive-level panel included 11 generals, 4 colonels, and the Sergeant Major of the Marine Corps. The advisory panel included representatives from different ranks of officers and enlisted personnel.

The Corps scheduled monthly meetings between the metaevaluators and each panel. Each meeting was scheduled for at least two hours. The Corps required the metaevaluators to deliver printed reports at least 10 working days in advance of each meeting and required the panelists to read and prepare to discuss the reports. Collectively, these reports spanned all major steps in the metaevaluation, including selection of standards for judging the Corps' personnel evaluation system; plans and instruments for obtaining information; diagnoses of strengths and weaknesses in the Corps' current system; assessments of alternative personnel evaluation systems used in business, industry, and six other military organizations; generation and evaluation of three alternative new evaluation plans; and a plan for operationalizing and testing the selected new personnel evaluation system. A general officer chaired each meeting for both groups.

Each meeting began with an overhead projector briefing by the metaevaluators, with copies of the transparencies distributed to all persons present. A period of questions, answers, and discussion followed. At the meeting's end the presiding general officer asked each panelist to respond to a bottom line question. The lead general then summarized the meeting's main outcomes. Subsequently, an assigned officer prepared and distributed a report of all conclusions reached at the meeting. These meetings were highly substantive and productive, with one going more than five hours without a break. The Marine Corps clients were an evaluator's dream. They read, understood, critiqued, and used the metaevaluation reports.

A down side was that the stakeholder panels were top heavy with general officers. This is an especially serious limitation, considering that they had all been promoted by the personnel evaluation system under review. Also, all members of the panels worked in the DC area, not, for example, in California, Hawaii, or Saipan. There was risk that voices and concerns of rank and file members throughout the Corps would not be sufficiently represented and heard. The metaevaluators convinced the lead general that marines beyond Quantico and Washington should be consulted and involved. With this accomplished through surveys and site visits, the stakeholder involvement aspect of this metaevaluation was good. The structure involved in this work with the Marine Corps' stakeholder panels could be beneficially applied in a wide range of metaevaluations.

2. Establish a Qualified Metaevaluation Team

Turning to the second metaevaluation step, the metaevaluation team must be credible. The members must be both competent and trusted by the stakeholders. In setting up the team for the Marine Corps metaevaluation, it was important to include persons with military personnel evaluation experience, as well as expertise in the different aspects of a metaevaluation. The metaevaluation for the New York City School District basic education program included the perspectives of educational research, program evaluation, educational policy, and school district operations, as well as the perspectives of women and minorities. This team also could have used at least another perspective representing school and classroom-level operations and possibly others. Generally, the leader of a metaevaluation needs to project the type of metaevaluation to be done and interact with an appropriate range of stakeholders to set up an appropriately qualified and acceptable metaevaluation team.

Of course, there will be cases where the client for the metaevaluation can afford to employ only one metaevaluator. Then, one must engage the most credible, capable metaevaluator one can find. For example, Dr. Bill Wiersma conducts metaevaluations for the Appalachia Regional Educational Laboratory and meets this need exceptionally well. He is a highly accomplished research methodologist, with extensive successful experience in schools. He is thoroughly familiar with professional standards for evaluation and measurement. He writes easily and well. He understands education at all levels and relates effectively to educators, students, parents, and policymakers. Dr. Wiersma's qualifications give an indication of the characteristics one should seek out for a "lone ranger" metaevaluation assignment.

3. Define the Metaevaluation Questions

The fundamental consideration in selecting appropriate questions for a metaevaluation are to assess the subject evaluation for (1) the extent to which it meets its audience's needs for evaluative information (worth) and (2) how well it meets the requirements of a sound evaluation (merit).

The metaevaluator should carefully deliberate with the client and other stakeholders to assure that the metaevaluation will address their important questions. For example, in the referenced metaevaluation of the National Assessment Governing Board's attempt to set achievement levels of "basic, proficient, and advanced" on the National Assessment of Educational Progress, the metaevaluators and the NAGB Board defined more than 20 particular metaevaluation questions.

Two examples illustrating clients' specific metaevaluation questions are as follows:

1.1 Is the membership of NAGB duly constituted, sufficiently representative of the National Assessment's constituencies, and effectively in touch with stakeholders so that it enjoys sufficient authority and credibility to set and secure use of achievement levels on the National Assessment?

2.1 Are NAGB's policy framework and specifications for setting achievement levels sufficiently clear and consistent with the state of the relevant measurement technology to assure that an appropriately representative group of standards setters can consistently and effectively set sound achievement levels on the National Assessment?

In general, the metaevaluator should carefully assure that the metaevaluation will address the audience's most important questions and also determine the quality and the overall value of the subject evaluation. A useful means of focusing metaevaluations on an appropriate range of questions is to key them to professional standards for judging the evaluations.

4. Agree on Standards to Judge the Evaluation System or Particular Evaluation

Evaluation is a professional activity. As such, it is appropriate to judge evaluations against the professional standards of the evaluation field. The APA (1985) *Standards for Educational and Psychological Tests* are especially useful for assessing testing programs. Other standards are those developed by the National Center for Education Statistics (1991) for conducting large-scale surveys and the American Evaluation Association (Shadish, Newman, Scheirer, & Wye, 1995) guiding principles for program evaluations across the full range of disciplines.

The standards most used in The Evaluation Center's metaevaluations are the program and personnel evaluation standards issued by the North American Joint Committee on Standards for Educational Evaluation (1988, 1994). They have been widely applied in American educational evaluations. For example, the Hawaii State Board of Education adopted the Joint Committee's program and personnel evaluations as state policy, stipulating that these standards be used to assess and strengthen Hawaii's system of educational accountability. While the Joint Committee's standards were developed for use in evaluating North American educational evaluations, they have been shown to apply in other areas. For example, with minor modifications, the U.S. Marine Corps (The Evaluation Center, 1995) adopted the Joint Committee *Personnel Evaluation Standards* for use in assessing and reforming the Corps' personnel evaluation system. Similarly, General Motors (Orris, 1989) used the Joint Committee's *Personnel Evaluation Standards* to assess GM's system for evaluating executives.

5. Negotiate the Metaevaluation Contract

As with any evaluation, a metaevaluation should be firmly grounded in a sound memorandum of agreement or formal contract. According to the Joint Committee on Standards for Educational Evaluation (1994), evaluators and their clients should negotiate and document evaluation agreements that contain ". . . mutual understandings of the specified expectations and responsibilities of both the client and the evaluator" (p. 87). Such an agreement clarifies understandings and helps prevent misunderstandings between the client and metaevaluators and provides a basis for resolving any future disputes about the evaluation. The Committee further states, "Having entered into such an agreement, both parties have an obligation to carry it out in a forthright manner or to renegotiate it. Neither party is obligated to honor decisions made unilaterally by the other" (p. 87). Written agreements for metaevaluations should be explicit but should also allow for appropriate, mutually agreeable adjustments during the evaluation. Advance agreements can mean the difference between a metaevaluation's success and failure. Without such agreements, the metaevaluation process is constantly open to misunderstandings, disputes, efforts to compromise the findings, attacks, and/or the client's withdrawal of cooperation and funds.

In one high-stakes metaevaluation, the absence of an updated contract aided the client to try to discredit a valid, but negative metaevaluation report. The National Assessment Governing Board, (NAGB), under a requirement from the U.S. Congress, had contracted for a metaevaluation of NAGB's attempt to set achievement levels on the National Assessment of Educational Progress (NAEP). Pursuant to the contract, the metaevaluation team assessed NAGB's first two attempts to set levels on the NAEP and issued formative metaevaluation reports, noting, among other shortcomings, that the attempts had failed to achieve acceptable levels of reliability and validity. NAGB thanked the team and said their work was completed.

However, NAGB soon contacted the team on an emergency basis. The Congress had wanted, beyond the external formative metaevaluations of the achievement levels-setting effort, an external summative metaevaluation of the work. NAGB asked the metaevaluators to undertake this on short notice in order to meet the Congressional mandate and the imminent reporting deadline. NAGB officials said that the summative metaevaluation could not wait for a new contract to proceed through the government channels and asked the metaevaluators to proceed immediately. NAGB officials promised that the contract would arrive later. The metaevaluators agreed to this good faith arrangement and proceeded post haste.

Having drafted the summative metaevaluation report, they sought to assure its accuracy and clarity before finalizing it. They sent it to about a dozen members of NAGB and about 10 others with specialized expertise in measurement and policy analysis. These persons were asked to keep the report confidential and to promptly return their criticisms and recommenations. Consistent with the previous formative metaevaluation reports, this summative metaevaluation report noted that NAGB's achievement levels-setting procedure was fatally flawed and could only mislead the public and the Congress about students' performance on the NAEP.

Upon seeing the draft report, NAGB promptly fired the metaevaluators, even though there still was no contract. The metaevaluators used the obtained critiques to finalize their report and sent it in anyway. Their findings were vindicated when the Congress directed the General Accounting Office (GAO) to assess this report and make its own assessment. GAO also found that NAGB's achievement levels-setting process was "fatally flawed," as did several subsequent metaevaluations, including one by the National Academy of Education (Shepard, Glaser, Linn, & Bohrnstedt, 1993).

NAGB never paid the previously agreed on price of $5,000 for this summative metaevaluation. Because the legal process would have cost more than the amount to be recovered, the metaevaluators did not sue for payment. In retrospect, the metaevaluators probably should have refused to proceed with this summative metaevaluation without a written contract.

6. Collect and Review Pertinent Available Information

After negotiating the contract, the metaevaluator needs to examine the subject evaluation against pertinent evidence. Initially, this involves collecting and assessing existing information. In some metaevaluations, this is the only information used to reach the metaevaluation conclusions. Legitimate reasons for collecting additional information are that the existing information is technically inadequate, insufficient, and/or not sufficiently credible to answer the metaevaluation questions. When the existing information is fully acceptable for producing a sound metaevaluation report, further data collection is wasteful.

My metaevaluation of the evaluation of the Open Learning Australia distance education program is instructive about the kinds of extant information from which to begin a metaevaluation and how to handle that information. It was in the interest of Open Learning Australia to control the metaevaluation costs, since travel from the U.S. to Australia could entail a sizable expense. Thus, it was agreed that Open Learning Australia would send pertinent information to Kalamazoo, where I could assess it to reach at least tentative judgments about the adequacy of the evaluation of Open Learning Australia. A wide array of documents was involved. These included letters, plans, budgets, contracts, data collection forms, journal and newspaper articles, field notes, reports, and responses to reports. Substantive foci were the nature of Open Learning Australia, the background of the evaluation, the evaluation plans and procedures, the evaluation process, the findings, publicity for the program, and guidelines for the metaevaluation.

The client for the metaevaluation emphasized that all judgments of the evaluation should be grounded in references to the pertinent evidence. This, they thought, would distill any notion of stakeholders that the metaevaluation from afar was only a set of ill-informed opinions. Accordingly, I catalogued every piece of information used in the metaevaluation, giving its year of origination and a unique number within that year. In reporting a judgment for each of the 30 Joint Committee standards, I referenced each catalogued information item used in reaching the judgment. Thus, the client group and its constituents could review essentially all the evidence I used to reach the metaevaluation conclusions.

7. Collect New Information as Needed, Including, for example, On-site Interviews, Observations, and Surveys

While the extant information for evaluating the evaluation of Open Learning Australia (OLA) was substantial, it was insufficient to produce the needed metaevaluation report. Thus, I went to Australia to fill in some important information gaps. In addition to talking with OLA's leaders and participating faculty, I also met with OLA students and with leaders and faculty in the more traditional higher education programs. This additional input led to the determinations that the assumed need for Open Learning Australia was questionable, the quality of OLA offerings was highly variable, and these findings were at variance with the evaluation of OLA. In retrospect, the additional information obtained by making a site visit to Australia was vital to the validity of the metaevaluation report.

Another example of supplementing extant information with new information in order to reach metaevaluation conclusions occurred in an assessment of Hawaii's teacher evaluation system. The metaevaluator first used extant information to judge the Hawaii system against each of the 21 standards in the Joint Committee's (1988) *Personnel Evaluation Standards*. He then supplemented this information with surveys, keyed to the 21 personnel evaluation standards, of representative samples of Hawaii's public school teachers and administrators. The additional information not only corroborated the initial judgments but provided an even stronger statement that the existing teacher evaluation system was badly in need of reform.

8. Analyze the Findings and Judge the Evaluation's Adherence to the Selected Evaluation Standards

The wide array of information used in metaevaluations requires a correspondingly wide range of qualitative and quantitative analysis procedures. In The Evaluation Center's metaevaluations, we have, among other techniques, used line and bar graphs, pie charts, and computer-assisted content analysis. It is particularly important to analyze judgments in the context of standards that are adopted.

The rubrics in Table 1 were used to determine the degree to which the Marine Corps personnel evaluation system had satisfied standards in the four categories of Utility, Feasibility, Propriety, and Accuracy. All available relevant evidence was then used to identify the personnel evaluation system's strengths and weaknesses related to each standard. Using these lists, judgments were made about whether the system met, partially met, or failed to meet each standard. These judgments were portrayed as seen in Figure 1. Then, to summarize the Figure 1 results, the rubrics from Table 1 were used to prepare the summary matrix in Table 2. Based on this analysis, the Marine Corps decided to replace its personnel evaluation system with one that would better meet the standards.

9. Write the Needed Reports

Following the analysis of metaevaluation information, the metaevaluator prepares and submits the report. In some situations, there will be several reports. For example, in the Marine Corps metaevaluation, successive reports were presented to evaluate the Corps' existing system, to evaluate the personnel evaluation systems used by industry and other military services, to present and evaluate three competing and newly designed systems, and to present a field test plan for operationalizing and testing the selected new system. For each report there was an executive summary,

Table 1. Rubrics Used to Determine Whether the USMC Personnel
Evaluation System Satisfies the Conditions of Utility, Feasibility, Propriety, and Accuracy[1]

Categories of Standards	Degree of Fulfillment of Requirements[2]		
	Not Met	Partially Met	Met
Utility	1. Three or more standards are not met.	2. At least 3 of the 5 standards are met or partially met, and at least 1 standard is not met. or 3. Fewer than 4 standards are met, all 5 are either met or partially met, and no standard is unmet.	4. At least 4 of 5 standards are met, and none is unmet.
Feasibility	5. Three or 4 standards are not met.	6. At least 2 of the standards are met or partially met, and at least 1 standard is not met. or 7. Fewer than 2 standards are met, and no standard is unmet.	8. At least 2 of the 4 standards are met, and none is unmet.
Propriety	9. Three or more standards are not met.	10. At least 3 of the 5 standards are met or partially met, and 1 or 2 standards are unmet. or 11. Fewer than 4 standards are either met or partially met, and no standard is unmet.	12. At least 4 of the 5 standards are met, and none is unmet.
Accuracy	13. Four or more standards are not met.	14. At least 5 of the 8 standards are met or partially met, and at least 1 standard is not met. or 15. Fewer than 5 standards are met, at least 4 are either met or partially met, and no standard is unmet.	16. At least 5 of the 8 standards are met, and none is unmet.

[1] This form is designed for use in judging the overall utility, propriety, feasibility, and accuracy of an evaluation. Use of the decision rules on this form requires that the user first judge whether the evaluation meets, partially meets, or fails to meet the detailed requirements of each of the 21 standards as they appear in Joint Committee on Standards for Educational Evaluation, *The Personnel Evaluation Standards* (Sage, 1988) and an additional standard (Transition to the New Evaluation System) developed for this project.

[2] In some cases, a standard may appropriately be judged as not applicable, and such standards would have no impact on determining which of the above rubrics fits the pattern of judgments.

a full-length report, an appendix of relevant materials, and copies of supporting transparencies. All reports were presented in both oral and written form. Moreover, all reports were first presented in draft form and then finalized on the basis of discussions with clients. Generally, this experience provides a useful model for presenting metaevaluation findings.

10. Help the Client and Other Stakeholders Interpret and Apply the Metaevaluation Findings

Delivering metaevaluation reports does not conclude the metaevaluator's responsibilities to make the metaevaluation successful. One role of a metaevaluator is to

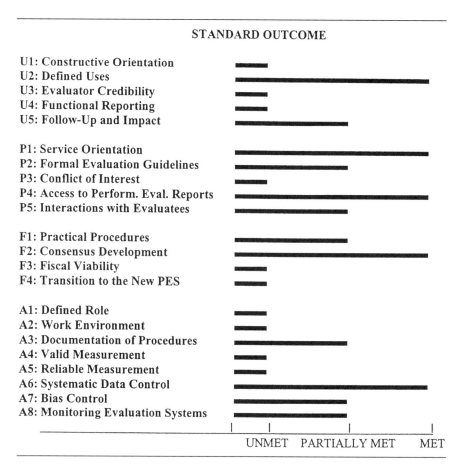

Figure 1. Summary of the degree to which the adapted Personnel Evaluation Standards have been satisfied by the Marine Corps Personnel Evaluation System

Table 2. Conclusions on the Degree to Which the Marine Corps
PES Satisfies Standards of Utility, Propriety, Feasibility, and Accuracy

Category of Standards	Conclusion	Rubric From Table 1
Utility	Not Met	1
Propriety	Partially Met	10
Feasibility	Partially Met	6
Accuracy	Not Met	13

promote and assist appropriate use of the metaevaluation findings. The groundwork for this should be laid at the outset of the metaevaluation.

A metaevaluation for the Hawaii Department of Education illustrates some of the procedures metaevaluators can employ to promote and assist uses of the metaevaluation findings. At the outset of this metaevaluation, the department of education established a metaevaluation review panel. This panel represented the various interests in the state's public education system. Included were the president of the state board of education, the majority leaders of the two houses of the state legislature, a representative of the military establishment, the president of the state teachers' union, the state superintendent of public instruction, the chief executive officer of one of the state's largest industries, two school principals, other school teachers and staff members, the head of the Pacific Regional Educational Laboratory, and representatives of parents and the general public. The metaevaluator and members of Hawaii's Department of Education regularly met with this group to discuss and obtain input for the ongoing metaevaluation of Hawaii's systems for evaluating students, teachers, administrators, and schools. The review panel helped to clarify the metaevaluation questions, provided valuable critiques of draft reports, and used the findings to generate recommendations for improving the state's systems of educational accountability. By being involved in the metaevaluation process, the review panel developed ownership of the findings and became a powerful, informed resource for helping to chart and obtain support for the needed reforms.

Parallel to the review panel's involvement, the metaevaluators worked with teams of Hawaii educators to conduct metaevaluations of the department's systems for evaluating teachers, administrators, students, and schools. These stakeholders also made valuable inputs to the metaevaluation process and developed interest and confidence in the findings.

As seen in these examples, metaevaluation can and often should be a collaborative effort. This is especially so when the aim is to help an organization assess and reform its evaluation systems. When the aim is to protect the public from being misinformed by evaluations of specific entities, the evaluator must maintain proper distance to assure an independent perspective. Even then, however, metaevaluators should communicate appropriately with audiences for the metaevaluation reports to secure their contributions, confidence, interest, understanding, and informed uses of findings.

CONCLUSION

Metaevaluations are important to all segments of society. They are important to both the users and producers of evaluations. Parents need to know whether they are getting reliable and valid evaluations of the schools and colleges where they might send their children and of their children's' performance. Students are entitled to know whether their efforts and achievements have been fairly and validly graded. School board members and school administrators need assurances that they are getting relevant and technically defensible evaluations of schools, programs, and personnel. Taxpayers need to know whether they are getting dependable information on the needs and performance of their town's schools and other service organizations in order to intelligently decide on levels of support. In all of these cases, users of evaluations are helped to see the relevance and quality of evaluative information by means of sound metaevaluations.

Metaevaluations also have significance for developers and providers of services and products. Teachers, chief executive officers, factory workers, and others deserve to know whether their contributions have been fairly and validly assessed. Military personnel need to know that they are being retained in the service and promoted based on impartial and valid assessments. In all such cases, metaevaluations can be appropriately applied to assess personnel evaluation systems.

As professionals, evaluators themselves need to regularly subject their evaluation services to independent review. Sound metaevaluations provide evaluators with a quality assurance mechanism they can use to examine and strengthen evaluation plans, operations, draft reports, and means of communicating the findings. Also, the prospect and fact of metaevaluations should help keep evaluators on their toes and push them to produce defensible evaluation conclusions.

Metaevaluation is as important to the evaluation field as is auditing to the accounting field. Society would be seriously at risk if it depended only on accountants for its financial information, without acquiring the scrutiny of independent auditors. Likewise, parents, students, educators, business and military employees, and others are at risk to the extent they cannot trust evaluation results. Clearly, metaevaluations are needed to scrutinize state assessment systems; evaluations of new, expensive curricula; evaluations of equipment and technology; evaluations of hospitals and other organizations; and evaluations of teachers, administrators, and others. For these reasons, metaevaluations are very much in the public interest.

This article's main thrust has been to sketch a general methodology for metaevaluation. It is seen in the 10 general steps for metaevaluations. In addition, selected procedures were provided to give practical ideas of how metaevaluators can carry out each step. Undergirding this presentation was the strong recommendation that metaevaluations be grounded in professional standards for evaluations. This helps to assure that evaluations will be useful, feasible, proper, and accurate.

REFERENCES

A "class act": More money, more teachers. (1996). *Salt Lake Tribune*, February 23, A1.

Achilles, C. M., Nye, B. A., Zaharias, J. B., & Fulton, B. D. (1993). *The Lasting Benefits Study (LBS) in grades 4 and 5 (1990–91): A legacy from Tennessee's four-year (K-3) class-size study (1985–89), Project STAR.* Paper presented at the North Carolina Association for Research in Education. Greensboro, North Carolina. January 14, 1993.

Adams, J. A. (1971). *A study of the status, scope and nature of educational evaluation in Michigan's public K-12 school districts.* Unpublished doctoral dissertation, Ohio State University, Columbus.

AEA Task Force on Guiding Principles for Evaluators. (1995). Guiding principles for evaluators. *New Directions for Program Evaluation, 66,* 19–34.

Agranoff, R., & Radin, B. A. (1991). The comparative case study approach in public administration. *Research in Public Administration, 1,* 203–231.

Aguaro, R. (1990). *R. Deming: The American who taught the Japanese about quality.* New York: Fireside.

Airasian, P. W. (1983). Societal experimentation. In G. F. Madaus, M. S. Scriven, & D. L. Stufflebeam (Eds.), *Evaluation models: Viewpoints on educational and human services evaluation* (pp. 163–176). Boston, MA: Kluwer-Nijhoff.

Alexander, D. (1974). *Handbook for traveling observers.* National Science Foundation systems project. Kalamazoo, MI: Western Michigan University Evaluation Center.

Alkin, M. C. (1969). Evaluation theory development. *Evaluation Comment, 2,* 2–7.

Alkin, M. C. (1995, November). *Lessons learned about evaluation use.* Panel presentation at the International Evaluation Conference, American Evaluation Association, Vancouver, British Columbia.

Alkin, M. C. (1997). Stakeholder concepts in program evaluation. In A. Reynolds & H. Walberg (Eds.), *Evaluation for educational productivity.* Greenwich CT: JAI Press.

Alkin, M. C., Adams, K. A., Cuthbert, M., & West, J. G. (1984). *External evaluation report of the Caribbean Agricultural Extension Project, Phase II.* Minneapolis: CAEP.

Alkin, M., Daillak, R., & White, P. (1979). *Using evaluations: Does evaluation make a difference?* Beverly Hills, CA: Sage.

Allison, G. T. (1971). *Essence of decision: Explaining the Cuban missile crisis.* Boston: Little, Brown.

American Educational Research Association and National Council on Measurements Used in Education. (1955). *Technical Recommendations for Achievement Tests.* Washington, D.C.: Author.

American Educational Research Association, American Psychological Association, & National Council on Measurement in Education. (1985). *Standards for educational and psychological tests.* Washington, D.C.: Author.

American Evaluation Association Task Force on Guiding Principles for Evaluators. (1995). Guiding principles for evaluators. In W. R. Shadish, D. L. Newman, M. A. Scheirer, & C. Wye (Eds.), *Guiding principles for evaluators. New Directions for Program Evaluation, 34,* 19–26.

American Psychological Association. (1954). *Technical recommendations for psychological tests and diagnostic techniques.* Washington, D.C.: Author.

American Psychological Association. (1966). *Standards for educational and psychological tests and manuals.* Washington, D.C.: Author.

American Psychological Association. (1973). *Ethical principles in the conduct of research with human participants.* Washington, D.C.: Author.

American Psychological Association. (1974). *Standards for educational and psychological tests.* Washington, D.C.: Author.

American Psychological Association. (1985). *Standards for educational and psychological tests.* Washington, D.C.: Author.

American Psychological Association. (2000). *Standards for educational and psychological tests.* Washington, D.C.: Author.

Anderson, J. R., Reder, L. M., & Simon, H. (1996). Situated learning and education. *Educational Researcher, 25*(4), 5–21.

Argyris, C., & Schoen, D. (1978). *Organizational learning: A theory of action perspective.* Harlow: Addison-Wesley.

Armstrong, I. (1995). *New feminist discourses.* London: Routledge.

Australian Commonwealth Department of Finance. (1998). *Lessons learned from others. Discussion Paper 2. International experience on the identification of outputs and outcomes.* Canberra: Author.

Bahm, A. J. (1981). Science is not value-free. *Policy Sciences, 2,* 391–396.

Baker, E. L, O'Neil, H. R., & Linn, R. L. (1993). Policy and validity prospects for performance-based assessment. *American Psychologist, 48,* 1210–1218.

Baker, R. (1982). *Growing up.* New York: Signet.

Bakker, S. A. (1999). Educational assessment in the Russian Federation. *Assessment in Education: Principles, Policy and Practice, 6,* 291–303.

Ball, S., & Bogatz, G. A. (1970). *The first year of Sesame Street: An evaluation.* Princeton, N.J.: Educational Testing Service.

Ballart, X. (1998). Spanish evaluation practice versus program evaluation theory. *Evaluation, 4,* 149–170.

Ballou, F. A. (1916). Work of the Department of Educational Investigation and Measurement, Boston, Massachusetts. In G. M. Whipple (Ed.), *Standards and tests for the measurement of the efficiency of schools and school systems.* National Society for the Study of Education Fifteenth Yearbook, Part I. Chicago: University of Chicago Press.

Bandura, A. (1977). *Social learning theory.* Englewood Cliffs, N.J.: Prentice-Hall.

Banta, M. (1993). *Taylored lives: Narrative productions in the age of Taylor, Veblen, and Ford.* Chicago: University of Chicago Press.

Barkdoll, G. (1980). Type III evaluations: A method to strengthen evaluation in smaller programs with similar purposes. *Evaluation Practice, 14*(2), 141–147.

Barnett, W. S. (1985). *The Perry Preschool Program and its long term effects: A benefit-cost analysis.* Early Childhood Policy Papers, No. 2. Ypsilanti, MI: High/Scope Educational Research Foundation.

Barnett, W. S. (1993). Benefit-cost analysis of preschool education: Findings from a 25-Year follow-up. *American Journal of Orthopsychiatry, 63,* 500–508.

Barnett, W. S. (1995). Long-term effects of early childhood programs on cognitive and school outcomes. *Future of Children, 5*(3), 25–50.

Barnett, W. S. (1996). *Lives in the balance: Age-27 benefit-cost analysis of the High/Scope Perry Preschool Program.* Monograph Number 11. Ypsilanti, MI: High/Scope Educational Research Foundation.

Barnett, W. S. (1998). Long-term cognitive and academic effects of early childhood education on children in poverty. *Preventive Medicine, 27,* 204–207.

Barnett, W., Frede, E., Cox, J., & Black, T. (1994). Using cost analysis to improve early childhood programs. In W. Barnett (Ed.), *Advances in educational productivity: Vol. 4. Cost analysis for education decisions (pp. 145–181).* Greenwich, CT: JAI Press.

Barone, T. (1983). Things of use and things of beauty: The story of the Swain County High School Arts Program. *Daedalus, 112*(3), 1–28.

Barone, T. (1989). Ways of being at risk: The case of Billy Charles Barnett. *Phi Delta Kappan, 71*, 147–151.

Barone, T. (1993, April). *Qualitative research its socially committed literature.* Paper presented at the Annual Meeting of the American Educational Research Association, Atlanta, GA.

Bass, G., & Kirst, M. W. (1976). *Accountability: What is the federal role?* Santa Monica, CA: RAND Corporation.

Basseches, M. (1980). Dialectical schemata. *Human Development, 23*, 400–421.

Batterham, R., Dunt, D., & Disler, P. (1996). Can we achieve accountability for long-term outcomes? *Archives of Physical Medicine and Rehabilitation, 77*, 1219–1225.

Battistich, V., Watson, M., Solomon, D., Lewis, C., & Schaps, E. (1999). Beyond the three Rs: A broader agenda for school reform. *Elementary School Journal, 99*, 415–432.

Bayless, D., & Massaro, G. (1992). *Quality improvement in education today and the future: Adapting W. Edwards Deming's quality improvement principles and methods to education.* Kalamazoo, MI: Center for Research on Educational Accountability and Teacher Evaluation.

Beath, L. (1991a, April). *A local habitation and a name: The authorial "I" and narrative voice.* Paper presented at annual meeting of the American Educational Research Association, Chicago, IL.

Beath, L. (1991b). Stories of connected teaching. *Dissertation Abstracts International, 52*, 2384. (University Microfilms No. 91-37, 332).

Becker, M. H. (Ed.) (1974). The health belief model and personal health behavior. *Health Education Monographs, 2*, 324–473.

Benbasat, I., Goldstein, D., & Mead, M. (1987). *The case research strategy in studies of information systems. MIS Quarterly, 11*, 369–386.

Bennett, C. F. (1982). *Reflective appraisal of programs.* Ithaca, NY: Cornell University.

Berger, P. L., & Luckmann, T. (1967). *The social construction of reality.* New York: Doubleday.

Bertalanffy, L. V. B. (1968). *General systems theory: Foundations, development, applications.* New York: George Braziller.

Bhola, H. S. (1965). A theory of innovation diffusion and its application to Indian education and community development. *Dissertation Abstracts International, 27/01A*, 135.

Bhola, H. S. (1973). Making evaluation operational in functional literacy programs. *Literacy Discussion, 4*, 457–493. (ERIC Clearinghouse No. EJ 094 233).

Bhola, H. S. (1975). *The India education project: A case study of institution building and organizational conflict.* Bloomington, IN: International Development Research Center.

Bhola, H. S. (1979). *Evaluating functional literacy.* Amersham, Bucks, U.K.: Hulton Educational Publications.

Bhola, H. S. (1988). The CLER model of innovation diffusion, planned change and development: A conceptual update and applications. *Knowledge in Society: An International Journal of Knowledge Transfer, 1*, 56–66.

Bhola, H. S. (1989). Training evaluators in the Third World: Implementation of an Action Training Model (ATM). *Evaluation and Program Planning, 12*, 249–258.

Bhola, H. S. (1990). *Evaluating "literacy for development": projects, programs and campaigns.* Hamburg: UNESCO Institute for Education/Bonn: German Foundation for International Development.

Bhola, H. S. (1991). *Designing from the heart of an epistemic triangle: Systemic, dialectical, and constructivist strategies for systems design and systems change.* Paper presented at the systems conference organized by the International Systems Institute, Asilomar, CA. [ERIC Document No. ED 345 700].

Bhola, H. S. (1995a). *A policy analysis and program evaluation: National Literacy Program in Namibia.* Windhoek, Namibia: Directorate of Adult Basic Education, Ministry of Basic Education and Culture, Government of the Republic of Namibia.

Bhola, H. S. (1995b). Informed decisions within a culture of information: Updating a model of information development and evaluation. *Adult Education and Development, 44*, 75–84.

Bhola, H. S. (1996). Between limits of rationality and possibilities of praxis: Purposive action from the heart of an epistemic triangle. *Entrepreneurship, Innovation, and Change, 5*, 33–47.

Bhola, H. S. (1998a). Constructivist capacity building and systemic evaluation of adult basic education and training in South Africa: One discourse, two scripts. *Evaluation, 4*, 1–22.

Bhola, H. S. (1998b). Program evaluation for program renewal: A study of the national literacy program in Namibia (NLPN). *Studies in Educational Evaluation, 24*, 303–330.

Bhola, H. S. (1998c). They are learning and discerning: Evaluation of an adult education project of the National Literacy Cooperation of South Africa. *Studies in Educational Evaluation, 24*, 153–177.

Bickman, L. (Ed.) (1987). *Using program theory in evaluation. New Directions in Program Evaluation.* San Francisco: Jossey-Bass.

Bickman, L. (Ed.) (1990a). *Advances in program theory. New Directions in Program Evaluation.* San Francisco: Jossey-Bass.

Bickman, L. (1990b). Using program theory to describe and measure program quality. In L. Bickman (Ed.), *Advances in program theory* (pp. 61–72). *New Directions in Program Evaluation.* San Francisco: Jossey-Bass.

Bickman, L. (1996). The application of program theory to the evaluation of a managed mental health care system. *Evaluation and Program Planning, 19,* 111–119.

Bickman, L., Guthrie, P., Foster, E. W., Summerfelt, W. T., Breda, C., & Heflinger, C. A. (1995). *Evaluating managed mental health care: The Fort Bragg Experiment.* New York: Plenum.

Biddle. B. J., & Ellena. W. J. (Eds.) (1964). *Contemporary research on teacher effectiveness.* New York: Holt, Rinehart, & Winston.

Blalock, A. B. (1999). Evaluation research and the performance management movement. From estrangement to useful integration? *Evaluation, 5,* 117–149.

Blanchard, K. (1986). *Situational leadership* (Cassette Recording). Escondido, CA: Blanchard Training and Development, Inc.

Blatchford, P., & Mortimore, P. (1994). The issue of class size for young children in schools: What can we learn from research? *Oxford Review of Education, 20,* 411–428.

Bloom, B. S. (1961). Quality control in education. *Tomorrow's teaching.* Oklahoma City: Frontiers of Science Foundation, pp. 54–61.

Bloom, B. S. (Ed.) (1956). *Taxonomy of educational objectives.* New York: Longmans, Green.

Bloom, B. S., Englehart, M. D., Furst, E. J., Hill, W. H., & Krathwohl, D. R. (1956). *Taxonomy of educational objectives: Handbook I: Cognitive domain.* New York: David McKay.

Bloom, B. S., Madaus, G. F., & Hastings, I. T. (1981). *Evaluation to improve learning.* New York: McGraw-Hill.

Bogatz, G. A., & Ball, S. (1971). *The second year of Sesame Street: A continuing evaluation.* 2 vols. Princeton, N.J.: Educational Testing Service.

Borg, W. R., & Gall, M. D. (1989). *Educational research* (5th ed.). New York: Longman.

Boruch, R. F. (1994). The future of controlled randomized experiments: A briefing. *Evaluation Practice, 15,* 265–274.

Boruch, R. F. (1997). *Randomized experiments for planning and evaluation: A practical guide.* Thousand Oaks, CA: Sage.

Bottoms, C. L. (1977). Reanalysis by individual of Harvard Project Physics Data. Qualifying Paper, Harvard Graduate School of Education.

Bowers, D. (1977). *Survey-guided development: Data-based organizational change.* La Jolla, CA: University Associates.

Boyce, A. C. (Ed.) (1915). *Methods for measuring teachers' efficiency.* Fourteenth Yearbook of the National Society for the Study of Education, Part 11. Chicago: University of Chicago Press.

Bracht, G. H., & Glass, G. V. (1968). The external validity of experiments. *American Educational Research Journal, 5,* 437–474.

Bray, M. (1995). Community financing of education. In M. Carnoy (Ed.), *International encyclopedia of economics of education* (2nd ed.) (pp. 430–433). Oxford: Pergamon.

Brickell, H. M. (1976). Needed: Instruments as good as our eyes. *Occasional Paper Series, #7.* Kalamazoo, MI: Western Michigan University Evaluation Center.

Brightman, H., & Noble, C. (1979). On the ineffective education of decision scientists. *Decision Sciences, 10,* 151–157.

Brinkerhoff, R. (1983). Evaluation Technical Assistance: Reflections on a National Effort. *CEDR Journal.*

Brinkman, P., & Leslie, L. (1987). Economies of scale in higher education: Sixty years of research. *Review of Higher Education, 10*(1), 1–28.

Browder, L. (1975). *Who's afraid of educational accountability?* Denver, CO: Cooperative Accountability Project.

Bryant, D., & Bickman, L. (1996). Methodology for evaluating mental health case management. *Evaluation and Program Planning, 19,* 121–129.

Bryk, A. S. (Ed.) (1983). *Stake holder-based evaluation.* New Directions for Program Evaluation. San Francisco: Jossey-Bass.

Bullen, P., & Weller, S. (1992). Applying an expanded outcomes hierarchy model in the evaluation of the National Migrant Access Projects Scheme. *Proceedings of the Australasian Evaluation Society International Conference, Melbourne,* pp. 19.1–19.7.

Bunda, M. A. (1980). *Catalog of criteria for evaluating student growth and development.* Toledo, OH: Toledo, Ohio Public Schools and the Western Michigan University Evaluation Center.

Bunker, J. P., Barnes, B. A., & Mosteller, F. (Eds.) (1977). *Costs, risks, and benefits of surgery.* New York: Oxford University Press.

Burkhead, J. (1973). Economics against education. *Teachers College Record, 75,* 193–205.

Buros, O. K. (Ed.) (1953). *The fourth mental measurements yearbook.* Highland Park, N.J.: Gryphon Press.

Callahan, R. E. (1962). *Education and the cult of efficiency.* Chicago: University of Chicago Press.

Campbell, D. T. (1975). Degrees of freedom and the case study. *Comparative Political Studies, 8,* 178–193.

Campbell, D. T., & Stanley, J. C. (1963). Experimental and quasi-experimental designs for research on teaching. In N. L. Gage (Ed.), *Handbook of research on teaching* (pp. 171–246). Chicago: Rand McNally.

Campbell, D. T., & Stanley, J. C. (1966). *Experimental and quasi-experimental designs.* Boston, MA: Houghton Mifflin.

Campbell, D. T. (1969). Reforms as experiments. *American Psychologist, 24,* 409–429.

Campbell, F. A., & Ramey, C. T. (1994). Effects of early intervention on intellectual and academic achievement: A follow-up study of children from low-income families. *Child Development, 65,* 684–698.

Campbell, F. A., & Ramey, C. T. (1995). Cognitive and school outcomes for high risk African-American students at middle adolescence: Positive effects of early intervention. *American Educational Research Journal, 32,* 743–772.

Candoli, I. C., Cullen, K., & Stufflebeam, D. L. (1997). *Superintendent performance evaluation: \Current practice and directions for improvement.* Boston: Kluwer-Nijhoff.

Cash, J. I., & Lawrence, P. R. (Eds.). *The information systems research challenge: Qualitative research methods, Vol. 1.* Boston: Harvard Business School.

Catterall, J. (1987). On the social costs of dropping out of school. *High School Journal, 71*(October–November), 19–30.

Cell, E. (1984). *Learning to learn from experience.* Albany, NY: SUNY Press.

Centra, J. A. (1979). *Determining faculty effectiveness.* San Francisco: Jossey-Bass.

Chambers, J. (1994). Career oriented high schools. In W. Barnett (Ed.), *Advances in educational productivity: Vol. 4. Cost analysis for education decisions* (pp. 75–111). Greenwich, CT: JAI Press.

Chase, F. (1980). *Educational quandries and opportunities.* Dallas, TX: Urban Education Studies.

Checkland, P. (1981). *Systems thinking, systems practice.* New York: Wiley.

Chelimsky, E., & Shandish, W. R. (Eds.). *Evaluation for the 21ˢᵗ Century. A handbook* (pp. 177–188). Thousand Oaks, CA: Sage.

Chen, H. (1980). Special issue: The theory-driven perspective. *Evaluation and Program Planning, 12,* 2.

Chen, H. (1990). *Theory driven evaluation.* Newbury Park, CA: Sage.

Chinapah, V. (1997). *Handbook on monitoring learning achievement. Towards capacity building.* Paris: UNESCO.

Cicirelli, V. G., et al. (1969). *The impact of Head Start: An evaluation of the effects of Head Start on children's cognitive and affective development.* Study by Westinghouse Learning Corporation and Ohio University. Washington, D.C.: Office of Economic Opportunity.

Clarke, J. (1995). Evaluation of the Road Whys program: A road safety education program targeting secondary school students. *Proceedings of the Australasian Evaluation Society Conference, Sydney.*

Clune, W. H. (1987). *Institutional choice as a theoretical framework for research on educational policy.* New Brunswick, N.J.: Center for Policy Research in Education.

Coffey, A., & Atkinson, P. (1996). *Making sense of qualitative data: Complementary research strategies.* Thousand Oaks, CA: Sage.

Cohen, D., & Murnane, R. (1985, summer). The merits of merit pay. *Public Interest 3,* 30.

Cohn, E. (Ed.) (1996). *Market approaches to education: Vouchers and school choice.* Oxford: Pergamon.

Coleman, J. S., Campbell, E. Q., Hobson, C. J., McPartland, J., Mood, A. M., Weinfeld, F. D., & York, R. L. (1966). *Equality of educational opportunity.* Washington, D.C.: Office of Education, U.S. Department of Health, Education, and Welfare.

Coleman, J. S., & Karweit, N. L. (1972). *Information systems and performance measures in schools.* Englewood Cliffs NJ: Educational Technology Publications.

Conner, R., Mishra, S., Lewis, M., Bryer, S., Marks, J., Lai, M., & Clark, L. (1990). Theory-based evaluation of AIDS-related knowledge, attitudes, and behavior changes. In L. Leviton, A. Hegedus, & A. Kubrin (Eds.), *Evaluating AIDS prevention: Contributions of multiple disciplines. New Directions for Program Evaluation.* San Francisco: Jossey-Bass.

Cook, D. L. (1966). *Program evaluation and review techniques. Applications in education.* U.S. Office of Education Cooperative Monograph, 17 (OE-12024).

Cook, T. D., & Campbell, D. T. (1979). *Quasi-experimentation: Design and analysis issues for field settings.* Chicago: Rand McNally.

Cook, T. D., Reichardt, C. I. (Eds.) (1979). Qualitative and quantitative methods in evaluation research. Beverly Hills, CA: Sage Publications.

Cook, D. L., & Stufflebeam, D. L. (1967). Estimating test norms from variable size item and examinee samples. *Educational and Psychological Measurement, 27,* 601–610.

Cooley, W., & Bickell, W. (1986). *Decision-oriented educational research.* Boston, MA: Kluwer-Nijhoff.

Coombs, A. (1972). *Educational accountability.* Washington, DC: Association for Supervision and Curriculum Development.

Coombs, P., & Hallak, J. (1987). *Cost analysis in education: A tool for policy and planning.* Baltimore MD: Johns Hopkins University Press.

Cordray, D. S. (1982). An assessment of the utility of the ERS standards. *Standards for evaluation practice. New Directions for Program Evaluation, 15.* San Francisco: Jossey-Bass.

Cousins, J. B., & Earl, L. M. (Eds.) (1995). *Participatory evaluation in education: Studies in evaluation use and organizational learning.* London: Falmer.

Cousins, J. B., & Whitmore, E. (1998). Framing participatory evaluation. In E. Whitmore (Ed.), *Participatory evaluation approaches. New Directions in Evaluation.* San Francisco: Jossey-Bass.

Covert, R. W. (1995). A twenty-year veteran's reflections on the guiding principles for evaluators. In W. R. Shadish, D. L. Newman, M. A. Scheirer, & C. Wye (Eds.), *Guiding principles for evaluators. New Directions for Program Evaluation, 34,* 35–45.

Cremin, L. A. (1962). *The transformation of the school.* New York: Knopf.

Crisp, N. J. (1982). *The brink.* New York: Viking Press.

Cronbach, L. J. (1963). Course improvement through evaluation. *Teachers College Record, 64,* 672–683.

Cronbach, L. J. (1975). Beyond the two disciplines of scientific psychology. *American Psychologist, 30,* 116–127.

Cronbach, L. J. (1982). *Designing evaluations of educational and social programs.* San Francisco: Jossey-Bass.

Cronbach, L. J. (1983). Ninety-five theses for reforming program evaluation. In G. F. Madaus, M. S. Scriven, & D. L. Stufflebeam (Eds.), *Evaluation models. Viewpoints on educational and human services evaluation* (pp. 405–412). Boston: Kluwer-Nijhoff.

Cronbach, L. J., Ambron, S. R., Dornbusch, S. M., Hess, R. D., Hornick, R. C., Philips, D. C., Walker, D. F., & Weiner, S. S. (1981). *Toward reforms of program evaluation.* San Francisco: Jossey-Bass.

Cronbach, L. J. and Associates. (1980). *Toward reform of program evaluation.* San Francisco: Jossey-Bass.

Cronbach, L. J., & Snow, R. E. (1969). *Individual differences in learning ability as a function of instructional variables.* Stanford, CA: Stanford University Press.

Cronbach, L. J., & Suppes, P. (1969). Research for tomorrow's schools: Disciplined inquiry in education. New York: Macmillan Company.

Cuban, L. (1990). Reforming again, again, and again. *Educational Researcher, 19*(1), 3–13.

Cunningham, A. (1988). Eeny, meeny, miny, moe: Testing policy and practice in early childhood. Commissioned paper for the National Commission on Testing and Public Policy. Chestnut Hill MA: Boston College.

Danzberger, J. et al. (1986). *Improving grassroots leadership: School boards.* Washington, D.C.: Institute for Educational Leadership.

Darling-Hammond, L. (1988). Accountability and teacher professionalism. *American Educator,* Winter, 9–10.

Davies, D. (1990). Shall we wait for the revolution? A few lessons from the Schools Reaching Out Project. *Equity and Choice, 6*(3), 68–73.

Davies, I. C. (1999). Evaluation and performance management in government. *Evaluation, 5,* 150–159.

Davis, B. G., Scriven, M., & Thomas, S. (1981). *The evaluation of composition instruction.* Iverness, CA: Edge-Press.

Davis, H. R., & Salasin, S. E. (1975). The utilization of evaluation. In E. L. Struening & M. Guttentag (Eds.), *Handbook of evaluation research, Vol. 1* (pp. 621–666). Beverly Hills, CA: Sage.

Debus, M. (1995). *Methodological review: A handbook for excellence in focus group research.* Washington, DC: Academy for Educational Development.

Delago, R. R. (1988). Applications of systems dialectics to integrated development. *Systems Practice, 1,* 259–295.

Deming, W. E. (1982). *Out of the crisis.* Cambridge, MA: Center for Advanced Engineering Study, Massachusetts Institute of Technology.

Deming, W. E. (1986). *Out of the crisis.* Cambridge, MA: Center for Advanced Engineering Study, Massachusetts Institute of Technology.

Denny, T. (1978, November). *Story telling and educational understanding.* Occasional Paper No. 12. Kalamazoo, MI: Evaluation Center, Western Michigan University.

Denzin, N. K. (1978). The logic of naturalistic inquiry. In N. K. Denzin (Ed.), *Sociological methods: A sourcebook.* New York: McGraw-Hill.

Denzin, N. K., & Lincoln, Y. S. (Eds.) (1994). *Handbook of qualitative research.* Thousand Oaks, CA: Sage.

Devine, E. C. (1992). Effects of psychoeducational care with adult surgical patients: A theory-probing meta-analysis of intervention studies. In T. D. Cook, H. Cooper, D. S. Cordray, H. Hartman, L. V. Hedges, R. J. Light, T. A. Louis, & F. Mosteller (Eds.), *Meta-analysis for explanation: A casebook* (pp. 35–82). New York: Russell Sage Foundation.

Dewey, J. (1934). *Art as experience.* New York: Perigee.

Dewey, J. (1939). *Theory of valuation.* Chicago: University of Chicago Press.

Donmoyer, R. (1980). Alternative conceptions of generalization and verification for educational research. *Dissertation Abstracts International, 41,* 4592. (University Microfilms No. 81-08, 914).

Doray, B. (1988). *From Taylorism to Fordism: A rationale madness.* London: Free Association Books.

Dougherty, K. C. (1993). *Looking for a way out: Women on welfare and their educational advancement.* Unpublished doctoral dissertation. University of Colorado, Boulder, CO.

Doyle, D. P. (1991, September). *Empowering teachers. Atlantic Monthly,* p. 15.

Drews, E. M. (1963). Student abilities, grouping patterns, and classroom interaction: Final report of Cooperative Research Project. East Lansing, MI: Office of Research and Publication, College of Education, Michigan State University.

DuBois, P. H., & Mayo, D. (Eds.) (1970). *Research strategies for evaluating training* (AERA Monograph Series on Curriculum Evaluation). Chicago: Rand McNally.

Duran, P., Monnier, E., & Smith, A. (1995). Evaluation à la française. Towards a new relationship between social science and public action. *Evaluation, 1,* 45–63.

Durlak, J. A., & Wells, A. M. (1997). Primary prevention mental health programs for children and adolescents: A meta-analytic review. *American Journal of Community Psychology, 25,* 115–152.

Ebel, R. L. (1965). *Measuring educational achievement.* Englewood Cliffs, N.J.: Prentice-Hall.

Education Board Asks Budget Delay. (1995). *Atlanta Journal and Constitution,* August 10, 1B.

Education Commission of the States. (1989). *Choice: Options for state policymakers.* Denver, CO: Author.

Eicher, J. (1995). International educational expenditures. In M. Carnoy (Ed.), *International encyclopedia of economics of education* (2nd ed.) (pp. 443–450). Oxford: Pergamon.

Eisner, E. W. (1967). Educational objectives: Help or hindrance? *School Review, 75,* 250–260.

Eisner, E. W. (1969). Instructional and expressive educational objectives: Their formulation and use in curriculum. In W. J. Popham, E. W. Eisner, H. J. Sullivan, & R. Tyler, *Instructional objectives* (AERA Monograph Series on Curriculum Evaluation). Chicago: Rand McNally.

Eisner, E. W. (1975, March). *The perceptive eye: Toward a reformation of educational evaluation.* Invited address, Division B, Curriculum and Objectives, American Educational Research Association, Washington, DC.

Eisner, E. W. (1979). *The educational imagination.* New York: Macmillan.

Eisner, E. W. (1983). Educational connoisseurship and criticism: Their form and functions in educational evaluation. In G. F. Madaus, D. L. Stufflebeam, & M. S. Scriven (Eds.), *Evaluation models: Viewpoints on educational and human services evaluation* (pp. 335–348). Boston: Kluwer-Nijhoff.

Eisner, E. W. (1985). *The educational imagination* (2d ed.). New York: Macmillan.

Eisner, E. W. (1991). *The enlightened eye.* New York: Macmillan.

Eisner, E. W. (1992). Objectivity in educational research. *Curriculum Inquiry, 22*(1), 9–15.

Elashoff, J. D., & Snow, R. E. (1971). *Pygmalion reconsidered.* Worthington, OH: Charles A. Jones.

Elias, D. (1993). *Educating leaders for social transformation.* Doctoral dissertation. New York: Teachers College, Columbia University.

Elmore, R. (1996). Getting to scale with good educational practice. *Harvard Educational Review, 66,* 1–26.

Elmore, R., & McLaughlin, M. (1988). *Steady work: Policy, practice, and reform of education.* Santa Monica, CA: Rand Corporation.

Elster, J. (1983). *Sour grapes: Studies in the subversion of rationality.* Cambridge: Cambridge University Press.

Epstein, T. (1989). An aesthetic approach to the teaching and learning of the social studies. *Dissertation Abstracts International,* 50, 2368 (University Microfilms No. 89-15, 413).

ERS Standards Committee. (1982). Evaluation Research Society standards for program evaluation. *Standards for Evaluation Practice. New Directions for Program Evaluation, 15.* San Francisco: Jossey-Bass.

Esslin, M. (1966). *The theater of the absurd.* London: Eyre & Spotteswoode.

European Commission. (1997). *Evaluating EU expenditure programmes: A guide to ex post and intermediate evaluation.* Luxembourg: Author.

Evaluation News. Sponsored by the Evaluation Network, Sage Publications, no. 2, 2.

Evers, J. (1980). *A field study of goal-based and goal-free evaluation techniques.* Unpublished doctoral dissertation. Kalamazoo, MI: Western Michigan University.

Ewert, G. (1991). Habermas and education: A comprehensive overview of the influence of Habermas in educational literature. *Review of Educational Research, 61,* 345–378.

Feagin, J. R., Orum, A. M., & Sjoberg, G. (Eds.). *A case for the case study.* Chapel Hill, N.C.: University of North Carolina Press.

Ferguson, G. A. (1954). On learning and human ability. *Canadian Journal of Psychology, 8,* 95–112.

Ferguson, R. (1999, June). Ideological marketing. *The Education Industry Report.*

Ferris, F. L. Jr. (1962). Testing in the new curriculums: Numerology, tyranny, or common sense? *School Review, 70,* 112–131.

Fetterman, D. (1989). *Ethnography: Step by step.* Thousand Oaks, CA: Sage.

Fetterman, D. M. (Ed.) (1993). *Speaking the language of power: Communication, collaboration and advocacy.* London: Falmer Press.

Fetterman, D. M. (1994). Empowerment evaluation. *Evaluation Practice, 15*(1), 1–15.

Fetterman, D., Kaftarian, S. J., & Wandersman, A. (Eds.) (1996). *Empowerment evaluation.* Thousand Oaks, CA: Sage.

Fetterman, D., Shakeh, J. K., & Wandersman, (Eds.) (1996). *Empowerment evaluation: Knowledge and tools for self-assessment & accountability.* Thousand Oaks, CA: Sage.

Filstead, W. J. (1979). Qualitative methods: A needed perspective in evaluation research. In T. D. Cook & C. I. Reichart (Eds.), *Qualitative and quantitative methods in evaluation research.* Beverly Hills, CA: Sage.

Finn, J. D., & Achilles, C. M. (1990). Answers and questions about class size: A statewide experiment. *American Educational Research Journal, 27,* 557–577.

Finn, J. D., & Achilles, C. M. (1999). Tennessee's class size study: Findings, implications, misconceptions. *Educational Evaluation and Policy Analysis, 21,* 97–110.

Finn, C. E., Stevens, F. I., Stufflebeam, D. L., & Walberg, H. J. (1997). The New York City Public Schools Integrated Learning Systems Project: A meta-evaluation. *International Journal of Educational Research, 27,* 159–174.

Finnan, C., & Davis, S. C. (1995). *Linking school-wide evaluation and goals-based teacher evaluation: Act 135, the Accelerated Schools Project and ADEPT.* Paper presented at the annual meeting of the American Educational Research Association.

Firestone, W. A. (1990). Accommodation: Toward a paradigm-praxis dialectic. In E. G. Guba (Ed.), *The paradigm dialog.* Newbury Park, CA: Sage.

Fischer, F. (1980). *Politics, values, and public methodology: The problem of methodology.* Boulder CO: Westview.

Fisher, R. A. (1951). *The design of experiments* (6th ed.) New York: Hafner.

Flanagan, J. C. (1939). General considerations in the selection of test items and a short method of estimating the product-moment coefficient from data at the tails of the distribution. *Journal of Educational Psychology, 30,* 674–680.

Fletcher, J. (1966). *Situation ethics: The new morality.* London: John Knox.

Flexner, A. (1910). *Medical education in the United States and Canada.* A report to the Carnegie Foundation for the Advancement of Teaching. New York: Carnegie Foundation. (Reprint. New York: Arno Press, 1970).

Flinders, D. J. (1989). *Voices from the classroom.* Eugene, OR: University of Oregon, ERIC Clearinghouse on Educational Management.

Flinders, D. J. (1991, April). *Narrative reconsidered: On the implications of frame analysis for curriculum research.* Paper presented at the Annual Meeting of the American Educational Research Association, Chicago, IL.

Floden, R. E. (1983). Flexner, accreditation, and evaluation. In G. F. Madaus, M. S. Scriven, & D. L. Stufflebeam (Eds.), *Evaluation models: Viewpoints on educational and human services evaluation* (pp. 261–278). Boston: Kluwer-Nijhoff.

Funnell, S. (1990). Developments in the use of the New South Wales approach to analysing program logic. In *Evaluation: Making it work. Proceedings of the Australasian Evaluation Society International Conference, Sydney.*

Funnell, S. (1997). Program logic: An adaptable tool. *Evaluation News & Comment, 6*(1), 5–17.

Funnell, S. (1998). Generic program models. Unpublished paper.

Funnell, S., & Lenne, B. (1990). Clarifying program objectives for program evaluation. *Program Evaluation Bulletin* 1/90. Office of Public Management, New South Wales Premiers Department, Sydney.

Gallagher, J., Nuthall, G. A., & Rosenshine, B. (1970). *Classroom observation* (AERA Monograph Series on Curriculum Evaluation). Chicago: Rand McNally.

Galtung, J. (1990). Theory formation in social research: A plea for pluralism. In E. Oyen (Ed.), *Comparative methodology* (pp. 96–112). Newbury Park, CA: Sage.

Garber, E. K. (1988). "My Kinsman Major Molineux": Some interpretive and critical probes. In B. F. Nelms (Ed.), *Literature in the classroom* (pp. 83–104). Urbana, IL: National Council of Teachers of English.

Gardner, H. (1983). *Frames of mind: The theory of multiple intelligences.* New York: Basic Books.

Gardner, H. (1989). Balancing specialized and comprehensive knowledge. In T. Sergiovanni (Ed.), *Schooling for tomorrow: Directing reforms to issues that count.* Boston, MA: Allyn & Bacon.

Garraway, G. B. (1995). Participatory evaluation. *Studies in Educational Evaluation, 21,* 85–102.

Geske, T., Davis, D., & Hingle, P. (1997). Charter schools: A viable public school choice option? *Economics of Education Review, 16*(1), 15–23.

Gilgun, J. F. (1994). A case for case studies in social work research. *Social Work, 39,* 371–380.

Ginsburg, P. B., & Fasciano, N. J. (Eds.) (1996). *The Community Snapshots Project: Capturing health system change.* Princeton, N.J.: Robert Wood Johnson Foundation.

Gintis, H. (1971). Toward a political economy of education. *Harvard Educational Review, 42,* 70–96.

Glaser, B. G., & Strauss, A. L. (1967). *The discovery of grounded theory.* Chicago: Aldine.

Glaser, R. (1963). Instructional technology and the measurement of learning outcomes: Some questions. *American Psychologist, 18,* 519–521.

Glass, G. V. (1969). *Design of evaluation studies.* Paper presented at the Council for Exceptional Children Special Conference on Early Childhood Education, New Orleans, Louisiana.

Glass, G. V. (1974, May). *Excellence: A paradox.* Speech presented at the second annual meeting of the Pacific Northwest Research and Evaluation Conference sponsored by the Washington Educational Research Association.

Glass, G. V. (1975). A paradox about excellence of schools and the people in them. *Educational Researcher, 4*(3), 9–13.

Glass, G. V. (1976). Primary, secondary, and meta analysis of research. *Educational Researcher, 10*(5), 3–8.

Glass, G. V., & Maguire, T. O. (1968). *Analysis of time-series quasi-experiments.* (U.S. Office of Education Report No. 6-8329.) Boulder: Laboratory of Educational Research, University of Colorado.

Glass, G. V. et al. (1970). Data analysis of the 1968–69 Survey of Compensatory Education, Title I, Final Report on Grant No. OEG8-8-961860 4003-(058). Washington, D.C.: Office of Education.

Goals 2000: Educate American Act of 1994, Public Law No 103–227.

Greaney, V., & Kellaghan, T. (1996). *Monitoring the learning outcomes of education systems.* Washington, D.C.: World Bank.

Green, L. W., & Kreuter, M. W. (1991). In *Health promotion planning: An educational and environmental approach* (2nd ed) (pp. 22–30). Mountain View, CA: Mayfield Publishing.

Greenbaum, T. L. (1993). *The handbook of focus group research.* New York: Lexington Books.

Greene, J. C. (1988). Stakeholder participation and utilization in program evaluation. *Evaluation Review, 12,* 91–116.

Greene, J. C. (1990). Technical quality versus user responsiveness in evaluation practice. *Evaluation and Program Planning, 13,* 267–274.

Greene, J. C. (1997). Evaluation as advocacy. *Evaluation Practice, 18*(1), 25–35.

Grissmer, D. (1999). Introduction to special issue on class size: Issues and new findings. *Educational Evaluation and Policy Analysis, 21,* 93–96.

Grobman, H. (1968). *Evaluation activities of curriculum projects* (AERA Monograph Series on Curriculum Evaluation). Chicago: Rand McNally.

Guardini, R. (1994). *Letters from Lake Cuomo: Explorations in technology and the human race.* Grand Rapids, MI: William B. Eerdmans. (Original work published 1923).

Guba, E. G. (1966, October). A Study of Title III activities: Report on evaluation. Indiana University, National Institute for the Study of Educational Change.

Guba, E. G. (1969). The failure of educational evaluation. *Educational Technology, 9*(5), 29–38.

Guba, E. G. (1976). *Alternative perspectives on evaluation.* Keynote speech at the annual meeting of the Evaluation Network, St. Louis, Missouri.

Guba, E. G. (1978). *Toward a methodology of naturalistic inquiry in evaluation.* Monograph Series, no. 8. Los Angeles, CA: Centre for the Study of Evaluation, University of California.

Guba, E. G. (1981a). Criteria for assessing the trustworthiness of naturalistic inquiries. *Educational Communication and Technology Journal, 29,* 75–92.

Guba, E. G. (1981b). Investigative journalism. In N. L. Smith (Ed.), *New techniques for evaluation* (pp. 167–262). Beverly Hills, CA: Sage.

Guba, E. G. (1982, April). *The search for truth: Naturalistic inquiry as an option.*

Guba, E. G., & Lincoln, Y. S. (1981). *Effective evaluation: Improving the usefulness of evaluation results through responsive and naturalistic approaches.* San Francisco: Jossey-Bass.

Guba, E. G., & Lincoln, Y. S. (1989). *Fourth generation evaluation.* Newbury Park, CA: Sage.

Guba, E. G., & Lincoln, Y. S. (1990). Can there be a human science? Constructivism as an alternative. *Person-Centered Review, 5*(2), 130–154.

Guskey, T. R., & Kifer, R. (1990). Ranking school districts on the basis of statewide results: Is it meaningful or misleading? *Educational Measurement: Issues and Practice, 9*(1), 11–16.

Hahn, A. J., Greene, J. C., & Waterman, C. (1994). *Educating about public issues.* Report from the Kellogg Foundation, Cornell University, Ithaca, NY.

Hambleton, R. K., & Swaminathan, H. (1985). *Item response theory.* Boston: Kluwer-Nijhoff.

Hammond, R. L. (1967). *Evaluation at the local level.* Address to the Miller Committee for the National Study of ESEA Title Ill.

Hammond, R. L. (1972). *Evaluation at the local level.* (Mimeograph). Tucson, AZ: EPIC Evaluation Center.

Hansson, F. (1997). Critical comments on evaluation research in Denmark. *Educational Evaluation and Policy Analysis, 21*, 111–126.

Hanushek, E. A. (1997). Assessing the effects of school resources on student performance: An update. *Educational Evaluation and Policy Analysis, 19*, 141–164.

Hanushek, E. A. (1999). Some findings from an independent investigation of the Tennessee STAR experiment and from other investigations of class size effects. *Educational Evaluation and Policy Analysis, 21*, 143–164.

Hanushek, E., & Jorgenson, D. (Eds.) (1996). *Improving America's schools:. The role of incentives.* Washington, D.C.: National Academy Press.

Harmon, M. (1992). *Evaluation report: Washington Comity School-Based High Risk Youth Substance Abuse Prevention Program.* College Park, MD: Institute of Criminal Justice and Criminology, University of Maryland.

Hart, D. (1994). *Authentic assessment: A handbook for educators.* Menlo Park, CA: Addison-Wesley.

Hartman, W. (1990). Supplemental/replacement: An alternative approach to excess costs. *Exceptional Children, 56*, 450–459.

Harvey, D. (1990). *The condition of postmodernity: An enquiry into the origins of cultural change.* Oxford: Blackwell.

Hastings, T. (1976). *A portrayal of the changing evaluation scene.* Keynote speech at the annual meeting of the Evaluation Network, St. Louis, Missouri.

Haug, P. (1996). Evaluation of government reforms. *Evaluation, 2*, 417–430.

Hawthorne, R. K. (1992). *Curriculum in the making.* New York: Teachers College Press.

Heflinger, C., Bickman, L., Northrup, D., & Sonnichsen, S. (1997). A theory-driven intervention and evaluation to explore family caregiver empowerment. *Journal of Emotional and Behavioral Disorders, 5*(3), 184–191.

Heleen, O. (1992). Is your school family-friendly? *Principal, 72*(2), 5–8.

Herman, J. L., Gearhart, M. G., & Baker, E. L. (1993). Assessing writing portfolios: Issues in the validity and meaning of scores. *Educational Assessment, 1*, 201–224.

Hersey, P. (1985). *Situational leader.* Charlotte, N.C.: Center for Leadership.

Hirsch, E. D., Jr. (1987). *Cultural literacy: What every American needs to know.* Boston: Houghton Mifflin.

Hofstadter, D. R. (1979). *Göder, Escher, Bach: An eternal golden braid.* New York: Basic Books.

Homans, G. A. (1978). What kind of a myth is the myth of a value free social science? *Social Science Quarterly, 58*, 530–541.

Hong, H., & Rist, R. C. (1997). The development of evaluation in the People's Republic of China. In E. Chelimsky & W. R. Shadish (Eds.), *Evaluation for the 21st century. A handbook.* Thousand Oaks, CA: Sage.

Hopfenberg, W. S., Levin, H. M., & Associates. (1993). *The accelerated schools resource guide.* San Francisco, CA: Jossey-Bass.

Hoskins, K. (1968). The examination, disciplinary power and rational schooling. *History of Education, 8*, 135–146.

Hough, J. (1994). Educational cost-benefit analysis. *Education Economics, 6*(1), 1–14.

House, E. R. (1977a). *Fair evaluation agreement.* Urbana-Champaign, IL: University of Illinois Center for Instructional Research and Curriculum Evaluation.

House, E. R. (1977b). *The logic of evaluative argument.* Center for the Study of Evaluation, UCLA, Monograph 1.

House, E. R. (1980). *Evaluating with validity.* Beverly Hills, CA: Sage.

House, E. R. (1983). Assumptions underlying evaluation models. In G. F. Madaus, M. S. Scriven, & D. L. Stufflebeam (Eds.), *Evaluation models. Viewpoints on educational and human services evaluation* (pp. 45–64). Boston, MA: Kluwer-Nijhoff.

House, E. R. (1993). *Professional evaluation–Social impact and political consequences.* Newbury Park, CA: Sage.

House, E. R., Glass, G. V., McLean, L. D., & Walker, D. F. (1977). No simple answer: Critique of the "Follow Through Evaluation." Urbana-Champaign, IL: Center for Instructional Research and Curriculum Evaluation.

House, E. R., & Howe, K. R. (forthcoming). *Values in evaluation.* Thousand Oaks, CA: Sage.

House, E. R., Rivers, W., & Stufflebeam, D. L. (1974). A counter-response to Kearney, Donovan, and Fisher. *Phi Delta Kappan, 56,* 19.

Huenecke, D. (1992). An artistic criticism of Writing-to-Read, a computer-based program for beginning readers. *Journal of Curriculum and Supervision, 7,* 170–179.

Huey-Tsyh Chen. (1994). Current trends and future directions in program evaluation. *Evaluation Practice, 15,* 229–238.

Husén, T. (Ed.) (1967). *International study of achievement in mathematics* (2 vols). New York: Wiley.

Ingram, D. (1990). *Critical theory and philosophy.* New York: Paragon House.

Inter-Agency Commission for Basic Education for All. (1990). *Meeting basic human needs. A background report for the World Conference on Basic Education for All.* New York: InterAgency Commission, United Nations.

Ireland. Royal Commission of Inquiry into Primary Education. (1870). *Report of the Commissioners.* (H.C. xxviii, part i).

Jackson, P. W. (1981a). Comprehending a well-run comprehensive: A report on a visit to a large suburban high school. *Daedalus, 110*(4), 81–96.

Jackson, P. W. (1981b). Secondary schooling for children of the poor. *Daedalus, 110*(4), 39–58.

Jackson, P. W. (1981c). Secondary schooling for the privileged few: A report on a visit to a New England boarding school. *Daedalus, 110*(4), 117–130.

Jackson, P. W. (1990). *Life in classrooms* (2nd ed). New York: Holt, Rinehart & Winston.

Jackson, P. W. (1992). *Untaught lessons.* New York: Teachers College Press.

Jalil, N., & McGinn, N. (1992). Pakistan. In R. Thomas (Ed.), *Education's role in national development plans.* New York: Praeger.

James, H. T. (1968). *The new cult of efficiency and education.* Pittsburgh, PA: University of Pittsburgh Press.

Jamieson, D., Klees, S., & Wells, S. (1978). *The costs of educational media: Guidelines for planning and evaluation.* Beverly Hills, CA: Sage.

Janz, N. K., & Becker, M. H. (1984). The health belief model: A decade later. *Health Education Quarterly, 11,* 1–47.

Jimenez, E., Lockheed, M., & Wattanawaha, N. (1988). The relative efficiency of public and private schools: The case of Thailand. *World Bank Economic Review, 2,* 139–164.

Johnson, R. (1980). *Directory of evaluators and evaluation agencies.* New York: Exxon Corporation.

Johnston, L., & Mermin, J. (1994). Easing children's entry to school: Home visits help. *Young Children, 49*(5), 62–68.

Joint Committee on Standards for Educational Evaluation. (1981a). *Principles and by-laws.* Kalamazoo MI: Western Michigan University Evaluation Center.

Joint Committee on Standards for Educational Evaluation. (1981b). *Standards for evaluations of educational programs, projects, and materials.* New York: McGraw-Hill.

Joint Committee on Standards for Educational Evaluation. (1988). *The personnel evaluation standards.* Newbury Park, CA: Sage.

Joint Committee on Standards for Educational Evaluation. (1994). *The program evaluation standards. How to assess evaluations of educational programs.* Thousand Oaks, CA: Sage.

Jorgensen, D. (1989). *Participant observation: A methodology for human studies.* Thousand Oaks, CA: Sage.

Kaagan, S., & Coley, R. (1989). *State education indicators.* New Brunswick, N.J.: Center for Policy Research in Education.

Kahneman, D., Slovic, P., & Tversky, A. (1982). *Judgement under uncertainty: Heuristics and biases.* Cambridge: Cambridge University Press.

Kaplan, A. (1964). *The conduct of inquiry.* San Francisco: Chandler.

Kaplan, R. S., & Norton, D. P. (1996). Linking the balanced scorecard to strategy. *California Management Review, 39*(1), 1, 3 & 4.

Karlsson, O. (1996). A critical dialogue in evaluation: How can interaction between evaluation and politics be tackled? *Evaluation, 2,* 405–416.

Karlsson, O. (1998). Socratic dialogue in the Swedish political context. In T. A. Schwandt (Ed.), *Scandinavian perspectives on the evaluator's role in informing social policy. New Directions for Evaluation, 77,* 21–38.

Kaufman, R. A. (1969, May). Toward educational system planning: Alice in educationland. *Audiovisual Instructor, 14,* 47–48.

Kee, J. E. (1995). Benefit-cost analysis in program evaluation. In J. S. Wholey, H. P. Hatry, & K. E. Newcomer (Eds.), *Handbook of practical program evaluation* (pp. 456–488). San Francisco: Jossey-Bass.

Kellaghan, T., & Grisay, A. (1995). International comparisons of student achievement: Problems and prospects. In *Measuring what students learn* (pp. 41–61). Paris: Organisation for Economic Co-operation and Development.

Kellaghan, T., & Madaus, G. F. (1982). Trends in educational standards in Great Britain and Ireland. In G. R. Austin & H. Garber (Eds.), *The rise and fall of national test scores* (pp. 195–214). New York: Academic Press.

Kellaghan, T., Madaus, G. F., & Airasian, P. W. (1982). *The effects of standardized testing.* Boston: Kluwer-Nijhoff.

Kellaghan, T., Weir, S., Ó hUallacháin, S., & Morgan, M. (1995). *Educational disadvantage in Ireland.* Dublin: Combat Poverty Agency / Department of Education / Educational Research Centre.

Kelman, H. C. (1979). *Time to speak: On human values and social research.* San Francisco, CA: Jossey-Bass.

Kemple, J. J., & Rock, J. L. (1996). *Career academies: Early implementation lessons from a 10-site evaluation.* New York: Manpower Demonstration Research Corporation.

Kemple, J. J., & Snipes, J. C. (2000). *Career academies: Impacts on students' engagement and performance in high school.* New York: Manpower Demonstration Research Corporation.

Kendall, C. N. (1915). Efficiency of school and school systems. In *Proceedings and addresses of the fifty-third annual meeting of the National Education Association,* pp. 389–395.

Kentucky Department of Education. (1993). *Kentucky results information system, 1991–92 technical report.* Frankfort, KY: Author.

Kidder, T. (1989). *Among schoolchildren.* New York: Avon.

Kidder, L., & Fine, M. (1987). *Qualitative and quantitative methods: When stories converge. Multiple methods in program evaluation. New Directions for Program Evaluation, 35.* San Francisco: Jossey-Bass.

King, J. (1994). Meeting the educational needs of at risk students: A cost analysis of three models. *Educational Evaluation and Policy Analysis, 16,* 1–19.

Kirst, M. W. (1975). The rise and fall of PPBS in California. *Phi Delta Kappan, 56,* 535–538.

Kirst, M. W. (July, 1990). *Accountability: Implications for state and local policymakers.* Policy Perspectives Series. Washington, DC: Information Services, Office of Educational Research and Improvement, U.S. Department of Education.

Kirst, M. W., & Meister, G. (1985). Turbulence in American secondary schools: What reforms last? *Curriculum Inquiry, 15,* 169–186.

Klass, C. S. et al. (1993). Home visiting: Building a bridge between home and school. *Equity and Choice, 10*(1), 52–56.

Klees, S. (1995). Economics of educational technology. In M. Carnoy (Ed.), *The international encyclopedia of economics of education* (2nd ed.) (pp. 398–406). Oxford: Pergamon.

Kliebard, H. M. (1972). Metaphorical roots of curriculum design. *Teachers College Record, 73,* 403–404.

Koretz, D. (1986). *The validity of gains in scores on the Kentucky Instructional Results Information System (KIRIS).* Santa Monica, CA: Rand Education.

Koretz, D. (1994). *The evolution of a portfolio program: The impact and quality of the Vermont portfolio program in its second year (1992–93).* Los Angeles, CA: National Center for Research on Evaluation, Standards, and Student Testing.

Koretz, D. (1996). Using student assessments for educational accountability. In R. Hanushek (Ed.), *Improving the performance of America's schools* (pp. 171–196). Washington, DC: National Academy Press.

Koretz, D. (1997). *The assessment of students with disabilities in Kentucky.* CSE Technical Report 431. Los Angeles: Center for the Study of Evaluation, University of California.

Koretz, D. M., & Barron, S. I. (1998). *The validity of gains in scores on the Kentucky Instructional Results Information System (KIRIS).* Santa Monica, CA: Rand Corporation.

Koretz, D., Barron, S., Mitchell, K., & Stecher, B. (1996). *The perceived effects of the Kentucky Instructional Results Information System (KIRIS)*. Santa Monica, CA: Rand Corporation.

Koretz, D., Klein, S., McCaffrey, D., & Stecher, B. (1994). *Interim report: The reliability of Vermont portfolio scores in the 1992–93 school year*. Santa Monica, CA: Rand Corporation.

Koretz, D., Mitchell, K., Barron, S., & Keith, S. (1996). *The perceived effects of the Maryland School Performance Assessment Program*. CSE Technical Report No. 409. Los Angeles: Center for the Study of Evaluation, University of California.

Koretz, D., Stecher, B., Klein, S., McCaffrey, D., & Deibert, E. (1993). *Can portfolios assess student performance and influence instruction? The 1991–92 Vermont experience*. Santa Monica, CA: Rand Corporation.

Krathwohl, D. R. (1972). Functions for experimental schools evaluation and their organization. In G. V. Glass, M. L. Byers, & B. R. Worthen (Eds.), *Recommendations for the evaluation of experimental schools projects of the U.S. Office of Education* (pp. 174–194). Report of the Experimental Schools Evaluation Working Conference, Estes Park, CO, December 1971. University of Colorado Laboratory of Educational Research, Boulder.

Krathwohl, D. R. (1980). The myth of value-free evaluation. *Educational Evaluation and Policy Analysis, 2,* 37–45.

Krathwohl, D. R., Bloom, B. S., & Masia, B. B. (1964). *Taxonomy of educational objectives: The classification of educational goals. Handbook II: Affective Domain*. New York: David McKay.

Kritzman, L. D. (Ed.) (1990). *Michel Foucault: Politics, philosophy, culture: Interviews and other writings 1977–1984*. New York: Routledge.

Krol, R. A. (1978). *A meta analysis of comparative research on the effects of desegregation on academic achievement*. Unpublished doctoral dissertation, Western Michigan University.

Kuhn, T. S. (1970). The structure of scientific revolutions. *International Encyclopedia of Unified Science*. Vol. 2, no. 2 (2nd ed.). Chicago: University of Chicago Press.

Kvale, S. (1995). The social construction of validity. *Qualitative Inquiry, 1,* 19–40.

Lakoff, G., & Johnson, M. (1980). *Metaphors we live by*. Chicago: University of Chicago Press.

Langer, J. A., & Allington, R. L. (1992). Curriculum research in writing and reading. In P. W. Jackson (Ed.), *Handbook of research on curriculum* (pp. 687–725). New York: Macmillan.

Lau, L. (1979). Educational production functions. In *Economic dimensions of education* (pp. 33–69). Washington, DC: National Academy of Education.

Lawrence-Lightfoot, S. (1981a). Portraits of exemplary secondary schools: George Washington Career Comprehensive High School. *Daedalus, 110*(4), 17–39.

Lawrence-Lightfoot, S. (1981b). Portraits of exemplary secondary schools: Highland Park. *Daedalus, 110*(4), 59–80.

Lawrence-Lightfoot, S. (1981c). Portraits of exemplary secondary schools: St. Paul's School. *Daedalus, 110*(4), 97–116.

Lemke, J. L. (1995). *Textual politics: Discourse and social dynamics*. London: Taylor & Francis.

Lenne, B., & Cleland, H. (1987). Describing program logic. *Program Evaluation Bulletin 2/87*. New South Wales Public Service Board.

Leonard-Barton, D. (1987). Implementing structured software methodologies: A case of innovation in process technology. *Interfaces, 17,* 6–17.

Lessinger, L. M. (1969, June–July). Accountability for results. *American Education*. Washington, D.C.: U.S. Office of Education.

Lessinger, L. M. (1970). *Every kid a winner: Accountability in education*. New York: Simon & Schuster.

Levin, H. (1972, January 10). *New York Times*, Education Supplement.

Levin, H. (1974). A conceptual framework for accountability. *School Review, 82,* 363–391.

Levin, H. (1983). *Cost-effectiveness analysis: A primer*. Beverly Hills, CA: Sage.

Levin, H. (1988). Cost effectiveness and educational policy. *Educational Evaluation and Policy Analysis, 10,* 51–69.

Levin, H. (1989). An accountability model for the accelerated school. Stanford University, Unpublished paper.

Levin, H. (1995). Cost-effectiveness analysis. In M. Carnoy (Ed.), *International encyclopedia of economics of education* (2nd ed.) (pp. 381–386). Oxford: Pergamon.

Levin, H. (1996). Economics of school reform for at risk students. In E. Hanushek & D. Jorgenson (Eds.), *Improving America's schools: The role of incentives*. Washington, DC: National Academy Press.

Levin, H., Glass, G., & Meister, G. (1987). A cost-effectiveness analysis of computer-assisted instruction. *Evaluation Review, 11,* 50–72.

Levine, M. (1973). Scientific method and the adversary model: Some preliminary suggestions. *Evaluation Comment, 4*, 1–3.

Levine, M. (1974). Scientific method and the adversary model: Some preliminary thoughts. *American Psychologist, 29*, 666–677.

Lewis, A. C. (1997). Shrinking pains: California's initiative to reduce class size is off to a bumpy start. *Harvard Education Letter, 13*(4), 7.

Lightfoot, S. L. (1983). *The good high school.* New York: Basic Books.

Lincoln, Y. S. (1982, April). *The utility of naturalistic inquiry for special education studies.* Paper presented at the annual meeting of the Council on Exceptional Children, Houston, Texas.

Lincoln, Y. S., & Guba, E. G. (1981, September). *Do evaluators wear grass skirts? Going native and ethnocentrism as problems of utilization in evaluation.* Paper presented at the Joint annual meeting of the Evaluation Network and the Evaluation Research Society, Austin, Texas.

Lincoln, Y. S., & Guba, E. G. (1982, April). *Establishing dependability and confirmability in naturalistic inquiry through an audit.* Paper presented at the American Educational Research Association, New York.

Lincoln, Y. S., & Guba, E. G. (1985). *Naturalistic inquiry.* Beverly Hills, CA: Sage.

Lindquist, E. F. (Ed.) (1951). *Educational measurement.* Washington, D.C.: American Council on Education.

Lindquist, E. F. (1953). *Design and analysis of experiments in psychology and education.* Boston: Houghton-Mifflin.

Lindvall, C. M., & Cox, R. (1970). *Evaluation as a tool in curriculum development* (AERA Monograph Series on Curriculum Evaluation). Chicago: Rand McNally.

Linn, R. L., Baker, E. L., & Dunbar, S. B. (1991). Complex, performance-based assessment: Expectations and validation criteria. *Educational Researcher, 20*(8), 15–21.

Linney, J. A., & Wandersman, A. (1991). *Prevention plus III (Assessing alcohol and other drug prevention programs at the school and community level: A four-step guide to useful program assessment).* Rockville, MD: Office of Substance Abuse Prevention, U.S. Department of Health and Human Services.

Lipsey, M. (1993). Theory as method: Small theories of treatments. In L. Sechrest & A. Scott (Eds.), *Understanding causes and generalizing about them.* New Directions for Evaluation. San Francisco: Jossey-Bass.

Lipsey, M. (1997). What can you build with thousands of bricks? Musings on the cumulation of knowledge in program evaluation. In D. Rog & D. Fournier (Eds.), *Progress and future directions in evaluation: Perspectives on theory, practice and methods.* New Directions for Evaluation. San Francisco: Jossey-Bass.

Lipsey, M., & Pollard, J. (1989). Driving towards theory in program evaluation: More models to choose from. *Evaluation and Program Planning, 12*, 317–328.

Lloyd, A. (1967). *Folksong in England.* London: Lawrence & Wilshart).

Lofland, J., & Lofland, L. H. (1995). *Analyzing social settings: A guide to qualitative observation and analysis* (3rd ed.). Belmont, CA: Wadsworth.

Lord, F. M. (1962). Estimating norms by item-sampling. *Educational and Psychological Measurement, 22*, 259–268.

Lord, F. M., & Novick, M. R. (1968). *Statistical theories of mental test scores.* Reading, MA: Addison-Wesley.

Love, A. J. (1983). Editors Notes. In A. J. Love (Ed.), *Developing effective internal evaluation* (pp. 1–3). New Directions For Program Evaluation No 20. San Francisco: Jossey–Bass.

Lyotard, J. (1984). *The postmodern condition.* Minneapolis: University of Minnesota Press.

MacDonald, B. (1975). Evaluation and the control of education. In D. Tawney (Ed.), *Evaluation: The state of the art.* London: Schools Council.

MacDonald, B. (1977). A political classification of evaluation studies. In D. Hamilton (Ed.), *Beyond the numbers game.* London: Macmillan.

MacDonald, B., & Sanger, J. (1982). Just for the record? Notes towards a theory of interviewing in evaluation. *Evaluation Studies Review Annual, 7*, 175–198.

Madaus, G. F., Airasian, P. W., & Kellaghan, T. (1980). *School effectiveness. A reassessment of the evidence.* New York: McGraw-Hill.

Madaus, G. F., Clarke, M., & O'Leary, M. (in press). A century of standardized mathematics testing. In G. M. Stanic & J. Kilpatrick (Eds.), *A recent history of mathematics education in the United States and Canada.* Reston, VA: National Council of Teachers of Mathematics.

Madaus, G. F., & Kellaghan, T. (1992). Curriculum evaluation and assessment. In P. W. Jackson (Ed.), *Handbook of research on curriculum* (pp. 119–154). New York, Macmillan.

Madaus, G. F., & Raczek, A. E. (1996). The extent and growth of educational testing in the United States: 1956–1994. In H. Goldstein & T. Lewis (Eds.), *Assessment: Problems, developments and statistical issues* (pp. 145–165). New York: Wiley.

Madaus, G. F., Scriven, M. S., & Stufflebeam, D. L. (1983). *Evaluation models: Viewpoints on educational and human services education*. Boston: Kluwer-Nijhoff.

Maeroff, G. I. (1991). Assessing alternative assessment. *Phi Delta Kappan, 73*, 272–281.

Manning, P. R., & DeBakey, L. (1987). *Medicine: Preserving the passion*. New York: Springer-Verlag.

Mark, M. M., & Shotland, L. R. (1987). Stakeholder-based evaluation and value judgments. *Evaluation Studies Review Annual, 11*, 131–151.

Martin, D. T. et al. (1976). *Accountability in American education*. Princeton, NJ: Princeton Book Publishers.

Massachusetts Department of Education. (1998). *Report of the 1988 statewide results: The Massachusets Comprehensive Assessment System (MCAS)*. Malden, MA: Author.

May, P. (1971). Standardized Testing in Philadelphia, 1916–1938. Unpublished manuscript.

Mayoya, M. (1997). *Private costs and access to secondary education in Burundi*. Unpublished doctoral dissertation, College of Education, Michigan State University, East Lansing.

McConney, A. (Ed.) (1994). *Toward a unified model: The foundations of educational personnel evaluation*. Kalamazoo, MI: Center for Research on Educational Accountability and Teacher Evaluation, Western Michigan University Evaluation Center.

McDonnell, L., & Elmore, R. (1987). *Alternative policy instruments*. Santa Monica, CA: Rand Corporation, Center for Policy Research in Education.

McDonnell, L. (1987). Educational accountability. Presentation to the California Commission on Educational Quality, Sacramento, CA, October 9.

McKenna, B., Nevo, D., Stufflebeam, D., & Thomas, R. (1994). *The school professional's guide to improving teacher evaluation systems*. Kalamazoo, MI: Center for Research on Educational Accountability and Teacher Evaluation, Western Michigan University Evaluation Center.

McLean, R. A., Sanders, W. L., & Stroup, W. W. (1991). A unified approach to mixed linear models. *American Statistician, 45*, 54–64.

Mehrens, W. A. (1972). Using performance assessment for accountability purposes. *Educational Measurement: Issues and Practice, 11*(1), 3–10.

Mehrens, W. A., & Lehmann, I. J. (1987). *Using standardized tests in education*. (4th ed.). New York: Longman.

Meier, P. (1972). The biggest public health experiment ever: The 1954 field trial of the Salk poliomyelitis vaccine. In J. M. Tanur et al. (Eds.), *Statistics: A guide to the unknown* (pp. 2–13). San Francisco: Holden-Day.

Merton, R. K., Fiske, M., & Kendall, P. L. (1990). *The focused interview: A manual of problems and procedures* (2nd ed.). New York: Free Press.

Messick, S. (1994). The interplay of evidence and consequences in the validation of performance assessments. *Educational Researcher, 23*(3), 13–23.

Metfessel, N. S., & Michael, W. B. (1967). A paradigm involving multiple criterion measures for the evaluation of the effectiveness of school programs. *Educational and Psychological Measurement, 27*, 931–943.

Mezirow, J. (1991). *Transformative dimensions of adult learning*. San Francisco: Jossey-Bass.

Miles, M. B., & Huberman, A. M. (1994). *Qualitative data analysis: An expanded sourcebook*. Thousand Oaks, CA: Sage.

Mill, J. S. (1843). *A system of logic*. New York: Longmans Green (reprinted 1947).

Millman, J. (Ed.) (1981). *Handbook of teacher evaluation*. Beverly Hills, CA: Sage.

Millman, J., & Darling-Hammond, L. (Eds.) (1990). *The new handbook of teacher evaluation: Assessing elementary and secondary school teachers*. Newbury Park, CA: Sage.

Milne, C. (1993). Outcomes hierarchies and program logic as conceptual tools: Five case studies. *Proceedings of the Australasian Evaluation Society Annual Conference, Brisbane*.

Milne, C., & Brooks, M. (1996). Programlogic. Sydney: ARTD Software.

Miron, G. (1998). Chapter in L. Buchert (Ed.), *Education reform in the south in the 1990s*. Paris: UNESCO.

Mithaug, D. (1991). *Self-determined kids: Raising satisfied and successful children*. New York: Macmillan.

Mitroff, I. I., & Mason, R. O. (1981). *Creating a dialectical social science: Concepts, methods, and models*. Boston: Reidel.

Modell, W. (1963). Hazards of new drugs. *Science, 139*, 1180–1185.

Moll, L. C. et al. (1992). Funds of knowledge for teaching: Using a qualitative approach to connect homes and classrooms. *Theory into Practice, 31*, 132–141.

Morris, B., & Stronach, I. (1993). *Evaluation of the management of change: Tayside TVEI*. Stirling, Scotland: Department of Education, University of Stirling.

Mosteller, F. (1995). The Tennessee study of class size in the early school grades. *Future of Children, 5*(2), 113–127.

Mosteller, F., Light, R., & Sachs, J. (1996). Sustained inquiry in education: Lessons from ability grouping and class size. *Harvard Educational Review, 66,* 797–842.

Mullen, P. D., Hersey, J., & Iverson, D. C. (1987). Health behavior models compared. *Social Science and Medicine, 24,* 973–981.

Murphy, J. K., & Cohen, D. (1974). Accountability in education. *Public Interest 2, 36* (summer), 53–81.

Nathan, J. (1984). *Free to teach.* New York: Harper & Row.

National Center for Education Statistics. (1991). *SEDCAR (Standards for Education Data Collection and Reporting).* Rockville, MD: Westat, Inc.

National Commission on Excellence in Education. (1983). *A nation at risk: The imperative of educational reform.* Washington, D.C.: U.S. Government Printing Office. (No. 065-000-00177-2)

National Science Foundation. (1993). *User-friendly handbook for project evaluation: Science, mathematics, engineering and technology education.* NSF 93–152. Arlington, VA: Author.

National Science Foundation. (1997). *User-friendly handbook for mixed method evaluations.* NSF 97–153. Arlington, VA: Author.

Natriello, G. (1996). Diverting attention from conditions in American schools. *Educational Researcher, 25*(8), 7–9.

Nevo, D. (1974). *Evaluation priorities of students, teachers, and principals.* Unpublished doctoral dissertation, Ohio State University, Columbus.

Nevo, D. (1993). The evaluation minded school: An application of perceptions from program evaluation. *Evaluation Practice, 14,* 39–47.

Nevo, D., & Stufflebeam, D. L. (1993). *Toward a theory of teacher evaluation.* Kalamazoo, MI: Center for Research on Educational Accountability and Teacher Evaluation, Western Michigan University Evaluation Center.

Newcomer, K. E., & Wholey, J. S. (1989). Conclusion: Evaluation strategies for building high-performance programs. In J. S. Wholey & K. E. Newcomer (Eds.), *Improving government performance: Evaluation strategies for strengthening public agencies and programs* (pp. 195–208). San Francisco: Jossey-Bass.

Nowakowski, A. (1974). *Handbook for traveling observers.* National Science Foundation systems project. Kalamazoo, MI: Western Michigan University Evaluation Center.

Nuttall, D. L., & Goldstein, H. (1990). The 1988 examination results for ILEA. Paper presented to the Inner London Educational Authority Committees.

Nyberg, L. M. (1991). Dynamics of excellence in science education: The state of the art. *Dissertation Abstracts International,* 52,1280. (University Microfilms No. 91-25, 228)

Nye, B., Hedges, L. V., & Konstantopoulos, S. (1999). The long-term effects of small classes: A five-year follow-up of the Tennessee class size experiment. *Educational Evaluation and Policy Analysis, 21,* 127–142.

Oakes, J. (1985). *Keeping track.* New Haven, CN: Yale University Press.

OECD (Organisation for Economic Co-operation and Development) (1997). *Education at a glance.* Paris: Author.

Office of Public Management. (1992). *Planning and monitoring your program: First steps in program evaluation.* Sydney: New South Wales Premiers Department.

Orris, M. J. (1989). *Industrial applicability of the Joint Committee's Personnel Evaluation Standards.* Unpublished doctoral dissertation. Western Michigan University, Kalamazoo.

Owen, J. M., & Lambert, F. (1994). Roles for evaluation in learning organizations. *Evaluation, 1*(2), 21–43.

Owen, J. M., & Rogers, P. J. (1998). *Program evaluation: Forms and approaches.* Beverly Hills, CA: Sage.

Owens, T. (1973). Educational evaluation by adversary proceeding. In E. House (Ed.), *School evaluation: The politics and process.* Berkeley, CA: McCutchan.

Owens, T. R., & Stufflebeam, D. L. (1964). An experimental comparison of item sampling and examinee sampling for estimating test norms. *Journal of Educational Measurement, 6,* 75–83.

Parlett, M., & Hamilton, D. (1972). *Evaluation as illumination: A new approach to the study of innovatory programs.* Edinburgh: Centre for Research in the Educational Sciences, University of Edinburgh, Occasional Paper No. 9.

Parlett, M., & Hamilton, D. (1977). Evaluation as illumination: A new approach to the study of innovatory programmes. In D. Hamilton et al. (Eds.), *Beyond the numbers game* (pp. 6–22). London: Macmillan Education.

Patton, M. Q. (1978). *Utilization-focused evaluation.* Beverly Hills, CA: Sage.

Patton, M. Q. (1980). *Qualitative evaluation methods.* Beverly Hills, CA: Sage.

Patton, M. Q. (1982). *Practical evaluation.* Beverly Hills, CA: Sage.

Patton, M. Q. (1986). *Utilization-focused evaluation.* (2nd ed.). Beverly Hills, CA: Sage.

Patton, M. Q. (1990). *Qualitative evaluation and research methods* (2nd ed.). Newbury Park, CA: Sage.

Patton, M. Q. (1994). Developmental evaluation. *Evaluation Practice*, *15*, 311–319.

Patton, M. Q. (1996). *Utilization-focused evaluation*. (3rd ed.). Thousand Oaks, CA: Sage.

Patton, M. Q. (1997). *Utilization-focused evaluation: The new century text* (3rd ed.). Newbury Park, CA: Sage.

Pawson, R., & Tilley, N. (1997). *Realistic evaluation*. London: Sage.

Peck, H. (1981, Fall). *Report on the Certification of Evaluators in Louisiana*. Paper presented at the meeting of the Southern Educational Research Association, Lexington, Kentucky.

Perrin, B. (1998). Effective use and misuse of performance measurement. *American Journal of Evaluation*, *19*, 367–379.

Peters, R. S. (1970). Must an educator have an aim? In R. S. Peters (Ed.), *Authority, responsibility, and education* (pp. 122–131). London: George Allen & Unwin.

Peters, T. (1982). *In search of excellence: Lessons from America's best-run companies*. New York: Harper & Row.

Peters, T. J., & Waterman, R. H. (1982). *In search of excellence*. New York: Warner Books.

Peterson, P. (1996). School choice in Milwaukee. *Public Interest*, *125*, 38–56.

Peterson, P., & Hassel, B. (Eds.) (1998). *Learning from school choice*. Washington, D.C.: Brookings Institution Press.

Phi Delta Kappa Commission on Evaluation. (1971). *Educational evaluation and decision making*. Itasca, IL: Peacock.

Phillips, D. C. (1990). Postpositivist science: Myths and realities. In E. G. Guba (Ed.), *The paradigm dialog*. Newbury Park, CA: Sage.

Picariello, H. (1968). *Evaluation of Title I*. Washington, D.C.: American Institute for the Advancement of Science.

Pinker, R. (1971). *Social theory and social policy*. London: Heinemann.

Platt, J. (1992). Case study in American methodological thought. *Current Sociology*, *40*, 17–48.

Pollitt, C. (1993). Occasional excursions: A brief history of policy evaluation in the UK. *Parliamentary Affairs*, *46*, 353–362.

Polanyi, M. (1966). *The tacit dimension*. New York: Doubleday.

Popham, W. J. (1969). Objectives and instruction. In R. Stake (Ed.), *Instructional objectives*. AERA Monograph Series on Curriculum Evaluation, Vol. 3. Chicago: Rand McNally.

Popham, W. J. (1971). *Criterion-referenced measurement*. Englewood Cliffs, N.J.: Educational Technology Publications.

Popham, W. J., & Carlson, D. (1983). Deep dark deficits of the adversary evaluation model. In G. F. Madaus, M. S. Scriven, & D. L. Stufflebeam (Eds.), *Evaluation models* (pp. 205–213). Boston: Kluwer-Nijhoff.

Postlethwaite, T. N. (1987). Comparative educational achievement research: Can it be improved? *Comparative Education Review*, *31*, 150–158.

Powell, A. G., Farrar, E., & Cohen, D. K. (1985). *The shopping mall high school*. Boston: Houghton Mifflin.

Prochaska, J. O., & DiClemente, C. C. (1992). Stages of change in the modification of problem behaviors. In M. Hersen, R. M. Eisler, & P. M. Miller (Eds.), *Progress in behavior modification 28*. Sycamore, IL: Sycamore Publishing Company.

Proppe, O. (1979). *Dialectical evaluation*. Urbana, IL: Center for Instructional Research and Curriculum Evaluation. Mimeo.

Provus, M. (1969). *Discrepancy evaluation model*. Pittsburgh, PA: Pittsburgh Public Schools.

Provus, M. (1971). *Discrepancy evaluation*. Berkeley, CA: McCutchan.

Psacharopoulos, G. (1994). Returns to investment in education: A global update. *World Development*, *22*, 1325–1343.

Pursley, L. C. (1996). *Empowerment and utilization through participatory evaluation*. Unpublished doctoral dissertation, Cornell University, Ithaca, NY.

Radaelli, C. M., & Dente, B. (1996). Evaluation strategies and analysis of the policy process. *Evaluation*, *2*, 51–66.

Ragin, C. C., & Becker, H. S. (Eds.) (1992). *What is a case? Exploring the foundations of social inquiry*. New York: Cambridge University Press.

Ramey, C. T., & Campbell, F. A. (1984). Preventive education of high-risk children: Cognitive consequences of the Carolina Abecedarian Project. *American Journal of Mental Deficiency*, *88*, 515–523.

Ramey, C. T., & Campbell, F. A. (1991). Poverty, early childhood education, and academic competence: The Abecedarian experiment. In A. C. Huston (Ed.), *Children in poverty: Child development and public policy* (pp. 190–221). New York: Cambridge University Press.

Ramey, C. T., & Smith, B. J. (1977). Assessing the intellectual consequences of early intervention with high-risk infants. *American Journal of Mental Deficiency*, *81*, 319–324.

Rappaport, J. (1987). Terms of empowerment/exemplars of prevention: Toward a theory for community psychology. *American Journal of Community Psychology, 15,* 121–148.

Reed, M. (1989). *WMU traveling observer handbook* (5th ed.). Kalamazoo, MI: Western Michigan University Evaluation Center.

Reed, M. (1991). *The evolution of the Traveling Observer (TO) role.* Paper presented at the annual meeting of the American Educational Research Association, Chicago.

Reinhard, D. (1972). *Methodology development for input evaluation using advocate and design teams.* Unpublished doctoral dissertation, Ohio State University, Columbus.

Rhyne, R. F. (1972). Communicating holistic insights. *Fields Within Fields—Within Fields, 5,* 93–104.

Rice, J. K. (1997). Cost analysis in education: Paradox and possibility. *Educational Evaluation and Policy Analysis, 19,* 309–317.

Rice, J. M. (1897). The futility of the spelling grind. *Forum, 23,* 163–172.

Rice, J. M. (1914). *Scientific management in education.* New York: Hinds, Noble & Eldredge.

Richards, C. (1989). *State sponsored school performance incentive plans.* New Brunswick, N.J.: Center for Policy Research in Education.

Rickey, G. (1995). *Constructivism: Origins and evolution.* New York: George Braziller.

Ridings, J. (1980). *Catalog of criteria for evaluating administrative concerns in school districts.* Toledo, OH: Toledo, Ohio Public Schools and the Western Michigan University Evaluation Center.

Rippey, R. M. (Ed.). (1973). *Studies in transactional evaluation.* Berkeley, CA: McCutchan.

Ritter, G. W. (1997). The political and institutional origins of a large scale education experiment; Tennessee's Project STAR: A randomized experiment in elementary class-size. Unpublished manuscript.

Ritter, G. W., & Boruch, R. F. (1999). The political and institutional origins of a randomized controlled trial on elementary school class: Tennessee's Project STAR.

Rogers, P. J., & Huebner, T. A. (1998). *Using program theory for formative evaluation and organizational learning.* Paper presented at the Canadian Evaluation Society National Conference.

Rosenthal, R. (1994). Interpersonal expectancy effects: A 30-Year perspective. *Current Directions in Psychological Science, 3*(6), 176–179.

Rosenthal, R., & Jacobson, L. (1968). *Pygmalion in the classroom: Teacher expectation and pupils' intellectual development.* New York: Holt, Rinehart & Winston.

Rossi, P. H., & Freeman, H. E. (1993). *Evaluation: A systematic approach* (5th ed.). Newbury Park, CA: Sage.

Roth, I. E. (1978). *Theory and practice of needs assessment with special application to institutions of higher learning.* Unpublished doctoral dissertation, University of California, Berkeley.

Roth, J. (1977). Needs and the needs assessment process. *Evaluation News, 5,* 15–17.

Rubin, A., & Babbie, E. (1993). *Research methods for social work* (2nd ed.). Pacific Grove, CA: Brooks/Cole.

Rychlak, J. F. (Ed.). (1976). *Dialectics: Humanistic rationale for behavior and development.* New York: Karger.

Salkie, R. (1995). *Text and discourse analysis.* London: Routledge.

Sandberg, J. (1986). *Alabama educator inservice training centers traveling observer handbook.* Kalamazoo, MI: Western Michigan University Evaluation Center.

Sanders, J. R. (1995, Summer). Standards and principles. In W. R. Shadish, D. L. Newman, M. A. Scheirer, & C. Wye (Eds.), *Guiding principles for evaluators. New Directions for Program Evaluation, 34,* 47–53.

Sanders, J. R., & Nafziger, D. H. (1977). *A basis for determining the adequacy of evaluation designs.* Occasional Paper Series, Paper No. 6. Kalamazoo, MI: Western Michigan University Evaluation Center.

Sanders, J. R., & Sachse, T. P. (1977). Applied performance testing in the classroom. *Journal of Research and Development in Education, 10,* 92–104.

Sanders, W. L. (1989). *Using customized standardized tests.* Washington, DC: Office of Educational Research and Improvement, U. S. Department of Education. (ERIC Digest No. ED 314429).

Sanders, W. L., & Horn, S. P. (1994). The Tennessee Value-Added Assessment System (TVAAS): Mixed-model methodology in educational assessment. *Journal of Personnel Evaluation in Education, 8,* 299–311.

Sartorius, R. (1996). The Third Generation Logical Framework Approach: Dynamic management for agricultural research projects. *European Journal of Agricultural Education and Extension, 2*(4), 49–62.

Schatzman, L., & Strauss, A. L. (1973). *Field research.* Englewood Cliffs, N.J.: Prentice-Hall.

Schmidt, W. H., McKnight, C. C., & Raizen, S. A. (1996). *Splintered vision: An investigation of U.S. science and mathematics education—Executive summary.* U.S. National Research Center for the Third International Mathematics and Science Study, Michigan State University.

Schmoker, M., & Mazano, R. J. (1999). Realizing the promise of standards-based education. *Educational Leadership, 56*(6), 17–21.

Schnee, R. (1977). Ethical standards for evaluators: The problem. *CEDR Quarterly, 10*(1), 3.

School Curriculum and Assessment Authority. (1994). *Value-added performance indicators for schools*. London: Author.

Schwandt, T. A. (1984). *An examination of alternative models for socio-behavioral inquiry*. Unpublished Ph.D. dissertation, Indiana University.

Schwandt, T. A. (1993). Theory for the moral sciences: Crisis of identity and purpose. In D. J. Flinders & G. E. Mills (Eds.), *Theory and concepts in qualitative research* (pp. 5–23). New York: Teachers College Press.

Schwandt, T. A. (1997). Evaluation as practical hermeneutics. *Evaluation, 3*, 69–83.

Schweinhart, L. J., & Weikart, D. P. (1997). The High/Scope preschool curriculum comparison study through age 23. *Early Childhood Research Quarterly, 12*, 117–143.

Schweinhart, L. J., Barnes, H. V., & Weikart, D. P. (with W. S. Barnett & A. S. Epstein). (1993). *Significant benefits: The High/Scope Perry Preschool study through age 27*. Ypsilanti, MI: High/Scope Press.

Scriven, M. S. (1966). *The methodology of evaluation*. Publication #110 of the Social Science Education Consortium, Purdue University, Lafayette, IN.

Scriven, M. S. (1967). The methodology of evaluation. In R. Tyler, R. Gagne, & M. Scriven (Eds.), *Perspectives of curriculum evaluation* (pp. 39–83). (AERA Monograph Series on Curriculum Evaluation). Chicago: Rand McNally.

Scriven, M. S. (1969a, February). An introduction to meta-evaluation. *Educational Products Report, 2*(5), 36–38.

Scriven, M. S. (1969b). *Evaluation skills* [Audiotape No. 6B]. Washington, D.C.: American Educational Research Association.

Scriven, M. S. (1971). Objectivity and subjectivity in educational research. In L. G. Thomas (Ed.), *Philosophical redirection of educational research*. Seventy-first Yearbook of the National Society for the Study of Education, Part 1. Chicago: University of Chicago Press.

Scriven, M. S. (1972). An introduction to metaevaluation. In P. A. Taylor & D. M. Cowley (Eds.), *Readings in curriculum evaluation*. Dubuque, IA: W. C. Brown.

Scriven, M. S. (1973). Goal-free evaluation. In E. House (Ed.), *School evaluation: The politics and process*. Berkeley, CA: McCutchan.

Scriven, M. S. (1973, July). Maximizing the power of causal investigations—The modus operandi method. (Mimeo).

Scriven, M. S. (1974a). Evaluation perspectives and procedures. In W. J. Popham (Ed.), *Evaluation in education: Current applications*. Berkeley, CA: McCutcheon.

Scriven, M. S. (1974b). Pros and cons about goal-free evaluation. *Evaluation Comment, 3*, 1–4.

Scriven, M. S. (1975). *Evaluation bias and its control*. Occasional Paper Series no. 4. Kalamazoo, MI: Western Michigan University Evaluation Center.

Scriven, M. (1980a). *Evaluation thesaurus* (2nd ed.). Pt Reyes, CA: Edgepress.

Scriven, M. (1980b). *The logic of evaluation*. Inverness, CA: Edgepress.

Scriven, M. (1981a). *Evaluation thesaurus* (3rd ed.). Inverness, CA: Edge-Press.

Scriven, M. (1981b). Product evaluation. In N. Smith (Ed.). *New models of program evaluation*. Beverly-Hills, CA: Sage.

Scriven, M. (1981c). Summative teacher evaluation. In J. Millman (Ed.), *Handbook of teacher evaluation*. Beverly Hills, CA: Sage.

Scriven, M. (1991). *Evaluation thesaurus (4th ed.)*. Newbury Park, CA: Sage.

Scriven, M. (1993). *Hard-won lessons in program evaluation. New Directions for Program Evaluation, 58*. San Francisco: Jossey-Bass.

Scriven, M. (1994a). Evaluation as a discipline. *Studies in Educational Evaluation, 20*, 147–166.

Scriven, M. (1994b). Product evaluation: The state of the art. *Evaluation Practice, 15*, 45–62.

Scriven, M. (1994c). The final synthesis. *Evaluation Practice, 15*, 367–382.

Scriven, M. S., & Roth, J. E. (1977). Needs Assessment. *Evaluation News, 2*, 25–28.

Scriven, M. S., & Roth, J. E. (1978). Needs Assessment: Concept and Practice. *New Direction for Program Evaluation, 1*, 1–11.

Seidman, I. E. (1991). *Interviewing as qualitative research: A guide for researchers in education and social sciences*. New York: Teachers College Press.

Senge, P. (1990). *The fifth discipline: The art & practice of the learning organization*.

Senge, P., Kleiner, A., Roberts, C., Ross, R., & Smith, B. (1994). *The fifth discipline fieldbook: Strategies and tools for building a learning organization*. New York: Doubleday.

Shadish, W. R., Cook, T. D., & Leviton, L. C. (1991). *Foundations of program evaluation*. Newbury Park, CA: Sage.

Shadish, W. R., Newman, D. L., Scheirer, M. A., & Wye, C. (1995). Guiding principles for evaluators. *New Directions for Program Evaluation, 66.*

Shavelson, R. et al. (1989). *Indicators for monitoring math and science education.* Santa Monica, CA: Rand Corporation.

Shepard, L. A. (1977). *A checklist for evaluating large-scale assessment programs.* Occasional Paper Series, Paper No. 9. Kalamazoo, MI: Western Michigan University Evaluation Center.

Shepard, L., Glaser, R., Linn, R., & Bohrnstedt, G. (1993). *Setting performance standards for student achievement: A report of the National Academy of Education panel on the evaluation of the NAEP trial state assessment: An evaluation of the 1992 achievement levels.* Stanford, CA: National Academy of Education.

Simpson, J., & Weiner, S. (Eds.). (1989). *The Oxford English dictionary* (2nd ed.). Oxford: Oxford University Press.

Singer, M. J. (1991, April). *Must educational criticism be literary?* Paper presented at the annual meeting of the American Educational Research Association, Chicago, IL.

Sizer, T. R. (1984). *Horace's compromise: The dilemma of the American high school.* Boston: Houghton Mifflin.

Sizer, T. (1992). *Horace's school.* Boston: Houghton Mifflen.

Smith, E. R., & Tyler, R. W. (1942). *Appraising and recording student progress.* New York Harper.

Smith, H. L., & Judd, C. M. (1914). *Plans for organizing school surveys.* Thirteenth Yearbook of the National Society for the Study of Education, Part II. Bloomington, IL: Public School Publishing Co.

Smith, L. M., & Pohland, P. A. (1974). Educational technology and the rural highlands. In L. M. Smith (Ed.), *Four examples: Economic, anthropological, narrative, and portrayal.* (AERA Monograph on Curriculum Evaluation). Chicago: Rand McNally.

Smith, M. F. (1989). *Evaluability assessment: A practical approach.* Boston: Kluwer-Nijhoff.

Smith, M. R. (1987). Army ordnance and the 'American system' of manufacturing: 1815–1861. In M. R. Smith (Ed.), *Military enterprise and technological change* (pp. 39–86). Cambridge, MA: MIT Press.

Smith, N. L. (1981a). *Metaphors for evaluation: Sources of new methods.* Beverly Hills, CA: Sage.

Smith, N. L. (1981b). *New techniques for evaluation.* Beverly Hills, CA: Sage.

Smith, N. L. (1987). Toward the justification of claims in evaluation research. *Evaluation and Program Planning, 10,* 309–314.

Smith, N. L. (1992). *Aspects of investigative inquiry in evaluation. New Directions for Program Evaluation No 56.* San Francisco: Jossey-Bass.

Snyder, J., Bolin, F., & Zumwalt, K. (1992). Curriculum implementation. In P. W. Jackson (Ed.), *Handbook of research on curriculum* (pp. 402–435). New York: Macmillan.

Spitz, H. H. (1999). Beleaguered Pygmalion: A history of the controversy over claims that teacher expectancy raises intelligence. *Intelligence, 27,* 199–234.

Sroufe, G. E. (1977). Evaluation and politics. In J. D. Scribner (Ed.). *The politics of evaluation.* Seventy-sixth Yearbook of the National Society for the Study of Education, Part II (pp. 287–318). Chicago: National Society for the Study of Education.

Stake, R. E. (1967). The countenance of educational evaluation. *Teachers College Record, 68,* 523–540.

Stake, R. E. (1970). Objectives, priorities, and other judgment data. *Review of Educational Research, 40,* 181–212.

Stake, R. E. (1971). *Measuring what learners learn.* (mimeograph). Urbana, IL: Center for Instructional Research and Curriculum Evaluation.

Stake, R. E. (1974). *Nine approaches to evaluation.* Unpublished chart. Urbana, IL: Center for Instructional Research and Curriculum Evaluation.

Stake, R. E. (1975a). *Evaluating the arts in education: A responsive approach.* Columbus, OH: Merrill.

Stake, R. E. (1975b, November). *Program evaluation, particularly responsive evaluation.* Kalamazoo: Western Michigan University Evaluation Center, Occasional Paper No. 5.

Stake, R. E. (1976). A theoretical statement of responsive evaluation. *Studies in Educational Evaluation, 2,* 19–22.

Stake, R. E. (1978). The case-study method in social inquiry. *Education Researcher, 7*(2), 5–8.

Stake, R. E. (1979). Should educational evaluation be more objective or more subjective? *Educational Evaluation and Policy Analysis, 1,* 46–47.

Stake, R. E. (1981). Setting standards for educational evaluators. *Evaluation News No 2,* 148–152.

Stake, R. E. (1986). *Quieting reform: Social science and social action in an urban youth program.* Chicago: University of Illinois Press.

Stake, R. E. (1988). Seeking sweet water. In R. M. Jaeger (Ed.), *Complementary methods for research in education* (pp. 253–300). Washington, DC: American Educational Research Association.

Stake, R. E. (1994). Case studies. In N. K. Denzin & Y. S. Lincoln (Eds.), *Handbook of qualitative research* (pp. 236–247). Thousand Oaks, CA: Sage.

Stake, R. E. (1995). *The art of case study research.* Thousand Oaks, CA: Sage.

Stake, R. E., & Easley, J. A., Jr. (Eds.) (1978). *Case studies in science education, 1*(2). NSF Project 5E-78–74. Urbana, IL: CIRCE, University of Illinois College of Education.

Stake, R. E., & Gjerde, C. (1974). *An evaluation of TCITY: The Twin City Institute for Talented Youth.* AERA Monograph Series in Curriculum Evaluation, no. 7. Chicago: Rand McNally.

Staudemaier, J. (1985). *Technology's storytellers: Reweaving the human fabric.* Cambridge, MA: MIT Press.

Staudenmaier, J. (1989). U.S. technological style and the atrophe of civic commitment. In D.L. Gilipi (Ed.), *Beyond individualism toward a retrieval of moral discourse in America* (pp. 120–152). South Bend: Notre Dame Press.

Steinmetz, A. (1983). The discrepancy evaluation model. In G. F. Madaus, M. S. Scriven, & D. L. Stufflebeam (Eds.), *Evaluation models* (pp. 79–100). Boston: Kluwer-Nijhoff.

Stenner, A. J., & Webster, W. J. (Eds.) (1971). *Technical auditing procedures. Educational product audit handbook,* 38–103. Arlington, VA: Institute for the Development of Educational Auditing.

Stern, J. D. (1986). *The Educational Indicators Project at the US Department of Education.* Washington, DC: US Department of Education.

Stillman, P. L., Haley, H. A., Regan, M. B., Philbin, M. M., Smith, S. R., O'Donnell, J., & Pohl, H. (1991). Positive effects of a clinical performance assessment program. *Academic Medicine, 66,* 481–483.

Stronach, I., & MacLure, M. (1997). *Educational research undone: The postmodern embrace.* Philadelphia: Open University Press.

Stufflebeam, D. L. (1966). A depth study of the evaluation requirement. *Theory Into Practice, 5,* 121–34.

Stufflebeam, D. L. (1967). The use of and abuse of evaluation in Title III. *Theory Into Practice, 6,* 126–33.

Stufflebeam, D. L. (1969). Evaluation as enlightenment for decision making. In A. Walcott (Ed.), *Improving educational assessment and an inventory of measures of affective behavior.* Washington, DC: Association for Supervision and Curriculum Development.

Stufflebeam, D. L. (1971). The relevance of the CIPP evaluation model for educational accountability. *Journal of Research and Development in Education, 5*(1), 19–25.

Stufflebeam, D. L. (1974). *Meta-evaluation.* Occasional Paper Series, Paper No. 3. Kalamazoo, MI: Western Michigan University Evaluation Center.

Stufflebeam, D. L. (1977, September). *Needs assessment in evaluation.* Audio-tape of presentation at meeting of the American Educational Research Association, San Francisco.

Stufflebeam, D. L. (1978). Meta evaluation: An overview. *Evaluation and the Health Professions, no. 2, 1.*

Stufflebeam, D. L. (1982). A next step: Discussion to consider unifying the ERS and Joint Committee standards. In P. H. Rossi (Ed.), *Standards for evaluation practice. New Directions for Program Evaluation, 15,* 27–36. San Francisco: Jossey-Bass.

Stufflebeam, D. L. (1983). The CIPP model for program evaluation. In G. F. Madaus, M. S. Scriven, & D. L. Stufflebeam (Eds.), *Evaluation models: Viewpoints on educational and human services evaluation* (pp. 117–141). Boston: Kluwer-Nijhoff.

Stufflebeam, D. L. (1995). Evaluation of superintendent performance: Toward a general model. *Studies in Educational Evaluation, 21,* 153–225.

Stufflebeam, D. L. (1997). A standards-based perspective on evaluation. In R. L. Stake, *Advances in program evaluation, 3,* 61–88.

Stufflebeam, D. L. et al. (1971). *Educational evaluation and decision making.* Itasca, IL: Peacock.

Stufflebeam, D. L., Foley, W. J., Gephart, W. J., Guba, E. G., Hammond, R. L., Merriman, H. O., & Provus, M. M. (1971). *Educational evaluation and decision making.* Itasca, IL: Peacock.

Stufflebeam, D. L., Jaeger, R. M., & Scriven, M. S. (1992, April). *A retrospective analysis of a summative evaluation of NAGB's pilot project to set achievement levels on the National Assessment of Educational Progress.* Paper presented at the annual meeting of the American Educational Research Association, San Francisco.

Stufflebeam, D. L., & Madaus, G. F. (1988). *Educational evaluation: The classical writings of Ralph W. Tyler.* Boston: Kluwer-Nijhoff.

Stufflebeam, D. L., & Shinkfield, A. J. (1985). *Systematic evaluation.* Boston: Kluwer-Nijhoff.

Stufflebeam, D. L., & Webster, W. (1983). An analysis of alternative approaches to evaluation. In G. F. Madaus, M. S. Scriven, & D. L. Stufflebeam (Eds.), *Evaluation models: Viewpoints on educational and human services evaluation* (pp. 23–44). Boston, MA: Kluwer-Nijhoff.

Suarez, T. (1980). *Needs assessments for technical assistance: A conceptual overview and comparison of three strategies.* Unpublished doctoral dissertation. Western Michigan University.

Suchman, E. A. (1967). *Evaluative research*. New York: Russell Sage Foundation.

Sumida, J. (1994). *The Waianae self-help housing initiative: Ke Aka Ho· ona: Traveling observer handbook*. Kalamazoo, MI: Western Michigan University Evaluation Center.

Swanson, D. B., Norman, R. N., & Linn, R. L. (1995). Performance-based assessment: Lessons from the health professions. *Educational Researcher, 24*(5), 5–11.

Tax, S. (1958). The fox project. *Human Organization, 17*, 17–19.

Taylor, F. (1947). *Scientific management comprising shop management*. New York: Harper & Row.

Tennessee Board of Education. (1992). *The master plan for Tennessee schools 1993*. Nashville, TN: Author.

Thompson, D. (1950). *England in the nineteenth century (1815–1914)*. Baltimore: Penguin.

Thompson, T. L. (1986). *Final synthesis report of the life services project traveling observer procedure*. Kalamazoo, MI: Western Michigan University Evaluation Center.

Thorndike, R. L. (Ed.) (1971). *Educational measurement* (2nd ed.). Washington, DC: American Council on Education.

Thornton, S. J. (1988). Curriculum consonance in United States history classrooms. *Journal of Curriculum and Supervision, 3*, 308–320.

Thornton, S. J. (1991, April). *Identifying issues in the criticism of social studies textbooks*. Paper presented at the annual meeting of the American Educational Research Association, Chicago, IL.

Tibi, C. (1986). The determinants of educational cost. *IIEP Newsletter, 4*, 1–2.

Tiffany, C. R., & Lutjens, L. R. J. (1998). *Planned change theories for nursing*. Thousand Oaks, CA: Sage.

Timar, T. (1989). The politics of restructuring. *Phi Delta Kappan, 71*, 264–275.

Toffolon-Weiss, M. M., Bertrand, J. T., & Terrell, S. S. (1999). The results framework—An innovative tool for program planning and evaluation. *Evaluation Review, 23*, 336–359.

Torrance, H. (1993). Combining measurement-driven instruction with authentic assessment: Some initial observations of national assessment in England and Wales. *Educational Evaluation and Policy Analysis, 15*, 81–90.

Toulmin, S. (1958). *The uses of argument*. Cambridge: Cambridge University Press.

Toulmin, S. (1982). The construal of reality: Criticism in modern and post-modern science. In W. J. T. Mitchell (Ed.), *The politics of interpretation* (pp. 99–118). Chicago: University of Chicago Press.

Tracking Health System Change. (1996). *Health Affairs, 15* (entire issue 2).

Tranel, D. D. (1981). A lesson from the physicists. *Personnel and Guidance Journal, 59*, 425–428.

Travers, R. W. (1977). Presentation in a seminar at the Western Michigan University Evaluation Center, Kalamazoo, Michigan, October 24.

Tsang, M. (1994a). *Cost analysis of educational inclusion of marginalized populations*. Paris: International Institute for Educational Planning, UNESCO.

Tsang, M. (1994b). Costs of education in China: Issues of resource mobilization, equality, equity, and efficiency. *Education Economics, 2*, 287–312.

Tsang, M. (1995). Public and private costs of education in developing countries. In M. Carnoy (Ed.), *International encyclopedia of economics of education* (2nd ed.) (pp. 393–398). Oxford: Pergamon.

Tsang, M. (1997). The costs of vocational training. *International Journal of Manpower, 18*, 63–89.

Tsang, M., & Taoklam, W. (1992). Comparing the costs of government and private primary education in Thailand. *International Journal of Educational Development, 12*, 177–190.

Turner, D. (1998). Evaluation and organizational learning under uncertainty. Proceedings of the 1998 International conference of the Australasion Evaluation Society: Vol. 1 (pp. 375–390). Canberra: Australasian Evaluation Society.

Tyack, D. B. (1974). *The one best system: A history of American urban education*. Cambridge MA: Harvard University Press.

Tyack, D., & Hansot, E. (1982). *Managers of virtue*. New York: Basic Books.

Tyler, R. W. (1934). *Constructing achievement tests*. Columbus, OH: Ohio State University Bureau of Educational Research.

Tyler, R. W. (1942a). Eight-year study. In E. R. Smith & R. Tyler (Eds.), *Appraising and recording student progress*. New York: Harper.

Tyler, R. W. (1942b). General statement on evaluation. *Journal of Educational Research, 35*, 492–501.

Tyler, R. W. (1949). *Basic principles of curriculum and instruction*. Chicago: University of Chicago Press.

Tyler, R. W. (1951). The functions of measurement in improving instruction. In E. F. Lindquist (Ed.), *Educational measurement* (pp. 47–67). Washington, D.C.: American Council on Education.

Tyler, R. W. (1966). The objectives and plans for a National Assessment of Educational Progress. *Journal of Educational Measurement, 3*, 1–10.

Tyler, R. W. (1967). Changing concepts of educational evaluation. In R. Tyler, R. Gagne, & M. Scriven

(Eds.), *Perspectives of curriculum evaluation*, (pp. 13–18). (AERA Monograph Series on Curriculum Evaluation). Chicago: Rand McNally.

Tyler, R. W. et al. (1932). *Service studies in higher education*. Columbus, OH: The Bureau of Educational Research, Ohio State University.

Tymms, P. (1995). *Setting up a national "valued added" system for primary education in England: Problems and possibilities*. Paper presented at the National Evaluation Institute Center for Research on Educational Accountability and Teacher Evaluation (CREATE), Kalamazoo, MI.

Uhrmacher, B. (1991). Waldorf schools marching quietly unheard. *Dissertation Abstracts International, 52*, 3172. (University Microfilms No. 92–05, 736).

Uhrmacher, B., & Green, G. (1991, April). *Educational criticism and the theory of the avant garde*. Paper presented at the annual meeting of the American Educational Research Association, Chicago, IL.

UNESCO. (1976). *The experimental world literacy programme: A critical assessment*. Paris: Author.

U.S. Departments of Education and Labor. (1993). *Preamble to Goals 2000: Education America Act*, Washington, DC: Authors.

U.S. General Accounting Office, Program Evaluation and Methodology Division. (1990). *Case study evaluations*. Washington, D.C.: Government Printing Office.

U.S. Office of Education. (1970). *Education of the disadvantaged: An evaluation report opt Title I, Elementary and Secondary Education Act of 1965, Fiscal Year 1968*. Washington, D.C.: Author.

Vallance, E. (1973). *Aesthetic criticism and curriculum description*. Ph.D. dissertation, Stanford University.

Van der Walt, H., & Hoogendoorn, L. (1993). *Training for self-evaluation at Ithusheng health centre*. Tygerber: Centre for Epidemiological Research in Southern Africa, Medical Research Council.

Van Dijk, T. A. (1995). Discourse semantics and ideology. *Discourse and Society, 6*, 243–289.

Vinovskis, M. (1999). Overseeing the nation's reportcard: The creation and evolution of the National Assessment Governing Board (NAGB). Washington, DC: National Assessment Governing Board.

Wadsworth, Y. (1991). *Everyday evaluation on the run*. Melbourne, Victoria: Action Research Issues Centre.

Wallerstein, N. (1992). Powerless, empowerment, and health: Implications for health promotion programs. *American Journal of Health Promotion, 6*(3), 197–205.

Walters, J. (1996). Auditor power! *Governing*, April, 25–29.

Webb, E. et al. (1966). *Unobtrusive measures*. Chicago: Rand McNally.

Webster, W. J. (1975). *The organization and functions of research and evaluation in large urban school districts*. Paper presented at the annual meeting of the American Educational Research Association, Washington, DC.

Webster, W. J. (1994). *Use of assessments of student progress to evaluate school effectiveness*. Honolulu, HI: Hawaii State Department of Education, Institute on Assessment & Accountability.

Webster, W. J. (1995). The connection between personnel evaluation and school evaluation. *Studies in Educational Evaluation, 21*, 227–254.

Webster, W. J., Mendro, R. L., & Almaguer, T. O. (1994). Effectiveness indices: A 'value added' approach to measuring school effect. *Studies in Educational Evaluation, 20*, 113–145.

Weir, E. (1980). Types of explanation in educational evaluation. *Paper and Report Series*, no. 34. Research on Evaluation Project, Northwest Regional Educational Laboratory, Portland, OR.

Weiss, C. H. (1972). *Evaluation*. Englewood Cliffs, N.J.: Prentice Hall.

Weiss, C. H. (1983). Toward the future of stakeholder approaches in evaluation. In A. S. Bryk (Ed.), *Stakeholder-based evaluation. New Directions for Program Evaluation*. San Francisco: Jossey-Bass.

Weiss, C. H. (1995). Nothing as practical as good theory: Exploring theory-based evaluation for comprehensive community initiatives for children and families. In J. Connell, A. Kubisch, L. B. Schorr, & C. H. Weiss (Eds.), *New approaches to evaluating community initiatives*. New York: Aspen Institute.

Weiss, C. H. (1996). *Why is theory-based evaluation not making headway?* Paper presented at the Annual Meeting of the American Evaluation Association, Atlanta.

Weiss, C. H. (1997a). *Evaluation*. (2nd ed.). Upper Saddle River, N.J.: Prentice Hall.

Weitzman, E. A., & Miles, M. B. (1995). *A software sourcebook: Computer programs for qualitative data analysis*. Thousand Oaks, CA: Sage.

Welch, W. W., & Walberg, H. J. (1972). A natural experiment in curriculum innovation. *American Educational Research Journal, 9*, 373–383.

Wheelock, A. (1992). *Crossing the tracks*. New York: New Press.

Wholey, J. S. (1979). *Evaluation: Promise and performance*. Washington, D.C.: Urban Institute.

Wholey, J. S. (1995). Assessing the feasibility and likely usefulness of evaluation. In J. S. Wholey, H. P. Hatry, & K. E. Newcomer (Eds.), *Handbook of practical program evaluation* (pp. 15–39). San Francisco: Jossey-Bass.

Wiggins, G. (1989). A true test: Toward more authentic and equitable assessment. *Phi Delta Kappan, 70,* 703–713.

Wiles, D. K. (1981). The logic of Y = f(X) in the study of educational politics. *Educational Evaluation and Policy Analysis, 3,* 67–74.

Wiley, D. E., & Bock, R. D. (1967). Quasi-experimentation in educational settings: Comment. *School Review, 75,* 353–366.

Wolcott, H. F. (1994). *Transforming qualitative data: Description, analysis and interpretation.* Thousand Oaks, CA: Sage.

Wolf, R. L. (1974). *The application of select legal concepts to educational evaluation.* Unpublished doctoral dissertation, University of Illinois.

Wolf, R. L. (1975). Trial by jury: A new evaluation method. *Phi Delta Kappan, 3,* 185–187.

Wolf, R. L. (1983). The use of judicial evaluation methods in the formulation of educational policy. In G. F. Madaus, M. S. Scriven, & D. L. Stufflebeam (Eds.), *Evaluation models: Viewpoints on educational and human services evaluation* (pp. 189–203). Boston, MA: Kluwer-Nijhoff.

Womer, F. (1970). *What is national assessment?* Ann Arbor, MI: National Assessment of Educational Progress.

Woodhouse, G., & Goldstein, H. (1996). The statistical analysis of institution-based data. In H. Goldstern & T. Lewis (Eds.). *Assessment: Problems, developments and statistical issues* (pp. 135–144). New York: Wiley.

Word, E., Johnston, J., Bain, H. P., et al. (1990). *Student/teacher achievement ratio (STAR): Tennessee's K-3 class size study. Final summary report 1985–1990.* Nashville, TN: Tennessee Department of Education.

World Bank. (1995). *Priorities and strategies for education: A World Bank review.* Washington, DC: Author.

Worthen, B. R., & Sanders, J. R. (1987). *Educational evaluation: Alternative approaches and practical guidelines.* White Plains, NY: Longman.

Worthen, B. R., Sanders, J. R., & Fitzpatrick, J. L. (1997). *Program evaluation (2nd ed).* New York: Longman.

Wynne, E. (1972). *The politics of school accountability.* Berkeley, CA: McCutchan.

Yin, R. K. (1981a). The case study as a serious research strategy. *Knowledge: Creation, Diffusion, Utilization, 3,* 97–114.

Yin, R. K. (1981b) The case study crisis: Some answers. *Administrative Science Quarterly, 26,* 58–65.

Yin, R. K. (1989). *Case study research: Design and method.* Newbury Park, CA: Sage.

Yin, R. K. (1992). The case study as a tool for doing evaluation. *Current Sociology, 40,* 121–137.

Yin, R. K. (1993). *Applications of case study research.* Thousand Oaks, CA: Sage.

Yin, R. K. (1994a). *Case study research: Design and methods* (2nd ed.). Thousand Oaks, CA: Sage.

Yin, R. K. (1994b). Evaluation: A singular craft. In C. S. Reichardt & S. F. Rallis (Eds.), *The qualitative-quantitative debate: New perspectives.* New Directions for Program Evaluation, no. 61. San Francisco: Jossey-Bass.

Yin, R. K. (1997). The abridged version of case study research. In L. Bickman & D. Rog (Eds.), *Handbook of applied social research methods.* Thousand Oaks, CA: Sage.

Yin, R. K. (1997). Case study evaluations. In D. Rog & D. Fournier (Eds.). *Progress and future directions in evaluation: Perspectives on theory, practice and methods. New Directions for Evaluation.* San Francisco: Jossey-Bass.

Yin, R. K., & Bickman, L. (forthcoming). Reforms as non-experiments: A new paradigm. In L. Bickman (Ed.), *Validity and social experimentation: Donald Campbell's legacy.* Thousand Oaks, CA: Sage.

Zigler, E., & Styfco, S. J. (1994). Is the Perry Preschool better than Head Start? Yes and no. *Early Childhood Research Quarterly, 9,* 269–287.

Zimmerman, M. A., & Rappaport, J. (1988). Citizen participation, perceived control, and psychological empowerment. *American Journal of Community Psychology, 16,* 725–750.

INDEX